Artificial Intelligence and Robotics in Sports Industry

Past, Present, and Future

Ekaterina Glebova
Higher Colleges of Technology
Dubai, UAE

Université Paris-Saclay, CIAMS
Orsay, France

CRC Press
Taylor & Francis Group
Boca Raton London New York

CRC Press is an imprint of the
Taylor & Francis Group, an **informa** business
A SCIENCE PUBLISHERS BOOK

First edition published 2027
by CRC Press
2385 NW Executive Center Drive, Suite 320, Boca Raton FL 33431

and by CRC Press
4 Park Square, Milton Park, Abingdon, Oxon, OX14 4RN

CRC Press is an imprint of Taylor & Francis Group, LLC

Library of Congress Cataloging-in-Publication Data (applied for)

ISBN: 978-1-032-85335-2 (hbk)
ISBN: 978-1-032-87659-7 (pbk)
ISBN: 978-1-003-53379-5 (ebk)

DOI: 10.1201/9781003533795

Typeset in Times New Roman
by Prime Publishing Services

Preface

Sport is entering an exciting tech era. AI and robotics are changing training, games, and fan experiences. This book explains these changes clearly. It cuts through hype to show real uses.

What

This book explores artificial intelligence (AI) and robotics in the sports industry. It covers how these technologies transform training, coaching, officiating, fan experiences, and business operations.

From historical origins to futuristic scenarios, it uses examples from soccer, basketball, tennis, and esports, while clarifying concepts like automation versus autonomy.

It covers historical origins to futuristic scenarios, it uses examples from soccer, basketball, tennis, and esports, while clarifying concepts like automation versus autonomy.

It dives into training where wearables predict injuries before they happen and robots spar with athletes.

It examines coaching where AI dashboards reveal hidden fatigue patterns and suggest tactics.

It shows officiating where VAR and Hawk-Eye deliver unblinking precision.

It explores fan experiences where VR stadiums and AR overlays turn spectators into participants.

It maps business operations where dynamic pricing and sponsorship analytics reshape revenue.

Starting from early stopwatches to tomorrow's digital twins and embodied AI, the book connects past innovations to future possibilities. It clarifies key ideas: automation repeats fixed rules, while autonomy adapts like a thinking teammate; machine learning spots patterns, while deep learning mimics human brain layers. These distinctions cut through hype, showing what truly works in soccer's Wyscout tactics, basketball's shot analytics, tennis' Hawk-Eye calls, and esports' real-time

AI coaches. The goal is simple: turn complex tech into clear tools that honor sport's spirit while pushing its boundaries.

Why

Sport faces rapid tech changes, but confusion surrounds terms like AI, machine learning, and smart systems. This book cuts through hype to provide clarity, frameworks (e.g., human-machine teamwork), and ethical guidance. It equips readers to spot real innovations and apply them responsibly, drawing from research collaborations.

This book has been written because sport is at a tipping point. AI and robotics are no longer experiments—they are live in stadiums, training grounds, and boardrooms worldwide. Yet confusion reigns: Is that "smart" system truly intelligent or just automated? Are we enhancing fairness or deepening divides between rich clubs and grassroots teams? The stakes are massive—billions in revenue, athlete careers, fan trust—and the window to shape this future responsibly is narrow. The global expertise in sports management shows that leaders lack clear frameworks to turn tech into strategic advantage without ethical pitfalls. This book delivers those frameworks now, when they matter most.

When

Now, as AI and robotics enter a revolution in sports—seen in tools like VAR, wearables, and predictive analytics. The timing aligns with 2026's digital transformation, bridging today's applications to tomorrow's possibilities like digital twins and embodied AI. The moment is now—2026, as AI and robotics surge from labs into live stadiums, training pitches, and global broadcasts. VAR and Hawk-Eye already judge offsides with laser precision; wearables predict injuries before a muscle twinges; predictive analytics shape NBA trades and FIFA tactics daily. This isn't tomorrow's promise—it's today's game. The timing aligns with a digital transformation cresting toward 2030, where digital twins will clone your perfect swing in real time, embodied AI robots will spar as adaptive partners, and autonomous systems will manage stadiums that breathe with crowd energy. Before hype hardens into habit—is vanishingly small. This book captures that fleeting, electric now, bridging what works today to what will define champions tomorrow.

Where

Across global sports ecosystems: elite Olympics, professional leagues (FIFA, NBA), grassroots teams, smart stadiums, and UAE higher education contexts. It applies from local pitches to international events, emphasizing accessibility and fairness.

Where does this revolution strike? It strikes in Olympic villages where AI wearables don't merely track—they predict an athlete's collapse before the first twinge of pain. It strikes in FIFA and NBA arenas where VAR and predictive analytics don't assist coaches—they dictate strategy in real-time, turning intuition into data-driven command. It strikes on grassroots pitches where a single smartphone doesn't just level the field—it obliterates the chasm between elite academies and neighborhood kids. It strikes in smart stadiums that don't host fans passively—they manipulate emotions with crowd-sensing robotics and surge pricing that weaponizes loyalty. From Dubai's cutting-edge labs to European clubs where Wyscout's tactical wizardry decides million-dollar signings, to U.S. courts where sentiment analytics don't measure fan passion—they engineer it from scratch. This book doesn't apply from local fields to world stages; it weaponizes both, demanding accessibility and fairness so innovation doesn't lift a privileged few—it liberates every player with a dream.

Who

Coaches, athletes, managers, policymakers, sports scientists, and enthusiasts. Ideal for academics in sports technology and practitioners seeking practical tools for ethical tech integration.

Who is this for? It's for you—the coach burning midnight oil over fatigue data, desperate to know when to rest a star before injury strikes. It's for you—the athlete whose career hinges on trusting AI insights while owning your biometric destiny. It's for you—the manager calculating ROI on smart stadiums and the policymaker drafting AI governance that doesn't crush innovation. It's for you—the sports scientist hunting frameworks to validate predictive models, and the enthusiast craving to see beyond the scoreboard into the digital soul of sport. It's for you—my academic peers in sports technology and higher education—who need teaching tools that bridge theory and practice. If you're a practitioner seeking ethical tech integration that actually works, not just dazzles, this is your playbook.

Contents

Chapter 1

Emarking on the Journey

"*The best way to predict the future is to invent it.*" – Alan Kay
"*Sport has the power to change the world. It has the power to inspire.*" – Nelson Mandela
"*Machines take me by surprise with great frequency.*" – Alan Turing

History reminds us that visionaries often see the seeds of tomorrow in the movements of today. From the stadiums of ancient Olympia to the smart arenas of the 21st century, sport has mirrored humanity's greatest ambitions—discipline, excellence, creativity, and progress. And now, standing at the threshold of a new era, we witness an unprecedented convergence: the fusion of sport's enduring spirit with the precision and intelligence of machines.

This book is a journey across time—examining how Artificial Intelligence (AI) and robotics have entered the realm of sport, not as distant science fiction fantasies, but as real, transformative forces. From early mechanical tools that tracked performance to today's autonomous referees and AI-powered coaching assistants, technology has evolved from supporting roles to central players on and off the field. How these innovations are reshaping the way athletes train, how fans engage, how decisions are made, and how competitions unfold? But beyond functionality lies a deeper question: What does it mean for sport—rooted in human struggle and triumph—to share its space with non-human intelligence? To answer that, we'll travel across the past, where mechanical ingenuity met muscle and tradition. We'll analyze the present, where algorithms dissect performance, and robots throw first pitches. And we'll glimpse into the future, where the line between human and machine becomes a shared space of possibility, tension, and redefinition.

In the words of Aristotle, "*We are what we repeatedly do. Excellence, then, is not an act but a habit.*" As AI and robotics reshape what we can do, this book invites you to consider: how will they reshape who humans are in the world of sport? How AI and robots change the way how sport is played, watched, consumed, managed, determined, perceived, and understood?

1.1. Why Dive into AI and Robotics in Sports?

At the first glance, sport and technology might seem like strange teammates.

Sport is sweaty, passionate, unpredictable. It's about instinct, emotion, and pushing the human body to its limits. AI and robotics, on the other hand, are cold, calculated, and tireless. They don't feel pressure. They don't choke in the final minutes. They don't cheer when they win or cry when they lose.

DOI: 10.1201/9781003533795-1

So why are we bringing them together?

The short answer: because sport is changing—and rapidly.

1.1.1. A New Kind of Athlete, Coach, and Fan

AI and robotics are not replacing sport. They're **reshaping it**—in subtle and radical ways. AI doesn't just crunch data. It's becoming an invisible coach, a digital scout, a real-time analyst whispering insights in an athlete's ear. Robotics isn't just about mechanical arms; it's about machines that move, respond, and even learn alongside humans.

Whether it's AI detecting early signs of injury before an athlete feels pain, or a robot helping paralympic athletes train with precision, the impact is already profound. Coaches no longer rely solely on experience and instinct; they have dashboards of predictions and probabilities. Fans don't just watch; they interact with the game through apps, wearables, and augmented reality—often enhanced by AI.

In short, technology is now a teammate.

The Athlete: Precision, Prevention, and Personalization

Eliud Kipchoge, the legendary marathon runner; Eliud Kipchoge's sub-two-hour marathon on October 12, 2019, in Vienna, known as the INEOS 1:59 Challenge, was a groundbreaking blend of human endurance and technology. Advanced AI algorithms dynamically controlled the pace using a rotating team of elite pacemakers who adjusted their speed precisely to maintain the ideal target pace for Kipchoge, minimizing energy waste. The route was carefully chosen for its flat, straight course with minimal turns, and the event took place during optimal weather conditions. AI models helped predict and select conditions that would minimize wind resistance and temperature stress. Kipchoge wore smart sensors that captured detailed data on his running form, cadence, stride length, and fatigue levels. Coaches and data scientists used this information in real-time to provide feedback and make adjustments as needed. Data analysis influenced the design and selection of Nike's Vaporfly shoes worn by Kipchoge, optimized for energy return and lightweight performance. This fusion of elite athleticism with data-driven insights pushed the limits of human performance, turning a seemingly impossible goal into reality. AI algorithms were used to optimize pace, route, and environmental conditions. Smart sensors tracked his form, fatigue, and stride dynamics to fine-tune every aspect of his performance.

Eliud Kipchoge's historic sub-two-hour marathon wasn't merely a feat of physical endurance—it was a precision-engineered performance where artificial intelligence, human physiology, and psychological mastery worked in unison. At the heart of the achievement was a pace strategy powered by machine learning. Sophisticated algorithms, trained on vast datasets of race performances, energy expenditure patterns, and environmental variables, produced a finely tuned pacing blueprint. This was not just theoretical. The data-driven plan was put into action by an elite rotation of pacemakers who took turns running in front of Kipchoge, shielding him from wind resistance and maintaining an unyielding rhythm throughout the race.

The environment, too, was curated for success. Vienna's flat, straight course along the Danube River was deliberately chosen to minimize the muscular strain caused by elevation changes and sharp turns. AI contributed here as well, forecasting weather conditions with remarkable precision to select a day with optimal temperature, humidity, and wind conditions. Even minor atmospheric advantages were leveraged to conserve Kipchoge's energy over the full distance.

Throughout the run, real-time biomechanical feedback kept his body operating at peak efficiency. Kipchoge wore smart insoles and sensors embedded in his shoes and gear, which streamed live data on stride length, ground contact time, and muscle fatigue to a support team monitoring every movement. Small, mid-race adjustments—such as a shift in cadence or posture—helped reduce strain and extend endurance without disrupting the flow of the run.

The shoes themselves were a masterpiece of innovation. Nike's Alphafly Next combined carbon fiber propulsion with ZoomX foam that delivered exceptionally high energy return. Every element of the footwear was optimized through biomechanical trials to enhance running economy while keeping the design ultra-lightweight, minimizing the metabolic cost of each step.

None of this would have been possible without a meticulously data-informed training regimen. Kipchoge's preparation integrated physiological metrics—like lactate thresholds, VO2 max, and heart rate variability—to tailor every aspect of his workouts. AI tools played a central role in dynamically adjusting training intensity and recovery, ensuring the perfect balance between pushing limits and avoiding injury. Long endurance runs were combined with interval and tempo work targeted at race-pace precision, with recovery periods guided by wearable technologies that constantly assessed fatigue and readiness. Supporting this physical mastery was an equally strategic approach to nutrition and mental conditioning. Kipchoge's fueling plan was personalized down to the gram and minute, ensuring sustained energy through calculated doses of carbohydrate gels and fluids, informed by sweat rate analyses and electrolyte profiling. Pre-race meals were optimized to fill glycogen stores without digestive discomfort, and AI modeling helped fine-tune intake to match his individual metabolism and anticipated effort level.

Mentally, Kipchoge was equally prepared. Daily visualization and mindfulness routines helped him rehearse victory in his mind before it played out on the pavement. Techniques like meditation and controlled breathing grounded his focus, while his iconic mantra—"No human is limited"—acted as a mental anchor, reinforcing resilience and belief. Psychological data, too, were measured and analyzed, with indicators like heart rate variability used to track and fine-tune his stress levels and emotional state.

It is forming a seamless, interdisciplinary system—where data science, cutting-edge technology, nutrition, and psychology fused into a singular objective: transcending what was once thought humanly possible. Kipchoge's run was more than athleticism—it was a masterclass in how the future of sport is being redefined by the integration of science, innovation, and the human spirit.

Meanwhile, in basketball, NBA teams like the Golden State Warriors use and AI models to monitor players' stress loads and predict injury risk. Devices such as Catapult Sports' GPS vests and sensors embedded in compression shirts track every acceleration, deceleration, directional change, and jump during practices. Sensors record forces on joints, particularly knees and ankles, helping identify high-risk movement trends before they lead to overuse injuries. Real-time monitoring of metrics like heart rate variability (HRV) and exertion levels uncovers signs of fatigue and incomplete recovery.

Wearables such as Whoop straps measure sleep cycles and recovery scores, feeding data into AI platforms for individualized load management. AI systems compile data from wearables, video analysis, training logs, and even medical test results to build a holistic picture of each player's condition. Machine learning models analyze these patterns to spot early warning signs—such as a drop in sprint speed or changes in joint mechanics—that might signal brewing injuries due to overexertion or improper recovery. For instance, subtle declines in a player's vertical leap or unusual favoring of one leg can indicate muscle fatigue or compensation after minor strains. The AI platform alerts trainers and coaches when a player nears risk thresholds, enabling changes in training intensity, rest schedules, or even playing time before minor strains escalate into serious tears or ruptures.

The Warriors have reported up to a 25% reduction in soft tissue injuries after adopting wearable tech and data-driven interventions. Catapult vests and tools like Athos' smart clothing give real-time readings, which medical staff combine with player-reported soreness and sleep data to inform decisions. The NBA is rolling out a centralized AI platform to aggregate and analyze injury risk leaguewide, with a particular focus on preventing Achilles, ACL, and hamstring injuries. This system integrates everything from wearable data to MRI imaging for enhanced injury prediction (Russell et al., 2021).

Impact on Player Health: Trainers now intervene earlier, adjusting practice intensity or recommending rest based on AI-driven insights, reducing both short-term and chronic injury rates. The combined use of wearables and AI covers physical, biomechanical, and recovery factors—including sleep, which is a strong predictor of injury risk. Technology lets teams tailor programs for each athlete, ensuring readiness and minimizing unnecessary time lost to preventable injuries (Table 1).

Table 1: Table Summary on Technologies and Metrics

Technology	Key Metrics Tracked	Example Use
Catapult Sports	Acceleration, force, HRV	Monitors fatigue, injury trends
Whoop Straps	Sleep, HRV, recovery	Guides rest and recovery plans
SportVu Cameras	Position, movement on court	Analyzes game/pattern fatigue
AI Models	Aggregated multi-metric	Flags early risk, suggests actions

In Paralympic sports, athletes are training with robotic resistance machines like RoboGym and Motek, which adapt to user's capabilities in real time. These machines offer personalized, data-driven training that helps athletes push boundaries safely and efficiently. Advanced robotic training systems like RoboGym and Motek are transforming the way Paralympic athletes prepare for competition, offering a blend of precision, personalization, and safety that conventional training methods often cannot match. These technologies allow for real-time adaptation to an athlete's unique physical condition, responding moment by moment to performance data. For instance, robotic resistance and assistance mechanisms continuously assess force output, range of motion, and movement speed, adjusting automatically to ensure that each exercise remains appropriately challenging without causing undue strain. This intelligent responsiveness enables athletes to train at the edge of their capacity while significantly reducing the risk of overexertion or injury.

At the heart of these systems lies an ecosystem of embedded sensors that capture a wealth of biomechanical data—joint angles, muscle activation patterns, symmetry of movement—all of which feed into AI algorithms that analyze performance in real time. This allows training programs to be dynamically tailored to the individual, targeting weaker muscles or inefficient movement patterns while progressively increasing the complexity and intensity of exercises. As the athlete improves, the system evolves with them, fine-tuning the training load, recommending changes in form or posture, and even modifying the exercise itself to match new capabilities. These robotic platforms create an environment where Paralympic athletes can safely push their limits. Immediate feedback ensures that any deviation in movement, onset of fatigue, or asymmetry is quickly detected and corrected, whether during upper body resistance exercises with RoboGym or functional gait training on Motek's motion-sensing treadmills. Trainers and therapists benefit from this constant stream of feedback, using it to make split-second decisions or refine long-term training plans.

Crucially, these technologies also offer powerful tools for tracking progress over time. Data is not only used to fine-tune performance in the moment but is also compiled into detailed reports that highlight trends, improvements, or areas that require more focus. This holistic view supports smarter goal setting, enables more effective communication between athlete and coach, and helps ensure that every stage of development is evidence-based.

Beyond athletic performance, the same technologies are a powerful ally in rehabilitation. For athletes recovering from spinal cord injuries, amputations, or neurological impairments, robotic platforms provide both mechanical assistance and therapeutic guidance. These systems promote neuroplasticity and help reestablish functional movement through repetitive, task-specific training. Whether it's relearning to walk, mastering balance on uneven terrain, or strengthening key muscle groups for competition, the technology facilitates meaningful recovery alongside performance enhancement. AI plays a vital role in sustaining this intelligent training ecosystem. It analyzes real-time movement and physiological data to spot inefficiencies or early signs of fatigue, adjusting resistance or exercise patterns accordingly. Machine learning models predict optimal progression rates for each athlete, reducing the likelihood of plateaus or overtraining. In some cases, AI systems also flag potential risks, such as emerging compensatory movements, allowing coaches to preemptively revise sessions to prevent injury. Even outside traditional training spaces, these technologies extend their reach. Remote monitoring capabilities allow therapists and coaches to track progress from afar. Athletes can engage in high-quality training from home, with AI-generated dashboards providing insight into performance trends and suggested adjustments for future sessions. Together, these robotic and AI-driven innovations are setting new standards for inclusivity and excellence in sport. They don't just compensate for physical impairments—they empower Paralympic athletes to train smarter, recover more efficiently, and reach their full competitive potential in ways that are scientifically grounded, technologically advanced, and deeply personalized.

The Coach: From Gut Feeling to Predictive Strategy

Coaching is becoming a high-tech symphony of real-time feedback, AI-generated insights, and strategic simulations. Liverpool FC, under manager Jürgen Klopp, uses an AI system known as RedZone, which combines match data, GPS tracking, and player health information to guide training loads and match tactics. AI not only identifies who needs rest but even suggests optimal formations based on opponent tendencies. Liverpool FC has emerged as a trailblazer in modern football by integrating AI into its coaching, tactical planning, and player development. But central to Liverpool's AI strategy is its partnership with Zone7, an advanced platform designed to detect injury risks and optimize player performance. Since adopting the system in the 2021/2022 season, Liverpool has used it to analyze a wide range of biometric and performance data—from GPS tracking and match stats to sleep patterns and stress indicators. Zone7 synthesizes this information to flag potential injury risks, helping coaches and medical staff adapt training loads, plan rest periods, and fine-tune recovery. The impact has been measurable: the club has reported a significant reduction—over a third—in lost player days due to injury since implementing the technology.

Another groundbreaking innovation has come through a collaboration with Google DeepMind, resulting in TacticAI—an AI tool developed to optimize set-piece execution, especially corner kicks. By analyzing thousands of scenarios, TacticAI identifies patterns, predicts player movements, and suggests strategic formations that often outperform human-devised plans. In blind testing, experts preferred its recommendations 90% of the time, highlighting AI's growing influence on football tactics. Although the full extent of its use within Liverpool's matches remains closely guarded, it's clear the coaching staff increasingly consult AI-driven insights in tactical planning.

Liverpool's digital transformation doesn't stop at training grounds or matchday tactics. The club also employs tools like All Red and Wasabi AiR to enhance media operations and game analysis. These AI platforms can instantly sort through extensive video archives, recognize faces, club logos, and key moments, making it easier for analysts, coaches, and even fans to interact with the club's rich trove of match content. This kind of rapid, automated indexing accelerates film review for tactical purposes and strengthens fan engagement through more dynamic content delivery. The role of AI in shaping training decisions is particularly influential. Algorithms monitor biometric signals—such as heart rate, sleep quality, and muscle fatigue—to ensure each player receives a tailored recovery and conditioning plan. AI doesn't just react; it anticipates, offering coaching staff predictive models of player readiness and adjusting workloads accordingly. On the tactical front, AI analyzes opposition data and in-game trends to propose lineup adjustments, defensive shapes, or pressing strategies. Simulations known as "ghosting" models can forecast how different player configurations might respond to specific plays or scenarios, giving coaches a virtual test run before taking real-time action.

Player development, too, benefits from this data-rich environment. AI pinpoints individual strengths and weaknesses within broader team tactics, allowing for targeted training that aligns physical readiness with strategic intent. Whether it's sharpening a defender's response time or enhancing a midfielder's pressing efficiency, the focus is always on refining performance through intelligent, personalized coaching. Yet, Liverpool's success is not just the product of machines. The magic lies in the balance between technology and human judgment. Klopp's leadership and emotional intelligence remain the glue that binds data insights to team unity and motivation. Figures like Ian Graham, who heads the club's research and analytics team, have played a pivotal role in applying data science to everything from scouting to in-game decision-making. But it is Klopp's ability to translate this wealth of information into high-performing, emotionally cohesive squads that completes the equation.What Liverpool FC represents is a glimpse into the future of football, where coaching extends beyond the pitch into a complex, dynamic system of AI-enhanced decision-making. As technology continues to evolve, its role in tactical innovation, injury prevention, and personalized training will only expand—turning elite football clubs into ecosystems of human talent and machine intelligence working in harmony.

In tennis, SlamTracker by IBM analyzes thousands of data points from past matches and delivers predictive analytics in real time—helping coaches and broadcasters alike anticipate pivotal moments. IBM SlamTracker is changing the way we experience tennis—not just for coaches and players, but for broadcasters and fans too. At its heart, SlamTracker is about using data to tell a better story. It pulls from a massive archive of tennis history—tens of millions of points collected over more than eight years of Grand Slam action—to help us understand what's really happening on the court, often before we even realize it ourselves. One of SlamTracker's most impressive features is what it calls the "Keys to the Match." These are three crucial performance stats tailored to each player—specific things they need to get right if they want to win. What makes this so powerful is that it's not just historical guesswork. The system updates these keys in real time during a match, helping coaches tweak strategy on the fly, giving commentators more to talk about, and helping fans understand the "why" behind the action, not just the "what." SlamTracker's AI tools can also estimate each player's chance of winning as the match unfolds. This isn't a static prediction—it changes point by point, factoring in stats, momentum, and even expert insights. For fans watching live, there's the "Match Chat" feature: a real-time assistant that can answer questions during play, making the entire experience more interactive and a lot more fun.

Behind the scenes, SlamTracker is tracking up to 25 different match variables for every single point—things like rally length, serve type, how often a player breaks serve, and how much they move. But it doesn't just dump this information into charts. Instead, it turns it into easy-to-follow visuals that help everyone—from tennis novices to seasoned analysts—spot momentum shifts and game-changing moments as they happen. For coaches, this means more than just numbers. It's a practical tool they can use to make real-time decisions and plan smarter training based on what the data says their players need. For broadcasters, it adds color and depth to their storytelling, turning stats into insights that bring viewers closer to the game. And for fans, it opens up a new layer of understanding—making it easier to follow the ebb and flow of a match and appreciate the skill and strategy involved.

SlamTracker's reach is global. You'll find it powering the digital experience at all the Grand Slams—Wimbledon, the US Open, the Australian Open—bringing its insights to millions of people around the world. And it's not standing still. IBM is constantly updating the system with new features: automated match reports, better predictive tools, and even generative AI that helps interpret the data in new ways. Virtual coaching systems are also emerging.

Startups like OliveX and A-Champs have developed interactive coaching platforms where athletes receive instant, AI-driven feedback on their drills—transforming how talent is developed at youth and amateur levels. These platforms offer immediate feedback on performance, allowing young athletes to make real-time adjustments while staying engaged through gamified challenges. Their contribution is particularly significant in contexts where access to expert coaching may be limited, as they provide structured, adaptive guidance that mirrors aspects of professional-level training.

OliveX, for instance, has carved out a space in fitness-focused gamification by linking physical activity to immersive digital experiences. Through technologies such as augmented reality, blockchain rewards, and audio-based games like Dustland Runner, it transforms traditional workouts into interactive adventures. While its focus leans more toward fitness motivation than technical sport training, it still supports the development of fundamental movement skills and promotes consistency in physical activity—essential building blocks for athletic progression, especially at younger stages.

A-Champs, on the other hand, has taken a more direct route into sport-specific skill development. Its platform uses sensors and machine learning to monitor drills and deliver personalized feedback during training sessions. This kind of feedback, typically reserved for athletes in elite academies, becomes instantly available to those training in schools, local clubs, or even at home. Though public information about A-Champs is somewhat limited, its commitment to using AI for practical coaching applications is well recognized within the sport tech community.

What makes these tools so impactful is their ability to combine real-time performance tracking with accessible design. Athletes receive immediate, tailored insights about how to improve a movement or approach a drill more efficiently. Over time, this allows for more refined training strategies, better self-awareness, and improved performance without requiring constant one-on-one coaching. Coaches benefit too from data dashboards that help them identify trends, monitor athlete development, and adjust training plans accordingly. Another key advantage lies in the motivational design of these platforms. Gamified experiences, achievement tracking, and challenge-based progression make the training process more engaging and fun—especially important when working with young athletes. These elements encourage consistent participation and build a positive relationship with sport and physical activity.

In a broader sense, platforms like OliveX and A-Champs help democratize access to quality coaching tools. With mobile apps, , and intuitive interfaces, athletes from a wide range of backgrounds can benefit from technology that was once exclusive to professional environments. This not only supports long-term athlete development but also increases the potential for early talent identification, even in communities with fewer training resources. From an educational standpoint, early research points to positive outcomes related to skill retention, motivation, and self-directed learning when using interactive training technologies. As AI continues to evolve, we can expect these systems to deliver more precise feedback, generate custom drills, and even help prevent injuries through predictive analytics.

The Fan: Immersive, Interactive, and Intelligent

Fans, too, have transformed from passive viewers into interactive participants. FC Barcelona's Barça Innovation Hub enables fans to interact with matches through AI-enhanced second-screen apps offering tactical breakdowns, real-time stats, and augmented reality (AR) overlays. In the NFL, the Next Gen Stats platform allows fans to access advanced analytics previously reserved for analysts and scouts. FC Barcelona's transformation of the fan experience through its Barça Innovation Hub is a prime example of how sports organizations are using advanced technology and data strategies to create an immersive, interactive, and intelligent connection with fans worldwide. Here are some detailed real-life facts and insights about this:

Established in 2017, the Barça Innovation Hub is part of FC Barcelona's strategic plan to lead innovation in sports, leveraging the club's vast ecosystem—including over 300 million fans globally, a stadium with nearly 100,000 seats, and thousands of athletes across professional and amateur levels—to develop cutting-edge products that greatly enhance fan engagement and sports performance. It functions as a living lab for innovation, collaborating with startups, universities, and major brands in the sports sector. The Innovation Hub develops AI-enhanced second-screen applications that allow fans to interact with live matches in real time. Features include tactical breakdowns, detailed player stats, AR overlays, and personalized content delivery. This interactivity transforms passive viewing into an active, engaging experience. For example, fans can access match insights that were once limited to analysts, deepening their understanding of game strategies and player performance. Barça Innovation Hub collects and analyzes vast amounts of data to create detailed fan profiles. This enables the club to tailor communication and content based on individual fan preferences, timing, and location. They also use automation technologies like chatbots for multilingual interaction and gamification elements such as Daily Fantasy Sports to further engage fans.

The fan-centric digital strategy targets both global audiences and specific fan segments, aiming to deepen relationships and provide fans with relevant Barça products and services. FC Barcelona is the most followed sports club worldwide, with over 502 million social media followers, around 314 million dedicated fans, and matches viewed by approximately 434 million people across 180+ countries. Their digital ecosystem includes Barça Studios (content creation), Barça Vision (utilizing AR, virtual reality (VR), AI, and blockchain), and Barça Games, which engages younger audiences through platforms like Fortnite and Roblox. The club's new Camp Nou stadium, opening fully in 2026 and accommodating 105,000 spectators, is also being developed with smart stadium technologies to integrate digital and physical fan experiences seamlessly. Data analytics is a core pillar of Barça Innovation Hub, not only enhancing sports performance and health science but also transforming fan engagement through advanced big data techniques. The club employs a Fan Relationship Management (FRM) system to collect and analyze fan data, which informs content, product development, and marketing strategies that resonate personally with fans. Beyond commercial and technological innovation, FC Barcelona views sport as a force for social good. Their foundation and Innovation Hub collaborate on projects focused on social responsibility, including youth engagement and community support initiatives, emphasizing that innovation should positively impact society.

AR apps like NBA AR or Bundesliga Match Facts let fans visualize player heatmaps, ball trajectories, and live win probabilities by simply pointing their phone at the screen. During the Tokyo 2020 Olympics, NHK broadcasted select events in ultra-realistic 3D with robotic camera systems, offering a deeply immersive experience for fans at home. NBA AR app lets fans stand courtside virtually and engage with 360-degree AR portals. While it started primarily as an interactive game where users can "pop-a-shot" with a virtual backboard and court inserted into their real environment, NBA AR (available on iPhone 6s and later) is evolving to deliver richer AR experiences integrating real-time game analytics and immersive views of the court using ARKit technology. Emerging NBA AR features include a 3D tabletop mode, showcased on platforms like Apple Vision Pro, that gives viewers a miniature, real-time 3D diorama of the game with live player positioning, shot trajectories, and puck or ball movement heatmaps. These overlays provide fans with new visual perspectives, such as shot heatmaps or zones of player activity, making game data more interactive and understandable. The AR visualizations extend to live win probabilities and player stats, offering fans situational insights usually reserved for analysts. For instance, AR overlays during broadcasts can highlight player shooting efficiencies with heatmaps or display projected plays, enhancing both entertainment and informed viewing regarding Bundesliga Match Facts, similar AR tools also allow fans to visualize tactical data such as player heatmaps and ball trajectories on their device screens by pointing them at the live broadcast. This application is part of a broader trend in football (soccer) broadcasting to integrate AI and AR-driven tactical insights into fan experiences, enabling fans to access details that enrich their understanding of team strategies and individual player performances.

At the Tokyo 2020 Olympics, NHK went further by broadcasting select events in ultra-realistic 3D using robotic camera systems. This technology captured multiple angles and depths to provide home viewers deeply immersive experiences, simulating being present at the event with spatial depth and perspective shifts that AR and 3D enable. This innovation represents a leap in broadcast technology, offering more lifelike and engaging ways to experience live sports remotely.

Wearables are also entering the fan experience. Devices like Whoop and Oura Ring allow fans to monitor their own fitness while comparing data with their favorite athletes—blurring the line between professional and recreational sport. These include heart rate variability, sleep quality, recovery status, and overall fitness levels. What makes this trend particularly compelling is the ability for fans to compare their own data with that of professional athletes, forging a more personal and interactive connection to the elite performance. This convergence of professional and recreational sport is made possible through several evolving dynamics. Athletes are increasingly open about their biometric and training data, sharing it through official apps or team platforms. This transparency allows fans to go beyond the surface of match-day excitement and access behind-the-scenes insights into how athletes train, rest, and recover. By using the same wearable technology, fans can benchmark their own fitness levels against these shared metrics, which not only deepens their engagement but also adds a layer of authenticity to their connection with the sport.

Motivation is a central aspect of this interaction. When fans align their personal health goals with the performance metrics of their sports heroes, they often find a new sense of drive. Many platforms now integrate elements of gamification—offering challenges, leaderboards, and social groups that turn personal fitness into a shared journey. This transforms fandom into a more participatory experience where striving for better performance becomes part of supporting one's favorite team or player. Teams and leagues are also taking full advantage of the aggregated data from wearables to create more personalized fan experiences. These may include sending tailored motivational messages, fitness tips, or even creating competitions based on fans' activity profiles. Reward systems tied to activity levels—such as steps taken, heart rate zones achieved, or consistent sleep patterns—unlock exclusive digital content, merchandise discounts, or in-game perks, strengthening fan loyalty through real-time, data-driven interactions. Live events are also being enhanced by this technology. Some sports organizations now overlay biosensor data from athletes during live broadcasts, allowing fans to compare their own physiological responses to high-stakes moments in the game. In stadiums, interactive apps are being used to link wearable data to fan engagement tools like in-game leaderboards and performance-based challenges. Clubs such as FC Barcelona and the Los Angeles Dodgers have pioneered these integrations, turning match attendance into an immersive, gamified experience. Yet, as wearable tech becomes more deeply embedded in the fan-athlete relationship, questions around ethics and privacy are becoming more important. Sports organizations and wearable brands are collaborating to ensure that biometric data—both from athletes and fans—is handled responsibly, with transparent consent processes and robust data protection measures in place.

As AI and robotics continue to mature, the distinctions between athlete, coach, and fan are becoming more fluid. Technology enhances intuition with insight, memory with machine learning, and emotion with immersion. It empowers athletes to go further, coaches to see deeper, and fans to feel closer.

This is not the future of sport. It is the new present.

1.1.2. Beyond Performance: Changing the Game Itself

We're not just talking about performance or coaching. AI and robotics are affecting every layer of the sports ecosystem (Laykute, 2020; Glebova et al., 2024). In the realm of recruitment, AI is helping teams and scouts move beyond traditional performance statistics to identify emerging talent with high potential. Algorithms can now analyze thousands of data points—from movement patterns and decision-making under pressure to physiological trends over time—offering a more nuanced, predictive view of an athlete's future capabilities. This allows for more inclusive, data-informed scouting strategies that recognize hidden potential, even in athletes who may not yet stand out by conventional metrics. It redefines what it means to be "talented," opening new doors for players who might otherwise be overlooked.

Meanwhile, in officiating, AI and robotics are reducing human error by offering precise, real-time decision support. Robotic systems and computer vision technologies assist in everything from offside calls in football to line judgments in tennis. While these systems improve accuracy and consistency, they also stir controversy. Questions of fairness, authenticity, and the human element in sports remain central to public discourse. Some fans and professionals express concern that the increasing reliance on machines diminishes the spontaneity and emotional depth that come with human decision-making. As a result, the debate isn't just about efficiency—it's about what we value in sport itself.

Fan engagement, too, is undergoing radical change through AI-driven personalization and interactive technologies. From curated content streams tailored to individual fan preferences to AI-generated avatars that interact with supporters in real time, the fan experience is becoming more immersive and individualized than ever before. These tools do more than deliver information—they build emotional connections, allowing fans to feel closer to teams, players, and the game itself. In many ways, technology is enabling a more intimate and participatory relationship between fans and sport, one that transcends physical presence or scheduled broadcasts.

Even stadium operations are being transformed behind the scenes. Robotic cleaners, AI-managed entry systems, and predictive crowd flow analysis are making sporting events smoother, safer, and more efficient. These technologies are not just cost-saving tools; they reshape the entire atmosphere of attending a live game. For example, AI can anticipate crowd congestion and redirect foot traffic in real time, enhancing both security and spectator comfort. From lighting systems that adjust based on crowd behavior to automated concession services, the "game behind the game" is becoming increasingly intelligent.

And this raises some big questions:

- Can machines understand fairness?
- Can algorithms replace intuition?
- What happens to human emotion when decisions are made by code?

In the past, scouting was rooted in tradition—watching tapes, following instincts, and trusting a coach's "gut." it was traditionally a craft rooted deeply in human judgment and experience rather than data or technology. Scouts and coaches would analyze hours of video tapes, looking for standout moments, skills, and performance during matches and training sessions. This was a time-consuming process reliant on what could be seen rather than measured. Coaches often trusted their "gut feeling" or intuition about a player's potential, character, and fit within a team. This subjective approach depended heavily on personal experience and observation. Talent identification was also based on recommendations from trusted contacts, other scouts, or local coaches. Scouting often had a strong regional or localized focus. Before modern technology, detailed statistical data on player movements or physiological metrics were scarce or nonexistent. Performance evaluation was usually limited to goals, assists, and visible technical skills. Much of scouting was done live, attending matches and practices to see players in action and assess their attitude, work ethic, and social dynamics. This traditional scouting model was inherently limited by subjectivity, bias, and accessibility. It was difficult to evaluate large numbers of athletes or forecast future development accurately. The potential for overlooking promising talent was high, especially if a player's skills didn't immediately stand out in highlight reels or if scouting networks didn't reach certain regions. This past reliance on "watching tapes, following instincts, and trusting a coach's gut" has been the foundation of sports talent discovery for most of the 20th century until the recent infusion of AI and analytics started to transform these practices into more scientific and predictive processes.

Today, AI platforms are helping clubs and federations spot talent based on predictive potential, not just highlight reels. AI platforms are now revolutionizing talent identification by introducing data-driven, predictive analytics that assess a player's potential. Modern AI scouting tools analyze vast datasets including player movement patterns, physiological data, performance metrics across multiple games, and contextual factors like opposition strength. They use machine learning algorithms to identify patterns that predict future success—such as consistency, adaptability, and growth trajectory—which human scouts might miss due to cognitive biases or limited observation time.

This shift toward predictive potential analysis allows clubs and federations to (a) identify promising athletes who may not yet have standout highlight moments but exhibit underlying traits linked to high future performance, (b) make recruitment decisions based on statistical evidence rather than subjective judgment, minimizing expensive transfer mistakes, (c) tailor training and development programs based on predictive insights, focusing resources effectively to maximize player growth, (d) process and analyze data on thousands of players globally in real time, accelerating scouting processes and broadening talent pools. Examples include platforms that aggregate tracking data (GPS, biometric, video) and run AI models that generate player potential scores or performance forecasts. Such systems are increasingly integrated with club scouting departments and federations, complementing traditional methods to create a hybrid, intelligence-led scouting approach.

AiSCOUT, an AI-driven talent identification app used by clubs like Chelsea FC. It analyzes a player's movement, decision-making, and physical aptitude through video submissions and benchmarks them against professional standards. This opens the door for previously overlooked athletes—especially those outside elite academies or major markets—to be discovered based on data-driven insights. AiSCOUT is an innovative, AI-powered talent identification platform that is redefining the way football clubs discover and recruit new players. Trusted by elite organizations such as Chelsea FC, AiSCOUT is designed to make the scouting process more equitable and accessible by harnessing AI to evaluate players based on objective performance data rather than traditional, often exclusive, scouting methods. At its core, AiSCOUT allows aspiring footballers to record and submit videos of themselves performing a series of structured drills or match-specific scenarios. These videos are then analyzed by the app's proprietary AI technology, which examines key aspects of player performance. It assesses movement qualities such as agility, speed, positioning, and coordination, while also evaluating decision-making abilities including tactical awareness and game intelligence. Physical aptitude is measured through parameters like explosiveness, endurance, and strength. What sets AiSCOUT apart is that all submitted data is benchmarked against performance standards derived from professional athletes and academy-level players, ensuring that the evaluation is not only consistent but rigorously aligned with elite expectations.

One of AiSCOUT's most transformative impacts lies in its ability to widen access to scouting opportunities. Players from remote or underserved regions, who might otherwise never be seen by professional scouts, can participate in virtual trials with nothing more than a smartphone. This removes traditional geographic and financial barriers, making the pathway to professional football more inclusive. A compelling example of this is Ben Greenwood, who was discovered via AiSCOUT, earned a trial with Chelsea FC, and eventually signed with AFC Bournemouth, even representing Ireland at the U19 level. Cases like this underscore the platform's ability to uncover overlooked talent and provide life-changing opportunities based solely on merit. For clubs, AiSCOUT offers a powerful complement to traditional scouting. It provides a robust layer of AI-driven insights, enhancing talent evaluation with data that supports more informed decision-making. Chelsea FC, for instance, has integrated AiSCOUT into its official recruitment framework and academy research for a five-year term, demonstrating the club's commitment to blending innovation with legacy scouting systems. The platform is also gaining momentum globally, with dozens of professional clubs and national football federations now using it as part of their scouting pipelines. Notably, AiSCOUT is the only digital scouting technology to have been selected for FIFA's Innovation Programme, affirming its status as a leading-edge solution in football tech.

What makes AiSCOUT especially dynamic is the real-time feedback and guidance it provides. Players receive ratings and comments from coaches and sports scientists, helping them track their development and understand where they stand in comparison to professional standards. Through virtual open trials hosted by top clubs, athletes gain visibility that was once limited to those within privileged networks or elite academies. The platform fosters a more transparent, data-driven ecosystem where talent alone can open doors to professional pathways. Ultimately, AiSCOUT represents a major evolution in football recruitment. By shifting the focus to objective, AI-analyzed performance metrics, it challenges long-standing biases in scouting and creates opportunities for a wider, more diverse pool of players. Its growing network of success stories—over 65 athletes trialed or signed by professional teams—proves that technology can be a powerful tool in democratizing access to the game, elevating both the quality and fairness of football talent identification on a global scale.

In baseball, the have used machine learning models to predict future performance by analyzing minor league data, biomechanics, and even psychological resilience. The Houston Astros have established themselves as trailblazers in Major League Baseball through their forward-thinking application of machine learning to enhance player evaluation and development. Rather than relying solely on traditional scouting or performance stats, the Astros have embraced a deeply analytical model that draws on a wide spectrum of data—from minor league metrics and biomechanical assessments to psychological profiling. This comprehensive, data-rich approach allows them not only to identify emerging talent with greater precision but also to accelerate development and maintain competitive excellence at the highest levels of the game.

One of the foundational components of their system is the analysis of minor league player data. By collecting detailed performance metrics such as batting averages, on-base percentages, isolated power, and WHIP, the Astros feed these inputs into machine learning models trained on years of historical player trajectories. These algorithms aren't just designed to evaluate a player's current performance; they're built to forecast long-term potential, helping decision-makers anticipate, who is likely to succeed at the major league level. This has enabled the organization to make data-informed choices that often uncover undervalued players, ultimately contributing to a more cost-effective and strategically assembled roster. The Astros have also turned to biomechanics as a vital layer of their analytics ecosystem. Using sensor-based technologies like Blast Motion, they gather sophisticated data on swing mechanics, including metrics such as bat path, hand speed, and rotational efficiency. Through machine learning, this biomechanical information is transformed into a detailed understanding of a player's swing profile. Coaches are then equipped to deliver personalized, data-driven feedback, tailoring training interventions to target weaknesses or optimize strengths. This shift from intuition-based observation to quantifiable motion analysis has allowed the Astros to enhance skill acquisition and reduce the developmental timeline for many prospects. Equally groundbreaking is their emphasis on the psychological dimension of performance. The Astros recognize that raw athletic talent alone isn't enough to succeed in the pressure-cooker environment of professional baseball. They conduct behavioral and mental skills assessments to gauge attributes such as resilience, discipline, and mental clarity—qualities that often separate good players from great ones. These psychological insights influence recruitment strategies and player development plans, ensuring the organization prioritizes individuals capable of maintaining composure, focus, and adaptability under high-stress conditions. It's no coincidence that the Astros have repeatedly demonstrated the ability to sustain performance through injuries and setbacks—mental toughness is part of their DNA. All of these innovations converge into a holistic talent evaluation model that has yielded tangible results. The Astros' predictive systems have consistently surfaced undervalued prospects, widening the pool of MLB-ready talent and minimizing traditional scouting biases. By incorporating biomechanics and psychological metrics into their decision-making, they've not only improved player performance and retention but also enhanced the team's resilience during critical stretches, such as playoff runs or injury-heavy seasons. The outcome of this integrated strategy is clear: consistent postseason appearances, a robust farm system, and multiple World Series titles—all underpinned by a data-first philosophy.

Refereeing: Precision, But at What Cost?

From VAR (Video Assistant Referee) in football to Hawk-Eye in tennis and cricket, AI-powered officiating systems have already reduced human error significantly. Semi-automated offside detection, tested at FIFA World Cup Qatar 2022, uses multiple cameras and body-mapping AI to deliver near-instant decisions.

But this new accuracy has sparked debate. Fans and players often question the **authenticity** of decisions made by machines. A perfectly valid call may still feel unfair if it contradicts the human rhythm of the game. Can a robot understand **intentional handball**, or **sportsmanship**? And when a goal is ruled out by a pixel-thin margin, is that justice—or an overreach of precision?

These systems don't just add clarity; they change the flow and feel of the game itself.

Fan Engagement: Interactive, Personalized, and Algorithmically Designed

Today's fans don't just passively watch—they interact, co-create, and even shape the narrative. AI personalizes content streams in real time. Platforms like IBM Watson in Wimbledon generate highlight reels based on player emotion, crowd noise, and in-game drama. At Wimbledon 2025, IBM Watson significantly enhances fan engagement through AI-powered platforms that generate highlight reels and provide real-time insights based on player emotion, crowd noise, and in-game drama.

An interactive AI assistant built on IBM's watsonx Orchestrate and large language models like IBM Granite. Accessible via the official Wimbledon app and website, it answers fan questions during live singles matches—such as "Who has converted more break points?" or "Who is performing better?"—delivering instant, context-aware tennis analysis that reflects the tournament's editorial voice. This interaction enriches the viewing experience by providing deeper understanding beyond traditional commentary. Likelihood to Win Tool enhanced AI-driven feature continuously updates and visualizes a player's win probability in near real-time during matches. It analyzes player stats, momentum shifts, and expert data to dynamically reflect the match's ebb and flow. This probabilistic insight helps fans grasp the drama and changing stakes of every point. IBM's AI automatically generates highlight reels by processing multimodal data—such as player expressions, crowd reactions, and pivotal in-game moments—without human intervention. These highlights have driven millions of additional views across Wimbledon platforms, freeing editors to focus on other content while delivering emotionally resonant recaps that capture the intensity and atmosphere of matches. These technologies are part of IBM's 35-year partnership with Wimbledon, aiming to blend tradition and innovation in a seamless digital fan experience worldwide. By leveraging AI to analyze emotional and contextual cues from matches, IBM Watson personalizes and intensifies how fans experience one of tennis's most prestigious events.

Technical Workings Behind IBM Watson at Wimbledon (Table 2)

1. Multimodal Data Processing

IBM Watson leverages multimodal AI, meaning it processes multiple types of data simultaneously:

- *Video and Image Analysis:* Computer vision models analyze player facial expressions, gestures, and body language to detect emotional intensity, fatigue, or frustration.
- *Audio Analysis:* Speech recognition and sound analysis detect crowd noise levels, cheers, gasps, and commentator excitement.
- *Match Statistics:* Integration with live match data feeds (serve speeds, unforced errors, break points) provides objective inputs about key moments.

These data streams are fused to create a rich contextual understanding of the match's "emotional arc." For example, high crowd excitement combined with a player's tense expression and a crucial break point increases the chance that a moment will be marked as a highlight.

2. Natural Language Processing (NLP) and Large Language Models

- IBM's Match Chat uses large language models (like variants of GPT architectures tailored for sports) combined with Watson Orchestrate and IBM Granite to understand and generate natural language responses.
- It combines real-time tennis statistics with historical and contextual knowledge embedded in the model, enabling it to answer fan queries in an engaging, conversational manner that reflects the Wimbledon brand voice.
- The system continually updates as the match progresses, utilizing fast data pipelines and real-time analytics.

3. Real-Time Predictive Analytics

- The Likelihood to Win tool uses machine learning models trained on historical tennis match data to calculate the probability of each player winning at any given point.
- Models incorporate dynamic factors like current score, momentum swings, player fatigue patterns, and historical head-to-head records.
- Probabilities update in near real-time using streaming data architectures that can process live scoring and point statistics with millisecond latency.

4. Highlight Generation Pipeline

- IBM's AI uses **automated video editing algorithms** to select clips based on the importance and excitement detected via emotional and statistical cues.
- Selected clips are sequenced and trimmed automatically, requiring minimal human input.
- This pipeline dramatically reduces turnaround time for highlights while delivering emotionally powerful recaps that resonate with fans.

5. Scalability and Integration

- The AI systems are deployed on IBM's cloud infrastructure designed for scalability, able to handle millions of concurrent users accessing the Wimbledon app and web platforms globally.
- APIs enable seamless integration into existing Wimbledon digital assets for smooth user experiences across broadcast, streaming, and mobile.

Table 2: Comparison with Other Sports AI Highlights Platforms

Feature	IBM Watson @ Wimbledon	AI Highlights in Other Sports
Multimodal Inputs	Video, audio, live stats, emotion	Often limited to video and stats
Natural Language Interaction	Integrated conversational assistant	Few platforms offer live NLP chatbots
Real-Time Predictive Metrics	Dynamic win probability updated live	Some (e.g., NFL Next Gen Stats) provide live stats but fewer probabilistic insights
Emotional Context Awareness	High—integrates crowd/player emotions	Varies; some focus mainly on data-driven moments
Automation Level	High—near real-time highlight reels	Emerging; varies by sport and provider
Brand-Specific Voice	Yes—tailored responses and tone	Rarely customized

IBM Watson's approach is one of the most advanced in combining deep AI multimodal analysis with natural, interactive fan engagement, going beyond data-driven highlight generation to create a more immersive and emotionally resonant fan experience.

To this end, IBM Watson's platforms at Wimbledon are powered by a blend of advanced AI models, flexible cloud architectures, and leading-edge data engineering that deliver real-time, emotionally aware experiences for fans.

1. Core AI Models and Techniques

- *Computer Vision: Convolutional Neural Networks (CNNs)*
  - CNNs scan frame-by-frame video to detect key events in matches, such as aces, break points, rallies, or player celebrations.
  - These models recognize facial expressions, body language, and gestures, quantifying emotional responses and intense moments.
- *Audio Analysis: Signal Processing and Deep Learning*
  - Recurrent neural networks (RNNs) and convolutional models process soundtracks, isolating patterns associated with crowd noise, applause, or commentator pitch changes.
  - These audio cues are fused with video signals to gauge emotional crescendos—when tension or excitement is at its peak.
- *NLP: Transformer Models*
  - AI chatbots like Wimbledon's Match Chat use transformer architectures (descendants of models like GPT or BERT) specially trained with sports data.
  - These models generate and understand conversational queries, seamlessly integrating real-time stats, historical facts, and editorially approved language.
- *Real-Time Predictive Modeling*
  - Gradient boosted decision trees, logistic regression, and deep learning models analyze match statistics to compute live "Likelihood to Win."
  - These models are trained on years of match data, considering serve percentages, points won, and trends to dynamically update probabilities with each shot.

2. Cloud-Based Data Pipelines and Scalability

- *Stream Processing Frameworks*
  - Technologies such as Apache Kafka, Apache Spark, and IBM Cloud Pak enable continuous ingestion and low-latency processing of score feeds, audio, and video.
  - This infrastructure is essential for real-time updating of stats, highlights, and AI-generated insights for millions of users worldwide.
- *Automated Video Editing and Delivery*
  - The highlight reel pipeline stitches key event clips detected by AI into concise videos, using predefined editorial rules and emotional analysis.
  - These tools deliver highlights across platforms—apps, web, broadcast TV—within seconds of live play.

3. Trends in AI-Driven Fan Engagement

- *Hyper-Personalization*
  - Platforms now tailor content to user preferences, such as favorite players or preferred match types, offering customized highlight reels and notification.
- Expansion Beyond Tennis
  - Similar AI architectures are being used in the NFL, NBA, soccer's Bundesliga, and cricket to drive real-time highlight packages, predictive analytics, and interactive conversational assistants.
- *Cloud-Native and Serverless Innovations*
  - Cloud-native deployments, including serverless functions, auto-scale to meet audience demands during peak moments, optimizing costs and performance.

4. Ethical and Editorial Curation

- Human oversight remains, ensuring highlights meet editorial standards and reflect the unique "voice" and heritage of events like Wimbledon.

IBM's Wimbledon platform is a leading showcase for the marriage of deep learning, scalable cloud, and editorial best practices. Athletic organizations globally are building on these advancements, integrating AI-powered highlights, conversational analysis, and emotional sensing to make fan experiences smarter, more interactive, and more personalized than ever before (Table 3).

Table 3: Example AI/ML Architecture for Wimbledon

Layer	Key Technologies/Models	Purpose
Data Ingestion	API feeds, Kafka, video/audio capture	Ingest live match data, broadcast streams
Data Processing	Spark, Watson AI models, custom pipelines	Real-time data fusion of vision, audio, stats
Analysis/Prediction	CNNs, transformers, gradient boosting	Event, emotion, and outcome modeling
Application/Delivery	IBM Cloud, web/mobile APIs, chatbots	Generate highlights, serve chat responses, update apps

LaLiga's Mediacoach platform offers fans tactical insights once exclusive to coaches, while AR experiences let viewers visualize player stats, sprint speeds, and heatmaps in their own living room. Originally launched in 2010 and evolving continuously since, Mediacoach collects real-time data from perimeter cameras installed around stadiums, capturing player movements at speeds exceeding 25 frames per second. This high-resolution tracking covers thousands of data points, including player positioning, sprint speeds, distance covered, ball trajectories, and tactical patterns.

For coaches and clubs, Mediacoach has long been a vital tool for detailed tactical analysis and match preparation, enabling them to make data-driven decisions about player positioning and strategy. Over 430 staff members across all 42 LaLiga clubs regularly use the platform, which has been credited with helping teams achieve remarkable competitive success, including 16 European titles during the platform's period of influence. In recent seasons, LaLiga has expanded the use of Mediacoach to enhance the fan experience dramatically through immersive augmented reality (AR) and real-time broadcast graphics. Fans watching from home can now see dynamic visualizations such as:

- Player heatmaps showing zones of activity and movement intensity during a match.
- Sprint speed data rendered live, illustrating how fast players move during key moments.
- Ball trajectories and tactical overlays that highlight attacking routes or defensive formations.
- Real-time statistics and predictive insights, such as the probability of a pass leading to a goal or the likelihood of a successful corner kick.

These AR elements allow fans to visualize the game's tactical depth as if they were in the coach's seat or inside a sports analytics lab—right in their living rooms. This represents a democratization of advanced sports intelligence previously restricted to insiders. The system's integration with broadcast partner Mediapro enables these graphics to be deployed centrally and delivered in near real-time to all matches, ensuring a consistent, enriched viewing experience. LaLiga's continuous innovation also includes expanding camera arrays—for example, using up to 37 cameras with super slow-motion and cinematic angles—to complement data analytics with high-fidelity video production. These measures together elevate match storytelling and fan engagement by merging cutting-edge AI, AR, and visual technology. In short, LaLiga's Mediacoach exemplifies a leading-edge fusion of AI-powered tactical insight and immersive AR visualization, making the sport's intricate data accessible and engaging for fans worldwide. It shifts traditional passive viewership into an active, intelligent experience where fans can (a) understand player roles and strategies visually, (b) track athlete's physical performance live (speed, distance, positioning), (c) access predictive analytics in an intuitive, graphical form during broadcasts.

LaLiga's Mediacoach platform represents a cutting-edge fusion of data analytics, broadcast technology, and augmented reality, transforming not only how football is played and analyzed but also how it is experienced by fans. Rather than merely tracking numbers behind the scenes, Mediacoach turns complex tactical insights into visually rich content that enhances viewers' understanding and enjoyment of the game.

A central strength of the platform lies in how it translates raw performance data into intuitive, engaging visuals. During broadcasts, fans are presented with heatmaps that color-code each player's movement across the pitch, instantly revealing positional trends, tactical roles, and shifts in formation. These aren't static summaries—they evolve in real time, helping viewers see, for instance, how a winger adjusts positioning depending on game tempo or how midfield control shifts across halves. Further elevating the broadcast experience are visualizations of physical performance. When a player sprints, on-screen graphics trace their path, display their speed, and place these metrics into context—whether to highlight a critical run or compare athleticism across the squad. Meanwhile, AR overlays demonstrate tactical elements such as ball trajectories, pressing patterns, or defensive setups. These graphics pause and dissect plays as they unfold, offering viewers an inside look at how coaches structure match strategy, and how players execute or respond to those plans. Adding another dimension, predictive visuals such as win probability meters and chance creation percentages are now standard elements of the viewing experience. These real-time insights turn abstract probabilities into accessible visual cues, allowing even casual fans to interpret game momentum and the likely outcomes of specific plays or formations.

Behind the scenes, the technological infrastructure supporting Mediacoach is both robust and precise. More than 16 high-definition cameras surround each LaLiga stadium, capturing over 25 frames per second of every player and the ball. This detailed visual data is continuously streamed into cloud-based systems where advanced AI models process it for key insights—generating everything from movement heatmaps to sprint speed, pass likelihood, and expected goal (xG) metrics. These insights are not only accurate but delivered at a pace fast enough to support real-time integration into broadcasts.

The augmented reality layer is where all this data becomes an immersive experience. Working closely with broadcast partners such as Mediapro, LaLiga overlays tactical graphics and analytical data directly onto the live television feed. Viewers see visual cues like passing lanes highlighted, player tracers activated, or attacking sequences paused and dissected—all with an immediacy and fluidity that brings fans closer to the tactical dimensions of the sport.

Importantly, this isn't confined to television. Fans can engage with the data on mobile apps or second screens, choosing their favorite players to track or revisiting key plays with interactive tools. This fan-facing interactivity is what distinguishes Mediacoach from traditional analytics platforms—it democratizes access to tactical knowledge, offering fans the ability to observe matches through a lens once reserved for analysts and coaches. The technical architecture behind this experience includes four core layers: data capture via in-stadium camera arrays and tracking systems; AI-based processing in the cloud, which analyzes positional and event-based data; real-time visualization with AR overlays and 3D graphics; and delivery through television, streaming services, and interactive apps. This pipeline ensures speed, accuracy, and usability across platforms and audiences.

In Asia, Rakuten's AI-powered avatars let fans attend matches virtually, interacting with other fans via custom avatars that mirror their gestures and reactions. At events like Rakuten Optimism 2023 in Yokohama, attendees could create highly realistic 3D avatars of themselves in less than a minute using advanced body scanning technology equipped with about 40 infrared sensors and cameras. These personalized avatars then interact within virtual sports scenes alongside digital versions of real athletes from teams such as the Tohoku Rakuten Golden Eagles (baseball) and Vissel Kobe (football). Fans can even download videos of their avatars performing iconic sports moments, effectively immersing them as participants rather than spectators. This technology replicates fans' gestures and reactions in real-time, enabling social interaction with other virtual fans in shared digital spaces. The platform behind this, developed with Kyoto-based digital studio 1 to 10 and the 3D avatar tech company VRC, combines rapid 3D scanning, AI-powered animation, and video generation to deliver personalized, immersive experiences. Beyond festivals, Rakuten Mobile has also demonstrated AR and VPS (visual positioning system) technologies in stadiums, enabling spectators to overlay real-time player and match stats using smartphones, which can complement the avatar experience at live events. Such AI-powered virtual attendance lets fans connect deeply with their favorite sports and communities—particularly valuable amid geographic or mobility constraints—blurring the boundary between physical presence and digital engagement (Glebova et al., 2020). This approach integrates well with Rakuten's broader innovation efforts to use AI for personalized fan content, real-time analysis, and enhancing both pre-game and in-game experiences across multiple sports.

Platforms like Sorare and FanCraze combine blockchain, fantasy gaming, and AI to make fans stakeholders in their favorite athletes' careers. Sorare is a leading fantasy sports platform launched in 2018 that uses non-fungible tokens (NFTs) on the Ethereum blockchain to represent collectible digital player cards. Fans buy, sell, and trade these NFT cards to build fantasy teams that compete in leagues where points are awarded based on real-world player performances. Sorare's ecosystem allows users to truly own their digital cards with verifiable scarcity and security on the blockchain—meaning rare cards can hold significant monetary and sentimental value. For example, highly sought-after player cards such as Cristiano Ronaldo's have sold for over 50 ETH (around $100,000+). The platform supports over 300 partnered football clubs and leagues worldwide, including the Premier League, LaLiga, Bundesliga, NBA, and MLB, giving fans access to official licensed content and players. Sorare's use of AI helps enhance the gameplay by dynamically scoring teams weekly based on real player statistics, fostering a data-driven fantasy competition. Importantly, Sorare recently introduced a "Cash Wallet" feature that allows users to transact in fiat currency without needing to handle cryptocurrency directly, lowering barriers for mainstream sports fans to participate. FanCraze operates in a similar space, blending blockchain, fantasy sports, and fan engagement, though it is somewhat less prominent than Sorare in reach and scale. FanCraze focuses on allowing fans to participate in fantasy leagues and collectible card trading while leveraging blockchain to verify ownership and enable peer-to-peer trading. The platform aims to give fans a stake in athletes' careers by tying game outcomes and collectibles with real-world sports data. However, detailed specifics on AI integration and scale compared to Sorare are more limited publicly. Both platforms reflect a growing trend where sports fans evolve from passive consumers to active participants and stakeholders by leveraging blockchain for digital collectibles, AI for smart gaming mechanics, and fantasy sports as the engagement framework.

Stadium Operations: Smart, Safe, and Silent

Behind the scenes, AI and robotics are running the show—quietly but powerfully. During the pandemic, Japanese stadiums used disinfecting robots and thermal imaging AI to maintain public health standards.

Smart stadiums like Tottenham Hotspur Stadium in London are equipped with AI-based crowd flow systems, predictive maintenance software, and dynamic pricing algorithms. AI manages not just parking and concessions but energy consumption, helping reduce the venue's environmental impact. Tottenham Hotspur Stadium in London embodies the future of venue management by integrating AI-driven technologies to optimize operations, enhance fan experience, and minimize environmental impact.

AI-Based Crowd Flow and Safety

The stadium uses an integrated network of more than 700 CCTV cameras and advanced surveillance systems, allowing real-time monitoring of crowd movement through AI-based analytics. Mobile ticketing and contactless entry eliminate bottlenecks at gates, while digital wayfinding and crowd management tools provide dynamic updates to staff and fans. AI-driven monitoring ensures rapid incident response, boosts safety, and helps manage the flow of more than 62,000 visitors efficiently.

Predictive Maintenance and Operational Reliability

Tottenham Hotspur partners with Schneider Electric to deploy the EcoStruxure platform, which offers real-time monitoring and predictive maintenance across all stadium systems. The system checks critical infrastructure (like electrical supply, HVAC, and lighting) every five minutes—a total of 60,000 automated checks per hour. Data from IoT sensors is sent to a remote field services bureau and analyzed with AI, enabling early fault detection and preventive interventions that reduce downtime and extend equipment life. Robotic cleaning technologies further automate and streamline maintenance tasks.

Dynamic Pricing Algorithms

The club employs dynamic pricing for tickets and concessions, adjusting prices in real time based on factors such as demand, match significance, and seat location. Complex algorithms analyze purchase patterns and inventory, maximizing attendance and revenue while offering flexibility for fans. These systems ensure that the stadium is almost always full, delivering strong atmosphere and commercial value.

AI Management of Parking, Concessions, and Connectivity

All food and beverage outlets are cashless, ensuring smooth and speedy service for visitors. Parking and in-stadium navigation are optimized using digital sensors, mobile apps, and automated guidance systems, helping reduce congestion and waiting times. Under-seat Wi-Fi access points provide broad, high-speed connectivity for every attendee, supporting app-based services, live stats, and interactive fan experiences.

Energy Consumption and Environmental Sustainability

Schneider Electric's EcoStruxure system actively manages the stadium's energy consumption, using predictive analytics to optimize lighting, heating, and cooling according to occupancy and weather forecasts. Continuous monitoring cuts waste and adjusts energy use in response to real-time stadium needs. The stadium's energy management strategy contributes to reduced carbon emissions, operational cost savings, and delivers on Tottenham Hotspur's commitment to environmental sustainability. The stadium is certified to international standards for sustainable event management (ISO 20121), highlighting its environmental leadership

The Mercedes-Benz Stadium in Atlanta uses AI for real-time crowd sentiment analysis, allowing staff to respond quickly to incidents, adjust music or lighting, and even predict post-game congestion patterns. The stadium, managed by Arthur M. Blank Sports and Entertainment (AMBSE), integrates AI-powered tools that analyze various forms of fan feedback, including voice interactions, social media sentiment, and on-site behavior, allowing staff to quickly detect and respond to incidents, adjust environmental factors such as music and lighting, and predict post-game congestion patterns to optimize crowd flow. AMBSE has deployed Solgari's AI-powered platform, integrated into Microsoft's Azure environment, to give customer service agents a unified view of fan interactions, including real-time sentiment analysis from calls and messages. This allows a faster, personalized response tailored to fan emotions and needs during events. Real-time insights from AI-driven sentiment and behavior analytics enable stadium staff to adapt the atmosphere dynamically—such as changing music playlists or lighting intensity—to enhance fan mood and safety. AI models analyze crowd movement data collected via Wi-Fi, proximity beacons, and video feeds to forecast congestion levels in exits and transit points after events. This predictive capability helps staff optimize crowd dispersal strategies, improving safety and reducing wait times. The stadium features voice-command AI interfaces and augmented reality experiences (e.g., MBUX technology) that further enrich fan engagement, allowing personalized interaction and immersive experiences with Atlanta Falcons and Atlanta United players. Through comprehensive mobile data tracking and AI insights, the stadium continuously monitors live fan activity across ticketing, concessions, and social engagement to improve both operational efficiency and marketing effectiveness.

But With Great Innovation Comes Deep Questions

As technology permeates the soul of sport, we face urgent philosophical and ethical dilemmas:

- **Can machines understand fairness?**
  Algorithms are designed to optimize, but fairness is a deeply human concept. Is fairness just accuracy? Or does it include empathy, context, and spirit?
- **Can algorithms replace intuition?**
  When AI suggests a substitution or lineup, does a coach trust the model—or their gut? And what happens when both are right in different ways?

- **What happens to human emotion when decisions are made by code?**
  A thrilling goal ruled out by a few pixels. A record broken with help from predictive pacing tech. When machines govern the margins, does joy become diminished—or more secure?

Sport has always been about more than performance. It's about drama, identity, emotion, and community. As AI and robotics infiltrate deeper layers of the ecosystem, the challenge isn't just technical—it's cultural, emotional, and existential.

The question is not just how far the technology can go, but how much of sport's soul we choose to carry forward with it.

1.1.3. Sport as a Mirror of Society

Sport has always mirrored the big shifts in society (Glebova and Desbordes, 2021)—gender equality, global politics, commercialism, and now... AI. If we want to understand how society is grappling with AI, look at what's happening in sports. It's a microcosm, a testing ground, and a global stage all rolled into one.

To dive into AI and robotics in sports is to explore how technology is influencing not just how we play—but who we are when we play.

This is a story about science, yes. But it's also a story about people. About decisions, consequences, dreams, and dilemmas.

And just like the greatest games ever played, this story is still unfolding.

What unfolds is a complex interplay between human aspiration and machine augmentation. AI and robotics are not merely tools that enhance athletic performance or optimize training regimes; they are reshaping the ontological boundaries of sport itself (Breivik, 2020). These technologies challenge deeply embedded notions of authenticity, fairness, and even what it means to be an "athlete." In doing so, they prompt an urgent reexamination of the values and identities that sport has historically celebrated: effort, resilience, skill, and the unpredictability of human performance (Bertolini and Episcopo, 2022).

At the heart of this transformation is a paradox. While AI and robotics offer unprecedented precision, consistency, and data-driven insights, they also raise critical questions about spontaneity and human error—elements long considered essential to the drama and spirit of sport (Glebova and Madsen, 2024). For instance, when robotic systems are used to officiate games, removing human referees from the equation, they may reduce bias and error but at the potential cost of reducing the game's emotional complexity. Similarly, when AI algorithms prescribe optimal training loads and tactical decisions, they may eclipse the role of intuition, creativity, and in-the-moment judgment that define elite athleticism.

The story is also socio-political. The deployment of AI-driven scouting systems or robotic training partners does not occur in a vacuum—it reflects broader inequities in access to technology (Glebova et al., 2023b). Wealthier clubs and nations are more likely to benefit from cutting-edge tools, thus widening the gap between resource-rich and resource-poor competitors. This technocentric stratification risks undermining the ideal of a level playing field, which remains a foundational ethos of modern sport.

Moreover, the growing reliance on machine intelligence introduces new dilemmas related to surveillance, autonomy, and agency (Kosta, 2022). Athletes are increasingly embedded in systems of continuous biometric monitoring, where every movement, heartbeat, and neural signal can be quantified and analyzed. While such data can prevent injury and enhance performance, it also exposes athletes to a regime of hypervisibility that may erode their privacy and psychological well-being. The athlete becomes a cyborg subject: part biological performer, part data-producing node (Barker and Parker, 2024).

Yet, amid these tensions lies potential. AI and robotics can be democratizing forces when used ethically and inclusively. They can empower athletes with disabilities, improve safety protocols, and enable personalized coaching that was once reserved for the elite. They can bring fans closer to the action through immersive technologies and help governing bodies detect fraud and enhance integrity. In these capacities, technology does not displace the human—it amplifies it.

Thus, this evolving narrative of AI and robotics in sport is not one of technological determinism, but of human agency entangled with algorithmic logic. It is a story where each innovation presents a choice, and each choice reflects deeper questions about the kind of future we want for sport—and for ourselves.

So, why dive into AI and robotics in sports?

Because the next chapter of sport isn't just about who wins—it's about how we play the game.

Sport has always been more than just a game. It's been a mirror to society, reflecting our triumphs, tensions, values, and transformations. From the fight for gender equality on the pitch to protests for racial justice on the podium, sport has consistently acted as a global stage for the biggest conversations of our time.

Now, that stage is being illuminated by a new kind of spotlight: AI and robotics.

If you want to understand how society is grappling with the promises and perils of AI, look at sports. Here, decisions are made in split seconds. Emotions run high. Stakes are personal and public. It's where data meets drama, and where every technological advancement must contend with deep-rooted traditions and the human spirit.

A Microcosm, A Testing Ground, A Global Arena

In sports, we see machine-human interaction not just as a technical process, but as a social experiment—an open debate about trust, authenticity, and fairness. Should a referee be replaced by an algorithm? Should a scout trust a neural network over their own eyes? Should a robot that trains with athletes be considered part of the team?

These are not just questions for coders or coaches. They're questions for all of us.

Sport, in this context, becomes a laboratory of ethics, a testing ground for public acceptance, and a barometer of cultural change. If fans won't accept a robotic referee's decision in a World Cup final, what does that say about our readiness for algorithmic judgment in a courtroom, classroom, or clinic?

Not Just How We Play, But Who We Are When We Play

To explore AI and robotics in sport is to confront some of the most profound questions of the 21st century:

- What does it mean to compete?
- Where do we draw the line between enhancement and interference?
- How do we define human excellence in a world increasingly mediated by machines?

This isn't just a story about science or engineering. It's a story about people. About how athletes, coaches, fans, and entire communities navigate change—sometimes embracing it, sometimes resisting it, but always grappling with its implications.

It's about the tension between tradition and transformation, emotion and efficiency, instinct and intelligence.

It's about dreams and dilemmas, played out on a field, in a ring, across a court.

The Game is Still Being Written

Like the greatest matches ever played, the story of AI and robotics in sport is still unfolding. There's no clear winner yet. Just endless possibilities.

We're watching—and shaping—a new era where technology doesn't just assist the game; it redefines it. And how we respond to that will echo far beyond stadiums and scoreboards.

1.2. Building the Solid Theoretical Background

The term **Artificial Intelligence** (AI) was coined in 1956, but its essence goes back further—back to ancient myths of mechanical beings with minds of their own. In modern terms, AI refers to the ability of machines to perform tasks that normally require human intelligence. This includes learning, reasoning, recognizing patterns, understanding language, and even making decisions.

At its core, AI is not about creating robots that "think" like humans—it's about enabling systems to solve problems, adapt to new information, and automate decisions at scale.

In sport, AI shows up in many ways, including predictive models that forecast player injuries, video analysis tools that recognize patterns in gameplay, chatbots that simulate fan interactions, AI-enhanced scouting systems that discover future stars…

AI is a collection of tools, methods, and philosophies, constantly evolving.

1.2.1. Robotics: Beyond the Sci-Fi

In the world of sports, robotics is divers.

A robot, broadly speaking, is a machine capable of carrying out a complex task automatically. It may be physical, like a robotic assistant helping with rehabilitation, or digital, like an AI-driven avatar interacting with fans in virtual environments.

Robot Classification and Taxonomy

1. Mechanical Structure (Morphology)

- *Cartesian Robots:* Used in pick-and-place tasks or 3D printing; e.g., 3-axis CNC machine.
- *SCARA Robots*: Widely found in assembly lines requiring fast, precise lateral movements, such as electronics manufacturing.
- *Articulated Robots:* Common in car manufacturing (e.g., ABB IRB and KUKA arms), capable of flexible movement.
- *Parallel (Delta) Robots:* Efficient for quick packaging and sorting in food or pharmaceuticals.
- *Cylindrical Robots:* Used for welding and material handling; combine linear and rotary movements.

2. Control System Examples

- *Open-Loop:* Basic conveyor belt robots that follow timed cycles.
- *Closed-Loop:* Industrial arms using feedback sensors to ensure precision, like robotic welders.
- *Hybrid:* Automated guided vehicles (AGVs) in warehouses, blending simple instructions with feedback from the environment.

3. Function or Sector In-Depth

- *Industrial Robots:* Welding, painting, assembly, material handling; e.g., FANUC robot arms in automotive factories.
- *Service Robots:* Hospital delivery robots (Aethon TUG), hotel room service robots.
- *Military Robots:* Drones, bomb-disposal robots (e.g., Northrop Grumman's Andros).
- *Medical Robots:* Da Vinci surgical robot, exoskeletons for rehabilitation.
- *Educational Robots:* LEGO Mindstorms kits for schools and STEM competitions.
- *Domestic Robots:* iRobot Roomba vacuum, window-cleaning robots.
- *Autonomous Mobile Robots (AMRs):* Amazon warehouse robots navigating inventory aisles.
- *Cobots:* Universal Robots' collaborative arms working directly beside humans on production lines.

4. Behavior or Autonomy

- *Manual Handling:* Jib cranes or simple exoskeletons that amplify but do not automate movement.
- *Fixed Sequence:* Automated bottling lines—exact, unchanging sequences.
- *Variable Sequence:* Robots that adjust for different packaging sizes or custom assembly.
- *Playback Robots:* Painting robots taught by demonstration, replicating paths.
- *Numerical Control:* CNC machines executing G-code for part fabrication.
- *Intelligent Robots:* Autonomous vehicles identifying and adapting to road conditions, or warehouse AGVs rerouting in real time.

5. Detailed Taxonomic Example (Table 4)

Table 4: Detailed Taxonomic Example

Taxonomic Rank	Example Robot	Description
Kingdom	Autonomous System	Broad robot classification
Phylum	Industrial Robot	Used in manufacturing
Class	Robotic Arm	Manipulator type
Order	Serial Robot	Linked joints in series
Family	SCARA Robot	Selective Compliance Assembly Robot Arm
Genus	Industrial SCARA Robot	For precise assembly
Species	Epson G6 SCARA	Specific commercial model

Some robots today integrate several classification aspects (e.g., collaborative articulated cobots for medical surgery with feedback and AI-based autonomy). The taxonomy outlined helps map the evolution, structure, and purpose of each type, improving clarity—from basic task automation to advanced, environment-adaptive robots (Table 5).

Table 5: Types of Robots

Mechanical Type	Sector Example	Autonomy Example	Practical Use
Articulated Arm	Industrial welding robot	Closed-loop	Automotive paint shop
SCARA	Electronics assembly robot	Variable sequence	Printed circuit board placement
Delta (Parallel)	Food packaging robot	Intelligent	High-speed sorting of pastries
Mobile Platform	Autonomous warehouse robot	Autonomous mobile	Amazon storage/ retrieval
Humanoid	Research and development robot	Playback/Intelligent	Toyota's T-HR3 assisting humans

Modern sport robotics includes (but not limited to):

- Ball-collecting bots on practice courts.
- Exoskeletons used in injury recovery.
- Robots that perform precision movements (e.g., for training drills).
- Semi-autonomous camera systems following athletes in real time.

The line between AI and robotics is increasingly blurred—many robots use AI to make decisions and learn over time. And that's where things get interesting.

1.2.2. Theories and Concepts Behind the Tech

There are key theoretical frameworks that help us understand the relationship between technology and human activity—especially in performance settings like sport.

1. **Technological Determinism**

   This theory suggests that technology shapes society, not the other way around (Schut and Glebova, 2022). Applied to sport, it asks: Are athletes changing because of technology? Or is sport evolving to adapt to technology?

   Technological determinism is a theoretical framework suggesting that technology is the primary driving force shaping society and culture, rather than society shaping technology. It posits that technology advances autonomously and inevitably, with profound and often irreversible effects on social structures, human behavior, and institutions.

   Applied to sport, technological determinism prompts the question of whether athletes are changing because of technological innovations or if the sport itself evolves in response to technology. In this context, technology can influence athletic performance directly (e.g., through improved equipment or training tools) and shape how sports are played, judged, and experienced. This often leads to debates over fairness, ethics, and the essence of human skill in sport, as technology can create greater performance opportunities but also raise concerns about alienating the human element of competition. Thus, technological determinism in sport highlights the idea that technology drives changes in athlete capabilities and sport practices, sometimes autonomously from social or cultural factors. However, this view contrasts with social constructivist perspectives that emphasize society's role in shaping technology and its uses.

2. **Sociomateriality**

   This idea views technology and humans not as separate entities, but as deeply entangled (Leonardi, 2012; Mutch, 2013). A smart wearable isn't just a device; it becomes part of how an athlete trains, thinks, and even feels. It's not just a tool—it's part of the practice. So, sociomateriality is a theoretical framework that emphasizes the inseparable entanglement of technology and humans, rejecting the idea that they are independent or separable entities. In the context of sport, this means that technologies like smart wearables are not merely neutral tools but become integral to athletes' practices, influencing how they train, make decisions, and experience their own bodies and performance.

Rather than viewing technology as external or just an aid, sociomateriality considers how human and technological elements are co-constitutive—they mutually shape and are shaped through their interactions over time. For example, a smart wearable embeds itself in an athlete's routine, providing data that affects not only physical training but cognitive and emotional aspects such as motivation, confidence, and awareness. Thus, technology and human activity form a dynamic entangled system. This approach contrasts with technological determinism, which sees technology as driving change autonomously, and with purely social constructivist views that focus mainly on human agency shaping technology. Sociomateriality bridges those perspectives by highlighting the materiality of technology as active and relational, inseparable from human practices and meanings. In sport performance settings, this means analyzing how technologies and athletes co-evolve in practice, how technology redefines what it means to train or compete, and how new forms of embodiment and skill emerge from this entanglement.

3. **Human-Machine Interaction (HMI)**

   This field studies how people engage with intelligent systems (Agah, 2000). In sport, it can include how coaches trust—or resist—AI recommendations, or how players emotionally respond to robotic feedback (Glebova and Desbordes, 2022; Glebova et al., 2023a). It studies these interactions in performance, training, and decision-making contexts, highlighting the complex and dynamic relationship between human users and technological systems designed to assist or augment sport practices.

4. **Ethics of Automation**

   While not a traditional "theory," ethical considerations—privacy (Wu, 2024), bias, transparency, fairness—are now central to discussions about AI in all industries, especially one as emotionally charged and public as sports. The ethics of automation in sport emphasizes protecting athlete rights, fairness, transparency, and accountability while ensuring human agency in AI's use, particularly given the scale of data collection and the high stakes involved in competitive sports. Continuous ethical oversight and updated governance frameworks are vital to responsibly harness AI's benefits without undermining integrity or participant wellbeing.

5. **Social Constructivism (SCOT—Social Construction of Technology)**

   This view stresses that social groups and cultural values shape technology's development and use (Pinch, 2012). In sport, decisions about which technologies get accepted (like VAR in soccer) depend on social negotiations, power dynamics, and cultural acceptance rather than pure technological capability. Social Constructivism, specifically the SCOT framework, emphasizes that technology's development and adoption are not determined solely by technical features but are significantly shaped by social groups, cultural values, and power relations. In the context of sport, this means that technologies such as VAR in soccer are accepted, modified, or rejected based on social negotiations among stakeholders like players, coaches, officials, fans, and sporting bodies.

Key aspects of SCOT in sport include the following:

- *Social Groups as Interpretive Communities:* Different groups hold varying interpretations and interests regarding a technology. For example, referees may value VAR for accuracy, while fans or players might resist it fearing it disrupts the flow of the game or the traditional human element.
- *Negotiation and Meaning-Making:* The acceptance of technologies involves ongoing negotiations over their meaning, appropriateness, and practical application. Those with more influence or power within sport governing structures often shape these negotiations.
- *Cultural and Contextual Influences:* Broader cultural factors, such as attitudes toward fairness, tradition, or innovation, affect whether a technology is embraced. VAR's global rollout has encountered cultural resistance in some regions, reflecting these dynamics.
- *Non-Deterministic View:* Unlike technological determinism, SCOT argues that technology is malleable and its adoption depends on collective human choices, not technological inevitability.

6. Actor-Network Theory (ANT)

ANT highlights how humans (athletes, coaches, officials) and non-humans (equipment, software) form networks in which each actor influences outcomes. Here, technology and humans co-construct sporting outcomes—technology is neither purely deterministic nor passive (Kerr, 2016).

ANT offers a compelling lens for understanding the evolving relationship between sport and technology. Rather than viewing technology as a passive tool or a deterministic force, ANT positions both humans (such as athletes, coaches, and officials) and non-humans (including equipment, software, and analytics systems) as equally important "actors" in networks that shape the production and experience of sport.

At the core of ANT is the principle of symmetry: the idea that humans and technologies contribute equally to the outcomes of sporting practices. This challenges traditional distinctions between the social and the technical, instead emphasizing how practices emerge from networks of interaction between diverse elements. For example, a GPS tracking device used in training does not merely collect data—it becomes a central actor in how performance is measured, understood, and even how training regimes are designed.

These actor-networks are inherently complex. Technologies in sport—whether GPS units, video replay systems, or doping detection methods—operate within broader assemblages involving athletes, coaches, data analysts, media, governing bodies, and even fans. Their introduction is never straightforward; it involves what ANT calls enrolment and translation, meaning that multiple stakeholders must be brought into alignment, and the technology's role must be negotiated within existing practices.

A telling example is the use of GPS tracking in the Australian Football League (AFL). Far from being a neutral innovation, the technology created a new network of actors: athletes wearing the devices, coaches interpreting the data, analysts processing metrics, and ethical debates around privacy and surveillance. The GPS units had agency in shaping how players trained, how strategies were formulated, and how performance was assessed—demonstrating ANT's idea that technologies can generate unintended consequences and actively reshape the sporting landscape.

Other applications of ANT in sport include the integration of video technologies in gymnastics, which allow performances to circulate beyond the live event, altering how routines are judged and remembered. Similarly, officiating systems like Hawk-Eye in tennis or VAR in football form hybrid networks where human decision-making and technological input coalesce—transforming not only rule enforcement but also how legitimacy and fairness are perceived by players and spectators alike.

As Roslyn Kerr's *Sport and Technology: An Actor-Network Theory Perspective* (2016) illustrates through multiple case studies, ANT helps move beyond simplistic narratives of technology as either savior or threat. Instead, it emphasizes that sporting realities are co-produced through dynamic, negotiated, and evolving interactions between human and non-human actors. By doing so, ANT offers a more nuanced understanding of how innovation, resistance, adaptation, and transformation unfold in the world of sport.

7. **Critical Theory**

Focused on power relations, critical perspectives analyze how technology can reinforce inequalities (e.g., access to advanced training tech) or challenge traditional norms in sport (gender, nationality, socio-economic status). At its core, this perspective interrogates how power relations influence who benefits from sport technologies and how their implementation might either reinforce or challenge existing social inequalities. Rather than treating technology as a neutral or purely performance-enhancing tool, Critical Theory situates it within broader systems of economic, political, and cultural domination (Giulianotti and Thiel, 2023). Drawing from the Frankfurt School tradition, it views sport technology as shaped by capitalist imperatives and institutional power structures. This orientation draws attention to the ways in which technological access is often stratified along lines of gender, nationality, and socio-economic status. Elite athletes and wealthy nations typically enjoy disproportionate access to advanced technologies—such as biomechanical sensors, AI-driven analytics, or custom performance gear—while grassroots or underfunded competitors are left behind, deepening existing inequities.Moreover, technology in sport is frequently entangled with dominant norms and ideologies. For instance, performance measurement tools and standards are often gendered in ways that disadvantage female athletes, while media technologies may reinforce traditional narratives of national superiority or racial stereotyping. At the same time, critical theorists highlight technology's potential to challenge such norms. Devices that track and amplify female athletic performance, or platforms that democratize access to coaching and training, represent instances where technological tools might be reoriented toward progressive and inclusive ends. Ethical concerns are also central to critical inquiries into sport technology. Issues such as privacy, data ownership, algorithmic bias, and athlete surveillance underscore the need for transparency and participatory governance in how technologies are designed and deployed. For critical theorists, the question is not only whether a technology is effective, but also whose interests it serves, who gets to decide its uses, and with what social consequences.

While critical theory is often associated with critique, it also offers a transformational vision. Sport technologies, if consciously designed and governed with equity in mind, can become instruments for emancipation rather than domination. This might involve rethinking funding models to ensure broader access, challenging commercial logics that prioritize profit over athlete well-being, or creating inclusive innovation ecosystems that amplify marginalized voices in sport.

Examples that illustrate this approach include the unequal distribution of smart wearables between high-income and low-income athletes, the gendered impacts of performance-tracking standards, and the dominance of commercial agendas in the development of fan-engagement technologies that often overlook ethical implications. Each case demonstrates that technology is not merely technical—it is deeply political and social, requiring critical reflection and deliberate action to align its development with values of justice, inclusion, and human dignity.

8. **Postphenomenology**

This approach examines how technology mediates human experiences—for example, how wearable tech changes an athlete's perception of their own body or how virtual reality reshapes training experiences (Ritter, 2021). Rooted in phenomenology (Glebova et al., 2023c) but moving beyond its classical formulations, postphenomenology emphasizes that technologies are not external instruments acting on a stable human subject; rather, they actively co-constitute how humans perceive, interpret, and inhabit their environments (Mykhailov and Liberati, 2023).

In the context of sport, postphenomenology explores how athletes' relationships with their bodies, training routines, and competitive environments are mediated through technological artifacts. For example, wearable devices such as heart rate monitors, GPS trackers, or motion sensors do more than collect data—they alter how athletes experience exertion, fatigue, and performance. When an athlete begins to train based on biometric feedback, their sense of bodily limits is no longer solely intuitive or embodied; it becomes hybridized with external data streams. The body becomes not just something one feels, but something one reads and interprets through screens and metrics. Similarly, VR and AR systems in sport training do not merely simulate scenarios for practice—they construct new experiential realities. A goalkeeper training with VR may come to understand the timing of penalty shots not only through embodied practice, but through mediated perception shaped by immersive visual and auditory cues. The athlete's sense of space, anticipation, and reaction becomes restructured through the interface.

Postphenomenology also draws attention to the idea of technological multistability—the notion that any given technology can be experienced and interpreted in multiple ways depending on context, intention, and cultural framing. A fitness tracker may serve as a motivational companion for one athlete, a tool of surveillance for another, or a source of anxiety for someone obsessively monitoring performance. These differences highlight the interpretive flexibility of technological mediation and the centrality of human-technology-world relations. Moreover, postphenomenology is concerned with embodiment relations, where technologies become transparent extensions of the body (e.g., a cyclist's aerodynamic helmet or a swimmer's suit that feels "like skin"), and hermeneutic relations, where technologies interpret or visualize phenomena otherwise inaccessible to human perception (e.g., blood lactate data or heat maps of player movement). Each of these relations shapes how sport is practiced, understood, and experienced. This approach invites us to rethink sport technology not merely as enhancement or efficiency tools, but as co-creators of meaning, subjectivity, and embodied knowledge. It helps explain why some athletes resist certain technologies—not because they reject innovation per se, but because such tools fundamentally reconfigure their lived experience in ways that may feel alienating, unnatural, or overly instrumental.

1.2.3. Why This Matters in Sport

You may wonder—why not just focus on cool gadgets and AI tricks? Why dig into theory?

Because without a theoretical lens, we risk seeing AI and robotics as mere novelty or magic. With a foundation, we can ask deeper questions:

- What kind of knowledge does AI produce—and what does it miss?
- Who benefits from robotics in sports, and who might be left out?
- How do these technologies shape the very meaning of competition, fairness, and human performance?

AI in sports, for example. It can enhance training, reduce injury risks, and provide real-time analytics. But theory compels us to ask: what kind of knowledge is being prioritized? Is it only quantifiable metrics—speed, force, trajectory? What about tacit, intuitive, emotional, or relational forms of knowledge that athletes draw upon? When AI becomes the arbiter of performance, certain ways of knowing the body—particularly those less easily measured—may be devalued or erased.

Who benefits from robotics in sports—and who might be left out? This question moves us from tech hype into questions of equity. Elite teams with more funding can afford biomechanical exosuits, real-time neural feedback systems, and AI-driven strategy models. But what about youth leagues, underfunded schools, or athletes from marginalized communities? Theory helps expose the political economy of technology: how power, access, and inequality are woven into its very deployment.

Moreover, these technologies are not neutral. They shape the very meaning of competition, fairness, and human performance. Consider debates around prosthetics and "cyborg" athletes—at what point does assistive technology become an unfair advantage? Or think about biometric tracking: if an AI coach knows your stress levels, hydration, and sleep cycle, are you still competing against others, or against your own algorithm-optimized potential? Theory helps us parse such questions—not to reject innovation, but to make its stakes visible.

We need theory not to drain the wonder from AI and robotics, but to ground that wonder in ethical, philosophical, and social reflection. Without it, we are spectators dazzled by spectacle. With it, we become critical participants—able to imagine technologies not just as tools, but as forces shaping who we are, how we play, and what we value.

1.2.4. How Can We Ensure That the Future of Sport—Powered by Machines—is Still Fundamentally Human?

Understanding the Key Terms—and How They Interact

To truly follow the trajectory of AI and robotics in sport, we need a clear understanding of the core concepts—and how they differ or overlap. Let's unpack the big terms and important distinctions, and then connect them back to sport (Figure 1).

A. Artificial Intelligence vs. Machine Learning vs. Deep Learning

These three terms are often used interchangeably, but they're not quite the same. Think of them as layers in a Russian nesting doll:

- *Artificial Intelligence* (*AI*) is the broadest concept: any machine that mimics human cognitive functions like reasoning, learning, or decision-making. AI can be symbolic (rule-based) or adaptive (data-driven).
- *Machine Learning* (*ML*) is a subset of AI where systems learn from data rather than being explicitly programmed. ML allows computers to improve performance based on experience—like a tennis AI that gets better at predicting serves the more footage it sees.
- *Deep Learning* (*DL*) is a subset of machine learning that uses neural networks inspired by the human brain. Deep learning powers things like pose detection, gesture recognition, and voice interaction—tools increasingly used in smart gyms and AR coaching.

📌 **In Sport:**

- AI = a video assistant referee system
- ML = the algorithm that learns to detect fouls
- DL = the neural network that classifies player body movements in real time

AI is the overall system that acts smart—like a video assistant referee helping make calls. ML is a part of AI that improves by learning from data—like an algorithm trained to recognize fouls by analyzing past games. DL goes even deeper; it uses complex, layered neural networks to spot subtle patterns—like analyzing real-time body movements to classify actions with high precision. In short: AI is the broad goal of smart decision-making, ML is how systems learn from experience, and DL is the most advanced way of learning, mimicking the brain to handle complex tasks like real-time motion analysis.

B. Automation vs. Autonomy

Another critical contrast: automation is not the same as autonomy.

- Automation means pre-programmed actions that follow a fixed set of rules. Think of a robotic ball launcher that shoots at set speeds and angles.
- Autonomy implies that the system can make decisions on its own based on its environment or new data—like a robot that adjusts its passes based on player position and weather conditions.

📌 **In Sport:**

An automated treadmill maintains a set pace.

An autonomous treadmill adjusts speed based on your heart rate and form in real time.

C. Robotics vs. AI: Complementary, Not Competing

As we mentioned, robotics is about physical systems that act in the world. AI is about decision-making, pattern recognition, and learning. The magic happens when they work together.

A robot without AI follows commands blindly. AI without a robotic body might live entirely in a digital world. But together? They create adaptive, intelligent agents that can train, assist, or even challenge athletes.

📌 **In Sport:**

A robot referee may use AI to recognize offside positions and make real-time rulings.

A training robot sparring with a boxer uses both physical sensors (robotics) and pattern prediction (AI) to offer reactive, strategic practice.

D. Smart Systems vs. Intelligent Agents

Let's get a bit more conceptual.

- A smart system responds efficiently to user inputs—like a wearable that tracks steps and shows data.
- An intelligent agent not only collects data but also makes decisions or suggestions—like a training AI that tells a coach when to pull an athlete based on fatigue patterns.

📌 **In Sport:**

A smart system says: "You ran 8.2 km."

An intelligent agent says: "*Y*ou should rest tomorrow; your performance curve is dipping."

E. Embodied AI: When Intelligence Has a Body

One of the most exciting developments in sport is the rise of embodied AI—where learning algorithms are integrated with physical systems, allowing them to interact with and learn from the world.

This is key in sport, where movement, space, and touch matter. An embodied AI robot goalie learns not just from visual data but from actual saves and movements. It learns the physics of sport in a more human-like way.

📌 **In Sport:**

Embodied AI is the foundation for humanoid robots playing exhibition matches or robotic arms assisting with disabled athlete training.

```
ARTIFICIAL INTELLIGENCE
│
├── Machine Learning
│   └── Deep Learning
│
├── Smart Systems       → Data-driven responses
├── Intelligent Agents  → Decision-making entities
└── Embodied AI         → AI with physical bodies

ROBOTICS
│
├── Automation          → Fixed, repeatable actions
└── Autonomy            → Adaptive, responsive actions
    └── Uses AI for decision-making
```

Figure 1: Concept Map How These Fit Together

❗ **Where they meet:** In training robots, performance-enhancing exosuits, AI-driven coaching platforms, and smart stadium infrastructure.

1.2.5. Final Link: From Theory to Practice

Why do these distinctions matter? Because when we talk about "AI in sport," we're not talking about a single tool or system. We're talking about an ecosystem—where software (AI), hardware (robotics), human behavior, various stakeholders, and ethical design all intersect in many complex ways (Glebova et al., 2024a).

Understanding these relationships will help to:

- Evaluate claims (Is this truly intelligent, or just automated?).
- Spot innovation (What's actually new and meaningful?).
- Ask the right questions (How does this affect performance, access, fairness?).

AI in sport is multifaceted (Gao and Liu, 2023; Glebova et al., 2024b): it involves machine learning models trained on player data (Wang, 2021), robotic exoskeletons enhancing physical rehabilitation (Xu and Tang, 2021), neural networks powering predictive scouting tools, and computer vision systems facilitating real-time performance analytics (Eid et al., 2024). Each of these applications operates within its own domain logic, yet they are increasingly converging, producing hybrid systems whose impacts extend far beyond the playing field (Glebova et al., 2024a,b).

Evaluating claims, for instance, becomes a matter of epistemological rigor. The line between automation and intelligence is not always clear, and the language used to describe systems can obscure more than it reveals (Chamberland, 2024). A wearable device that records heart rate data might appear "smart," but without adaptive learning or context-aware feedback, it does not qualify as AI in a meaningful sense. Distinguishing between mere data processing and genuine machine learning is essential for avoiding both technological hype and conceptual slippage. Overstating the intelligence of such systems risks not only misleading stakeholders but also misallocating resources and attention (Glebova and Desbordes, 2022).

Spotting innovation requires an appreciation of both the technical architecture and the socio-technical environments in which these technologies operate (Glebova et al., 2024b). Novelty is not always in the code—it may lie in how existing systems are repurposed or integrated. For example, AI-powered motion capture has existed for years, but its use in generating real-time tactical feedback for youth athletes represents a shift in the cultural accessibility of elite-level insight. Innovation, then, must be understood as relational and situated—embedded in practices, norms, and user communities rather than isolated in patents or prototypes. In other words, what makes something "new" or "innovative" in sport is often not the invention of a completely new algorithm or robotic platform, but the creative application or combination of known technologies to solve problems in a way that is meaningful and impactful within a specific sporting context.

Another example is video analysis platforms like Playermaker, Hudl, or HomeCourt. The underlying technologies—computer vision, basic machine learning, and motion tracking—have been around for years and are widely used in elite sport and surveillance applications. The novelty does not lie in the foundational code that enables object detection or pose estimation, but in how these systems have been reconfigured and integrated into low-cost, mobile platforms accessible to youth athletes, amateur coaches, and school teams.

In elite football (soccer), such technologies were traditionally limited to clubs with substantial financial and technical resources, often requiring fixed multi-camera setups, proprietary software, and dedicated analysis staff. What is novel about contemporary applications is that these tools now work with a single smartphone, leveraging cloud computing and user-friendly interfaces to make high-quality performance feedback available at scale.

This repurposing of existing technology achieves several important things:

- It democratizes access to data-driven insights, narrowing the gap between elite and grassroots levels.
- It supports developmental coaching in underserved communities, where traditional scouting might be minimal or absent.
- It fosters a culture of self-analysis and reflection among young athletes, empowering them to engage critically with their own performance.

Crucially, no single breakthrough in AI or robotics was required to make this possible. Instead, the innovation was systemic—a rethinking of how to combine available tools (camera, AI models, cloud infrastructure, mobile UX) into a coherent, affordable, and user-centric product. It illustrates that technological novelty can emerge from new configurations and use cases, rather than from the invention of entirely new algorithms. In sport—as in other domains—innovation is often most powerful when it shifts who can use a technology, how it can be used, and what problems it can help solve.

Equally important is the formulation of appropriate, critical questions—questions that do not merely inquire about efficiency or performance enhancement but probe deeper ethical and institutional consequences. How might algorithmic bias manifest in AI-driven talent identification platforms? What assumptions are embedded in the data sets used to train these systems, and whose bodies are excluded or misrepresented? How do such technologies reinforce or challenge existing power structures within sports organizations, from youth development programs to international federations?

Furthermore, the intersection of AI and sport also invites a rethinking of temporality and embodiment (Thorpe et al., 2021). Technologies that monitor and forecast athletic performance are not only reactive but increasingly predictive. This predictive turn shifts the logic of coaching and competition from the present to the future, where decisions are based on probabilistic simulations rather than experiential judgment. It reframes athletes as temporal subjects—understood through a lens of anticipated outcomes rather than present capacities. This, in turn, has implications for how careers are managed, how training loads are allocated, and even how potential is defined and nurtured.

In this ecosystem, ethical design is not an afterthought—it is a foundational requirement. Decisions about transparency, accountability, inclusivity, and consent must be baked into the development process. This is especially pertinent when AI systems influence athlete health, career trajectories, or access to opportunities. The governance of such systems must therefore involve not only engineers and data scientists but ethicists, legal scholars, coaches, and athletes themselves. Interdisciplinary dialogue is essential to ensure that innovation aligns with the values of fairness, dignity, and justice that sport, at its best, seeks to uphold.

The distinctions matter because they help us see clearly in a rapidly evolving landscape. They allow us to separate signal from noise, identify genuine breakthroughs, and critically engage with the changing conditions of sport. Ultimately, they shape how we respond to a fundamental question: not just what AI can do in sport, but what it should do—and for whom.

1.3. What's in Store: Adventure Map

This book offers a comprehensive exploration of how AI and robotics are reshaping the global sports industry. It combines historical analysis, current applications, future perspectives, and critical reflections to guide readers through the key developments and implications of these technologies across various domains of sport.

The structure of the book is designed to take readers on a logical and engaging journey, beginning with foundational concepts and culminating in practical applications and future opportunities (Figure 2).

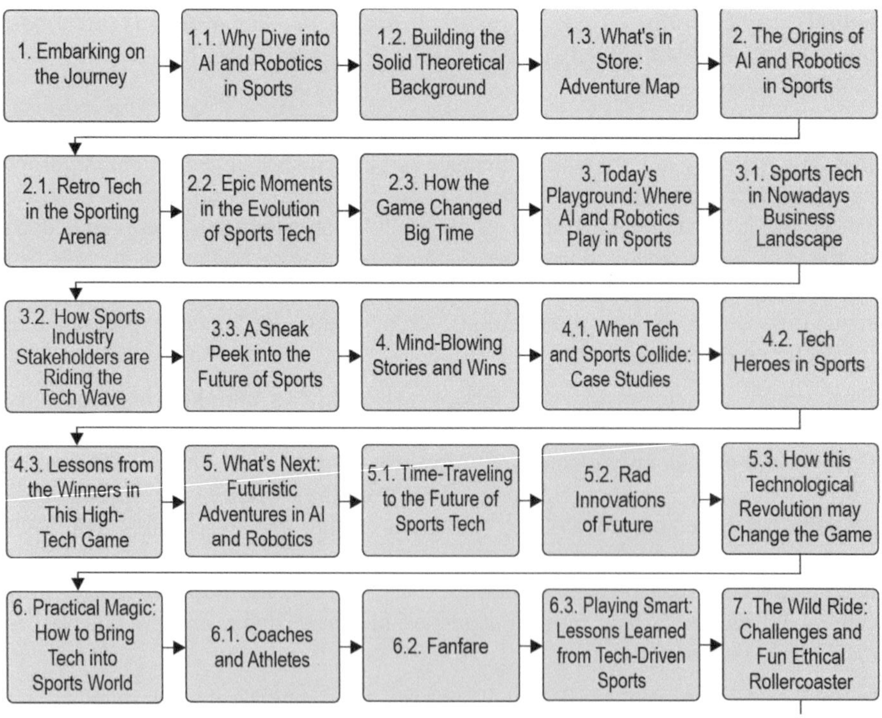

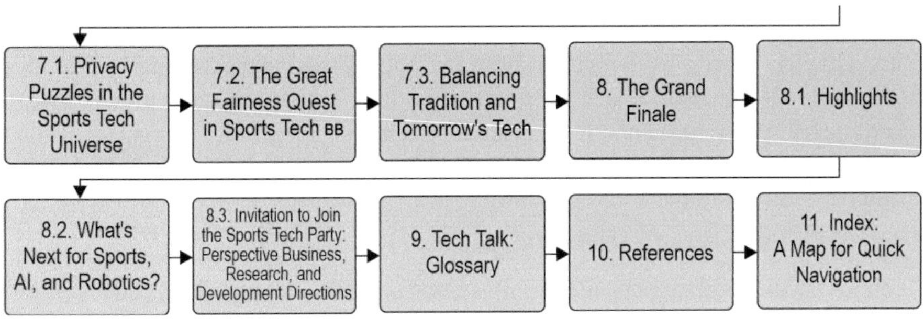

Figure 2: Book Map

Chapter 2: The Origins of AI and Robotics in Sports

This chapter traces the historical emergence of technological innovation in sport. It explores the early stages of AI and robotic integration, including early mechanical devices, analog innovations, and the pivotal moments that led to the digital transformation of sports. The discussion highlights how technological experimentation initially entered the athletic space and began to influence training, officiating, and equipment design.

Chapter 3: Today's Playground—Contemporary Applications

The focus here shifts to the present-day landscape. The chapter surveys the current use of AI and robotics in various sectors of the sports industry, including athlete performance optimization, injury prevention, fan engagement, and sports business analytics. It also maps how different stakeholders—athletes, coaches, organizations, and spectators—are navigating and integrating these emerging technologies in practice.

Chapter 4: Case Studies and Success Stories

To ground the discussion in real-world evidence, this chapter presents a series of illustrative case studies demonstrating the successful deployment of AI and robotics in sport. These narratives showcase both the achievements and challenges encountered, emphasizing the transformative potential of technology when effectively implemented. The chapter also reflects on the critical success factors and strategic approaches that have led to innovation-driven outcomes.

Chapter 5: Futuristic Scenarios and Emerging Trends

Anticipating what lies ahead, this chapter presents speculative and research-based projections about the future roles of AI and robotics in sport. It introduces upcoming innovations, anticipated industry disruptions, and novel use cases—such as immersive fan experiences, autonomous systems in athlete management, and the integration of sport into the broader digital-physical ecosystem. These insights are grounded in current trajectories while allowing space for visionary thinking.

Chapter 6: From Vision to Implementation—Practical Guidance

This chapter serves as a bridge between theory and application. It provides actionable insights for coaches, sport scientists, managers, and entrepreneurs seeking to implement AI and robotic solutions in their respective contexts. Lessons learned from prior applications are presented, along with frameworks for evaluating feasibility, ethical impact, and scalability.

Chapter 7: Ethical and Societal Challenges

Technological advancement inevitably raises complex ethical, legal, and cultural questions. This chapter critically examines the dilemmas associated with AI and robotics in sport, including data privacy, algorithmic bias, fairness in competition, and the preservation of tradition. It encourages a reflective approach to innovation, advocating for responsible and inclusive design.

Chapter 8: Conclusion and Future Outlook

The final chapter synthesizes the key findings and thematic insights of the book. It outlines emerging directions for research, business development, and public policy, inviting stakeholders to contribute to the future of sport technology. The chapter emphasizes the importance of interdisciplinary collaboration in shaping a future that balances performance enhancement with integrity and social value.

Chapters 9–11: Glossary, References, and Index

To support readers in navigating the terminology and concepts introduced throughout the book, a comprehensive glossary is provided. References include scholarly sources, industry reports, and technical documentation. The index offers quick access to key topics and themes.

Chapter 2

The Origins of AI and Robotics in Sports

The intersection of sport, technology, and human performance has a longer history than one might expect. Long before artificial intelligence (AI) and robotics became common buzzwords in athletic discourse, early forms of technological assistance were already taking root—quietly transforming the way sports were played, measured, and experienced. The origins of AI and robotics in sports are best understood as a slow and cumulative process, shaped by innovations in data collection, mechanical engineering, and computational logic that gradually converged with athletic performance needs.

In many ways, sport has always served as a testing ground for innovation. The inherent desire to push human limits—faster, stronger, more accurate—has consistently motivated athletes, coaches, and engineers to seek tools that provide a competitive edge. Even before the digital age, this pursuit led to the development of performance-enhancing technologies: precision stopwatches, motion analysis cameras, and biomechanical feedback systems. These tools, while not "intelligent" in the modern sense, laid the foundation for today's more sophisticated AI and robotic systems by generating and interpreting data in structured ways.

The initial applications of AI in sport were largely focused on pattern recognition, prediction, and decision support. Early computer models were developed to simulate game strategies, assess player movement, and even evaluate the probability of success in specific plays or matchups. These systems—though limited by the computing power and algorithmic simplicity of their time—represented a significant shift from intuition-based decision-making to data-informed strategy.

Robotics, on the other hand, began to emerge in the field of training and repetition-based skill development. Machines were built to simulate opponents, replicate playing conditions, or assist in controlled drills, particularly in sports like tennis, baseball, and table tennis. While these machines lacked autonomy or adaptive capabilities, they introduced the notion that physical training could be augmented by non-human actors—an idea that would eventually evolve into today's use of intelligent robotic systems capable of real-time feedback and personalization.

Importantly, the adoption of these early technologies was not always linear or uniform across sports. Certain disciplines—such as motor racing, baseball, and

DOI: 10.1201/9781003533795-2

tennis—were more amenable to quantification and technological experimentation, whereas others, particularly those rooted in more subjective or aesthetic judgment (e.g., gymnastics or martial arts), were slower to integrate such tools. Nevertheless, the growing interest in performance metrics, fairness, and spectator engagement created an environment ripe for technological innovation.

In tracing this historical evolution, we see how the precursors to AI and robotics in sport were deeply entwined with broader technological trends: the rise of computing in the mid-20th century, advances in sensor technologies, and the emergence of systems thinking in both engineering and physiology. These developments gradually redefined what it meant to train, compete, and evaluate performance, setting the stage for the more advanced systems we examine in subsequent chapters.

As we delve deeper into the formative years of AI and robotics in sports, it becomes clear that the driving forces behind their development were not merely technological, but philosophical. The idea that human performance could be measured, optimized, and perhaps even replicated by machines reflects a broader fascination with mastery, precision, and the potential of human-machine collaboration.

Leonardo da Vinci, often regarded as a pioneer of both engineering and biomechanics, once said: "The human foot is a masterpiece of engineering and a work of art." This reverence for the body's design prefigured modern attempts to capture and model athletic movement. Centuries later, engineers and scientists would use motion capture systems and biomechanical simulations to analyze an athlete's stride, swing, or jump—not only to understand it, but to improve it. While da Vinci sketched ideas for flying machines and robotic knights, today's sport technologists build data-driven avatars and robotic training partners. Leonardo da Vinci's profound admiration for the human body as a masterwork of design continues to resonate in today's efforts to optimize athletic performance through AI and robotics. His meticulous anatomical drawings and mechanical innovations reflected not only artistic genius but also a foundational philosophy: that the human form, in all its complexity, is both a source of inspiration and a subject for engineering inquiry. This blend of aesthetics, scientific curiosity, and technological ambition forms a historical-philosophical lineage that still shapes the evolution of sport technologies today. At the heart of this lineage lies the belief that athletic performance is not merely a series of movements to be measured but an integrated, expressive system worthy of detailed understanding. Da Vinci's approach to the body—as both an artistic subject and a biomechanical structure—prefigures contemporary efforts to model performance using technologies that combine engineering precision with a respect for the complexity of human physiology. From AI-driven simulations to robotic interfaces, modern sport technology strives to capture the richness of embodied movement without reducing it to mere data points. This holistic orientation reflects a philosophical commitment in honoring the full experience of the athlete—emotion, cognition, and kinesthetic intelligence included.

Equally central is the quest for mastery and precision—a desire not only to measure but to refine, not only to analyze but to elevate. This pursuit, evident in da Vinci's own technical drawings and prototypes, is echoed today in tools such as motion capture systems, biomechanical analysis platforms, and AI-based coaching assistants. These technologies do more than quantify—they enable insights that were once available only to the most expert eyes. They break down the nuances of a sprinter's stride, the arc of a tennis serve, or the posture in a gymnast's vault, translating them into actionable feedback. The human drive toward perfection, once guided by intuition and observation, now finds support in sophisticated digital allies. These technologies often function as collaborators—extensions of the body and mind that support, adapt, and respond. This idea of human–machine collaboration, rooted in da Vinci's mechanical explorations, has evolved into a design philosophy wherein AI systems, robotic devices, and virtual environments become dynamic partners in training and performance. Such entanglement between athlete and technology aligns with conceptual frameworks like sociomateriality and Human–Machine Interaction (HMI), which stress the co-evolution of human practices and technological systems. It is not simply about adding machines to sport, but about co-constructing new forms of embodied knowledge and capability through their presence.

Crucially, these developments are not merely technical achievements—they are also guided by enduring philosophical questions about what it means to perform, to excel, and to evolve. The increasing use of AI and robotics in sport forces us to revisit values that da Vinci himself implicitly championed: the balance between precision and creativity, between enhancement and integrity. As such, contemporary sport technologies are not purely tools of optimization; they are manifestations of a long-standing dialogue between philosophy, ethics, and engineering. They invite us to ask not only how far we can go in improving performance, but how we do so in ways that remain human-centered, ethically sound, and aesthetically meaningful. In this sense, the integration of AI and robotics in sport can be seen as a continuation—not a rupture—of a historical trajectory that began with thinkers like da Vinci. It represents a continuum of human ingenuity that values the body not just as a machine to be improved, but as a marvel to be understood, celebrated, and augmented in thoughtful, respectful partnership with technology.

The spirit of continuous improvement that drives sport also mirrors the relentless curiosity of early scientists and inventors. Isaac Newton, whose laws of motion underpin nearly every physics-based analysis in sports performance, famously noted: "If I have seen further, it is by standing on the shoulders of giants." Likewise, the evolution of sports technology has advanced not through isolated leaps, but through layered innovations—each generation building on the tools and ideas of those before. This sentiment captures a truth that extends beyond scientific discovery into the domain of sport technology: progress is rarely achieved in isolation. Instead, it unfolds through a cumulative process, where each breakthrough builds upon prior knowledge, methods, and tools. From rudimentary timing devices to today's AI-powered performance analytics, the evolution of sport technologies represents a layered history of innovation—each generation refining and reimagining the contributions of the past. This lineage not only honors the foundational insights of figures like Newton but also reinforces the inherently collaborative nature of technological advancement in sport.

In the mid-20th century, as computational technologies became more accessible, sports scientists began using early computers to analyze game strategies and optimize training plans. These developments, modest by today's standards, were revolutionary in their time. The ability to simulate different match outcomes or assess tactical decisions based on historical data introduced a form of rudimentary AI that began to supplement human judgment. The integration of computational tools into sport during the mid-20th century marked a foundational shift—one that laid the intellectual and technological groundwork for today's AI and robotic systems. At the time, these innovations were not described in the language of AI or automation, yet they introduced a mindset that favored algorithmic thinking, simulation, and data-driven decision-making—an orientation that continues to shape contemporary sport technologies.

In the 1950s and 1960s, game theory and operations research began entering the realm of sport strategy, primarily through the use of simulation models. These early tools enabled coaches and analysts to experiment with hypothetical scenarios, allowing them to model possible outcomes of strategic decisions in sports like American football and basketball. Although the simulations were relatively simplistic, they represented a crucial departure from intuition-based coaching toward a more probabilistic and calculated approach. This gradual analytical turn seeded the core logic behind modern AI systems—learning from data, anticipating behavior, and optimizing performance under uncertain conditions. Parallel developments in statistical computing provided new opportunities for deeper analysis of individual and team performance. Early mainframe software—such as those developed by IBM—enabled sports researchers to process data quantitatively, leading to a more scientific study of games. In baseball, these methods fueled the emergence of sabermetrics, a data-centric approach to player evaluation and game management that would later be popularized through the "Moneyball" narrative. Although still limited by computational power and data availability, these efforts set a precedent for performance metrics that go far beyond box scores and basic stats.

In the 1960s and 70s, computer-assisted video tools allowed for the detailed breakdown of an athlete's movements frame-by-frame. Coaches and scientists could finally move beyond subjective assessments and into measurable biomechanics—an advancement that had a profound effect on training methodologies in sports such as sprinting, throwing, and jumping. These early ventures into biomechanical computation prefigured the AI-powered motion capture and feedback systems now embedded in elite training environments. The impact of these computational tools was particularly visible in several sports. Baseball became an early proving ground for systematic data analysis, transforming how teams scouted talent and planned strategies. In American football, simulation-based decision tools contributed to the evolution of playbooks, introducing new levels of tactical complexity. In track and field, biomechanical modeling influenced coaching by identifying efficient movement patterns, optimizing start techniques, and minimizing injury risks—all using computer-generated visual and statistical insights. These early innovations were more than just historical curiosities; they established conceptual and technological principles that would be carried forward into the AI era. The basic practice of using data to inform human judgment—a hallmark of today's sports analytics—originated in these mid-century experiments. Likewise, the shift from passive data recording to active, real-time feedback foreshadowed the development of intelligent systems capable of adapting and responding dynamically during play or training.

Perhaps most critically, these developments initiated a reimagining of the relationship between humans and machines in sport. While early tools merely supplemented human expertise, they opened the door to deeper forms of collaboration where technology doesn't just assist but interacts—seen today in AI-driven coaching systems, robotic training partners, and adaptive wearables. Alongside these advancements, however, came philosophical and ethical questions that continue to challenge the field: To what extent should computational tools influence human performance? What constitutes fair use of technology in competition? These questions began surfacing as soon as computers entered the sporting domain, and they remain central in current debates over AI's role in preserving the integrity and humanity of sport. In retrospect, the computational turn of the mid-20th century marked a quiet revolution. Although primitive by modern standards, these early tools introduced a mode of thinking and a set of practices that have become foundational to the modern sports ecosystem. The legacy of that era endures in every algorithm that predicts injury risk, every model that optimizes strategy, and every robotic system that refines movement with sub-millimeter precision. AI and robotics in sport are not sudden disruptions—they are the sophisticated descendants of a decades-long journey toward intelligent performance enhancement.

Meanwhile, robotics—though still limited in complexity—found their place in skill development. Devices such as ball-serving machines, used in tennis and baseball, offered consistent, programmable repetitions for athletes aiming to refine their reflexes and techniques. While these machines were not "intelligent," they embodied the earliest notions of what we now call augmented training environments—spaces where human athletes and mechanical systems co-exist to enhance performance. By the late 20th century, a growing awareness of data as a strategic asset prompted professional sports organizations to invest in performance analytics. This laid the groundwork for the integration of AI algorithms capable of pattern recognition, injury risk forecasting, and even biometric monitoring. Though these systems were not yet autonomous, they demonstrated that machines could not only record information—but interpret it in ways that influenced decision-making.The stage was set for a technological renaissance in sport. The building blocks—data collection, mechanical augmentation, and algorithmic modeling—were already in place. What followed was a gradual but profound transformation of how sport was trained, watched, governed, and even understood. The late 20th century marked a critical turning point in the technological evolution of sport—a transition from isolated tools and mechanical aids to more interconnected systems that laid the groundwork for today's AI-driven and data-intensive sporting landscape. During this period, technology was no longer viewed merely as an external support but increasingly became an embedded and influential part of the athletic experience. One of the clearest manifestations of this shift was the introduction of mechanical training aids, such as tennis ball-serving machines and baseball pitching machines. These devices, though simple by today's standards, fundamentally changed how athletes trained. By providing consistent, programmable repetitions, they enabled athletes to refine their reflexes and techniques in ways previously reliant on human partners. Importantly, these machines began to blur the line between tool and training partner, contributing to a new form of HMI where mechanical systems became co-actors in performance development rather than passive equipment.

At the same time, professional sports organizations increasingly recognized the strategic value of data. The collection and interpretation of performance metrics began to influence decisions at all levels, from recruitment and training to game-day strategy and injury prevention. Early algorithmic models, though still limited in sophistication, offered a new way of thinking about sport—not as a domain governed solely by intuition and experience, but as one where patterns could be detected, risks anticipated, and outcomes optimized. This emerging reliance on data signaled a growing shift toward analytical and computational forms of knowledge that would soon become foundational. What ultimately defined this era was the convergence of mechanical systems, data infrastructures, and computational modeling. Together, they created a technological ecosystem that transformed not just how sport was practiced and managed, but how it was conceptualized. Training methods became more personalized and targeted, fan engagement evolved through data-driven broadcasting innovations, and even officiating and governance were reshaped by the integration of technology. These transformations were not just functional—they also introduced new questions about fairness, authenticity, and the boundaries of human enhancement. This period represents more than a step toward technical sophistication; it signifies a cultural and epistemological shift in sport. It connected the early experimental uses of computation and biomechanics to the current era of intelligent systems, marking the moment when sport began to evolve into a complex sociotechnical domain in which human expertise and machine intelligence are increasingly intertwined.

2.1. Retro Tech in the Sporting Arena

Before AI and robotics became embedded in the very fabric of contemporary sport, there existed a wide array of analog and mechanical innovations that shaped how athletic performance was understood, measured, and enhanced. This "retro tech" period marked a transitional phase—one in which the pursuit of athletic excellence began to intersect more consistently with tools designed not just to observe performance, but to structure and optimize it. "Retro tech" in sport refers to the era of mechanical and analog technologies that predated the digital revolution, representing a crucial bridge between intuitive coaching practices and the data-driven, AI-powered systems of today. This period was defined by innovations that introduced systematic measurement, standardization, and structured training methods, transforming sport from an art guided by experience into a science grounded in empirical data. These technologies operated without digital processing, relying instead on mechanical engineering, analog electronics, and manual input, yet they played an essential role in shaping modern sports science.

One defining characteristic of retro tech was its ability to quantify athletic performance. Devices such as mechanical stopwatches, photo-finish cameras, and analog timing gates allowed for precise measurement of race times, reaction speeds, and split intervals. These innovations provided athletes and coaches with objective, repeatable assessments, establishing benchmarks that were critical for performance comparison and improvement. Similarly, tools for biomechanical analysis—such as film cameras for frame-by-frame motion analysis, goniometers for measuring joint angles, and early force plates for tracking ground reaction forces—introduced an analytical dimension to movement and technique. These methods, though manual and labor-intensive, marked the beginning of biomechanical science in sport, enabling a deeper understanding of athletic form and efficiency.

Retro tech was not limited to observation; it actively augmented training environments. Mechanical training devices such as tennis ball-serving machines and baseball pitching machines provided athletes with consistent, controlled repetitions, essential for refining reflexes and honing technique without the constant presence of a coach. Early treadmills, stationary bikes, and pneumatic resistance machines further advanced structured conditioning by allowing athletes to train in controlled, measurable settings. These tools mirrored modern principles of overload and periodization, emphasizing the importance of precision and repeatability in training.

Physiological monitoring also evolved during this period through analog heart rate monitors, spirometers for measuring lung capacity, and early electromyography systems to track muscle activation. Although data collection remained manual—coaches and scientists meticulously recording measurements by hand—the insights gained from these instruments informed strategies for endurance, recovery, and injury prevention. Combined with early computational aids like mechanical calculators, these technologies laid the foundation for systematic data analysis long before the advent of sophisticated software.

The significance of retro tech goes beyond technical innovation. It signaled a philosophical and cultural shift in sport, legitimizing technology as an integral partner in performance optimization. By introducing objective measurement and repeatable protocols, retro tech created trust in technological aids, a relationship that would later expand into the AI-driven systems of today. However, these developments also raised early ethical questions about fairness and authenticity—debates that echo in current discussions around Video Assistant Referee (VAR), AI coaching, and robotic training aids. For instance, the introduction of photo-finish cameras sparked controversies about whether technology undermined the human element of officiating, foreshadowing similar debates in contemporary sport.

Retro tech marked a transformative phase in the evolution of sport technology. It provided the conceptual and practical groundwork for the digitization of performance metrics, real-time analytics, and intelligent systems. By formalizing methods for measuring time, motion, and physiological output, it allowed future technologies to build upon an established framework of precision and standardization. Understanding this era is essential because it illustrates that the integration of technology into sport has always been incremental, shaped by human values, cultural acceptance, and ongoing negotiations between tradition and innovation. From mechanical stopwatches to robotic training partners, the trajectory of sport technology reflects a continuous dialogue between human aspiration and technological possibility—one that began with the analog devices of the retro tech era.

One of the earliest examples of technological integration in sport was the mechanical stopwatch, introduced in the late 19th century. Though simple in design, the stopwatch radically altered the concept of performance by introducing precise, standardized timekeeping into competitive sport. Timed races became more than just contests of physical ability—they became measurable challenges, paving the way for objective comparison, record-keeping, and the emergence of performance analytics.

Another pivotal innovation was the development of photo finish cameras in track and field events during the 1930s. Initially devised to eliminate disputes at the finish line, these high-speed cameras captured sequential images that could be analyzed frame by frame, offering visual clarity and temporal precision. The ability to determine outcomes at the level of milliseconds not only enhanced fairness but also demonstrated the growing role of optical technologies in decision-making processes. Before these devices, close finishes in races were often determined by human judgment, leaving room for error and dispute. The introduction of cameras capable of capturing a strip of film at the finish line provided analog proof that validated results with unprecedented precision. This technology did more than improve fairness—it introduced philosophical debates about the role of machines in adjudicating human competition, foreshadowing current discussions surrounding video-assisted refereeing systems and automated decision-making in sport.

In parallel, sports like baseball and cricket began experimenting with manual data collection systems—scorecards, shot charts, and play diagrams—that allowed for more systematic performance tracking. These analog databases, often compiled by hand, represented an early form of sports informatics, long before the advent of digital data storage or automated analysis. While the insights they provided were limited, they laid the conceptual groundwork for today's expansive performance databases and predictive models. By providing athletes with hundreds of programmable, controlled practice shots, these machines created training environments where repetitive drills could be executed without the fatigue or variability of human feeders. This innovation dramatically increased training efficiency and technical refinement, but it also sparked cultural conversations about the influence of mechanical aids on authenticity, creativity, and the essence of sporting skill. Such discussions resonate with modern theories of sociomateriality and HMI, which interrogate how technology becomes embedded in human practice rather than functioning as a neutral tool.

Physiological monitoring also advanced significantly during this period, most notably with the advent of analog heart rate monitors in the 1960s and 1970s. For the first time, athletes and coaches could systematically track cardiovascular load and recovery, enabling individualized training plans grounded in empirical data rather than intuition alone. This innovation reinforced the growing medicalization and quantification of the athletic body, opening pathways for sports physiology but also introducing ethical questions about bodily surveillance and the construction of the "self-monitoring" athlete—issues that continue in today's discussions on wearable technologies and biometric data privacy. Equally transformative was the use of film and early video analysis for biomechanical research. Coaches and scientists began capturing athlete movements frame-by-frame, employing projectors and overlays to identify inefficiencies and refine technique. This practice introduced a new kind of technological gaze that mediated the athlete's experience of their own body, emphasizing representation and correction over immediate, embodied perception. These early imaging practices foreshadowed today's sophisticated motion-capture systems and the philosophical inquiries of postphenomenology, which explore how technology reshapes human perception and experience.

Collectively, these innovations positioned humans and machines as collaborators in the sporting process. Technologies of this era did not replace human expertise but extended and augmented it, offering new tools for optimization while maintaining a degree of transparency and control absent from the opaque algorithms of contemporary AI systems. Yet, their adoption was not without cultural negotiation; debates over fairness, authenticity, and the human element surfaced with every major technological leap, signaling an enduring tension that defines sport's relationship with technology.

The retro tech era thus represents more than a collection of mechanical devices; it reflects a profound philosophical and cultural transition. It transformed sport into a domain of scientific inquiry and standardization while laying the groundwork for later developments in digital analytics, AI, and robotics. Understanding this phase reveals that technological integration in sport is neither abrupt nor purely technical—it is a process deeply entangled with social values, ethical considerations, and evolving notions of what it means to compete, improve, and remain human in an increasingly technologized world.

While none of these tools qualify as "artificially intelligent" or autonomous by contemporary standards, they established a fundamental shift in how sport was conceptualized: from a purely physical endeavor to one that increasingly engaged with technology as a strategic and operational partner.

As we reflect on the technological milestones of the pre-digital era, we must recognize that these early tools—however simple by today's standards—were more than mere accessories. They were catalysts for a cultural shift in sport: from instinct to evidence, from spontaneity to strategy, from tradition to transformation.

Yet, as with all innovations, these early integrations raise important questions that continue to echo in today's high-tech sports environment:

- **To what extent did retro tech preserve or disrupt the 'spirit of the game'?** While many of these tools enhanced fairness and precision, some purists argued they diminished the human drama and spontaneity that made sport compelling in the first place. Does increased objectivity always equate to better sport?
- **Were these early technologies neutral, or did they subtly favor certain athletes or teams?** Access to film equipment, motion analysis, and even reliable timekeeping was not equally distributed. Might this unequal access have contributed to competitive imbalances or shaped the dominance of particular countries, institutions, or clubs?
- **Did the use of such tools begin to redefine what it meant to be 'talented'?** When training aids and performance feedback became standard, the definition of talent expanded beyond natural ability to include one's capacity to respond to technology, to learn through data, and to optimize performance through feedback. Was this the beginning of the data-driven athlete?
- **And finally, do these analog systems truly belong to a bygone era, or do they still echo in the technologies of today?** Many foundational concepts, like motion capture, performance tracking, and training simulation, are not new, only their implementation has evolved. In what ways are we still building on the legacy of retro tech, rather than discarding it?

These questions remind us that technological change in sport is never purely technical, it is deeply cultural, economic, and philosophical. The roots of today's intelligent systems lie not only in lines of code or robotic arms but in the analog tools that first taught us to measure motion, assess skill, and believe that improvement could be engineered.

2.2. Epic Moments in the Evolution of Sports Tech

The history of technological evolution in sport is not a smooth continuum, but rather a sequence of pivotal moments—milestones where a new invention or system dramatically altered the way games were played, managed, judged, or consumed. These "epic moments" highlight how sport has often served as a dynamic testing ground for broader technological shifts.

1. The 1968 Mexico City Olympics: The Rise of Electronic Timing

One of the earliest breakthroughs came during the 1968 Summer Olympics, where fully automatic timing systems were used for the first time in track and field events. Prior to this, races were often timed by hand, subject to human error and inconsistencies. The new Omega electronic timing system could measure to the hundredth of a second, decisively ending many long-standing disputes over finishes. This event marked a global turning point—from human estimation to mechanical precision in sport.

Real-world impact: The use of fully automatic timing systems became standard practice in elite competitions, reshaping how athletes trained, and even redefining records. A difference of 0.01 seconds became the line between gold and silver.

2. The Hawk-Eye System in Tennis (2006 Onward)

The introduction of Hawk-Eye, a computer vision system that tracks the trajectory of a ball, revolutionized officiating in tennis. Initially met with skepticism, it was soon embraced by players, fans, and governing bodies for its ability to settle controversial line calls with high-speed camera triangulation and 3D modeling.

Real-world impact: Hawk-Eye didn't just improve accuracy—it also changed player behavior. The challenge system it enabled introduced a psychological dimension, requiring players to be strategic about when to contest calls. Over time, it became a symbol of trust in technology over human referees.

3. VAR in Football (2018 FIFA World Cup)

After years of debate, the VAR system was officially introduced at the 2018 FIFA World Cup. VAR allows referees to review decisions using multiple camera angles and slow-motion footage—ushering in a new era of accountability and precision in football officiating.

Real-world impact: VAR has significantly reduced controversial decisions in high-stakes matches. However, it also sparked debates about the pace and emotion of the game, highlighting tensions between technological correctness and the fluid nature of live sport.

4. Wearable Technologies and Biometric Tracking

The early 2010s saw the proliferation of wearable devices in both training and live competition. From GPS vests to heart rate monitors and sleep trackers, these tools allowed coaches and medical teams to monitor real-time physiological data. Elite clubs like FC Barcelona and national teams in cycling, rugby, and basketball have heavily integrated these technologies into their training regimes.

Real-world impact: Wearable tech has redefined the boundaries between training and recovery, enabling individualized coaching plans, early injury detection, and even predictive analytics that forecast fatigue levels and performance risks.

5. The Emergence of AI-Powered Scouting and Game Analysis

Companies like Stats Perform and Second Spectrum have deployed AI systems capable of breaking down hours of game footage into actionable insights. These platforms can recognize patterns, suggest tactical shifts, and identify player strengths and weaknesses—all in real-time.

Real-world impact: In sports like basketball and American football, AI analysis has become a cornerstone of strategic planning, influencing roster decisions, game-day tactics, and player development.

Linking the Moments: More Than Milestones

Each of these events represents more than a technological advancement—they mark phases of cultural acceptance. In many cases, the technology existed long before it was widely implemented. What changed was the attitude of stakeholders, the regulatory landscape, and the evidence of benefit. Together, these moments reveal that successful tech integration in sport is not just about capability—it's about credibility, transparency, and timing.

These epic shifts have now laid the foundation for a more automated, data-driven, and interconnected sports ecosystem. In the next section, we explore how the game itself has been fundamentally transformed—not just on the surface, but in its rules, rhythms, and rituals—through the evolving partnership between humans and intelligent machines.

2.3. How the Game Changed Big Time?

Technology in sport has evolved from simple aids and digital enhancements to becoming a core driver of how sport is played, judged, monetized, and experienced. This shift isn't just about better equipment or faster analysis—it marks a structural transformation of the entire sporting experience, from grassroots to elite levels, from athlete to audience, from locker room to global stage.

The Athlete Redefined—From Natural Talent to Technological Hybrid

Traditionally, athletes were praised for their raw physical ability, mental fortitude, and technical skill. Today, that profile has expanded. Modern athletes are part biological, part digital. They train with smart wearables, analyze their biomechanics using AI-powered video breakdowns, and follow sleep and nutrition regimens informed by real-time data. Modern athletes are no longer just users of technology; rather, they are entangled with it in their daily practice, embodying the sociomateriality concept. Smart wearables become extensions of their bodies, collecting continuous physiological and biomechanical data that shape how they train, recover, and compete. AI-powered video breakdowns and biomechanical analysis allow incredibly precise feedback on technique and movement, surpassing what coaches or athletes could perceive unaided. This technology amplifies human skill by exposing subtle patterns, asymmetries, or inefficiencies in real time. Modern athletes benefit from continuous monitoring of sleep quality, nutrition, hydration, and even psychological states through integrated sensors and AI algorithms, creating 360-degree performance profiles. This level of detail enables individualized regimens optimized for peak performance and injury prevention. The athlete and technology operate in a dynamic interactive loop—athlete behavior influences AI recommendations, which in turn inform athlete decisions and adjustments. This highlights the bidirectional relationship central to HMI theory. Furthermore, the athlete's identity shifts toward a hybrid self, part biological organism and part digital entity shaped by data streams. This raises new questions about authenticity, fairness (technology access disparities), and the essence of human competition. This transformation aligns with the broader historical arc from retro tech's mechanical aids to today's intelligent, integrated systems that deeply reshape what it means to be an athlete and how sport is practiced.

In sports like cycling, Formula 1, and even baseball, the athlete is now seen as a data point in a complex system—where performance is optimized not only through effort and talent, but through insightful interpretation of physiological and tactical metrics. Continuous data collection through wearables, sensors, and telemetry enables real-time tracking of variables like heart rate variability, power output, fatigue, and even environmental conditions. This constant stream of information transforms the athlete into a dynamic data point, with performance analyzed and refined at levels of granularity unimaginable in earlier eras.

The shift reflects a systems-based approach, where success depends not only on individual capability but on the interaction between athletes, technology, and environmental factors. In cycling, for instance, power meters and aerodynamic sensors provide insights that allow coaches to optimize pacing strategies and select equipment tailored to race conditions. Recovery metrics, derived from physiological monitoring, ensure that training loads are precisely calibrated to avoid overtraining. Similarly, Formula 1 epitomizes the integration of human and machine: drivers' biometric data are fused with car telemetry, tire conditions, and track analytics to inform race tactics and car setup in real time. Baseball, too, has embraced this paradigm by applying data analytics to pitching and batting performance, using metrics like spin rate, launch angle, and player positioning to refine strategies and predict outcomes.

Interpreting this wealth of data requires advanced computational tools, often powered by AI and machine learning. These technologies sift through complex patterns to generate actionable insights, from designing personalized training programs to predicting injury risks and optimizing in-game tactics. Human expertise remains essential, but it now works symbiotically with algorithmic intelligence—a model that exemplifies the HMI frameworks discussed earlier. This creates an athlete identity that is no longer purely physical but increasingly hybrid, merging biological capability with digital augmentation. The implications are profound, raising questions about fairness, access to technology, and the nature of competitive advantage in a bio-digital sporting landscape. Central to this model is the feedback loop: data collection, analysis, and application occur in near real time, allowing athletes and teams to adapt strategies dynamically as physiological and tactical variables shift. The result is a sport environment where decisions are driven by a fusion of intuition, experience, and empirical evidence, enhancing precision, efficiency, and performance outcomes. This transformation redefines the logic of competition. Athletes are no longer isolated performers but nodes in an interconnected network of systems, tools, and analytics that collectively shape sporting outcomes. Success, therefore, hinges not only on talent and effort but on the capacity to interpret and leverage complex data ecosystems—an evolution that positions technology as an inseparable partner in the pursuit of excellence.

In cycling, performance optimization revolves around a suite of interconnected tools designed to quantify and refine every aspect of the rider's effort. Power meters mounted on cranks, pedals, or hubs measure output in watts, allowing riders and coaches to tailor pacing strategies to the demands of terrain and competition.

Heart rate monitors and wearable devices track cardiovascular load and recovery, helping prevent overtraining and supporting sustainable progress. GPS systems and environmental sensors capture variables such as speed, cadence, elevation, and wind conditions, with data relayed in real time to coaches through cloud-based platforms. Advanced software like TrainingPeaks and WKO analyzes this data to produce nuanced metrics—such as Training Stress Score and fatigue indices—enabling precision in periodized training. Complementing these physiological and performance insights, biomechanical sensors and motion capture technologies refine body positioning and pedal stroke efficiency to improve aerodynamics, reduce energy loss, and mitigate injury risks. Together, these innovations promote holistic health management, enhance tactical decision-making, and expand the horizon of personalized coaching. However, the reliance on high-end technologies also raises ethical questions around equity, as access remains uneven across regions and resource levels.

Formula 1 represents perhaps the most extreme embodiment of human-machine symbiosis in sport. Telemetry systems embedded within vehicles collect hundreds of data points every second, capturing everything from driver biometrics, such as heart rate and breathing patterns, to intricate details of car performance, including engine temperature, tire degradation, and G-force exposure. These data streams feed into machine learning models that optimize race strategies in real time, guiding decisions about pit stops, tire choices, and fuel management. Driver assisted algorithms, while carefully regulated, provide haptic and visual feedback to refine steering, braking, and acceleration inputs, enhancing performance without compromising regulatory integrity. Beyond the racetrack, simulator training immerses drivers in high-fidelity virtual environments, replicating competitive conditions with AI-driven feedback to refine technique and responsiveness. While these systems amplify precision and safety, they also foreground pressing ethical issues such as data ownership, driver privacy, and the reliability of algorithmic recommendations, especially in a sport where milliseconds—and lives—are at stake. Looking ahead, we can anticipate innovations such as augmented reality head-up displays, AI coaching assistants, and more granular real-time biomechanical monitoring, deepening the already intricate entanglement between human drivers and their technological ecosystems.

Baseball offers another rich context where technology and analytics converge to transform tradition. The Statcast system, deployed across professional stadiums, uses radar tracking and high-speed cameras to capture detailed metrics on pitching velocity, spin rates, ball trajectories, and player positioning. Biomechanical sensors attached to pitchers provide insights into arm angles, joint stress, and release points, reducing injury risk and improving technical efficiency. AI-powered scouting platforms analyze historical datasets to predict player potential, optimize lineups, and simulate game scenarios, complementing traditional talent evaluation with algorithmic precision. Video analysis tools, driven by computer vision and machine learning, pinpoint inefficiencies in batting mechanics or pitching techniques, enabling highly individualized coaching interventions. These advancements not only elevate performance but also foreground questions of fairness, as resource-rich teams may outpace competitors by leveraging superior technologies. Future developments may include robotic pitching systems capable of replicating specific pitching styles for batting practice and immersive AI simulations for strategic preparation, further redefining the boundaries of performance enhancement.

Across these three sports, the implications extend far beyond performance optimization. Continuous data monitoring supports proactive injury prevention and personalized recovery protocols, yet it also risks imposing psychological strain when overemphasis on metrics fosters pressure or erodes athlete autonomy. Ethical considerations loom large, particularly regarding data privacy, consent, and ownership, alongside concerns about competitive equity in a landscape where technological access remains uneven. Transparency in algorithmic decision-making and governance frameworks will be essential to safeguard integrity and trust.

Ultimately, athletes in these contexts emerge as bio-digital hybrids, inseparable from the technological infrastructures that surround them. Success is no longer defined solely by physical ability or mental resilience but by the capacity to navigate and capitalize on complex, data-rich systems. The integration of AI, robotics, and advanced analytics signals a future where human and machine collaborate in unprecedented ways—redefining not only performance but also the very identity of the athlete within the global sporting ecosystem.

The Coach as a Data Strategist

Gone are the days when coaching was based solely on intuition and experience. Coaches now rely heavily on predictive analytics, video analysis tools, and machine learning dashboards. AI provides suggestions on formations, substitution timing, injury prevention, and even mental readiness. This reshapes the coaching role into that of a strategic interpreter of data as much as a motivator or tactician.

The modern coaching role has undergone a profound transformation as AI, predictive analytics, and data-driven technologies have become integral to sport. No longer confined to the realm of intuition and experience alone, the coach now operates as a data strategist—synthesizing traditional expertise with cutting-edge technological insights to optimize team and individual performance.

Central to this evolution is the strategic interpretation of complex datasets. Coaches are expected to navigate predictive models, AI-powered video breakdowns, wearable sensor outputs, and machine learning dashboards, converting raw numerical patterns into actionable plans. These insights shape everything from game-day tactics to individualized training loads and recovery strategies, ensuring that decisions are not only evidence-based but contextually relevant to team dynamics and athlete profiles. Predictive analytics has shifted coaching from a reactive to a proactive discipline. Advanced AI systems anticipate opponent strategies, forecast injury risks, and monitor fatigue levels, allowing coaches to plan substitutions, adjust formations, and tailor recovery interventions with unprecedented precision. These capabilities are complemented by tools that integrate physiological and psychological indicators, enabling holistic performance management where physical readiness is aligned with mental resilience. Tactical planning has likewise entered a new era. AI-enhanced video analysis reveals patterns in opposition play and uncovers exploitable weaknesses, empowering coaches to craft nuanced strategies and make real-time adjustments during competition. This blend of human insight and machine intelligence reflects a paradigm of collaboration rather than replacement: AI amplifies rather than supplants the coach's role, while human judgment remains indispensable in interpreting data within the fluid, unpredictable context of sport. To thrive in this environment, coaches require an expanded skillset that includes data literacy, technological fluency, and continuous learning, layered upon their traditional expertise in leadership and motivation. They serve as mediators between intelligent systems and human athletes, ensuring that algorithmic recommendations are harmonized with team chemistry, emotional dynamics, and ethical considerations (Glebova et al., 2024a). This shift exemplifies the principles of HMI and sociomateriality: coaches are no longer peripheral users of technology but central nodes in a network where human agency and machine intelligence co-produce outcomes. In this sense, the future of coaching is defined by hybridity—an evolving fusion of art, science, and digital systems that is reshaping what it means to lead in the sporting arena.

Postphenomenology emphasizes that technology mediates human experience rather than acting as a neutral tool. In the coaching context, AI systems and wearable analytics shape how coaches perceive athletes and performance itself. For example, biometric dashboards alter the coach's sense of athlete readiness—no longer just observed through body language or verbal cues, but quantified through recovery scores and stress indices. This mediates the coach-athlete relationship, reframing trust and authority through data transparency while introducing new ethical questions: Does reliance on technology diminish embodied intuition, or does it enhance decision-making by revealing otherwise invisible dimensions of performance?

Actor-Network Theory (ANT) positions coaches as actors within a socio-technical network that includes players, AI systems, wearables, video platforms, governing bodies, and even the algorithms themselves. Decisions are not made in isolation but negotiated across this network. For instance, implementing an AI-driven load management tool involves enrolling athletes, sports scientists, and organizational stakeholders who trust and accept its role. The agency here is distributed: a predictive model influences substitution decisions just as much as an athlete's physical signals or a physiotherapist's recommendations. This symmetry between human and non-human actors underscores that modern coaching is a product of dynamic, constantly evolving networks rather than a linear hierarchy of authority. These theoretical perspectives highlight that the role of the coach is not simply technologically enhanced; it is ontologically transformed. Coaches are no longer mere motivators or tacticians—they are interpreters of mediated realities, balancing embodied experience with algorithmic insight. Their authority now depends on hybrid expertise that spans data literacy, ethical governance, and relational intelligence, making them mediators in a complex ecosystem where human values and machine logic continuously interact.

The integration of AI-driven data strategies is transforming coaching practices across a wide range of sports, reshaping how decisions are made and performance is optimized. In football, for instance, platforms like Wyscout, InStat, and StatsBomb employ machine learning to dissect opponent formations, anticipate passing lanes, and reveal tactical vulnerabilities. Coaches increasingly rely on these systems to design game plans and adapt strategies dynamically during matches. AI also supports real-time decision-making by analyzing wearable data—such as heart rate and distance covered—to predict fatigue and recommend optimal substitutions, reducing injury risks and maintaining peak performance. Similar predictive algorithms combine training loads, biomechanical assessments, and historical records to forecast injuries, enabling tailored recovery protocols and personalized training adjustments.

In basketball, AI-driven analytics refine both technical and strategic dimensions. Advanced dashboards evaluate shooting efficiency across court zones and against different defenders, guiding coaches in developing offensive plays that maximize scoring probability. Machine learning applied to video analysis identifies tendencies in opposing teams' offensive sets, while sentiment analysis of interviews, social media activity, and biometric stress markers provides insights into players' psychological readiness—helping coaches balance physical preparation with mental resilience.

American football has also embraced AI, particularly in predictive modeling. By analyzing historical play data, AI systems anticipate likely opponent moves based on game context, allowing defensive strategies to be preemptively structured. Wearable devices integrated with AI monitor impact forces and workloads, crucial for concussion management and recovery planning. Even esports, inherently digital, leverages AI for real-time strategic feedback, scenario simulation, and performance optimization, reinforcing the role of the coach as both analyst and strategist.

While these technologies offer unprecedented advantages, their integration introduces significant challenges. The sheer volume of available data risks overwhelming coaches unless filtered into actionable insights. Equally critical is the issue of interpretability: opaque, "black box" models can foster distrust if coaches cannot understand the rationale behind AI recommendations. Moreover, the human dimension remains irreplaceable—data-driven decisions must complement, not substitute, intuition, team chemistry, and psychological nuance. Financial disparities also create uneven access to advanced tools, amplifying competitive imbalances between resource-rich and smaller organizations. Furthermore, privacy and ethical governance around athlete data represent a growing concern, necessitating robust frameworks for consent, security, and responsible usage. Best practices for overcoming these challenges begin with building data literacy among coaches, enabling them to interpret outputs critically and understand limitations. Successful integration involves a gradual approach, often starting with specific applications such as injury prevention before expanding to broader tactical or psychological analytics. Crucially, AI should remain a supportive instrument within a human-centered coaching philosophy, preserving motivational leadership and empathetic engagement. Collaboration between coaches, sports scientists, data analysts, and AI specialists is essential to ensure that insights are contextualized and ethically applied.

Refereeing: The Era of Digital Authority

One of the most profound changes has been in officiating. As systems like VAR, Hawk-Eye, and goal-line technology have become more sophisticated and widespread, human referees are now supported—or sometimes overridden—by AI-powered systems. One of the most transformative developments in modern sport is the rise of digital authority through AI-driven officiating systems such as VAR, Hawk-Eye, and goal-line technology. These innovations signify a profound shift from a model where referees served as the sole arbiters of truth to one where decision-making occurs within a hybrid human-machine framework. Referees today operate not in isolation but in partnership with sophisticated technologies that augment, verify, and sometimes even override their judgments.

The introduction of systems like VAR and Hawk-Eye enhances accuracy and fairness by providing referees with multiple camera angles, ball trajectory simulations, and real-time sensor data. These tools reduce human error in critical decisions, such as determining offsides, validating goals, or assessing fouls. In certain cases, the authority of the machine surpasses that of the official, as with goal-line technology that delivers definitive proof of whether the ball crossed the line. This redistribution of decision-making power provokes important debates about the balance between human agency and technological authority, as well as the extent to which trust should be placed in algorithmic systems.

The promise of greater precision has undeniably improved fairness and transparency in officiating, but its adoption has not been free from controversy. The negotiation of technological acceptance involves players, officials, fans, and governing bodies, each weighing the benefits of error reduction against concerns over game flow disruption, loss of spontaneity, and the diminishing of the "human element" traditionally seen as intrinsic to sport. These debates are amplified when technological malfunctions or ambiguous interpretations lead to contentious outcomes, reminding us that even advanced systems are not infallible.

What makes this transformation particularly significant is the agency these technologies exert within the sporting network. From an Actor-Network Theory perspective, technologies like VAR and Hawk-Eye are not passive instruments but active participants shaping the reality of the game. They co-construct outcomes alongside human referees, players, and institutional frameworks, creating a new sociotechnical ecology in which authority is distributed rather than centralized.

This new officiating paradigm brings both opportunities and challenges. While technology provides empirical data, it often lacks the capacity to interpret contextual nuances such as player intent or situational ethics, leaving complex judgments within the human domain. At the same time, reliance on automated systems introduces vulnerabilities to technical failure, algorithmic opacity, and questions of accountability—issues that demand ongoing ethical scrutiny.

The evolution of refereeing into a digitally augmented practice exemplifies a symbiotic relationship between human and machine actors. Modern officials must not only master the traditional skills of interpretation and decision-making but also acquire technological literacy and the ability to communicate technology-assisted judgments clearly to stakeholders. This development raises broader implications for sport integrity and fan experience. While accuracy reinforces the legitimacy of outcomes, it also challenges cherished notions of unpredictability and human fallibility that many consider integral to the spirit of sport. Looking ahead, as AI decision-support systems become more advanced, the possibility of semi-autonomous or fully automated officiating looms, prompting profound questions about human control, technological determinism, and the essence of competitive play.

This raises key philosophical and regulatory questions:

- Can a game be fair if its decisions rely on algorithms hidden from public scrutiny?
- Should a system that guarantees technical accuracy also consider the rhythm and emotion of live sport?

The answers are still evolving, but what's clear is that trust in machines is now central to the integrity of competition.

The integration of AI-powered officiating systems into sport brings profound ethical and philosophical challenges, particularly regarding fairness, transparency, and the cultural essence of the game. At the heart of these debates lies the problem of algorithmic opacity. Can a game truly be considered fair when its most consequential decisions depend on proprietary algorithms hidden from public scrutiny? Fairness in sport is not solely about producing unbiased outcomes; it also entails procedural justice—ensuring that decision-making processes are transparent and comprehensible. When algorithms operate as "black boxes," stakeholders—players, coaches, fans, and officials—are left in the dark, unable to verify the validity or integrity of the judgments rendered. This opacity risks eroding trust, especially if errors or biases go unchecked.

Sport regulators increasingly face calls to impose standards for algorithmic explainability or, at the very least, independent audits to ensure accountability. These pressures mirror broader societal debates about algorithmic governance and ethical AI, where transparency is viewed as a prerequisite for legitimacy. Yet practical tensions persist, as technology providers often guard algorithmic designs as intellectual property, and excessive disclosure could invite system manipulation or hacking.

Beyond questions of fairness and accountability, the technological pursuit of absolute accuracy confronts the intangible yet vital qualities that define the spirit of sport. Should systems that deliver technical perfection also respect the rhythm and emotional flow of live competition? VAR reviews, for example, can interrupt momentum, dampen spontaneity, and reduce the dramatic tension that makes sport compelling to spectators. Philosophically, sport has always embraced an element of unpredictability and human fallibility, qualities that infuse games with drama and authenticity. Excessive reliance on mechanistic precision risks sanitizing these qualities, challenging the cultural and social meaning of sport itself. Recognizing this, governing bodies have sought compromises—limiting review times, applying technology only to "clear and obvious errors," and introducing protocols designed to preserve continuity without sacrificing fairness.

Central to this evolving landscape is the concept of trust. Where once trust rested solely in human referees, it now extends to machines and those who operate them. If technological systems are perceived as opaque, error-prone, or inconsistently applied, confidence in the integrity of competition can falter. Building and sustaining trust requires more than technical reliability; it calls for transparent communication, consistent application, and frameworks that allow for human oversight and, where appropriate, override. Ethical frameworks for sport increasingly draw from AI governance principles—fairness, accountability, transparency, and inclusivity—as essential foundations for sustaining sport integrity.

Looking forward, several pathways emerge for navigating these dilemmas. Advocates of open algorithmic governance propose that leagues adopt standards for algorithmic transparency or enable third-party audits, striking a balance between accountability and the protection of proprietary details. Hybrid decision-making models, where human referees retain ultimate authority while using AI as a decision-support tool, offer another approach to preserving contextual judgment alongside technological accuracy. Efforts to educate and engage fans about how decisions are reached may further enhance acceptance and trust, while dynamic rule-making ensures that regulations evolve in tandem with technological capabilities, maintaining both fairness and the essence of the game. The incorporation of digital authority in officiating is not merely a technical development but a cultural and ethical transformation. It forces sport to negotiate between two imperatives: the pursuit of accuracy and the preservation of meaning. The challenge is to design systems and governance structures that uphold fairness without stripping sport of its human drama, unpredictability, and emotional intensity—the very qualities that make it more than a game.

Global sporting bodies have adopted varied strategies to reconcile the benefits of AI-assisted officiating with the philosophical and regulatory concerns surrounding fairness, transparency, and the preservation of sport's cultural essence. These approaches reveal a common emphasis on balancing accuracy with rhythm, machine precision with human judgment, and technological authority with procedural justice.

FIFA's introduction of the VAR exemplifies this balancing act. Although the underlying AI algorithms that assist with offside calls and foul evaluations remain proprietary, FIFA has sought to enhance transparency by openly communicating decision rationales during matches. Stadium announcements and broadcast graphics now explain why decisions are overturned or upheld, reducing the sense of technological opacity. To maintain the natural flow of play, FIFA restricts reviews to "clear and obvious errors" and mandates that on-field referees retain ultimate authority, even when VAR evidence is compelling. This hybrid governance approach underscores the principle that technology should augment, not replace, human decision-making. Importantly, FIFA continues to refine VAR protocols through workshops, feedback loops, and iterative updates, signaling a commitment to adaptive regulation.

Cricket's Decision Review System (DRS) demonstrates a parallel yet distinct model. The International Cricket Council (ICC) has incorporated elements of transparency by publishing performance accuracy studies for ball-tracking technologies like Hawk-Eye. Teams are allowed a limited number of reviews, a mechanism designed to discourage frivolous challenges and ensure technology does not overshadow the game's rhythm. Umpires play an active communicative role, clearly signaling and explaining decisions to players and spectators, thereby fostering trust and understanding.

The NBA's use of replay review technologies illustrates a strong commitment to transparency and entertainment value. The league ensures that review outcomes are explained during broadcasts and summarized in post-game reports. Teams have a restricted number of challenges per game, and specialized committees oversee technological consistency and integrity. These measures protect both fairness and the pacing that defines the spectator experience.

Tennis, an early adopter of Hawk-Eye, has gone further in fan engagement by broadcasting real-time visualizations of ball trajectories on stadium screens. This transparency not only legitimizes calls but also enhances the drama and theater of the game. Players retain agency through limited challenges per set, reinforcing human control within a technologically mediated framework. Hawk-Eye's credibility rests on rigorous accuracy testing and frequent calibration, which is critical for maintaining trust among athletes and audiences.

Globally, regulatory approaches vary according to cultural and institutional priorities. European frameworks often stress independent oversight and standardized communication protocols, whereas North American leagues prioritize entertainment value and continuity of play. In Asia and Oceania, experimental hybrid models combine AI decision-support with human discretion, coupled with education initiatives to build stakeholder trust. Across all regions, however, algorithmic transparency remains a persistent point of tension. Technology vendors guard proprietary systems for competitive advantage, while critics call for independent audits and algorithmic explainability to ensure accountability.

Emerging practices suggest possible resolutions. Some leagues are piloting third-party audits to validate fairness and detect systemic biases, while researchers advocate for explainable AI models capable of producing human-readable justifications for decisions. Efforts to involve player unions and fan representatives in governance discussions aim to democratize decision-making and legitimize technology use. Furthermore, there is growing momentum toward sport-specific

AI ethics frameworks, emphasizing fairness, transparency, privacy, and human oversight as foundational principles.

Fan Engagement: The Immersive Turn

From real-time stats on mobile apps to augmented reality replays, fans are no longer passive spectators. Technologies like AI chatbots, immersive camera angles, and sentiment-based broadcasting are making the fan experience more personalized, interactive, and gamified. The landscape of fan engagement in sports has undergone a profound transformation, driven by the integration of advanced digital technologies such as AI, augmented reality (AR), and sophisticated real-time data analytics. No longer confined to passive spectatorship, fans today are active participants, immersed in highly personalized and interactive experiences that blur the lines between the physical and digital realms.

At the core of this immersive turn is the capability to access real-time statistics and personalized content through mobile applications and digital platforms. These systems ingest vast quantities of live data—ranging from traditional metrics like scores and player stats to advanced analytics such as player efficiency ratings, expected goals (xG), and biometrically informed fatigue indices. Machine learning algorithms power recommendation engines that tailor content feeds, delivering individualized insights according to a fan's preferred teams, players, or statistical interests. This personalization is achieved through pattern recognition in user behavior, preference clustering, and real-time feedback loops that dynamically adjust content relevance.

Simultaneously, augmented reality applications are revolutionizing how fans experience live and recorded sporting events. Utilizing sophisticated computer vision and 3D spatial mapping technologies, AR platforms overlay rich, contextual visualizations onto live broadcasts or within stadiums themselves. These overlays include player movement trajectories, shot heat maps, biomechanical analyses, and tactical zone highlights. For example, in basketball, AR can project interactive shot charts during replays, while in cycling, a virtual "ghost" rider representing an opponent's pace functions as a visual benchmark. These AR experiences rely on high-precision tracking systems that synchronize positional data from multiple cameras and sensors with the real-time video feed, processed using graphics rendering pipelines and low-latency streaming architectures to ensure seamless integration.

Moreover, immersive camera technologies such as 360-degree 4K ultra-high-definition cameras, multi-angle robotic camera rigs with AI-controlled framing, and drone-mounted platforms provide unprecedented viewing perspectives. This data is streamed via content delivery networks optimized for bandwidth-intensive VR and AR experiences. Viewers utilizing virtual reality headsets or AR-enabled devices can freely navigate the virtual stadium environment or switch dynamically between camera angles. The backend integrates real-time spatial audio processing and low-latency networking to maintain an immersive, synchronized sensory experience for remote audiences.

AI-powered chatbots and virtual assistants further deepen fan interaction by providing conversational interfaces that deliver live updates, answer inquiries, suggest merchandise, and explain rules or tactics. These systems employ natural language processing (NLP) models trained on extensive sport-specific corpora to understand context, detect sentiment, and generate coherent, contextually relevant responses. Chatbots are integrated into team apps, social media channels, and smart home devices, offering persistent, on-demand engagement that can respond adaptively to the unfolding sport narrative.

In broadcasting, sentiment analysis and social media mining play pivotal roles in shaping dynamic content delivery. Using real-time text and emotion recognition algorithms, broadcasters analyze audience reactions on platforms like Twitter or fan forums to gauge sentiment polarity and intensity. This data feeds into adaptive broadcasting systems that modulate camera focus, commentary tone, graphics animation, and even playlist sequencing to align with the mood of the audience. For example, during periods of high excitement or controversy, the broadcast may shift to more intense, fast-paced coverage and include interactive polls or prediction games, thereby enhancing emotional resonance and sustained viewer involvement.

Gamification frameworks embed interactive challenges, predictive contests, and social competition mechanics directly within streaming apps and stadium platforms. Real-time telemetry and gameplay data are fed into cloud-based game engines that track fan participation, award points, and enable social sharing. Leaderboards and achievement systems incentivize continuous engagement, converting spectatorship into an active, competitive community experience.

Despite these advances, the immersive fan experience raises important technical and sociotechnical challenges. The collection and processing of large-scale behavioral and biometric data require robust architectures ensuring privacy, consent management, and secure data transmission. Edge computing and federated learning techniques are increasingly adopted to minimize latency while safeguarding sensitive information. Furthermore, digital inclusion issues emerge, as the availability of high-performance devices and high-speed internet access varies globally, potentially creating engagement disparities.

The NBA's use of Second Spectrum allows fans to choose camera angles and see advanced player tracking data during games—blurring the line between viewer and analyst. The NBA has transformed fan engagement by integrating Second Spectrum, an advanced AI-powered player tracking and video analytics platform that brings cutting-edge technology traditionally reserved for professional analysts directly to the hands of fans. Utilizing a sophisticated network of high-resolution cameras strategically placed around the arena, Second Spectrum's AI algorithms process live video feeds at over 30 frames per second to accurately track the precise position, speed, and trajectories of every player and the ball on the court. This continuous flow of spatiotemporal data is then analyzed using advanced machine learning models to generate detailed statistics, including player speeds, distances traveled, shot probabilities, defensive pressures, and advanced impact metrics such as player impact estimate (PIE) or defensive box plus-minus. These metrics are visualized dynamically through intuitive graphics that overlay live or replay footage.

What makes this technology especially compelling is how it empowers fans with interactive features such as choosing from multiple camera angles during games. Through the NBA's "Lyriq" viewing experience, spectators can seamlessly switch between traditional broadcast views, player-focused cameras, or overhead court maps that reveal tactical player positioning, giving them nuanced insights into game strategies. This access to near real-time contextual data—like heat maps pinpointing where a player excels, live-updating shot charts, or pass prediction overlays—elevates fans beyond passive spectatorship, effectively turning them into analysts who can explore the intricate details of basketball tactics and player behaviors alongside professional commentators. This immersive experience relies on low-latency data pipelines, real-time AI inference, and robust cloud infrastructures that synchronize the delivery of player tracking data and multiple video streams. Content delivery networks optimize this rich multimedia content to ensure smooth and responsive viewing across various devices, including mobile platforms.

The Business of Sport: From Sponsorships to Smart Stadiums

AI and robotics are indeed reshaping the commercial landscape of sport in profound ways, transforming how teams, leagues, venues, and brands operate beyond just athletic performance.

AI-driven marketing in sports leverages machine learning and big data analytics to predict consumer behavior with greater accuracy. This enables sports organizations and sponsors to target audiences much more effectively than before. Instead of generic mass messages, marketing campaigns are now highly personalized, tailored to fans' preferences, purchasing histories, and engagement patterns. AI systems continuously analyze social media, ticket sales, and merchandise interactions, enabling real-time optimization of promotions and ad placements. This precision marketing enhances fan loyalty and drives higher conversion rates while also uncovering new revenue streams.

Smart stadiums illustrate another critical dimension where AI and robotics underpin the fan experience and operational efficiency. These venues integrate technologies such as facial recognition for seamless ticketing and security, crowd movement analytics that optimize ingress, egress, and concession line management, and robotic food and merchandise delivery systems that improve service speed and reduce staffing costs. Sensors and IoT devices stream continuous data about crowd density and environmental conditions, allowing stadium managers to improve safety and comfort dynamically. AI-powered predictive models guide staffing schedules, resource allocation, and emergency response, making stadiums not only high-tech venues for spectators but also intelligent infrastructures that support commercial success.

At the organizational level, machine learning models assist clubs and leagues in commercial decision-making. Sophisticated algorithms analyze multifactor data—

ranging from player performance and injury risk to social media popularity and market trends—to estimate player market worth more accurately than traditional scouting alone. Teams also apply AI to optimize sponsorship valuing by assessing audience exposure across platforms and predicting sponsor return on investment (ROI) more reliably. Additionally, ticket pricing strategies dynamically adjust based on demand forecasts, competitor pricing, event importance, and even external factors like weather, maximizing revenue while maintaining accessibility.

AI and robotics have become the core infrastructure that supports athletic competition not just on the field but across fan engagement, venue operations, commercial partnerships, and revenue generation. As AI advances, we see sports not only evolving in how they are played and watched but being continuously redefined by data-driven, intelligent ecosystems that monetize and project the industry into the future.

The game has changed—not subtly, but fundamentally. We're no longer merely watching players on a field; we are witnessing the unfolding of a cyber-physical theatre, where human capacity meets AI in a constant feedback loop of measurement, optimization, and adaptation. As Marshall McLuhan once said, "*We shape our tools and thereafter our tools shape us.*" In sport, AI and robotics are not just enhancing performance—they're reshaping what performance means.

In the next chapter, we move from this high-level transformation to a grounded, contemporary view: how AI and robotics are currently being deployed across sports disciplines, what roles they play in the business landscape, and what the early indicators suggest about their long-term impact?

Chapter 3

Today's Playground: Where AI and Robotics Play in Sports

Sport has always reflected the society in which it thrives. From the introduction of radio broadcasts to instant replays and wearable sensors, the playing field has constantly evolved through technology. Today, we stand at the cusp of a transformation driven by artificial intelligence (AI) and robotics. These technologies are not only augmenting the way games are played and managed but are also redefining the very experience of sport for athletes, coaches, fans, and administrators alike.

The world of sport has always been about pushing limits, but now, those limits are being redefined by AI and robotics. These technologies aren't just tools anymore—they're teammates, analysts, and even game-changers in their own right.

For athletes, training isn't what it used to be. Gone are the days when progress relied solely on instinct or a coach's sharp eye. Today, wearable sensors and AI-powered cameras track every movement, heartbeat, and strain, offering instant feedback that helps players train smarter, stay healthier, and avoid injuries. Robotic partners have entered the scene too—machines that deliver perfect passes, flawless serves, and endless repetitions, helping athletes sharpen their skills with precision no human could maintain.

Coaches, too, are adapting to this new reality. They're still motivators and tacticians, but now they're also data strategists. AI crunches mountains of game footage and player stats to spot patterns that even the most experienced eye might miss—predicting opponent moves, identifying weaknesses, and even suggesting the perfect moment to make a substitution. Scouting has gone digital as well: instead of relying on word-of-mouth or limited highlight reels, coaches now have AI-driven platforms that comb through global data to find the next rising star.

For fans, the game feels more alive than ever. AI serves up personalized highlights, interactive stats, and replays that focus on what you love the most. Robotics adds some fun too, with automated cameras capturing action from incredible angles and even robotic mascots entertaining the crowd. Watching a game today isn't just about cheering for your team—it's an immersive experience tailored to you.

Administrators are feeling the impact as well. AI makes event management smoother than ever, from ticketing and security to predicting crowd movements for safety. Robotics handles field maintenance and even assists with setting up training

DOI: 10.1201/9781003533795-3

equipment. And when it comes to fairness, technologies like Video Assistant Referee (VAR) and Hawk-Eye have changed the rules of trust. Decisions aren't left to human judgment alone anymore—machines are there to make sure the right call is made.

This partnership between humans and machines is rewriting the story of sport. It's no longer just about strength, speed, or skill—it's about the harmony between instinct and intelligence, emotion and precision. As AI and robotics continue to evolve, they promise even more: smarter strategies, safer training, and unforgettable experiences for players and fans alike. The future of sport isn't human versus machine—it's human with machine, working together to make the game better than ever.

This chapter explores how AI and robotics are actively shaping contemporary sport. It moves beyond hype to examine concrete applications, industry trends, and ethical considerations, offering a critical overview of the "playground" where humans and machines now co-exist.

1. Enhancing Athlete Performance Through AI and Robotics

a. *Intelligent Wearables and Data-Driven Training*

Athlete training is increasingly data-informed. Wearables such as Whoop, Catapult, and Garmin track physiological and biomechanical parameters in real time. AI algorithms process this data to identify patterns, optimize training loads, and reduce injury risk. For example, AI can detect signs of overtraining by correlating sleep quality, heart rate variability, and exertion levels.

b. *Robotic Assistants in Practice Environments*

Robotic technologies offer consistent, fatigue-free training partners. Tennis ball machines, robotic sparring partners in martial arts, and football passing robots are becoming standard tools. These devices are integrated with vision and motion systems, allowing real-time feedback and adaptation to athlete performance.

c. *AI in Rehabilitation and Recovery*

AI-driven diagnostics can support tailored rehabilitation plans. Vision-based gait analysis or robotic exoskeletons assist with controlled physical therapy, while predictive models assess recovery trajectories. Tools like Sparta Science or Kinduct blend performance data with medical history to monitor readiness.

2. Game Analysis, Tactics, and Strategy Optimization

a. *Real-Time Game Intelligence*

In elite sports, teams use AI to derive tactical insights during live play. Tools like Second Spectrum in the NBA or StatsBomb in football provide spatial analytics, tracking player positioning, movement efficiency, and decision-making in real time.

b. *Predictive Modeling and Opponent Scouting*

Machine learning models forecast game outcomes, player matchups, or substitution strategies based on historic and current performance data. Coaches now use AI-generated scouting reports to detect weaknesses in opponents with unprecedented precision.

c. *Simulation and Virtual Twin Technology*
Digital twins of athletes and matches are used to test strategies under various conditions. This technique allows teams to simulate fatigue scenarios, adjust formations, and plan for contingencies without stepping onto the field.

3. Stadiums, Fan Experience, and Robotic Operations

a. *Smart Stadiums and AI Infrastructure*
AI powers dynamic ticket pricing, crowd flow analytics, and energy optimization in modern venues. Facial recognition enables personalized access control and enhances security. In Tokyo 2020, robots welcomed guests and assisted individuals with limited mobility.

b. *Robotic Service and Logistics*
Stadium robots now handle food delivery, sanitation, and merchandise restocking. These functions improve operational efficiency and reduce physical contact—particularly relevant in post-pandemic sporting environments.

c. *Immersive Fan Engagement*
AI curates personalized fan experiences through augmented reality (AR) overlays, real-time stats, and gamified content. Platforms like Genius Sports or IBM Watson enhance live broadcasts with interactive storytelling and data visualizations.

4. AI and Robotics on the Field of Play

a. *Automated Officiating*
Computer vision and AI are now integral to officiating. The VAR and Hawk-Eye systems use frame-by-frame image analysis to make critical decisions with minimal delay. In tennis and cricket, line calls are now largely automated.

b. *Robot Athletes and Competitive Robotics*
Events like RoboCup or autonomous drone racing challenge our definition of "sport." These competitions simulate strategic play and coordination, acting as laboratories for AI development while entertaining new fan bases.

c. *Robotic Integration in Practice Matches*
Robots are being tested in roles like ball retrieval, tactical modeling, or even as opposition players in training environments. These AI agents mimic certain patterns of play, aiding in scenario-based learning.

5. Esports, Virtual Training, and AI Opponents

a. *AI-Powered Esports Engines*
AI is foundational to the development and fairness of esports titles. It governs game physics, player matching, and anti-cheating systems. Moreover, AI bots trained via reinforcement learning now serve as high-quality sparring partners, as seen in OpenAI's Dota 2 experiments.

b. *Virtual Coaching and Simulation*
Young athletes can now train against AI-generated avatars. Through virtual reality (VR) headsets and simulated environments, they experience immersive

drills that adjust to their skill level in real time. This is especially valuable for cognitive training and decision-making under pressure.

c. *AI-Enhanced Youth Development*
Gamification powered by AI enhances engagement and skill acquisition in youth sports. Apps track progress, deliver feedback, and motivate continued participation—helping to bridge the gap between play and high-performance development.

As AI and robotics become deeply embedded in sport, they bring with them a host of ethical, legal, and philosophical challenges. While these technologies enhance performance, efficiency, and fan engagement, they also raise difficult questions about fairness, bias, and the nature of human agency in competition. The playground may be smarter, but it is also more complex—and navigating it responsibly requires careful consideration of the rules that govern this new game.

One of the most pressing challenges in this domain is data ownership and privacy. Modern athletes are surrounded by an array of data-capturing technologies—wearable devices, video analysis platforms, GPS trackers, and AI-powered monitoring tools that collect everything from biometric signals to behavioral patterns and emotional states. While these insights can improve training and performance, they also raise a fundamental question: who owns this data? Is it the individual athlete, the team, the league, or the technology provider? The answer is often murky. Without clear regulatory frameworks or athlete-centered data governance, there is a risk that personal information will be commodified or exploited without proper consent. Athletes may feel pressured to share intimate health data for fear of losing their competitive edge or professional opportunities. In such a scenario, the line between voluntary participation and coercion becomes dangerously thin.

Equally critical is the issue of bias and inequality in AI systems. Algorithms are not neutral—they reflect the assumptions, values, and blind spots of the data they are trained on. If the training datasets used in scouting, recruitment, or performance evaluation are skewed—favoring certain genders, ethnicities, or socioeconomic groups—then the decisions made by these systems will reflect and amplify existing inequalities. For instance, a predictive tool that recommends promising young athletes might overlook talent from underrepresented communities simply because they are underrepresented in the historical data. Similarly, AI-driven performance metrics may favor certain playing styles or body types, unintentionally marginalizing athletes who do not conform to those models. In this way, technology can entrench discrimination under the guise of objectivity. Preventing this requires not only technical audits and algorithmic transparency, but also a deeper commitment to inclusive design and ethical accountability in sport tech development.

A third ethical frontier lies in the human-machine boundary. As AI begins to influence everything from in-game tactics to officiating decisions, we must ask ourselves: where should we draw the line between legitimate technological assistance and an unfair advantage? There is a delicate balance between augmentation and automation. Tools that help athletes understand their performance can be empowering, but tools that start making strategic decisions on their behalf raise questions about the authenticity of competition. For example, if a football coach uses AI to determine the optimal substitution pattern, does that enhance the coach's insight—or diminish their role altogether? Likewise, if AI-driven officiating becomes standard, do we lose the human element of judgment, context, and interpretation that makes sport both unpredictable and engaging?

This debate is especially heated in contexts where technology appears to "tilt" the competitive playing field. Wealthier teams and nations with access to cutting-edge AI and robotics may be able to train, recover, and strategize more effectively than their less-resourced counterparts. This creates a technological arms race that could further polarize global sport ecosystems and undermine the principle of fair play. As sport increasingly becomes a hybrid of physical talent and computational advantage, governing bodies must grapple with difficult regulatory decisions: Which technologies should be allowed? When do they enhance the spirit of the game, and when do they distort it?

In sum, while AI and robotics offer tremendous potential to elevate sports, they also challenge us to rethink core values that have long defined competition—fairness, equality, integrity, and human excellence. The future of fair play will not be determined by machines alone, but by the choices we make about how to design, regulate, and integrate those machines into the world of sport. Ultimately, the question is not just what technology can do, but what we want sport to be in an era where human and AI increasingly play side by side.

The fusion of AI and robotics with sport is not a distant dream—it is today's reality. From training to tactics, officiating to fan engagement, machines are no longer just watching the game—they're playing alongside us. As we embrace this transformation, we must also guard the human essence of sport: its unpredictability, emotion, and spirit of fair play. The future of sports will be shaped not just by how well athletes are trained, but by how thoughtfully the rules are designed — where AI and robotics are no longer in the stands, but very much in the game.

3.1. Sports Tech in Nowadays Business Landscape

The sport industry is undergoing a profound transformation, fueled by the rapid evolution of technology and its deepening integration into all facets of the industry. Sports technology—once limited to performance wearables and video replay systems—has now become a foundational pillar of modern sports business. From athlete management and fan engagement to sponsorship valuation and digital merchandising, sports tech is no longer a supporting function; it is central to operational efficiency and global competitiveness. At the center of this shift lies the convergence of multiple digital technologies: AI, machine learning, computer vision, the Internet of Things (IoT), blockchain, and immersive media such as virtual and augmented reality. Together, these technologies are transforming the sport industry into a dynamic, data-driven ecosystem. This evolution is not only changing how sports are played and watched—it is redefining the economic logic of the entire sector. For professional clubs, leagues, and federations, adopting sports technology is no longer a choice—it is a competitive necessity. Digitally mature organizations are leveraging advanced analytics to make smarter decisions, from player recruitment and health monitoring to game-day tactics and opponent scouting. At the same time, these organizations are using digital tools to build stronger brand identities and deeper connections with fans.

For example, the use of fan data analytics in professional football. Clubs like Manchester City, FC Barcelona, and Bayern Munich invest heavily in customer relationship management (CRM) systems that aggregate behavioral and transactional data across touchpoints—ticket sales, mobile apps, social media interactions, and e-commerce platforms. AI-powered analytics allow clubs to segment fans, personalize communications, and increase lifetime value through targeted merchandising, loyalty programs, and digital memberships. In essence, sports tech is enabling a shift from mass broadcasting to individualized fan journeys. On the field, the integration of real-time performance data through wearable sensors and vision tracking has revolutionized coaching and medical support. Athlete management platforms now offer consolidated dashboards that track training load, recovery cycles, nutrition, sleep, and even cognitive performance. These insights not only reduce injury risk but also extend player careers and maximize return on investment. In an era where elite athletes are multimillion-dollar assets, the value of precision health and performance optimization cannot be overstated.

Perhaps most significantly, sports technology is unlocking new revenue streams and catalyzing the emergence of innovative business models. Digital broadcasting, over-the-top (OTT) streaming platforms, and direct-to-consumer content are challenging traditional media rights structures. Platforms like DAZN, Amazon Prime Sports, and Apple TV+ have disrupted the monopoly of legacy broadcasters by offering flexible, subscription-based models that reach global audiences at scale.

Simultaneously, immersive technologies are creating entirely new forms of content monetization. AR and VR offer fans interactive, gamified experiences—from virtual stadium tours to live 360-degree match streams and mixed-reality viewing parties. These innovations are not only enhancing the fan experience but also opening up branding and sponsorship opportunities in digital environments. Virtual billboards, branded in-game assets, and interactive advertisements are generating new value in both physical and virtual arenas.

The rise of blockchain and NFTs (non-fungible tokens) is further redefining ownership and monetization in sport. Platforms like Sorare, NBA Top Shot, and Socios.com have introduced digital collectibles, fan tokens, and decentralized governance structures that allow fans to invest in and interact with their favorite teams in unprecedented ways. While still nascent, these models are shifting the economics of fandom—from passive consumption to participatory engagement.

The surge in sports tech innovation has created fertile ground for startups and attracted significant venture capital investment. Global accelerators and incubators—such as Stadia Ventures, HYPE Sports Innovation, and leAD Sports—are nurturing a new generation of tech entrepreneurs focused on sport-specific solutions. These startups range from AI scouting platforms and biometric training tools to fan engagement apps and venue management systems.

Major sports organizations are not only investing in these startups but also forming joint ventures and corporate innovation labs to accelerate adoption. For instance, the NBA has partnered with Microsoft to create a cloud-based digital platform for personalized fan content, while the NFL has collaborated with Amazon Web Services to develop advanced game statistics. These partnerships underscore a strategic shift in how sport properties see themselves—not just as entertainment providers, but as tech-driven media enterprises.

Despite the opportunities, the rise of sports tech also introduces new challenges. Data privacy, cybersecurity, ethical AI, and digital exclusion are critical concerns that must be addressed. The increasing reliance on data raises questions about consent, surveillance, and control, especially when it comes to young athletes or underserved fan communities with limited digital access. Moreover, the growing role of automation in decision-making, from recruitment algorithms to AI referees, necessitates strong governance frameworks to preserve fairness, transparency, and human oversight. The sport industry must also remain vigilant about the risk of over-commercialization, where technology undermines the authenticity and emotional resonance that make sport so compelling in the first place. Finally, the digital divide between well-funded professional organizations and resource-constrained amateur or community clubs must not be allowed to widen. Democratizing access to sports technology—through scalable, low-cost solutions and inclusive design—should be a guiding principle for developers and governing bodies alike.

In the current business landscape, sports technology is more than a suite of tools—it is a driving force of transformation. It touches every stakeholder in the sport ecosystem: athletes seeking peak performance, fans craving immersive experiences, executives pursuing growth, and investors betting on the next big platform. The organizations that thrive in this environment will be those that not only adopt technology but embed it strategically, ethically, and creatively into their operations and vision.

Sport has always adapted to the tools of its time. In the digital age, the playing field is no longer just grass or court, it is also a network of sensors, code, data streams, and intelligent systems. Understanding and mastering this new terrain is essential for any stakeholder aiming to stay relevant in the fast-evolving world of sports business.

3.2. How Sports Industry Stakeholders are Riding the Tech Wave

In the past decade, technology has reshaped nearly every aspect of the sports industry, from performance optimization and fan engagement to revenue generation and media distribution. But this transformation isn't occurring in a vacuum—it's being actively driven, adapted, and leveraged by a diverse group of stakeholders. Each actor within the sports ecosystem—athletes, coaches, teams, leagues, broadcasters, sponsors, fans, and governing bodies—has found distinct ways to ride the tech wave, often with overlapping goals but different strategies. This chapter explores how these stakeholders are embracing digital innovations, and how their actions collectively redefine the business and culture of sport.

For today's athletes, technology is both a performance enhancer and a personal brand amplifier. From wearables that track biomechanical efficiency to neurofeedback tools and AI-generated training regimens, elite athletes are optimizing every aspect of their preparation and recovery. Platforms like WHOOP, Catapult, and STATSports provide granular insights into workload, fatigue, and injury risk, giving athletes and their support teams real-time data to inform smarter decisions.

But the use of tech extends beyond the field. Social media platforms, athlete-centric content hubs like Uninterrupted, and monetization tools such as Cameo or NFTs empower athletes to become media producers and global influencers. With the rise of personal analytics dashboards, athletes can now quantify not only their physical performance but also their digital reach—allowing them to negotiate more favorable contracts and sponsorship deals.

Coaches and sports scientists are increasingly operating in a data-rich environment. Match footage is no longer reviewed manually; instead, AI-powered video analysis platforms such as Hudl, Spiideo, and Wyscout generate automated breakdowns of player movements, tactical formations, and opponent behavior. Decision-making has become both more evidence-based and more granular. Training programs are now hyper-personalized, supported by biometric and GPS data, sleep monitoring, and nutrition tracking. The line between coaching and science is blurring, with many elite clubs employing multidisciplinary teams of analysts, data scientists, and biomechanists to complement traditional coaching expertise. The challenge? Balancing human intuition with machine intelligence. While data provides unprecedented visibility, interpreting it meaningfully and translating it into actionable insights still requires domain knowledge and experience.

Sports clubs, particularly at the professional level, have evolved into tech-enabled media businesses. Clubs like Manchester United, Real Madrid, and the Golden State Warriors have invested heavily in CRM systems, content production studios, e-commerce platforms, and app-based fan engagement ecosystems. These organizations view technology not just as a tool, but as a growth engine. From using AI for dynamic ticket pricing to launching AR experiences for fans, clubs are diversifying revenue streams while building deeper fan relationships. Behind the scenes, they are adopting ERP systems, blockchain-based merchandise authentication, and digital twins of stadiums to streamline operations and create scalable business models. Moreover, global expansion strategies are increasingly digital-first. Clubs are creating region-specific social media content, launching virtual fan zones, and signing eSports teams to reach younger audiences. The club of the future is both physical and digital—a hybrid institution with fans as much in Seoul or São Paulo as in the hometown.

Leagues and federations act as both regulators and innovators. On the one hand, they must maintain the integrity of sport—ensuring fairness, enforcing anti-doping measures, and adjudicating disputes. On the other, they are embracing technology to enhance competitiveness, grow audiences, and protect the sport's long-term value. The NBA's use of AI for real-time statistics, the NFL's partnership with Amazon Web Services for predictive analytics, and FIFA's adoption of semi-automated offside technology exemplify how governing bodies are at the forefront of innovation. These institutions are also investing in broadcast innovations—360-degree replay, biometric overlays, and interactive viewing modes—designed to create more immersive fan experiences. Importantly, they also serve as gatekeepers. By defining the rules for acceptable tech use (e.g., VAR protocols, wearable approval), they determine how innovation is integrated into the sport without undermining competitive balance or tradition.

In a saturated media landscape, broadcasters are turning to technology to offer differentiated experiences. The traditional one-size-fits-all live feed is giving way to customizable viewing options, multi-camera angles, data-rich overlays, and second-screen experiences. OTT platforms such as DAZN, ESPN+, and Amazon Prime have disrupted conventional broadcasting by offering on-demand access, dynamic pricing, and algorithm-driven recommendations. These services also allow for better audience segmentation, enabling personalized content and targeted advertising. Tech also underpins innovation in rights management and content creation. AI-generated highlight reels, automated commentary, and real-time translation services are lowering costs and enabling global distribution. In the age of digital sport consumption, content is king—but personalization and interactivity are the new emperors.

Sponsors are no longer satisfied with static logos on kits or billboards. Technology has allowed them to move from brand awareness to brand engagement. Through digital activations—like branded AR filters, interactive fantasy leagues, and shoppable content—brands are embedding themselves into the fan experience. Data analytics also allow for better return on investment (ROI) tracking. Sponsors can now measure not only impressions, but engagement rates, purchase behavior, and social sentiment. This accountability is raising the bar for what constitutes a successful partnership. In some cases, sponsors are becoming co-creators of content and innovation. Consider how Red Bull blurs the line between sponsor and sport property, producing high-tech sporting events and media in-house. This evolution suggests that the brand's role in sport is no longer peripheral—it is increasingly central and strategic.

Perhaps the most important stakeholder riding the tech wave is the fan. Today's fans are not passive spectators but active participants—streaming games on mobile devices, engaging with athletes on social media, trading digital collectibles, and even influencing decisions through fan tokens or interactive polls. Technology has democratized access to sport. A teenage fan in Nairobi can watch La Liga matches live, interact with players on TikTok, and join a Discord community around his favorite team. Simultaneously, fans have become data sources themselves, as clubs and platforms collect behavioral and transactional data to personalize experiences. However, this increased connectivity raises questions about digital fatigue, surveillance, and commercialization. Fans are at the heart of the sport experience—but as stakeholders, they must be treated with respect, transparency, and value.

The tech wave in sport is not a single phenomenon—it is a networked movement, shaped by a complex interplay of stakeholder goals, innovations, and values. Athletes seek peak performance and personal empowerment. Coaches want actionable insights. Clubs aim for global growth. Leagues pursue innovation and integrity. Brands look for relevance and returns. Fans crave authenticity and engagement. Technology is the common thread weaving these ambitions together. But its success depends not only on the tools themselves, but on how they are used, governed, and aligned with the human spirit of sport. In this rapidly evolving environment, one thing is clear: those who understand the unique position of each stakeholder—and design tech strategies that respect and amplify their roles—will be the true game-changers of the industry.

3.3. A Sneak Peek into the Future of Sports

The future of sports promises to be both disruptive and exhilarating. The game is evolving not just in how it's played or consumed, but in how it's imagined. From AI-driven strategies to immersive fan experiences and bio-enhanced athletes, the next chapter in the story of sport will be written by those who embrace change while safeguarding its essence. The future of sports is poised to be a groundbreaking fusion of technology, human potential, and cultural evolution, reshaping not just how games are played or watched but fundamentally transforming what we imagine sport to be. At the heart of this transformation lies the integration of AI, immersive technologies, and bio-enhancement, a convergence that promises to elevate athletic competition and fan engagement to unprecedented heights.

AI is becoming indispensable in redefining the intellectual fabric of sports strategy and performance. No longer merely a support tool, AI systems now analyze massive datasets—from detailed player biometrics to nuanced opponent behaviors—to craft hyper-personalized training programs and execute real-time in-game decisions. By simulating countless scenarios and predicting outcomes with remarkable accuracy, AI empowers athletes and coaches to anticipate moves, optimize performance, and reduce injury risks. This evolution effectively transforms sport from a primarily physical contest into a sophisticated strategic science that blends data-driven precision with human skill and intuition. Meanwhile, the spectator experience is undergoing a dramatic metamorphosis. Immersive technologies such as AR and VR are revolutionizing how fans connect with the game. Rather than passive observers, fans become active participants, receiving personalized content tailored to their interests, accessing real-time statistics, and engaging in interactive, virtual courtside experiences that were once impossible outside stadium walls. This democratization of premium perspectives fosters stronger emotional bonds between fans, teams, and athletes, creating vibrant, participatory communities that transcend geographic and social boundaries. On the athlete side, the integration of bio-enhancement technologies marks a new frontier in optimizing human performance. Continuous health monitoring through wearables and advancements in bioengineering allow athletes to fine-tune every aspect of their physical condition—from recovery rates to endurance and movement mechanics. This wealth of biometric data feeds into AI systems that not only personalize training with unparalleled specificity but also predict potential injuries before they occur. While pushing the limits of human capability, these technologies also raise profound ethical questions about the nature of athleticism and fairness, underscoring the need for thoughtful regulation and ongoing dialogue.

This future is not about supplanting the core spirit of sport but about amplifying it. The challenge lies in balancing technological innovation with the timeless values that make sports meaningful: fair competition, unpredictability, human creativity, and emotional resonance. Embracing AI and bio-innovation should enhance athletes' efforts rather than diminish their agency or the game's integrity. Maintaining this balance requires vigilance around ethical considerations and data privacy, as well as a commitment to preserving the cultural essence that makes sports a uniquely human endeavor.

Hyper-Personalized Fan Experiences

The future fan won't just watch sport—they will co-create it. Advances in AI, AR, and VR are enabling fans to step into digital arenas, choose custom camera angles, receive real-time stats tailored to their preferences, and interact with players and other fans in immersive virtual environments. Live sports may increasingly become a hybrid event—simultaneously taking place in physical stadiums and the metaverse. Imagine fans donning VR headsets to experience a courtside seat at the NBA Finals, or using AR apps to play along with athletes in real time. Subscription models may evolve toward dynamic pricing based on engagement levels, device types, and gamified loyalty. AI will anticipate fan behavior, recommend content, and drive digital storytelling experiences tailored to individual tastes and emotions.

The concept of hyper-personalized fan experiences represents a profound shift in how sports consumption will evolve, moving fans from passive observers to active co-creators of their own sport engagement. Grounded in advances in AI, AR, and VR, this future revolves around flexibility, immersion, and individualization at an unprecedented scale.

With VR and AR, fans will no longer be confined to fixed, limited viewpoints of a game. Instead, they can step into fully immersive digital arenas where they control their experience—selecting camera angles, zooming in on detailed plays, or observing athletes' biometric data in real time. This multi-perspective participation allows fans to engage deeply as never before, effectively transforming each game into a customizable, interactive narrative. For example, imagine donning a VR headset to gain courtside access to the NBA Finals from your living room, feeling as if you're inside the stadium, hearing crowd reactions and players communicate, all while interacting with other virtual attendees. Meanwhile, AR apps will allow fans on-site or at home to "play along" with athletes through overlayed virtual objects—a real-time, mixed-reality game layered atop physical events, blurring boundaries between watching and participating.

The sporting event of the future may exist simultaneously across physical stadiums and metaverse environments—a hybrid model expanding both accessibility and engagement. Fans unable to attend in person will experience the thrill virtually, complete with social interaction, exclusive viewpoints, and augmented content. This creates new fan communities that are global, diverse, and deeply connected, as geography becomes less a barrier to participation. AI will analyze individual fan preferences, emotions, and past behavior to deliver tailored real-time stats, commentary, and digital storytelling that resonate personally. This personalization can range from recommending highlight reels that match a fan's favored player's style, to customizing interactive narratives that respond dynamically to game developments and fan reactions. Subscription and monetization models will evolve accordingly. Instead of flat fees, dynamic pricing could vary based on engagement intensity, device capabilities, and loyalty program participation. Gamification elements—such as loyalty rewards, leaderboards, and customizable avatars—will foster ongoing engagement and community-building, incentivizing deeper investment emotionally and financially.

This future creates new revenue streams for leagues and broadcasters by expanding their market beyond physical tickets and traditional broadcasts to virtual attendance and micro-transactions within fan experiences. Moreover, younger generations, particularly Gen Z and Gen Alpha, who naturally gravitate toward interactive, tech-enhanced entertainment, are likely to embrace and drive these models.

Culturally, this transformation democratizes access to elite sports experiences, allowing fans worldwide to participate meaningfully despite physical or economic barriers. However, it also raises challenges around data privacy, digital equity, and preserving authentic social connections among fans. Hyper-personalized fan experiences represent a convergence of AI intelligence, immersive tech, and innovative business models that redefine what it means to be a sports fan. The fan becomes a co-author of the sporting event's narrative, navigating a borderless, richly interactive, and emotionally engaging landscape that is tailored, dynamic, and deeply social. This reimagining not only enhances enjoyment but broadens the cultural and economic impact of sports in the digital age.

One of the most striking examples of this shift is the partnership between the NBA and Meta (formerly Facebook). Through the Meta Quest platform, fans can now enjoy select NBA games in virtual reality. By wearing a VR headset, they are transported courtside, with the ability to select custom camera angles, interact with other spectators' avatars, and access real-time 3D stat overlays. This creates an environment that closely mimics the in-stadium experience, extending it to fans across the globe who may never step foot in an arena.

Similarly, Spain's LaLiga has embraced advanced technology through its collaboration with Microsoft. Together, they have launched an AI-powered application that goes beyond standard match broadcasts. Fans can receive personalized highlight reels, access real-time tactical statistics, and even project holographic replays of key moments into their living rooms using AR. This not only enhances the viewing experience but also merges digital innovation with physical space, allowing fans to experience the game as if the action were unfolding right in front of them.

Sony's Hawk-Eye Innovations provides another example of how technology is deepening engagement. Originally designed as an officiating tool for sports like tennis and cricket, Hawk-Eye has evolved into a fan-centric platform. Today, it offers real-time augmented stats, play simulations, and interactive replay features available through mobile applications and AR stadium displays. Fans can analyze granular details of player performance and tactical execution, empowering them to engage with the game in unprecedented ways.

Beyond AR and VR, blockchain technology is also transforming fan engagement. Platforms such as Sorare blend fantasy sports with digital collectibles and gamification. Fans can collect and trade player cards, compete in fantasy leagues, and earn tokens that unlock exclusive digital content or metaverse-based experiences. This fusion of digital ownership and competition incentivizes long-term engagement and introduces entirely new revenue models for sports organizations.

The push toward hyper-personalization is another defining trend. Formula 1's F1 TV service exemplifies this by allowing viewers to fully customize their race-watching experience. Subscribers can choose onboard cameras from any driver, follow real-time data feeds, and access predictive AI modules that highlight dramatic moments involving their favorite teams or drivers. Personalized audio commentary further enhances the sense of individualization, making the fan feel as though the broadcast was created specifically for them.

Major League Baseball (MLB) has also ventured into the virtual realm with its Virtual Ballpark. This immersive platform enables fans to create custom avatars, attend games in a 3D virtual stadium, interact with other fans and AI-powered bots, and participate in live trivia and gamified challenges projected onto the VR field. Similarly, the NFL has experimented with AR-driven interactivity through "Play-Along" apps. These tools let fans overlay a coach's tactical perspective during live games, predict plays in real time, and compete on leaderboards, blending strategy with entertainment.

At the core of these innovations lie two powerful principles: deep personalization and immersive participation. AI enables highly tailored experiences—ranging from custom content and personalized stats to adaptive commentary—while AR and VR transform spectators into active participants rather than passive viewers. These technologies not only redefine fan engagement but also open new pathways for monetization, including flexible subscription tiers, gamified loyalty programs, microtransactions, and exclusive digital merchandise. The real-world impact of these developments is significant. Platforms that incorporate AR and VR features report nearly double the average engagement time compared to traditional viewing formats. Virtual experiences also enable leagues and brands to expand their global fan base, reaching audiences who cannot physically attend live events. Furthermore, new digital revenue streams—stemming from virtual goods, premium interactive content, and blockchain-based collectibles—are strengthening the economic ecosystem of sports. As the boundary between physical and digital worlds continues to blur, the future of sports fandom appears increasingly participatory and personalized. Sports organizations that successfully leverage these technologies will not only enhance fan loyalty but also secure a competitive advantage in an industry where engagement is the ultimate currency.

The Rise of the Cyborg Athlete

Wearable tech, biometric implants, and AI-driven coaching are already changing how athletes train, but what lies ahead may blur the boundary between human and machine. The elite athlete of the future could benefit from neurofeedback implants for focus control, gene editing for injury resistance, and exoskeleton-assisted training for strength development. While controversial, these advancements could redefine physical limits, forcing leagues and governing bodies to draw new ethical lines around "natural" performance. This era may also witness the expansion of technologically modified sports—competitions specifically designed for enhanced or synthetic athletes. Paralympic and adaptive sports, often pioneering in tech-driven performance, may become a model for how innovation and inclusion can thrive together.

The rise of the cyborg athlete represents a profound evolution in sports, where the integration of wearable technology, biometric implants, AI-driven coaching, and advanced bioengineering is pushing human performance beyond traditional boundaries. The elite athlete of the near future could harness neurofeedback implants that enhance mental focus and cognitive control, gene editing technologies that increase resistance to injuries and optimize physical traits, and powered exoskeletons that accelerate strength and recovery during training. These innovations collectively blur the boundary between the biological body and machine augmentation, fundamentally shifting notions of human athleticism.

Neurofeedback implants, for instance, would allow athletes to regulate stress and maintain peak concentration during competition, effectively providing a mental edge grounded in direct neural interface rather than solely psychological training. Gene editing, potentially utilizing techniques related to CRISPR (Clustered Regularly Interspaced Short Palindromic Repeats), could reduce susceptibility to common sports injuries such as ligament tears or improve muscle repair and endurance capacities. Meanwhile, exoskeleton-assisted training systems could provide targeted resistance and support, enabling athletes to develop muscular strength and stamina more efficiently and safely.

This convergence invites critical ethical and regulatory challenges. Leagues and governing bodies will face unprecedented decisions about what constitutes "natural" performance and fair competition. Current anti-doping frameworks may prove inadequate when enhancements are technologically embedded or genetically programmed. Questions arise such as: Should neuro-augmentation or genetic modification be allowed? At what point does an enhanced athlete compete in a fundamentally different category than unmodified peers? These considerations imply the need for new, nuanced ethical guidelines and possibly entirely new classes of competition.

Technologically modified sports, which are emerging alongside these developments, offer a forward-looking model for how innovation and inclusivity coexist. Paralympic and adaptive sports have long been leaders in integrating cutting-edge prosthetics, assistive devices, and tailored training technologies to empower athletes with disabilities. These arenas may serve as a blueprint for hybrid or enhanced athlete competitions that embrace synthetic augmentations as part of their core identity, celebrating human-machine collaboration rather than viewing it as an unfair advantage.

This evolution could eventually spawn new sporting categories or leagues dedicated to cyborg athletes, where augmented capabilities are standardized and compete on equal footing under regulations specifically designed for such enhancements. This may foster a richer diversity of athletic expression, pushing the limits of possibility while balancing fairness and spectacle.

Mark Daniel, paralyzed from the waist down, became a global symbol of advanced athletic augmentation when he competed in the Cybathlon, an international event specifically designed for athletes who use cutting-edge assistive devices. He trained daily with a 75-pound robotic exoskeleton, which he used for mobility after a spinal cord injury. Pilots like Daniel participate in tasks such as walking courses and navigating obstacles, effectively blending human willpower with robotic augmentation. In other Cybathlon events, paralyzed athletes used brain-computer interfaces (BCIs) to control avatars via thought alone, demonstrating the frontier of neurotech in sport.

Neurofeedback—training that measures and modulates an athlete's brainwaves—has been leveraged by champions in various sports. Andrea Dovizioso (MotoGP), Gabriella Papadakis (Olympic figure skating), Chris Kaman and Tobias Harris (NBA), and entire teams like Italy's national football squad ahead of their 2006 World Cup win. These athletes use neurofeedback systems to optimize focus, control stress, and improve real-time decision-making. Such techniques have measurably improved performance and are integrated into both individual and team training regimens at the world-class level.

Sports-specific exoskeletons—wearable robotic devices—are now used by both professional able-bodied and paralympic athletes for rehabilitation and, in some cases, competition.

- Barcelona FC and U.S. basketball franchises utilizing exoskeletons for rapid recovery from knee and back injuries, seeing recovery speed up by up to 30%.
- The U.S. Paralympics Team using robotic suits for athletes with spinal injuries, which improved their mobility and functional independence by 50%.
- Marathon runners and European footballers returning to competition much faster and with fewer re-injuries, thanks to lower-body exoskeletons.

Athletes like Oscar Pistorius and Markus Rehm have gained prominence for competing internationally with advanced prosthetic limbs, sparking debates about where to draw ethical lines on "natural" vs. technologically enhanced abilities. Pistorius made history as a double-amputee runner using carbon-fiber blades in both the Paralympics and the Olympic Games, fundamentally shifting public perception of what is possible with biomechanical augmentation.

While widespread, officially sanctioned gene editing for performance enhancement has not yet occurred, concern about "gene doping" is rising. Anti-doping agencies have banned the use of CRISPR and other gene-editing technologies, as the basic scientific capability for such enhancements already exists. No specific case of successful gene-doping in elite sports has been confirmed to date, but the field is actively monitored as genetic modification could soon move from science fiction into reality, fundamentally altering what it means to be an athlete.

Beyond competitive sport, pilot programs and research trials now use BCIs to help athletes—especially those with severe paralysis—interact with digital avatars and devices using only brain signals. These systems have been showcased at events like the Cybathlon and as therapeutic tools for regaining movement, coordination, and confidence after traumatic injury or neurological disease.

Smart Stadiums and Sustainable Infrastructure

Stadiums of the future will be intelligent ecosystems—autonomous, data-rich, and sustainable. Integrated with IoT sensors and edge computing, these venues will optimize everything from crowd flow and waste management to energy use and real-time security monitoring. Fans will enjoy seamless experiences—biometric entry, AI concierge services, drone food delivery, and climate-adaptive seating. These future stadiums are expected to leverage massive real-time data flows from sensors to manage crowd movements efficiently, reduce environmental impact through sustainable energy and waste strategies, and bolster safety via advanced monitoring. Fan engagement will be transformed by technologies such as biometric entry systems that speed up access, AI concierge services providing personalized assistance, drone-based food delivery for convenience, and adaptive seating that responds to climate conditions for comfort.

In 2022, Purdue Athletics partnered with Levy (a hospitality provider), Valqari, and USOG to pilot the first drone-delivered food and beverage service at a sports venue. During select baseball games, fans could pre-order combo meals such as hot dogs, chips, and bottled water. The food was prepared at a nearby location and loaded onto drones, which then flew over the campus, avoiding crowds and parking lots, and delivered the orders to secure lockers at the stadium. Fans retrieved their orders using digital codes, resulting in a fast, touchless, and convenient service. This pilot was intended to test efficiency and service quality for possible future large-scale implementation. Also, Google's Wing Aviation showcased a live drone delivery demonstration at Coors Field, home of MLB's Colorado Rockies. Drones autonomously delivered beer and peanuts directly to the field during an event attended by over 1,000 people. Though this was a demonstration and not a regular service during games, it highlighted the technical potential and logistical challenges of drone-based delivery in densely populated sports environments.

Thermavance has developed and deployed personal climate-control stadium seats, which enable spectators to heat or cool their own seats regardless of outdoor weather. This technology uses conductive heating and cooling, providing direct personal comfort without having to heat large open spaces. The adaptive seats are waterproof, dust-repellent, and robust enough for power-washing, making them suitable for football, baseball, tennis stadiums, and concert venues. This approach has been piloted in outdoor settings to reduce overall stadium operating costs and improve fan experience, especially in regions with extreme climate variability. Several stadiums have explored or implemented advanced microclimate cooling systems, with patented designs integrating climate control into both the seating structures and stadium architecture. For example, some systems use tiered seating with built-in air ventilation—a combination of air handling units and vent-diffusers can direct cooled or heated air down from seats to the field, maintaining comfortable conditions even in open-roof or partially open environments. Phase change materials embedded in stadium seats have also been tested to absorb and release heat, smoothing temperature extremes and enhancing spectator comfort.

Such intelligent venues epitomize the convergence of digitization, sustainability, and user-centric innovation in sport infrastructure, offering a rich area for exploration in studies or chapters focusing on AI and robotics in sports industry innovation. Crucially, these infrastructures will also become testbeds for sustainable development. Powered by solar energy, constructed with recycled materials, and digitally monitored for carbon output, stadiums will need to align with global climate goals. Sport as a spectacle and sport as a sustainability leader can—and must—coexist.

Mercedes-Benz Stadium (MBS) in Atlanta stands as a global benchmark for intelligent, sustainable sports venues, where digitization, sustainability, and user-centric innovation seamlessly converge. From its inception, the stadium was envisioned as an "intelligent ecosystem" designed not only to exceed fan expectations but also to set an unparalleled standard for environmental and operational excellence. Driven by owner Arthur Blank's vision, the stadium aimed to achieve and surpass LEED Gold certification, ultimately becoming the first professional sports venue in North America to earn the prestigious LEED Platinum status. This was achieved through a record 88 points awarded for green building innovation. At the core of MBS's sustainable design is an emphasis on energy efficiency and renewable power. The stadium uses 29% less energy than comparable venues, thanks in large part to over 4,000 rooftop solar panels that generate about 1.6 million kWh annually—enough to power the stadium for nine football games or thirteen soccer matches, greatly offsetting its operational carbon footprint. Energy-saving measures extend to the exclusive use of LED lighting and video boards, which consume up to 60% less electricity compared to traditional systems. Water stewardship is another pillar of the stadium's green credentials. With an extensive cistern system capable of holding between 680,000 and 2 million gallons, MBS captures and reuses rainwater for landscape irrigation and cooling, simultaneously mitigating urban flooding risks in Atlanta's Westside neighborhood. Complemented by water-efficient fixtures, these measures reduce the stadium's water usage by 47% compared to standard benchmarks. Sustainability is further reflected in the choice of materials and a commitment to circular economy principles. During construction and ongoing operations, recycled and recyclable materials were prioritized, including durable porcelain tiles sourced from 25 international manufacturers to reduce environmental impact. A dedicated Resource Recovery Room rigorously sorts and diverts waste, supporting the stadium's zero-waste goals (Mercedes-Benz Stadium, n.d.).

This commitment to waste reduction culminated in 2023 when MBS became the first sports stadium worldwide to earn TRUE Platinum certification for zero waste. The stadium consistently diverts over 90% of its waste from landfills through recycling, composting, and sophisticated waste sorting. Innovation in the supply chain, with the use of compostable and recyclable packaging, alongside widespread sorting bins, engages both fans and vendors in sustainability efforts. The stadium's comprehensive "zero waste playbook" now serves as a model for other venues globally. Technology plays a major role in enhancing both user experience and operational efficiency. Fans benefit from biometric entry, digital ticketing, and app-based services designed to optimize flow and convenience. The stadium's iconic retractable roof, made of ETFE—a lightweight, highly efficient polymer—maximizes natural daylight and supports natural ventilation, while lowering energy consumption and operational costs. Advanced IoT sensors and edge computing systems monitor and manage crowd safety, energy use, and other resources dynamically, creating a smart, responsive environment.

Beyond the stadium's walls, MBS integrates deeply with its community, offering urban gardens and edible landscaping that provide local jobs and educational opportunities. Sustainability programs encourage low-carbon transportation through biking valets, electric car charging stations, and pedestrian-friendly pathways, reinforcing the venue's role as a community asset. Since its opening, Mercedes-Benz Stadium has hosted over 50 major events annually, welcoming more than three million visitors while steadfastly upholding its stringent sustainability standards. Its efforts contribute to Atlanta's broader urban resilience by reducing heat islands, managing stormwater effectively, and providing surplus solar energy and educational outreach for local neighborhoods. The stadium not only sets a new industry standard but offers a scalable blueprint for large-scale sustainable infrastructure projects worldwide.

The Evolution of Governance and Digital Fair Play

As sports become more technology-driven, governance models must evolve to ensure fairness, transparency, and inclusion. Issues like data ownership, AI bias, and digital doping will require new regulatory frameworks. The introduction of AI refereeing systems and algorithmic match decisions will need to be accompanied by oversight protocols and ethical safeguards.

Modern governance in sport is shifting towards models that emphasize transparency, accountability, stakeholder engagement, and inclusivity. Successful frameworks clarify roles between boards and executives, foster open decision-making processes, and create avenues for diverse participation—ensuring governance bodies reflect the communities they serve. New codes such as the UK's "Code for Sports Governance" offer templates for transparency, diversity, and integrity, while federations like Badminton Denmark demonstrate the value of multi-tiered, democratic structures with explicit ethical standards.

With the explosion of biometric and performance data, the question of who owns athlete and game data has become critical. Leagues and teams often claim data ownership as a business asset, while players assert rights over their own performance and health information. This tension can lead to legal disputes and requires clear, athlete-centered policies that balance commercialization with individual rights. AI-driven algorithms now shape scouting, officiating, and performance analytics, but they are vulnerable to bias if trained on non-representative data. This can perpetuate or amplify inequalities in player recruitment, game decisions, or even injury predictions. Recent research suggests that strategies like "blind" AI scouting—where identifying features are hidden—can reduce human and algorithmic bias, but oversight is needed to ensure diverse, representative datasets. Continuous evaluation and human review remain essential safeguards.

The emergence of "digital doping"—where athletes may exploit wearable tech, AI-enhanced analytics, or data manipulation for unfair advantage—requires extension and adaptation of existing frameworks like the World Anti-Doping Code (World Anti-Doping Agency). E-sports, for example, now mandates similar anti-doping protocols as physical sports, expanding definitions and compliance requirements as needed.

The adoption of AI-based refereeing systems (such as Hawk-Eye, VAR, or smart foul detection) offers consistency and precision but also raises significant concerns about transparency, reliability, and ethical oversight. AI officials are subject to both technical errors and algorithmic biases, sometimes reflecting social or demographic prejudices embedded in their training data. Best practice dictates three key safeguards, namely: (a) all automated or AI-enhanced decisions should be validated by trained human referees, (b) AI officiating systems must be regularly audited for fairness, inclusive of diverse and representative datasets, (c) transparent feedback loops and stakeholder involvement—players, coaches, experts—ensure continuous improvement and public trust.

Ethical governance for tech-driven sports infrastructure should adhere to the following core principles:

1. Respect for human autonomy (Keeping humans at the center of decision-making, using AI to support—not replace—judgment).
2. Justice and non-discrimination (Ensure systems do not perpetuate or introduce new inequities).

3. Transparency and accountability (Make decision processes open to scrutiny; document and explain the logic behind automated rulings).
4. Privacy and security (Protect athlete and stakeholder data rigorously, with clear rules for usage, consent, and storage).

Blockchain may also play a growing role in creating trust and traceability, from smart contracts for athletes and agents to tamper-proof performance records and anti-corruption systems in match fixing. Sport's legal and ethical playbook will need to be rewritten—just as it was with the advent of professionalism or global broadcasting. Blockchain is poised to become a foundational technology for trust and transparency in the evolving landscape of sports governance. By enabling secure, immutable digital records and decentralized verification, blockchain can address many of the novel legal and ethical challenges that arise in the tech-driven era of sport. Blockchain-based smart contracts can automate and enforce agreements between athletes, agents, and organizations. These contracts are self-executing and transparent, ensuring that payment terms, transfer clauses, and performance incentives are carried out exactly as agreed—without the ambiguity or loopholes that can lead to disputes. For example, blockchain can guarantee automatic salary payments triggered by performance milestones, or instantly register image rights and endorsement deals. This reduces the risk of contractual fraud and streamlines negotiations. One of the most promising uses of blockchain is for the secure storage of athletes' performance data—from match statistics to biometric results. Once recorded, these data cannot be altered or forged, providing a trusted source for contract negotiations, anti-doping agencies, and scouting decisions. For athletes, this offers added protection of their professional history and a means to prove their credentials across leagues and borders.

Blockchain can also underpin monitoring systems that document every step in the organization and execution of matches. Transactions—from ticket sales to officiating decisions—can be logged transparently, making it far more difficult for bad actors to manipulate results or siphon off funds without leaving an indelible record. In betting and anti-match fixing, smart contracts can monitor wagering flows in real time and flag suspicious patterns for investigation. Just as professionalism and global broadcasting once forced wholesale change in sport's legal frameworks, blockchain now demands new standards for compliance, dispute resolution, and stakeholder engagement. Leagues, federations, and player associations will need to collaborate on protocols for digital identities, dispute mediation via smart contracts, and cross-jurisdictional enforcement. The challenge will be in designing systems that protect individual rights while promoting radical transparency.

The Expanding Role of Esports and Virtual Competitions

Digital-native sports such as esports, drone racing, and sim racing will continue to grow, not just as spectator events but as participatory platforms. With the rise of digital twins and AI-generated athletes, future competitions may blend real and virtual players in hybrid tournaments. What was once a niche subculture is becoming an integral part of the sport industry's identity, creating new career paths, fan communities, and business models. Virtual training environments may also become part of athlete development pipelines, particularly for cognitive training and scenario simulation.

Esports and virtual competitions are rapidly expanding their role within the broader sports industry, evolving from niche subcultures into mainstream, integral components of sport's identity. Digital-native sports such as esports, drone racing, and sim racing are increasingly recognized not only as spectator events but also as participatory platforms that engage diverse global audiences.

The integration of technologies such as digital twins—virtual replicas of real-world players or environments—and AI-generated athletes is driving innovation in competition formats. Future tournaments may feature hybrid ecosystems where human players and AI-driven or virtual competitors coexist and compete, blurring the lines between physical and digital sport. This fusion opens possibilities for novel spectator experiences and competitive dynamics.

Esports leagues continue to formalize their governance by adopting models inspired by traditional sports, ensuring structures for fairness, transparency, and professionalism. Established sports clubs like Paris Saint-Germain and FC Schalke 04 investing heavily in competitive gaming signal the convergence of traditional and digital sport sectors, expanding career paths for athletes, coaches, and related professionals. Moreover, virtual training environments are becoming increasingly relevant for athlete development—not just within esports but also for traditional sports. These platforms offer controlled, data-rich scenarios ideal for cognitive training, strategic decision-making, and scenario simulation, enhancing preparation and performance analysis.

Looking Ahead

The future of sports is not a destination but a process—an ever-evolving playground where innovation meets tradition. While uncertainty remains, what's clear is that the sports industry is becoming more connected, intelligent, and participatory. Those who embrace the coming changes with curiosity, responsibility, and a human-centered approach will help ensure that technology enhances rather than erodes the joy, drama, and fairness that make sport a global passion.

In the end, sport's most enduring power lies not in its tools, but in its ability to inspire. The challenge ahead is to ensure that technology doesn't just make sport faster or smarter—but more inclusive, more sustainable, and more meaningful for generations to come.

Chapter 4

Mind-Blowing Stories and Wins

The fusion of sports and technology has already produced unforgettable moments—some astonishing, others controversial, but all undeniably transformative. These stories don't just showcase what tech can do; they reveal how it is reshaping the very soul of competition, preparation, fandom, and performance. Whether through data-driven miracles, artificial intelligence (AI)-powered comebacks, or game-changing gadgets, these moments are the proof that the future of sport is not just on the horizon—it's already here.

The AI-Engineered Marathon Record

One of the most iconic moments in recent sports history was Eliud Kipchoge's sub-two-hour marathon run in 2019. While not officially recognized as a world record due to controlled conditions, the feat was a masterclass in how data, biomechanics, and precision engineering can align with human potential. Every element—from Kipchoge's shoe design and stride frequency to the timing of his pacers and the aerodynamic formation—was optimized using AI models and simulation tools. This wasn't just a run; it was a real-time experiment in human-machine symbiosis. Although this attempt, known as the INEOS 1:59 Challenge, was not eligible for official record recognition due to controlled pacing and course conditions, it showcased how technology can amplify elite human performance in unprecedented ways.

Key numerical and technological details highlight the depth of AI integration underlying this historic run:

- *Pace Optimization Using AI Models:* Kipchoge maintained an average pace of 2 minutes and 50 seconds per kilometer, a blistering speed sustained flawlessly over 42.195 kilometers. AI-driven simulations modeled his optimal stride length, cadence, and even energy expenditure, ensuring efficiency at every step.
- *Advanced Footwear Technology:* He wore Nike's ZoomX Vaporfly Next%, which integrate a carbon-fiber plate and a proprietary foam designed via biomechanical data analysis to maximize energy return. Lab tests suggest these shoes can improve running economy by approximately 4%, translating to significant time gains over marathon distances.

DOI: 10.1201/9781003533795-4

- *Aerodynamic Pacing Formations:* Pacers ran in a V-shaped aerodynamic configuration, minimizing air resistance for Kipchoge. Computational fluid dynamics (CFD) analyses informed the optimal positioning and speed synchronization—the "drafting" effect reduced energy expenditure by an estimated 2–3%.
- *Real-Time Monitoring and Adjustments:* Sensors on Kipchoge's body and pacers collected biometrics such as heart rate, oxygen levels, and running mechanics. AI algorithms processed this data instantaneously, guiding subtle tactical adjustments communicated via earpieces to pacers to maintain ideal pacing and formation.
- *Course and Environmental Control:* The route was meticulously planned using geospatial data to ensure minimal elevation change and wind interference, along with optimal temperature (approx. 13°C), humidity, and air quality—factors all modeled for peak physiological performance.

These AI-engineered factors contributed to a pace that surpassed previous marathon bests by nearly three minutes—the official world record at the time (2:01:39 by Kipchoge himself in Berlin 2018). Such precision alignment of human and machine showcases how technology is not merely adjunct but an integral partner in redefining athletic limits. The achievement didn't diminish Kipchoge's greatness—it amplified it. It showed how athletes and technology, when ethically and intelligently combined, can push the boundaries of what's considered physically possible.

Smart Helmets Save Lives

In American football and cycling, smart helmets embedded with impact sensors are now playing a crucial role in concussion prevention. One high school football game in Texas made headlines when a helmet sensor alerted coaching staff to a collision that looked harmless but triggered dangerous G-force levels. The athlete was benched and later diagnosed with a concussion that could have been catastrophic if ignored. Smart helmets embedded with advanced impact sensors represent one of the most significant technological breakthroughs in sports safety, fundamentally changing how we detect, prevent, and respond to head injuries. These devices transform seemingly harmless collisions into life-saving data, ensuring that athletes receive immediate medical attention when their brains are at risk—often before symptoms become apparent.

Smart helmet technology centers on sophisticated sensor systems that monitor G-force impacts in real-time. Modern systems like the Riddell InSite Impact Response System utilize five-zone sensor pads within helmet liners that measure linear and rotational acceleration. When a player experiences an impact, these sensors instantly analyze the force, direction, and duration of the collision.

The Shockbox sensor system operates through Bluetooth-enabled accelerometers that attach directly to helmet interiors, measuring impacts exceeding predetermined thresholds—typically 20g to 50g of peak linear acceleration. These devices can monitor up to 128 players simultaneously, with alerts transmitted up to 325 feet away to coaches' smartphones or tablets.

Advanced systems like BYU's XOnano smartfoam technology go even further, measuring composite data including acceleration, impact energy, and velocity with 90% accuracy—metrics that traditional acceleration-only systems cannot capture. This comprehensive approach provides coaches and medical staff with unprecedented insight into the severity of head impacts.

Research has established that concussions in high school and college football typically occur within a range of 70 to 120 G's of linear acceleration and 5,500 to 9,500 radians per second squared of rotational acceleration. However, the biomechanical properties of concussive injuries show that even impacts at the lower end of this spectrum can cause significant brain trauma.

Studies utilizing the Head Impact Telemetry System (HITS) have revealed that 75% of concussions result from impacts exceeding 96g linear acceleration and 7,235 rad/s^2 rotational acceleration. More concerning, research shows that for every diagnosed concussion, football players average 341 head impacts of greater strength than the concussion itself, highlighting the cumulative nature of brain injury risk.

Liberty Christian High School in Texas became an early adopter of helmet sensor technology, installing sensors in all varsity and junior varsity helmets to monitor impact force and frequency. When sophomore running back Andre Washington's sensor triggered after what appeared to be a routine play, coaches immediately pulled him from the game. The subsequent medical evaluation confirmed a concussion that could have been catastrophic if the athlete had continued playing.

The Riddell InSite system has been deployed across more than 25 colleges and hundreds of high school programs nationwide. At Port Neches-Groves High School in Texas, athletic trainer Ricardo Serna noted that the system provides "more eyes on the field," alerting medical staff to impacts they might otherwise miss during the chaos of gameplay.

Madison Plains High School in Ohio became the first football team in the state to implement Shockbox sensors after an alumnus funded the $149.99-per-unit devices for the entire team. Coach Jason Hunt emphasized the technology's role in protecting athletes' long-term cognitive health, stating, "*They're not going to make a living playing football, but what they are going to make a living at is using their brains, and we want to protect them.*"

Smart helmet technology extends far beyond American football. Cycling applications have seen significant innovation with devices like the HIT Impact system, which uses G-force measurements up to 140 across X, Y, and Z axes. Professional mountain bikers are now using these systems to monitor both major crashes and cumulative smaller impacts that occur during regular riding.

In ice hockey, research has shown that sport-related traumatic brain injuries occur at a rate of 160 concussions per 1,000 hours of play time. The G-Force Monitoring System (GFMS) developed for hockey players achieved a 6-millisecond sampling rate, providing real-time indication of impacts exceeding predetermined thresholds.

Cutting-edge research has produced fiber Bragg grating (FBG) sensors embedded within helmet structures, capable of detecting not only impact magnitude but also direction and location with unprecedented accuracy. These systems utilize machine learning algorithms to analyze transient signal "fingerprints" that reflect the physical deformation of helmet structures during impact.

Smart textile impact sensors (STIS) represent another breakthrough, using semiconducting polymer composites that can be integrated directly into helmet cushioning. These flexible sensors provide distributed impact measurement across the entire helmet interior, offering more comprehensive protection than traditional single-point accelerometers. Smart helmet technology operates on the principle that real-time objective data can overcome the subjective nature of concussion symptoms and athlete reporting. Research indicates that nearly one-third of athletes sustain undiagnosed concussions, often because they minimize symptoms to avoid being removed from competition.

The Minus Tau system, developed by Texas Tech medical students, exemplifies this approach by focusing on preventing tau protein buildup in the brain—a key factor in chronic traumatic encephalopathy (CTE). The technology aims to provide immediate smartphone notifications to parents when their child experiences a significant head impact, ensuring prompt medical evaluation.

Cycling helmets have evolved beyond traditional foam protection to incorporate sophisticated rotational force mitigation systems. MIPS (Multi-directional Impact Protection System) technology allows helmets to move 10-15 millimeters during crashes, reducing rotational energy transmission to the brain. Studies show MIPS helmets consistently reduce rotational acceleration across various impact conditions.

WaveCel technology represents a revolutionary approach, using a collapsible cellular structure that flexes, crumples, and glides to absorb up to 73% more rotational force than standard helmet linings. Independent testing has shown WaveCel helmets reduce concussion risk by up to 48 times compared to traditional expanded polystyrene (EPS) foam helmets.

Stanford University's inflatable helmet system takes protection even further, using an airbag-like mechanism that deploys around the cyclist's head during impacts. Drop tests demonstrate this system reduces head accelerations five to six times more effectively than traditional bicycle helmets.

The transformative power of smart helmet technology lies not in its visibility but in its silent vigilance. Unlike traditional safety measures that rely on obvious symptoms or coach observations, these systems continuously monitor every practice and game, creating an objective safety net that operates independently of human judgment or athlete self-reporting.

This technology represents a fundamental shift from reactive to proactive safety management. Instead of treating concussions after they occur, smart helmets enable prevention through early detection, removing athletes from harm's way before catastrophic damage occurs. The case of the Texas high school player whose sensor detected dangerous G-forces from an apparently harmless collision exemplifies this paradigm shift—technology identifying what the human eye cannot see.

As research continues to reveal the long-term consequences of repetitive head impacts, smart helmet technology stands as a critical tool in preserving the cognitive health of current and future generations of athletes. These devices transform every helmet into a sophisticated monitoring system, ensuring that the next generation of athletes can pursue their passion with unprecedented protection for their most valuable asset: their brain. This life-saving intervention wasn't televised or celebrated, but it marked a quiet, revolutionary shift: technology isn't just improving sport; it's safeguarding the future of athletes.

A Virtual Comeback on the Tennis Court

The COVID-19 pandemic fundamentally transformed how professional athletes approached training, creating an unprecedented need for innovative solutions when traditional court access was limited. While specific claims about individual players using VR training require verification, the broader story of virtual reality revolutionizing tennis training represents one of the most significant technological advances in modern sport. During the COVID-19 pandemic, professional tennis players faced extraordinary challenges. Fabio Fognini, like many of his peers, experienced significant disruption to his training routine. According to his own account, "*In the beginning, the first 10 days were really tough... I was not there with my mind, if I have to be honest. I had my home list and I talked to my physical therapist and he sent me something different every week because I would get bored.*" He ended 2020 ranked 17th in the world with a 6-10 win-loss record, having played only five tournaments before the tour shutdown.

However, when tennis resumed, Fognini demonstrated remarkable resilience. At the 2021 Australian Open, he reached the fourth round after undergoing arthroscopic surgery on both ankles in 2020. His performance against Alex de Minaur showcased clinical precision, winning 6-4, 6-3, 6-4, and eventually facing Rafael Nadal in the fourth round.

Virtual reality (VR) tennis training has emerged as a transformative technology that addresses the exact challenges athletes faced during the pandemic. The ATP Tour's official partnership with Sense Arena in August 2023 demonstrates the legitimacy and potential of VR training platforms. This multiyear partnership made Sense Arena the Official VR Tennis Training Tool of the ATP Tour, providing complimentary access to the top 100 singles players and top 25 doubles players.

The ATP Tour Sense Arena platform features groundbreaking capabilities including "Master Your Return," powered by real match data and analytics from ATP and WTA tours. This revolutionary feature enables users to analyze and return true-to-life serves in VR from top professional players, creating an unprecedented training experience that mirrors real competition.

Modern VR tennis training platforms utilize sophisticated technologies that create remarkably realistic experiences. Sense Arena's systems operate via Meta Quest 2 headsets paired with haptic racquets, offering immersive training applications for players at all levels. The platform enables users to "visualize, process and react to the real speed and ball rotation" from professional players like Jack Sock, whose 138+ mph serve has been replicated virtually.

Research validates the effectiveness of VR tennis training. A 2025 study found that VR training with real-time swing data visualization led to improved performance behaviors and enhanced situational awareness. Ten participants wearing sensor devices showed increased swing consistency and strategic decision-making when their swing data was displayed in real-time via VR overlay.

The mental aspects of tennis receive particular emphasis in VR training systems. Sense Arena's "Active Mental Training" philosophy enables players to simulate decision-making scenarios necessary for higher-level play, helping develop coping mechanisms needed to perform at their potential. Unlike traditional mental training approaches, VR allows athletes to be active participants in their own mental health development on court.

A groundbreaking pilot study involving 23 adolescent tennis players demonstrated that combined VR and tablet-based cognitive training resulted in significant improvements in Universal Tennis Rating (UTR) scores. The intervention group showed an increase of 0.5 UTR points compared to 0.02 for the control group—a 38% greater improvement.

Advanced VR tennis systems create authentic experiences through several key technologies:

- *Physics-Accurate Simulation:* Modern VR tennis platforms like those developed at University of Washington focus on modeling ball physics and racket interactions, carefully tuned to replicate authentic tennis gameplay dynamics. The systems demonstrate compelling virtual tennis experiences with accurate ball trajectory and responsive gameplay.
- *Real-Time Performance Analytics:* Recent advances integrate wearable sensor technology with VR environments, capturing motion data including swing speed and power while players engage in virtual tennis scenarios. This data is processed to provide instant feedback, allowing players to make adjustments during training sessions.
- *Professional-Grade Motion Capture:* Companies like Sense Arena use motion capture technology to import serves from professional players, enabling users to face virtual opponents that replicate real playing styles and serve characteristics.

Several professional players have become advocates for VR tennis training. Jennifer Brady, the 2021 Australian Open finalist, used VR training during her 14-month injury recovery, stating: "*It has allowed me to be able to submerse myself back in the tennis world and swing the racquet without hindering my rehab process.*" Jack Sock, a four-time Grand Slam doubles winner, described VR training as "pretty eye-opening" and "a game changer."

The COVID-19 pandemic significantly accelerated VR adoption in sports training. Research indicates that 25% of athletes used innovative or modern ways to maintain fitness during lockdown, including virtual reality and tracking devices, with World-Class level athletes showing the highest adoption at 30%. Professional athletes perceive the virtualization of sport as positive, recognizing its supportive role in maintaining training continuity during disruptions.

A comprehensive study of 2,300 individuals found that virtual reality fitness had profound effects on participants' mental and physical wellbeing during COVID-19 home isolation periods. The technology served as an effective substitute for traditional training environments while maintaining engagement and motivation.

The integration of VR technology in tennis training raises fundamental questions about the future of athletic preparation. If athletes can develop skills more efficiently in virtual environments than through traditional methods, this could revolutionize training paradigms across all sports. Virtual reality represents more than a stopgap solution—it embodies a fundamental shift toward smarter, more targeted training methodologies. The technology enables athletes to train their cognitive abilities through immersive visual platforms that can benefit athletic performance beyond traditional physical preparation. As VR technology continues advancing, with improvements in haptic feedback, visual fidelity, and motion tracking accuracy, the distinction between virtual and real training environments will continue to blur. The pandemic demonstrated that innovative training solutions are not just conveniences but necessities for maintaining competitive edge in an unpredictable world.

The story of virtual reality in tennis training—whether through verified professional adoptions or conceptual possibilities—illustrates how technology can transform athletic preparation. VR training systems provide athletes with tools to maintain and enhance their skills regardless of external circumstances, fundamentally changing how we think about the relationship between practice, preparation, and performance in professional sport. It also raised important questions: If players can train smarter in VR than in reality, what does that mean for the next generation of athlete preparation?

Drones Deliver Victory in Cricket Strategy

In the Indian Premier League (IPL), one team used a drone data capture system during pre-season training that allowed coaches to map every player's position, movement efficiency, and reaction time during practice sessions. Using this data, they adjusted player placements and bowling strategies in real time during the actual match. The result? A shocking win over a dominant favorite, credited largely to this behind-the-scenes tech integration. The evolution of cricket from intuition-based strategy to data-driven intelligence represents one of the most transformative shifts in modern sports. This transformation is perhaps nowhere more evident than in the IPL, where drone technology and tactical analysis systems have revolutionized how teams prepare, strategize, and execute game plans. The story of drone-assisted training creating shocking victories over dominant favorites illustrates how technology has fundamentally altered the competitive landscape of professional cricket.

The integration of drone technology in cricket represents a significant leap beyond traditional coaching methods. Research has demonstrated that drone-based position detection systems can achieve remarkable accuracy, with static accuracy showing root mean square errors of just 0.02 meters on clay surfaces and 0.15 meters on grass surfaces. When compared to established GPS systems, drone-based tracking shows only 2.78% difference in Ultimate Frisbee and 2.36% difference in soccer, with an overall consistency value of 0.998.

The Mumbai Indians pioneered this approach as early as 2015, when they introduced drone cameras with Go-Pro attachments to capture team training sessions from aerial perspectives. This initiative marked the beginning of a technological revolution that would fundamentally change how cricket teams approach tactical preparation and real-time strategy adjustment.

Modern cricket analytics now utilize sophisticated systems that can efficiently collect real-time data on each fielder's position for each ball bowled, ensuring minimal error and streamlined processes. Cricket Australia has specifically identified the challenge of developing systems that can generate X/Y coordinates and corresponding fielding positions of each fielder at the point of ball delivery, highlighting the strategic importance of precise positional data. The power of drone-assisted tactical analysis lies in its ability to provide coaches with comprehensive bird's-eye views that reveal formation lines, spaces between players, and potential avenues of attack. This perspective enables teams to identify tactical opportunities and defensive vulnerabilities that are invisible from ground-level observations.

The IPL has become a laboratory for cutting-edge cricket technology, with teams increasingly utilizing advanced data to analyze player statistics, predict performance trends, and develop opponent-specific game plans. This data-centric approach affects multiple facets of team strategy, from player selection to match-specific tactical adjustments.

Real-time analysis using wearable tech and Internet of Things (IoT) devices, combined with ball tracking and strike zones, enables coaches and captains to make informed tactical decisions with unprecedented precision. The integration of these technologies allows teams to predict player match-ups, optimize batting orders and bowling rotations, and execute strategic adjustments during live matches.

A prime example of this technological evolution is Quidich Innovation Labs' development of the Quidich Tracker (QT), a proprietary player tracking and visualization solution that uses optical tracking and computer vision to display an always-live field plot. This system captures and highlights field changes often missed by traditional cameras, providing real-time insights into player positioning and tactical adjustments.

For IPL 2025, Quidich introduced "QT-Always Live," a compact field plot that appears on the bottom-left of viewers' screens after every ball during live cricket matches. Powered by AI, this system delivers real-time tracking of player positions and field changes, seamlessly integrated into broadcasts through clean, easy-to-follow field plots.

The Science of Drone-Based Performance Analysis

Scientific validation of drone technology in sports has demonstrated remarkable capabilities. Studies show that drone systems can achieve 95%+ tracking accuracy with minimal identity switching and 60 FPS processing speed for real-time analysis. These systems utilize advanced algorithms including DeepSORT and Fast R-CNN for player and ball detection, with CNN-based feature embeddings for object re-identification. The technological infrastructure supporting drone analytics includes:

- YOLOv8/Fast R-CNN models for player and ball detection.
- Kalman Filter algorithms for object motion prediction.
- Hungarian Algorithm for optimal assignment matching.
- Trajectory smoothing and heatmap generation capabilities.

The transformation from intuition to intelligence in cricket strategy is exemplified by AI-driven systems that can analyze opponents' formations and player performance metrics instantly, allowing for timely substitutions and strategic shifts. These systems monitor key performance indicators like fatigue levels, heat maps, and ball possession ratios, providing actionable insights for tactical adjustments. Advanced cricket analytics now enable teams to assess live match data and recommend formations that can counter opposing tactics effectively. The integration of predictive modeling allows teams to foresee potential in-game scenarios and prepare strategic responses in advance.

The Mumbai Indians' approach to technology integration provides a compelling example of how drone-assisted analysis can deliver competitive advantages. The franchise has consistently invested in cutting-edge analytics, using aerial footage from drones to change field positions according to batting orders. During their championship seasons, this technological edge proved crucial in tactical decision-making.

The team's use of drone technology extends beyond simple footage capture. AI algorithms are employed to identify players with specific attributes that might otherwise go unnoticed, such as raw pace in fast bowlers or revolutions on the ball for spinners. This comprehensive approach to data-driven player analysis and tactical preparation represents the evolution from traditional scouting to scientific performance evaluation.

In 2023, Chennai Super Kings (CSK) became the first IPL team to establish an official drone partnership, collaborating with Garuda Aerospace, an MS Dhoni-backed drone startup. This partnership represents a significant milestone in the integration of drone technology within professional cricket franchises. As CSK CEO Kasi Viswanathan noted, "*As a team that considers innovation an important part of our success and growth, we are thrilled to partner with a company like Garuda Aerospace that shares our values and commitment to excellence.*"

The revolution in cricket analytics extends far beyond simple data collection. Modern systems can automatically detect events like sprints, passes, presses, accelerations, and decelerations using machine learning models with increasing accuracy. This capability enables tactical adaptability through real-time monitoring of press triggers, spatial structures, and strategic implementations. Research in sports analytics demonstrates that reinforcement learning algorithms can develop intelligent decision models that dynamically adjust tactics and strategies in response to changing game conditions and opponent behaviors. These systems enable teams to optimize performance, exploit opponent weaknesses, and capitalize on opportunities during competitions. The transformation of cricket from intuition-based decision-making to intelligence-driven strategy represents a fundamental paradigm shift. Teams now leverage comprehensive context-aware frameworks that collect data, extract insights from commentary, identify player strengths and weaknesses, and propose bowling and fielding strategies according to given contexts. These frameworks have demonstrated the ability to reduce batsman score rates by an average of 33% in simulated scenarios. The integration of AI in cricket enables performance analysis through AI algorithms that sift through extensive match data, allowing coaches to tailor training sessions and match strategies based on opponents' weaknesses. AI tools now predict player fatigue, injury risks, and potential match outcomes, enabling teams to optimize player selection and gameplay dynamics.

The impact of drone-assisted training and tactical analysis on competitive outcomes cannot be overstated. Teams that embrace these technologies gain access to detailed footage that helps identify strengths, weaknesses, and areas for improvement, leading to better training outcomes and enhanced athletic performance. The ability to capture overhead views, follow action closely, and offer perspectives previously unattainable with traditional cameras results in more engaging analysis and strategic insights. Modern cricket analytics platforms now provide comprehensive live data feeds including player statistics, match developments, and strategic insights in real-time. These systems help coaches and analysts make well-informed judgments about player replacements, tactical changes, and game strategy based on real-time data.

The story of drone-delivered victory in cricket strategy represents more than technological advancement—it signifies the complete transformation of how professional sports teams approach competition. What once relied on intuition, experience, and gut feeling now depends on precise data analysis, real-time intelligence, and scientifically-validated strategic decisions. The IPL's embrace of drone technology and tactical analysis systems has created a new competitive landscape where teams utilize advanced data to analyze player statistics, predict performance trends, and develop opponent-specific game plans. This data-driven approach enables more informed decisions about player selection, tactics, and strategy, based on real-time data and insights. As drone technology continues advancing with improvements in AI-powered analytics, real-time processing capabilities, and integration with machine learning algorithms, the distinction between traditional coaching methods and technological intelligence will become increasingly pronounced. The teams that successfully integrate these systems—combining human expertise with technological precision—will define the future of cricket strategy and competitive success.

Fan-Led Wins Through Technology

In a lesser-known but equally powerful story, a semi-professional soccer club in England turned its struggling financial future around by launching fan engagement initiatives using blockchain-based fan tokens. Fans voted on jersey designs, match-day music, and even lineup selections. The club sold over $1 million in digital tokens within the first year and saw both revenue and fan loyalty skyrocket.

The emergence of blockchain-based fan tokens represents a seismic shift in the relationship between sports organizations and their supporters, transforming passive spectators into active stakeholders with genuine decision-making power. While the story described highlights a semi-professional English club's remarkable transformation, this phenomenon extends far beyond hypothetical scenarios to documented cases of clubs generating substantial revenue and fundamentally reimagining fan ownership.

FC Barcelona set a powerful precedent when the club generated $1.3 million in less than two hours during their initial fan token offering in June 2020. The 600,000 $BAR fan tokens were sold at €2 each on a first-come, first-served basis, with demand exceeding the initial supply by over five times, resulting in more than $6 million deposited across platforms during the sale period.

The broader fan token ecosystem demonstrates the substantial financial impact of this technology. Top European football clubs have collectively earned around $204 million through fan token sales, while the global fan token market cap has reached over $440 million. Socios.com, the leading fan token platform, claims to have generated more than $150 million for partner clubs in a single year.

Apollon Limassol (Cyprus) partnered with Socios.com to launch their $APL fan token in 2021, allowing supporters to vote on team decisions including bus designs and matchday experiences. The initiative generated over €100,000 in new revenue and increased digital engagement by over 35%—crucial funding for a club operating in a smaller market.

BSC Young Boys (Switzerland) launched their $YBO fan token, offering fans VIP matchday access and signed memorabilia through the platform. The initiative led to a 25% increase in fan engagement online and brought in approximately CHF 250,000 in additional revenue since launch, with funds reinvested in youth development programs.

Levante UD (Spain), while competing in La Liga but not among the financial giants, launched their $LEV fan token to connect more closely with their global fanbase. Within months, the club reported a 40% increase in international fan engagement and generated around €150,000 from token sales, enabling investments in digital transformation initiatives.

Fan tokens operate on blockchain technology, creating transparent, secure digital assets that grant holders voting rights on club decisions, access to exclusive rewards, and participation in gamified loyalty programs. Unlike traditional cryptocurrencies, fan tokens are designed specifically for engagement rather than speculation, with their value tied to fan participation and team success rather than market speculation alone.

The democratic aspect of fan tokens is particularly compelling. Research analyzing 3,576 fan token polls revealed that fan tokens engage an average of 4,003 participants per poll, representing around 50% of token holders. This engagement level demonstrates the technology's effectiveness in transforming fans from passive consumers into active community participants.

The scope of fan token voting extends far beyond superficial decisions. Documented examples include:

- Juventus fans voting on goal celebration songs, with Blur's "Song 2" winning the first-ever binding poll and being played during a 4-0 victory.
- Galatasaray allowing fans to choose squad numbers for new signings.
- Young Boys of Switzerland enabling fans to vote on new kit designs.
- Valencia CF organizing "take the pitch" events where token holders experience exclusive stadium access.
- Apollon FC (Cyprus) permitting fans to vote on match line-ups and formations.

The financial model creates mutual benefit for both clubs and supporters. Clubs can use funds raised from token sales to invest in infrastructure, player development, or community projects, while fans gain access to exclusive opportunities that deepen their connection to the team. The tradability of fan tokens adds an economic dimension, allowing fans to potentially gain value as their team's popularity or success grows.

Barcelona's fan token success exemplifies this model: fans who purchased $BAR tokens gained voting rights on artwork for the first-team's locker room at Camp Nou, while the club received immediate capital injection during financially challenging times.

Critics have raised legitimate concerns about fan tokens, including lack of buyer protections, market volatility, and questions about the significance of voting rights. The UK's Advertising Standards Authority ruled that Arsenal FC had to remove fan token advertisements for being "misleading", while supporter organizations have expressed concerns about exploitation and insufficient crypto education.

However, proponents argue that fan tokens represent genuine innovation in democratizing team governance. Alexandre Dreyfus, CEO of Socios.com, emphasizes that "innovation requires education, education, education" and stresses the importance of transparency in communicating the technology's potential.

Fan tokens represent a fundamental shift toward co-created sporting experiences where supporters become genuine stakeholders in their clubs' identity and culture. This democratization of influence empowers fans with real decision-making power while maintaining the integrity of sporting competition.

The technology enables clubs to overcome geographical barriers when communicating with fans and engaging younger, digitally native audiences. FC Barcelona, with an estimated 450 million fans worldwide, can now reach supporters globally through blockchain-enabled fan tokens.

The integration of blockchain technology in sports extends beyond simple tokenization. Watford FC became the first major English football club to offer true ownership shares through digital equity, allowing fans to purchase actual club shares using fiat currency while gaining access to exclusive benefits and potential dividends based on financial performance.

As Socios.com CEO Alexandre Dreyfus envisions, within five years "hundreds, potentially thousands, of major sporting organizations and some of the biggest entertainment franchises from film and music" will fully embrace fan tokens as "a core part of their digital engagement strategy."

The blockchain revolution in sports represents more than technological innovation—it embodies a fundamental reimagining of the relationship between organizations and their communities. By transforming fans from passive spectators into active stakeholders with genuine voting power and financial investment, fan tokens create sustainable revenue streams while preserving the authentic passion that drives sports culture.

The documented success stories, from Barcelona's million-dollar token sales to smaller clubs like Apollon Limassol generating crucial revenue, demonstrate that this technology transcends hype to deliver tangible benefits. As blockchain-based fan engagement continues evolving, it promises to create more inclusive, democratic, and financially sustainable models for sports organizations worldwide.

In a world where audiences increasingly demand interaction and authentic engagement, fan tokens prove that sport can indeed become a truly co-created experience without sacrificing its fundamental integrity. The future of sports fandom is not just about watching from the sidelines—it's about actively shaping the teams and experiences that inspire passionate loyalty across the globe. This wasn't a tech gimmick—it was a radical rethinking of fan ownership. In a world where audiences are increasingly demanding interaction, this case shows how sport can become a co-created experience without sacrificing its integrity.

4.1. When Tech and Sports Collide: Case Studies

The integration of technology into sport is no longer speculative—it's concrete, measurable, and transformative. Across disciplines, levels, and continents, the collision between tech and sport has birthed new paradigms in training, strategy, fan engagement, and commercial models. This chapter delves into select case studies where technology has not only complemented but redefined the game.

Case Study 1: FC Barcelona's Innovation Lab—Data as a Competitive Weapon

Context

One of the most storied football clubs in the world, FC Barcelona, has shifted from relying solely on talent and tradition to becoming a pioneer in sports innovation through its Barça Innovation Hub.

What Happened

The club invested heavily in a high-performance data analytics infrastructure. From GPS tracking to neuromuscular performance assessments, every aspect of player movement, sleep, nutrition, and even emotional well-being is monitored and analyzed. Training loads are now adjusted using predictive models to reduce injury risk, and recruitment is influenced by behavioral analytics.

Impact

Injuries reduced significantly in key seasons, youth player development became more efficient, and the club attracted tech partnerships with global brands seeking innovation credibility. Barça's lab is now a commercial and educational asset, hosting international sports science conferences and publishing white papers.

FC Barcelona's transformation from a tradition-bound football club into a cutting-edge sports innovation powerhouse represents one of the most compelling examples of technology-driven competitive advantage in modern athletics. When the club launched the Barça Innovation Hub (BIHUB) in 2017, it wasn't merely adding a tech department—it was fundamentally reimagining how one of the world's most storied football institutions could leverage data science, predictive analytics, and cross-disciplinary research to maintain its competitive edge in an increasingly analytical sport.

The genesis of BIHUB emerged from a recognition that talent and tradition, while invaluable, were no longer sufficient guarantees of success. The club's leadership understood that the future belonged to organizations capable of converting daily training sessions, match performances, and even fan interactions into actionable intelligence. This vision materialized as a comprehensive "knowledge and innovation campus" that now manages more than 70 research projects simultaneously, collaborates with eight startup companies through equity partnerships, and hosts the annual Sports Tomorrow Congress—an event that has welcomed over 2,300 global delegates from across the sports technology ecosystem.

The technological infrastructure underlying Barcelona's transformation operates through multiple interconnected layers. At the foundational level, every player across the first team, academy, and women's squads wears WIMU PRO multi-sensor GPS vests that capture granular data on velocity, metabolic load, accelerations, and positional movement patterns. This data streams continuously into centralized analytics platforms where machine learning algorithms process millions of data points to identify performance trends, fatigue indicators, and tactical patterns that would be impossible for human observers to detect.

Beyond simple performance tracking, Barcelona has pioneered the integration of neuromuscular diagnostics through advanced techniques including tensiomyography and electromyography (EMG). These assessments feed into longitudinal muscle-fatigue models that track individual players' physiological adaptation over time. The club's "Sportomics" initiative takes this approach even further, utilizing metabolomic profiling to monitor biochemical adaptation and identify early warning signs of overtraining syndrome—a condition that can sideline elite athletes for months if not detected early.

The predictive power of Barcelona's analytics infrastructure became evident through their injury prevention initiatives. Machine learning pipelines now link weekly training loads, sleep quality metrics, and individual injury histories to sophisticated survival-analysis models that predict injury risk windows for each player. A comprehensive 2025 study focusing on the women's first team demonstrated a 14% improvement in player availability compared to traditional heuristic approaches. More dramatically, club-wide injury totals plummeted from 1,463 days in the 2021–22 season to just 704 days in 2022–23—a remarkable 52% reduction directly attributed to data-driven load management protocols.

The democratization of performance technology extends far beyond Barcelona's professional squads. The club's Barça GPS Tracker, developed in partnership with OLIVER Sports, places a coin-sized sensor on academy players' dominant legs, providing AI-generated feedback, detailed heat maps, and gamified training challenges. This system now serves more than 10,000 global users, creating a worldwide network of young players who train using the same technological principles as Barcelona's professional stars.

Barcelona's innovation extends into the digital infrastructure realm through partnerships with the Barcelona Supercomputing Center and GSMA to create a comprehensive digital twin of Camp Nou. This virtual replica models crowd flow patterns, energy consumption optimization, and 5G-enabled fan services, allowing the club to optimize stadium operations while enhancing supporter experiences. The digital twin serves as a testing ground for new technologies and services before implementation in the physical stadium environment.

The club's startup ecosystem represents another dimension of their technological transformation. Through BIHUB equity stakes in companies such as Visualfy, which develops stadium accessibility technology, and Metrica Sports, which provides advanced video-tracking analytics, Barcelona embeds external innovation directly into its operational framework. This approach allows the club to access cutting-edge technologies while maintaining strategic influence over their development and application.

The measurable impact of Barcelona's technological transformation extends across multiple dimensions of club performance. Player injury days decreased by more than half, research projects expanded from fewer than 20 in 2016 to over 70 by 2025, and the club developed entirely new revenue streams through educational programs and technology licensing. The annual Sports Tomorrow Congress has become a significant commercial and reputational asset, while startup investments have created a diversified technology portfolio that positions Barcelona at the forefront of sports innovation.

This transformation has fundamentally redefined core club functions across performance, recruitment, commercial operations, and brand positioning. Performance improvements are evident not only in reduced injury rates but also in enhanced sprint efficiency among La Masía graduates and more precise training load management across all squads. Recruitment processes now incorporate behavioral and physical "360-degree profiles" that inform scouting algorithms, ensuring potential signings align with both tactical requirements and injury-resilience thresholds.

Barcelona's approach to monetizing intellectual capital through online educational programs has enrolled over 8,000 students across 100 countries, converting research and development expenses into sustainable revenue streams while cultivating the next generation of sports science practitioners. This educational initiative reinforces the club's position as a global authority on sports innovation while strengthening grassroots development pathways worldwide.

The brand equity implications of Barcelona's technological leadership have attracted partnerships with tier-one technology firms who view association with the club as validation of their sports-focused innovations. These relationships create mutually beneficial arrangements where Barcelona gains access to cutting-edge technologies while partners benefit from real-world testing environments and the credibility that comes with powering one of the world's most prestigious football clubs.

Perhaps most significantly, Barcelona's transformation represents a fundamental cultural shift from intuition-based decision-making to evidence-driven processes. Coaching decisions, medical clearances, tactical adjustments, and even match-day logistics now rely on data-supported hypotheses rather than traditional wisdom alone. This cultural evolution has created an organizational learning environment where continuous improvement is embedded in daily operations rather than relegated to periodic review cycles.

The Barcelona Innovation Hub exemplifies how legacy sports organizations can leverage comprehensive data integration, machine learning, and open innovation partnerships to build sustainable competitive advantages. By treating the club as a living laboratory for sports science advancement, Barcelona has created a model that generates immediate performance benefits while contributing to the broader advancement of athletic science and sports technology development.

Case Study 2: Hawk-Eye in Tennis and Beyond – Trusting the Machine

Context

Hawk-Eye technology began as a line-calling system in professional tennis and quickly revolutionized officiating across multiple sports.

What Happened

The system uses high-speed cameras and sophisticated computer vision algorithms to track ball trajectory with remarkable accuracy. Initially adopted to review contentious calls, it eventually replaced line judges altogether in some tournaments.

Impact

Match flow improved, human error decreased, and fan trust in officiating increased. Beyond tennis, Hawk-Eye expanded into cricket, football (VAR), and even baseball, proving that high-stakes decisions could be reliably handed to machines—provided transparency and accountability were built into the process.

Key Lesson

When technology can clearly outperform the human eye, the cultural resistance to its adoption fades—especially when fairness is improved.

Hawk-Eye's journey from experimental television tool to global officiating standard is a vivid illustration of how technology can fundamentally redefine trust, fairness, and flow in competitive sport. The story begins in the early 2000s, at a time when disputed line calls in professional tennis matches often triggered controversy and, occasionally, injustice. The increasing speed of the modern game and relentless slow-motion scrutiny on television exposed the limitations of even the most skilled line judges—a missed call could sway not just a match, but a career. Sensing an opportunity, Dr. Paul Hawkins, a British computer scientist, drew upon advances in computer vision and triangulation algorithms to build a solution that could track a tennis ball's flight path with extraordinary precision.

Originally introduced during television broadcasts at Wimbledon in 2001, Hawk-Eye debuted as a way for audiences to visualize ball bounces and clarify contentious calls. Its impact was immediate: the vivid, computer-generated "traces" allowed both commentators and viewers to see exactly where the ball landed, erasing doubt and speculation. Soon, the tennis authorities recognized the system's wider potential—for not only improving the fan experience, but fundamentally increasing the fairness and integrity of the game itself.

The heart of the Hawk-Eye system lies in an array of high-speed cameras—ten to twelve in a typical tennis setup—carefully positioned around the court, each capturing the ball up to 340 times per second. Sophisticated algorithms stitch these images together, reconstructing the three-dimensional trajectory of the ball and pinpointing its landing spot, often with accuracy to within two or three millimeters. Before every tournament, the system is meticulously calibrated; surface geometry and environmental variables are incorporated to ensure maximal fidelity.

When the Hawk-Eye system was first officially introduced to tennis competition at the 2006 Miami Open, players were permitted a limited number of challenges per set to contest line calls. The moment of challenge became an arena drama—everyone in the crowd could watch the digital replay unfold on stadium screens in real time. Far from undermining umpires, the technology democratized the officiating process: players trusted the outcome, fans enjoyed the suspense, and heated arguments all but vanished from the sport. Match interruptions diminished, and matches proceeded with a new rhythm and integrity.

The technology's decisiveness and transparency—its propensity to make correct calls and display the evidence to everyone—shifted cultural perceptions quickly. Veteran players accustomed to skepticism began to rely on the system, sometimes requesting challenges just for peace of mind in pivotal moments. By the late 2010s, major tournaments like the US Open and Australian Open had begun abolishing human line judges on several courts, relying exclusively on Hawk-Eye's live calls. During the COVID-19 pandemic, this full automation proved its value further, ensuring continuity even with reduced on-site staffing.

Empirical analysis bore out Hawk-Eye's superiority: studies found that while human error rates in line judging could approach 10% during the fastest rallies, Hawk-Eye's error rate was consistently under 1%. The trust that athletes and fans placed in the system further legitimized its authority. Surveys and behavioral studies confirmed that both players and chair umpires came to accept Hawk-Eye determinations as final, even in climactic, high-tension scenarios.

Success in tennis created a blueprint for other sports. In cricket, Hawk-Eye became part of the Decision Review System (DRS), guiding crucial leg-before-wicket decisions and aiding in boundary and fielding assessments. In football (soccer), its visual tracking underpinned Goal-Line Technology, determining with laser clarity whether the ball had fully crossed the line—ending years of heartbreak for teams denied by officiating errors. The system evolved into a core component of Video Assistant Referee protocols. Major League Baseball turned to Hawk-Eye for both ball/strike calls and comprehensive player tracking. Even newer frontiers, such as e-sports and snooker, have embraced the technology for objective event adjudication.

Yet, Hawk-Eye's enduring legacy is not just its technical excellence, but its transparent, auditable operation. By making its decisions—and the underlying evidence—visible and open to scrutiny, the technology earned legitimacy and minimized cultural resistance to automation. Its adoption compelled sports federations to refine official protocols, balancing machine precision with human oversight and ensuring that error tolerances, appeal protocols, and data integrity standards were meticulously defined and maintained. Hawk-Eye's rise marks a milestone in sport's digital transformation. It stands as proof that when technology clearly and transparently outperforms the human eye, even the most traditional institutions will adapt. And in doing so, the sport becomes not just faster or more precise, but fundamentally fairer and more trustworthy—a testament to how digital evolution, carefully managed, can elevate the very soul of competition.

Case Study 3: WHOOP Wearables and Athlete Longevity

Context

Wearable fitness tech has exploded, but few have made as big an impact in elite sport as WHOOP.

What Happened

Initially used by CrossFit athletes and endurance runners, WHOOP gained traction in the NBA, NFL, and PGA. The device continuously measures heart rate variability (HRV), respiratory rate, sleep cycles, and recovery levels. It helped athletes like Patrick Mahomes and Rory McIlroy optimize training and rest with personalized data.

Impact

Athletes reported better sleep, lower injury rates, and smarter scheduling. Teams began using aggregate data to adjust practice intensity. During COVID-19, WHOOP even predicted early signs of infection based on respiratory anomalies—an unintended but critical health application.

The ascent of WHOOP wearables in elite sports captures a new era where continuous physiological monitoring guides not only performance but also health, longevity, and team strategy. Though the wearable fitness technology market is crowded, WHOOP has become singularly influential among professionals by focusing on invisible wellness variables—like HRV, sleep quality, and recovery—that traditional training metrics often overlook.

WHOOP's early adoption came via endurance athletes and the CrossFit community, who valued granular, 24/7 data over simple step counts or activity tracking. The device's strap, worn nonstop (even in water), collects a stream of biometric data: HRV, resting heart rate, respiratory rate, skin temperature, sleep stages, and movement patterns are algorithmically analyzed to create a personalized "recovery" score each morning. For pro athletes, this unbroken window into physical readiness transformed how they approach everything from practice intensity to scheduling days off.

The uptake accelerated as high-profile figures in major leagues embraced the platform. NBA players found that tracking overnight recovery and strain helped reduce soft-tissue injuries by enabling smarter load management. Patrick Mahomes cited WHOOP as a crucial tool in adjusting training routines for optimal quarterback performance, while Rory McIlroy attributed improvements in both focus and consistency on the golf course to his sleep and recovery data from WHOOP.

Perhaps the most profound validation of the technology arrived during the COVID-19 pandemic. By monitoring abnormal changes in respiratory rate—a metric often overlooked in sports settings—WHOOP's data flagged early warning signs that presaged COVID-19 diagnoses in multiple users, sometimes days before overt symptoms appeared. A study published in the British Journal of Sports Medicine (BJSM) in 2021 detailed how WHOOP was able to detect subtle deviations in baseline respiratory rates, enabling athletes and staff to seek prompt medical care and prevent outbreaks among teams.

Beyond individual benefits, professional teams have leveraged aggregated WHOOP data to inform collective decisions. Coaches use population-level trends to modulate practice loads, adjust travel plans, and manage rest—reducing the likelihood of overuse injuries and burnout across an entire roster. Elite organizations in the NBA, MLB, NFL, and PGA Tour increasingly view wearable-driven insights as competitive assets that enhance player safety and career longevity. The impact of WHOOP lies in its synthesis of continuous personal data with actionable, individualized feedback. Athletes report better, more restorative sleep, sharper focus, reduced risk of injury, and more rational scheduling—a holistic approach that reframes longevity as achievable through daily optimization, not just dramatic interventions. WHOOP's evolution from niche fitness monitor to essential health infrastructure during a global pandemic cements its status as a sport-technology paradigm, demonstrating the immense potential of smart wearables to transform the art and science of athletic performance and well-being.

Case Study 4: Manchester City's Augmented Reality Fan Experience

Context

As stadiums closed during the pandemic, clubs scrambled to find new ways to connect with fans. Manchester City responded with innovation.

What Happened

Partnering with digital agency Unit9, City launched an AR-enhanced app that allowed fans to project players into their homes, explore 3D match highlights, and take part in interactive challenges. The app used spatial computing and fan data to deliver personalized content.

Impact

Fan engagement skyrocketed despite empty stadiums. Merchandise sales saw a digital uptick, and fans from markets like Southeast Asia and North America reported increased loyalty. The campaign became a case study in immersive fan marketing.

The COVID-19 pandemic struck at the heart of Manchester City's relationship with its global fanbase, forcing the Premier League champions to confront an existential challenge. With the Etihad Stadium's 55,000 seats sitting empty for months, the club faced the potential erosion of fan loyalty and commercial partnerships that had taken decades to build. Rather than accepting this digital vacuum, Manchester City embarked on an ambitious technological transformation that would ultimately redefine how sports organizations worldwide approached fan engagement through immersive technologies.

The cornerstone of City's digital revolution emerged through their partnership with creative agency Unit9, a collaboration that demonstrated how spatial computing could transcend traditional sports marketing boundaries. The AR-enhanced mobile application they developed represented far more than a stopgap solution for pandemic-era restrictions; it became a blueprint for the future of sports entertainment technology. Through sophisticated spatial computing algorithms, the app created seamless interactions between physical and digital environments, allowing fans to project life-sized player avatars directly into their living spaces with photorealistic detail.

The technological architecture underpinning this experience showcased the convergence of multiple cutting-edge systems working in harmony. Spatial computing, which seamlessly blends digital and physical worlds, formed the foundation that enabled fans to experience interactive 3D match highlights from any angle they desired. The app's advanced rendering engine processed real-time environmental data, anchoring virtual elements convincingly onto users' coffee tables and floors while delivering instant responsiveness that made interactions feel natural and engaging.

What distinguished Manchester City's approach from conventional sports apps was its sophisticated integration of fan data analytics with personalized content delivery. The system analyzed individual user profiles, incorporating everything from geographical location and preferred players to previous purchase history and viewing patterns. This data fusion enabled the platform to deliver bespoke experiences for each supporter, whether they were longtime season ticket holders from Manchester or newly converted fans discovering the club from Southeast Asia. The technology could dynamically adjust content formatting, language preferences, and even cultural references to resonate with diverse global audiences spanning over 75 countries.

The impact on the broader sports technology ecosystem proved transformative across multiple dimensions. Augmented reality (AR) experiences in retail environments have demonstrated the potential to increase conversion rates by up to 94% compared to traditional digital interactions, and Manchester City's application of these principles to sports merchandise created new pathways for digital commerce integration. Fans who engaged with AR player projections showed significantly higher propensity to purchase official merchandise, particularly limited-edition items that felt more personally connected to their virtual experiences.

Manchester City's technological innovation extended beyond individual fan experiences to reshape the entire sports marketing landscape. The success of their AR initiatives prompted other major clubs and sports organizations to accelerate their own digital transformation programs. The NFL, for instance, began implementing Wi-Fi 6E infrastructure specifically to support future AR and VR applications in stadiums, recognizing that high-bandwidth, low-latency networks form the essential foundation for immersive fan experiences. Similarly, German football leagues experimented with AR smart glasses that overlay real-time statistics and player information directly onto live match viewing.

The technological ecosystem Manchester City created fundamentally altered how sports organizations understand audience engagement metrics. Traditional fan engagement measurement relied on attendance figures, television viewership, and social media interactions. The AR platform introduced granular behavioral analytics that tracked how long users interacted with specific players, which viewing angles they preferred for match highlights, and even how they customized their personal AR environments. This wealth of engagement data enabled the club to refine their digital offerings continuously while providing unprecedented insights into fan preferences across different global markets.

The ripple effects throughout the sports technology industry became evident as Manchester City's approach influenced everything from stadium design to broadcast production. The concept of "virtual perimeter advertising" emerged, where AR overlays could display sponsor messages and promotional content without requiring physical changes to stadium infrastructure. This innovation opened entirely new revenue streams for sports organizations while creating more targeted advertising opportunities that could be customized for different viewer segments simultaneously.

Manchester City's partnership with Sony to develop the Virtual Etihad Stadium further demonstrated how immersive technologies could create persistent digital environments that complement rather than replace physical experiences. Using Hawk-Eye Innovations technology, the virtual stadium enables fans to experience 3DCG match highlights, participate in community events, and explore digital merchandise collections through personalized avatars. This technological advancement represents a fundamental shift from event-based engagement to ecosystem-based fan communities that operate continuously throughout the season.

The broader implications for the sports industry ecosystem extend to how organizations approach fan retention and acquisition in increasingly competitive entertainment markets. Manchester City's AR initiatives proved particularly effective in markets like Southeast Asia and North America, where traditional stadium attendance presents logistical challenges but digital engagement offers unlimited scalability. The club's Southeast Asian fanbase of 80 million supporters demonstrates how immersive technologies can transcend geographical boundaries and create emotional connections that rival in-person experiences.

The technological foundation Manchester City established through spatial computing and AR integration has become a template for sports organizations seeking to build resilient, technology-enabled fan ecosystems. Their approach proved that immersive technologies could maintain and even strengthen fan loyalty during periods when traditional engagement methods became impossible, while simultaneously creating new revenue opportunities and deeper insights into supporter behavior across global markets. This case study ultimately illustrates how innovative technological adoption can transform crisis-driven necessity into long-term competitive advantage, reshaping an entire industry's approach to fan engagement and digital experience design.

Case Study 5: MLB and the Statcast Revolution

Context

Baseball has long been a numbers game, but Statcast turned it into a tech playground.

What Happened

MLB introduced Statcast—a player and ball tracking system that uses radar and cameras to provide real-time data on virtually every play. Exit velocity, launch angle, sprint speed, and catch probability became broadcast staples.

Impact

Broadcasters began using advanced stats to narrate games in new ways. Front offices transformed scouting and game strategy, and players used the data to tweak mechanics and boost performance. For fans, the once-opaque world of player development became a visual, data-rich experience.

Key Lesson

When data becomes entertainment, it builds deeper engagement and transparency without alienating traditionalists.

The technological transformation of Major League Baseball reached its inflection point on April 21, 2015, when MLB Network's broadcast of the Cardinals-Nationals game unveiled Statcast to television audiences for the first time. What viewers witnessed that Tuesday evening represented the culmination of a decade-long technological odyssey that had begun quietly in 2011 under layers of non-disclosure agreements and secretive development protocols. The system's emergence marked not merely an upgrade to baseball's statistical infrastructure, but a fundamental reimagining of how athletic performance could be measured, understood, and communicated to audiences spanning from front office executives to casual fans experiencing their first exposure to advanced metrics.

The technological foundation supporting Statcast's revolutionary capabilities emerged from an intricate marriage of optical tracking systems and cloud computing infrastructure that pushed the boundaries of sports analytics. The current iteration of Statcast, powered by Hawk-Eye Innovations technology since the 2020 season, employs a sophisticated network of twelve high-resolution cameras strategically positioned throughout each of MLB's thirty ballparks. This optical array represents a dramatic evolution from the original hybrid system that combined TrackMan radar technology with Pitchf/x camera systems, demonstrating how rapidly advancing computer vision and machine learning capabilities could enhance data collection accuracy while expanding the scope of measurable athletic phenomena.

The technical architecture of Hawk-Eye's implementation showcases the precision engineering required to capture the fleeting moments that define baseball performance. Five specialized cameras operating at 300 frames per second focus exclusively on the critical zone between the pitcher's mound and home plate, capturing every aspect of pitch delivery and batter interaction with microscopic precision. These high-frame-rate cameras generate what MLB technologists describe as a "veritable biography" for each individual pitch, documenting velocity, spin rate, seam orientation, horizontal and vertical break patterns, and release point coordinates within tolerances of plus or minus 0.1 inches. The remaining seven cameras, operating at 50 frames per second with 11-megapixel resolution, maintain continuous surveillance over the entire playing field, tracking every player movement, batted ball trajectory, and defensive positioning adjustment.

The data processing infrastructure underlying Statcast represents an equally impressive feat of technological coordination, requiring real-time analysis of approximately 10 gigabits of raw visual information generated every second during game play. This massive data stream flows through on-premises Kubernetes clusters deployed via Google's Anthos platform at each ballpark, enabling local processing capabilities that can function independently of network connectivity while maintaining seamless integration with Google Cloud's centralized analytics infrastructure. The system's ability to maintain operational continuity even during network disruptions reflects MLB's recognition that real-time data delivery had become as critical to game operations as electricity or lighting systems.

The technological sophistication extends beyond simple data collection to encompass advanced pose tracking capabilities that monitor eighteen skeletal points on each player's body thirty times per second. This biomechanical analysis opens unprecedented windows into the mechanical foundations of athletic performance, enabling coaches and analysts to correlate body positioning with performance outcomes in ways that traditional statistics could never achieve. The pose tracking system's ability to capture subtle variations in pitcher delivery mechanics, batter stance adjustments, and fielder reaction patterns provides insights that transcend basic outcome metrics to examine the underlying physical processes that generate those outcomes.

Cloud computing integration through Google Cloud services transforms the raw camera data into accessible insights through a complex pipeline of data processing and storage systems. The infrastructure stores pose tracking data in Google's Bigtable system while maintaining other game statistics in Cloud SQL for PostgreSQL databases, with nightly batch processing jobs using Dataflow to transfer information to Cloud Storage buckets and BigQuery for long-term analysis. This architectural approach enables MLB to manage the enormous data volumes generated throughout each season, which accumulate to over 25 terabytes of information annually while supporting real-time access for broadcast applications and front office analysis.

The technological evolution of Statcast reflects broader trends in sports analytics toward increasingly granular measurement capabilities. The 2023 upgrade to 300 frames-per-second cameras represented recognition that even 100 frames per second proved insufficient for capturing the complete dynamics of pitched baseballs traveling from mound to plate in less than half a second. This continuous pursuit of enhanced temporal resolution demonstrates how technological capabilities drive demand for ever-more-detailed athletic measurement, creating feedback loops between available technology and analytical curiosity that push the boundaries of what constitutes meaningful performance data.

The system's accuracy specifications reveal the engineering precision required to transform visual tracking into reliable quantitative measurements. Strike zone detection maintains accuracy within plus or minus one-quarter inch horizontally and even better precision vertically, while batted ball landing point measurements achieve accuracy within approximately one foot across the entire field of play. These precision levels represent significant improvements over previous tracking systems and approach the measurement tolerances required for official game decisions, suggesting potential future applications in automated officiating systems.

The integration of AI and machine learning capabilities amplifies Statcast's analytical potential beyond simple data collection toward predictive and prescriptive insights. Google Cloud's machine learning services process the continuous streams of positional and biomechanical data to identify patterns and correlations that inform player development strategies, injury prevention protocols, and strategic decision-making processes. This technological integration demonstrates how sports analytics has evolved from descriptive statistics toward predictive modeling that can anticipate performance trends and optimize training methodologies.

The technological infrastructure's impact extends throughout baseball's organizational ecosystem, fundamentally altering how teams approach player evaluation, strategic planning, and fan engagement. Front offices utilize the comprehensive data streams to build sophisticated player valuation models that incorporate previously unmeasurable elements of defensive positioning, reaction time, and biomechanical efficiency. The availability of precise sprint speed measurements, route efficiency calculations, and arm strength quantification enables scouts to evaluate players based on objective performance metrics rather than subjective observations, though the integration of traditional scouting expertise with technological insights remains an ongoing organizational challenge.

The broadcasting integration of Statcast technology exemplifies how advanced analytics can enhance rather than replace traditional storytelling approaches. Television producers can access real-time exit velocity measurements, launch angle calculations, and defensive positioning data to provide viewers with immediate context for every play's outcome. The system's ability to generate volumetric video replays and augmented reality visualizations creates immersive viewing experiences that help audiences understand the physical dynamics underlying exceptional athletic performances.

The technological foundation established through Statcast has created ripple effects throughout the broader sports technology industry, demonstrating how comprehensive tracking systems can generate insights that transcend their original applications. The integration of wearable technology, biomechanical analysis, and computer vision capabilities showcases convergent technological trends that are reshaping athletic performance measurement across multiple sports. The success of baseball's implementation provides a roadmap for other professional sports leagues seeking to leverage similar technological capabilities for enhanced fan engagement and competitive intelligence.

Statcast's technological architecture ultimately represents more than an incremental improvement in sports statistics; it embodies a fundamental shift toward data-driven understanding of athletic performance that bridges the gap between subjective observation and objective measurement. The system's ability to capture, process, and communicate complex physical phenomena in real-time demonstrates how advanced technology can enhance rather than diminish human appreciation for athletic excellence. By making visible the previously invisible elements of baseball performance through sophisticated optical tracking and data processing capabilities, Statcast has established a new paradigm for sports analytics that continues to evolve with advancing technological capabilities and expanding analytical curiosity.

Collision or Convergence?

These cases don't reflect tech disrupting sports — they show a convergence where both domains elevate each other. Whether the goal is winning, entertaining, or protecting athletes, the synergy between smart innovation and human talent is clear. What matters most is the intentionality behind the tech—used to enhance, not replace; to connect, not divide. As more organizations look to replicate these models, the challenge will be scale, equity, and ethics. But one thing is certain: the frontier of sports will be shaped not just on the field, but in labs, code, and digital ecosystems where the next breakthroughs are already taking shape.

4.2. Tech Heroes in Sports

While athletes often stand in the spotlight, behind many of today's biggest breakthroughs in sports performance, safety, and fan engagement are a growing group of innovators—engineers, scientists, designers, and entrepreneurs. These tech heroes are reshaping the playing field not by scoring goals or breaking records, but by building the tools, platforms, and systems that enable those moments to happen. This section celebrates some of the unsung figures whose tech-driven vision has changed the game—from wearables to AI coaching to immersive experiences. Their stories show that the heroes of modern sport aren't always wearing jerseys—they're often wearing lab coats or coding in hoodies.

4.2.1. Sam Robertson—The Performance Predictor

Hero move: Designing predictive algorithms that help teams prevent injuries before they happen.

A leading sports data scientist and professor at Victoria University in Australia, Dr. Sam Robertson is known for blending machine learning with human performance analytics. His models are used to predict injury risk, optimize training loads, and even support draft picks across professional leagues. Robertson advocates for a balance between human expertise and machine intelligence, warning against both over-reliance on AI and resistance to its integration. His work has helped bridge the gap between academics, coaches, and data engineers—creating systems that are both rigorous and practical.

Sam Robertson's journey from the Mornington Peninsula to the cutting edge of sports technology reads like a manifesto for a new breed of data-driven coach-scientist. After early stints in biomechanics and skill-acquisition research, he landed at Victoria University and the Western Bulldogs, where he began weaving machine-learning models into the everyday rhythms of elite sport.

He designed systems that forced numbers to converse with coaches, athletes, and even sceptical executives, insisting that contextual intuition finish every sentence that the algorithm started. In 2014 he published one of the first calls to fuse training-load monitoring with predictive modelling, warning that raw correlations alone could never capture the messy realities of a full season's campaign. Those ideas eventually crystallized into injury-risk dashboards that medical teams could trust in real time, cutting soft-tissue layoffs for several AFL clubs and saving six-figure payroll costs each year.

Despite the technophile résumé, Robertson's public talks are peppered with cautionary tales. He recalls models that "predicted" a rookie's ACL tear—after it had happened—and draft algorithms that seduced scouts into overlooking intangible grit. His answer is a "co-adaptive loop" in which algorithms surface probabilities and humans decide acceptable risk, a philosophical middle ground that has become standard doctrine across Australian sport.

The hero moment came when one of his injury-prediction suites flagged a marquee forward at 72 per cent risk three days before a preliminary final. Robertson convened coach, physio, and player, translated the coefficients into plain language, and persuaded all parties to trim a sprint block in training. The forward played pain-free, scored twice, and the club advanced. For Robertson, the victory was less about the model's accuracy than about engineering trust between silicon and sweat—a template now copied across professional leagues from Barcelona to Kansas City.

In the decade since, Robertson has evolved from in-house scientist to global consultant and podcast host, but his mission remains fixed: merge human know-how with computational foresight so seamlessly that, one day, preventing an injury feels as instinctive as taping a wrist—not because the data replaced experience, but because it amplified it.

4.2.2. Prof. Dr. Daniel Memmert: Redefining Sport Intelligence

Prof. Dr. Daniel Memmert serves as Professor and Executive Head at the Institute of Exercise Science and Sport Informatics at the German Sport University Cologne (Figure 3). Internationally recognized as a pioneer in the digital transformation of sport, he has significantly influenced the field through groundbreaking research in AI, machine learning, and big data analytics applied to sports. Ranked among the top ten sport scientists worldwide, Prof. Memmert has authored over 300 peer-reviewed articles and 45 books and has secured more than €10 million in third-party funding for his projects.

Figure 3: Prof. Dr. Daniel Memmert (source: own archives)

His research uniquely bridges theory and practical application, focusing on developing innovative tools for tactical analysis, predictive modeling, and decision-making support in elite performance settings. Collaborating with major organizations such as UEFA, FIFA, Bundesliga teams, and national federations, he remains driven by the question of how intelligent systems can help athletes, coaches, and sports organizations make faster, more accurate, and fairer decisions.

His academic journey began with studies in mathematics and sport education, leading to doctoral research on cognition and creativity in team games and investigations into athletes' attention and cognitive processes under pressure. Around 2003, his collaboration with Prof. Perl introduced neural network modeling to simulate decision-making in soccer, marking a significant shift toward data-driven sport analysis. Under his leadership, the institute has launched numerous projects funded by the German Research Foundation (DFG), including innovative 'e-science' initiatives that utilize deep learning to detect strategic patterns and anomalies in team sports.

Among his recent accomplishments is the "SportVid" project, a €500,000 initiative designed to automate tactical video analysis using computer vision, enabling near real-time extraction of positional data and comprehensive performance metrics beyond conventional stats like goals or passes. Real-world application is a core priority, with tailored systems developed for clubs and federations to streamline training, match analysis, and scouting workflows.

Education is another cornerstone of Prof. Memmert's work. He established a postgraduate program in match analysis and developed an AI curriculum for sport science students. In 2022, he launched the uLKIS project (University Teaching Concept for AI in Sport Science) to train educators across Germany in AI tools for coaching, tactical analysis, and decision support.

Throughout his career, Prof. Memmert has observed that innovation requires overcoming resistance, highlighted by initial skepticism toward AI technologies like neural networks in football. He emphasizes that sport's complexity and dynamic nature make it an ideal domain for AI to address challenges such as context sensitivity, anticipation, and noisy data. His approach relies on interdisciplinary collaboration combining expertise from cognitive science, engineering, computer science, and high-performance coaching.

Looking forward, Prof. Memmert envisions AI not only analyzing games but also designing personalized training, monitoring cognitive fatigue, and delivering real-time feedback directly to athletes via wearables. However, he stresses the importance of ethical AI development prioritizing transparency, explainability, and inclusivity to avoid biased outcomes and maintain trust. Prof. Memmert's vision for the future of AI and robotics in sport centers on three priorities: prioritizing explainability over complexity for users, integrating AI tools seamlessly into existing coaching practices, and addressing ethics before efficiency to secure credibility and equitable access. He anticipates advancements in personalized rehabilitation, adaptive training systems, and hybrid intelligence—AI systems that learn collaboratively with athletes.

In sum, Prof. Memmert champions a human-centered digital transformation of sport, where intelligent technology elevates rather than replaces the human element, making the game more insightful and strategically sophisticated without losing its essential human spirit.

4.2.3. Mounir Zok—Olympian Optimization

Hero move: Turning tech into an invisible ally for Olympic athletes chasing peak performance.

As the former Director of Technology and Innovation for the U.S. Olympic Committee, Mounir Zok led efforts to bring performance-enhancing technologies to American athletes ahead of the Rio 2016 and PyeongChang 2018 Olympic Games. Zok championed wearable tech, real-time motion analysis, and decision-support tools that allowed Team USA to tailor training at an individual level. His approach was athlete-centered, ensuring that innovation didn't overwhelm but empowered performance. His journey from Beirut to Olympic training centers and Silicon Valley boardrooms represents a remarkable story of innovation, perseverance, and visionary leadership that continues to shape the future of sports technology.

Mounir Zok's story begins in Beirut, Lebanon. Following his passion for physics and scientific exploration, Zok enrolled at the American University of Beirut, where he pursued a Bachelor of Science degree in Physics from 1994 to 1998, graduating Magna Cum Laude. At the University of Surrey, he completed a Master of Science degree in Biomedical Engineering from 1998 to 1999. The University of Surrey's Centre for Biomedical Engineering, one of the most respected programs in the field, provided him with expertise in human movement analysis, biomechanics, and the application of engineering principles to biological systems. His academic journey culminated with doctoral studies at the University of Bologna in Italy, where he earned his PhD in Biomedical Engineering from 2000 to 2003. Zok's dissertation focused on the functional analysis of the human musculoskeletal system through minimally invasive techniques. This research would prove foundational to his later work in developing wearable sensors and motion capture technologies for elite athletes. During his doctoral studies, Zok also spent time as an exchange scholar at the University of Virginia from 2002 to 2003, where he conducted sports biomechanics research at the Physical Medicine and Rehabilitation Department. This international exposure broadened his perspective on applying biomedical engineering principles to athletic performance optimization.

After completing his PhD, Zok embarked on a diverse career path that would establish him as a pioneer in both academic research and commercial applications of biomedical technology. His early post-doctoral work took place at prestigious institutions including the Santa Lucia Foundation in Rome and the University of Rome "Foro Italico," where he advanced wearable inertial sensor methods for gait and sports analysis.From 2003 to 2004, Zok worked as a post-doctoral researcher at the IRCCS Fondazione Santa Lucia, focusing on clinical rehabilitation, biomechanics modeling, and gait analysis. His research involved developing mathematical models of the human musculoskeletal system and working closely with orthopedic surgeons and physical therapists to assist in clinical decision-making processes. Simultaneously, Zok began exploring the intersection of biomechanics and performance arts through his role as Motion Capture Director at The POOL Factory from 2003 to 2012. This innovative company pioneered the application of real-time motion capture technology in contemporary dance and stage performances, creating immersive experiences that combined choreography, sound, light, and motion graphics.

In 2008, recognizing the commercial potential of his research, Zok co-founded Sensorize, a startup focused on developing GPS and inertial measurement unit (IMU) systems for elite football clubs across Europe. As the company's Business Development Director for healthcare and sports applications, he led the development of sensor-based solutions that provided unprecedented insights into athlete performance and movement patterns. Sensorize represented a significant milestone in Zok's career, as it demonstrated his ability to translate cutting-edge academic research into practical, market-ready solutions. The company's success in securing contracts with major European football clubs validated the commercial viability of wearable sports technology and established Zok's reputation as an innovator in the field.

In 2012, Zok received a career-defining opportunity when the United States Olympic Committee (USOC) recruited him as a Senior Sports Technologist. This role would transform not only his career but also the way American Olympic athletes trained and competed on the world stage. As Director of Technology and Innovation from 2016 to 2018, Zok brought a distinctive athlete-centered approach to sports technology. His philosophy centered on the principle that technology should empower rather than overwhelm athletes, ensuring that innovations seamlessly integrated into existing training routines without creating distractions or complications.

Zok's approach was grounded in what he called the "1% question"—identifying the one percent advantage that could mean the difference between winning and losing in Olympic competition. This philosophy drove his team to focus on technologies that provided meaningful, actionable insights rather than impressive but impractical innovations. Zok championed the integration of wearables that could provide real-time physiological and biomechanical monitoring without interfering with athletic performance. For cyclists, his team developed AR glasses that delivered cadence, speed, and heart rate data directly into the athlete's field of view, allowing them to maintain their aerodynamic position while receiving critical performance information.

Paralympic athletes benefited from high-tech wheelchairs developed in collaboration with BMW, which tracked metrics like stroke frequency and distance traveled. These innovations demonstrated Zok's commitment to inclusive technology development that served athletes across all Paralympic categories. The development of smart fabrics represented one of Zok's most forward-thinking initiatives. Working with companies like Google, his team explored weaving sensors directly into garments, creating truly seamless integration between clothing and data collection. These smart textiles maximized the available surface area of an athlete's body for data collection while maintaining comfort and performance.

Zok's background in biomechanics proved invaluable in developing sophisticated motion analysis systems. For archers, his team implemented high-speed cameras capable of capturing arrow flight at 16,000 frames per second, revealing the flex and trajectory characteristics invisible to the naked eye. This technology enabled athletes and coaches to make precise adjustments to technique based on previously unattainable data.Divers and gymnasts used sensors embedded in their training gear to track performance metrics in real-time, providing immediate feedback on elements like jump height, rotation speed, and landing accuracy. This instant feedback loop accelerated skill development and reduced the time required to perfect complex movements.

Recognizing that data collection was only valuable when properly analyzed and applied, Zok emphasized the development of decision-support tools that leveraged the IoT, AI, and centralized databases. These systems aggregated data from multiple sensors into real-time dashboards, enabling coaches to make informed, rapid adjustments to training and strategy. The integration of various data streams—from heart rate and GPS tracking to video analysis and environmental sensors—provided a comprehensive view of athlete performance that had never before been possible. This holistic approach enabled more nuanced and effective training interventions.

Among Zok's most innovative initiatives was the exploration of neuropriming technologies, which used controlled energy pulses to increase motor neuron excitability. These advanced methods aimed to accelerate both skill acquisition and strength gains, potentially reducing the time required for athletes to master new techniques or improve physical capabilities. The effectiveness of Zok's technology initiatives became evident in Team USA's performance at major international competitions. The 17-medal increase from 104 medals at London 2012 to 121 at Rio 2016, along with similar improvements for the Paralympic team, was partially attributed to these technological advancements and data-driven training methods. The success of the USA Women's Track Cycling team exemplified the transformative potential of Zok's approach. After earning silver medals at the 2012 London Olympics, the team embraced technology integration as a pathway to improved performance. Their training incorporated a sophisticated velodrome system that automatically recognized athletes, logged data points, and provided coaches with real-time dashboards displaying heart rate, oxygen levels, speed, and video analysis.

The cycling team's use of IBM's Watson IoT to track power, speed, energy consumption, and other factors in real-time, combined with heads-up displays on Solos SmartGlasses, demonstrated the seamless integration of multiple technologies into a comprehensive training ecosystem. Zok's innovations at the USOC earned widespread recognition within the sports technology community. In 2013, his team received the High Performance Team of the Year award from the Sports Analytics Innovation Summit, specifically recognizing their work with USA Boxing's sensor program. This recognition validated the practical impact of his technology initiatives on athlete performance.

His expertise led to frequent invitations to speak at major international conferences, where he shared insights about the intersection of technology and human performance. His 2018 keynote lecture at the International Society of Biomechanics in Sports, titled "The Rise of the Super-Athletes, and Why There Is No Turning Back," articulated his vision for the future of technology-enhanced athletic performance. In 2018, recognizing the broader potential for digital transformation across the entire sports industry, Zok co-founded N3XT Sports with a mission to modernize organizations at all levels of the sporting ecosystem. The company, initially conceived in Silicon Valley but headquartered in Barcelona, represents the next evolution of his career from athlete-focused technology development to comprehensive organizational transformation.

N3XT Sports operates on the principle that the sports industry faces a "tectonic shift" driven by changing consumer habits, technological advances, and revenue fragmentation. The company positions itself as a bridge between traditional sports organizations and emerging technologies, helping clients navigate complex digital transformations while maintaining their core sporting values. The firm's ecosystem approach connects endemic stakeholders like rights holders, commercial partners, and athletes with non-endemic players including investment funds, technology companies, and startups. This comprehensive perspective enables N3XT Sports to deliver solutions that address both immediate operational needs and long-term strategic objectives.

The company's most significant client relationship involves United World Wrestling, the international governing body for Olympic wrestling. Since 2021, N3XT Sports has supported UWW's comprehensive digital transformation, helping the organization evolve from a primarily social media-focused entity into a sophisticated digital media house. In February 2025, UWW appointed N3XT Sports as its Global Digital Transformation Partner, recognizing the success of their multi-year collaboration and expanding the scope of their partnership to include AI integration and enterprise-level optimization.

N3XT Sports has worked with multiple International Federations in preparation for major events like the Paris 2024 Olympics, helping centralize digital and data infrastructure while maximizing fan engagement and optimizing internal operations. Client relationships have included the International Olympic Committee (IOC), Union Cycliste Internationale (UCI), Fédération Equestre Internationale (FEI), and World Triathlon.Recognizing the rapid growth of the Middle East and North Africa sports market, N3XT Sports has established strategic partnerships to serve this emerging region. In 2025, the company expanded its collaboration with Link Development to create MENA-specific fan and member engagement solutions. This partnership includes the development of Arabic-language CRM tools and fan engagement platforms designed specifically for clubs, leagues, and federations in the region.

The company regularly publishes comprehensive reports on digital trends in the sports industry, providing insights into audience retention, data simplification, and technology integration. Their annual Digital Trends reports have become essential reading for sports industry professionals seeking to understand emerging technologies and best practices. N3XT Sports has formed strategic alliances with organizations like ThinkSport's CHANGE Project, which focuses on promoting integrity and good governance in grassroots sport through digital innovation. These partnerships demonstrate the company's commitment to democratizing sports technology and extending its benefits beyond elite-level organizations.

The company is actively exploring how AI can optimize sports organizations' operations at the enterprise level, from automated content generation to predictive analytics for fan engagement. This work builds on Zok's longstanding interest in using technology to enhance decision-making processes. N3XT Sports is developing scalable digital platforms that help federations improve fan engagement through personalized, localized content delivery. These platforms leverage first-party data collection to create more meaningful connections between sports organizations and their audiences. Recognizing that successful digital transformation requires human capital development, N3XT Sports focuses on helping organizations diversify their workforces to include dedicated technology managers, data engineers, and AI specialists. This emphasis on human development reflects Zok's understanding that technology is only as effective as the people who implement and manage it.

The company is actively expanding its geographic reach, with particular focus on emerging sports markets in the Gulf region and potential expansion into Asian markets. This growth strategy reflects Zok's vision of democratizing sports technology access across diverse cultural and economic contexts. From his early work with Team USA to his current client projects, Zok prioritizes user experience and practical functionality over technological complexity. This approach ensures that innovations genuinely enhance performance and operations rather than creating additional burdens or distractions.

Zok advocates for rapid prototyping, small-scale testing, and iterative development processes that allow for quick validation and course correction. This methodology reduces risk while enabling organizations to adapt quickly to changing needs and circumstances. Rather than focusing solely on individual technologies or isolated solutions, Zok emphasizes the importance of creating integrated ecosystems that connect various stakeholders and data sources. This holistic approach enables more comprehensive and sustainable transformations. Through his work with N3XT Sports and partnerships with organizations like the CHANGE Project, Zok demonstrates commitment to making elite-level sports technology accessible to grassroots organizations and emerging markets. This philosophy reflects his belief that technology should serve the entire sports ecosystem, not just elite levels.

He holds patents for innovations in sports technology, including the "Method for Measuring Muscular Power and Apparatus Thereof," granted in 2010. This patent reflects his ongoing commitment to developing practical, implementable solutions for sports performance measurement. His initiatives at the USOC demonstrated that technology could provide meaningful competitive advantages when properly implemented. The success of Team USA's technology-enhanced training programs has influenced similar initiatives by Olympic committees worldwide.Through his consulting work and thought leadership, Zok has helped establish industry standards and best practices for sports technology implementation. His emphasis on athlete-centered design and lean validation has become widely adopted across the sports technology sector.

By founding N3XT Sports and working with organizations at all levels of the sports ecosystem, Zok has helped make sophisticated sports technology accessible to a broader range of organizations, from grassroots federations to emerging market sports properties. His early work in biomechanics and sensor technology helped establish the foundation for the modern sports analytics industry. The data collection and analysis methodologies he pioneered continue to influence how sports organizations approach performance optimization and fan engagement.

4.2.4. Angela Ruggiero—The Blockchain Visionary

Hero move: Bringing the athlete's voice into boardrooms shaping the future of sport tech.

A former U.S. ice hockey Olympian and a member of the International Olympic Committee, Angela Ruggiero co-founded the Sports Innovation Lab to track how emerging technologies are changing the fan and athlete experience. Through her work, Ruggiero became one of the first voices to advocate for blockchain and digital identity systems in athlete contract management, endorsement tracking, and fan engagement. She's now a global advocate for Web3 in sports, helping leagues explore how NFTs, DAOs, and decentralized media can empower both athletes and supporters.

4.2.5. Will Ahmed—The Sensor Whisperer

Hero move: Making invisible physiological signals visible—and actionable.

David Lee, co-founder of sports wearable company WHOOP, helped transform how elite athletes understand recovery. WHOOP started as a sleep and strain tracker but evolved into a powerful health-monitoring platform used by pros in the NFL, PGA, and beyond. Lee's team pushed the limits of non-invasive biometrics, developing devices that could track heart rate variability and respiration 24/7 without interfering with performance. During COVID-19, WHOOP gained recognition for detecting early signs of illness—turning a performance tool into a public health ally.

4.2.6. Catapult Sports Engineers—The Invisible Coaches

Hero move: Building the "black box" of athlete movement.

Catapult, founded in Australia, became a quiet revolution in elite sports by embedding GPS and inertial sensors into lightweight vests worn by athletes during training and matches. Behind this success is a team of engineers and sports scientists who have made it possible to measure performance in ways that were once unimaginable. Used in the NFL, NBA, Premier League, and national teams across disciplines, Catapult's devices track explosive power, fatigue, sprint distances, and even acceleration patterns—giving coaches a second-by-second breakdown of what's happening beyond the scoreboard.

4.2.7. Prof. Dr. Sebahattin Devecioğlu: A Distinguished Academic Profile

Prof. Dr. Sebahattin Devecioğlu was born on May 19, 1968, in Elazığ, Turkey, where he completed his primary, secondary, and high school education. His athletic journey began during high school in 1983 when he played for both the Elazığ Vocational and Technical High School Team and the Elazığ Sürsürüspor Youth Team. In 1986, he enrolled at Gazi University's Faculty of Education, Department of Physical Education and Sports, graduating in 1990 with a specialization in football. That same year, he obtained his Class B Football Coaching License.

In 1991, Prof. Devecioğlu successfully passed the National Teaching Qualification Exam and was appointed as a Physical Education Teacher at Muş High School under the Muş Provincial Directorate of National Education. Following completion of his mandatory service, he transferred in 1993 to Elazığ İmam Hatip High School.

His academic pursuits advanced in 1994 when he began Master's studies in the Department of Physical Education and Sports at Fırat University's Institute of Health Sciences. The following year, he was appointed as a Research Assistant in the Department of Physical Education and Sports at the Faculty of Science and Letters. Under the supervision of Prof. Dr. Eyüp İspir, he completed his Master's thesis in 1996, titled "The Contribution of Sports Organizations in the Euphrates Basin to the Popularization of Sports." After serving as a reserve officer from 1997 to 1998, he embarked on his doctoral journey.

In 1998, Prof. Devecioğlu was admitted to the PhD program in Physical Education and Sports at Gazi University's Institute of Health Sciences while simultaneously being appointed as a Research Assistant at Gazi University School of Physical Education and Sports, Department of Sports Management. In 2002, under the supervision of Prof. Dr. Güner Ekenci, he completed his doctoral dissertation entitled "The Economic Dimension of Autonomy in Sports Management: The Case of the Turkish Football Federation (TFF)" and was subsequently appointed as a faculty member at Fırat University's School of Physical Education and Sports.

Between 2002 and 2008, Prof. Devecioğlu served as Vice Director of the School of Physical Education and Sports and Founding Head of the Sports Management Department at Fırat University. His international experience expanded significantly when he served as a visiting professor in the Department of Sports Management at Dowling College, USA, in 2011. He participated in Erasmus programs as a visiting academic at universities in Poland and Romania, and in 2012, attended the "International Sport Security" conference organized by ICSS and Paris Panthéon-Sorbonne University. From 2010 to 2020, he actively participated in international conferences on Sports Economics across the USA, Russia, the UK, India, and China, as well as the Football Biennale in Germany.

Prof. Devecioğlu was appointed Associate Professor in 2014 and achieved the rank of Professor in 2019 at Fırat University's Faculty of Sports Sciences, Department of Sports Management. During 2014–2015, he conducted significant postdoctoral research at the University of Maryland, Baltimore County (UMBC), Department of Economics, focusing on "The Contribution of Sports to the Economy in Turkey and the USA." In 2017, he participated in the "Value Education in Sports" Erasmus+ project in Spain.

Throughout his career, Prof. Devecioğlu has demonstrated exceptional leadership, serving on the University Senate, Quality Board, Incentive Committee, and Ethics Boards at Fırat University. His contributions extend to numerous national and international events, including the National Congress on Football and Science, Sport Business Chain, World Health and Sports Tourism Congress, National Sports Policy Workshop, Istanbul Bar Association's Sports Law Panel, International Football Economy Forum 2020, Turkish Sports Summit, 17th Council of Europe Conference of Ministers Responsible for Sport, and various Ministry of Youth and Sports workshops.

His practical experience in sports administration includes significant roles at Elazığspor Club, where he served as Manager (2008–2009), Chairman of the Board of Trustees, and Caretaker President in 2019. He also held positions as Manager and Head of the Football Department for the Fırat University Youth and Sports Club between 1995 and 2010, and was the founding president of the University Neighborhood Youth Sports Club. His involvement spans various sports federations and associations, and he was a candidate for the presidency of the Turkish Football Federation in both 2023 and 2024.

Prof. Devecioğlu has made substantial contributions to policy development, participating in the Elazığ Economic Congress and the 2014 Elazığ Development Congress as a member of the Sports Sector Commission. He contributed to the Ministry of Development's 10th Development Plan Special Expertise Commission on Sports and worked with strategic research centers like FESAM. His service extends to the Ministry of Youth and Sports' Economic Working Group, the Youth and Sports Council, and UNESCO's Committee on Physical Education and Sports. As a founding member of the Youth and Sports Commission of The Light Millennium, a New York-based NGO, he represented the organization at the United Nations in 2015.

His commitment to social responsibility is evident through numerous projects including Campus Sports, Elazığ Giants League, Peace and Sport, New York Street Football, Turkey's Search for Football Stars, International Hazar Sports Festival, Peace Ball Project, and Anatolian Informatics Meetings. He served as secretary of the 10th International Physical Education, Sports and Physiotherapy Congress and founding chair of the International Congress on Sports and Health.

From 2018 to 2025, Prof. Devecioğlu served as a member of the Scientific Board of the Sports Education Department at the General Directorate of Sports within the Ministry of Youth and Sports. In 2023, he was elected to the Education Committee and in 2025 to the Sponsorship and Marketing Committee of the Turkish University Sports Federation.

His international memberships include the International Association of Sports Economists, the Professional Committee and Turkish representation of the International Catchball Federation, the New European Media Initiative (NEM), and the Asgardia Independent Space Research Center (AIRC). He serves as Vice President of the Anatolian Informatics Meetings and represents Turkey in the European Platform for Sports Innovation (EPSI). As founder of the Turkish Sports Managers Platform and Ekospor portals, he continues to shape the digital landscape of sports in Turkey.

Prof. Devecioğlu's extensive academic portfolio includes editorial and authorial roles in numerous publications covering Sports Management and Sports Economics. His notable works include "The Economics of Autonomy in Football," "Elazığspor Belongs to the People of Elazığ," "Sports Technologies," "Postmodern Football," and "Turkish Football in its 100th Year," among others addressing games, football management, sports innovation, new trends in sports economics, social media in sports, the political economy of football, and the global football economy. He has also published book chapters, national and international journal articles, and presented papers at conferences, with research funded by FÜBAP and TÜBİTAK.

Currently, Prof. Devecioğlu continues his distinguished career as a faculty member at Fırat University's Faculty of Sports Sciences, Department of Sports Management, while also teaching in the Institute of Health Sciences. He lectures across undergraduate, master's, and doctoral programs in Sports Management and Sports Economics, maintaining his contributions to academic journals, newspapers, and magazines at local, national, and international levels as a sports editor and columnist.

Prof. Dr. Sebahattin Devecioğlu stands as a distinguished academic and thought leader in Sports Management and Sports Economics. His career seamlessly bridges athletic practice with academic excellence, connecting sport, innovation, and social responsibility. What began as an early interest in football has evolved into a lifelong passion for understanding sport's broader societal and economic impacts.

Currently serving as a professor at Fırat University's Faculty of Sports Sciences, he conducts research and teaches courses on sports policy, economics, innovation, and technology-driven change in global sports systems. His international scholarly experience includes positions at Dowling College (USA), The University of Maryland, Baltimore County (UMBC), and various European universities, where he has contributed to international dialogues on sport and society.

His pioneering research examines how digital transformation, sponsorship, and new media are reshaping sports economics, with particular focus on football governance, e-sports, and social innovation through sport. He has authored and edited numerous books addressing the political economy of football, social media in sports, and technology's evolving role in athletic development.

As a member of international organizations including the European Platform for Sports Innovation (EPSI), New European Media (NEM), and the International Association of Sports Economists, he actively contributes to cross-disciplinary projects linking academia, policy, and industry. He also serves on several national and international sports advisory boards and editorial committees.

Prof. Devecioğlu's work is inspired by sport's transformative power in communities and economies, integrating sports economics, technological innovation, policy reform, and education. His mission focuses on developing sustainable, inclusive, and future-oriented sports ecosystems both in Turkey and globally.

Reflecting on his journey through sports and academia, Prof. Devecioğlu identifies technology as both companion and catalyst. From grassroots football in Elazığ to international symposiums on sports economics and innovation, the evolving landscape of sports technology has shaped his path, defined his challenges, and inspired his vision for the future.

His introduction to sport was deeply personal and practical. As a young football player in high school, he was fascinated not only by the game's physicality but by its organizational structure: coaches, systems, communication, and metrics. This early curiosity established the foundation for his lifelong inquiry into how systems, strategies, and increasingly, technologies affect athletic performance, governance, and society.

During his undergraduate studies at Gazi University, where he specialized in football within the Department of Physical Education and Sports, he began thinking critically about sport as a field of study. At that time, digital technologies were emerging in sports analytics, training equipment, and media broadcasting. Although limited, these tools sparked his realization that sport was no longer merely a physical act; it was becoming a data-driven and media-saturated phenomenon.

The transformative moment of his career occurred during his postdoctoral research at the University of Maryland, Baltimore County (UMBC), where he examined the economic contributions of sport in both the U.S. and Turkey. This comparative perspective revealed how countries with strong innovation ecosystems were integrating sports technology not only into athlete training but into policymaking, urban planning, and education. This experience solidified his belief in technology's role as a tool for inclusion, transparency, and growth in sport.

He began working more intensively on technology-related themes: smart stadiums, e-sports, digital sponsorship models, and the intersection of social media and sports governance. Collaborations with international organizations like EPSI and NEM refined his understanding of how digital platforms were democratizing access to sports content and how AI-driven tools were enhancing both fan experience and strategic decision-making in clubs and federations.

Despite progress, the path presented challenges. In Turkey, budgetary constraints, institutional inertia, and lack of interdisciplinary integration often slowed technological adoption in sports systems. He encountered skepticism from traditionalists, resistance from policy circles, and logistical barriers when implementing innovation-driven projects. However, each obstacle became a lesson, teaching him the importance of building coalitions across disciplines, piloting small initiatives to demonstrate impact, and maintaining patience while advocating for change.

As an academic deeply rooted in both theory and practice of sport, Prof. Devecioğlu has witnessed firsthand, how AI and robotics are transforming athletic performance, coaching, fan engagement, and governance. These technologies are no longer theoretical ambitions; they are being implemented through AI-driven performance analytics, robotic rehabilitation devices, and even automated officiating systems.

His vision centers on human-centered innovation. AI and robotics should enhance rather than replace coaches, referees, or athletes. He advocates for augmented intelligence, where human expertise and machine precision complement each other. While AI may predict an athlete's fatigue threshold, the coach interprets that data within the context of the athlete's mental state and long-term development plan.

In Turkey and globally, he envisions sport innovation hubs—ecosystems where sports scientists, engineers, data analysts, and ethicists collaborate to develop AI applications tailored to local needs and values. He sees potential in robotics being used not only for elite performance but also for inclusive physical education, especially for individuals with disabilities or limited access to traditional training environments.

Academically, he encourages interdisciplinary research bridging sports sciences with computer science, engineering, and behavioral psychology. He mentors students exploring projects ranging from AI-based talent scouting to virtual reality-driven training simulations. Through his work with international platforms like EPSI and the New European Media initiative, he contributes to shaping policy and funding priorities that support ethical and equitable innovation in sport.

Prof. Devecioğlu views AI and robotics as critical tools—not ends in themselves, but means to create more resilient, transparent, and accessible sports ecosystems. Guided by ethical frameworks and collaborative practice, these technologies can help sport evolve without losing its essence.

His current focus represents this frontier: a future where technology doesn't define sport, but where sport defines how we use technology—for better humans, better athletes, and a better world.

Tech Heroes Are Rewriting the Playbook

These figures, and countless others like them, remind us that the biggest revolutions in sport often begin far from the pitch. They are the ones who anticipate needs, challenge norms, and build tools that allow athletes to do what they do best—with greater safety, efficiency, and joy. In a world where technology is no longer a novelty but a necessity, recognizing these tech heroes is essential. They are not supporting cast members—they are key players in the evolution of sport.

4.3. Lessons from the Winners in This High-Tech Game

In the fast-evolving world of sports technology, success isn't just measured in medals or match scores—it's reflected in adaptability, innovation, and long-term vision. The stakeholders who've embraced the digital shift aren't simply using technology—they're rethinking what performance, connection, and leadership mean in the 21st-century sports landscape. From elite athletes to visionary coaches, club managers to tech developers, the winners of this high-tech game share certain key mindsets and strategies. Here are the core lessons they're teaching the industry—and the world. Elite sport has always rewarded physical brilliance and tactical ingenuity, yet in the past decade a quieter contest has unfolded off the field—one in which the decisive factors are data fluency, digital empathy, and ethical foresight. The coaches, athletes, executives, and engineers who now set the pace in this high-tech arena do not merely install new devices; they re-define what it means to perform, to connect, and ultimately to lead in the twenty-first century. The following continuous narrative traces the mindsets and strategies through which these pioneers are reshaping the global sports landscape.

Walk into a top-flight training center today and the first impression is often silence. No shouted lap counts, no stop-watches snapping. Instead, a hum of sensors quietly captures each stride, swing, or dive. Companies such as Catapult have woven miniature GPS and inertial units into compression vests so light that National Hockey League skaters forget they are wearing them. As the athlete accelerates, decelerates, cuts, and collides, more than 80 live metrics shoot to a cloud dashboard where a performance scientist monitors workload and flags red zones long before muscle fibers fray.

The payoff becomes clear over a season. Soft-tissue injuries, once dismissed as bad luck, fall by double-digit percentages on squads that calibrate training load with these systems. When the same principles migrate to baseball, an algorithm capable of distinguishing a full-power pitch from a casual warm-up throw spares hundreds of ligament-straining repetitions, saving millions of dollars in salary protection for healthy rosters. The lesson is simple but profound: personalization wins where generalization once ruled.

Yet raw data alone does not orchestrate victory. In the analytics hub at an English Premier League club, an AI platform named AlphaPlay parses the last three seasons of opponent tendencies before the assistant coach has emptied his morning coffee. The software offers a shortlist of counter-press triggers and substitution windows—but crucially, it offers them in plain language, inviting rather than eroding human judgment. "AI becomes a highly productive assistant coach," concludes a recent Forbes profile, "while coaches retain control".

That framing—AI as collaborator, not overlord—has diffused earlier angst that algorithms might sideline intuition. Even mainstream technology vendors echo the theme. Microsoft's coaching guides emphasize real-time video breakdowns that augment but never replace a trainer's eye. Meanwhile, start-ups such as MetaBrain position conversational AI as a 24/7 mindset counselor, capturing biometric and mood cues so that the next face-to-face meeting between player and psychologist starts at a deeper level. Across disciplines, the winners treat code as co-pilot: indispensable in crunching possibilities, yet subordinate to human context.

Outside the locker room, a parallel transformation unfolds among supporters. Deloitte's global surveys show that today's spectators—especially the Gen Z cohort—expect their club to remember birthdays, predict merch tastes, and host live trivia during halftime. The International Olympic Committee's new Fan Data Platform met those expectations in Paris 2024, delivering 12 billion social engagements and 300 million web-app users around the Summer Games.

What distinguishes the leaders is persistence. When the Women's National Basketball Association relaunched its mobile app with Deloitte Digital, the guiding premise was a year-round dialogue, not a seasonal content push. Personalized highlight reels blend seamlessly with exclusive behind-the-scenes footage; loyalty wallets sync ticket scans with sponsor discounts. The more the system learns, the more each swipe feels like a one-to-one conversation—a relationship that outlasts the buzzer, drives lifetime value, and feeds new commercial models.

Such ambition succeeds only when the corner office treats technology as a cultural mandate rather than an IT add-on. Forward-looking executives declare a north-star vision, unify data silos, and link return-on-investment metrics to both engagement and efficiency. National governing bodies have begun to codify the practice: the United Arab Emirates, for instance, aligned federation, club, and government KPIs under a single AI-powered infrastructure, elevating digital transformation from department to doctrine. The International Olympic Committee went further, publishing an Olympic AI Agenda that enshrines excellence, respect, and fairness as guardrails for every machine-learning pilot.

Inside these digitally mature organizations, a psychological shift accompanies the technical one. Athletes who once feared scrutiny learn to embrace continuous feedback when coaches frame data as a growth opportunity. Sports psychologists note that performers steeped in growth mindset cope better with stress, treat mistakes as information loops, and sustain motivation deeper into their careers. The same ethos permeates analytics labs where data scientists iterate model versions overnight, celebrate small wins, and treat each failed prediction as fuel for refinement.

The expanding role of AI has also sharpened focus on ethics. Scholars warn that algorithmic bias could skew talent identification, or that opaque injury-risk scores might jeopardize careers. The IOC agenda therefore mandates athlete co-creation, transparent audit trails, and human oversight: AI must serve, not supplant, the people at the heart of sport. Clubs with foresight bake privacy protocols into onboarding sessions, clarify data ownership, and invite player unions to help shape governance. By treating trust as non-negotiable, these actors future-proof their innovations against legal and reputational backlash.

Finally, the most disruptive breakthroughs seldom emerge from isolated silos. At Rice University, a collaboration with alumni-founded BeOne Sports turns a simple smartphone camera into a motion-capture studio. Collegiate athletes compare their biomechanics against a global database, receiving pro-level insights without Hollywood budgets. BeOne's willingness to share data with third-party developers accelerates product cycles and spreads risk; the university, in turn, gains a research sandbox that attracts talent and funding. Similar triads—teams, tech firms, and academic labs—have sprung up worldwide, illustrating that cross-domain partnership is now a competency in its own right.

Success today is the capacity to translate streams of data into human empowerment, to convert fleeting fan attention into enduring community, and to anchor every innovation in ethical clarity. It demands leaders who champion digital literacy from boardroom to bench, cultures that prize experimentation over certainty, and alliances that dissolve boundaries between sport, science, and society.

The scoreboard still matters, of course. Yet the organizations that master this playbook discover that the numbers lighting up their arenas are mirrored by healthier athletes, richer fan relationships, and reputations for principled stewardship. In an industry where speed and spectacle often overshadow substance, the real winners are those who fuse technological audacity with a steadfast commitment to people. They are redefining what it means to triumph—not only today, but in every season the future unfolds.

1. Data is Only Power if it's Actionable

Elite teams and athletes don't just collect data—they translate it into meaningful insights. Whether it's biomechanics, sleep cycles, or opponent tendencies, winners invest in systems and people who know how to interpret and apply data in real time. The lesson? Data without interpretation is noise. Smart integration of analytics into decision-making is what turns potential into performance.

The NBA's Toronto Raptors have become leaders in performance analytics, using AI to manage player load, predict injury risk, and fine-tune game plans—resulting in one of the league's most data-driven championship runs in 2019.

2. Innovation Requires a Culture of Trust

Tech adoption isn't just a hardware or software issue—it's cultural. Coaches must trust AI-assisted recommendations. Players must believe in the efficacy of wearables and VR training. Executives must support experimentation even if ROI isn't immediate. The most successful organizations foster psychological safety around innovation: they encourage questions, allow for failure, and reward curiosity.

This mindset shift separates traditionalists from trailblazers. It's not about replacing human instinct with machines—but about creating an environment where the two complement each other.

3. Digital Transformation Must Be Human-Centered

No matter how powerful a new tool is, it won't succeed if it ignores the needs of the user. The best tech solutions in sports are those designed with empathy—for the athlete's body, the coach's workflow, or the fan's emotional journey. Successful stakeholders work closely with designers, psychologists, and performance experts to ensure tech enhances, rather than disrupts, human experience.

The Liverpool FC, whose player-focused tech stack prioritizes emotional well-being as much as physical metrics. They've proven that when technology respects the human behind the data, results follow.

4. Adaptability Outperforms Legacy

Champions in the tech-enabled era are often not the richest or most storied organizations—they are the most adaptable. From small federations using drones to scout talent in remote regions, to women's leagues leveraging social media algorithms to grow global audiences, the common thread is agility.

As the pace of technological change accelerates, the ability to pivot—strategically, creatively, and operationally—will be the defining trait of sustainable success. Legacy is no longer a shield; it must be constantly re-earned.

5. Inclusion is the Engine of Innovation

Many of the biggest leaps in sports tech have come from efforts to solve challenges for underrepresented groups. Adaptive sports and Paralympic innovations have led to breakthroughs in biomechanics and prosthetic design. Grassroots apps built for rural coaching have been scaled into enterprise-level scouting tools. When tech is developed with inclusivity in mind, it tends to be more robust, more creative, and more widely adopted.

Winners know that diversity isn't a box to check—it's a strategic advantage.

6. Fan Engagement is a Two-Way Street

In the digital age, successful organizations treat fans not just as spectators, but as co-creators. Winners in the fan experience space invest in personalization, interactivity, and digital storytelling. Whether through AR-enhanced game days, NFT collectibles, or fan-voted team decisions, the shift is from broadcasting to participation.

Lesson learned: In a world of infinite content, attention is earned—not assumed. The future belongs to those who know how to listen to their fans and build meaningful connections.

The winners in this high-tech game aren't just embracing gadgets—they're embracing change. They understand that technology is not a magic fix but a powerful enabler of human potential. They don't chase trends for optics, but align innovation with purpose. And above all, they remember that while machines can optimize performance, it's people—athletes, coaches, fans, communities—who give sport its meaning.

As the line between physical and digital continues to blur, these lessons will serve as a compass. Not every team or athlete will have the same tools or budgets—but mindset, openness, and strategic vision are universal currencies in the new era of sports.

Chapter 5

What's Next: Futuristic Adventures in AI and Robotics

The future of artificial intelligence (AI) and robotics is unfolding at a pace that challenges conventional frameworks of thought, innovation, and ethics. As machines become more capable of autonomous reasoning, perception, and physical interaction, they are increasingly embedded in domains that were once considered uniquely human. From healthcare to space exploration, the convergence of AI and robotics promises not only technical advancement but also fundamental shifts in how societies function, relate, and evolve. Intelligent systems are now integral to processes such as medical diagnostics, surgical assistance, and rehabilitation. Their capacity to process vast amounts of data with speed and precision allows for early detection of diseases, personalized treatment plans, and even emotional support through conversational agents. Looking ahead, developments in neurotechnology and human-machine interfaces suggest a future in which AI may not only assist but also augment cognitive and emotional functioning, raising deep ethical questions around agency, consent, and the nature of personhood (Figure 4).

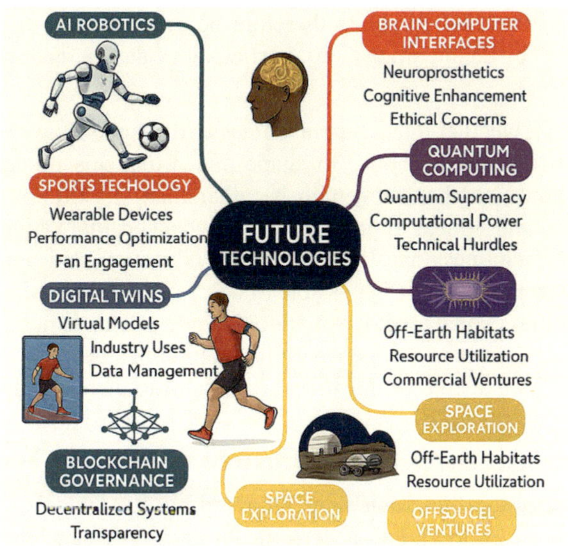

Figure 4: Future Technologies in Sports

DOI: 10.1201/9781003533795-5

In the domain of mobility, autonomous vehicles and aerial drones are reshaping how people and goods move through space. These technologies, supported by sensor networks and real-time data processing, promise to reduce traffic accidents, improve delivery systems, and create more efficient urban environments. However, the deployment of such systems also introduces risks, including algorithmic bias, exclusion of marginalized communities, and the expansion of surveillance infrastructures. The smart cities of the future must therefore balance technological efficiency with principles of equity, transparency, and public accountability. Equally transformative is the emergence of AI in the creative industries. Machines capable of composing music, generating art, and writing narratives blur the lines between tool and co-creator. While some celebrate this as a democratization of creativity, others worry about the loss of cultural authenticity, the dominance of corporate-owned algorithms, and the displacement of human artists. This tension highlights the need for new frameworks that recognize hybrid authorship and ensure inclusive access to creative tools.

Beyond Earth, robotics is extending human presence into space. Autonomous systems are already conducting planetary exploration, collecting data, and testing the feasibility of extraterrestrial habitats. As space missions become more ambitious, swarms of intelligent robots may one day construct infrastructure on the Moon or Mars, or mine asteroids for rare materials. These developments, while technologically exciting, invite reflection on the ethics of space colonization, environmental stewardship, and global equity in access to off-world resources. Despite these opportunities, the proliferation of intelligent machines also poses significant governance challenges. As AI becomes embedded in legal, financial, military, and educational systems, there is growing concern over accountability, transparency, and the erosion of human oversight. Automated decision-making can amplify social inequalities, especially when trained on biased or incomplete data. The future of AI and robotics must therefore be governed not only by technical standards but also by democratic values, participatory design, and interdisciplinary collaboration.

The question is not whether intelligent machines will change the world, they already are, but how societies will choose to shape and direct this transformation. The path forward should emphasize symbiosis rather than substitution, augmentation over automation, and ethical alignment over unchecked innovation. By fostering dialogue across disciplines, investing in inclusive education, and embedding human values into design processes, it is possible to co-create a future where humans and intelligent machines evolve together in mutual support. This is not a utopian vision but a necessary endeavor in an age where the boundaries between the organic and the artificial, the human and the machine, are becoming increasingly porous.

5.1. Time-Traveling to the Future of Sports Tech

Imagine stepping into a time machine calibrated not by dates, but by innovation. As you activate the controls and accelerate through the years, the scenery blurs until the doors slide open into the year 2045. You step into a world where the boundaries between sport, science, and storytelling have collapsed into a seamless, intelligent ecosystem. On the surface, the stadium looks familiar—grandstands, fans, a pitch—but as you approach, subtle signs of change appear. Entry is managed by facial recognition, replacing traditional tickets. Personalized greetings flash on digital walls, tailored to your favorite teams, players, and even your mood, detected through biometric scans. The crowd is no longer a passive mass. Each person wears lightweight AR glasses, turning the live match into an individualized dashboard. Some fans are tracking players' real-time oxygen levels, others are toggling between camera angles, and a few are watching with historic overlays comparing today's match to iconic games from decades past.

As the game begins, the players' jerseys double as biometric monitors, streaming continuous data to their coaches' AI dashboards. These systems don't just analyze—they advise. One player's sprint pattern has subtly shifted, signaling early signs of fatigue and prompting a substitution before injury strikes. Another receives real-time haptic feedback in their smart shoes, subtly correcting their posture to avoid strain. These are not robots in disguise, but humans whose every movement is enhanced by invisible algorithms, trained not only on personal data but on millions of hours of gameplay across eras, sports, and continents. On the sidelines, a retired athlete is not just a commentator but a digital twin trainer—guiding simulations that allow upcoming talents to train against hyper-realistic projections of legendary opponents. Practice no longer happens only on the field. It happens in virtual domes, with AI-generated weather, crowd noise, and pressure conditions that mimic future tournaments down to the psychological stress of penalty shootouts.

Elsewhere in this future landscape, fans from different continents participate in matches through remote haptic suits, letting them feel the rhythm of the game—every tackle, every heartbeat. These immersive experiences don't just replicate reality; they personalize it. A child in Nairobi watches a goal unfold from the perspective of her favorite striker. A grandfather in Buenos Aires relives his youth by stepping into a full-sensory recreation of the 1986 World Cup. Sport becomes not only a shared cultural moment, but a reprogrammable memory, a participatory narrative. Behind the scenes, blockchain infrastructures handle everything from player contracts and fantasy leagues to ticket resale and merchandise authenticity. Smart contracts eliminate corruption, ensure fair revenue distribution, and give fans micro-shares in their favorite clubs. Athlete branding is now co-managed with AI agents that analyze market trends and public sentiment in real time. Influencer-athletes don't just post—they co-create dynamic content experiences with generative media tools.

Yet amid this dazzling future, friction remains. As AI becomes the silent coach, strategist, and judge, questions arise about fairness, authenticity, and control. Who decides how much technology is too much? What happens when enhancements threaten the purity of natural talent? And who owns the flood of data that flows through every jump, swing, and breath of the modern athlete? As you return to the time machine, you realize that the journey to the future of sports tech is not just a technological one—it's philosophical. It's about redefining the meaning of play, competition, and human limits in a world where machines no longer sit on the sidelines.

Governing bodies face their toughest challenge yet: defining the rules for enhancement. International treaties emerge, stipulating limits on in-game augmentation—how much biometric feedback from smart jerseys, AI-driven coaching analysis, or wearable technology can be used before it crosses from "permitted innovation" to "unfair advantage." This ongoing debate echoes down to the grassroots, forcing youth leagues and amateur clubs to grapple with questions once reserved for the pros.

In this hyperconnected arena, the vital question becomes: who owns an athlete's body data? Olympic-level encryption standards guard biometric streams from smart clothing sensors, but legal battles flare between players' unions, leagues, and tech companies. Project Red Card—where over 2000 professional footballers have challenged betting companies over data usage—represents this new battleground. New rights emerge, granting athletes lifelong control over how their data is used, and even the ability to license their own digital twins for future compensation.

Ultra-personalized AR experiences challenge the sanctity of "the shared moment." Sports purists argue that technology risks creating parallel realities—where fans watching the same game through different AI-powered lenses experience entirely different narratives. In response, leagues introduce "authenticity zones" within arenas: sections where only non-augmented, real-time experiences are allowed, preserving the spontaneity that defines live sports.

Meanwhile, haptic suits allow fans from different continents to feel the rhythm of the game—every tackle, every heartbeat. These immersive experiences don't just replicate reality; they personalize it. A child in Nairobi watches a goal unfold from the perspective of her favorite striker. A grandfather in Buenos Aires relives his youth by stepping into a full-sensory recreation of the 1986 World Cup through VR training environments that now is extended to fan experiences.

Behind the scenes, blockchain infrastructures handle everything from smart contracts for athlete payments to ticket authenticity and fantasy league operations. Smart contracts eliminate corruption, ensure fair revenue distribution through tokenized systems, and give fans micro-shares in their favorite clubs. Athlete branding is now co-managed with AI agents that analyze market trends and public sentiment in real time, while tokenization allows fans to invest directly in player performance bonuses.

Retired athletes are no longer just commentators but digital twin trainers—guiding simulations that allow upcoming talents to train against hyper-realistic projections of legendary opponents. Practice happens in virtual domes with AI-generated weather, crowd noise, and pressure conditions that mimic future tournaments down to the psychological stress of penalty shootouts. These digital replicas create personalized training plans that adapt in real-time, predicting optimal recovery times and preventing injuries before they occur.

Yet amid this dazzling future, friction remains. Smart contracts and blockchain manage the money, but deeper equity problems persist. Will advanced training technologies and AI coaching exacerbate the gap between wealthy clubs and underfunded local teams? Global federations invest in "Equalize Tech Funds"—resource pools that subsidize access to the latest wearable and simulation gear for developing nations, ensuring that talent, not tech budget, remains the sport's true currency. As AI becomes the silent coach, strategist, and judge, questions arise about fairness, authenticity, and control. Who decides how much technology is too much? The consensus among experts suggests that AI should enhance rather than replace human expertise, with successful implementations requiring coaches, judges, and medical professionals working alongside technological systems rather than being displaced by them.

Finally, a new breed of ethicists and fan-philosophers steps onto the field to debate the future of play itself. Is the joy of victory greater when hard-won by flesh and will, or when aided by flawless algorithms? As champions hoist trophies, they do so not just for their physical prowess, but for their choices—to embrace, adapt, or resist the push of the machine age.

5.2. Radical Innovations of Future

Envisioning the future through the lens of radical innovation invites us to consider how transformative technologies might reconfigure the foundations of society, economy, and the environment. The term "rad" in this context signals not only extremity or novelty but a fundamental departure from incremental development toward paradigm shifts that challenge existing systems. As one projects forward, the built environment emerges as a central site of innovation. Cities are no longer merely dense concentrations of infrastructure and human activity, but responsive ecosystems embedded with sensor networks, adaptive materials, and distributed intelligence. Smart architecture utilizes energy-harvesting materials, climate-reactive facades, and modular construction systems that self-optimize according to environmental inputs. Urban mobility is redefined by frictionless multimodal transport solutions, including autonomous electric vehicles, personal air transport drones, and high-speed underground transit systems driven by magnetic levitation and vacuum technologies. These are integrated into a predictive infrastructure governed by AI capable of anticipating user needs in real time.

At the individual level, the interface between humans and technology becomes increasingly intimate and seamless. Wearable and implantable devices transition from tools of convenience to extensions of cognition and health management. Brain-computer interfaces allow for direct communication with machines, enhancing accessibility, decision-making speed, and even creativity. Personalized medicine is enabled by bioinformatics and gene-editing technologies, leading to tailored therapeutics, regenerative treatments, and preventative care optimized by predictive analytics. The integration of synthetic biology with nanotechnology further opens the door to programmable organisms and self-healing materials that operate at the molecular level.

Education and work undergo parallel transformations, facilitated by immersive learning environments powered by virtual and augmented reality, intelligent tutoring systems, and AI-driven skill acquisition platforms. The workplace evolves into a hybrid of physical and digital domains, where distributed teams collaborate across time zones in persistent, shared virtual spaces. In these environments, human and machine intelligences co-create outputs, with generative systems augmenting human creativity across fields from architecture to policymaking.

Radical innovation also reshapes social and economic systems. Blockchain-based governance models promote decentralization, transparency, and participatory decision-making. Digital currencies and smart contracts facilitate frictionless transactions while reducing dependency on traditional financial institutions. Meanwhile, ecological imperatives push technology towards regenerative design, circular economies, and carbon-negative practices. Materials sourced through green chemistry and 3D-printed at scale reduce environmental degradation while enabling localized, resilient production chains.

Despite these advancements, radical innovation is not without its tensions. Ethical, legal, and cultural frameworks must evolve to address issues of equity, surveillance, autonomy, and sustainability. The rapid pace of transformation risks exacerbating existing inequalities, privileging those with access to digital capital and infrastructure while leaving others behind. Furthermore, the blending of human and machine raises existential questions around identity, agency, and the limits of technological intervention.

The future envisioned through the lens of radical innovation is not merely one of novel gadgets or digital efficiency. It is a comprehensive reimagining of how we live, learn, work, heal, and govern—marked by a convergence of technologies that alter the very architecture of possibility. The challenge lies not only in the design and deployment of such innovations, but in ensuring they serve inclusive, ethical, and sustainable ends. This is the promise and paradox of radical futures: they compel us to think beyond continuity, while demanding a deeper commitment to collective stewardship.

5.3. How This Technological Revolution may Change the Game?

The current technological revolution is more than an era of rapid advancement—it is a structural reset that is altering the very game board on which economic, social, and cultural life unfolds. Unlike earlier industrial shifts that mechanized labor or digitized processes, today's transformation is characterized by intelligence that learns, systems that evolve autonomously, and tools that blend the physical and digital worlds. These are not incremental upgrades; they are paradigm-shifting disruptions. Consider healthcare: once reliant on routine diagnostics and manual expertise, it is now increasingly governed by AI-driven imaging systems capable of detecting diseases like cancer years earlier than human doctors. In some hospitals, robotic surgical assistants are now so precise they can perform complex procedures on microscopic tissue, guided by real-time data from 3D imaging and haptic feedback. In rural parts of India and Africa, telemedicine platforms powered by AI triage tools are giving people access to care for the first time, effectively redrawing the global healthcare map.

In education, the classroom is being redefined. A student in São Paulo no longer learns from a static textbook, but through immersive, adaptive software that responds to their pace, challenges their assumptions, and connects them with peers in Tokyo, Nairobi, or Berlin. Virtual reality allows learners to step inside a molecule, explore ancient cities as they once stood, or rehearse future careers in simulated environments. Platforms like Labster are already enabling students to conduct full-scale chemistry and biology experiments virtually, making expensive lab infrastructure less of a barrier. Meanwhile, companies like Duolingo or ScribeSense use machine learning not just to assess performance but to predict where learners are likely to struggle next, turning education into a dynamic, constantly evolving feedback loop.

In the world of work, automation has upended traditional career trajectories. Warehouse robots in Amazon's fulfillment centers navigate thousands of square feet in perfect coordination, reducing fulfillment time to minutes. In law, AI platforms like ROSS scan millions of legal documents in seconds to support case preparation. In finance, high-frequency trading algorithms now execute decisions at speeds impossible for any human to match. But rather than replacing all jobs, technology is transforming the nature of work itself: human-machine teams are now the new norm in logistics, journalism, and even architecture. For instance, architects increasingly use generative design tools—powered by AI—to create building blueprints that consider light, energy flow, material usage, and sustainability goals, offering options that human intuition alone might miss.

Entertainment and media are similarly being revolutionized. AI-generated art and music are challenging long-held definitions of creativity. Platforms like Runway and OpenAI's Sora can now generate cinematic video from text prompts, allowing filmmakers to visualize entire scenes before even stepping on set. In esports, competitions are not just digital representations of games—they're billion-dollar ecosystems with AI coaches, real-time performance analytics, and fans interacting through virtual stadiums using VR headsets and haptic wearables. Meanwhile, the rise of digital fashion houses—like The Fabricant—has introduced a world where garments are worn entirely in virtual spaces, used in social media posts, gaming avatars, or metaverse events, reducing physical waste while opening new dimensions of self-expression.

Governance and civic life are also being transformed. Estonia's digital citizenship system allows residents to vote, access healthcare, and manage taxes entirely online through secure, blockchain-supported identities. In Taiwan, digital platforms enable real-time public consultation on legislation, turning policymaking into a participatory, iterative process. Simultaneously, questions of surveillance, algorithmic bias, and data ownership are becoming central to public discourse, as seen in debates over facial recognition bans in San Francisco or the EU's AI Act, which seeks to regulate high-risk applications of AI.

These examples illustrate that this technological revolution is not merely about innovation—it is about redefinition. What it means to be skilled, educated, creative, employed, or even free is being rewritten by technologies that adapt faster than many institutions can regulate. The rules of the game are changing, but so too are the values that underpin them. In this new world, adaptability, ethical reasoning, interdisciplinary thinking, and emotional intelligence are not soft skills—they are essential competencies. As societies navigate this complex and often uneven transformation, the central question is not simply how fast we can innovate, but how thoughtfully we can design systems that prioritize inclusivity, sustainability, and human dignity. The game has changed, and with it, the stakes have never been higher.

Chapter 6

Practical Magic: How to Bring Tech into Sports World

In global sport, technology is no longer a peripheral enhancement—it is the engine driving transformation across performance, operations, fan engagement, and ethics. The idea of "practical magic" captures the essence of how applied innovation—when embedded thoughtfully into the real-world context of sport—can elevate every layer of the experience, from grassroots training sessions to elite-level competitions. Bringing technology into the sports world is not simply a matter of integrating gadgets or chasing trends; it requires strategic alignment, cultural adaptability, and a clear understanding of how sport functions as both industry and emotion.

The most visible arena for technological integration is athlete performance. Wearable sensors, GPS trackers, and biomechanical analysis tools now provide coaches and trainers with real-time insights into player workload, injury risk, and recovery patterns. These devices transform abstract data into actionable intelligence. For instance, in professional football (soccer), wearable vests embedded with accelerometers and heart-rate monitors allow teams to optimize training loads, customize rest protocols, and even predict muscular fatigue before an injury occurs. The practical outcome is not just peak performance—it is longevity, resilience, and a new ethic of care. But this is only one part of the story.

Behind the scenes, AI-powered video analysis tools are revolutionizing game preparation. Platforms that once required hours of manual tagging now use computer vision to identify formations, movements, and tactical weaknesses in minutes. In basketball, for example, AI can analyze thousands of plays to generate individualized scouting reports for each player. This not only enhances coaching precision but democratizes strategic insight—smaller clubs with fewer staff can now access the same level of analysis as elite teams. The result is a more competitive and intellectually rich environment where performance is shaped as much by data fluency as by raw talent.

For fans, the intersection of technology and sport is most palpable through immersive experiences and hyper-personalized content. Augmented reality overlays allow spectators to access live statistics during games, while virtual reality offers 360-degree replays and even virtual seats in iconic stadiums. In Formula 1, fans can now ride along with drivers using helmet cam feeds enhanced by real-time telemetry. The boundary between viewer and participant is dissolving, transforming

DOI: 10.1201/9781003533795-6

passive audiences into interactive communities. Social media algorithms now tailor highlights, fantasy league insights, and behind-the-scenes content based on fan behavior, while blockchain-enabled tokens grant supporters voting rights on minor club decisions, deepening their sense of belonging.

Operationally, stadiums and arenas have evolved into smart environments. From biometric ticketing to AI-powered crowd flow management, the infrastructure of sport is increasingly built on systems designed for efficiency, safety, and sustainability. Some venues are integrating environmental sensors and dynamic lighting systems to reduce energy use, while others deploy drone technology for security and maintenance. Logistics teams now use AI forecasting to manage everything from concession inventory to staff rotations. This practical deployment of tech behind the curtain ensures that the spectacle on the field is matched by seamless orchestration off it.

However, the introduction of technology also reshapes the ethical and regulatory frameworks of sport. The use of VAR (Video Assistant Referee) in football, or Hawk-Eye in tennis and cricket, has stirred debate about the sanctity of human judgment versus the accuracy of machine precision. These systems raise questions not only about fairness but about rhythm, emotion, and the perceived authenticity of the game. At the same time, the growing use of biometric and performance data introduces complex issues of consent, data ownership, and surveillance. Who controls the information collected from athletes? How is it stored, shared, or monetized? As sport adopts more sophisticated technologies, it must also develop robust governance models that protect individual rights while fostering collective innovation.

Implementing technology in sport is not a plug-and-play process. It requires sensitivity to the unique rhythms, rituals, and resistances of different sporting cultures. A successful integration often begins with experimentation—pilot projects, co-design with athletes, and feedback loops with coaches and fans. For example, Major League Baseball's cautious rollout of pitch-tracking systems was accompanied by years of testing and adjustment, ensuring that human umpires remained part of the ecosystem. Similarly, e-cycling platforms like Zwift have grown by collaborating directly with athletes to simulate physical conditions accurately and build credibility in competitive communities.

Perhaps the most critical success factor is education. Coaches, athletes, administrators, and fans all need to understand not just how the technology works, but what it means. Without digital literacy, even the most powerful tools can become sources of frustration or misuse. Investing in upskilling across the sports workforce—through workshops, certifications, and partnerships with tech companies—is essential to bridge the gap between innovation and implementation.

Bringing technology into the world of sport is both a technical challenge and a cultural project. The magic lies not in the machines themselves, but in how thoughtfully they are woven into the fabric of training, competition, and community. When done well, technology does not replace the soul of sport—it amplifies it. It makes the invisible visible, the complex actionable, and the future attainable. The real power of innovation in sport is not in creating something entirely new, but in unlocking the full potential of what already exists—human effort, team spirit, and the universal desire to push the boundaries of what is possible.

6.1. Coaches and Athletes

The relationship between coaches and athletes is being reshaped by technological advancement, shifting expectations, and new performance paradigms. While the foundational elements of trust, communication, and mutual respect remain central, the dynamics of coaching and athlete development are now deeply influenced by data-driven insights, digital platforms, and the expanding reach of sports science. The role of the coach is no longer confined to tactical instruction and motivational leadership; it increasingly encompasses data interpretation, mental health management, and the capacity to guide individuals through highly complex, technology-enhanced performance environments. Today's coaches must be part strategist, part psychologist, and part analyst. The athlete, likewise, is no longer a passive recipient of instruction but an active participant in co-creating their performance trajectory—armed with personal metrics, wearable technology, and on-demand access to feedback.

The integration of technology into training regimens has transformed how coaches observe, evaluate, and interact with athletes. Motion capture systems allow for granular biomechanical analysis, enabling subtle adjustments to technique that would be impossible to detect with the naked eye. High-speed cameras break down movement into millisecond frames, supporting injury prevention and efficiency improvements. Platforms like Catapult or Kinexon generate real-time data on player load, acceleration, and fatigue, equipping coaches with continuous feedback loops that enhance decision-making. As a result, coaching sessions have become more individualized, responsive, and precision-focused, fostering environments where athletes can develop with greater insight into their own capabilities and limits. However, the human element remains essential—data must be contextualized through relational knowledge and experiential wisdom to avoid reducing performance to mere numbers.

Athletes, meanwhile, are expected to possess an increasingly sophisticated understanding of their own training and development. Elite performers often collaborate with multidisciplinary teams that include not only coaches but also data analysts, nutritionists, mental performance consultants, and biomechanists. This ecosystem empowers athletes to take a more autonomous and informed role in shaping their routines, recovery, and preparation. In sports such as cycling or triathlon, athletes now self-monitor their performance using power meters, heart rate variability trackers, and sleep analysis tools, making micro-adjustments based on daily physiological responses. The relationship with the coach becomes a collaborative exchange—less about issuing commands and more about synthesizing information, discussing strategy, and co-designing growth pathways.

However, this shift also introduces new complexities. The abundance of data can lead to information overload, decision fatigue, or misinterpretation if not carefully curated. Moreover, technology may challenge the emotional and relational core of the coach-athlete bond. With so much information flowing through screens and platforms, there is a risk that human intuition, empathy, and trust—the cornerstones of effective coaching—become secondary to digital evidence. Successful coaches today must therefore learn not only how to use technology, but how to preserve and even enhance the personal connection in a digitized environment. The most effective coaching is not algorithmic; it is empathetic and adaptive, drawing upon both evidence and emotional intelligence to support athletes as whole persons.

Furthermore, the psychological landscape of both coaches and athletes is changing. Performance pressure, public scrutiny, and the mental toll of constant optimization can erode well-being. The coach's role has expanded to include fostering mental resilience, balancing ambition with care, and recognizing signs of burnout or distress. In response, many sports organizations are embedding psychological support into coaching frameworks, emphasizing the importance of athlete-centered practices. This broader duty of care reshapes the ethical dimensions of coaching, making well-being and personal development as important as winning and skill acquisition. The evolving relationship between coaches and athletes mirrors the larger transformation of sport itself—more collaborative, more data-informed, and more attuned to the complexities of human development. The best coaching today is no longer about control but about guidance; not about authority but about partnership. In this new paradigm, success is measured not only in medals or metrics but in the sustainability of performance, the growth of character, and the depth of mutual respect between those who teach and those who strive. The future of sport will depend not just on new technologies or innovative strategies, but on how well coaches and athletes continue to grow together—adapting to change, embracing complexity, and never losing sight of the human connection at the heart of competition.

6.2. Fanfare

The world of sports fanfare is filled with legendary composers and musicians who have created some of the most iconic and recognizable themes in athletic competition. These figures have become legends in their own right through their contributions to the musical landscape of sports. John Williams stands as perhaps the most legendary figure in Olympic fanfare composition. Williams, already famous for his film scores including Star Wars, Jaws, and E.T., was commissioned to write the Olympic Fanfare and Theme for the 1984 Los Angeles Olympics. His composition became synonymous with Olympic competition and continues to be used in Olympic broadcasts decades later. Williams didn't stop with one Olympic composition—he created multiple legendary works for the Games, including Olympic Spirit (1988), Summon the Heroes (1996), and Call of the Champions (2002). Each piece has contributed to his status as a legend in sports music composition. Leo Arnaud is another true legend of Olympic fanfare. The French-American composer created Bugler's Dream in 1958, which became the de facto Olympic theme music for television broadcasts starting with the 1964 Tokyo Olympics. What makes Arnaud's story particularly fascinating is that his famous Olympic fanfare was actually based on a 19th-century French military bugle call, Salut aux étendards, composed by Joseph-David Buhl. Arnaud's arrangement of this historical piece became one of the most recognizable sports fanfares in the world.

The world of sport has always been as much about the spectators as the athletes. The roar of the crowd, the colors of the jerseys, the chants, and the rituals—these elements transform games into spectacles and performances into cultural phenomena. "Fanfare" is more than a word denoting celebration or noise; it is the heartbeat of sport's public identity, the emotional crescendo that gives athletic achievement its resonance. In today's digital and increasingly immersive world, the concept of fanfare is being redefined. No longer confined to stadiums or match days, fanfare now spans social media platforms, streaming services, virtual fan zones, and interactive technologies that allow supporters to participate, engage, and even influence their favorite teams and athletes. The future of fanfare is about amplification—not just of sound or presence, but of access, personalization, and emotional connection.

At the core of this transformation is technology. Augmented reality allows fans to experience the thrill of walking through a stadium from their living room. Live chats and fan forums integrated into streaming platforms enable shared viewing experiences across continents. Wearable merchandise, connected via the Internet of Things, can vibrate or light up when a goal is scored or a record is broken. In American football, franchises have introduced "fan cams" that allow viewers to control their viewing angle in real-time. Meanwhile, AI-curated content pushes goal replays, highlight reels, and player interviews tailored to individual fan behavior and preferences. This reimagining of fanfare moves beyond cheering from the sidelines—it transforms fandom into a participatory and dynamic relationship, powered by data and designed to intensify loyalty.

The economics of fanfare have also evolved. Fans are not only consumers but contributors to brand equity. Through social media, they generate vast amounts of content that circulate globally, reinforcing team narratives and amplifying sponsorship visibility. Memes, reaction videos, fantasy leagues, and TikTok challenges are all part of a decentralized fanfare economy. Sports organizations have begun recognizing this power, investing in fan engagement strategies that treat supporters as co-creators rather than passive recipients. In some cases, fans now have a voice in team decisions, from jersey designs to playlist selections, facilitated by blockchain-based voting systems or interactive apps. This co-creation blurs the line between spectator and stakeholder, redefining what it means to "belong" to a club or community.

Yet, the evolution of fanfare is not without its tensions. The pursuit of constant engagement can lead to digital fatigue, over-commercialization, or the loss of traditional fan rituals. The ultra-curated digital experience may lack the unpredictability, spontaneity, and rawness that define live sporting atmospheres. Moreover, the monetization of fan attention through microtransactions, NFTs, and premium content tiers raises questions about inclusivity—will the future of fanfare be accessible to all, or will it privilege only those with the financial means to engage? These concerns call for a thoughtful balance between innovation and tradition, between revenue generation and authenticity.

Cultural diversity adds further layers to the notion of fanfare. In some regions, fan rituals are deeply intertwined with local identity, politics, or religion. Ultras groups in Europe, samba bands in Brazil, and choreographed cheers in South Korea illustrate how fanfare can be a form of storytelling, resistance, or collective memory. Preserving this diversity is crucial as globalized sports leagues seek to unify fanbases across different geographies. The challenge is to build platforms and experiences that respect local traditions while offering new modes of interaction. Technology can assist in this task—through language localization, fan-submitted content, and tools that allow global supporters to connect with hyperlocal practices.

Fanfare, in its future form, will continue to be a vital force shaping the spirit of sport. It is not just noise—it is narrative. Not just applause—but affirmation. The voices of fans, amplified through both human presence and digital infrastructure, lend emotional weight and cultural meaning to every pass, sprint, or goal. In this sense, fanfare is both a mirror and a motor of sport's evolution: it reflects societal shifts, technological possibilities, and emotional investments, while simultaneously propelling sport into new realms of relevance and reach. The stadium of tomorrow may be dispersed across millions of screens, but the collective joy, heartbreak, and exhilaration that define fanfare will remain the same—boundless, passionate, and powerfully human.

6.3. Playing Smart: Lessons Learned from Tech-Driven Sports

The integration of technology into sport has done more than transform how games are being played—it has fundamentally reshaped how athletes train, how teams operate, and how performance is understood and optimized. "Playing smart" no longer refers solely to strategic acumen or tactical brilliance on the field; it now encompasses a sophisticated interplay between human intelligence and digital systems, between instinct and insight. As technology becomes increasingly embedded in the everyday practices of athletes and coaches, a new set of lessons emerges—lessons about resilience, adaptability, innovation, and the balance between efficiency and intuition. From elite competitions to grassroots development, tech-driven sports offer a laboratory for observing how intelligence—both artificial and human—can be leveraged to achieve excellence.

One of the most powerful lessons from tech-enhanced sport is the value of real-time feedback and data-informed decision-making. In elite tennis, for example, athletes now train with smart rackets that analyze swing speed, angle, and spin. These metrics are fed back to coaches instantly, allowing immediate technical corrections and customized drills. In track and field, sprinters wear sensors that capture every stride, joint angle, and force application—turning movement into a digital language that can be optimized with precision. The lesson here is clear: when feedback loops are shortened and insights are made actionable in the moment, the learning curve accelerates dramatically. Coaches, in turn, shift from being observers to interpreters—translating complex datasets into accessible, performance-enhancing guidance.

The tennis industry has embraced sensor technology with remarkable innovation. Smart rackets from companies like HEAD, Babolat, and emerging players feature integrated sensors that provide comprehensive swing analysis. These devices track multiple metrics simultaneously: racket speed, ball impact location, spin generation, swing timing, and stroke consistency. The Zepp Tennis 2 system, for instance, can store up to 2,000 swings and automatically categorizes shots into forehands, backhands, and serves while measuring power output and sweet spot contact.

Modern smart rackets operate through various mounting systems—from plug-in sensors that attach to the racket handle to fully integrated systems built into the racket frame. The PIQ Robot and Sony Smart Tennis Sensor represent cutting-edge developments that attach directly to the string bed, acting as both performance trackers and vibration dampeners. These systems connect via Bluetooth to smartphone apps that provide instant 3D swing analysis and real-time coaching feedback. The technological sophistication extends beyond basic metrics. Advanced systems now offer AI-powered stroke comparison, allowing players to benchmark their technique against professional players. Tennis AI, for example, uses computer vision to analyze strokes in real-time and provides color-coded feedback—red for areas needing improvement, yellow for acceptable performance, and green for professional-level execution.

Track and field is experiencing its most significant technological transformation in nearly 60 years through sensor-enabled surfaces and wearable technology. Feldspar Limited is pioneering the world's first sensor-enabled running track that captures athletes' footsteps directly through embedded sensing technology. This revolutionary system measures stride length, foot placement, ground contact time, acceleration rates, and maximum velocity in real-time. The innovation represents a fundamental shift from traditional video-based analysis to direct, ground-level data collection. Athletes running on these smart tracks receive immediate feedback through wearable devices like smartwatches, providing comprehensive performance data that was previously accessible only to elite athletes with extensive support teams. The system can identify potential injury risks by analyzing biomechanical patterns and alerting coaches to adjust training intensity or technique modifications. Complementing track-based sensors, athletes now wear sophisticated motion capture devices that provide detailed biomechanical analysis. These systems use inertial measurement units (IMUs) containing gyroscopes and accelerometers to capture movement in three-dimensional space. Unlike traditional marker-based systems that require laboratory settings, modern wearable sensors enable real-time analysis during actual training and competition. The impact extends beyond individual performance monitoring. Research demonstrates that real-time tibial acceleration feedback can reduce peak tibial acceleration and vertical ground reaction forces by significant margins, with benefits lasting from five minutes to twelve months after feedback removal. This technology enables coaches to provide immediate gait retraining, reducing injury risk while optimizing running efficiency.

The integration of advanced technology has fundamentally transformed the coaching profession, shifting coaches from intuitive observers to sophisticated data interpreters. Modern coaches must now possess the ability to translate complex datasets into actionable training interventions, bridging what experts call "the interpretation gap" between data collection and practical application (Ahi, 2025). Performance analysts have become crucial intermediaries in this process, serving as "technology translators between coaches and players." They provide coaches with objective quantitative and qualitative information to address the natural limitations of human observation—studies show elite coaches can only recall 59% of critical events in matches when relying on memory alone. The analyst's role involves selecting relevant video clips, generating targeted statistical reports, and creating visual feedback that coaches can use for detailed discussions with athletes. The most successful coaching-analytics partnerships occur when domain experts—coaches with deep sport knowledge—learn to interpret and apply data insights rather than relying solely on data scientists. Examples include NBA coaches like Del Harris, who served as a translator between analytics teams and head coaches who were less comfortable with data. Similarly, successful coaches like Eric Spoelstra and José Mourinho built their careers by understanding both the technical and analytical aspects of their sports. This evolution requires coaches to develop new competencies in data communication. They must learn to provide visual rather than purely verbal feedback, as research shows visual feedback of kinematic data produces statistically greater improvements in performance than verbal feedback alone. The most effective coaches now use real-time displays showing metrics like bar velocity, movement patterns, or biomechanical data to create immediate, actionable feedback loops.

The psychology behind real-time feedback reveals why it's so effective in accelerating athletic development. When athletes receive immediate performance data, their brains associate successful behaviors with instant reinforcement through dopamine release, strengthening the likelihood of repeating optimal movements. This neurochemical response is significantly more powerful than delayed feedback provided hours or days later. Real-time feedback systems create what researchers call "gamified training environments" that increase enjoyment, boost adherence to training programs, and encourage consistent participation. Athletes can compete against their own personal records, teammates, or established benchmarks, introducing elements of fun and competition that enhance motivation. Systems like velocity-based training platforms allow coaches to create team leaderboards or recognize athletes who maintain optimal performance metrics across training sets.

The technology also enhances both extrinsic and intrinsic motivation. While external validation from coaches and peers remains important, real-time feedback primarily builds intrinsic motivation by allowing athletes to monitor their own progress. This self-directed improvement reduces dependence on coach approval and creates more autonomous, self-regulating athletes who take ownership of their development.

Studies demonstrate that externally focused feedback—such as focusing on display metrics or performance outputs—leads to better movement efficiency than internally focused cues about form or muscle activation. When athletes have clear targets and can measure results immediately, they train with greater intent and precision, leading to accelerated skill acquisition and performance improvements.

Previously, detailed biomechanical analysis and real-time feedback were available only to professional athletes with extensive support teams. Now, club-level athletes and even recreational players can access similar technologies through affordable wearable devices and smartphone applications. Virtual and augmented reality integration represents the next frontier in real-time feedback systems. Research shows that combining virtual reality (VR) environments with wearable sensors creates immersive training experiences where athletes can visualize their performance data while practicing, leading to improved technique consistency and enhanced situational awareness. The integration of artificial intelligence (AI) is enabling more sophisticated real-time coaching. AI systems can now provide immediate verbal and visual feedback during training sessions, analyzing movement patterns and comparing them to ideal techniques in real-time. These systems offer both instant feedback for immediate corrections and comprehensive performance analysis for long-term development planning.

Another key takeaway from tech-driven sport is the elevation of individualization. No two athletes are the same, and technology has made it possible to design hyper-personalized training programs based on physiology, psychology, and performance goals. In professional cycling, riders undergo lactate threshold testing, power-to-weight analysis, and biomechanical assessments to fine-tune their routines. In swimming, video analysis allows for micro-adjustments in underwater technique that are specific to each athlete's body shape and strength profile. This individualized approach not only maximizes performance but also fosters athlete agency. Athletes become more engaged when they understand how and why their programs are tailored—a powerful motivator that reinforces commitment and trust in the process.

Technology-driven individualization in sports fundamentally recognizes that each athlete is unique and must be approached as an individual rather than as part of statistical averages. This individualization revolution centers on the profound understanding that athletes possess distinctly different physiological responses, genetic predispositions, biomechanical patterns, and psychological characteristics that demand precisely tailored training approaches.

Athletes demonstrate remarkable interindividual differences in training responses, with research showing that response to exercise training can vary by more than 50% between individuals, even within homogeneous groups. These variations stem from fundamental differences in muscle fiber composition, cardiovascular capacity, metabolic efficiency, and hormonal profiles that are largely determined by genetic factors.

Each athlete's unique physiological makeup creates distinct training adaptations. For instance, 66% of athletic performance variance can be explained by genetic factors, while the remaining variance reflects environmental influences. This genetic foundation manifests in measurable differences in muscle fiber types, with some athletes naturally possessing higher proportions of fast-twitch fibers suited for explosive movements, while others have predominantly slow-twitch fibers optimized for endurance activities. Modern genetic research has identified specific polymorphisms that create individual athletic profiles. Studies demonstrate that athletes with different genetic makeups respond dramatically differently to identical training protocols. For example, athletes with "power genotypes" showed 7.1% improvements in explosive power when matched with high-intensity training, while the same training produced only 3.2% improvements in athletes with "endurance genotypes."

The complexity of the athletic phenotype involves intricate interactions between multiple genetic variants affecting oxygen transport, muscle contraction, energy metabolism, and recovery capacity. Each athlete carries a unique combination of these variants, creating individualized physiological signatures that determine optimal training strategies. Every athlete possesses unique movement patterns and compensations that serve as both advantageous traits and potential inefficiencies. These individual biomechanical signatures result from variations in skeletal structure, joint mobility, muscle architecture, and neuromuscular coordination patterns that cannot be standardized across athletes. Athletes develop distinct muscular phenotypes that reflect their individual anatomical adaptations. Research analyzing 35 different muscles in athletes revealed that athletes exhibit heterogeneous lower limb muscle volumes that can be characterized as individual muscular phenotypes, with these patterns reflecting factors beyond their specific sports.

Modern technology enables unprecedented measurement of individual athlete characteristics. In cycling, each rider undergoes comprehensive physiological profiling including lactate threshold testing that identifies their unique metabolic transition points. Power-to-weight analysis reveals individual efficiency patterns, while biomechanical assessments using motion capture technology map each cyclist's specific movement signatures. Swimming employs sophisticated video analysis systems that capture underwater and above-water technique patterns specific to each swimmer's body dimensions and strength profile. These systems analyze frame-by-frame movements to identify micro-adjustments in technique that are tailored to individual anatomical characteristics.

Technology now enables continuous monitoring of how each athlete responds to training stimuli. Wearable sensors and AI-powered platforms collect real-time data on individual physiological responses, allowing for immediate program adjustments based on each athlete's unique adaptation patterns. This individualized monitoring recognizes that identical training loads produce vastly different responses in different athletes. Genetic testing platforms now analyze multiple polymorphisms to create individual genetic profiles that guide training decisions. These profiles consider each athlete's unique predispositions for power development, endurance capacity, injury susceptibility, and recovery requirements. When athletes understand that their training programs are designed specifically for their unique characteristics, they develop enhanced motivation and commitment. This individual recognition creates a powerful psychological effect where athletes feel valued as unique individuals rather than generic members of a training group.

Individual attention and customized feedback significantly improve athlete engagement by addressing each person's specific learning style and motivational triggers. Athletes respond more positively to training when they understand how their individual characteristics influence program design. Individualized training fosters athlete agency by involving athletes in understanding their unique physiological and psychological profiles. When athletes comprehend their individual lactate thresholds, power profiles, biomechanical patterns, and genetic predispositions, they become active participants in their development rather than passive recipients of generic programming.

This understanding creates intrinsic motivation as athletes see the direct connection between their individual characteristics and training outcomes. They develop ownership of their development process when they understand how their unique traits influence training adaptations.

Effective individualization begins with thorough assessment of each athlete's unique characteristics. This includes physiological testing that identifies individual metabolic patterns, biomechanical analysis that reveals unique movement signatures, genetic profiling that uncovers individual predispositions, and psychological assessment that determines individual motivational patterns.

The most effective individualized programs continuously evolve based on each athlete's unique responses. They incorporate regular individual assessment to adjust training loads, exercise selection, and recovery protocols based on how each specific athlete responds to different stimuli.

Contemporary individualized training recognizes that each athlete requires a unique combination of physical, psychological, and lifestyle interventions. This approach acknowledges that optimal performance requires individualized optimization across all dimensions of each athlete's unique profile, not standardized application of generic principles.

Technology-driven individualization represents a fundamental acknowledgment that athletic excellence emerges from understanding and optimizing each athlete's unique biological and psychological characteristics. By embracing individual differences rather than attempting to standardize them, modern training approaches unlock each athlete's distinctive potential while fostering the deep engagement that comes from being recognized and developed as a unique individual (Figure 5).

Equally important are the lessons about injury prevention and recovery. Wearable technologies and predictive algorithms can now flag signs of fatigue or overuse before they manifest as injuries. In football and basketball, player load monitoring systems alert staff to changes in performance patterns that may signal elevated risk. Sleep trackers and wellness apps offer insights into recovery quality and readiness. These developments have led to a broader understanding that playing smart means

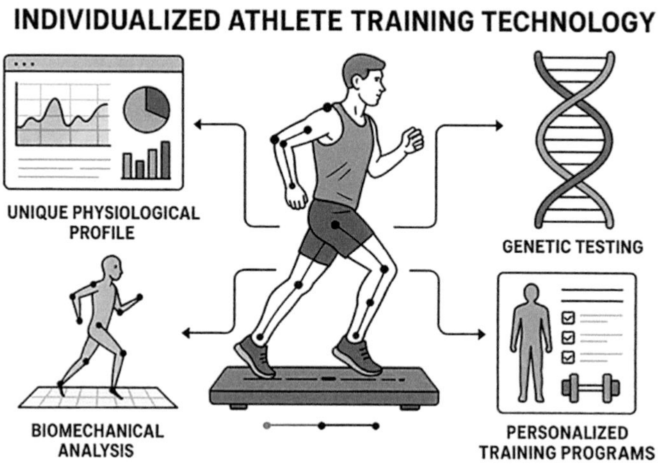

Figure 5: Technology-Driven Individualization

listening to the body, using data to inform rest as well as exertion. The culture of glorifying overtraining is gradually giving way to a more sustainable, holistic view of athletic development—where longevity and well-being are treated as indicators of success, not obstacles to it.

Wearable technologies and predictive algorithms represent a fundamental shift in how athletes approach injury prevention and recovery. These sophisticated systems have moved beyond simple activity tracking to become comprehensive health monitoring ecosystems that can detect subtle physiological changes before they manifest as performance-limiting injuries. The integration of machine learning algorithms with biometric data has created powerful predictive models capable of analyzing complex patterns in athlete health. Research demonstrates that AI-powered systems can achieve up to 90% accuracy in predicting performance outcomes and injury risks by incorporating multiple data streams including heart rate variability, biomechanical patterns, and psychological factors. These models significantly outperform traditional statistical approaches, which typically achieve only 77% accuracy.

In professional football and basketball, player load monitoring systems have become essential tools for maintaining athlete health throughout demanding seasons. These systems utilize advanced sensors including GPS trackers, accelerometers, and inertial measurement units to capture real-time data on player movements, impacts, and physiological responses. Modern load monitoring platforms can track multiple variables simultaneously, including PlayerLoad metrics, acceleration patterns, deceleration frequencies, and change-of-direction movements. Research shows that these comprehensive monitoring systems help prevent both acute and chronic injuries by identifying training load imbalances before they result in tissue breakdown.

The effectiveness of these systems lies in their ability to process vast amounts of data in real-time. Manchester City, for example, uses advanced analytics and monitoring systems to track performance data and assess injury risks, enabling strategic player rotation that minimizes fatigue-related injuries while maintaining competitive performance throughout packed schedules.

Advanced motion capture technology and biomechanical modeling have revolutionized how teams assess injury risk at the movement level. AI algorithms can now detect minute changes in biomechanical patterns that are imperceptible to human observation, such as subtle alterations in stride length, gait symmetry, or joint angles during exercise.

These systems analyze movement efficiency and identify faulty mechanics that could lead to injuries. For instance, AI-powered biomechanical analysis can detect a baseball pitcher's repetitive motion patterns that generate excessive shoulder stress or identify poor landing mechanics in basketball players that increase knee injury risk.

Sleep tracking technology has evolved from simple duration measurement to comprehensive analysis of sleep architecture and recovery quality. Modern sleep monitoring systems analyze multiple sleep stages including deep sleep, REM sleep, and light sleep phases, each contributing uniquely to athletic recovery. Deep sleep is particularly crucial for athletes as it's when the body releases growth hormones essential for muscle repair and strength building. Research indicates that athletes sleeping less than 7 hours per night experience decreased physical performance and higher rates of fatigue and burnout. Elite athletes who extended their sleep to 10 hours per day for 5-7 weeks showed significant improvements in sprint times and shooting accuracy, demonstrating the direct performance benefits of optimized sleep.

Modern athlete monitoring platforms integrate sleep data with broader wellness metrics including stress levels, mood states, fatigue indicators, and heart rate variability. These systems can detect early signs of overtraining or under-recovery by identifying patterns in subjective wellness questionnaires combined with objective physiological markers. Self-reported wellness feedback has proven to be a reliable predictor of injury risk, with elevated fatigue and poor sleep quality serving as significant predictors of future injuries. This integration allows coaching staff to make proactive adjustments to training loads before problems escalate to injury levels.

AI is transforming recovery by creating highly personalized protocols that adapt to individual athlete responses. AI systems analyze multiple data streams including sleep quality, heart rate variability, training loads, and subjective wellness reports to generate customized recovery recommendations. Companies like Amatra use sophisticated machine learning algorithms to identify what factors statistically correlate with better or worse recovery for each individual athlete. Their system can quantify the impact of variables like caffeine intake, morning sunlight exposure, meditation practices, and stress levels on recovery quality, providing personalized recommendations that go far beyond generic recovery protocols.

The most advanced AI systems are developing predictive capabilities that can forecast recovery needs before fatigue sets in. These models analyze patterns in metrics like heart rate variability, resting heart rate, and sleep quality to predict when an athlete will need additional recovery time. This predictive approach represents a fundamental shift from reactive to proactive recovery management. Instead of responding to fatigue after it occurs, teams can now anticipate recovery needs and adjust training schedules preemptively to maintain optimal performance while preventing overtraining.

The integration of comprehensive monitoring systems is facilitating a broader cultural shift in athletic development. Traditional approaches that prioritized immediate performance gains often came at the expense of long-term athlete health and sustainability. Modern data-driven approaches demonstrate that optimizing recovery and preventing overtraining actually enhances performance outcomes. Research on holistic athlete development emphasizes that sustainable performance requires attention to multiple domains including physical, psychological, academic, and social development. This multidimensional approach recognizes that an athlete's performance is influenced by complex interactions between all aspects of their life, not just their physical training.

Data is revealing that sustainable approaches to athletic development may actually enhance longevity both in sport and in life. Research on elite athletes shows that those participating in mixed sports incorporating both aerobic and anaerobic components tend to experience the greatest extensions in lifespan compared to the general population. This suggests that balanced, comprehensive training approaches benefit not only competitive performance but also long-term health outcomes. The shift toward evidence-based sustainability is also changing how success is measured in athletic programs. Instead of focusing solely on short-term competitive results, organizations are increasingly tracking metrics related to athlete well-being, injury rates, career longevity, and post-competition health outcomes. While the technological capabilities for comprehensive athlete monitoring continue to expand, the challenge lies in effectively integrating diverse data streams into actionable insights. Successful implementation requires sophisticated algorithms capable of processing physiological, biomechanical, psychological, and contextual data simultaneously while accounting for individual athlete differences. The most effective systems combine multiple monitoring modalities including wearable sensors, video analysis, subjective wellness reports, and environmental factors to create comprehensive athlete profiles. This integration enables more accurate risk assessment and more personalized intervention strategies than any single monitoring approach could provide.

As AI-powered monitoring systems become more sophisticated, there's growing recognition of the need to make these technologies accessible beyond elite professional sports. The development of cost-effective monitoring solutions is enabling amateur athletes, youth sports programs, and recreational athletes to benefit from advanced injury prevention and recovery optimization strategies. It represents a significant opportunity to improve athlete safety and performance across all levels of sport participation, potentially reducing injury rates and enhancing the overall sports experience for millions of participants worldwide.

The convergence of wearable technology, predictive analytics, and comprehensive wellness monitoring represents more than just technological advancement—it signifies a fundamental evolution in how we conceptualize athletic development. By prioritizing data-driven insights into recovery, fatigue management, and holistic athlete well-being, the sports community is moving toward a more sustainable model that recognizes peak performance and long-term health as complementary rather than competing objectives. This transformation promises not only to enhance competitive outcomes but also to ensure that the pursuit of athletic excellence contributes to rather than detracts from lifelong health and well-being.

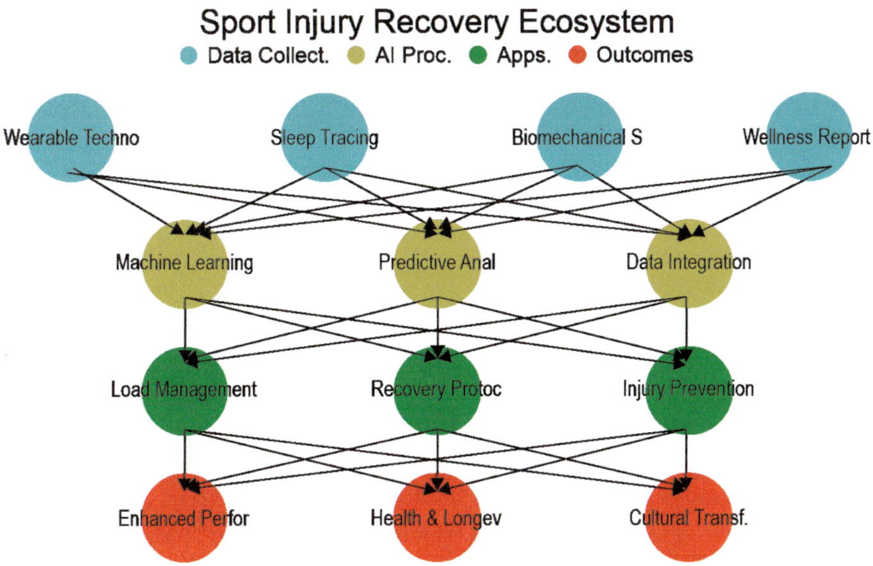

Figure 6: Modern Sports Injury Prevention and Recovery Ecosystem, Integrated Technology Framework

Figure 6 illustrates the integrated technology framework that is revolutionizing injury prevention and recovery in modern sports. The visualization demonstrates how data flows through four distinct layers:

- Data Collection Layer captures comprehensive athlete information through wearable technologies, sleep tracking devices, biomechanical sensors, and subjective wellness reports. This foundational layer provides the raw data necessary for advanced analysis.
- AI Processing Layer transforms raw data into actionable insights using machine learning algorithms that achieve 90% prediction accuracy, predictive analytics for fatigue forecasting, and sophisticated data integration systems that analyze multiple data streams simultaneously.

- Applications Layer translates AI insights into practical interventions including PlayerLoad management systems, personalized recovery protocols, and proactive injury prevention strategies that address risks before they manifest as injuries.
- Outcomes Layer represents the ultimate benefits: enhanced performance through consistent output and peak readiness, improved health and longevity with reduced injury rates and extended careers, and a cultural transformation toward sustainable, holistic athletic development.

The arrows in the diagram emphasize the systematic flow from data collection through intelligent processing to practical applications that generate measurable improvements in athlete health and performance. This integrated approach represents the evolution from reactive injury treatment to proactive, data-driven athlete management that prioritizes both immediate performance and long-term well-being.

Tech-driven sport has also revealed the critical role of mental performance and cognitive training. In high-pressure environments like Formula 1 or Olympic archery, athletes use neurofeedback headsets, VR simulations, and reaction-time software to train their minds alongside their bodies. Visualization exercises can now be augmented with immersive environments that mimic competition settings, enhancing psychological readiness and decision-making under stress. These tools reinforce the idea that smart play is not just physical—it's deeply mental. Athletes who cultivate focus, emotional regulation, and cognitive agility often outperform more physically gifted peers, especially in the clutch moments that define victory.

But the journey toward playing smart also involves ethical reflection and cultural adaptation. The flood of data available to coaches and sports organizations raises questions about privacy, consent, and data ownership. Who controls the insights generated by an athlete's body? How are those insights stored, shared, and potentially monetized? Lessons from tech-driven sport include the importance of establishing transparent, fair, and athlete-centered data governance frameworks. Additionally, the adoption of technology must be inclusive and context-sensitive. Not all teams or regions have equal access to cutting-edge tools, and imposing a one-size-fits-all model risks widening the performance gap rather than leveling the playing field.

Finally, perhaps the most enduring lesson from tech-enhanced sport is that technology alone is not enough. Tools, platforms, and devices are only as effective as the people who use them. The human element—creativity, intuition, empathy—remains irreplaceable. In fact, some of the most innovative uses of sport tech arise when coaches and athletes repurpose tools in unexpected ways, blend insights from different domains, or challenge the limits of conventional analytics. Playing smart means knowing when to follow the data and when to trust your gut, when to lean on automation and when to lean into lived experience. It is a mindset as much as a methodology—a continuous process of learning, experimenting, and adapting.

As the sports world continues to evolve, these lessons become increasingly valuable beyond the field. Corporate leaders, educators, healthcare professionals, and policy-makers are now looking to sport as a model for integrating technology in human-centered, high-performance environments. Playing smart is no longer just a competitive advantage—it is a framework for thriving in complexity, for navigating change with purpose, and for unlocking the full potential of people through the intelligent use of technology.

This paradigm of tech-enhanced intelligence in sport is not just theoretical—it is playing out vividly across disciplines. Consider the case of FC Barcelona, one of the pioneers in embedding analytics into every layer of club operations. Beyond the tactical data used by coaches, the club's use of GPS vests and heart rate monitors during training allows performance staff to analyze each player's workload. When Lionel Messi was at his peak, the club's analysts tracked his sprint patterns, deceleration moments, and even walking phases to manage his energy distribution. The lesson here is subtle but profound: playing smart doesn't always mean playing more. It means playing in tune with one's capabilities, rhythm, and strategic goals.

In American football, the NFL has adopted the Zebra Motion tracking system, which places RFID chips in players' shoulder pads to gather real-time data on speed, distance, acceleration, and even orientation. This data is not just used for post-game analysis; it is fed live to coaching staff to inform substitutions, evaluate fatigue, and shape mid-game decisions. Quarterbacks, for example, review 3D video simulations based on this data to adjust their reads and release timing. Patrick Mahomes, known for his creative improvisation, has worked with analysts to simulate unpredictable defensive patterns—sharpening his cognitive agility while still maintaining his natural instincts.

Another powerful illustration comes from the world of long-distance running. Eliud Kipchoge's historic sub-two-hour marathon in 2019 was not only a feat of human endurance but also of technological orchestration. The pacing strategy was meticulously modeled using data science, his nutrition was delivered with second-by-second planning, and the Nike Vaporfly shoes he wore were designed using biomechanical testing to maximize energy return. Drones, wind shields, and laser pacing helped maintain optimal positioning. While the performance itself was Kipchoge's, the ecosystem of precision engineering around him underscored the potential of playing smart as a collective, interdisciplinary endeavor.

In women's sport, too, smart performance tech is reshaping outcomes. The U.S. Women's National Soccer Team (USWNT), in their 2019 World Cup campaign, employed menstrual cycle tracking as part of player performance planning. Working with sports scientists, coaches tailored individual training and recovery protocols based on hormonal fluctuations. This recognition of biological rhythms within a high-tech framework exemplifies how playing smart includes listening to the body at a deeper, more personalized level. The USWNT's dominance was not only athletic but strategically intelligent, fueled by a blend of science, advocacy, and responsiveness to female athletes' specific needs.

In esports, where mental processing speed and precision are paramount, tools like Aim Lab are used to train reflexes, eye-hand coordination, and situational awareness. Professional players log thousands of hours using these platforms, analyzing heat maps of their cursor movements, measuring reaction times, and adjusting decision trees based on simulated match scenarios. For them, "smart" is digital fluency, knowing how to interpret interface feedback, optimize equipment setup, and preserve mental focus under sustained pressure. In this case, technology is not just an enhancement—it is the sport itself, with cognition and control as the primary currencies.

Even in youth sports, smart play is beginning to take hold. Grassroots basketball programs in the U.S. are integrating shot-tracking apps like HomeCourt, which uses a smartphone camera and AI to analyze shooting form, foot placement, and consistency. Young players receive instant feedback and engage in self-coaching practices, allowing them to accelerate skill acquisition independently. The democratization of this technology—available from a mobile device—illustrates how smart sport is becoming more accessible, flattening hierarchies that once privileged only elite institutions.

However, smart play also brings necessary cautionary tales. In professional baseball, the Houston Astros scandal involving sign-stealing via electronic surveillance raised ethical concerns about the misuse of technology. It served as a stark reminder that intelligence in sport must be accompanied by integrity. Similarly, the pressure to constantly measure and optimize can be overwhelming for some athletes, leading to anxiety or a reductionist view of performance. Naomi Osaka's openness about the mental strain of professional tennis highlights how even in a tech-forward era, emotional intelligence and mental well-being remain paramount.

Whether in stadiums, labs, or living rooms, the intersection of performance and innovation is producing a new generation of athletes, coaches, and fans who are more informed, more connected, and more reflective. The frontier is not just physical performance but cognitive agility, emotional resilience, and strategic awareness—all of which are amplified when sport embraces its most intelligent potential.

Chapter 7

The Wild Ride: Challenges and Fun Ethical Rollercoaster

As the world of sport accelerates into a high-tech future, the path forward is anything but smooth. It's a thrilling, unpredictable, and often disorienting ride—where breakthroughs in performance and entertainment are accompanied by equally intense ethical dilemmas and cultural disruptions. The integration of AI, biometrics, immersive experiences, and real-time data has made sport smarter, faster, and more interconnected than ever before. Yet with every advancement comes a question, a tension, or an unintended consequence. The landscape resembles a rollercoaster: exhilarating, full of promise, but also demanding careful navigation. The wild ride of tech-driven sports is as much about innovation as it is about responsibility, and understanding this balance is key to shaping a future that is not only exciting but also just and inclusive.

One of the most compelling challenges is data ownership. Athletes today generate an immense volume of personal data—heart rate variability, hormonal cycles, sleep patterns, injury history, brain activity—collected through wearables, apps, and sensors. But who owns this data? The athlete? The team? The sponsoring company? The issue becomes more complex when third-party platforms monetize or analyze this information without full transparency. A football player might wear a GPS tracker during practice, only to discover that the data has been sold to betting companies or used to negotiate a contract against them. The fun of optimizing performance with smart tech is quickly shadowed by the need to establish ethical boundaries, data rights, and mechanisms of consent. It's a digital gold rush, and without regulation, the athlete's body risks becoming the most exploited terrain.

Then comes the question of fairness. Technology has created new competitive edges—but not all athletes, clubs, or nations have equal access to these tools. When an elite rowing team trains with AI-powered biomechanics labs while their rivals rely on handheld stopwatches, the playing field begins to tilt. Even innovations as subtle as carbon-plated running shoes or cryotherapy chambers can have disproportionate impact, raising concerns about technodoping. Where do we draw the line between innovation and unfair advantage? The rollercoaster gets even steeper when governing bodies scramble to adapt—delayed rulings, inconsistent standards, and grey areas become part of the terrain. What was once fun—breaking records, setting new standards—turns into ethical ambiguity that tests the very spirit of sport.

DOI: 10.1201/9781003533795-7

This high-speed ride also twists through privacy concerns. Imagine a scenario where a tennis academy installs biometric surveillance to monitor pupil stress levels, hydration, and micro-expressions during practice. While intended to improve coaching, such systems may also create a culture of hyper-surveillance, where young athletes feel perpetually watched, judged, and compared. In youth sport especially, where development and confidence-building matter more than metrics, the risk of turning play into performance theater is real. There's a fine line between informed training and invasion of selfhood, and the fun of tech must not override the fundamental human need for autonomy, trust, and space to fail.

Another loop in this ethical ride is the impact on identity and representation. AI-driven highlighted reels, automated commentary, and virtual fan avatars are transforming how sport is consumed and performed—but they can also reinforce biases. Facial recognition systems might misclassify athletes of certain ethnicities, and algorithmic editing might disproportionately feature male players or overlook para-sports altogether. These issues aren't mere glitches—they reflect deeper systemic biases baked into the data and design. As sport becomes more automated, who gets seen, celebrated, and supported may be influenced by code more than conscience. If we are not careful, the rollercoaster of innovation will leave behind those who do not match its default template.

Yet, despite the challenges, there's also joy, creativity, and wonder in this ride. The fusion of tech and sport has opened new frontiers of inclusion—such as virtual reality environments that allow people with mobility challenges to participate in simulated sport, or AI translators that help multicultural teams communicate more effectively. Esports and digital competitions have created spaces where neurodiverse athletes can shine, and remote coaching platforms have made high-quality training available to communities once excluded from elite pathways. The ethical questions don't diminish the fun—they make it richer, more complex, and more human. They remind us that the real power of sport lies not just in winning, but in how we choose to play, collaborate, and imagine new futures.

The wild ride of tech and ethics in sport is about learning to steer with both hands on the wheel—one gripping innovation, the other gripping integrity. The future will not be navigated by avoiding hard questions but by leaning into them, with curiosity, courage, and collective responsibility. Sport has always been a mirror of society's aspirations and contradictions. Now, as it mirrors our digital selves, we must ask: What kind of game do we want to play, and who gets to play it? If we can answer that with empathy and foresight, then the ride, wild as it may be, will be well worth it.

7.1. Privacy Puzzles in the Sports Tech Universe

As data-driven innovation becomes a cornerstone of athletic performance enhancement, fan engagement, and operational efficiency, questions surrounding data collection, ownership, usage, and protection have become both urgent and unavoidable. The contemporary sports ecosystem, infused with artificial intelligence (AI), wearable technologies, biometric tracking systems, and immersive digital environments, now operates in a framework where personal data has become a central asset. Navigating the privacy implications of these developments constitutes one of the most critical ethical and regulatory issues in sport today.

The theoretical foundations of privacy law begin with the seminal 1890 Harvard Law Review article "The Right to Privacy" by Samuel Warren and Louis Brandeis. Written in response to technological advances in photography and mass printing that enabled unprecedented intrusions into private life, their work established the conceptual groundwork for modern privacy protection that remains remarkably relevant to today's sports data challenges.

Warren and Brandeis articulated privacy as the "right to be let alone" and grounded this right in the concept of "inviolate personality". They argued that individuals possess an inherent right to control when and how their thoughts, emotions, and personal information are shared with others. This foundational theory established privacy as instrumental to personal autonomy and dignity, creating the intellectual foundation for what would become the control theory of privacy.

Their prescient observation that "numerous mechanical devices threaten to make good the prediction that 'what is whispered in the closet shall be proclaimed from the house-tops'" eerily anticipates the current sports analytics environment where every heartbeat, movement, and performance metric can be captured and broadcasted.

Contemporary Privacy Theories

The control theory of privacy, which evolved from Warren and Brandeis's work, holds that privacy consists in an individual's ability to control access to information about themselves. Charles Fried argued that privacy involves the right to "grant or deny access to others," while Julie Inness defined privacy as existing when individuals have a "reasonable probability that they could regulate the outcome of the situation."

In the sports context, control theory faces particular challenges. Athletes often must surrender significant control over their personal data as a condition of participation in organized sports. The theory's emphasis on individual choice becomes problematic when athletes face coercive circumstances—participate and surrender data rights, or forfeit competitive opportunities.

Recent developments in control theory have attempted to address these limitations through concepts like "negative control" (the ability to prevent others from accessing information) and "source control" (being the originator of information flows). However, these refinements still struggle with the collective bargaining context that characterizes professional sports, where individual control is often subordinated to institutional needs.

The access theory, also known as the limitation theory, defines privacy as the state of limited access to personal information. This theory focuses not on control per se, but on whether others actually have access to personal information about an individual. Privacy exists when access is appropriately restricted, regardless of whether the individual themselves controls that restriction.

For sports contexts, access theory offers certain advantages. It recognizes that privacy can be protected through institutional safeguards and technical measures even when athletes cannot exercise direct control over their data. However, it provides limited guidance for determining what constitutes "appropriate" access restrictions in the complex ecosystem of sports organizations, sponsors, broadcasters, and analytics companies.

Helen Nissenbaum's contextual integrity theory represents perhaps the most sophisticated framework for understanding privacy in complex institutional settings like professional sports. Rather than focusing on individual control or access restrictions, contextual integrity theory holds that privacy is about appropriate information flows within specific social contexts.

According to this theory, privacy violations occur when information flows violate contextual norms regarding five parameters: data subject, sender, recipient, information type, and transmission principle. Information sharing that might be perfectly appropriate in one context (medical data shared between team physician and athlete) becomes a privacy violation in another context (the same medical data shared with opposing teams).

Contextual integrity theory is particularly well-suited to sports environments because it recognizes that different contexts within the sports ecosystem have different legitimate information needs and different appropriate norms. The theory provides a framework for evaluating whether particular data practices respect the functional purposes and values of specific sports contexts while protecting individual privacy.

Philosophical Foundations of Privacy Rights

The philosophical foundation most commonly invoked for privacy rights is personal autonomy. This approach, rooted in Kantian philosophy, holds that privacy is essential for individual self-determination and the development of personal identity. Without privacy, individuals cannot engage in the reflection, experimentation, and relationship-building necessary for autonomous personhood.

Autonomy-based theories face particular challenges in sports contexts. Athletic participation inherently involves surrendering certain aspects of autonomy—submitting to coaching authority, following training regimens, accepting performance monitoring. The question becomes how much autonomy athletes must surrender as a condition of participation and where appropriate boundaries exist.

An alternative philosophical foundation grounds privacy rights in human dignity rather than autonomy. This approach, influential in European privacy law and embodied in the GDPR, holds that privacy protection is necessary to preserve the inherent worth and dignity of human persons.

Dignity-based theories are particularly relevant to sports contexts because they focus on preventing the instrumentalization of individuals. When athletes are reduced to data points for commercial exploitation or when their most intimate biological functions become commodified information, dignity-based theories provide strong grounds for privacy protection regardless of consent or autonomy considerations.

Privacy theory divides between approaches that treat privacy as an inherent right deserving protection regardless of demonstrable harm, and approaches that require showing concrete injury to justify legal intervention. This distinction is crucial for sports privacy because many athletic data practices may not cause immediate, tangible harm while still violating important privacy interests.

Ryan Calo's influential taxonomy identifies two categories of privacy harm: subjective harms (unwanted perception of observation, causing anxiety, embarrassment, or fear) and objective harms (unanticipated or coerced use of information against a person). In sports contexts, both categories are relevant—athletes may experience subjective harms from constant monitoring, while objective harms may result from data being used against their interests in contract negotiations, team selections, or public relations.

Some scholars have proposed treating personal data as property that individuals own and can control through market mechanisms. Under this approach, athletes would own their biometric and performance data and could license its use to teams, leagues, and commercial partners.

However, property-based approaches face significant theoretical and practical challenges. Personal data often involves overlapping interests of multiple parties. Moreover, property rights typically include the right to exclude others, transfer ownership, and destroy the property—rights that may be inappropriate for personal information that defines individual identity.

The property approach also risks commodifying personal information in ways that undermine rather than protect privacy. If athletes can sell their data rights, they may face economic pressure to surrender privacy protections, ultimately leaving them worse off than under regulatory approaches.

From computer science comes the mathematically rigorous framework of differential privacy, which provides formal guarantees that statistical analyses will not reveal information about specific individuals. Differential privacy works by adding calibrated noise to query results such that the presence or absence of any individual's data does not significantly affect the output.

For sports analytics, differential privacy offers a potential solution for conducting population-level analyses (identifying injury risk factors, performance trends) while protecting individual athletes. However, differential privacy's utility decreases as the granularity of analysis increases, potentially limiting its applicability to performance optimization that requires individual-level precision.

Information-Theoretic Approaches

Luciano Floridi's ontological theory of informational privacy approaches privacy through information ethics, defining privacy as a function of "ontological friction" in the "infosphere." According to this theory, privacy exists when there are barriers to information flow, and privacy is diminished when technologies reduce these barriers.

This approach is particularly relevant to sports contexts where technologies like wearable sensors, video analysis, and biometric monitoring have dramatically reduced the "ontological friction" that previously protected athletes' private information. The theory suggests that protecting privacy requires either increasing technological barriers to information access or redesigning information systems to create appropriate friction.

Athletic data presents several characteristics that complicate traditional privacy frameworks:

1. *Embodied Information*: Athletic data often involves the most intimate aspects of bodily function—heart rate, sleep patterns, hormonal levels, injury susceptibility. This biological information is simultaneously highly personal and directly relevant to athletic performance.
2. *Collective Benefits*: Unlike many privacy contexts where data collection primarily benefits the collector, athletic data analysis can provide genuine benefits to athletes themselves through improved performance, injury prevention, and health monitoring.
3. *Power Imbalances*: The sports context involves significant power imbalances between athletes and institutions, with career opportunities contingent on data sharing. Traditional consent models may be inadequate given these coercive circumstances.
4. *Temporal Dimensions*: Athletic data often has long-term implications, affecting not just current performance but future opportunities, career longevity, and post-career prospects.

The theoretical foundations outlined above suggest several key principles for addressing privacy in sports data contexts:

1. *Contextual Appropriateness*: Drawing from Nissenbaum's contextual integrity theory, privacy protection should focus on ensuring that information flows respect the norms and purposes of specific sports contexts while preventing inappropriate cross-context sharing.
2. *Dignity Preservation*: Grounding privacy protection in human dignity rather than individual autonomy provides stronger protection against exploitative practices even when athletes formally consent.
3. *Harm Recognition*: Adopting broader concepts of privacy harm that include subjective experiences of unwanted observation and dignitary injuries, not just economic or physical harms.
4. *Technical Implementation*: Incorporating privacy-preserving technologies like differential privacy wherever possible to enable beneficial uses of data while protecting individual privacy.
5. *Institutional Safeguards*: Recognizing that individual control may be inadequate in sports contexts, privacy protection must rely partly on institutional design, regulatory oversight, and collective bargaining processes.

This theoretical foundation provides the conceptual framework necessary for evaluating specific privacy practices in sports and developing appropriate regulatory responses to the challenges posed by data-driven athletic innovation. The convergence of these theoretical foundation approaches suggest that protecting privacy in sports requires moving beyond simple consent models toward more sophisticated frameworks that account for the unique characteristics of athletic contexts and the complex ecosystem of stakeholders involved in sports data utilization.

Conceptual Network of Privacy Theories Applied to Sports Data Context

The Figure 7 shows the interconnected nature of privacy theories and how they relate to each other and to sports-specific challenges. Rather than viewing these theories in isolation, this visualization shows how historical foundations influence contemporary approaches, how individual-focused and context-focused theories complement each other, and how technical solutions attempt to address practical challenges. The central positioning of the sports data privacy framework emphasizes how all these theoretical approaches must be synthesized to address the unique challenges of athletic data.

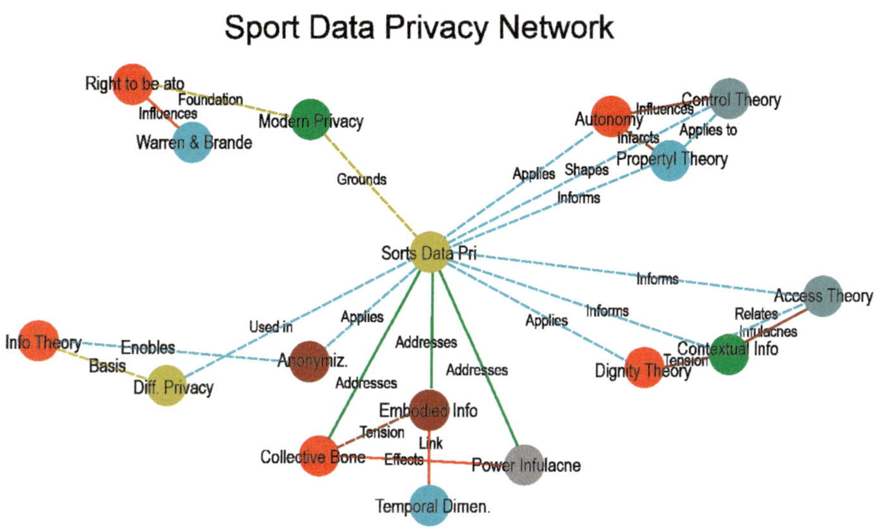

Figure 7: Conceptual Network of Relationships

Hierarchical Pyramid of Privacy Theory Application in Sports Data

This pyramid structure (Figure 8) demonstrates how abstract philosophical principles at the foundation increasingly support specific applications in sports contexts. The layered approach shows the progression from fundamental human rights concepts through established privacy theories to contemporary frameworks and finally to practical applications in athlete data protection. This visualization emphasizes how robust privacy protection in sports requires grounding in solid theoretical foundations while addressing the specific challenges of the athletic environment.

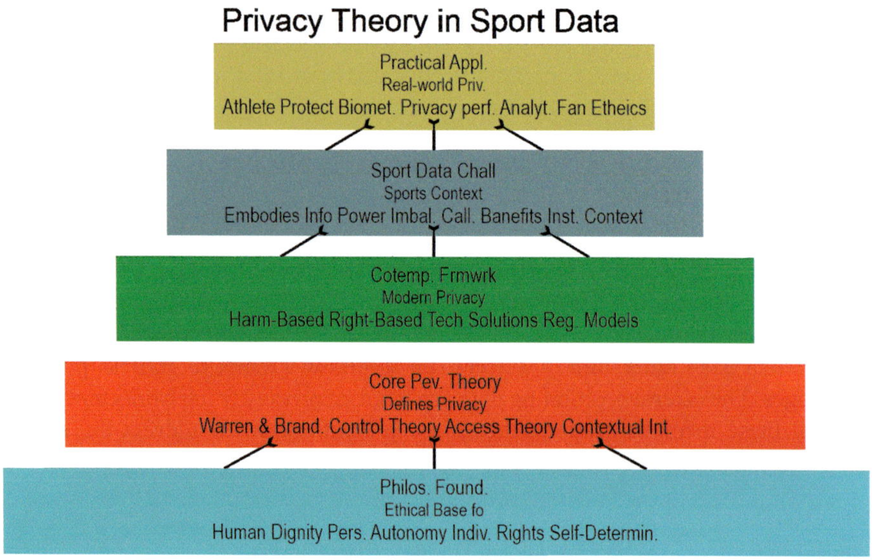

Figure 8: Implementation Hierarchy

At the core of privacy concerns is the collection of physiological and behavioral data from athletes. Modern performance tracking devices measure a wide range of parameters—including heart rate, blood oxygen saturation, muscular activity, hydration levels, sleep patterns, reaction times, and even mental focus—often in real time and continuously over extended periods. While these technologies have clear utility in optimizing training regimens, injury prevention, and tactical decision-making, they also expose highly sensitive personal data to potential misuse. For instance, if injury-related or mental health information is accessed without proper consent, it may negatively affect an athlete's career prospects, contract negotiations, or public image. Moreover, the ownership and governance of athlete data remain ambiguously defined in many sporting contexts. While some clubs and federations adopt centralized data management systems, the rights of athletes over their own biometric data are often unclear. This lack of clear legal and ethical frameworks raises questions about consent, access, and data monetization. In many cases, athletes may feel compelled to acquiesce to invasive data collection regimes under implicit or explicit pressure from employers, coaches, or sponsors, thereby undermining the principle of voluntary and informed consent.

The issue is particularly pronounced in youth and amateur sport, where regulatory oversight tends to be limited. Increasing numbers of youth programs and schools are employing performance-tracking applications and platforms that gather biometric data from minors. Given that children and adolescents are not legally capable of providing full consent, and that parents or guardians may not be fully informed of the data usage policies, this raises significant ethical concerns. Furthermore, the long-term storage and potential secondary uses of such data (e.g., by insurers, education institutions, or commercial entities) remain largely unregulated.

Beyond the athlete population, privacy challenges extend to fans and spectators. Smart stadiums and event environments now deploy a variety of surveillance and engagement technologies, including facial recognition for security, location tracking through mobile applications, and emotional analysis via AI-enhanced cameras. These systems are often justified by arguments relating to convenience, security, and personalized marketing. However, they can also facilitate extensive behavioral profiling and targeted advertising without sufficient transparency or control mechanisms for users. Spectators may not be fully aware that their in-venue actions and interactions are being recorded, analyzed, and potentially shared with third-party vendors.

Additionally, the rise of AI-generated media content in sport presents further risks to individual privacy. Deepfake technologies, voice synthesis, and generative imagery can create realistic but false representations of athletes and public figures, leading to reputational harm, misinformation, and identity manipulation. In this environment, athletes are increasingly required to protect their digital likenesses in addition to their physical performance, with limited legal recourse in some jurisdictions when their image or voice is misappropriated.

To address these multifaceted privacy challenges, a multi-stakeholder approach is essential. Sports organizations, technology developers, regulatory bodies, and athlete unions must collaborate to develop comprehensive data governance frameworks that balance innovation with ethical responsibility. These frameworks should include clear data ownership policies, enforceable consent procedures, rights to data access and deletion, and secure data storage protocols. Moreover, there is a growing need for data protection education initiatives targeting both athletes and fans to enhance digital literacy and awareness of individual rights in data-rich environments.

While technological advancements continue to reshape the structure and experience of sport, the associated privacy implications cannot be overlooked. The increasing dependency on biometric and behavioral data for competitive and commercial purposes necessitates the establishment of robust, rights-based protections. Only by embedding privacy considerations into the design and deployment of sports technologies can the sector ensure that technological progress does not come at the cost of individual autonomy and dignity. Addressing these privacy puzzles is not merely a legal obligation—it is a prerequisite for building a sustainable, trustworthy, and equitable sports technology ecosystem.

Below is a list of open questions that illustrate the key privacy puzzles in the sports tech ecosystem. These questions are organized thematically to reflect the most pressing issues currently facing stakeholders:

1. **Data Ownership and Control**

   Who owns the biometric and performance data collected from athletes—individuals, teams, leagues, or third-party tech providers?

   Do athletes have the right to access, transfer, or delete their data across clubs or organizations?

   Can organizations use historical athlete data for commercial purposes after the athlete has retired or left the team?

2. **Informed Consent and Voluntariness**

   How can informed consent be meaningfully obtained in high-pressure environments where athletes may feel compelled to comply?

   Are youth athletes (or their guardians) adequately informed about the extent and purpose of data collection?

   What mechanisms ensure that consent is freely given, revocable, and not a condition for participation or employment?

3. **Scope and Sensitivity of Collected Data**

   What are the ethical limits to data collection in sport—should psychological, cognitive, or emotional data be tracked?

   How should highly sensitive data (e.g., mental health, reproductive health, or injury risk) be handled to avoid misuse?

4. **Surveillance Culture and Behavioral Consequences**

   Does constant monitoring lead to self-censorship or undue psychological pressure among athletes?

   Could performance rankings or health scores based on biometric data create internal divisions, discrimination, or stigma within teams?

5. **Data Use by Third Parties**

   What access should insurers, sponsors, or betting companies have to athlete data?

   Are third-party platforms (e.g., wearables, fitness apps) transparent about how they use and share collected data?

6. **Fan Privacy and Smart Venues**

   Are fans adequately informed about the use of facial recognition, location tracking, and behavioral analytics in smart stadiums?

   How can stadium operators balance public safety with individuals' rights to anonymity and data protection?

7. **Deepfakes, Digital Likeness, and AI Manipulation**

   How can athletes protect their digital identities from AI-generated deepfakes or unauthorized reproductions?

   What legal and ethical frameworks govern the use of avatars, synthetic voices, or virtual representations in sports media?

8. Regulation and Compliance

Are existing data protection laws (e.g., GDPR, HIPAA) sufficient to address the unique contexts of sports data?

How should regulatory bodies respond to cross-border data transfers and the global operations of sport tech companies?

9. Data Retention and Legacy

For how long should athlete data be retained after it is collected?

What happens to a user's data once they leave a platform, retire from sport, or cease using a device?

10. Equity and Inclusion

Are privacy risks disproportionately affecting certain groups (e.g., minors, women, amateur athletes)?

How can we ensure equitable access to privacy-preserving technologies across different levels and types of sport?

The fundamental questions of data ownership reveal the need for hybrid ownership models that recognize multiple legitimate stakeholder interests while protecting athlete autonomy. Rather than seeking absolute ownership by any single party, emerging frameworks suggest tiered rights structures where athletes retain core privacy and commercial rights while allowing teams and leagues specific performance-related usage rights.

Legal frameworks are evolving toward contextual ownership models where data rights are distributed based on the purpose and sensitivity of information. The European GDPR model provides stronger athlete protections through data subject rights, while contractual models in the US emphasize negotiated agreements. Recent developments like MLB's 2022 Collective Bargaining Agreement demonstrate how collective bargaining can establish protective boundaries around sensitive biometric and medical data. Sports organizations should develop data governance frameworks that clearly delineate ownership and usage rights for different data categories. Implement data portability mechanisms allowing athletes to transfer their data across organizations, and establish sunset clauses for data retention that automatically limit commercial use of historical data after specified periods. Consider blockchain-based solutions for transparent, immutable data ownership records.

The challenge of obtaining meaningful consent in coercive environments requires structural reforms that go beyond traditional consent models. The power differential between athletes and institutions makes voluntary consent problematic when participation depends on data sharing. Legal scholars and practitioners are developing enhanced consent frameworks that account for coercive contexts. Solutions include independent consent advocates, opt-out alternatives that don't penalize non-participation, and granular consent mechanisms allowing athletes to consent to specific uses while refusing others. For youth athletes, guardian consent protocols must be supplemented with age-appropriate disclosure mechanisms and independent review processes. Establish cooling-off periods between contract negotiations and data consent decisions. Implement consent management platforms that allow athletes to modify permissions dynamically. Create athlete data ombudsman roles to advocate for individual privacy interests within organizational structures. For youth sports, develop simplified consent interfaces with clear explanations of data uses and establish regular consent renewal processes as athletes mature.

The expansion of data collection into psychological, emotional, and cognitive domains requires ethical boundary-setting frameworks that distinguish between performance-relevant and unnecessarily intrusive data collection. Emerging frameworks emphasize data minimization principles and purpose limitation-collecting only data necessary for specific, legitimate purposes. Mental health and reproductive health data receive special protection as “special category data” requiring explicit consent and enhanced security measures. Professional sports leagues are beginning to establish collective data collection standards that limit organizational overreach. Develop data collection impact assessments that evaluate the necessity and proportionality of each data type. Implement privacy-by-design principles in technology procurement, ensuring data collection capabilities align with ethical boundaries. Create athlete advisory committees to participate in decisions about expanding data collection scope. Establish independent ethics review boards for research involving sensitive athlete data.

The psychological and social impacts of constant monitoring require surveillance limitation frameworks and athlete wellbeing protections. Research demonstrates that pervasive monitoring can create chilling effects on athlete behavior and psychological harm through constant scrutiny. Solutions involve temporal and spatial boundaries on monitoring, data use restrictions that prevent punitive applications, and transparency measures that help athletes understand when and how they’re being monitored. Implement monitoring-free zones and monitoring-free times to provide athletes with private spaces. Develop algorithmic transparency requirements so athletes understand how their data influences decisions about them. Create data use policies that explicitly prohibit using performance data for disciplinary purposes outside of specific safety contexts. Establish athlete feedback mechanisms to identify and address surveillance-related stress.

The commercialization of athlete data by betting companies, insurers, and sponsors requires access control frameworks and benefit-sharing mechanisms. Legal challenges like “Project Red Card” are establishing precedents for athlete compensation when their data is used commercially. Regulatory frameworks are developing consent requirements for third-party data access and transparency obligations for data brokers. Insurance and betting companies face increasing access restrictions and fairness requirements in how they use athlete data. Develop third-party data sharing agreements that include athlete consent requirements and benefit-sharing provisions. Implement data usage auditing systems to track how third parties use athlete information. Create athlete data licensing collectives that can negotiate favorable terms with commercial users. Establish fairness review processes to ensure third-party uses don’t create discriminatory outcomes.

Stadium technology deployment requires proportionality frameworks that balance legitimate security needs with fan privacy rights. Smart venue privacy protection involves layered consent models, anonymization technologies, and purpose limitation for surveillance systems. Facial recognition systems face increasing regulatory restrictions and consent requirements. Solutions emphasize privacy-preserving technologies that can achieve security goals without creating comprehensive surveillance networks. Implement differential privacy techniques for crowd analytics that don't require individual identification. Develop granular opt-in systems for enhanced venue services versus basic access. Create data retention policies that automatically delete surveillance data after specified periods. Establish fan privacy advocates within venue operations.

The emergence of AI-generated content requires digital rights frameworks and authentication technologies to protect athlete digital identities. Legal frameworks are developing digital identity rights that extend traditional image rights to AI-generated content. Technical solutions include content authentication systems, deepfake detection technologies, and blockchain-based identity verification. Industry standards are emerging for consent requirements and attribution systems for AI-generated athlete content. Implement content authentication watermarking for official athlete content. Develop takedown procedures for unauthorized AI-generated content. Create digital identity monitoring services that can detect misuse of athlete likenesses. Establish licensing frameworks for legitimate AI applications involving athlete identities.

Current regulations require sports-specific adaptations and cross-border coordination to address the unique characteristics of athletic data. Legal frameworks are evolving toward sector-specific regulations that account for sports' unique characteristics while maintaining core privacy principles. Cross-border data transfer agreements and mutual recognition frameworks are being developed to address global sports operations. Regulatory sandboxes allow testing of new privacy approaches in sports contexts. Develop compliance management systems that track multiple jurisdictional requirements. Create privacy impact assessment templates specifically for sports contexts. Establish regulatory liaison roles to stay current with evolving requirements. Implement data localization strategies where required by specific jurisdictions.

The lifecycle management of athlete data requires temporal governance frameworks that address changing data sensitivity and athlete rights over time. Emerging frameworks establish differentiated retention periods based on data sensitivity and purpose. Right to be forgotten implementations require technical deletion capabilities and data minimization practices. Legacy data governance addresses questions of how historical data should be managed as privacy norms evolve. Implement automated data retention policies with clear deletion schedules. Develop data portability systems that allow athletes to export their data when leaving organizations. Create legacy data review processes to evaluate historical data against current privacy standards. Establish data estate planning for athlete career transitions.

Privacy protection must address differential impacts on vulnerable populations and ensure equitable access to privacy-preserving technologies. Research demonstrates that privacy risks disproportionately affect women athletes, minors, and amateur athletes who have less bargaining power and resource access. Solutions require targeted protection measures, accessible privacy technologies, and advocacy support for vulnerable populations. Develop tiered privacy protection systems that provide enhanced protections for vulnerable populations. Create privacy literacy programs to help athletes understand and exercise their rights. Establish privacy advocacy funds to provide legal support for privacy violations. Implement inclusive design principles that consider diverse athlete needs in privacy system design.

These privacy challenges require coordinated responses across legal, technical, and organizational domains. Successful implementation involves multi-stakeholder governance structures, privacy-by-design technologies, and adaptive regulatory frameworks that can evolve with technological development. The convergence of these approaches suggests that effective privacy protection in sports will require moving beyond simple compliance models toward comprehensive privacy ecosystems that embed protection into the fundamental structure of sports technology systems. This framework recognizes that privacy in sports is not merely a technical or legal problem, but a fundamental aspect of athlete dignity and autonomy that requires ongoing attention, resources, and institutional commitment to protect effectively.

7.2. The Great Fairness Quest in Sports Tech

As technological innovations transform the fabric of modern sport, the question of fairness has taken center stage in the ongoing evolution of athletic competition. The integration of performance-enhancing technologies, algorithmic decision-making systems, and data-driven training environments is revolutionizing how athletes compete, how officials judge, and how fans engage. Yet these same innovations are also challenging the traditional principles of equity, access, and integrity that underpin sport as a social institution. The pursuit of fairness—long considered a cornerstone of sporting culture—has entered a new era, marked by both promise and paradox.

The advent of wearable devices, motion capture systems, and real-time performance analytics has empowered athletes to train with unprecedented precision. Elite competitors now have access to custom-designed equipment, biomechanical modeling, and AI-powered coaching tools that optimize every aspect of performance—from foot placement to metabolic efficiency. While such tools can reduce injury risk and improve outcomes, they are unevenly distributed. Athletes from well-funded teams or countries can access high-end technologies that are financially out of reach for many others, particularly those in developing regions or amateur leagues. This growing disparity risks creating a technological divide that undermines the principle of a level playing field.

From motion capture systems that analyze movement with millimeter precision to AI-powered coaching platforms that customize training regimens in real-time, the modern athletic landscape is increasingly defined by technological sophistication. However, this technological revolution raises critical questions about fairness, accessibility, and the preservation of competitive integrity in an era where success is increasingly determined by access to cutting-edge equipment and data analytics.

The sports technology market is experiencing explosive growth, with the global wearable devices in sports market projected to reach $115.57 billion by 2030, growing at a compound annual growth rate of 4.18%. More broadly, the sports technology market is valued at $25.20 billion in 2025 and projected to surge to $86.22 billion by 2033, representing a CAGR of 16.62%. This rapid expansion reflects the increasing recognition of technology as essential infrastructure for athletic excellence and performance optimization. Elite athletes now have access to sophisticated performance monitoring systems that provide real-time biometric feedback, enabling split-second adjustments during training and competition. These technologies include advanced fitness trackers that monitor stress hormone levels and sleep architecture analysis, motion capture systems that provide precise biomechanical assessments, and AI-powered analytics that predict injury risks with up to 96.3% accuracy. The evolution from basic fitness tracking to comprehensive performance ecosystems is evident in the capabilities of modern sports technology. Contemporary systems can monitor continuous glucose levels, track heart rate variability, analyze movement efficiency, and even provide predictive fatigue modeling using machine learning algorithms. Motion capture technology, once confined to expensive laboratory settings, can now deliver real-time feedback from video footage without cumbersome sensor suits, democratizing access to previously elite-only biomechanical analysis tools.

For athletes with access to these technologies, the advantages are substantial and multifaceted. Performance enhancement through precision training has become the norm rather than the exception in elite sports. Wearable technology provides unprecedented insights into training loads, recovery patterns, and physiological responses, enabling highly personalized training regimens that maximize performance gains while minimizing injury risks. Motion capture systems allow for detailed analysis of technique refinement, with the ability to compare movements against professional benchmarks and identify inefficiencies that would be invisible to the naked eye. AI-powered biomechanical analysis can detect movement patterns that may lead to injury before they manifest, reducing injury rates by up to 30% in professional athletics. The integration of these technologies extends beyond individual performance optimization to encompass strategic advantages in team sports. Advanced analytics provide coaches with comprehensive performance intelligence that informs tactical decisions, player substitutions, and game strategies based on real-time physiological and performance data. This data-driven approach to coaching and competition has become a cornerstone of modern elite sports, where marginal gains often determine the difference between victory and defeat.

Despite these remarkable advances, access to high-end sports technology remains highly uneven, creating a technological divide that threatens the fundamental principle of fair competition. The disparity in access is most pronounced between developed and developing countries, where infrastructure limitations, financial constraints, and regulatory barriers prevent widespread adoption of advanced training technologies. Research indicates that investment in sports development in developing countries is significantly lower than in developed nations, as sport development is typically not prioritized in national budgets or education systems. This creates a "vicious cycle" where lower investment decreases the potential for athletes to develop their talents, leading to fewer prospects for professional sport careers and further limiting local investment in sports infrastructure.

The phenomenon of "muscle drain"—comparable to brain drain—sees talented athletes from developing countries migrate to industrialized nations where superior training facilities and technologies are available. This pattern not only depletes developing countries of athletic talent but also reinforces the technological advantages enjoyed by well-funded sports programs in wealthy nations.

The cost of high-tech sports equipment presents a significant barrier to entry for many athletes and organizations. Elite sports training facility startup costs can range from $275,000 to $805,000, with training equipment and technology representing $75,000 to $200,000 of this investment. Specialized equipment costs can be prohibitive: a basic powerchair football wheelchair costs nearly $18,000 USD, while additional modifications can add another $10,000 or more. Entry-level sit-skis range from $3,000 to $5,000 USD, far exceeding the cost of standard ski equipment. These financial barriers are particularly acute for athletes with disabilities, who often require specialized assistive technologies that are not covered by insurance schemes or funding programs. Even in countries with universal healthcare systems, assistive technologies often have significant coverage limits, creating additional financial burdens for athletes who need access to sport-specific equipment. The disparity in access creates competitive imbalances where "athletes or teams with greater financial resources may have an advantage, potentially exacerbating existing disparities within the sporting world." This technological divide challenges traditional notions of fair competition and raises questions about the inclusivity of modern sports technology.

Sports governing bodies face significant challenges in regulating the use of performance-enhancing technologies while maintaining competitive integrity. The regulatory environment for sports technology is not well-defined, with a patchwork of regulations that vary by sport, competition level, and geographic region. Unlike many other industries, the majority of sports technologies are not required to comply with statutory or regulatory requirements, leaving consumers to assume products have met quality standards before becoming commercially available.

The concept of "technological doping" (Bouillet, 2018) has emerged as governing bodies grapple with determining what constitutes fair technological enhancement versus unfair competitive advantage. Examples include the banning of full-body polyurethane swimsuits after the 2008 Olympics when records were rewritten by swimmers wearing the suits, and the restriction of Nike's Alphafly shoes by World Athletics after they were found to enhance running efficiency by 4% and speed by 3.4%.

International sports federations have begun implementing frameworks to address technology regulation. The Olympic Movement Code on the Prevention of the Manipulation of Competitions provides harmonized regulations for protecting competitions from manipulation, though it primarily focuses on match-fixing rather than technological advantages. The Sports Technology Research Network has developed a Quality Framework for Sports Technologies that includes 25 measurable features grouped under five quality pillars: Quality Assurance and Measurement, Established Benefit, Ethics and Security, User Experience, and Data Management. However, regulatory responses often lag behind technological innovation. Sport governing bodies frequently "put their heads in the sand" when faced with new innovations, instead of dealing with their ramifications proactively. This reactive approach leads to situations where advantages are gained and records set before regulations are implemented, creating precedents that may be difficult to address retroactively.

The integration of advanced technology in sports raises fundamental ethical questions about the nature of athletic competition and the definition of fair play. The challenge lies in balancing technological innovation with the preservation of competitive integrity and the values of sportsmanship that define athletic competition.

One of the primary ethical concerns relates to the potential inequality created by varying access to cutting-edge technologies. When success becomes increasingly dependent on technological advantages rather than athletic talent and training dedication, the fundamental premise of sports competition—that any athlete has the chance to emerge victorious on any given day—is undermined. The line between legitimate performance enhancement and unfair technological advantage continues to blur as innovations advance. Unlike traditional performance-enhancing substances, which are clearly prohibited, the use of advanced equipment and training technologies exists in a gray area where regulations struggle to keep pace with innovation. This creates situations where "you're seen as cheating because you're breaking the sets of rules and regulations that have been defined at one moment in time," even as those rules may become outdated by technological progress.

A critical concern in the technological evolution of sports is preserving the human element that makes athletic competition compelling. When competitions become more about "engineer versus engineer" rather than "athlete versus athlete," the fundamental appeal of sports may be diminished. The challenge for regulatory bodies is to harness the benefits of technology for safety, performance optimization, and injury prevention while maintaining the authenticity and human drama that defines sporting excellence. The use of predictive analytics and AI in sports decision-making also raises questions about the role of intuition, experience, and human judgment in athletic competition. As data-driven decision-making becomes more prevalent, there is a risk of reducing the complexity of athletic performance to quantifiable metrics, potentially overlooking intangible qualities that contribute to sporting success.

Addressing the technological divide in sports requires coordinated efforts from multiple stakeholders, including international sporting bodies, governments, technology companies, and sports organizations. Several approaches show promise for creating more equitable access to performance-enhancing technologies while maintaining competitive integrity.

Technology companies are beginning to recognize the market opportunity in making elite-level equipment accessible to broader audiences. ASICS, for example, has leveraged advanced manufacturing techniques to create customized shoe inserts using 3D foot scanning technology, making personalized equipment available to amateur athletes. Similar initiatives could expand access to technologies previously reserved for elite competitors.

The development of simplified versions of professional technologies offers another path toward democratization. Just as Video Assistant Referee (VAR) systems have been adapted into VAR Light and Football Video Support systems for competitions with limited resources, other sports technologies could be scaled and adapted for broader accessibility.

Sports governing bodies must develop proactive regulatory frameworks that anticipate technological developments rather than reacting to them after competitive advantages have been gained. This requires establishing clear criteria for evaluating new technologies, including their impact on competitive balance, safety, and the integrity of competition.

The development of standardized quality frameworks for sports technology evaluation, such as the one developed by the Sports Technology Research Network, provides a foundation for consistent assessment of new technologies across different sports and organizations. These frameworks can help ensure that technological innovations meet minimum standards for safety, effectiveness, and competitive fairness.

Bridging the global technological divide requires increased international cooperation and targeted support for developing nations. This could include technology transfer programs, shared training facilities, and international funding mechanisms specifically designed to support sports technology access in underserved regions. The establishment of regional technology hubs could provide shared access to expensive equipment and training systems, reducing individual costs while maintaining competitive opportunities. Such initiatives would require coordination between international sports federations, government agencies, and private sector partners.

The challenge is not to halt technological progress, but to shape its development and implementation in ways that enhance rather than diminish the values of fair competition, athletic excellence, and the inclusive spirit that sports at their best can embody. Only through thoughtful governance, innovative solutions, and international cooperation can the sports community navigate toward a future where technological advancement serves to elevate all athletes, rather than creating insurmountable barriers for those without access to the latest innovations.

Moreover, the use of technology in officiating has sparked its own fairness debates. Systems like VAR in football, Hawk-Eye in tennis, and goal-line technology have enhanced the accuracy of officiating and reduced human error. However, their inconsistent deployment across tournaments, leagues, or regions creates a fragmented landscape where fairness depends on whether a particular competition can afford the technology. A goal disallowed in a domestic league match due to the absence of VAR, while a similar situation is rectified in an international tournament, calls into question the uniform application of rules.

Another fairness concern arises in the design and use of algorithms. Predictive models used in talent scouting, injury forecasting, or game strategy may unintentionally reflect and perpetuate bias embedded in historical data. For example, AI tools trained on datasets that underrepresent certain groups—by race, gender, or region—may systematically undervalue talented athletes outside dominant categories. This introduces a form of structural inequity that is difficult to detect and even harder to correct without rigorous oversight, transparency, and inclusive data practices.

Gender fairness has also become a significant issue in sports technology. Many technologies are developed with male physiology as the default model, often neglecting the specific needs, biomechanics, and hormonal cycles of female athletes. This has led to misaligned training loads, poorly calibrated equipment, or wearable devices that inaccurately track metrics for women. As more female athletes adopt technology in elite and amateur contexts, the lack of gender-aware design is both a missed opportunity and a source of unfair disadvantage.

Furthermore, the commercialization of athlete data raises critical questions about fairness in terms of data ownership and exploitation. Athletes increasingly generate value through the data they produce—value that is often captured by clubs, leagues, or tech providers. Without clear frameworks for data rights, profit-sharing, or informed consent, athletes may contribute to systems that benefit others more than themselves. Fairness, in this context, means ensuring that those who produce value are also recognized and rewarded for it.

Fairness also intersects with fan engagement and access. Digital innovations such as augmented reality experiences, personalized live stats, and exclusive streaming services have enhanced how fans interact with sport. However, these services are often locked behind paywalls or limited to certain geographic regions, raising concerns about digital inequality. Fans in lower-income contexts may be unable to access the same content, perspectives, or interactivity, reinforcing divides in the global sports audience.

Addressing these fairness challenges requires a holistic, multi-stakeholder approach. Sports governing bodies, technology developers, regulators, and athlete advocacy groups must collaborate to establish ethical guidelines, technical standards, and accountability mechanisms. Fairness audits of algorithms, inclusive design protocols, and equitable funding models for tech access are just a few potential strategies. Moreover, efforts must go beyond technological fixes—embedding fairness as a cultural and institutional priority is essential for sustained progress.

The quest for fairness in sports technology is not about resisting innovation, but about shaping it with foresight, inclusivity, and ethical responsibility. Technology can elevate sport only if it is harnessed in ways that respect the values of equality, merit, and transparency. The great fairness quest is ongoing, and its outcomes will define not only the future of athletic competition, but also the role of sport as a driver of global justice and social cohesion. Thus nuanced perspective recognizes that while technological advancements can profoundly elevate performance, fan experience, and decision-making, they can also reinforce or introduce new inequities if left unchecked. Numerous real-world examples illustrate how fairness must be actively built into the design, deployment, and governance of sports tech to ensure that innovation contributes to equality, merit, and transparency.

Take the case of Nike's Vaporfly shoes, which caused widespread debate in distance running after several athletes wearing the model broke world records. While the shoes featured advanced carbon-fiber plates and responsive foam that undeniably enhanced performance, critics argued that their use skewed the principle of fair competition—particularly since not all athletes had access to them. World Athletics eventually regulated the sole thickness and availability of such footwear in elite competitions. This episode underscores how innovation must be guided by rules that ensure technological advantages do not become barriers to fair competition.

In football, the introduction of VAR technology has improved decision accuracy for offsides, fouls, and handballs. However, inconsistencies in its application—varying by league, country, or competition—have created a perception of unequal justice. A Premier League club may benefit from VAR reviews, while a lower-division team without such resources must contend with uncorrected human error. This disparity reveals the fairness problem not in the technology itself, but in its uneven distribution. A more ethically responsible approach would involve developing tiered or cost-accessible systems that support technological equity across leagues.

From a gender perspective, sports wearables and fitness apps often fail to serve female athletes properly. Devices like heart rate monitors, recovery trackers, and motion sensors have historically been calibrated based on male data sets, overlooking hormonal variations, menstrual cycle impacts, and different biomechanical profiles. This led to under-optimized training feedback or misleading health metrics. Recent responses, such as the introduction of "female-specific" performance tracking by companies like Whoop and Garmin, reflect growing foresight—but the initial oversight demonstrates why inclusive design is a non-negotiable element of fairness in sports tech.

Another illustrative case is Catapult Sports, a company providing athlete tracking systems used by top-tier clubs like Real Madrid, NFL teams, and Olympic federations. While such systems provide sophisticated performance and workload analytics, their adoption is expensive and therefore largely limited to elite programs. Amateur athletes, smaller federations, or athletes in the Global South often lack access to these data-driven tools. This deepens a technological divide in talent development and injury prevention. Ethical innovation would require not only open data standards but also affordable, scalable versions for broader adoption.

Algorithmic fairness is also a pressing concern. AI scouting platforms and predictive recruitment tools, such as those used in U.S. college sports or football academies in Europe, have the potential to accelerate talent identification. But they also risk perpetuating biases present in historical data—privileging athletes from well-known schools, certain body types, or dominant regions. Without transparency into how these models score athletes or what variables they prioritize, meritocracy is distorted. Calls for "algorithmic audits" and explainable AI systems in sport are now gaining traction to address these concerns.

Fan engagement technologies raise further issues. Dynamic ticket pricing algorithms, popular in the U.S. sports market, use AI to adjust prices based on demand patterns. While this increases revenue efficiency for clubs, it often prices out working-class fans, altering the social composition of stadiums and marginalizing traditional supporter bases. Similarly, geo-blocking of sports content limits access for fans in certain regions, reinforcing digital inequality. A fairer approach would involve balancing profit motives with accessibility strategies, such as subsidized streaming or universal access to key events.

Even privacy intersects with fairness. Consider facial recognition technologies deployed in venues like the Tokyo 2020 Olympics for access control and crowd monitoring. While efficient, such systems raise ethical concerns about surveillance, data use, and consent. These concerns are magnified when such tools are implemented without public debate or transparency, disproportionately affecting groups already marginalized by structural inequalities. Embedding privacy by design and ensuring participatory governance models can prevent technology from undermining trust and fairness.

In each of these examples, the central lesson is clear: technology does not automatically enhance fairness—it must be intentionally shaped to do so. Fairness in sports tech depends on designing systems that accommodate diversity, distribute benefits widely, and operate transparently. Regulation, standardization, participatory design, and digital literacy are all part of the ethical toolkit needed. Ultimately, the great fairness quest in sports tech is not just about optimizing competition but about defending sport's role as a global space for justice, unity, and aspiration. The future of sport will be defined not only by the speed of innovation but by the values guiding its application. How we resolve these fairness dilemmas will shape who gets to play, who gets to win, and who gets to belong.

7.3. Balancing Tradition and Tomorrow's Tech

In the unfolding narrative of sports innovation, a central tension emerges: how to harmonize centuries-old traditions with the accelerating march of tomorrow's technologies. Sport, by nature, is both ritualistic and progressive. It is built on deep-rooted customs, codified rules, and cultural meanings that span generations, yet it is increasingly shaped by data analytics, AI, wearable devices, and immersive media. The challenge, then, is not whether technology belongs in sport—it clearly does—but how to integrate it without eroding the essence of what makes sport meaningful, equitable, and human.

Tradition in sport goes beyond ceremonial anthems or historical venues. It encompasses intangible elements such as fair play, unpredictability, and the shared cultural memory of iconic moments shaped by human decisions and imperfections. These traditions allow fans to compare athletes across eras and to uphold a sense of continuity. But as technologies like AI-powered coaching, smart balls, and automated officiating become commonplace, they risk redefining what is "normal" in performance, training, and even storytelling.

One example of this balance in flux can be seen in tennis. The adoption of the Hawk-Eye line-calling system in professional tournaments has significantly improved accuracy and removed much of the controversy surrounding human error in officiating. Yet its use has also displaced the iconic, sometimes dramatic, role of the line judge—a longstanding feature of the sport's atmosphere. Some tournaments have gone further, removing all on-court judges in favor of fully automated systems. While technically precise, this shift raises the question: how much human presence and theatricality are we willing to sacrifice in the name of efficiency?

Another instructive case is Major League Baseball (MLB). Facing declining attention spans among younger fans, the league introduced a pitch clock to speed up the game, and is actively testing automated strike zones. These interventions are technologically sound and serve commercial interests, but they also alter the sport's rhythm and tactical nuance. Traditionalists argue that these changes compromise the soul of the game, which has long been defined by its unique tempo and strategic complexity. The debate highlights a deeper question: should tradition yield to technology for the sake of modern engagement, or should sport retain its historical pacing despite shifting audience expectations?

Similarly, in the realm of athlete training, the use of biometric sensors, AI video analysis, and predictive injury models is revolutionizing preparation and recovery. While these tools enhance performance and reduce risk, they also raise concerns about over-optimization. If every movement is algorithmically optimized, is there still room for creative improvisation, instinct, or the underdog narrative? The human element of sport—the surprises, the errors, the comebacks—often emerges from moments that defy logic and data. A future where machine learning dictates every decision risks flattening this rich emotional texture.

On the fan experience side, augmented reality (AR), virtual reality (VR), and AI-generated commentary are redefining how audiences consume sport. Fans can now project players into their living rooms or view matches through immersive 3D visualizations (Glebova, 2020). These tools offer exciting possibilities, particularly for global audiences unable to attend games in person. However, they also risk detaching fans from the communal, in-person rituals that anchor sport in shared physical space. Tailoring experiences too heavily to individual preferences could fragment collective fandom, replacing the roar of the stadium with isolated engagement.

To strike the right balance between tradition and tomorrow's tech, sports organizations must adopt a reflective, inclusive approach. Innovation should enhance—not replace—the human values and cultural significance embedded in sport. This means involving athletes, coaches, historians, fans, and technologists in the co-design of solutions. Regulatory bodies should develop frameworks that allow for experimentation while safeguarding the core principles of the game. Importantly, not every piece of technology needs to be implemented simply because it exists; selectivity, timing, and cultural sensitivity are essential.

Education also plays a key role. By equipping athletes, coaches, and fans with digital literacy and ethical awareness, sports institutions can ensure that new technologies are used not just effectively, but responsibly. Museums, documentaries, and archives should continue to preserve sporting heritage, helping new generations understand where their favorite games come from—and why their traditional roots matter. The path forward is not a binary choice between nostalgia and novelty. It is a continuous negotiation, a dynamic equilibrium. The true power of sport lies in its ability to evolve while remaining anchored in the values that made it significant in the first place. Balancing tradition and tomorrow's tech is less about compromise and more about synthesis: using innovation to reinforce the very traditions we cherish, and allowing those traditions to guide innovation's ethical and cultural compass.

Chapter 8

The Grand Finale

8.1. Highlights

As we reach the culmination of this journey through the evolving landscape of sports, artificial intelligence, and robotics, it's worth reflecting on the key insights and transformative moments that have defined our exploration. From the stadiums of the future to the ethical dilemmas posed by algorithmic decision-making, the intersection of sport and emerging technology is not just a frontier—it's a revolution already underway.

Throughout this book, several interconnected themes have woven together to tell the story of sports' technological transformation. At the heart of this evolution lies the reimagination of performance itself, where AI-driven analytics and robotic interventions are not merely reshaping how athletes train and perform, but fundamentally redefining the very limits of human achievement. Smart wearables, biomechanical feedback, and robotic rehabilitation tools now offer granular insights that were once unimaginable, creating new pathways to athletic excellence.

This technological revolution has simultaneously transformed the spectator experience, democratizing access and enriching fan engagement in unprecedented ways. Technology has elevated spectators from passive observers to active participants in the sports ecosystem through virtual reality replays, AI-generated commentary, personalized in-game statistics, and immersive fan platforms that blur the lines between watching and experiencing sport. Operational intelligence has become the backbone of modern sports organizations. Clubs, franchises, and governing bodies now leverage predictive analytics for everything from dynamic ticket pricing and security management to athlete health monitoring and climate control within venues. This data-driven approach has made decision-making smarter, faster, and more precise than ever before.

Yet this technological advancement brings with it profound ethical and social questions that cannot be ignored. The integration of AI and robotics in sport raises critical concerns about privacy, fairness, data ownership, algorithmic bias, and perhaps most importantly, the preservation of the human spirit in competition. These debates are not peripheral considerations but central challenges that will define the future character of sports. The transformation has also unleashed

DOI: 10.1201/9781003533795-8

entirely new economic opportunities, opening revenue streams that extend far beyond traditional models. Tech-driven innovation has birthed AI-generated virtual athletes, metaverse broadcasting experiences, blockchain-based fan tokens, and robotic sports competitions. These are not speculative futures but present realities already integrated into the business models of leading organizations worldwide.

This convergence represents more than just technological adoption—it serves as a bridge connecting where sports have been with where they are inevitably heading. The fusion of sports, AI, and robotics is not a passing trend but a fundamental, long-term evolution that will continue to challenge conventional thinking, inspire new possibilities, and transform the very essence of athletic competition and fan engagement for generations to come.

8.2. What's Next for Sports, AI, and Robotics?

Peering into the future, the fusion of sports, AI, and robotics promises not just incremental advances, but paradigm shifts. As technology evolves, so too will the boundaries of what is possible—on the field, in training centers, behind the scenes, and in the hearts of global audiences. What lies ahead is a dynamic, multi-dimensional ecosystem, shaped by continuous innovation, cross-sector convergence, and bold experimentation.

From Human-Centric to Hybrid Performance Models

Athletic performance will increasingly be seen through a hybrid lens, where human ability is continuously augmented by machine learning algorithms, exoskeletons, cognitive training systems, and emotion-recognition AI. The definition of "peak performance" will no longer be limited to physical ability but will encompass optimized decision-making, neuroplastic adaptability, and biometric harmony—achieved through symbiotic human-AI interaction.

AI-Designed Sports and Competitions

Beyond enhancing existing disciplines, we can expect the emergence of entirely new sports—some designed by AI, others played by robots, avatars, or even generative virtual athletes. Competitions in mixed-reality environments may become mainstream, challenging traditional notions of fairness, access, and physicality. These formats will redefine entertainment, accessibility, and even the way we measure excellence.

Hyper-Personalized Fan Ecosystems

The next generation of sports fandom will be personalized, predictive, and participatory. AI will tailor content feeds, merchandise, fantasy leagues, and loyalty programs based on real-time behavioral data. Fans will become co-creators of content and even stakeholders in decision-making processes through decentralized platforms.

Sustainability and Smart Infrastructure

As environmental concerns escalate, AI and robotics will be central to creating sustainable sports ecosystems—energy-efficient venues, intelligent transportation for events, autonomous maintenance robots, and data-driven sustainability monitoring. Green AI and circular robotics will emerge as key enablers for environmentally responsible growth in sport.

Ethics, Regulation, and the Human Element

With opportunity comes responsibility. The future will require robust frameworks around ethics, regulation, and inclusivity. Ensuring that AI and robotic systems uphold fairness, transparency, and human dignity will be paramount. Equally, the "soul of sport"—its spontaneity, emotion, and social bonding—must be preserved even as technology reshapes its every facet.

In short, the next frontier will not be defined solely by what technology can do for sport, but by what values we choose to embed in that transformation.

8.3. Invitation to Join the Sports Tech Party: Perspective Business, Research, and Development Directions

The curtain may be falling on this book, but the real show is just beginning. The convergence of sports, AI, and robotics is not a closed circle for tech giants or elite leagues—it is an open invitation for creators, thinkers, entrepreneurs, and innovators across disciplines. Whether you're a business leader, researcher, developer, policymaker, or passionate fan, there's a seat at the table—and a role to play in shaping the next era of sport.

For Business: Invest, Disrupt, Collaborate

The sports tech market is fertile ground for investment and innovation. Opportunities abound across smart equipment, AI-driven health diagnostics, immersive fan platforms, robotic officiating tools, and green infrastructure. Startups can challenge legacy models; established firms can pivot into new domains; brands can collaborate with tech labs to co-create unique consumer experiences.

But to succeed, the approach must go beyond gadgetry. Strategic vision, user-centered design, and ethical foresight will be key. The most successful ventures will be those that add value not only to performance and entertainment but to well-being, equity, and environmental sustainability.

For Researchers: Expand the Boundaries of Knowledge

Academia and research institutions have a critical role in examining, evaluating, and guiding this transformation. From biomechanics and computer vision to sociology and ethics, the questions are vast and complex:

- How does AI alter our concept of athletic identity?
- What psychological effects do robotic coaches have on athletes?
- Can machine learning predict injuries before they occur?
- How should AI-generated sport content be regulated?

There is room—and a need—for both theoretical inquiry and applied experimentation. Interdisciplinary collaboration will be the cornerstone of meaningful progress.

For Developers and Engineers: Build the Future Responsibly

Coders, data scientists, engineers, and roboticists are the architects of tomorrow's sports experience. Whether designing real-time analytics tools for coaches or developing autonomous camera systems for grassroots tournaments, your work is reshaping the game.

But with great power comes great responsibility. Developers must ensure their creations are inclusive, bias-aware, transparent, and respectful of the unique culture of sport. Open-source platforms, ethical AI standards, and collaborative sandboxes can help foster a healthier innovation environment.

The Grand Invitation

This book does not provide all the answers—nor should it. Instead, it offers a provocation, a framework, and a call to action. The real story is being written now, every day, across courts, labs, arenas, classrooms, and start-up hubs.

So, join the sports tech party—not just as a spectator, but as a co-creator.

Tech Talk: Glossary

This glossary provides quick-reference definitions of the core concepts, technologies, and terminology that have shaped our discussion of the evolving intersection between sport, artificial intelligence (AI), and robotics. Whether you're a seasoned expert or a curious newcomer, this section helps decode the language of sports tech.

The simulation of human intelligence processes by machines, especially computer systems. In sports, AI is used for performance analysis, injury prediction, fan engagement, and more.

Advanced Analytics

The autonomous or semi-autonomous examination of data or content using sophisticated techniques and tools that extend beyond traditional business intelligence. In sports contexts, advanced analytics involves the use of machine learning algorithms, predictive modeling, and statistical analysis to derive deeper insights from performance data, make predictions about future outcomes, and generate strategic recommendations. This includes techniques such as expected goals in football, player efficiency ratings in basketball, and injury prediction models that analyze biomechanical patterns to forecast potential health risks before they manifest.

Algorithm

A systematic set of rules, instructions, or mathematical formulas that computers follow to solve problems or complete specific tasks. In sports technology, algorithms form the foundation of machine learning models that analyze player performance, predict game outcomes, optimize training regimens, and automate decision-making processes. Examples include algorithms that determine optimal player substitutions based on fatigue patterns, calculate real-time win probabilities during matches, or identify tactical patterns in opponent gameplay through video analysis.

Algorithm: *A set of rules or instructions given to an AI system to help it learn from data and make decisions or predictions.*

Analytics: *The discovery, interpretation, and communication of meaningful patterns in data. In sport, analytics helps teams and coaches make informed decisions based on performance metrics.*

DOI: 10.1201/9781003533795-9

Artificial General Intelligence (AGI)

A theoretical form of artificial intelligence that possesses the ability to understand, learn, and apply knowledge across a wide range of tasks at a level comparable to or exceeding human cognitive abilities. Unlike narrow AI systems designed for specific functions, AGI would demonstrate flexible reasoning, creativity, and adaptability across diverse domains. While current sports AI applications represent narrow AI focused on specific tasks, the eventual development of AGI could revolutionize sports through systems capable of comprehensive strategic thinking, creative play design, and holistic athlete development programs.

Artificial Intelligence (AI)

The comprehensive field of computer science focused on creating digital systems capable of performing tasks that traditionally require human intelligence, including learning from experience, reasoning through complex problems, recognizing patterns, understanding natural language, and making informed decisions. In sports applications, AI encompasses everything from computer vision systems that track player movements to natural language processing that generates automated commentary, predictive analytics that forecast injury risks, and machine learning algorithms that optimize training protocols based on individual athlete characteristics.

Augmented Reality (AR)

An interactive technology that overlays digital information, graphics, or virtual objects onto the real-world environment, typically viewed through specialized devices such as smart glasses, mobile screens, or heads-up displays. In sports applications, AR enhances fan experiences by providing real-time statistics during live events, enables athletes to visualize tactical formations during training, allows coaches to analyze performance data overlaid on actual playing surfaces, and creates immersive educational experiences that help viewers understand complex strategies and rules.

> **Augmented Reality (AR)**: *An interactive experience where digital elements (like stats or visual overlays) are superimposed onto the real-world environment, enhancing live sports broadcasts anvd training experiences.*

Autonomous Robot

A sophisticated robotic system capable of performing complex tasks without direct human intervention, utilizing integrated sensors, artificial intelligence algorithms, and decision-making capabilities to navigate environments, respond to changing conditions, and execute programmed objectives. In sports contexts, autonomous robots serve as training partners that adapt to athlete skill levels, automated equipment managers that maintain playing surfaces, robotic referees that make consistent officiating decisions, and delivery systems that efficiently transport equipment and supplies during events.

Big Data

Extremely large and complex datasets that exceed the processing capabilities of traditional data management systems, typically characterized by the three V›s: volume (massive amounts of information), variety (diverse data types including text, images, video, and sensor readings), and velocity (rapid generation and processing requirements). In sports, big data encompasses comprehensive performance metrics collected from wearable devices, detailed video analysis of every player movement, fan engagement data across multiple platforms, and historical records spanning decades of competition that enable sophisticated predictive modeling and strategic insights.

Biomechanics

The scientific discipline that applies mechanical principles and engineering methods to understand the structure, function, and movement of biological systems, particularly human bodies in motion. In sports technology, biomechanical analysis utilizes motion capture systems, force sensors, and computer modeling to optimize athletic technique, prevent injuries through movement pattern analysis, design equipment that enhances performance, and develop rehabilitation protocols that restore optimal function following injury or surgery.

> **Biomechanics**: *The study of the mechanical laws relating to the movement or structure of living organisms. In sport, it's used to optimize technique and prevent injury.*

Blockchain

A distributed ledger technology that maintains a continuously growing list of records, called blocks, which are linked and secured using cryptographic principles, creating an immutable and transparent record of transactions without requiring a central authority. In sports applications, blockchain enables secure athlete data ownership and transfer, transparent fan voting systems, authenticated collectibles and memorabilia, smart contracts that automatically execute payment terms for athletes and agents, and decentralized governance structures that give stakeholders direct input in organizational decisions.

> **Blockchain**: *A decentralized digital ledger technology used to securely record transactions. In sports, it's often used for ticketing, NFTs, and fan tokens.*

Brain-Computer Interface (BCI)

Advanced neurological technology that establishes direct communication pathways between the brain and external devices, enabling users to control computers, prosthetics, or other systems through thought alone by detecting and interpreting neural signals. In sports contexts, BCIs facilitate cognitive training programs that enhance focus and decision-making speed, provide direct neural feedback for mental performance optimization, enable paralyzed athletes to compete using thought-controlled devices, and offer unprecedented insights into the psychological aspects of peak athletic performance.

Chatbot: *An AI-driven virtual assistant that interacts with users via text or voice. Chatbots in sports offer customer service, event updates, and personalized fan experiences.*

Computer Vision

A specialized field of artificial intelligence that enables machines to interpret, analyze, and understand visual information from digital images, videos, and real-world environments, mimicking human visual perception through sophisticated algorithms and pattern recognition techniques. In sports applications, computer vision powers automated player tracking systems, real-time tactical analysis, injury risk assessment through movement pattern recognition, automated highlight generation, and officiating assistance systems that provide instant replay analysis and rule violation detection. A field of AI that enables computers to interpret and process visual information from the world. Used in match analysis, player tracking, and referee assistance.

Conversational AI

Advanced artificial intelligence systems designed to engage in natural, human-like dialogue through text or voice interactions, utilizing natural language processing, machine learning, and contextual understanding to provide relevant responses and maintain coherent conversations over extended interactions. In sports contexts, conversational AI enables intelligent virtual assistants for fans seeking information, automated customer service systems for ticket and merchandise inquiries, personalized coaching advice delivered through chat interfaces, and interactive educational platforms that help newcomers understand complex sports rules and strategies.

CRISPR (Clustered Regularly Interspaced Short Palindromic Repeats)

is a powerful gene-editing technology originally discovered as part of a natural defense mechanism in bacteria. In simple terms, CRISPR allows scientists to precisely cut and modify DNA within living organisms, making it possible to turn genes on or off, insert new genetic material, or remove harmful mutations.CRISPR sequences in bacteria store fragments of viral DNA from past infections (like a genetic memory). When the virus attacks again, the bacteria use a protein (such as Cas9) guided by CRISPR RNA to find and cut the matching viral DNA, disabling it. Scientists adapted this system to edit genes in plants, animals, and humans by designing a guide RNA that targets a specific DNA sequence, and Cas9 acts as molecular scissors to cut the DNA at that spot. While CRISPR is revolutionary, it raises ethical and safety concerns about unintended mutations, gene drives in ecosystems, and human germline editing.

Data Analytics

The systematic computational analysis of data sets to discover patterns, correlations, and insights that inform decision-making processes, utilizing statistical methods, machine learning algorithms, and visualization techniques to transform raw information into actionable intelligence. In sports applications, data analytics encompasses performance analysis that identifies strengths and weaknesses, fan engagement metrics that optimize marketing strategies, injury prevention models that predict health risks, and strategic planning tools that inform coaching decisions and roster management.

Deep Learning

A sophisticated subset of machine learning that utilizes artificial neural networks with multiple hidden layers to automatically learn complex patterns and representations from large datasets, mimicking the hierarchical processing structure of the human brain to achieve superior performance in tasks such as image recognition, natural language processing, and decision-making. In sports technology, deep learning powers advanced video analysis systems that automatically recognize tactical patterns, enables real-time performance optimization through continuous learning from athlete data, and supports predictive modeling for injury prevention and performance forecasting.

Digital Twin

A comprehensive virtual replica of a physical object, system, or process that continuously updates with real-time data to mirror its physical counterpart›s current state, behavior, and performance characteristics, enabling simulation, analysis, and optimization without affecting the actual system. In sports applications, digital twins represent individual athletes with their complete physiological and performance profiles, enable virtual stadium management and crowd flow simulation, facilitate equipment testing and optimization in virtual environments, and support strategic planning through simulated game scenarios and training conditions.

Digital Twin: *A virtual model of a real-world object, system, or athlete. In sports, digital twins are used to simulate training, test strategies, and predict performance outcomes.*

Drone Technology: *Unmanned aerial systems used in sports for filming, broadcasting, and security surveillance.*

Edge Computing

A distributed computing paradigm that processes data closer to its source of generation rather than relying on centralized cloud servers, reducing latency, improving response times, and enhancing privacy by keeping sensitive information local while maintaining connectivity for necessary data sharing. In sports contexts, edge computing enables real-time performance feedback during training and competition, supports instant decision-making for autonomous systems like robotic referees, facilitates immediate injury detection and response protocols, and provides low-latency interactive experiences for fans using augmented reality applications.

Exoskeleton

A wearable robotic device that augments human physical capabilities by providing external support, strength enhancement, or mobility assistance through powered joints and mechanical structures that work in harmony with the user›s natural movements. In sports and rehabilitation applications, exoskeletons assist athletes recovering from injuries by supporting weakened limbs during movement, enhance training effectiveness by providing resistance or assistance as needed, enable individuals with disabilities to participate in competitive sports, and serve as research tools for understanding optimal movement patterns and biomechanical efficiency. A wearable robotic suit that supports and enhances body movement. Applied in athletic rehabilitation and performance training.

Facial Recognition

An advanced biometric technology that identifies or verifies individuals by analyzing unique facial features and characteristics through computer vision algorithms and machine learning models trained on extensive databases of facial images. In sports venues and events, facial recognition systems enhance security by identifying banned individuals or potential threats, streamline entry processes by replacing traditional ticketing methods, enable personalized fan experiences through automatic recognition and customized services, and support athlete monitoring for training attendance and performance correlation analysis.

Fan Tokens: *Digital assets that allow fans to engage with and influence their favorite teams through blockchain-based platforms.*

Generative Artificial Intelligence

Advanced AI systems capable of creating new, original content including text, images, videos, music, and other media by learning patterns and structures from training data and applying that knowledge to generate novel outputs that maintain coherence and relevance to given prompts or contexts. In sports applications, generative AI produces automated sports commentary and analysis, creates personalized training programs tailored to individual athlete needs, generates realistic virtual opponents for training simulations, develops strategic playbooks based on opponent analysis, and produces engaging content for social media and fan engagement platforms. AI systems capable of generating new content, such as text, video, or virtual athletes. In sports, it's used for simulations, commentary, and content creation.

GPS Tracking

Global Positioning System technology enhanced with additional sensors and analytics capabilities that provide precise location data, movement patterns, speed measurements, and spatial relationships in real-time, enabling comprehensive monitoring of objects or individuals across various environments. In sports contexts,

GPS tracking monitors athlete workload and movement patterns during training and competition, optimizes team tactics through positional analysis, prevents injuries by identifying overexertion or poor movement mechanics, supports referee decision-making through precise ball and player positioning data, and enhances fan experiences through detailed match analysis and statistics.

Haptic Feedback

Advanced tactile technology that provides users with physical sensations such as vibrations, forces, or motions to simulate the sense of touch and enhance interaction with digital environments, creating more immersive and intuitive user experiences through controlled mechanical stimulation. In sports applications, haptic feedback enables remote fans to feel the impact of plays through connected wearable devices, provides athletes with immediate physical cues for technique correction during training, enhances virtual and augmented reality sports experiences by adding realistic touch sensations, and supports rehabilitation programs by providing guided movement feedback through specialized equipment.

Human-Machine Interface (HMI)

The comprehensive system of hardware and software components that facilitate interaction and communication between humans and machines, encompassing input devices, output displays, control systems, and feedback mechanisms designed to optimize usability, efficiency, and safety in human-machine collaboration. In sports technology, HMIs enable intuitive control of training equipment and monitoring systems, provide coaches with accessible interfaces for analyzing complex performance data, support athlete interaction with wearable technology and biometric monitors, and facilitate seamless integration of AI-powered coaching tools into existing training methodologies.

Internet of Things (IoT)

A vast network of interconnected physical devices, sensors, and systems that collect, share, and analyze data through internet connectivity, creating intelligent environments capable of autonomous monitoring, control, and optimization across various applications and industries. In sports contexts, IoT encompasses smart stadiums with interconnected lighting, climate control, and security systems, wearable devices that continuously monitor athlete health and performance, intelligent equipment that adapts to user preferences and environmental conditions, and comprehensive facility management systems that optimize energy usage, maintenance schedules, and fan experiences.

IoT (Internet of Things): *A network of interconnected devices that collect and exchange data. In sport, IoT powers smart wearables and stadium technologies.*

Large Language Model (LLM)

Sophisticated artificial intelligence systems trained on extensive text datasets to understand, generate, and manipulate human language with remarkable fluency and coherence, capable of performing diverse language-related tasks including translation, summarization, creative writing, and complex reasoning through natural language processing. In sports applications, LLMs power automated sports journalism and commentary generation, provide intelligent analysis and insights from vast amounts of sports data and historical records, enable natural language interfaces for accessing complex statistical databases, and support fan engagement through conversational AI systems that can discuss games, players, and strategies in detail.

Machine Learning (ML)

A powerful subset of artificial intelligence that enables computer systems to automatically learn, improve, and make predictions or decisions from data without being explicitly programmed for each specific task, utilizing algorithms that identify patterns and relationships within datasets to develop predictive models and intelligent behaviors. In sports technology, machine learning analyzes player performance data to identify improvement opportunities, predicts injury risks through biomechanical pattern recognition, optimizes game strategies based on opponent analysis, personalizes fan experiences through preference learning, and continuously adapts training programs based on individual athlete responses and progress. A branch of AI focused on building systems that learn from data to improve over time without being explicitly programmed. Used for injury prediction, game strategy modeling, and personalization.

> **Metaverse**: *A collective virtual shared space where users can interact with digital environments and others in real time. In sports, this enables immersive viewing and virtual fan zones.*

Motion Capture

Advanced technology that records and analyzes the movement of objects or people through precise measurement of position changes over time, typically using multiple cameras, sensors, or markers to create detailed three-dimensional representations of movement patterns and biomechanical characteristics. In sports applications, motion capture systems provide comprehensive analysis of athletic technique for performance optimization, enable creation of realistic digital avatars for training simulations, support injury prevention through movement pattern assessment, facilitate equipment design and testing through detailed biomechanical data, and power video game development with authentic athletic movements.

> **Motion Capture**: *Technology used to digitally record movement. In sports, it's used to analyze athlete performance and develop animated simulations.*

Natural Language Processing (NLP)

A comprehensive branch of artificial intelligence that focuses on enabling computers to understand, interpret, and generate human language in meaningful ways, combining computational linguistics, machine learning, and statistical analysis to bridge the gap between human communication and computer understanding. In sports contexts, NLP powers automated sports reporting and commentary generation, enables sentiment analysis of fan reactions and social media discussions, supports intelligent search and query systems for sports databases, facilitates translation services for international sporting events, and enables voice-controlled interfaces for accessing sports information and statistics.

Natural Language Processing (NLP): *An AI field that enables machines to understand, interpret, and respond to human language. Used in chatbots, commentary systems, and sentiment analysis.*

Neural Network

A computational model inspired by the structure and function of biological neural networks in the human brain, consisting of interconnected processing nodes (neurons) organized in layers that can learn complex patterns and relationships from data through iterative training processes. In sports technology, neural networks enable sophisticated pattern recognition in video analysis systems, power predictive models for performance forecasting and injury prevention, support real-time decision-making in automated officiating systems, facilitate personalized training program development based on individual athlete characteristics, and enable advanced computer vision applications for tracking and analysis.

NFT (Non-Fungible Token): *A unique digital asset verified using blockchain, often used for owning exclusive sports memorabilia or digital collectibles.*

Predictive Analytics

Advanced analytical techniques that utilize historical data, statistical algorithms, and machine learning methodologies to identify patterns and forecast future events, behaviors, or outcomes with quantifiable probability estimates, enabling proactive decision-making and strategic planning. In sports applications, predictive analytics forecasts injury risks before symptoms appear, estimates game outcomes and player performance levels, optimizes training loads to maximize performance while minimizing overexertion risks, supports draft and recruitment decisions through talent evaluation models, and enables dynamic pricing strategies for tickets and merchandise based on demand predictions. The use of statistical algorithms and machine learning to identify future outcomes based on historical data. Widely used in scouting, training, and fan behavior forecasting.

Quantum Computing

Revolutionary computing technology that harnesses quantum mechanical phenomena such as superposition and entanglement to process information in fundamentally different ways than classical computers, potentially offering exponential speedups for certain computational problems through quantum bits (qubits) that can exist in multiple states simultaneously. In future sports applications, quantum computing could enable unprecedented optimization of complex training schedules and logistics, solve intricate strategic problems involving multiple variables and scenarios, accelerate machine learning processes for real-time performance analysis, and support advanced simulations of biomechanical systems for equipment design and injury prevention.

Radio Frequency Identification (RFID)

Wireless communication technology that uses electromagnetic fields to automatically identify, track, and collect data from tags or cards attached to objects, animals, or people, enabling efficient inventory management, access control, and location tracking without requiring direct line-of-sight contact. In sports applications, RFID technology tracks equipment and inventory management, monitors athlete attendance and movement patterns, enables contactless payment systems in venues, supports automated timing systems for races and competitions, and facilitates fan engagement through interactive experiences triggered by proximity to RFID-enabled locations or objects.

Robotics

The interdisciplinary field encompassing mechanical engineering, electrical engineering, computer science, and artificial intelligence to design, construct, operate, and maintain robots capable of performing tasks autonomously or under human guidance, integrating sensors, actuators, and intelligent control systems to create versatile and adaptable machines. In sports contexts, robotics includes autonomous training partners that adapt to athlete skill levels, robotic officials that ensure consistent rule enforcement, automated equipment maintenance systems, delivery robots for efficient venue operations, and specialized rehabilitation robots that assist in injury recovery and physical therapy protocols. The design, construction, and use of robots. In sport, robotics is applied in training equipment, refereeing systems, and venue maintenance.

Sensor Technology

Advanced electronic devices and systems that detect, measure, and respond to physical stimuli such as motion, temperature, pressure, light, or chemical composition, converting these inputs into electrical signals that can be processed, analyzed, and utilized for monitoring, control, and decision-making applications. In sports technology, sensors enable comprehensive athlete monitoring through wearable devices that track heart rate, movement patterns, and biomechanical data, provide environmental monitoring for optimal playing conditions, support equipment performance analysis and safety monitoring, facilitate automated officiating through ball and line sensors, and enable interactive fan experiences through motion-responsive systems.

Simultaneous Localization and Mapping (SLAM)

A sophisticated computational technique used in robotics and autonomous systems that simultaneously constructs a map of an unknown environment while tracking the system›s location within that environment, utilizing sensor data and probabilistic algorithms to build accurate spatial representations without prior knowledge of the surroundings. In sports applications, SLAM technology enables autonomous robots to navigate complex sports venues for maintenance and delivery tasks, supports augmented reality applications that overlay digital information on real sports environments, facilitates detailed venue mapping for security and crowd management purposes, and enables robotic camera systems to track action while maintaining optimal positioning.

Smart Stadium

A technologically advanced sports venue that integrates Internet of Things (IoT) devices, artificial intelligence, and data analytics to create intelligent, responsive environments that enhance fan experiences, optimize operations, and improve safety and sustainability through interconnected systems and real-time monitoring capabilities. Smart stadiums feature automated climate control and energy management, personalized fan services through mobile applications and beacon technology, advanced security systems with facial recognition and crowd monitoring, dynamic pricing and concession management, real-time crowd flow optimization, and sustainable practices through intelligent resource utilization and waste management. A technologically enhanced sports venue that uses data and connectivity to improve operations, fan experience, and sustainability.

Tibial Acceleration

Tibial acceleration measures the rapid change in velocity of the tibia (shin bone) during ground contact, typically captured by accelerometers on wearables. Peak tibial acceleration (PTA)—occurring milliseconds after footstrike—serves as a proxy for impact loading and bone stress in running/gait analysis.

Virtual Reality (VR)

Immersive technology that creates artificial, computer-generated environments that users can interact with in seemingly real or physical ways through specialized hardware such as headsets, controllers, and haptic feedback devices, providing complete sensory immersion that can simulate various experiences and scenarios. In sports applications, VR enables realistic training simulations that allow athletes to practice in various conditions and scenarios, provides immersive fan experiences that place viewers virtually at sporting events, supports injury rehabilitation through controlled, motivating exercise environments, facilitates coaching education through first-person perspective training scenarios, and enables tactical analysis through immersive replay systems. A fully immersive digital environment experienced through headsets. In sports, VR is used for fan engagement, athlete training, and simulations.

Wearable Technology

Devices worn on the body that collect real-time physiological and biomechanical data. These tools are essential for monitoring athlete health, load, and performance. Sophisticated electronic devices designed to be worn on the human body that continuously monitor, collect, and transmit data about the wearer's physical condition, activity levels, and environmental interactions, typically incorporating sensors, wireless connectivity, and data processing capabilities in compact, comfortable form factors. In sports contexts, wearable technology includes fitness trackers and smartwatches that monitor heart rate, sleep patterns, and activity levels, specialized sensors embedded in clothing or equipment that measure biomechanical data and performance metrics, GPS devices that track location and movement patterns during training and competition, and recovery monitoring systems that assess readiness for training and competition through physiological indicators.

References

Agah, A. 2000. Human interactions with intelligent systems: Research taxonomy. *Computers & Electrical Engineering*, *27*(1), 71–107.

Ahi, K. 2025. Risks & Benefits of LLMs & GenAI for Platform Integrity, Healthcare Diagnostics, Cybersecurity, Privacy & AI Safety: A Comprehensive Survey, Roadmap & Implementation Blueprint. *arXiv preprint arXiv:2506.12088*.

Barker, N. and Parker, H. 2024. Hybrid performances in sport: Cybathlon spectatorship for critically imagining technologies for disability futures. *Medical Humanities*, *50*(4), 657–669.

Bertolini, A. and Episcopo, F. 2022. Robots and AI as legal subjects? Disentangling the ontological and functional perspective. *Frontiers in Robotics and AI*, *9*, 842213.

Breivik, G. 2020. The sporting exploration of the world; toward a fundamental ontology of the sporting human being. *Sport, Ethics and Philosophy*, *14*(2), 146–162.

Bouillet, A. 2018, December. Technology doping. *In:* AIJA Conference. *https://brucherlaw.lu/wp-content/uploads/20181127-0000-Alexandre-Bouillet-Technology-doping-PPT-presentation-PROTECTED.pdf*

Chamberland, É. 2024. Automating the Science and Art of Judging. McGill University (Canada).

Eid, A.I.A., Miled, A.B., Fatnassi, A., Nawaz, M.A., Mahmoud, A.F., Abdalla, F.A., Mohamed, I.B. 2024. Sports prediction model through cloud computing and big data based on artificial intelligence method. *Journal of Intelligent Learning Systems and Applications*, *16*(2), 53–79.

Gao, L. and Liu, Z. 2023. Unraveling the multifaceted nexus of artificial intelligence sports and user willingness: a focus on technology readiness, perceived usefulness, and green consciousness. *Sustainability*, *15*(18), 13961.

Glebova, E., 2020. Définir la réalité étendue dans les sports: Limitations, facteurs et opportunités. *Manag Du Sport*, *3*, 271–93.

Glebova, E., Desbordes, M. and Geczi, G., 2020. Relocations of sports Spectators' customer experiences. *Phys. Educ. Sport Sci*, *1*, 44–49.

Glebova, E. and Desbordes, M. 2021. Technology innovations in sports: Typology, nature, courses and impact. *In:* Innovation and entrepreneurship in sport management, 57–72. Edward Elgar Publishing.

Glebova, E. and Desbordes, M. 2022. Smart sports in smart cities. Smart Cities and Tourism: Co-creating experiences, challenges and opportunities, 60 pages.

Glebova, E. and Madsen, D. Ø. 2024. Twin transformation as a strategic approach in sport management: the synergy of digitalization and sustainability in sports. *Frontiers in Sports and Active Living, 6*, 1403793.

Glebova, E., Book, R., Su, Y., Perić, M., and Heller, J. 2023a. Sports venue digital twin technology from a spectator virtual visiting perspective. *Frontiers in Sports and Active Living, 5*, 1289140.

Glebova, E., Desbordes, M., and Czegledi, O. 2024a. The "clockwork" model for deployment technology innovations in sports industry ecosystem: holistic approach. *Societies, 14*(2), 23.

Glebova, E., Madsen, D. Ø., Mihaľová, P., Géczi, G., Mittelman, A., and Jorgič, B. 2024b. Artificial intelligence development and dissemination impact on the sports industry labor market. *Frontiers in Sports and Active Living, 6*, 1363892.

Glebova, E., Terrien, M., and Desbordes, M. 2023b. Does digitalization accelerate the winner-takes-all effect in the sports industry? *Physical Culture and Sport, 101*(1), 17–24.

Glebova, E., Zare, F., Desbordes, M., and Geczi, G. 2023c. 'If there is no football, then we have nothing to discuss': A phenomenological study on football fandom and COVID-19 pandemic. *International Journal of Sport Management and Marketing, 23*(5), 373–390.

Giulianotti, R. and Thiel, A. 2023. New horizons in the sociology of sport. *Frontiers in Sports and Active living, 4*, 1060622.

Kerr, R. 2016. Sport and Technology: An Actor-Network Theory Perspective. Routledge.

Kosta, E. 2022. Algorithmic state surveillance: Challenging the notion of agency in human rights. *Regulation & Governance, 16*(1), 212–224.

Leonardi, P.M. 2012. Materiality, sociomateriality, and socio-technical systems: What do these terms mean? How are they different? Do we need them. *Materiality and Organizing: Social Interaction in a Technological World, 25*(10), 1093.

Mercedes-Benz Stadium. (n.d.). Sustainability at Mercedes-Benz Stadium. Retrieved July 28, 2025, *https://www.mercedesbenzstadium.com/news sustainability-at-mercedes-benz-stadium*

Mutch, A. 2013. Sociomateriality—Taking the wrong turning? *Information and Organization, 23*(1), 28–40.

Mykhailov, D. and Liberati, N. 2023. Back to the technologies themselves: Phenomenological turn within postphenomenology. *Phenomenology and the Cognitive Sciences*, 1–20.

Pinch, T. 2012. The social construction of technology: A review. *Technological Change*, 17–35.

Ritter, M. 2021. Philosophical potencies of postphenomenology. *Philosophy & Technology, 34*(4), 1501–1516.

Russell J.L., McLean B.D., Stolp S., Strack D., and Coutts A.J. 2021. Quantifying training and game demands of a national basketball association season. *Front. Psychol. 12*, 793216. *doi: 10.3389/fpsyg.2021.793216*

Schut, P.O. and Glebova, E. 2022. Sports spectating in connected stadiums: Mobile application Roland Garros 2018. *Frontiers in Sports and Active Living, 4*, 802852.

Thorpe, H., Brice, J., and Clark, M. 2021. New materialisms, sport and the environment: Imagining new lines of flight. *Sport, Education and Society*, *26*(4), 363–377.

Wang, L. 2021. Simulation of sports movement training based on machine learning and brain-computer interface. *Journal of Intelligent & Fuzzy Systems*, *40*(4), 6409–6420.

Wu, C. 2024. Data privacy: From transparency to fairness. *Technology in Society*, *76*, 102457.

Xu, T., and Tang, L. 2021. Adoption of machine learning algorithm-based intelligent basketball training robot in athlete injury prevention. *Frontiers in Neurorobotics*, *14*, 620378.

Index: A Map for Quick Navigation

F

H

I

L

M

P

R

S

For Product Safety Concerns and Information please contact our
EU representative GPSR@taylorandfrancis.com Taylor & Francis
Verlag GmbH, Kaufingerstraße 24, 80331 München, Germany

The Chagos Archipelago

This book is the story of the natural history of the Chagos Archipelago, and of the efforts of many to get it recognized as an important and protected wildlife reserve. Exploring its immense natural riches and biodiversity, both on islands and in the marine environment, this book addresses competing claims to its resources, its politics, and the desire of some commercial and political parties to exploit the area. It is about the fight to conserve a wonderland of biodiversity and obtain its protection from exploitation, especially of its reefs and other marine life. This book shows the importance of the Chagos Archipelago and why so much research was done there. Rather than being a typical research book, this work presents research in a narrative form and describes the now substantial Government, UN, and legal interest in the archipelago since the UK was told to 'decolonise' it. It is also the story of our planet in miniature: the archipelago encapsulates much of the world's conservation tribulations in a way we can much more easily understand. This narrative will explore the difficulties faced by the Chagos Archipelago, including displaced people, old and derelict industries (coconut in this case), the military, politics, rich and untouched ecosystems that some want to exploit, ruined habitats on land, climate change, and territorial claims. It will examine how all of these factors have affected the natural history, biodiversity, and conservation of the archipelago. With beautiful photography of the Chagos Archipelago coral reefs and islands, as well as graphs indicating their findings, this book offers professionals, researchers, academics, and students in conservation and biodiversity an insight into one of the world's most diverse ecosystems. It is also accessible for non-academic readers with an interest in climate change, biodiversity, and the importance of conservation.

The Chagos Archipelago

A Biological Biography

Charles Sheppard

Photos by Anne Sheppard

CRC Press
Taylor & Francis Group
Boca Raton London New York

CRC Press is an imprint of the
Taylor & Francis Group, an **informa** business

Photos by Anne Sheppard

First edition published 2024
by CRC Press
2385 NW Executive Center Drive, Suite 320, Boca Raton FL 33431

and by CRC Press
4 Park Square, Milton Park, Abingdon, Oxon, OX14 4RN

CRC Press is an imprint of Taylor & Francis Group, LLC

ISBN: 9781032713380 (hbk)
ISBN: 9781032729824 (pbk)
ISBN: 9781003423300 (ebk)

DOI: 10.1201/9781003423300

Typeset in Times
by codeMantra

Contents

About the Author

Charles Sheppard OBE is an Emeritus Professor whose work has focused on coral reefs and on impacts of marine exploitation and climate change on reefs and other marine habitats. He has researched in most Indian Ocean and Caribbean countries, written about 250 research articles and over a dozen books, receiving several awards for conservation.

Anne Sheppard has been his partner and scientific colleague throughout, a biologist, taxonomist and photographer. They first visited the Chagos Archipelago in the 1970s and then, with others, built up a series of research expeditions as the richness, condition and value of Chagos became apparent. This culminated in its declaration as the world's largest no-take ocean reserve.

Photo Jon Schlayer, with permission.

Introduction

In the middle of the tropical Indian Ocean lies the Chagos Archipelago: an enigmatic, beautiful but troubled place. It is a biological treasure, but when most people have heard of it, it is usually because of the episode that started in the late 1960s and early 1970s when the British Indian Ocean Territory (BIOT) was created as a political entity. The place is a collection of five atolls with islands, now covered by coconut plantations that had been in steady decline for several years, with about 1,000 inhabitants, reduced from probably double that number in its heyday. BIOT was created in 1969 by the UK to support a military facility on one of the atolls, and the local inhabitants were removed at that time from the plantations on all atolls in a way that is now seen to have been shoddy and careless. Books have been written, and documentaries have been made about the events at that time, most focussing on the Chagossian expulsion story and the people's continuing aim to return. Added to this has been the claim by Mauritius that the islands have always been theirs and were not British anyway. There is certainly sufficient material to make interesting stories, but some have exaggerated the events which later writers embellished further still.

In contrast to the exposure that these political events have received, this remote archipelago was scientifically very poorly known at the time of the depopulation. Only a few important but limited scientific visits had been made for over 100 years. Yet it was the environmental, economic, and social conditions of people living there that had a strong bearing on their fate. From the 1970s, however, scientific visits increased considerably so that the archipelago and the natural history of both the islands and of the coral reefs beneath the sea would become some of the best known and studied in the world.

This book is mainly a biological account of the archipelago told from a personal view by someone who has visited and worked in the place over a period of nearly half a century. It also explains the relevance of the story to the wider world, a story mainly of research leading to conservation during a time of massive global environmental change. Our world is far too complex for humans to comprehend, but this one part of it is much easier, and although relatively small, it has all the important attributes of the world at large: glorious marine life, some very degraded and shattered island life, angry politics, large-scale conservation, territorial claims, and military involvement and, coupled with these latter, some very unpleasant encounters with some parties who wish to exploit the place and therefore oppose its conservation, or who were opposed to government policy or to the military involvement.

The last half-century was a time when most of the waters of the Indian Ocean rim and its islands suffered severe degradation because a rapidly expanding population in all its countries severely over-exploited and abused its marine resources. More recently, this has been accompanied by damaging effects of climate change, including increases in terrestrial and marine temperatures, and changes to rainfall leading to floods in some countries and droughts in others, all accompanied by food crises. These times have sometimes been called the 'decades of destruction'. The seas of this archipelago initially avoided many of these depredations, though they have not avoided more recent damage from climate change. The wildlife of all inhabited islands, however, was badly damaged from 180 years of coconut plantations.

Almost all scientific knowledge of the place resides mainly in scientific journals and thus is limited to those relatively few people, mainly other scientists, who have access to and read scientific literature. The archipelago's remarkable natural history has never made it into the stories being told about it. This book fills that gap. It describes the natural history of the area, first of the islands and then of its far greater expanse of coral reefs, how people tried to make a living there for nearly 200 years, and, in the last few decades, how massive global environmental change has affected its marine habitats too. Being atolls, the islands rest upon, and indeed are made of, living coral reefs, which are now dying or dead from global warming.

This book also tells the story of the struggles that we had to conduct the science that turned out to be so important today. People depend on nature in one way or another, and how they use their environment will determine whether they will be prosperous or impoverished in the longer term. Usually, this is only apparent either from specialised science literature, which now has lots to say about the place, or perhaps when it is too late, when a place is damaged and supports only communities of impoverished people.

Aside from military matters, the place has never received much governmental support. The Chagos islands obviously needed friends, so several people got together in the 1990s to form *Friends of the Chagos*, later the *Chagos Conservation Trust*, started mainly by military or ex-military people who had an interest in the place and its natural history, along with a few scientists who had been lucky enough to go there in the 1970s. I had been one of the latter, accompanying some military adventure training expeditions that included magnificent scuba diving facilities, when we achieved a lot of early results about the islands and coral reefs. After these ended, there was a gap of several years before any scientist could return, but based on the visits in the 1970s, a small group of us developed an expanding series of scientific expeditions that then commenced from 1996. By the 2020s, we had ensured that Chagos had received more scientific attention than almost any other atoll group in the ocean. However, initially, it was still governed with less scientific input than most.

One research visit in 1996 was fortuitously timed. Just a couple of years after that visit had gathered much information about the ecology of the reefs, we saw the first of a series of major 'marine heatwaves' that caused massive destruction on tropical corals and reefs around the world. Scientists could observe this by satellite imagery and, in the case of inhabited regions (which is most of them), by direct observation of the reefs themselves too. However, most of Chagos was uninhabited. We could see that the reefs of the Chagos Archipelago lay right in the middle of a large slug of very warm water in the Indian Ocean. But any massive coral kill was quite unnoticed by anyone at the time, a point which should have been of passing interest since these British islands were wholly built by corals, and the islands themselves are maintained above sea level only by continued growth of healthy corals and their multitude of associated biota on the reefs. As the scientist who had organised most of the research there in the 1970s, I pointed out to BIOT's government that most other reefs in the Indian Ocean had died, so probably those of BIOT had died too. This idea was dismissed after someone BIOT asked told them that there had not been a mortality.

We did not believe it, so we found out by other means that there were indeed vast fields of dead corals around that atoll too. This led me to suggest to the BIOT Administration that a proper examination would perhaps be useful. They agreed.

I conducted a brief survey with just a snorkel in 1999, which showed that over 90% of Chagos' shallow corals had indeed died and were turning into rubble. The coral and reef mortality had occurred because of ocean warming, exacerbated by failure of the Indian Monsoon, which led to calm seas, leading to greater light penetration and even greater heating. Erosion of islands was mooted, and suggestions were made about what was needed. All the islands of BIOT are made by corals and are maintained by nothing else. If they are no longer living, then what?

But making such suggestions back then was not welcomed, at least not by those I could approach. However, who else might or could make scientific suggestions was unclear.

Britain had acquired the archipelago from France in 1814, during the conclusion of the Napoleonic War, and administered it from Mauritius, a colony at the time. This is why Mauritius claims it was Mauritian territory all along. In the late 1960s, after its separation to form the BIOT, its southernmost atoll, Diego Garcia, was turned into a defence facility with the United States. Diego Garcia is an important name in this story. It is a name perhaps associated more with a Mexican bandit from the 1800s, but it is now home to a very significant US Navy facility. However, its long runway and all other structures lie very close to sea level, and indeed, seats in bomber cockpits probably provide the highest vantage points on the island. A pilot awaiting clearance to take off could observe that the seaward reef, which formed the natural breakwater for his airfield, had been excavated in the early 1970s, mainly for fill material to build his runway. In other parts of the Indian Ocean, the digging of protective reefs by a few locals with crowbars for building material had been sufficient to cause erosion. Still, in Diego Garcia (DG for short), more determined contractors with explosives and bulldozers had made a much more thorough job of reef demolition. No environmental assessment was done in those secret, Cold War days: at least, not by anyone who knew what ocean storm waves did to soft coral rock after the latter had been dynamited. DG was suffering increasingly from erosion just as much as the other uninhabited atolls.

Following the discovery of massive coral mortality from warming, I proposed a larger scientific trip involving scuba. This was repeatedly stalled due to administrative and funding problems, but a small visit was eventually made in 2001 using scuba. Using observations from the 1970s and 1996, as well as aerial photos, we could see that erosion of some islands was clearly taking place, and that the reefs were changing very fast. However, because of the inaccessibility between about 1980 and the late 1990s, not many clear conclusions were possible, even from DG. That was a pity because DG contained a lot of very expensive stuff.

During that time, BIOT Administration gave much of DG and some northern islands a measure of environmental protection under the Ramsar convention and local BIOT laws. The whole archipelago benefitted also from being a military exclusion area, at least concerning terrestrial visits. Fishing, both legal and illegal, continued, and Russian 'trawlers' adorned with numerous antennae visited the waters of DG to see what was going on there. A proposal had been made for World Heritage status too, and its British Minister had agreed to that in writing, but then reversed his view, saying that instead, it would treat it 'as though' it had that status. After all, it was well known in the early 2000s that people cannot prosper if the environment around them is declining. This is almost a natural law, commonly observed.

Plantation workers had lived in the Chagos Archipelago for nearly 200 years by the time they were removed. This was done in a way for which the UK Government later expressed regret. Compensation had been paid to Mauritius, which received many of the displaced Chagossians, and by some measures, it was a lot of money. However, most of the money never reached the evicted Chagossians for quite a long time, during which they could have used it to develop a new life. The resulting fuss occupied legal teams and courts for many years after the turn of the Millennium. One lawsuit brought by lawyers for some Chagossians had even been for genocide caused by the eviction, but this had failed. A flurry of internet sites appeared expressing support for the Chagossians, and these were either devoid of information or presented 'information' in an often biased and inaccurate way. This did cause increasing demands on the time of a few interested people known to have some information, including the small band of scientists who had been there. But most media people at that time almost invariably mangled information to fit their own agendas. A few natural history film companies, including some highly acclaimed and leading ones, wanted to film the still extraordinary reefs and island wildlife they were now getting to hear about, but none received permission to film there for many years. Chagos' natural history had to remain secret, even though BIOT itself was becoming infamous.

The desire for resettlement and self-determination by many Chagossians persists strongly today. The matter of whether they can make a living there has exercised many minds, mostly minds of people who have never seen the place and do not understand it. If, or perhaps when, resettlement occurs, fishing would be the only likely occupation available to make a living there. Fish, after all, are the only resource available to them, other than coconuts priced several times higher than those obtainable on the global market. The state of the wildlife and global economics had a lot to do with the initial collapse of the way of life of the Chagossians by the mid-20th century.

Sea level continues to rise too, and we know that coral islands whose reefs have been damaged become much more quickly eroded and suffer periodic sea water incursions and inundations than do reefs with healthy coral communities. The US authorities in DG already spend hundreds of millions of dollars strengthening the shores of that atoll to keep their own military facilities protected. Would anyone spend this for returning Chagossians on the other atolls? This too has become a major issue worldwide: to build protective walls for coastal properties or to abandon the properties—under the dubious term 'managed retreat'? In the geographically very similar Maldives just to the north, even the World Bank has warned that 80% of its islands will be uninhabitable by 2050 [1], and the same applies to the islands of Chagos too.

The story of Chagos with its immense natural riches, its competing claims, its politics, and the desire of some commercial opportunists to exploit it, is thus the story of our planet in miniature. This archipelago encapsulates much of the world's tribulations in a way we can much more easily understand. It contains it all: displaced people, old and derelict industry (coconut in this case), the military, politics, rich ecosystems that some want to exploit, ruined habitats on land, climate change, and territorial claims.

The marine life of the archipelago is especially interesting scientifically because it remains perhaps the best example of a natural tropical system in the Indian Ocean that has been largely unaffected by local direct impacts and ongoing, local human interference (as opposed to climate change or warming effects, which are global). But it inevitably includes some politics because several political arguments have been used to try to undo or negate its protection and the complete conservation that it enjoys at the time of this writing. It reflects what happens in many, if not most, countries. The intensity of many arguments is significant, again mirroring the situation in the world generally. The arguments concern whether it should be conserved or exploited, and whether exploitation by any resettled Chagossians should really be called exploitation anyway. Who owns it? Do the needs of the ocean which sustains us all, count for more or less than the right of some to resettle there and exploit it? Such questions have no easy black-and-white answers. Much ignorant vitriol has been written, and several of us have come in for a lot of abuse merely because we have conducted marine and island research work there. One newspaper article said that I 'preferred the warty sea slug to people', (doubtless true in the case of that journalist) and so on. Threats have been made to those few Mauritian assistants we made a point of including in our research expeditions. Mauritius has written to the institutions of many participating scientists, threatening fines and imprisonment of anyone who has worked there on research and later visited Mauritius. Politics and global economics, along with cynical greed in some quarters, are all components of this story, as indeed it is elsewhere in the world. The problems of conservation can be understood better while looking at this relatively small part of the world. Whether this will help us to fix our global problem is, of course, another and bigger matter.

Today, there are over one hundred scientists whom I was privileged to introduce to the place via research expeditions, and this number is growing rapidly. The total of all the work achieved has been and continues to be impressive, and the knowledge gained has become globally important [2] at a time when environmental problems are increasing rapidly and mostly unsustainably in most places. In 2010, the whole area was proclaimed a marine protected area, at the time the largest in the world. The science contained here and the story of how that information was gained and developed over the years have involved many people. Most scientists who have visited have conducted important research, and most remain friends. To name them would burden this account with scores of names so, with the intention of making the text more easily readable, only very few are mentioned. However, most are listed in the over 200 citations to primary science literature listed in the Endnotes. In addition to these references, which inevitably need to be updated given continuing research there, members of the Chagos Conservation Trust have produced over 100 single-page 'Factsheets' that either summarise several of these scientific papers or introduce something new of interest. Pictorial identification guides of several groups, including corals, are on the CCT website and its newsletter *Chagos News*, which is also online [3]. Most photographs were taken just before the 2015–2016 heatwave that killed so much, and it is clear which ones were taken following it. This relates the natural history of the place in a narrative and sometimes personal form, from the early struggles, continued opposition to its conservation, up to the present time when substantial recognition and funding have become available. The story mirrors in many ways that of conservation of many species and habitats that we now know are essential to humanity's continued existence on this planet.

REFERENCES

[1] https://climateknowledgeportal.worldbank.org/country/maldives/impacts-sea-level-rise
And:
https://abcnews.go.com/International/facing-dire-sea-level-rise-threat-maldives-turns/story?id=80929487

[2] Koldewey H, Atchison-Balmond N, Graham N, Jones R, Perry C, Sheppard C, Spalding M, Turner J, Williams G. 2021. Key climate change effects on the coastal and marine environment around the Indian Ocean UK Overseas Territories. *MCCIP Science Review* 2021: 31 pp. https://doi.org/10.14465/2021.orc06.ind.

[3] https://chagos-trust.org/.

1 A Tour of the Archipelago

WHERE AND WHAT IS BIOT?

Several centuries ago, when European sailing traders headed East to cross the Indian Ocean en route to India and China, they encountered a formidable threat known to them as "the Archipelago." Many vessels foundered on reefs in the middle of the vast Indian Ocean during an era of poor and often very fictitious charts. The "archipelago" was depicted on some charts as enormous, forming a challenging barrier between the sailors and their desired destinations in India, Ceylon, or East Asia. Some charts from the 1600s even portrayed an ocean nearly filled with reefs. The dangers were real, and losses were frequent enough to instil a sense of dread among the sailors. While there was a barrier, it did not entirely fill the ocean. Part of the barrier was formed by the much larger Maldives chain of atolls further north, and the atolls, banks, and submerged reefs of the Chagos Archipelago at the southern end certainly contributed. In an era of poor navigation and unreliable charts, many boats and many lives were lost in this area. Mariners, such as the privateer, trader, and later the commander of the East India Company's fleets, Sir James Lancaster, vividly documented his experiences of being trapped in (now believed to be) the lagoon of an atoll in the Chagos. He struggled to find a way out for several days, and his fleet of traders suffered additional losses later on. In this supposedly reef-strewn ocean, the Chagos Archipelago lies entirely just south of the equator, with no land further south until Antarctica.

Sir James Lancaster's escape occurred in the 1590s, and today we know that these reefs are mere scraps of land in this ocean, separated by vast expanses of open sea. However, many of the reefs in the 900-nautical-mile-long Maldives-Chagos chain that extends south from India are submerged at all states of the tide, with no land or trees to warn a lookout on a sailing ship. In the Chagos group, these barely submerged reefs are, in fact, more numerous and widespread than the atolls that support land, and they still posed a threat to shipping into the 20th century. Unlike in the Pacific or in the Indian Ocean's Seychelles further west, there are no so-called high islands, that is, islands with hills or mountains of volcanic origin. All land here is composed of coral islands, rising a mere metre or two above high tide level and are less conspicuous from a distance. It remained a feared feature for over 200 years.

Now the Chagos Archipelago is well-mapped (Figure 1.1), with the first detailed charts produced in the 1830s by the remarkable Robert Moresby, a Captain of the East India Company's Bombay Marine/Indian Navy who had just completed mapping the reefs of the Red Sea and then the Maldives. Charted by means of teams rowing in longboats using weighted lines, his achievement is known to be remarkably accurate and close to modern satellite imagery. This work ensured that passage from Europe to India and the East Indies became far safer, preparing for the days when new steam vessels were taking over the routes.

DOI: 10.1201/9781003423300-1

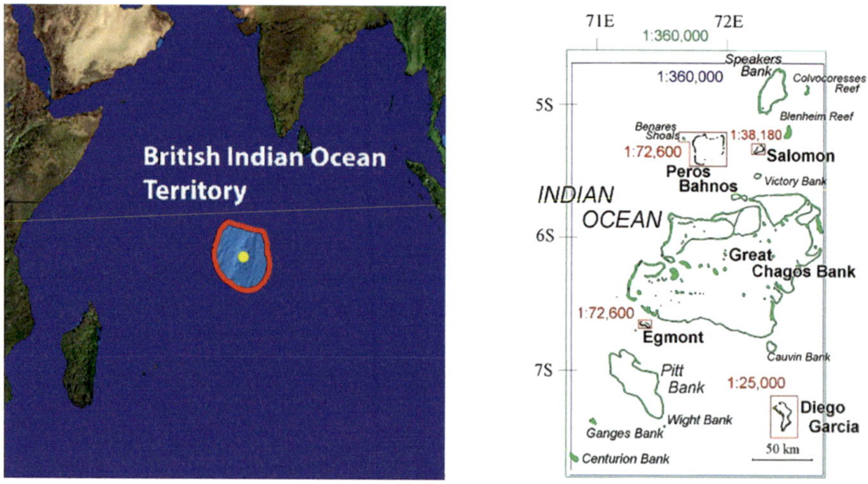

FIGURE 1.1 Location of BIOT, with its main atolls and banks.

At present, the entire Chagos Archipelago forms the British Indian Ocean Territory or BIOT, a political construct that originated from Western military defence requirements in the 1960s. Geographically, it is a group of five atolls whose islands emerge above the surface of the sea, along with a larger number of submerged atolls and reefs that may be awash at low tides or permanently submerged to a depth of 10 or 20 m, or even deeper. Initially, BIOT included some other places like Aldabra atoll, which later was ceded to the Seychelles and is now a World Heritage Site. The Chagos Archipelago lies almost exactly in the geographical centre of the Indian Ocean. Its 200 nautical mile territorial limit includes several hundred seamounts and an abyssal plain and trench that are very much deeper. The whole area encompasses about two-thirds of a million square kilometres.

In the 1960s, before the formation of BIOT, the British were withdrawing from East of Suez. Today, the Americans have assumed much of the guardianship of the West. During this period, there was significant nuclear sabre-rattling with the communist bloc. As a consequence, in short, America sought a reliable, unpopulated base in the Indian Ocean region, and a suitable atoll in the Chagos was one of two possible candidate sites. This underlay the decision to form the BIOT.

The other potential site for the base was Aldabra atoll, which briefly formed part of BIOT too. However, it was soon deemed unsuitable and was transferred to the Seychelles, where it remains today, receiving good protection and substantial scientific attention. One reason Aldabra was not chosen for the military facility was due to strong public and scientific objections arising from Aldabra's huge populations of giant tortoises. These animals are conservation icons, and the idea of their destruction to make way for facilities and an airfield was not palatable in the West. Jibes were made, both at that time and subsequently, suggesting that the British prioritised the welfare of giant tortoises over people, and that these animals were assigned greater value than the inhabitants of Chagos. Indeed, in the British Parliament, there were quips about the parliamentary benches being occupied by giant tortoises.

While I cannot be certain, I suspect that, although the presence of tortoises undoubtedly contributed to public opposition, Aldabra lacked one of the crucial perceived needs for a military base. This is quite evident but often overlooked: its lagoon is extremely shallow, averaging only 5 m in depth. Although an airfield might have been possible on the atoll rim, requiring a large area of tortoise-free habitat, an important requirement at the time was (and still is) a naval, forward positioning base for numerous very large cargo ships filled with military supplies and other materiel to support deployed troops. There was a need for a harbour that could safely shelter massive amounts of moveable equipment and weaponry. In contrast to the shallow Aldabra lagoon, the southern atoll of the Chagos Archipelago, Diego Garcia, boasts a deep, sheltered lagoon. By removing many of the inconvenient coral mounds in the lagoon (which was not too difficult using explosives), an ideal anchorage could be created. The lagoon's northern basin, where ships currently are located, reaches a depth of 30 m. Its suitability had been known for 100 years, as early visiting naturalists remarked on Diego Garcia's potential as a wonderful harbour for numerous ships [1]. For this reason: "This Island is one of the wonderful phaenomena of this globe." [2]. Aldabra, in contrast, has a lagoon that is entirely unsuitable for such ships. This key difference could have been observed simply by looking at a chart of the area. However, journalists never did, and still don't when they re-tell the same story about tortoises. The facility in Diego Garcia was principally, and remains, a Navy Support Facility, featuring a runway long enough for any bomber, and which was also long enough to serve as an emergency landing ground for the space shuttle. The administration building even bears the title NAVSUPFAC (Naval Support Facility in US military jargon) over its doorway. Aldabra could never have fulfilled this role, regardless of the presence of tortoises or not.

For any long-term strategic use, Diego Garcia would have been always the obvious choice for this purpose, there were no other available atolls (Figure 1.2).

Around 1970, the old and declining coconut plantations were abandoned, and the local population were removed from the atolls, mostly to Mauritius, and some to the Seychelles. This has led to a very long period of angst and legal cases with multiple dimensions. The Chagossians, as they came to be called, campaigned fervently for a return to the islands. The archipelago had been administered from Mauritius when the latter was a colony, and the Mauritian Government campaigned at least as much for a return of the archipelago to Mauritius, not recognising BIOT as the legal government. The way people were exiled left much to be desired, and the British Government later expressed regret for it. The legacy of this has resulted in many repercussions, which will be discussed in more detail later.

THE CAPITAL AREA

The main administration building at the military headquarters on the western side of Diego Garcia atoll has a large but rather uninspiring patch of grass in front of it. The administration building itself is unprepossessing too, enlivened only by a couple of old brass naval cartridges with mock wooden shells located just inside its doorway. They sit near a notice board holding photographs portraying the current 'Employees of the Month' in the manner seen inside most supermarkets. This building and its

FIGURE 1.2 Image from Google Earth of Diego Garcia, the only presently inhabited atoll, dated 2022. The military facility is located along the western side. Entry to the deserted plantations on the eastern arm requires special permission. Credit: Google Earth. Data SIO, NOAA, US Navy, NGA, GEBCO Image © 2022 Maxar Technologies.

grass front constitute the centre of the BIOT: its Houses of Parliament or its Capitol Hill. Set in an exceptionally sparkling and beautiful archipelago, to my mind, this building and its front lawn are the only mundane aspects in the Territory.

The rest of the downtown area of Diego Garcia resembles a small American mall, surrounded by accommodation blocks. The area features several fast-food outlets, a chapel, library, medical centre, and many other facilities, including a central food hall that serves good quality food with fresh produce flown in every few days. It has a supermarket (which also displays its Employee of the Month) and a shop where you can order different kinds of T-shirts with your own design on them. T-shirts seem to serve as a sort of currency on the island, coming only slightly second to the dollar. The downtown area is dominated by several huge dish antennae at the telecom station, one pointing nearly overhead to a geostationary satellite over the Indian Ocean and another pointing nearly horizontally to another satellite beyond Africa, somewhere over the Caribbean. Senior officers get accommodation in the more wooded, lagoon-facing side, while most accommodation is located where there are fewer trees and can be baking hot, though with so many air conditioners that scarcely matters.

There is nothing particularly attractive or historical about any of these buildings; they were built for purely functional purposes. There is no 'Old Quarter' as akin to what you find in, say, Zanzibar, and these are perfectly utilitarian, well-maintained buildings that appear to serve perfectly well the needs of servicemen and women based here, usually for one year at a time. On the eastern side of the atoll, there are some old stone plantation buildings, mostly a century old and now ruined, but there are some that have been well restored. These give a glimpse of the better-quality buildings constructed during those days long ago for managers or for warehousing. The workers mostly had huts made from timber and palm fronds.

There is a lot more to Diego Garcia than this 'Downtown' area, of course. Most infrastructure is located further south, down the western arm of the atoll. There are a few old guns pointing out to sea dating from before World War II to defend the island against the Japanese. Fortunately, they were never put to the test; they surely wouldn't have lasted ten minutes. They point out to sea on the western arm of the atoll, overlooking a lovely reef flat with spectacular reef slope descending to great depths beyond. Coincidentally, they now point exactly to the site of some of our temperature monitoring instruments. These old cannons, along with a beached and disintegrating Catalina Flying boat near a couple of radio huts on the eastern side of the atoll, are all that remain from that wartime era.

All the military and numerous supporting facilities are located on the western arm of the atoll, around the harbour and airfield, and further south. There is a GPS control facility. At the far south, there is a Space Command centre with its optical telescopes that track every object in orbit, including thousands of bits of junk that are stuck in space. At the latter, you can have a fascinating guided tour where you can see all the orbits in real time. However, you cannot actually look through the telescopes, as they are linked only to light sensitive chips. There are several other facilities, many with domes and various antennae, many with fences and 'Keep Out' notices all around, and some with notices saying things like 'Bomb Assembly Area'. All are located along very attractive shorelines (Figure 1.3). At the southern tip of the horseshoe-shaped atoll are several large antennae arranged in complex geometrical designs.

FIGURE 1.3 The ocean-facing western arm of Diego Garcia. With coral sand and rubble, this is typical of all the atolls. The protective reef flat extends seaward to a line of breakers before plunging to hundreds of metres deep.

These facilities have all developed steadily over the nearly 50 years that I have visited Diego Garcia, from visits in the 1970s as a youthful marine biologist and enthusiastic scuba diver, to today, when I am a much older marine biologist but still an enthusiastic scuba diver. I have organised and led numerous research expeditions to this and to the northern atolls and their reefs over many years, and these atolls contain, to a naturalist and ecologist, the most wonderful features of all. Most of this book is about these northern atolls.

I saw even more of the Diego Garcia facilities when, in 2003, I took on the additional task of being a scientific adviser to the British Commissioner for ten years. This mainly involved matters affecting development on the military facility itself: a sort of town and harbour environmental planning advisor. Both this role and my long-term role as a visiting scientist have been delightful—the area contains, after all, some of the best diving in the world and some of its least damaged coral reefs, at least until the marine heatwaves began. Visiting has always been an immense privilege, and I have had more than my fair share of this particularly glorious place.

The natural environment of this archipelago reveals an almost unexploited marine environment and a set of coral reefs that are changing rapidly now due to global climate change. Underwater, the vibrancy of the coral reefs that built the islands and atolls was especially dramatic, and if given a decade or two without repeated heatwaves, it will still be akin to most of the world's reefs would have been a century ago. In earlier days, I lost count of the number of times that visiting scientists surfaced from their first research dive there and uttered phrases on the lines of "wow", usually rather more expressively. This was especially gratifying to me because, many times early on when I was extolling the virtues of the place and pressing for its continued conservation, I felt that I was out on a lonely limb. When I heard leading scientists express amazement about, for example, the numbers and sizes of fish in Chagos, I was always reassured, especially when they are leaders in their subjects who have studied reef systems across much of the world. They could see the difference between Chagos and the ruined tropical environments of most other places, which many have come to assume are somehow normal (Figure 1.4). This "Chagos difference" occurs in many aspects of its natural history.

ENVIRONMENTAL PLANNING ON DIEGO GARCIA

Most of my own research has been on the uninhabited atolls of Salomon, Peros Banhos, Egmont, and the huge Great Chagos Bank, along with their dozens of tiny islands, forming the largest unexploited marine system left in the tropical world [3]. However, as we will see, climate change has badly affected these areas now. While I can freely discuss about any of that, I cannot talk similarly about most of the work that I have done for the military facility in Diego Garcia because of the Official Secrets Act. Though in truth, in the context of natural history, there is not much there that the other atolls don't have too. Where I do discuss Diego Garcia, in all cases, I have already seen that information publicly available in sources such as the internet or British parliamentary accounts, meaning that I have not revealed anything new, merely assembled it in one place for the purposes of this story. In Diego Garcia, my own work was, in fact, little different from what an environmental adviser might do

FIGURE 1.4 Rich and diverse corals on a typical reef of the archipelago, at about 10 m depth. This was taken in 2006, showing exceptional recovery of coral cover eight years after a mass mortality due to warming.

in any small commercial port or town in Europe or the USA. The difference lies in that the planes taking off or landing are sometimes bombers or in-flight refuelling tankers rather than commercial jets, and the cargo ship docking at the jetty might be unloading containers of munitions rather than cars from Japan, or because the vessel itself is a military one.

My work in Diego Garcia was to help ensure, along with several environmental scientist contractors stationed in that atoll, that the activities performed there do not cause pollution or other environmental damage, either in their construction or during the course of general day-to-day operation. Usually, this has not been difficult. The military does not want to cause unnecessary environmental damage. Their 'mission' is always their priority of course, and they will usually agree to look at different approaches concerning ground construction, for example, when they learn about alternatives. They have always been very receptive to suggestions and changes that avoid this or that problem—that is, when they know about it. Little environmental damage has been caused in Diego Garcia in the last 30 years knowingly, and likely none has been done capriciously, at least during my term of office, and it has generally been a pleasure to guide certain developments in ways that cause less ecological impact.

Sometimes getting a more environmentally benign course of action in Diego Garcia is, in fact, much easier than the civilian equivalent would be. In some countries where I do the same thing, I know from the start that avoiding environmental catastrophe will be a losing, uphill battle, especially in most Middle Eastern, Caribbean, and African countries. Even a small building plan in a British dockyard project might take years of sub-committees and 'stakeholder consultations', by which time it will be too late to save the habitat anyway. In this respect, Britain itself is rather poor in its ability to conserve important marine habitats (look no further than Britain's lack of properly protected marine areas for a very important example). In Diego Garcia, in contrast, the needed change can take only a phone call from the commander to his officer in charge of the relevant department to get the same thing done, once he has been briefed about it. One example was the phone call from the CO to his deputy, which essentially went: "I don't understand it, but it seems desirable, so do it. I'm sending this Brit round to tell you about it." That was three years consultations by-passed in one phone call! In that case, as in many others, the military achieved their needs and an environmental problem was solved—a win-win situation, in conservation jargon. In a similar case in Britain, the affected marine habitat almost certainly would have been 'sacrificed' during years of competing 'stakeholder' claims.

Doing research there and advising the government has had its drawbacks, however. The mere fact of going to what is essentially a military exclusion zone has meant that I and some colleagues have been accused of being used and "duped" by the military or by the 'imperialist-colonialist-capitalist-government machine', and so on, in excitable language reminiscent of the days when Chinese governments spoke of 'Imperialist paper tigers and running dogs'—all wonderful stuff. I was often accused of exaggeration and of talking 'hysterical nonsense' by people pushing for Chagossian return for example, and of being a 'conservation fascist' and 'imperialist lackey' (yes, really!) by antagonistic people who argued for resettlement of Chagossians or exploitation of its natural resources. Some argued that there is nothing special about the place anyway, presumably because this would make it less controversial to exploit.

Much hostility arose because of the claim by implacable opponents of our military that any research programmes there, and the marine reserve that was created in 2010, were only done in order to keep Chagossians out. This overlooked the point that while the marine reserve is relatively recent, Chagossians and just about everyone else have been excluded from most of the place for half a century now. No conservation arguments were needed throughout most of that time, so the argument that conservation was the main reason for continuing that policy is nonsense (as even British Courts have explained to some simple-minded opponents). But it is a useful, emotive tool for some.

THE REST OF THE ARCHIPELAGO

The rest of the archipelago, or 'Outer Islands' as they are called in Diego Garcia, comprises over 90% of its shallow seas. It is commonly forgotten, particularly by civilians, that the whole of BIOT, not just Diego Garcia, was created because of one thing only—the military facility. Diego Garcia is one part of it in its far south. The other reefs and banks are vastly larger and are all uninhabited. They lie between the military facility and the rest of the sometimes hostile world, and these areas are considered to be an important and integral part of the territory.

Although there may be big differences between the mind-set of military commanders and that of academic scientists such as myself, I have encountered no problems in the civilian-military relationship, British or Americans. Indeed, we have had substantial help from the military in our work there.

Most visitors and temporary residents in Chagos, at least 99% of them, will never leave the one atoll with the military facility. However, the territory is roughly

FIGURE 1.5 An island and its lagoonal reef flat off one of the islands in Salomon atoll. The area of reef is much greater than the area of islands.

650,000 km² in total. Most is very deep water, but in the centre of it the atolls in total extend over at least 60,000 km² of shallow and sunlit reef, containing coral reefs, their islands, seagrass beds, and other shallow areas, none of which have been significantly impacted by all the usual human activities seen in the rest of the populous Indian Ocean.

Perched precariously on a few parts of these reefs, there sits a mere 6 km² of land (Figure 1.5). Of this land, about half of it is in the atoll Diego Garcia with its military base. That leaves half of the land area for all the rest, and that land is split up into about 55 tiny islands in four other atoll groups.

Most of the islands, including all the larger ones, were ecologically ravaged in plantation days. Only the smallest islands, in contrast to the larger ones, were too small or difficult to convert into coconut plantations and avoided the attentions of the planters. So today, they survive in magnificent splendour.

The reefs, in contrast, were mostly left alone and as a result, their marine life remained glorious. However, the marine realm too is being ravaged now due to warming seawater. The phrase Global Warming today is giving way in several media outlets to Global Boiling which, while clearly grossly exaggerated, shows the perceived extent of the problem. But up to nearly the end of the 20th century, this marine area still supported some of the most spectacular reefs to be seen anywhere. Additional to the pleasure and satisfaction of doing research in such a wonderful place is the knowledge that the global human population will go up a further 2 billion in the next two or three decades, many of whom will be in countries in or bordering the Indian Ocean. All are countries whose own natural resources are becoming ever more depleted and degraded and unable to feed these burgeoning populations. As the need to feed such populations of people increases, so will the difficulties of maintaining this reservoir of life in the centre of the Indian Ocean.

REFERENCES

[1] Bourne GC. 1887. The atoll of Diego Garcia and the coral formations of the Indian Ocean. *Proceedings of the Royal Society of London* 43: 440–461.
[2] Horsburgh J. 1809. Directions for Sailing to and from the East Indies, China, New Holland, Cape of Good Hope, and the Interjacent Ports; Compiled Chiefly from Original Journals at the East India House, and from Journals and Observations, Made during Twenty-One Years' Experience Navigating in Those Seas. Part First. London, Black, Parry and Kingsbury, 397 pp.
[3] Spalding MD. 2007. Report for Howell resettlement report. Draft notes on Biodiversity, resettlement and the long term prospects for small populations on small tropical islands. 12 pp.

2 Geography, Origins, Human Use

The five groups of islands that constitute the archipelago are all atolls. These ring-shaped structures have island on their rims, each enclosing a relatively shallow lagoon, ranging from just a few metres deep in the case of Egmont to over 60 m deep in the case of both Peros Banhos and the largest atoll, the Great Chagos Bank. These atolls are the summits of submarine mountains rising from a deep ocean, which is hundreds of metres, and sometimes a few thousand metres, deep. Around the five islanded atolls are several more atoll-shaped reef structures rising from the deep ocean floor, but they are now totally submerged. Some of these are submerged to several metres deep, some are very shallow, and one of them, Blenheim Reef, apparently used to have three vegetated islands on it when first discovered but is now barely awash at high tide. The largest atoll, the Great Chagos Bank, is the largest atoll in the world in terms of area, but it is now mostly submerged, with only a half dozen islands on its western side and Nelsons Island in its north. Most of its rim is submerged to depths of as much as 30 m or more. The overall topography of these atolls and submerged banks is the present-day result of millions of years of geological processes: firstly, volcanoes forming and then slowly subsiding under their own weight back into the Earth's mantle; secondly, coral and reef growth on the flanks of the volcanoes in shallow water; and thirdly, of many subsequent rises and falls of sea level and erosion of the limestone coral reefs by waves and by rain (Figure 2.1, Table 2.1).

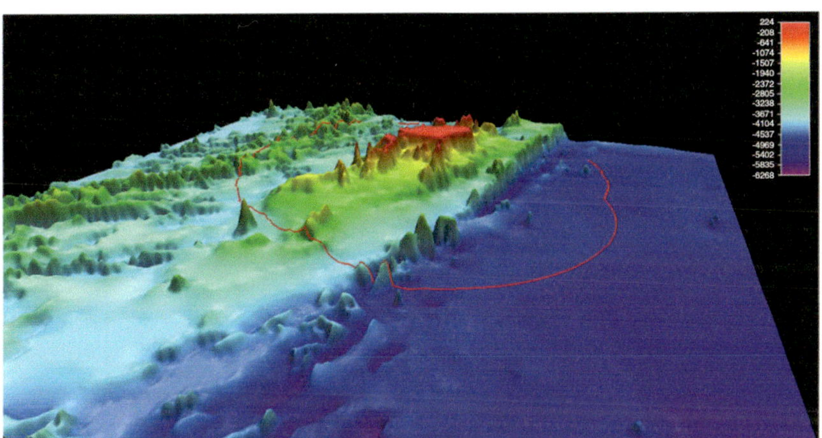

FIGURE 2.1 Bathymetric interpretation of BIOT and surrounding seamounts and abyssal regions. The thin red line marks the boundary, and the scale bar in metres. Courtesy of Dr C Yesson.

DOI: 10.1201/9781003423300-2

TABLE 2.1
Physical Characteristics of the Major or Larges Atolls and Banks

Atoll	Atoll Area (km^2)	Land Area (ha)	Number of Islands	Lagoon Greatest Depth (m)	Lagoon Mean Depth (m)	Shallowest Depth (If No Islands) (m)	% Rim Enclosure by Islands or Reef Flats
				Atolls			
Diego Garcia	<200	2,733	4	31	10		95
Salomon	38	311	11	33	25		85
Peros Banhos	463	920	24	80	38		60
Great Chagos Bank	18,000	445	8	84	50		<5
Egmont	40	~300	6	26	12		35
				Submerged Atolls			
Blenheim Reef	40	0	0	17	8	Awash	60
Victory Bank	16	0	0	33	25	5	0
Speakers Bank	680	0	0	35	44	7	0
Pitt Bank	~1,200	0	0	44	35	<10	0

Several small banks with atoll cross-section also exist but which have not been studied.

The whole archipelago originated approximately 45 million years ago when a volcanic hotspot under the Earth's mantle began pushing up lava to form volcanic mountains. This hotspot had been generating volcanoes for several million years already as the Earth's plates moved, starting under India's Deccan Traps and subsequently creating the chain of Lakshadweep and Maldives atolls extending southwards towards and then below the equator. Chagos, the youngest and southernmost of this long chain, followed. Basically, once formed, volcanoes are so heavy that they then subside slowly back into the Earth. However, during this subsidence, stony corals create reefs that grow upwards around them at roughly the same rate, remaining in the sunlit zone near the surface of the water. Over the past 45 million years, these extinct volcanoes have subsided back into the Earth's crust and mantle, sinking a total of about 1 or 2 km. The coral reefs have kept pace with this sinking, remaining near the sunlit surface of the ocean. Today, you would have to core down through this kilometre or two of coral rock, which is limestone, before reaching the igneous rock of its volcanic foundation. Since this process started, there have been many changes in sea level with varying degrees of growth and erosion. As a result, the atoll rims only roughly correspond to the flanks of the old volcanoes. It is too simplistic to assert that the atoll rims still match the rims of the old volcanoes, as many complex changes have taken place over this immense span of time. Throughout this long period, corals, in broad terms, have kept up their vertical growth to match the subsidence, remaining in the sunlit zone nearest the surface. There were times when the sea level remained constant for extended periods, and sometimes, sea levels were considerably lower than today. These areas are identifiable by lines of wave-cut caves many metres below the surface (Figure 2.2).

Subsequently, as the Earth's crust continued to slide slowly across the underlying hotspot deep within the Earth, the surface location of that hotspot moved southwest to form Mauritius. Presently, the hotspot lies under the French island of La Reunion, where a smoking volcano remains active.

FIGURE 2.2 The entrance of a cave system at 20 m deep on the ocean side of eastern Peros Banhos, cut by waves when sea level was 20 m lower than today.

The Chagos Archipelago, consisting of a few square kilometres of islands in the middle of the British Indian Ocean Territory (BIOT), appears as minute specks spread over an expanse of ocean approximately the size of southern England. It proves challenging for people in an office at home, and even for people in Diego Garcia itself, to visualise the small and widely scattered nature of these islands and atolls, along with their exposure to waves and the potential hazards associated with landing on them. The second-largest individual island, Eagle Island, situated on the western rim of the Great Chagos Bank, can be walked around in a very few hours. The smallest islands on all the atolls are little more than sandbanks that you can walk across in just minutes.

Most islands are found on Peros Banhos atoll in the northwest. Salomon atoll is smaller and is more enclosed by land (Figure 2.3). Egmont atoll in the south-east of the archipelago has a south-western rim with islands, though its north-eastern rim is totally submerged, usually to 4 or 5 m deep. Diego Garcia, the militarised atoll in the south, is unusual in this group in that its rim is a near-continuous strip of land, sometimes only 30 m across from the lagoon beach to the ocean side.

All larger islands in all the atolls were inhabited during plantation times that began in the late 18th century. Their conversion into coconut plantations involved clearing away the natural vegetation, along with much of the fauna. With the arrival of people came rats, and because of these two introduced species, the coconut and the rat, nothing much was left of the native flora and fauna after a very few years. While a beach adorned with palm trees leaning over it may appear more beautiful, these islands were mostly rendered about as natural as a modern wheat field.

About a dozen islands were deemed too small to bother with, and some others are very difficult to land on, maintaining a closer approximation to a natural (or at least pre-inhabited) undisturbed state today. Most of these islands do have a few coconut trees, scattered about or only around the rim, where coconuts have been

FIGURE 2.3 Part of the rim of Salomon atoll with a few islands and very shallow reefs forming part of the eastern rim.

FIGURE 2.4 Middle Brother on the Great Chagos Bank. The Three Brothers group was too small for much sustained coconut plantation, never had rats, and today, they are important seabird areas.

storm-tossed by the sea up onto land. These small islands are sometimes rat-free, largely coconut-free, and densely packed with many species of native plants and seabirds. Despite their size, they now house some of the most important seabird colonies left in the Indian Ocean. Indeed, today, the bird populations of Chagos serve as a globally important refuge and reservoir for several species of seabirds (Figure 2.4).

The atoll Diego Garcia is just one of five islanded atolls in the Chagos Archipelago, located far to the southeast of the rest. While it constitutes about half of the total land area of the entire archipelago, it was always considered the main atoll and still is. Diego Garcia is often synonymous with the whole BIOT, which is why, from that perspective, all the rest are sometimes called the 'outer islands'. However, in terms of geography and ecology, that is akin to a Londoner dividing Great Britain into London and the 'outer parts' or 'the rest' (many Londoners probably do!) (Figure 2.5). From the military point of view, such categorisation may be valid, but from a scientific point of view, Diego Garcia may well be relatively much *less* important than the rest. Nevertheless, it is crucial in the sense that the existence of the military base is the reason for the existence of all BIOT in the first place. This, together with the policy to keep the whole territory reserved for defence purposes, has had enormously beneficial ecological consequences for the rest of the territory.

In early days of our science expeditions, I was often left in no doubt that many of the military and political spheres regarded (or at least, used to regard) the scientific interest in the Chagos as somewhat of a nuisance. Nevertheless, they mostly indulged us where they could, firmly believing that their military mission is the important part. They certainly did not want science or conservation to interfere with that 'mission'. I, on the other hand, along with many other scientists who I know share my view, believe that, in the long run, the most important legacy of the military presence will be the inadvertent creation of this huge area of unexploited marine life in the

FIGURE 2.5 The atolls and reefs of the Chagos Archipelago overlying a map of England and Wales. Atolls and shallow banks are represented in green, with Diego Garcia located in the southeast.

Indian Ocean: a refuge, a reservoir, the last remaining place for unpolluted marine nature to thrive in a small part of our planet. Several opponents of science visits there have suggested that scientists are being used or manipulated by the military to sanitise the military activities. From my perspective, I see it in a more global context and a longer-term perspective. In this sense, we might be thought of 'using' the military to achieve something that, in many years' time, will be viewed as being far more important: ensuring that at least one decent sized bit of this planet's life has remained as intact as possible in today's rapidly changing tropical world. Many individuals in several organisations that have contributed to the protection of Chagos share this perspective. Only time will tell which viewpoint proves correct!

WHAT IS SO IMPORTANT ABOUT CORAL REEFS ANYWAY?

Coral reefs are the most biodiverse habitat in the oceans and, excluding beetles, the most biodiverse anywhere on the planet (the biologist Haldane quipped that God must be "inordinately fond of beetles"!). They are enormously productive, producing protein for countless millions of people. When abused and no longer able to supply that protein, millions of people starve. This is not just a forecast for the future; it is happening now. More than half of infant deaths in the tropics, for example, are now attributed to malnutrition, not disease [1]. While books have been written on the importance of reefs to mankind, it is sufficient to say here that they are as important to mankind as forests are on land.

In terms of construction, put quite simply: they construct the reefs on which the islands sit.

We have only just begun to explore this archipelago. A crucial aspect of understanding Chagos is that it can serve as an ecological reference point for other places. In those other places, reefs and other shallow marine habitats have been disturbed so much that reefs can no longer really provide the necessary information on how to manage, restore, or even bring them back to a condition of being valuable to people. Consider the quantity of fish, for example. Some colleagues, who have worked in Chagos as well as many other places, have demonstrated what quantities of fish a coral reef can supply when not abused. This number is 100 times greater than the quantity that is observed on heavily exploited reefs and even about 10 times greater than the amount found in most of the small, so-called marine protected areas of the world, areas where various forms of control are attempted on people's exploitative behaviour. Until this work reminded us, people had, quite simply, lost all folk knowledge of what a coral reef could and should be like, and what it could do for us when not heavily abused. In science, we have a name for this sort of loss of memory: the 'shifting baseline syndrome' [2]. What we usually consider natural or normal is often only what we observed around us when we ourselves started our scientific lives, making it challenging to appreciate what it was like a few generations earlier. Only a place like Chagos can show us what good conditions in the sea should really be like, and what they could do for us if not damaged (Figure 2.6).

FIGURE 2.6 Rich fish life, including huge schools of paddletail snappers, thrives over reefs of the Chagos Archipelago because there is an almost complete absence of reef fishing.

It took years of research and collaboration with many excellent scientists, science societies, and conservation bodies to get the place designated as a fully protected marine reserve in 2010. Several people had laid the groundwork in the Government, and then a meeting with the Foreign Secretary encouraged him to declare the whole territory a huge no-take Marine Protected Area (MPA). In fact, quite a lot of environmental legislation was already in place in BIOT, developed over the years, mostly in a rather piecemeal manner. The MPA consolidated all those efforts. Perhaps the only additional measure taken in 2010 was the termination of pelagic shark and tuna fishing. By about 2015, other marine protected areas were declared that exceeded ours in size, but usually not in protection because most still permit fishing—one of the most ecologically distorting activities of all. I, for one, hope that many more areas will achieve similar protection to that which exists in the Chagos Archipelago. We know the world needs this.

While most of the following chapters delve into the science and natural history of the Chagos Archipelago, a later chapter describes briefly the political and commercial opposition to total protection. The challenges faced by attempts to conserve the place are prevalent worldwide. In the Chagos, achieving total protection became possible because we developed the science to support it through a series of research expeditions starting in the early 1970s. Opposition has been fierce at times; commercial interests are strong after all, and they are far better funded than conservationists, even when their arguments are blatantly transparent and self-serving. The ultimate question, I believe, is not whether mankind can afford to leave a few places on our planet in near-natural conditions. Rather, can we afford not to?

REFERENCES

[1] Bryce J, Boschi-Pinto C, Shibuya K, Black RE. 2005. The WHO Child Health Epidemiology Reference Group. WHO estimates of the causes of death in children. *Lancet* 365: 1147–1152.

[2] Pauly D. 1995. Anecdotes and the shifting baseline syndrome. *Trends in Ecology & Environment* 10: 430. **And:**

Sheppard CRC. 1995. The shifting baseline syndrome. *Marine Pollution Bulletin* 30: 766–767.

3 Natural History of the Islands and Human Settlement

Usually, the islands are of the greatest interest to most people, but ecologically, most of these were very badly damaged from the earliest days of settlement and their conversion to plantations [1]. However, several small islands are still in spectacular condition (Figure 3.1).

The noise from the thousands of birds is deafening, and their flocks form a sight that most wildlife photographers would travel widely to find. Dense colonies of terns, perhaps 10,000 pairs in one colony of ground nesters, create a continuous racket over which you must shout to your colleague to make yourself heard. There will be scores of nests of Red-footed Boobies in the shore-fringing scrub vegetation or nests of brown boobies on grassy expanses, many occupied by chicks as well as by a parent, or perhaps by an egg being incubated. Frigate birds will be higher up in the trees, while in mid-air, other species of terns, including the translucently white fairy tern, flit between the trees (Figure 3.2a and b).

The trees will be different too, native hardwood trees, some with striking leaves and flowers, and with branching patterns that tree-nesting birds favour. On some

FIGURE 3.1 A corner of a colony of Sooty Terns, one of the ground-nesting terns, on South Brother Island.

DOI: 10.1201/9781003423300-3

FIGURE 3.2 (a) Noddy Tern nesting on the ground. (b) Fairy terns make very rudimentary nests in trees.

FIGURE 3.3 An abandoned coconut grove with dead fronds blanket the ground making an impenetrable barrier for other species to return.

islands, you must watch where you walk because other species nest in burrows: shearwaters, smaller birds with prodigious powers of long-distance flight. If you walk in those areas, you would likely go through the surface, possibly break your ankle, and doubtlessly crush a shearwater chick as well. In fact, people are prohibited from walking in these areas. More about all these will be discussed later.

In contrast, when you land on the larger, once-inhabited, and coconut-planted islands, it is ghostly silent, except for the rustling of rats through the fallen, dead coconut fronds (Figure 3.3).

ENVIRONMENTAL HISTORY IN PLANTATION DAYS

One of the persistent myths about life in plantation days is that the people who lived and worked the plantations did so in harmony with nature and were good guardians of the islands' environment. This notion is much emphasised today by those advocating for resettlement, arguing that having people there is necessary to look after it, for example.

But was it so enviable a life? After all, the plantations were created during days of slavery and then by labour that was initially free, mostly in name only. A visitor to Diego Garcia long after slavery was abolished, said in 1885: "The misery of life on a coral island can hardly be exaggerated... It rains every day. The mosquitoes are unequalled for size and ferocity, the only food is occasional fresh fish, with tinned meat and vegetables from England." [2]. This may, of course, have been one man's very jaundiced view, but several facts testify to the general accuracy of the statement. Mortality from malnutrition such as beriberi, at the end of the 19th century was high, for example, as was child and infant mortality of around 50% [3].

What was the environmental state of the islands in plantation days, and how did people live there? Environmental practices in plantation days were awful and destructive, as recorded by some of the earliest literate visitors such as magistrates. It might not need to be so if settlement happened now, of course, given prosperous inhabitants. It must be stressed at the outset that the conditions and practices in Chagos atolls were no different from many other places in the tropical world, and that difficult conditions were not only experienced by the inhabitants of this particular group of islands. Everywhere, thorough exploitation of the environment was the name of the game, and for many, it was a matter of survival. It was an essential requirement in the creation of coconut plantations.

We know that, in terms of birds and vegetation, the larger islands were once very like the smaller ones are today. However, in the late 1700s, the coconut plantations were established, creating a trade that became profitable for plantation owners due to human toil. All over the tropical world, islands were turned into factories for coconut production (and other crops too in islands of any size). On tiny islands like those in Chagos, native trees were felled, and those with suitable timber were used to construct buildings and sheds for various coconut products: the oil, copra, and coir, as well as homes for people. Islands were stripped clear, and coconut trees were planted in place of the native trees and shrubs. In all Chagos islands, the soil is thin and poor, and where there was no soil at all, circular pits were commonly carved out of the rock into which vegetation matter was placed along with a germinating coconut that was left to grow. Covering the larger islands without exception, ranks of palm trees grew upwards, turning the islands into profitable enterprises, but leaving them faunistically impoverished and botanically trashed.

The natural habitat vanished: "...the French, who with the assistance of slave labour probably derived directly from West Africa (where they were major participants in the slave trade in this time...) soon felled the majority of the native woodland and replaced it with exceptionally productive coconut plantations wherever there was room for them. Timber continued to be exported to Mauritius from the last and most luxuriant forest on Boddam Island in the Salomon group, well into the nineteenth century, and tree stumps could still be seen there very recently" [4].

Conversion of the natural habitat was thorough, and it was noted that in "1882-1888, [there was] a consequent increase in the human population and amount of disturbance to the environment" [5]. The human-powered industriousness needed for such near-total alteration of so many islands must have been prodigious in days before mechanical help was available. There is little detailed record of wildlife from then, but we can guess what conditions were like from other, similar examples elsewhere on small islands in the Indian and Pacific Oceans, or in Caribbean islands. Native plants mostly disappeared, and most birds went too. Birds, turtles, coconut crabs, and more were simply eaten.

Certainly a few native trees were left, and these were supplemented by an ever-increasing variety of plants such as fruit trees and ornamentals shipped in from Asia and Africa, but most land became a coconut monoculture. The environmental havoc wreaked on Chagos islands was extensive, though there was nothing different about the Chagos islands in this respect.

INTRODUCED PLANTS

Many more plants than animals appear to have been introduced. A survey in Diego Garcia, which at 2,700 ha contains approximately half of the total land area of the archipelago, showed about 280 'higher' plants, of which the original native flora present today is only about 45 species, with the rest being introduced [6]. Dates of the introductions are poorly documented. It doubtless started as early as 1784 when a considerable amount of soil (reportedly six ship-loads on one occasion) was imported from India to help horticulture; that soil inevitably would have contained a huge variety of non-native plant seeds [7]. Later, soil was imported from Mauritius too, and thus the islands received seeds and weeds from two continents. By the mid-20th century, the plantations were infested by weeds and pests, which by then contributed to the decline of coconut production [8].

Many plants were introduced for food, and although many survive and were doubtlessly invaluable in plantation days, none could remain abundant when neglected. The surveyor Moresby wrote that '...maize, tobacco, cabbages, "greens", sweet potatoes, onions, carrots, turnips, "leeks", garlic, existed, along with all the common vegetables cultivated in India, with limes and citrons' [9]. Even cotton was introduced in one optimistic but failed experiment. Moresby himself introduced the breadfruit tree and the yam. Sometime in the 1800s, bananas were introduced, along with some other tropical fruits. Along with these came numerous introduced insects, including the rhinoceros beetle, which became a severe pest of coconuts [10].

SEABIRDS

In the process of transforming the islands into coconut monocultures, the birds were largely destroyed, along with their nesting and roosting trees and shrubs. Tree nesters don't like palm trees because their fronds do not provide suitable nesting areas, and the ground-nesting birds never stood a chance against the disturbance, the conversion of their open spaces, and rats. What must have been one of the world's largest colonies of terns was on Diego Garcia, and that didn't last long at all—the ground they nested on was both turned into a plantation and quarried for guano (phosphate) too. Thousands of birds are needed over decades and centuries to make deposits worth quarrying.

The first two plantations to fail were on Egmont Atoll and the Great Chagos Bank; both of which closed during the 1930s. At the closure of the rest around the early 1970s, the ornithologist Bourne said about Diego Garcia: "[It] is now largely devastated from an ornithological point of view by nearly two centuries of the activities of man and other introduced animals. [It is] in urgent need of conservation…" [5]. In 1887, there were possibly 100,000 Sooty Terns in Diego Garcia, but the inhabitants were taking many of the terns' eggs and feathers [11]. "The early settlers found the frigate birds, boobies, noddies, terns, herons and tropicbirds to breed on these islands. They are considered good eating; the feathers too, make excellent bedding" [8].

It appears that most seabird colonies were wiped out before the early 20th century, so that: "Whereas when the islands were first described colonies of breeding seabirds, particularly terns, noddies and shearwaters, were important, these have now virtually disappeared on Diego Garcia and possibly on the other larger atolls also. The most conspicuous birds of Diego Garcia are now all introduced land birds…" [12]. It had even been suggested that there was once quite a rich land bird community, comparable to that of Christmas Island further east [13], but if there was, it was wiped out.

Birds were simply commodities. As late as the 1930s, booby chicks were taken to be dried in the sun for use as feathery powder puffs, after being left without food to die: "…very young booby chicks suffering the sad agonies of complete deprivation of food: feathered snowballs, … their starving beaks clacking like castanets..." (Figure 3.4) [14].

Conservation never received significant attention. In the 1870s, a manager named James Spurs took the first practical conservation measures. However, "in the absence of enforcing authority or of any clear need for conservation it is unlikely that much attention was paid to it" [10]. Only some tiny islands escaped.

FIGURE 3.4 Booby chicks were allowed to die and were then used as feathery powder puffs.

RATS AND OTHER INTRODUCED ANIMALS

If habitat destruction was not bad enough, humans introduced rats wherever they went. Consequently, chicks of ground nesters that had survived intense disturbance of their habitat were eaten by the rodents. For people, rats quickly became a problem and were recorded as existing in plague proportions in Diego Garcia as early as the late 1700s. Periodic 'rat drives' in Diego Garcia, using dogs, resulted in the killing of 30,000 rats each year [15]. All islands with significant human habitation still have abundant rats today, and their rustling in the undergrowth or climbing the coconut trees can be observed. In Diego Garcia today, the rat density is amongst the highest known for coral atolls, although there is a substantial ongoing baiting and eradication programme in the inhabited parts [16]. It has been supposed that there are two semi-independent populations of rats on any one island, with one living high in coconut trees, subordinate perhaps to another group that mainly live on the ground.

It was not only rats; with humans came domesticated animals. Birds were "confronted with the destruction of their habitat and the introduction of such predators as rats, cats, and hogs, all of which appear to have been widespread by the middle of the 19th century" [5]. In Egmont in the 1840s, conditions were very poor, and it was overrun by 600 pigs, together with dogs and cats [17]. That atoll has only about 300 ha of land in total, meaning pigs roamed freely at an average density of two pigs per hectare. Poultry was also abundant, probably in all atolls at that time, as recorded in sailing notes of the period [18]. Moresby, who was responsible in the 1830s for the first detailed charts of the whole archipelago [19], noted donkeys, rats, abundant pigs and poultry, feral cats and dogs, and labourers lived in "considerable intimacy" with their swine [9]. Bees were introduced too [20]. These factors were more than enough to extinguish most of the native wildlife, resulting in the silent islands of today.

Cattle and sheep were even tried, though these did not thrive [21]. Cattle were used for milk production, and it had been recommended in the 1930s that the pasturage be fertilised by about 50 kg of locally sourced guano per acre each year because the natural soil was "lacking in most essential plant food" [22]. Donkeys were introduced, brought to carry loads and to plod for hours in a small circle attached to a beam connected to the coconut presses. They were turned loose in the early 1970s. There is a residual population of donkeys in Diego Garcia today, and a smaller population persisted until at least the turn of the present century on Isle du Coin in Peros Banhos atoll. In Diego Garcia, these feral donkeys have inhibited attempts to rehabilitate native trees in the uninhabited eastern arm because they eat the tree seedlings.

TURTLES

Both the Green and Hawksbill turtles (Figure 3.5) used to nest here in some quantity, but the number caught in plantation days was prodigious. It seems that the total number of Hawksbills remaining in the archipelago when we first began to study these islands in the 1970s was roughly the same as the number that was recorded as being caught every year in the early 1900s. Turtle catch figures show a rapid decline from that time onwards (Figure 3.6) [23]. Turtles take about 30 years to show significant recovery from such depletion, and it is now clear that, from the number now seen on dives, we may be witnessing such a recovery.

FIGURE 3.5 A mature Hawksbill turtle, showing its lustrous shell. Their population is recovering following heavy exploitation.

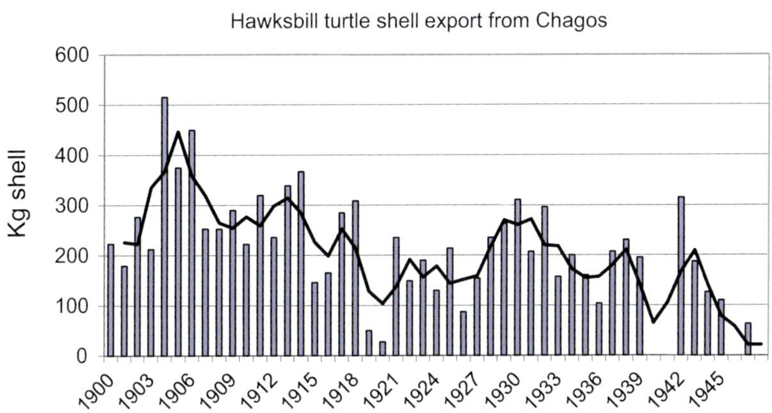

FIGURE 3.6 Hawksbill turtle shell export from the Chagos Archipelago during the first part of the last century. About 2 kg of shell comes from one turtle. From Mortimer J. 2008. History of turtle exploitation in Chagos. *Chagos News* 34: 14–16.

For turtles, treatment of animals was grim. Charles Darwin related in his *Voyage of the Beagle:*

> Captain Moresby informs me that in the Chagos archipelago… the natives, by a horrible process, take the shell from the back of the living turtle. 'It is covered with burning charcoal, which causes the outer shell to curl upwards; it is then forced off with a knife… After this barbarous process the animal is suffered again to regain its native element where, after a certain time, a new shell is formed; it is, however, too thin to be of any service, and the animal always appears languishing and sickly.' [24]

Green turtles, which do not have a saleable shell but are used for food, were kept in pens at the ends of jetties until needed for consumption or export.

Several scientists have conducted extensive research on the turtles during the expeditions. New discoveries resulting from attaching radio-satellite trackers to the shells of several green turtles show that they conduct huge migrations, reaching as far as East Africa and Somalia [25]. This is just one of many records for the natural world that involve the Chagos Archipelago.

There is no record of the Aldabra giant tortoise ever being in Chagos, other than a domesticated one [26].

COCONUT CRABS

In most of these islands, coconut crabs are now enormously abundant. When we first counted these in the mid- and late 1970s, we noticed, in broad terms, that the longer the interval that had elapsed since people had left the island, the more abundant were its coconut crabs and the larger were its individuals [27]. Recently abandoned islands still had none at all that we could see. It was obvious that recovery was taking place after people had left. For example, in islands such as Eagle Island, whose plantations had been abandoned in the 1930s, there were many huge specimens (Figure 3.7), while islands that had been abandoned only a few years previously had only a few young, or none.

These crabs are the largest land-living arthropods in the world and can reach a weight of 4 kg, being at the upper size limit for terrestrial animals with exoskeletons in the present Earth atmosphere with current oxygen concentrations. They release larvae into the sea for dispersal, but adults do not swim, and will, in fact, easily drown in water. Their problem is that people like eating them, and consequently, they are virtually extinct throughout most of their range: "…both the size and geographical distribution of coconut crab populations are significantly reduced and … localised extinction has occurred in areas where coconut crabs were sympatric with humans" [28]. However, the fact that these animals still lay eggs in the sea in the ancestral crab manner means that they can disperse on ocean currents, which allows their populations to recover, given protection.

FIGURE 3.7 The huge coconut crab *Birgus latro*, sometimes called the robber crab.

In 2011, the first quantitative survey found extraordinarily high numbers in parts of Diego Garcia [29]. On the Eastern, uninhabited side, their average density was 300 per hectare, with peak numbers in some survey areas of nearly 600 per hectare, densities quite unheard of elsewhere in modern times. Numbers to date have not been measured in the northern atolls but my own rough estimates suggest the numbers are at least as great in many northern islands too.

They were captured not only for food but also to help increase the number of nuts harvested because, in the early part of the 20th century, it had been estimated that an adult coconut crab could consume 250 nuts per year in these plantations [30].

Even in the now mostly protected Diego Garcia, it is not entirely a rosy story because the same study showed that numbers diminished in survey plots nearer to human habitation on the Western arm of that atoll. Without apportioning blame to any particular group of people, we know that some sectors of the very multinational civilian workforce regard them as a desirable food. During one of my annual visits to the military base, we heard rumours of a barbecue of coconut crabs being planned for the end of that week. We put it around that we were aware of this plan and reminded people that the penalty for harming these animals, let alone eating them, was immediate dismissal from their job and swift return to their country of origin. That particular barbecue did not happen. From the patterns of densities around the island, it is probably impossible to stop all consumption of coconut crabs in Diego Garcia, but it is strictly forbidden.

We have seen examples of coconut crab poaching in northern atolls too. Once, I received a copy of an article from a French yachting magazine about a family who had visited Salomon atoll on their yacht. They wrote about their adventures in Chagos, focussing on their own private barbecue of coconut crabs. They were very proud of their feast and advocated it, even sharing ways to cook them. Some visiting yacht owners, including these, delude themselves into thinking that living what they perceive as a noble, 'eco-friendly' type of existence, feeding off the land, is harmless. They clearly have no idea that it would not take very many of them long to obliterate the crabs completely. That particular crew was told never to return. And then again, in 2010, another visiting yacht owner publicised in his blog how good the eating of coconut crabs was in Chagos. Although reported at once, this was, surprisingly, not considered sufficient evidence to prosecute them so those people were merely asked to leave.

Such people are likely to be simply unthinking and ignorant, finding it convenient to believe that their own feasts do not make much difference. However, they can and do make a huge difference in such small islands. I have no doubt that poaching by visiting yachts continues, although, of course, most who do so have the sense not to boast about it in blogs and magazines. Not all yacht visitors are unaware of the fragile nature of the wildlife in the islands, and indeed, several have sent me emails telling me of poaching activities of other yachts that they had witnessed. Most know that the taking of turtles, coconut crabs, and indeed any wildlife, is illegal from these islands. Signs on the main islands of the permitted anchorages convey this information, as does new documentation sent to anyone who applies for a permit to visit. Still, during my visits as the Government's advisor, several individuals have been quite assertive, contending that I or the Government have infringed their 'human rights' of freely wandering the oceans and living off the land in any way they wish.

Genetic studies on these coconut crabs have indicated that a small but significant fraction of those in Chagos originate, every generation, from populations much further west in the Seychelles and East Africa (a generation here is about 5 years, which is their age of earliest maturity). Fewer crabs migrate from Chagos to the West, primarily due to the current direction during their breeding season, which appears to be around December. The numbers dispersing to Chagos are far greater than what is needed to ensure a thorough genetic mixing in these islands, and the genetic studies of this species were among the first to demonstrate that Chagos is an important reservoir for species. There, they have now recovered from their near extinction [31].

The other name for this huge crab is the robber crab. They are not only dependent on the coconut; they will eat most kinds of fruit or seed. They scavenge and will consume the occasional small bird and even a rat when available. I imagine that in the case of a rat, it would need to be either old or sick or taken very much by surprise. Combat between these giant crabs and rats is a not an uncommon sight, and a short film has been made in Chagos of a rat going for and apparently deliberately biting off the feelers of the crab, an act that would render the crab very vulnerable since the feelers contain many of its rich sensory organs.

While consumption of these giant crabs during plantation days reduced their population to nothing in many places, in Chagos, they were used for sport as well. Accounts exist of competitions in which crabs were held up to a rope onto which they clung, and the winner of a competition was the 'owner' of the crab which hung on longest; sometimes this 'sport' would go on all night, even with weights attached to the crab.

In 1996, attempts were made to artificially breed some in London Zoo, but despite best efforts, this failed [32]. For now, at least, the only way to conserve them is simply to leave them alone and let them repopulate their numbers by themselves. Quite obviously, in a hungry world, this is most unlikely to happen anywhere where there are people, so Chagos and the diminishing number of places like it are perhaps the only refuges left for these magnificent and huge crabs.

FINAL PLANTATION DAYS

By 1970, the coconut plantations were in decline in terms of both quantity and quality of produce [1], even though the proportion of land area used for coconut production by that time was very large. Regarding Diego Garcia, the coral island geographer David Stoddart remarked, "...almost the whole area of the atoll (6,250 out of 7,488 acres) was being cropped for coconuts" [10] and: "Little attention has been paid at Diego Garcia to conservation: the atoll has simply been used as a supplier of coconut products, and to a lesser extent of dried fish and turtles, for Mauritius". However, the plantations were producing less and less due to inefficient cultivation practices. Production became "derisory" and "absurdly low" [8], only half of that obtained from even poor soils in the Caribbean and one-third of that harvested from plantations in Ceylon and East Africa.

Plantation management was commonly incompetent, placing production in a perilous situation considering the much higher costs associated with their location in these distant central Indian Ocean islands, far from centres of trade. The plantations increasingly struggled throughout their last decades of existence, becoming close to

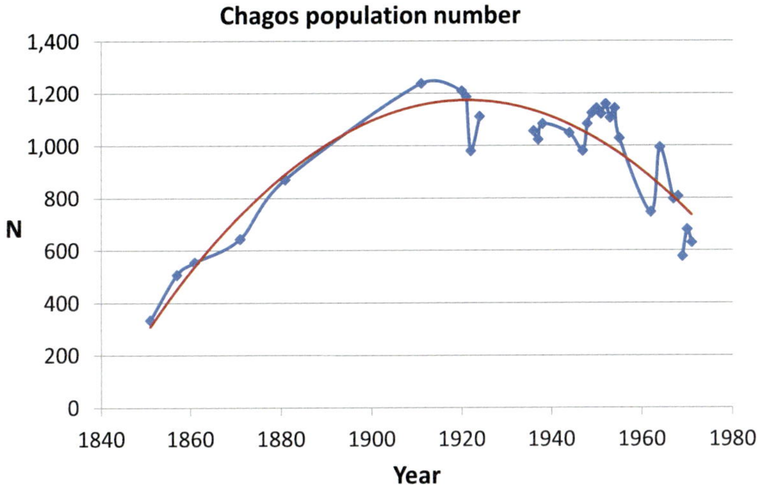

FIGURE 3.8 Human population on the islands over time, taken from censuses. There has been debate about the accuracy of these figure, and some suggest they were a bit higher. Whatever the numbers, however, the trend of a decline after about 1920 is clear. Red line is polynomial best fit to the data. From Wenban Smith N. 2012. Population of the Chagos. *Chagos News* 39: 18–22.

bankruptcy three times. As plantations declined, those on two atolls, Egmont and the Great Chagos Bank, closed in the 1930s for both economic reasons and because of social problems. The human populations declined too, so that increasingly, temporary workers were brought in to make up the labour shortfall, mostly from the Seychelles following plantation ownership changes (Figure 3.8) [33].

As a result, just before the creation of British Indian Ocean Territory (BIOT), Stoddart said, "The atoll was by then simply a coconut plantation. I had to say there was no case in the terrestrial ecology to object to the military plans" [34]. Emphasising the lack of ecological value that remained, he states, "The land vegetation of Diego Garcia consists almost entirely of coconut-dominated woodland, with some small areas of shrubs and occasional relict broadleaf trees. All parts of the atoll have been subject to continuous human interference for almost two hundred years, and man now actively controls vegetation growth in coconut plantations in many areas".

At the time, in a letter to the Commonwealth Office (1968), Stoddart said: "Diego is, of course, much altered by man, and there are few natural features remaining undisturbed. It is really an extended coconut plantation from end to end" [35]. He mentioned that the islets in the north are more natural. Although he did not visit other atolls, he added: "It does, however, seem unlikely that they will be of such biological interest as to require any measure of conservation at all…".

From the terrestrial point of view, in the larger, planted islands, most would agree with him. It cannot be too much of an exaggeration to say that the terrestrial ecology had been trashed by the time Diego Garcia became part of BIOT. Larger islands in the other atolls were no different. However, a dozen small islands remained that were not affected, and these remain today an example of a previous existence. They can also be the source islands for future restoration efforts.

ECONOMICS AND THE ISLAND ENVIRONMENT

Such destructive environmental behaviour was the norm throughout the tropical world during this period, and few would have thought to act differently. People did not, unfortunately, live in any kind of harmony with nature in Chagos, contrary to some now rather romantic ideas being suggested about people caring for their environment in those days. The Chagos was known as the 'Oil Islands' for a good reason.

Human existence throughout plantation days was clearly very difficult. During those times, visits to the smaller and more remote islands of Chagos from the villages on the larger atolls were made for more than coconut harvesting. They were made when supply ships failed to turn up, sometimes because they had sunk, necessitating the Chagossians to go elsewhere to collect birds and birds' eggs, turtles, and turtle shell. The need to do this arose simply because those on the inhabited islands had become heavily depleted. While protein was never a problem using the plentiful fish from the reefs, along with pigs, chickens, and other animals, agriculture was always poor. The basic carbohydrate foodstuff for people was rice, which had to be imported, mostly from Mauritius. It was paid for by the copra and, to a small extent, by selling turtle shell and bird feathers [22]. Fruit was grown to a probably sufficient extent, using introduced fruit trees such as pawpaw, guava, and banana.

By the 1930s, rats accounted for about a third of the already declining yields of coconuts. Collections of fallen nuts and clearing of undergrowth were carried out only infrequently, resulting in many more nuts being simply lost in the undergrowth [22].

Although coconut production was in decline throughout the Chagos Archipelago in the 20th century, the increasingly interconnected global economy was forcing an even greater change. By the 1970s, palm oil from Southeast Asia had started to sweep coconut oil off the world's supermarket shelves. Huge palm oil plantations were being developed in many places, such as Indonesia, starting a trend that has continued. (Today, clearance of tropical forest to create more plantations for the oil palm is one of the main drivers of deforestation in Southeast Asia.) Furthermore, those oil palm plantations are in countries with much closer access to major trade ports, more flexible labour markets, and an infinitely greater land area on which to plant. By the mid-1970s, global palm oil production overtook that of coconut oil [36], which became ever more relegated to being a curiosity or luxury item. Coconut plantations in Asia and the Caribbean became sufficient for world demand (Figure 3.9).

The trouble for Chagos was that it had no other industry to sustain it. The islands have too little soil for anything else, and they are too small anyway. Turtle shells and bird feathers, no matter how avidly they were exploited, were never more than a bit of cash on the side. Because of all these factors, the fate of this industry in Chagos was sealed.

There is an alternative, more attractive narrative for the lives of the plantation residents, and that is one of a delightful existence. Accounts in more recent years have focussed on several related things: the peaceful and pleasant lives lived on the islands, plentiful food, the miserable evacuations carried out brutally, sometimes resulting in miscarriages, and people 'dying of sadness', and of the very poor conditions and alleged neglect that the Chagossians then suffered later in Mauritius [37]. These accounts are evocative and moving. But even if life remembered from many

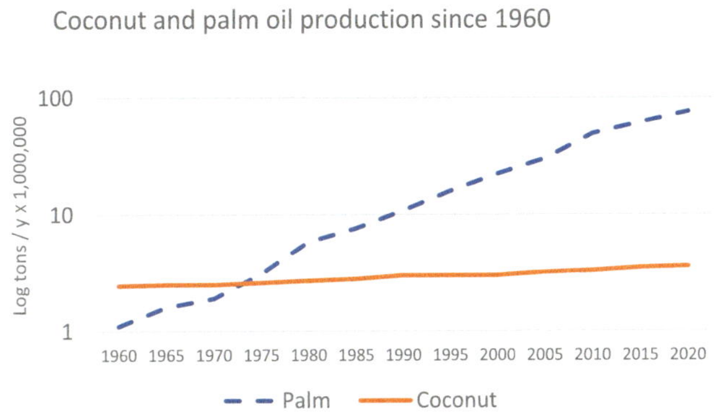

FIGURE 3.9 Log scale of annual production of palm oil (blue line) and coconut oil (red line). By the mid-1970s, coconut oil had been eclipsed by the cheaper and easier palm oil. Data from "Our Word in Data" Richie H, Rosand P, Roser M. *Agricultural Production*. https://ourworldindata.org/agricultural-production. Creative Commons.

years earlier has become rose-tinted, they are sincerely held. Most come from former residents who were children at the time, and poverty is a comparative thing; everybody lived under the same conditions with nothing to relate to in this respect.

REFERENCES

[1] Sheppard CRC. 2016. Changes to the natural history of islands of the Chagos atolls, central Indian Ocean, during human settlement (1780–1969), and prospects for restoration. *Atoll Research Bulletin* 612: 1–15.

[2] Anon. 1885. A coral island. Saturday Review of Politics, Literature, Science and Art 59 (1545): 746–747.

[3] Manson P. 1902. A discussion on beriberi. *British Medical Journal* 2177: 830–839. **And:**
Schott G. 1900. The oceanographical and meteorological work of the German "Valdivia" expedition. *Geographical Journal* 15: 518–528. **And:**
Chun C. 1903. *Aus den Tiefen des Weltmeeres*. Gustav Fischer Jena, Chapter XIX. **From:**
Carter M. 2022. The Chagos Archipelago. In: *Oxford Research Encyclopaedia of Asian History*. Oxford University Press. doi.org/10.1093/acrefore/9780190277727.013.739

[4] Stoddart DR. 1971. Geography and ecology of Diego Garcia atoll, Chagos Archipelago. *Atoll Research Bulletin* 149: 176.

[5] Bourne WRP. 1971. The birds of the Chagos group, Indian Ocean. *Atoll Research Bulletin* 149: 175–208.

[6] Topp JMW, Sheppard CRC. 1999. Higher plants of the Chagos Archipelago. In: Sheppard CRC, Seaward MRD (eds) *Ecology of the Chagos Archipelago*. Linnean Society Occasional Publications 2. Westbury Publishing, Otley, W. Yorkshire, pp. 225–240. **And:**
Topp JMW. 1988. An annotated checklist of the flora of Diego Garcia, British Ocean Territory. *Atoll Research Bulletin* 313: 1–21.

[7] Price R. undated. Bombay Secretariat Records Office, Secret Department, Vols. 30–39, in Stoddart DR, 1971 (ref 13 below).

[8] Lucie-Smith. File CO 1036/502 in the National Archives at Kew.

[9] Moresby R, Elwon T. 1845. *Sailing directions for the Red Sea*. Indian Navy. Printed by order of the Court of Directors of the East India Company. London, Allen and Co.
[10] Stoddart DR. 1971. Settlement and development of Diego Garcia. *Atoll Research Bulletin* 149: 209–217.
[11] Finsch O. 1887. Ein Besuch auf Diego Garcia im Indischen Ozean. *Deutsche geographische Blgtter Bremen* 1887: 30–42.
[12] Stoddart DR. 1971. Terrestrial fauna of Diego Garcia and other Chagos atolls. *Atoll Research Bulletin* 149: 163–170.
[13] Gibson-Hill CA. 1948. Field notes on the birds of Christmas Island. *Bulletin Raffles Museum* 18: 87–165.
[14] Dussercle R. 1936. *Dans les Zîles là-Haut*. Port Louis, General Printing and Stationery.
[15] Wenban Smith N, Carter M. 2016. *Chagos: A History. Exploration, Exploitation, Expulsion*. London, Chagos Conservation Trust, pp. 550.
[16] Carr P, Harper GA. 2015. The distribution of the Ship Rat *Rattus rattus* in the Chagos Archipelago. *Chagos News* 47: 20–31.
[17] Scott R. 1961. *Limuria: The Lesser Dependencies of Mauritius*. London, Oxford University Press, 308 pp.
[18] Horsburgh J. 1852. *India Directory, or Directions for Sailing to and from the East Indies*. Sixth edition. London, 2 vols. London, WMH Allen & Co.
[19] Moresby R. 1837 (and updated revisions). Admiralty Charts and Publications. Several covering the archipelago and its atolls. **Also**: *Transactions of the Bombay Geographical Society* 1: 307–310.
[20] Findlay. 1882. *A Directory for the Navigation of the Indian Ocean*. Fourth edition. London, R. H. Laurie, 1304 pp.
[21] Bourne GC. 1886. General observations on the fauna of Diego Garcia, Chagos group. *Proceedings Zoological Society London* 1886: 331–334.
[22] Weihe PO. 1939. Report on a visit to the Chagos archipelago. *Mauritius Department of Agriculture*, document from Kew archives.
[23] Mortimer JA. 2009. History of turtle exploitation in Chagos. *Chagos News* 34: 14–16.
[24] Darwin C. 1897. *Naturalist's Voyage Round the World*. Also known as *Voyage of the Beagle*. London, John Murray, pp. 441.
[25] Hays GC, Mortimer JA, Jerodiaconou D, Esteban N. 2014. Use of long-distance migration patterns of an endangered species to inform conservation planning for the world's largest marine protected area. *Conservation Biology* 28: 1636–1644.
[26] Stoddart DR, Peake JF, Gordon C, Burleigh R. 1979. Historical records of Indian Ocean giant tortoise populations. *Philosophical Transactions Royal Society London B* 286: 147–161.
[27] Sheppard CRC. 1979. Status of three rare animals on Chagos. *Environmental Conservation* 6: 310.
[28] FAO. undated. *Assessment of the status of the coconut crab Birgus latro*. Corporate Document Depository. http://www.fao.org/docrep/field/003/ac281e/ac281e03.htm.
[29] Vogt S. 2011. Population densities and demographics of the Coconut Crab, *Birgus latro*, on Diego Garcia, British Indian Ocean Territory. A report to NAVFACECFE. **And:** Carr et al. 2013. Chapter 20 Coral Islands of the British Indian Ocean Territory (Chagos Archipelago). In: Sheppard CRC (ed.) *Coral Reefs of the UK Overseas Territories*. Springer, Dordrecht, pp. 271–282.
[30] Gardiner JS, Cooper CF. 1907. Description of the expedition. (The Percy Sladen expedition to the Indian Ocean in 1905). *Transactions Linnean Society London, Zoology* 12: 1–56, 111–175.
[31] Sheppard CRC et al. 2012. Reefs and islands of the Chagos Archipelago, Indian Ocean: Why it is the world's largest no-take marine protected area. *Aquatic Conservation: Marine Freshwater Ecosystems* 22: 232–261.

[32] Barnet LK, Emms C, Clarke D. 1999. The coconut or Robber crab (*Birgus latro*) in the Chagos Archipelago, and its captive culture at London Zoo. In: Sheppard CRC, Seaward MRD (eds) *Ecology of the Chagos Archipelago*. Linnean Society Occasional Publications, pp. 273–284.
[33] Wenban Smith N. 2012. Population of the Chagos, 1820-1973. *Chagos News* 39: 18–22.
[34] Stoddart DR. 2001. Be of good cheer, my weary readers, for I have espied land. *Atoll Research Bulletin* 494: 235–272.
[35] Stoddart D. 1968. Letter to the Commonwealth Office, dated 24 July 1968.
[36] Our world in data agricultural production. https://ourworldindata.org/palm-oil#:~:text=In%202018%2C%20the%20world%20produced,across%20a%20number%20of%20countries.
[37] Sands P. 2022. The last colony: A tale of exile, justice and Britain's colonial legacy. Weidenfeld and Nicolson. **And:**
Mandarin F. 2015. Chapter 20 Living memories: A worker's view of the 1950s. In: Wenban Smith N, Carter M (eds) *Chagos: A History. Exploration, Exploitation, Expulsion*. London, Chagos Conservation Trust, pp. 550.

4 Restoration, Rats, and the Persistence of the Coconut

The islands that were too small to bother with, or which were too rocky and dangerous to land on, were also too difficult and dangerous to load and ship away boatloads of coconuts, even if they had been collected. These small scraps of land were left more or less alone (Figure 4.1).

Some were used for a very short time, maybe a few days per year with no permanent settlement and, fortunately, no introduction of rats. These are today's gems. They contain remnants of Indian Ocean hardwoods as well as huge bird colonies that have recovered where they can, though rarely where there are rats.

It is from these examples that we hope recovery can be stimulated in larger islands too. Restoration needs substantial human intervention to reverse the destruction. Restoration started in a very small way in the 1970s when, on an early expedition, we gathered numerous seedlings of several native hardwoods which, after propagaton for a few weeks, were planted in clearings we had made for our tents. Today, many of these live on as large established trees with seedlings of their own. However, they need help to initiate their growth; they need cleared areas because a thick layer of fallen coconut fronds on the ground is very inimical for new seeds. Several proposals

FIGURE 4.1 Several islands were too small or dangerous to land on, and North Brother Island on the Great Chagos Bank is one such example.

DOI: 10.1201/9781003423300-4

to extend this planting-out scheme failed to get off the ground until very recently. Three interlocking actions are needed: rat eradication, coconut tree reduction, and hardwood seedling planting, all of which need to be undertaken simultaneously.

We have an apparent contradiction here in the minds of many members of the public. We are brought up to consider palm-fringed tropical beaches to be a holiday paradise—and indeed they can be a paradise. Travel brochures are filled with images of stretches of sand, an azure sea... almost always with palm trees overhanging the sand, offering welcome and attractive shade. Tourism industries are built on such images, and the travel industry provides a substantial proportion of the hard currency for many tropical states. It must be natural, isn't it? A primordial Eden in fact? Well, no, it isn't really! Fringes along beaches are natural enough because the coconut is a huge seed that floats vast distances until being tossed by waves onto a suitable shore. The coconut palm originates, it is now believed, from a small part of Indonesia, and it has tremendous powers of dispersal. But only in very few cases will the coconut tree then manage to establish itself throughout the interior of an island. They do not compete well with the native vegetation when the latter is already established. Native Indian Ocean hardwoods were the natural flora of these islands, so before coconut trees can dominate them, it was necessary for man to chop the hardwoods down.

Doing so changed the balance completely, and coconuts became the new ecological 'stable state'. But does coconut forest revert by itself to native Indian Ocean hardwood forest when the plantations are abandoned, and can there be a natural return to 'original' conditions? The answer, unfortunately, seems to be no here too, at least not in a few human generations. For proof of this, we need look no further than the fact that some of these plantations have been abandoned for over 90 years, and all of them for over 50 years. Yet, although mature hardwood trees were left which continually shed copious seedlings onto the ground beneath them, there has been only very slow or no spread of these natives. In many places, the reverse happens: coconuts can readily extend their choking advance. A particularly important example of this is around the two diminishing mangrove patches that remain, one on Eagle Island in the Great Chagos Bank and the other on Moresby Island in Peros Banhos (Figure 4.2).

Even mangrove trees, which thrive in salt water, are losing the competition against encroaching coconut palms. These unusual areas are shrinking and will be lost completely in just a few more years if we do not intervene and cut back the coconut. The coconut palm is a very successful, aggressive invasive tree, once man has given it the head start it needs.

One reason why this is the case can be seen on the island floor, where fallen palm fronds cover the entire ground completely, up to as much as a metre deep. The ground becomes almost impenetrable and blocks out the light at ground level, preventing other plants from getting enough light to grow. The choking palm litter has been aptly described as "coconut chaos" [1].

Another problem for recovering island vegetation comes from the tree known as ironwood, whose botanical name is *Casurina*. This seems to be the exception to the rule. It lives in several places and seems to grow happily enough amongst the palms. It is durable, strong and is valuable for building. A few islands are covered with it,

FIGURE 4.2 The mangrove stand on Moresby Island hosts nesting Red-footed Boobies.

and it sheds needles that inhibit other plants every bit as effectively as coconut litter does. Nobody knows if this tree was introduced or whether it was there before man appeared, but man certainly planted it in some places for its timber. David Bellamy described in his book about the first two science expeditions of the 1970s [2] how he and others made a concerted effort in the early 1970s to rid Egmont atoll of it, which they succeeded in doing—for a while.

However, ridding the islands of both these invasive plants does not solve the problem on its own: rats remain. They can be heard rustling through the dried coconut fronds on the ground and seen in the tree canopies too. Rat eradication might be difficult in these islands but would be essential for restoration to permit the bird life to return to them.

Restoration is possible but is expensive and complicated. Chagos is one of the few places in the world where it might be achievable, where its results can be monitored and measured, and very importantly, where results can be used to aid other countries that are trying to unravel past damage to improve their own environment and living conditions for their people. The Chagos islands are perhaps the ideal places where we might be reasonably certain that past damages could be repaired for the benefit of the wider community, given a proper, integrated, and planned restoration programme.

POSSIBLE RESTORATION

The detailed history of the Chagos' discovery, settlement, and exploitation by Nigel Wenban Smith and Marina Carter [3] touches on environmental matters sufficiently to show, amongst much else, that there was sometimes interest and concern amongst some visiting magistrates and others about the rat infestation. However, this never led anywhere.

In 2006, we made the first concerted attempt to eradicate rats on Eagle Island. Eagle was chosen for several reasons. Firstly, it is large, the second largest after Diego Garcia, and so the largest island in the northern atolls; if the eradication attempt had been successful, the increased land area that was potentially available for birds would have roughly doubled. We did not have a massive tree restoration programme at the same time—we had not fully appreciated the degree to which that was necessary too, and anyway, that could be done later if the rat eradication was successful. We chose Eagle also because one of the first scientific expeditions to the Chagos (and my first experience of the archipelago) was based there in 1975, led by David Bellamy, the botanist, and Mont Hirons, an ornithologist, and consequently, it became, in Chagos terms, one of the best understood at that time. Finally, to either side of it are tiny islands with no rats that were teeming with bird colonies, one called Sea Cow just to the south, and the Three Brothers group to the northeast, both within sight of Eagle. If Eagle could be cleared of predatory rats, then the result might have been spectacular. It is a shortage of suitable land or nesting sites that restricts birds in Chagos, not shortage of food or current human disturbance. There were, and still are, about ten internationally 'Important Bird Areas (IBAs)' in the archipelago, a designation gained by fulfilling certain rules such as holding a significant proportion of the entire world population of a species. These could spread, given a chance.

So, Eagle was provisionally chosen. A sum of money was raised, and a reconnaissance party visited for a 'feasibility study', under the auspices of a well-known NGO. They concluded that it was possible and wrote a plan to guide how it should be done. A larger sum of over £100,000 was then raised for an eradication programme, and the same NGO ran that.

It was a failure. The people doing the work were not to blame—they were magnificent. They chopped paths through the palm trees at regular intervals just a few yards apart, back-breaking labour that took a couple of months, longer than anticipated. Additionally, they laid prodigious quantities of carefully spaced rat bait. However, even although it was soon realised that more time was clearly needed than the allocated three months, they were withdrawn at the end of the scheduled period. They had to leave just one day after a rat was seen still alive, despite their own feasibility study stipulating that baiting must continue for several weeks after the last rat was seen or detected from bait traps. The workers, mostly experienced field workers, were dismayed at having to leave, and several volunteered to stay on, unpaid, to fulfil the necessary requirements. But they were not allowed to do so. Money lost for changing non-refundable flight tickets home was one reason given. The primary funders, the UK's Foreign and Commonwealth Office (FCO), and several others amongst us would have made up the difference if only we had known about it in time.

In an attempt to salvage the precarious situation, we planned a return visit shortly afterwards to check on the situation. Stores of bait and traps had been left there, and possibly more bait laying might yet have reversed the failure. However, inexplicably, that was not permitted because the British Indian Ocean Territory (BIOT) ship which would again have transported the personnel was said to have other priorities. It would only have taken a couple of days or less to drop the team, and another couple later to remove them, but, for whatever reason, several months after that, rats were found again, and the island's rat population was back to square one. Naturally, recriminations ran strongly. The NGO chief was summoned to the FCO to explain but failed to turn up. Some in the FCO were dismayed (it was FCO money that had been wasted), and feelings ran high. Money is short in the conservation world.

There may be further reasons for failure, and it may be the case that these factors would have ensured failure in any case. The unavailability of the BIOT ship for a very few days was unclear. There were always other demands on its time, of course, but given the BIOT enthusiasm and support for this project, it did seem strange. There was a different team in charge in the BIOT Government by then, and a sense of continuity and historical memory is not a strong point in BIOT's Administration. Last year's wasted money is, well, a different accounting period after all!

A biological reason for the failure may come from the idea that there are two non-intermixing rat populations, or at least populations that don't mix very much: ground dwellers and tree dwellers. According to this hypothesis, even if the ground population had been eliminated, the subordinate tree dwellers could then colonise the ground over the next several weeks. Perhaps that is what happened, and even if baiting had continued for a month longer, a residue of rats living in the coconut canopy that seldom visited the ground might still have defeated the plan. We don't know.

What next? Rat eradication, initially on much smaller islands, is the answer, where all coconut trees are simultaneously felled to ensure no residual subordinate population hiding away high in the canopy. In 2013, we raised funding for a trial of this method, and a prime candidate, the much smaller Vache Marine island in Peros Banhos atoll, was selected. An eradication took place in 2014, and at the same time, the small number of coconut trees were all cut down too. Several years later, that island remained free of rats. We all hope that this island is well on the way to developing into another bird stronghold and refuge. A couple of tiny islands in eastern Salomon atoll were similarly cleared.

The Eagle Island episode highlighted how challenging it is to eradicate rats once they are established. We were not unusual in failing; other recent example is the failed attempt to remove them on Henderson atoll, part of the Pitcairn Island group in the Pacific, which is another UK Overseas Territory. Much more money was spent on that one. Efforts to eradicate a giant mouse on Gough Island, part of St Helena in the Atlantic, another UK Overseas Territory, appear to have failed too. These mice are just as predatory on the local birds, including albatross chicks in this case, as is the rat in Chagos islands. Plans now have been drafted to eradicate rats for all the islands in Chagos. Only a lack of funding that is preventing the execution of the plans. Carrying out this plan has, for a while, been the role of the Chagos Conservation Trust, under its banner of *Healthy Islands, Healthy Reefs*, a programme that "will rewild 30 islands, increasing the amount of suitable habitat available for nesting birds by 350%." [4].

In Diego Garcia, three large experimental plots on the eastern arm totalling several hectares were cleared of all their palm trees, thus allowing native trees to have a better chance of reaching maturity. Some bird species have slowly been recovering, especially the shrub-nesting Red-footed Booby. These birds seem able to nest successfully despite the presence of rats there. Seedlings of some of the native tree species have been gathered for planting out in the cleared plots. Due to the feral donkeys, descendants of those that used to trudge round and round grinding coconuts, many areas and individual trees were fenced off. Some of these enclosed trees are now several metres tall and flourishing. Some unexpected consequences occur, such as a sudden explosion in number of the vigorous tall shrub *Pipturus*, which is probably a native but usually is kept in check by other plants. In the open and cleared areas, the sudden bright light available to them allows them to swarm upwards by the thousand. These need to be hand pulled as well, which as I can attest, takes hours of hot and exhausting work.

These successful experiments, as well as lessons from the failures, all lead to the conclusion that restoration of the land from the ravages of plantation life can be done. The tiny islands that already allow Chagos islands to support internationally important bird areas could, given the chance, expand astronomically—an inspiring thought.

Is it 'natural' to intervene like this? No, of course, it is not. But nor was the planting of coconuts in the first place, and so it needs intervention again to help restore land to its pre-man condition and thus allow the once huge bird populations to recover. Presumably, the end result will be stability imposed by a mature hardwood forest, but we can expect several more surprises on the way.

As an aside, these experiments were valuable later in the inhabited area of Diego Garcia. There had been a thought that removal of the introduced palms from some areas of the plantations might improve the amount of water available to people from the water lens beneath, correctly assuming that the thousands of palm trees transpire large volumes of water, which is thus not available for human use. However, these experiments showed that the seed density of the *Pipturus* shrubs, which also transpire similar amounts of water, is everywhere very high. Therefore, this measure probably would not have achieved anything in this regard. Thus, a simple (though arduous) experiment in those experimental plots, done for minimal or no cost to any funding agency or government, saved a lot of work and money.

TODAY'S TINY ISLANDS

The Three Brothers on the Great Chagos Bank are my own favourite group of tiny islands in this archipelago, though Sea Cow and Nelsons are close behind. Over them all, thousands of terns form dense clouds above the islands, wheeling apparently pointlessly, landing and taking flight again, depending sometimes on the time of day and on whether they are breeding or not. Sooty terns, especially, flock like this. At times, especially early in the morning and late afternoon, you may see hundreds of boobies departing on fishing trips or returning from them, in huge streams. Accompanying them on their way back to their nests are frigate birds, known sometimes as pirate birds, which harass the boobies to make them disgorge their day's catch, which the frigates then scoop up in mid-air. It seems unfair, like many forms of parasitism, but curiously, these two unrelated bird species roost side by side in the hardwood trees during the day, the boobies making no effort at all to avoid the frigates. It is only when being raided in flight, when boobies are heavily laden with a day's catch, that they try their utmost to avoid the frigates. Often a cheer goes up from our ship when a booby successfully dodges a pursuing frigate and makes it back to its nest without having had to disgorge its fish. But that is a human reaction—the frigate has its own cute and hungry chicks to feed too!

On many of these tiny islands, there is a sandy beach on which to land an inflatable boat. Those islands that are sheltered enough may have large families of nurse sharks in the shallows adjacent to these beaches. However, on some islands, there is no sandy beach, and so landing requires a swim ashore, gripping the rock at the right time, hoping a rogue wave (which may seem to be most of them) doesn't throw you onto something sharp, and scrambling clear before the next breaker comes crashing in. Getting off is no easier either: you jump out as far as you can and swim rapidly outwards to the boat waiting a safe distance off. Only once in a while is the water calm enough to make landing or getting off these small islands perfectly free from risk of cuts, bruises, or even capsize. This difficulty of access is, of course, one reason why these scraps of land were never planted. Evidence of how important ease of access was comes from the fact that on some small and medium-sized islands with an easy landing spot, coconuts were planted for a time, from which coconuts were collected by short-term visiting parties. On Middle Brother, for example, old records show this, and there are also several circular cut pits that were carved out for coconut trees, now long abandoned. On this island, some of these pits are now submerged into the intertidal area due to rising sea levels.

Today, most people are not permitted onto any of these islands under the conservation laws of the Territory. However, botanists, ornithologists, and conservation advisors can visit with permissions, or perhaps someone working on a turtle nesting programme, or a coconut crab count. Occasionally, a marine scientist such as myself might accompany them (Figure 4.3).

Different islands have different populations of birds. North Brother has had a large colony of brown boobies for 40 years at least. These birds are ground nesters, with only

FIGURE 4.3 Tern colony at the eastern tip of Nelsons Island, Great Chagos Bank.

FIGURE 4.4 Part of the Brown Booby colony on North Brother, Great Chagos Bank.

small and untidy collections of twigs or driftwood to mark their lazily built nests. The colony is on the edge of North Brother, extending to the rocky edge, where chicks, eggs, and adults may equal each other in number. They are shy and won't let you get too close, so we walk around the colony, on the perimeter or, when possible, on the beach.

I visited this island and its brown booby colony shortly after the Boxing Day tsunami of 2004 [5]. It looked different. Only adults were there, many sitting on eggs, but there were no newly hatched chicks and no youngsters. I concluded that the tsunami had flooded the site, in which case adults would have flown upward and away from danger, but the flightless chicks and presumably all eggs were destroyed. Three months later, the adults were continuing their normal behaviour and laying eggs and, a year later, in 2006, all was back to normal with every stage of development visible, from eggs, chicks, and nesting adults (Figure 4.4).

North Brother is the island with the most shearwaters too, and this is why nobody should go into the limited amount of interior. The soil there is riddled with shearwater burrows, and you simply could not avoid crushing many chicks if you walked through.

Two islands that are home to the uncommon Masked Booby (Figure 4.5) are very different in character from all the other islands. They are both small, relatively bare rocks, apparently very inhospitable and devoid of anything much taller than a blade of grass, lacking shade and baking hot.

Some shearwaters have been found underground on one of them too, but otherwise, only the very elegantly patterned Masked Booby lives and nests here. In scorching areas such as this, it is particularly important not to disturb the nesting birds: if they fly away for more than a few minutes, their eggs would overheat, killing their embryonic chick. It is for good reasons that landing on such islands is prohibited to all but the fortunate few who have a valid reason to be there and who are fully aware of how to avoid causing disturbance.

However, the bird that has become almost the icon of this archipelago is the Red-footed Booby (Figure 4.6). This bird mainly nests in the shrubs that ring much

FIGURE 4.5 Part of the Masked Booby colony on Resurgent Island in the Three Brothers group.

FIGURE 4.6. Red-footed Boobies nest in shrubs that encircle most of the islands and also in hardwood trees further inland in dense colonies.

of the islands and in hardwood trees. Because they are relatively large birds and are not ground nesters like the other booby species, and perhaps because they have formidable beaks, they can co-exist with rats on islands to a much greater extent than the other species. Their recovery since the islands were depopulated has been remarkable, both in their total number on the islands and in terms of the number of islands that they now inhabit. Figure 4.7 shows the expansion in the number of the islands in Peros Banhos atoll on which this booby has been seen nesting. This atoll has the largest number of islands, most being fairly small. The range expansion now includes all islands except sandbanks, and the number of birds on each has also increased over time.

Another range expansion is seen on Diego Garcia's eastern arm. From about three pairs only in the mid-1980s, there has been a progressive rise in the number of

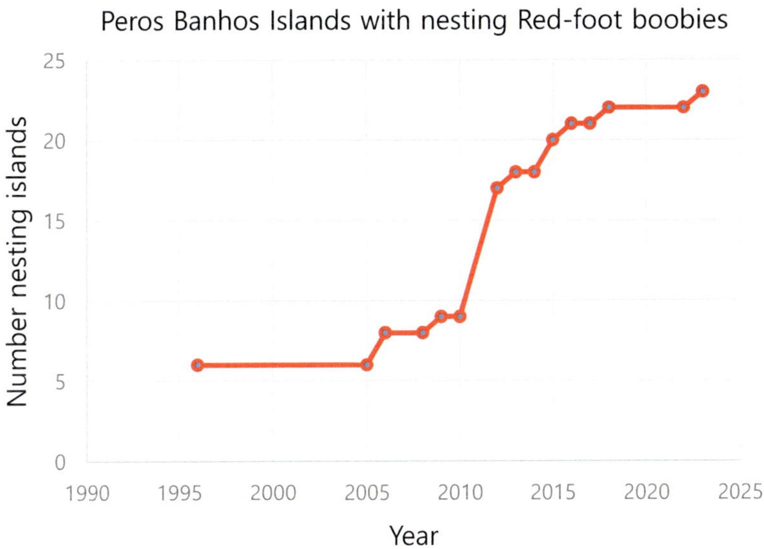

FIGURE 4.7 Graph of the number of islands in Peros Banhos atoll that have been colonised by Red-footed Boobies. Data provided by Dr Pete Carr.

nesting pairs since that region was put out of bounds to military staff and contractors on the military base, so that by 2018, there were about 10,000 breeding pairs. Exact numbers are difficult to plot because Red-footed Boobies show two breeding spikes per year, in about January and July, so both periods need to be added together for an accurate number, and censusing them has been very irregular.

This clearly leads to an important question: what limits the number that the archipelago, and the seas around it, can support? Are they limited by the availability of living space on which to breed and nest, or by the availability of food? Such questions are important in terms of whether it is worth restoring islands and removing rats and coconuts from the many medium-sized islands. To help resolve this, trackers have more recently been placed on Red-footed Boobies from three colonies so that their fishing areas can be determined (Figure 4.8). This shows that although these individual birds travel widely, these colonies do partition the ocean resources to a remarkable degree, with each colony almost reserving to itself different sectors of ocean.

For ground nesters, the predatory rats prevent breeding. By observing instances where this occurs naturally on the smallest islands, we can discern the enormous potential of this archipelago. Several small islands boast beautiful glades, through which numerous noddy terns flit, small brown birds with white caps. These inquisitive birds hover near any visitor. Even more attractive still to many people are the fairy terns, a startling white all over with large black beaks and eyes. These are the laziest nest builders of all, simply laying their eggs on almost any tree branch that provides a dent big enough to stop the egg rolling off. Many so-called nests appear impossibly precarious, but they clearly work because the fairy terns are abundant and widespread throughout the islands. Even on islands with rats, they may be found high in the trees.

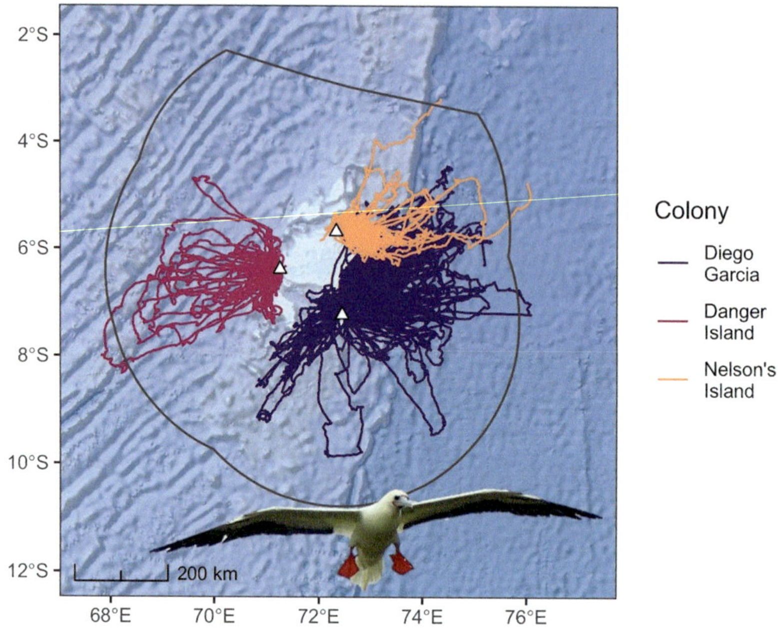

FIGURE 4.8 Radio tracks of radio-tagged members of three different colonies of Red-footed Booby, showing that each colony fishes over a different patch of ocean. Courtesy Prof. Graeme Hays. Published in Hays et al. 2020. *Marine Biology* 167: 159. https://doi.org/10.1007/s00227-020-03776-w.

These small, bird-packed islands have also yielded other important results, the nutrients that run-off from such islands exhibit a different balance compared to those from islands where there are no birds but only rats. On nearby reefs, the growth of corals and fish surpasses that on reefs near islands with no birds. All types of feeding fish benefit from the presence of birds, and recovery from the mass mortalities that follow warming events also witnesses improvement [6]. The benefits derived from maintaining robust bird populations are multiple.

POTENTIAL VALUE OF THE ISLANDS

If restoration of the island vegetation and the removal of rats can be achieved, the result will significantly increase the ornithological value of the archipelago. Very few examples remain anywhere of Indian Ocean Island native hardwood forest. Most have long since been felled or severely disturbed by mankind in their struggle to make a living from these places.

On several islands in the tropics, there have been attempts to open tourist areas and conservation areas that might attract a paying public. Many have been successful, though some have been rather sad efforts, as they begin with only small remnants of original fauna and flora. From giant islands like the heavily impacted Madagascar [7] to small ones throughout the world, numerous areas still contain fragments of pre-man fauna and flora. Sometimes, this might be extensive, but alleged 'primary forest reserves' can be secondary forests themselves, many started during colonial times from remnants and only now reaching some semblance of maturity with attractive wildlife abundance. However, even small-scale interference by humans has a significant impact, and it would be beneficial to leave some unimpacted or properly restored for the benefit of future generations. The smallest, unspoiled Chagos islands remain a beacon of hope in this regard.

The islands and their surrounding seas have been provisionally assigned monetary values as well [8]. "Estimated possible annual economic flows of several hundred million pounds, with an economic value in excess of £1 billion, with the benefits accruing both regionally in the southwest Indian Ocean and globally" have been calculated. We arrived at this assessment through clearly laid-out methods and reasoning because the important decision makers are, inevitably, accountants, politicians, and others, people who may not necessarily understand our world in any meaningful way. This value is attributed to the region as a whole and arises from Chagos serving as a reservoir set amid an ocean of 'biodiversity disasters'. It should not be assumed, for example, that tourist visits to the archipelago itself could bring in even a tiny fraction of this amount. It represents an ecological value.

REFERENCES

[1] Carr P. 2011. *Guide to Birds of the British Indian Ocean Territory*. Bedford, UK, Pisces Publications for Royal Society for the Protection of Birds, 110 pp.
[2] Bellamy DJ. 1979. *Half of Paradise*. London, Cassell Ltd, pp. 192.
[3] Wenban Smith N, Carter M. 2015. *Chagos: A History. Exploration, Exploitation, Expulsion*. London, Chagos Conservation Trust, pp. 550.
[4] https://chagos-trust.org/our-work/healthyislands.
[5] Sheppard CRC. 2007. Effects of the tsunami in the Chagos Archipelago. *Atoll Research Bulletin* 544: 135–148.
[6] Graham NAJ, Wilson SK, Carr P, Hoey AS, Jennings S, MacNeil MA. 2018. Seabirds enhance coral reef productivity and functioning in the absence of invasive rats. *Nature* 559: 250–253. **And:**
BenkwittCE, Wilson SK, Graham NAJ. 2019. Seabird nutrient subsidies alter patterns of algal abundance and fish biomass on coral reefs following a bleaching event. *Global Change Biology*. https://doi.org/10.1111/gcb.14643. **And:**
BenkwittCE, Carr P, Wilson SK, Graham NAJ. 2022. Seabird diversity and biomass enhance cross-ecosystem nutrient subsidies. *Proceedings of the Royal Society B: Biological Sciences* 289. https://doi.org/10.1098/rspb.2022.0195.
[7] WWF/ZSL. 2018. The Living Planet Index database. www.livingplanetindex.org.
[8] Gravestock P, Sheppard CRC. 2015. Valuing the ecosystem services of the Chagos: A review of challenges and estimates. *Marine Ecology Progress Series* 530: 255–270.

5 Coral Reefs of Chagos

British Indian Ocean Territory (BIOT) has a wealth of coral reefs. In fact, BIOT is made of them, and the territory exists only because of them. Apart from the odd fragment of pumice that has floated in from volcanoes in areas such as Indonesia, and apart from building materials and rocks imported to Diego Garcia to combat sea-level rise and shoreline erosion, there is no rock of any kind in the archipelago other than the limestone derived from both new and ancient coral reefs. Furthermore, the islands' continued existence is dependent upon their corals remaining healthy, as without them, they would not last long before becoming overwhelmed by the ocean (Figure 5.1).

The reefs and the abundant marine life have always been the main attraction of the place for most visiting scientists, and they are the primary focus of the research I have conducted there. These elements have been the central theme of the programme that we have developed over the years.

These extensive coral reefs provide a habitat for a much greater diversity of marine life than exists anywhere else in Britain and its widespread territories. This is because, at higher taxonomic levels, coral reefs have a greater diversity of life than any other ecosystem in the world. The tropics are richer than areas closer towards the poles, and Indian Ocean reefs contain many more species than those in the entire Caribbean. Britain's Territory of Pitcairn in the Pacific, the next richest, is simply too far east to match the diversity of life in the central Indian Ocean. BIOT comes out on top, by a considerable margin.

Reefs create a vast array of different niches for all forms of life, from fishes to a multitude of invertebrates. The reefs in the archipelago are spread over at least 60,000 km^2 of the photic zone, which is the zone of relatively shallow water down to

FIGURE 5.1 Many thousands of hectares of coral reef build the Chagos Archipelago.

DOI: 10.1201/9781003423300-5

about 50 or even 80 m deep. These depths are where light penetrates strongly enough to support photosynthesis. This shallow area is not only found around the islanded atolls but includes many reefs, banks, and submerged atolls too. We have visited most over the years.

The photic zone here contains lush coral gardens, seagrass beds, and associated ecosystems. Much of the floor of some Chagos atoll lagoons were (until recent ocean heatwaves) almost totally packed with living corals, mixed with sandy patches. A surprise in the 1970s was that the lagoon of Salomon appeared to be almost entirely coral-covered, and wide patches of corals also existed in the much larger lagoon of Peros Banhos down to all depths of 45–50 m. This contrasted with ideas at the time that held that lagoon floors were usually covered in sand and sediment.

There are few expanses of seagrass near the islands, but it covers large areas many kilometres away from land. Reasons for this distribution remain unknown but are possibly attributable to chemicals such as nitrates and phosphates in rainwater runoff from the islands. This has not been tested, but the presence and correct balance of these fertilising chemicals is known to be crucial to other processes too. Seagrasses are integral to a thriving coral reef. In the whole reef complex, the part dominated by coral itself might cover a relatively small portion of the total area. The sandy and seagrass areas may not look as colourful or vibrant as the reefs, but they are vital habitats to a range of life forms, many of which move between them and the reefs for different parts of their life cycle, or even daily. They are also important in terms of nutrient turnover and retention.

A vastly greater area of substrate lies deeper still, where light is dim, although that area remains almost completely unexplored at present. So-called 'soft sediments' of sands, muds, and clays made of ever smaller particles dominate in deeper water, but they are far from lifeless. These areas are churned continuously by animals living and burrowing within them and by predators hunting for those species. Contrast this huge area with only 60 km^2 of islands, and you can see why the main ecological importance of this archipelago lies in these submerged areas rather than the ecologically damaged islands. During our visits to the reefs in the 1970s, our daily surveys extended to 45 m depth. Very occasionally, several of us dived deeper where we saw, in these very clear waters, fields of corals covering about a third of the reef slope even to 60 m deep. We don't dive that deep now; we know much more about the dangers and risks of doing so, but in the 1970s, most health and safety issues were still in the future.

We keep finding new surprises every time we visit. It was on some reefs lying much further from islands where I first found huge beds of sea grass; these are flowering plants that evolved from terrestrial forms, developing dense 'lawns' over extensive areas. Being land plants, they have flowers, though these are inconspicuous, and seagrasses have extensive networks of roots that bind and stabilise the sediments. Amongst their blades, they provide another and different kind of habitat for more and different species. The areas of fine sand here are scarce in shallower waters because of the usually vigorous wave energy that would sweep it away; yet all these areas too are part of the greater reef system. The sand or mud plains have coverings of simple algae and are also highly productive when they are shallow enough to receive adequate light.

The area is so vast that we have only been able to explore a miniscule part of it. Our lack of widespread exploration is only partly due to its sheer size; another reason is that on our expeditions, we deliberately return mostly to the same places again and again for reasons of continuity. This is because although one-off observations are important, it is trends and changes over longer periods of time that provide us with much more information, and you need to return to the same place each time to get a fair comparison between years.

Determining trends and trajectories is important. For example, we might find out what the amount of coral is at a site, or perhaps the density of new corals that settled on reefs this year, but knowing the trend of these factors over long periods of time—whether it is declining or perhaps recovering—is much more important information for many scientific and management purposes than is a one-off 'snap shot' of what its condition is at the time of a single survey.

However, the archipelago is basically built by corals, specifically by their limestone skeletons which become ground down by waves and by boring animals and plants, and then bind together back into solid rock through several processes. It is these areas that have drawn most of our scientific attention.

THE EARLIEST SCIENTISTS

The earliest visits were carried out well before the invention of SCUBA, and these were a key starting point for us. New science builds on old, after all—no scientist works in isolation. These early visits were mostly to Diego Garcia, with the most notable amongst them being those by the reef geographers Bourne in the late 1800s [1], Gardiner and colleagues early in the 20th century [2], and then Professor David Stoddart and his team in 1968, which included several marine scientists [3]. Frazer came to study turtles [4], and Kohn [5] came to study molluscs in the mid-20th century. Of these visits, the largest was by J. Stanley Gardiner on the Percy Sladen Trust expedition. His write-up was contained in several volumes, which, however, did not appear until 30 years later. This delay was attributed, he said, to the war and other events (which is an interesting commentary on the more leisurely pace of ecological and biological science a century ago compared with today!) It contained several useful descriptions of the atolls and added greatly to the knowledge of atolls generally. However, none of these visits could look at the reefs below extremely shallow depths—they could explore little further than wading depths, in fact—which meant that they missed most marine life completely.

THE 1970s REEF EXPEDITIONS

A lot of work was achieved by a few of us in the 1970s during a series of three military expeditions. These expeditions were principally for joint services adventure training, but they also offered a few places to scientists. Our inclusion with the military added a significant benefit to the expeditions: the military divers gained an additional rational for participating, while scientists benefitted from the undreamed-of logistics and substantial quantities of equipment and manpower for research. Started by David Bellamy, the first expedition was based on Egmont atoll in 1972 in the southwest of the archipelago, and most members were scuba divers. Significant ornithological and botanical work was conducted, but of greatest interest to divers was the realisation of the incredibly rich, colourful, and thriving reefs and of the glorious diving experience available. A second expedition, based on Eagle Island on the Great Chagos Bank, was arranged for 1975, and this was my first visit to the place as Prof Bellamy's student. Our task was to initiate an inventory of the corals and to plot the zonation of the corals, which changes according to depth and exposure to waves.

I remember the first time I saw the island in early dawn from the deck of the ship taking us there: warm, covered with palms. It looked magical to me. We brought ashore all we would need in inflatable boats from the ship, including a recompression chamber in case of diving accidents (which fortunately wasn't needed). We were living in tents in this, the rainiest part of the Indian Ocean, and food for all 18 of us was basically tinned rations. We had several large inflatable boats from which to dive each day, and crucially, these first two expeditions were both supported by an extremely generous couple named Warren and Tue Blake, with their own yacht and crew. This ketch, the *Four Friends*, supplied inter-island transport, and we were taken to the archipelago on a Royal Fleet Auxiliary supply ship from Mauritius (which would not happen now!) It was called *Resurgent*, and a new island that we found, recorded as being just a shoal by Moresby over 100 years earlier, was named after her.

The diving was indeed fabulous, though I accept that I, like most people, might view past wonders with exaggerated views, and we managed to conduct much basic work on coral zonation. Subsequently, the military diving organisation wanted to repeat this expedition and again invited us to provide a scientific rationale to add to the adventure training element for the Forces.

This one was scheduled for 1978. With David Bellamy, we put forward a proposal that it should be a phased one lasting nearly a year. The justification I presented in a presentation given to the General in charge of the Joint Services Adventure Training was that Mother Nature works on annual cycles, so it would be good to observe changes that occurred over this time. That was rather naïve, I now know, because seasonal changes are not very great in this tropical region, much less than seasonal changes are in higher latitudes, but it was approved.

Then David Bellamy had to back out. I had obtained my doctorate by then, and I was asked to lead it—lead on the scientific side, that is, because it was still primarily a military adventure training expedition. It was a daunting task considering my youth and inexperience.

This took place in 1978–1979 to the two northern atolls of Peros Banhos and Salomon, and this also was made possible by another very generous person, Peter Winch, with his large yacht, the *Paille en Queue*, which is the Creole name for one of the Tropic Birds. This was used for all inter-island travel again and for changing personnel to Diego Garcia.

Much early reef science was facilitated, therefore, not by official funding but by a few benefactors at significant cost to themselves, especially the last one due to its length and the number of people involved. Significant funding was also generously given to us by David Bellamy from royalties on his book about the first two expeditions [6]. Some significant work was done, with several publications resulting from it. We filled several gaps in the knowledge of how reefs worked.

REEF CORALS IN THE SUNLIT CORAL GARDENS

Most of my own work was with corals in the mid-depths, where the turbulence that exists in the shallows has diminished but where light is still strong. One part of that was to improve the inventory of corals and their zonation again, now that more detailed taxonomy guides were available [7]. Coral taxonomy keeps progressing, however, so the list produced then has since been developed further. Results also provided an inventory of molluscs and revealed their broad distribution patterns too, in a way that matched coral zonation [8].

My main interest at this time was in the interactions between different coral species [9]. Aggressive interactions between coral species are a phenomenon that had been recently discovered in the Caribbean. These interactions occur where corals, when growing towards other species of corals, will engage in a battle with them for space (Figure 5.2). They can do this in several ways: the polyps closest to the encroaching species can open a cavity in their body wall and throw digestive filaments from their gut over the encroaching threat. This can happen overnight when one coral is knocked over by a fish, perhaps, and tumbles down the slope to land beside another. It is more easily studied when observed after one is placed next to another in an aquarium, such as those we constructed using sandbags, plastic sheeting, and pumps on Peros Banhos. Another way of fighting involves the development of very long sweeper tentacles around the colony's periphery that are loaded with poison-filled stinging darts. These sweeper tentacles then brush over the encroaching colony, killing the polyps on its advancing edge.

This method stops the encroachment, but the mechanism takes a couple of weeks to develop. When it does develop, however, it has a much longer reach than does the method of using digestive filaments. Corals whose normal tentacles are usually only a few

FIGURE 5.2 Several slow-growing massive forms of corals can prevent themselves from being overtopped and shaded by using long sweeper tentacles to kill and prevent themselves from being overgrown by the fast-growing table coral.

FIGURE 5.3 The Chagos Brain coral, *Ctenella chagius*, once common but now one of the world's most endangered coral species because of its limited distribution.

millimetres long may develop sweepers that are 10 cm long. This form of attack is longer range, slower, but quite fast enough to counter a coral growing slowly towards it. There is a consistent hierarchy between different pairs of species: species A might always kill B, but never the other way around. This is one reason why so many different corals can exist on one reef, why the fastest growers or those that produce the most larvae do not always dominate; a small one with slow growth, for example, may hold its own using these and other mechanisms. I took this work further later on [10] and showed that there is a continuous ebb and flow of different species on any point on the reef: there may be a similar per cent cover overall from one year to the next, but the colonies at any one point may change every few years. It is a constant battle with changing occupancy at every point. It may seem very slow to us, but the highly dynamic nature of the reef is maintained.

I also studied the beautiful brain coral *Ctenella chagius* (Figure 5.3) that was thought to live only in this group of reefs [11]. It has been found on the Saya de Malha Banks further to west but is basically a Chagos endemic. It was one of the commonest corals on reefs almost everywhere, both on reef slopes facing open ocean and in lagoons at most depths. It is somehow a very delicate species, and we found that no matter how hard we tried, it would not survive being moved into the large open water aquaria system we had constructed on land, an aquarium where all other species thrived.

CORALS AT THE EXTREMES: THE SHALLOWEST CORALS

On the reef flats of Chagos atolls, there are very few corals indeed. These flats are very broad in places and are always shallow; in places, they dry at low spring tides. The timing of when they dry and become exposed to the air is critical. In this central Indian Ocean region, this commonly happens late in the morning, not at solar noon but late enough in the morning when the sun is high. This is when water temperatures in these shallows can become very warm, even hot—over 40°C. Corals cannot live in these temperatures even if they remain covered by water. Sometimes, in a depression on the reef flat, near a pass perhaps, where water flow remains high, one or two species do manage to survive, but these are usually small. The main inhabitants here that live attached to the reef are a cup-shaped sponge called *Phyllospongia*, small grey whorls, the size of a teacup, and these can be quite abundant. Otherwise, moray eels, crabs, molluscs, and some trapped fish are most of what can be seen on the shallowest parts. Moray eel feeding behaviour here can be especially spectacular as they slither over the rocks to ambush and eat the crabs [12].

On reef flats where it is slightly deeper, some corals, notably the massive-shaped *Porites* boulders, develop growth forms called 'micro-atolls'. These may extend nearly 2 m in diameter. Because their growth form is usually hemispherical and because their tops cannot grow above the lowest tides, they cannot form their usual domed form and can only grow out laterally. Their tops stop at the tide level, and then become gradually eroded, resulting in a ring-shaped structure in the shallow water. Several species can grow in this shape, but it is the grey *Porites* that can take this to the greatest degree. Some of the species here are some of the most heat-resistant of all corals.

In the days before SCUBA diving, the reef flats were really the only part of the whole coral reef system that could be visited. Photos in old books exist of 19th-century naturalists working on reef flats dressed appropriately for the time but very impractically in boots, plus-fours, and hats, sheltering from the sun under an umbrella perhaps, measuring distances with a theodolite. Regardless of their undoubted skills, they cannot be described as studying the reefs per se. This is because they would have missed the vast bulk of the reef ecosystem and could not have observed most of the extensive biodiversity found a little deeper than their reachable depth. Perhaps, their limitations could be likened to studying the Amazon rainforest only from the edge of a roadside, never able to venture further in. The corals and other attached organisms on the reef flats differ significantly from those found in deeper waters where there are more favourable conditions. Some individuals did manage to peer deeper, usually from a boat, leading them to marvel at the richness and vibrancy of what they encountered. The advent of SCUBA allowed us to transform our understanding of reefs.

At the seaward edge of the reef flat, changes occur rapidly. The most turbulent and stormy areas on the reefs are those facing the open ocean rather than facing the lagoon, occurring where the reef flat meets the descending reef slope, known as the reef crest. Corals in this zone were the least studied anywhere in the world when we first went to the Chagos Archipelago, simply because of difficulties and even dangers of access. This area is where the spur and groove system on stormy reefs develops (Figure 5.4). These fascinating structures are constructed from calcareous red algae, sometimes called stony algae, and experiments on their strength and solidity have demonstrated that they can be as hard as concrete. Some say that it is this toughness and resistance to strong wave energy that permits reefs to exist at all, and some marine botanists used to suggest that coral reefs should really be renamed algal reefs. On the calmest days, I snorkelled amongst them and mapped the spur and groove system along with the corals that grew in them [13]. The algal-made spurs join onto and are confluent with a broad algal ridge, made of the same species of stony red algae, but which runs parallel to the edge of the reef flat. Together, these structures may encircle the entire atoll, except where one or two passes permit passage through into the lagoon.

FIGURE 5.4 From the broad red algal ridge in Diego Garcia, long spurs constructed from the same algae are seen projecting seawards.

They are not only highly resistant to strong wave energy, but these algae, in fact, require high turbulence. They do not grow in calmer waters. The spacing between the spurs and their size is intriguing: they are structured such that the back swash of one wave meets the next oncoming wave, dissipating much of the wave's energy. This spacing varies with the generally prevailing wave energy and seems to be a complicated function of the average wavelength. The result is that much of the incoming and very erosive wave energy of each wave is cancelled out by the backwash of the wave before it. Even on the calmest of days, snorkelling in this area is hazardous, and you may finish only when you start feeling a little seasick. Corals there are relatively sparse, with a much-reduced complement of different species. Those that can manage to grow there include, perhaps surprisingly, forms that are branching when they grow deeper. Their growth forms in this location are extremely squat and stunted.

CORALS AT THE EXTREMES: THE DEEPEST CORALS

During the expeditions of the 1970s, we routinely surveyed the reefs to 45 m depth, usually conducting surveys twice daily. At 45 m depth, coral cover was commonly still as high as 75% in these clear waters. From that depth we could see clearly further down another 15 m or more on the steep slopes, and noted coral cover was still 25% at about 60 m depth where light dimmed severely [14]. At these depths, there was only a little blue light remaining. Light progressively dims with increasing depth, but it changes in quality too because water differentially absorbs longer-wavelength light. Red disappears first, so nearly none is left at 10 m depth, followed by green wavelengths, leaving only blue at the greatest depths to which light can penetrate. This is why underwater photographs have a blue shade, unless strong flashlights or torches are used. Even then, only nearby objects can have their red colours 'painted' back.

FIGURE 5.5 Colonies of leafy corals grow out from the deeper reef slope. Growing horizontally would allow them to catch more light but would also catch more sediment and kill them. An angle of 45° is common.

Here, most corals take on leafy forms, spreading out their whorls to capture what remains of the sunlight at this depth (Figure 5.5). However, the whorls or leaves must still retain enough slope to help them shed settling sediment. Most corals still rely on sunlight for photosynthesis, and many contain high densities of algae cells for this purpose.

This gives most leafy corals a fairly dull grey-brown appearance. However, some corals, notably of the genus *Madracis*, stand out by glowing a startling bright orange in the dim blue. They resemble bright beacons in the general blue twilight. This occurs for two reasons: firstly, these corals were fluorescing. Fluorescence happens when pigments in the corals capture ambient light and then re-emit that energy in another colour. In shallow water, many, perhaps most corals develop fluorescent pigments that capture and re-emit light in this way, but usually, the algae in their tissues then capture it immediately and use it in their photosynthesis. Usually, this light is absorbed almost completely by the algae, so we do not see it. However, in these deep and dim waters, this species of *Madracis* does not contain symbiotic algae. Thus, the fluorescence escapes from the coral. Secondly, the overall light level here is so low that only a feeble glow becomes highly conspicuous when the divers' eyes are dark-adapted; in shallower water. Such dim fluorescence is simply swamped. Adding to the eerie sight in deep water, this species grew most commonly on dead branches of large seafans, elevated off the seafloor by a metre or so. Their preferred elevated location enables them to better trap any passing food since they cannot photosynthesise any for themselves. The effect is to produce a scene of glowing, orange beacons on the dim reef between 45 and about 60 m.

Some of us did dive occasionally to depths deeper than 45 m during days when decompression sickness (the 'bends') was less well understood. Our precautions were extensive, and our dive durations down there were very short, fortunately uneventful from a safety standpoint. We would not dive that deep now. However, at that time, dives to 45 m twice daily were our normal maximum depth and was designed into our weekly programme. Even this, we now know, can lead to a potentially hazardous build-up of nitrogen in our tissues. Indeed, some of us who had been engaging in this practice twice daily for over a week all developed 'niggles' after a while, indicating early stages of too much nitrogen in the blood trying to escape. A day or two of land-based camp duties without diving eliminated these symptoms.

Many years later when I was permitted to restart some expeditions, I was asked to propose a diving plan. This had to be very safe indeed, for I knew that any incident whatsoever would lead the authorities to immediately prevent any more diving from that time onwards; at that time, they were not enthusiastic about allowing us into the archipelago in any case. So, my rule was that nobody would be permitted to go beyond 25 m depth and, furthermore, no diving was permitted that would take a person into decompression requirements. Another rule was that on every dive, everybody would still do a decompression stop at 5 m deep for three minutes, to ease the rate at which nitrogen can leave the body. There were no incidents in several thousand dives.

LASTING IMPRESSIONS

The work we conducted during the extended trip from 1978 to 1979 not only advanced the understanding of Chagos but, I like to think, also expanded the knowledge of coral reefs in general. While the primary focus was on corals as they are the building blocks of the archipelago, we also had leading fish biologists and taxonomists [15], oceanographers, conservation ecologists [16], algae specialists and some island botanists. The number of resulting publications roughly reflects the scientific productivity of the team. The military personnel on the expeditions were almost all divers who provided support and undertook a significant portion of the logistics, administration, radio operation, and cooking.

We dived extensively, even on Christmas Day when the scientific work gave way to an underwater obstacle course and treasure hunt, a nice change from the routine recording work. The General in charge of adventure training had emphasised that the science recording work was the reason for allowing so many people to go on this expedition, as he had mentioned to me before departure. True to his words, the work was accomplished. On Christmas Day, mysteriously, some bow ties materialised—not necessarily accompanied by a shirt, but then you can't have everything.

A different General visited us for a couple of weeks about halfway through. I remember with some pain the amount of attention that was given to neatly arranging whitewashed rocks along the sides of the main paths we had cut. The General wanted to go diving and selected me to accompany him as his diving partner. Despite having no dive training, one does not say no to a General. Luckily for me, he survived, despite his tendency to dash off into deeper water to see this or that colourful fish. Consequently, he may not have been the most relaxing dive buddy, even though he was one of the most charming. The enthusiasm with which he spoke later about his experience was nice to hear.

On this long expedition, led by the late Major John Griffiths, we were based mainly in western Peros Banhos atoll. We also made extended trips to Salomon atoll, the smaller but very attractive atoll to the East, perhaps the most attractive, likely because it is small enough to see the islands all the way around its rim from any one

FIGURE 5.6 A reef slope in Chagos dominated by soft corals. These have skeletons made of a gelatinous substance rather than limestone, so they do not help build the reef structure.

point. However, both these atolls were mostly devoid of birds, turtles, and coconut crabs except, again on some smaller islands. These animals had mostly disappeared during the plantation days which, after all, had ended only a very few years previously, and these animals did not yet show much sign of recovery. However, underwater, the scene all around these atolls and around one or two of the offshore banks and drowned atolls was always one of dazzling richness, colour, and abundance of marine life. Colour comes particularly from a range of soft corals (Figure 5.6) as well as many of the stony corals, sponges, and algae.

In the 1970s, there seemed to be none of the problems and objections from three governments involved (the UK government, the USA, and the BIOT government) or from some in the military that we later encountered about going there and using Diego Garcia as our transit point. This was probably because these were basically military expeditions, with a few scientists tagging along for the ride. We were always made very welcome. Generous were the activities offered to us to help pass a few days while waiting to depart for home at the end, such as day-long flights in aircraft that circumnavigated much of the Indian Ocean, dropping listening and weather sets of instruments at regular intervals.

There were some oddities at that time in the main centre of activity: the developing military facility in Diego Garcia. No women were allowed on Diego Garcia amongst either the military or its numerous civilian contractors, and the few women passing through on our expeditions were kept in secure quarters. The construction battalions building the base on Diego Garcia were considered to be a somewhat rough lot. The women had several trips out each day, always escorted, and were also looked after very well by the British military stationed there. There were some amusing episodes as a result. My wife, Anne, was asked if she would do some live announcing on Diego Garcia's radio station. She happily agreed to do so, but the snag was, she said, that she was asked to read out letters from wives and girlfriends in a sexy, sultry voice from 5 o'clock in the morning. She obliged, but five in the morning, she said, was not her best time for sexy or sultry. Sleepy and groggy was more like it.

Anne was also asked to talk down an aircraft when visiting the control tower of the airfield. This would not be something you would normally do at a busy airport, I suspect, but flights were infrequent enough that it all seemed rather informal. On one aircraft's approach, she was handed the microphone and told "repeat after me" by the controller. She did exactly that and when the plane landed with a lot of bouncing the control tower staff remarked that it was the worst landing they had ever seen. The flight crew then ran up into the control tower, stared for a while, and exclaimed "it really is a woman".

Diego Garcia had a frontier town atmosphere. The construction work that the Seabees (Construction Battalions) were tasked with was clearly hard and very hot. Gradually, over the 1970s, the military base was built in the northwest part of the island, over land that had formerly been coconut plantations.

However, that was Diego Garcia nearly half a century ago. No longer a frontier construction site, service women abound today, now that it is a settled military facility. Even now though, nobody can have their married spouse there. We only went there at the beginning or end of an expedition or during a changeover of scientists. Almost all our research was done in the northern atolls.

Together with the events in Diego Garcia, the main impression that I retain from the 1970s, nearly a half century later, is the vibrancy and colour of the coral reefs.

In all atolls in the 1970s, particularly noteworthy was the number of sharks seen on almost every dive. Five, 10, 20 or even more would have been common, and the record number I saw on one dive exceeded 100, and I have photographs to prove it. On such occasions, we would cautiously leave the water. Every diving team, usually of two or three scientists, would have a dive leader who acted as shark guard, whose role was to get into the water first, leave last, and keep an eye out for trouble throughout. These shark guards were necessary. We soon learned what kind of things attracted them, such as noises, and we swiftly recognised their different behaviour as they either just cruised by or behaved in an agitated way, demonstrating an aggressive mood with depressed pectoral fins and an arched body. Luckily, we never had any attacks, though there were one or two worrying incidents as we left the water at the end of a dive. Sometimes, I took a turn as shark guard when I found I had to prod sharks away from my colleagues on several occasions using the 2 m-long 'bang stick' that the shark guard always carried. This had a single .303 rifle round at its tip, with a safety catch that was always securely locked, even when we had to prod away curious sharks. We sometimes would take the safety off when we became especially worried, at which point, the shark guard who was also the dive leader would signal to the others to wrap up the work and end the dive. But nobody ever had to hit a shark with safety off, which would detonate its single .303 round. This was fortunate; one wonders what might happen if several sharks were interested and one was killed or dying. A feeding frenzy would certainly ensue, as sharks would rapidly devour the killed or injured one. That this would happen was demonstrated on several occasions when our fish scientists used hook and line to collect some sharks. It was common for them to pull up just a portion of that shark after some of it had been eaten by others during the few seconds it took to land it on the boat. One Royal Navy colleague was fishing in the lagoon from an inflatable for something to supplement his military rations when a shark lunged at his latest catch, which he had pulled up to the inflatable side tube; three teeth punctured the tube causing him to paddle carefully and quickly home!

These expeditions took place before BIOT had any patrol vessel, which was why our transportation to the atolls from Diego Garcia and between atolls and offshore banks depended on private yachts on all three expeditions. Of the first two expeditions, David Bellamy writes a full and proper mention of the yacht and its crew in his book *Half of Paradise* [6]. Throughout the 1970s, the BIOT Administration was totally dependent on the generous acts of these private yacht owners for obtaining any environmental information on its territory. However, at that time, the BIOT Administration's only concern was about the military base in Diego Garcia. Because there was no patrol vessel in those early days, it did not even monitor its waters for poaching, for example, and this was before any satellites existed that might have been used for that purpose. Officers in Diego Garcia told me that Russian 'trawlers' festooned with antennae regularly passed by Diego Garcia during the height of the Cold War. In a biological sense, the BIOT Administration really had no idea what it had in terms of biological richness at that time—because nobody did. Most reefs in the Indian Ocean were probably in similarly good condition at that time, but until our research began, we were quite unaware that the UK had a biological treasure trove that was to become so important a few decades in the future.

REFERENCES

[1] Bourne GC. 1886. General observations on the fauna of Diego Garcia, Chagos group. *Proceedings Zooofical Society London* 1886: 331–334.

[2] Gardiner JS, Cooper CF. 1907. Description of the expedition. (The Percy Sladen Expedition to the Indian Ocean in 1905.) *Transactions Linnean Society London, Zoology* 12: 1–56, 111–175.

[3] Stoddart DR. 1971. Geography and ecology of Diego Garcia atoll, Chagos Archipelago. *Atoll Research Bulletin* 149: 176.

[4] Frazier J. 1980. Exploitation of marine turtles in the Indian Ocean. *Human Ecology* 8: 329–370. **And:**
Frazier J. 1982. Status of sea turtles in the central western Indian Ocean. In: Bjorndal KA (ed.) *Biology and Conservation of Sea Turtles.* Washington, DC, Smithsonian Institution Press, pp. 385–389.

[5] Kohn AJ. 1963. Notes on Indian Ocean atolls visited by the Yale Seychelles expedition. *Atoll Research Bulletin* 101: 12.

[6] Bellamy DJ. 1979. *Half of Paradise*. London, Cassell Ltd, pp. 192.

[7] Sheppard CRC. 1981. The reef and soft substrate coral fauna of Chagos, Indian Ocean. *Journal of Natural History* 15: 607–621.

[8] Sheppard ALS. 1984. The molluscan fauna of Chagos (Indian Ocean) and an analysis of its broad distribution patterns. *Coral Reefs* 3: 43–50.

[9] Sheppard CRC. 1979. Interspecific aggression between reef corals with reference to their distribution. *Marine Ecology Progress Series* 1: 237–247. **And:**
Sheppard CRC. 1982. "Reach" of aggressively interacting corals, and relative importance of interactions at different depths. *Proceedings of 4th International Symposium on Corals and Coral Reefs* 2: 363–368.

[10] Sheppard CRC. 1982. Coral populations on reef slopes and their major controls. *Marine Ecology Progress Series* 7: 83–115. **And:**
Sheppard CRC. 1985. Unoccupied substrate in the central Great Barrier reef: Role of coral interactions. *Marine Ecology Progress Series* 25: 259–268.
[11] Sheppard CRC, Drew E, Dinesen Z. 1984. Ecology and physiology of the scleractinian coral *Ctenella chagius* (Matthai). *Bulletin of Marine Science* 3: 905–918.
[12] Graham NAJ, Purkis SJ, Harris A. 2009. Diurnal, land-based predation on shore crabs by moray eels in the Chagos Archipelago. *Coral Reefs* 28: 397.
[13] Sheppard CRC. 1981. The groove and spur structures of Chagos atolls and their coral zonation. *Estuarine and Coastal and Shelf Science* 12: 549–560.
[14] Sheppard CRC. 1980. Coral cover, zonation and diversity on reef slopes of Chagos atolls, and population structures of the major species. *Marine Ecology Progress Series* 2: 193–205.
[15] Winterbottom R. 1984. A review of the gobiid fish genus *Trimma* from the Chagos Archipelago, central Indian Ocean, with descriptions of seven new species. *Canadian Journal of Zoology* 62: 695–715. **And:**
Winterbottom R, Emery AR. 1985. Review of the gobioid fishes of the Chagos Archipelago, Central Indian Ocean. *Royal Ontario Museum. Life Sciences Contributions 142*: 82. **And:**
Winterbottom R, Emery AR, Holm E. 1989. An annotated checklist of the fishes of the Chagos Archipelago, Central Indian Ocean. *Royal Ontario Museum. Life Sciences Contributions 145*: 226. **And:**
Winterbottom R, Anderson RC. 1997. A revised checklist of the epipelagic and shore fishes of the Chagos Archipelago, Central Indian Ocean. *Ichthyological Bulletin* 66: 1–28.
[16] Salm R. 1980. The genus-area relation of corals in reefs of the Chagos Archipelago, Indian Ocean. PhD thesis. John Hopkins University.

6 Dark Ages and Enlightenment

THE DARK AGES

There was a large gap of 17 years before we could revisit. It was 1996 before the next expedition, and if any science happened at all during that interval, even in Diego Garcia, nothing of significance was published. I don't know why expeditions stopped, but those were still Cold War days, and in any case, I think the Joint Services Expeditions scheme was suffering from economy cuts. Many other Joint Services Expeditions took place in nearer European locations, and I participated in a few to Gibraltar, France, Italy, and parts of the UK itself. I was not the only scientist who benefitted from this, and I wonder how many people are aware that the military, via this means, contributed significantly to marine ecological research in the UK during the early days of SCUBA diving!

However, no further expeditions were conducted to Chagos. Personally, I never thought that I would have the opportunity to return there, although I frequently spoke and lectured about the wonders of the place. In my own case, my research had shifted its focus to the Great Barrier Reef, Arabian countries including the full length of the Red Sea, some countries around the Indian Ocean rim, as well as several Caribbean islands and reefs. All areas were highly interesting from the point of view of marine science. Importantly, they provided the immense advantage of making me aware of the extent of regional differences in the quality or 'types' of marine habitats worldwide, their varying levels of exploitation and degradation, and the fact that different kinds of stresses affected coral reefs differently according to location and the kind and amount of exploitation they experienced. This variation is still far too commonly overlooked today by some institution-based scientists who work with a restricted geographical scope.

During this long 17-year period between visits to Chagos, numerous coastal environments around the world, especially coral reefs, experienced significant harm due to over-exploitation, overfishing, and various forms of pollution. In several locations, reefs were also affected by simple extraction of the reef fabric for use as building material. These 'decades of destruction', as others have called them, greatly depleted the productivity of many coral reefs in the Indian Ocean. They also reduced what we now call the 'ecosystem services' provided by reefs to human societies, notably protein. During the last decades of the old millennium, we became aware of the magnitude of the worldwide loss of reefs, a trend that had markedly accelerated and continues to this day [1]. Several countries, including the Maldives, which is British Indian Ocean Territory's (BIOT) nearest neighbour, became increasingly concerned about the very survival of their nation itself, and indeed, they have every reason to be. Their main concern was sea level rise, but in fact, some of their problems, both there

DOI: 10.1201/9781003423300-6

and elsewhere, were added to by their own essentially unmanaged 'development' of numerous islands and other facilities. When shorelines and reefs are damaged or killed, islands are left with reduced defence against waves and erosion from the rising sea.

Because the Chagos Archipelago had no permanent residents outside Diego Garcia, except for those on a few visiting yachts, it did not suffer the numerous direct human impacts experienced by most places. Despite containing Britain's highest marine biodiversity, it was totally neglected in a scientific way throughout these years. During this period, a 'Chagos difference' emerged between the condition of its reefs and those of the rest of the ocean, not because reefs in Chagos improved—in some respects, they did not—but because reefs almost everywhere else were undergoing severe decline. Back then, it was thought that the distance of the Chagos Archipelago from the rest of the world would ensure its continued good condition; after all, it faced none of the usual problems from fishing, pollution, and shoreline development. Was it immune from those sorts of problems, surely? No, it was not, as it turned out!

AGE OF ENLIGHTENMENT

One unassuming but remarkable man, John Topp, was the senior British Royal Navy officer stationed in Diego Garcia—the British Representative or 'Britrep'—for a couple of years in the 1980s. He was essentially in charge of the Territory. His mild manner was deceptive, and he had exceptional talents. He was a passionate botanist and conservationist. Several years after he leaving the Royal Navy, he founded a charity in the early-1990s called *Friends of the Chagos*, which I immediately joined, along with several others who had a connection with the archipelago. Some were interested scientists, some had been stationed there, and others had worked in the Foreign Office in connection with BIOT in various capacities. Around that time, the Administration decided it needed a conservation adviser, and John took on that role, one that would last for ten important years. John passed away in 2011 but will be remembered for his enormous contribution to conserving the Chagos Archipelago.

In 1993, John visited me and asked if I might try to obtain funding for a scientific expedition to end the 'dark ages'. I agreed to try, and it eventually came to fruition in 1996. It was not easy discovering who exactly, in government grant-providing circles, might fund such an expedition. After my outline of needs and of benefits that would accrue from a scientific investigation was eventually approved by the Government's agencies, I developed a more solid grant application and approached several science funding agencies. However, these agencies simply stated that they did not cover UK Overseas Territories; it was considered 'foreign' and not domestic in that respect. On the other hand, others, such as the UK's aid department, asserted that because it was a UK Overseas Territory, it was domestic and not foreign, and so outside their remit too. Moreover, since there were no starving local people (they had all been removed, of course), they weren't interested from that perspective either. The Department of Environment was not interested, and when they received my application, they passed it back to the BIOT Administration, stating that it looked very good but, as their remit did not include Overseas Territories, BIOT should fund it themselves or else find another entity willing to do so. Consequently, BIOT provided some core funding themselves.

Scientific work recommenced in 1996. The first of this purely civilian series was achieved despite a marked lack of enthusiasm from several authorities. Why they agreed at all is rather opaque—possibly some higher authority in government had a hand in it, or perhaps they simply had no idea what might develop. They had little idea about the biological and long-term worth of the archipelago, a trait that gradually changed over the following years.

At that time, the military also strongly opposed the involvement of civilian scientists going there, so with that kind of resistance, the 1996 expedition almost foundered even after being funded.

It took a long while to assemble all the stores needed to send to Diego Garcia for the 1996 expedition and to arrange the equipment needed for a large group of mostly diving scientists. Although BIOT had just engaged a Fisheries Patrol Vessel, they declined to make it available to us. As a result, we resorted to seeking private yachts and their benefactor owners once again. Two large yachts responded to my advert in the *Times*, and these sailed from northeast England to house and support us, using the same model that we had benefitted from in the 1970s. This was a massive undertaking on the part of the owner-skippers and their wives. It was enormously generous, and I, for one, have no idea what the real cost to them must have been. They, like their counterparts of two decades earlier, were unfailingly willing and helpful. One of the boats, *Inga Viola*, was a converted Danish trawler owned by Mike and Birgitta Pilling. The other, *Aztec Lady*, was a large steel ketch, belonging to John and Joan Heath. Both were lovely boats, as were their owners and crew. Without them, we would have had nothing at all.

The success of this expedition was entirely due to the calibre of the participants and to John Topp's tireless efforts in Diego Garcia to support us, even though he was no longer the Britrep. It had little to do with any local 'help'. We were allowed to use the first short-lived Fisheries Patrol Vessel to carry our stores from Diego Garcia, and we quickly discovered how fortunate we were not to be using that ship for any more than this ferry trip. Its skipper would not take his ship closer than about a couple of miles from shore, which meant we had to offload the stores into our small inflatable boats far out to sea and drive them a long way to a beach on an island. The ship itself was in a sorry state of repair, baking hot because its air conditioning was broken, which is a major problem in what is essentially a steel box in the tropical sun. This coincided with a very demoralised crew. We were glad not to be based on it.

However, the main obstacle, once we had arrived in Diego Garcia and before we ever got to the northern islands, was the attitude of some staff stationed there at that time. These officers usually rotate every year, and I would stress that this negative attitude was not at all typical. We quickly learned that someone had instructed the staff not to help us in any way and placed a guard on our jetty to monitor any movements to shops or other facilities that we might need to use. This was fine as far as it went because we were self-contained and didn't need any significant help. However, we found that this became active obstruction when it became clear that we would continue with our government-funded brief regardless. Fortunately, these instructions to the troops were obeyed for only a very short time. The problem seemed to be caused by an antipathy to 'bloody civvies', all this being related back to us over a beer or two by some of the troops placed to guard us. But John Topp, who was accommodated on the island itself, knew the system inside out and ensured we got

the supplies we needed in Diego Garcia. This ensured the success of that expedition. (After it was all over, I wrote that if this antipathy was going to be repeated in future, and if BIOT wished to learn a bit more about its remarkable territory, then we had better base our expeditions from somewhere else, rather than from Diego Garcia. The message got through.)

The reefs were every bit as wonderful underwater as I remembered from nearly 20 years previously. They did show some changes, though I did not yet know why. They contrasted starkly with reefs in those many other places that I had worked on and studied in the meantime elsewhere in the world, most of which were becoming over-exploited and degraded. The corals and fish were as abundant as I remembered, but there was one huge difference—there were hardly any sharks [2]! This low shark density was disturbing to those of us who had experienced the extraordinary numbers in the 1970s. Often, we would see none in an hour-long dive. This mirrored what was being reported in all the oceans at that time, but why was that the case in this remote place too? Even the very conservative Food and Agriculture Organisation of the UN had reported that, in the preceding couple of decades, so many sharks had been caught by industrial fishing fleets that only 10% of the world's stock of these key predators remained. This atrocious indictment of fishing behaviour throughout the world and during the heyday of 'fisheries management' demonstrated the lack of any meaningful high seas fisheries control.

Some of the reef scenes did look a little different. There was a significant reduction, for example, in the large colonies of that highly conspicuous and attractive branching coral called *Isopora palifera* in the extreme shallows (Figure 6.1). So abundant was this coral in the 1970s that we named these shallows the '*palifer*a

FIGURE 6.1 Compass plot of cover by Isopora palifera in 1979 and 1996. Combined data from atolls Peros Banhos and Salomon. Blue, 1978, red 1996. Always absent in the highest energy shores facing the SE Trades, it preferred the moderately turbulent northwest shores. Photo insets: Top: a dead colony two years after the 1998 mortality, showing colony almost 1m tall. Bottom: A young colony a few years old, taken in 2006.

zone' when referring to where we needed to return to. I could not explain it then, but measured the considerable decline and recorded it plainly [3]. In these zones, the effective height of the reef was effectively reduced by about a metre—the height of the colonies. We worked out later that probably the mortality was because episodic ocean warming events had killed them. These warming events were being recorded in some other places elsewhere, but because no one visited Chagos throughout its long 'dark ages', we could not be sure this was the reason there too.

This expedition focussed on the two northern atolls, although we visited several islands and reefs on the Great Chagos Bank and Egmont atoll, and even parts of Diego Garcia as well. The work done was very productive scientifically and led to a day-long conference hosted by the Linnean Society of London. The results from this expedition and conference filled a book published by the Linnean Society [4].

We took terrestrial biologists who visited numerous islands. I was very pleased that Professor David Bellamy, who had introduced me to Chagos nearly a quarter of a century earlier, was able to come along too and, with others, characterised the plant life of many of the islands [5], furthering the earlier botanical work of John Topp [6]. We had an ornithologist who began the systematic survey of the seabirds as well [7], and one of the remarkable findings he came up with, unsurprising in hindsight, is not only the inverse relationship of birds and rats, but the fact that where there still were some nesting birds on islands with rats, the birds' nests were found higher in trees and shrubs where they were less accessible. At the same time, others did significant work on the insects, discovering new subspecies and associating many with different plant types [8]. Together, these laid the foundations of what has now become an ongoing programme of research on the islands' flora and flora.

Underwater, we continued research on the corals. Assisted by Anne again, I commenced a sampling and survey protocol at many of the same sites that we had visited nearly two decades earlier, and which we still continue to visit today. Results on the coral work are related later, mainly in the context of impacts of climate change, a factor that has now become one of the main issues of our time.

For the first time, we started a programme of research on the soft corals too, which occupy a significant proportion of the reefs. We identified and mapped many of the main species [9]. Soft corals are important because they may occupy about 20% of reef surface, in some places up to 50% or even more in some reefs that experience heavy wave action, a space occupancy that has important consequences to the total amount of limestone laid down by the reef-building process (Figure 6.2).

Two more programmes started that year were on the subject of poaching. Our island exploration discovered nearly two dozen poachers' camps on islands throughout the archipelago. These were identified by the shacks built from local materials, by fresh-water wells that had been dug, and by discarded materials such as tarpaulins, bottles, and cooking utensils. Some looked old, while some looked as though they expected more visitors next season. Our research programmes included one on shark abundance and, using data on sharks from diver logbooks (divers commonly note the sharks they see), we determined trends of shark numbers over time [10]. We also began a survey of sea cucumber densities and of potential poaching of these very important animals. Both surveys continue to the present day. These showed very clearly the substantial extent of poaching that was taking place [11], and mostly, the

FIGURE 6.2 Much of the colour of a coral reef comes from the soft corals.

poachers were from the coastal villages and ports of Sri Lanka. We had colleagues in Sri Lanka, and with them, we estimated how large the total take was of both groups of animals. It was huge. BIOT had been wide open for poachers for the preceding couple of decades, during which supplies had become increasingly diminished elsewhere in the Indian Ocean.

SHIP EXPEDITIONS: A WAY TO DO SCIENCE

All this was most fortuitous in its timing because this survey, in 1996, was just two years before the first recorded massive marine heat wave. This event in 1998, a massive manifestation of the effects of warming oceans of the world on marine life, and one that would repeat again and again all over the world, then featured strongly in our work. This is discussed in later chapters.

Following these studies of 1996, we realised that broader surveys were needed. While our limited coverage was yielding very useful results, it was clear that the variety of marine habitats we had stumbled across merited much wider investigation. Ship-based expeditions are, we have found, the most useful and productive way to do science over such a large and dispersed area. It has been difficult sometimes to convey the size of the territory compared with that of the islands and atolls themselves, which occupy such a tiny fraction (see Figure 2.5). There is no other way to conduct the necessary ecological surveys. I have discussed with the authorities on several occasions since the late 1990s the merits of having a research station somewhere in Chagos, most sensibly Diego Garcia atoll, but this has always been discounted for a couple of reasons. To be economically viable, such a shore facility would need to be occupied by paying scientists for much of the time, and we were never sure that we could make this happen. Almost everywhere, environmental science funding has been poor for many years, and many marine stations have severe budget constraints already. People from several stations have told me that they would be unlikely to afford 'bench space' in another location as well. Secondly, people in research stations tend to focus their research in areas nearby simply because it is logistically easier, focussing perhaps on questions of organism physiology or biochemistry rather than ecology. However, Chagos is so vast, and we need to cover such a large area that a ship-based approach is the necessary and only sensible course of action. Some in the government also had been inquiring about wider environmental aspects at that time. Additionally, it made more sense, as by then, BIOT had a ship that could be used for reef research. The *Pacific Marlin*, for years, carried out border enforcement, mostly focussing on intercepting poachers and monitoring fishing boats during the periods when industrial-scale fishing was still permitted and licensed. It was a very friendly ship but eventually became uneconomic to run. After it was retired and scrapped in 2015, the *Grampian Frontier* took its place, until that vassel was scrapped too! We never had the newest, shiniest ships, but their very helpful crews always made up for that (Figure 6.3).

These ships have served as the platform from which we have conducted almost all the science in recent years. Today, the amount of science has significantly increased. This has enabled the number of peer-reviewed scientific publications arising from work using these ships to become substantial; several hundred science papers have now been written on many aspects of the place by a couple of hundred scientists. Collectively, these publications have turned Chagos from being little more than a blank on the scientific map to one of the best-known reefs systems in the world. This body of work has provided valuable insights into how this rich ecosystem functions and has offered information on long-term trends in the health of reefs, particularly during a period of climate change with its severe impacts. However, developing this programme all took time, and these two ships became invaluable in facilitating these scientific endeavours.

FIGURE 6.3 The Pacific Marlin supported dozens of scientists over the years before being scrapped. Initially, it was called the Fisheries Protection Vessel until licensed fisheries was stopped after which it was rebadged the BIOT Protection Vessel.

LATER EXPEDITIONS

Several expeditions took place over the ensuing years and continue to the present. These were funded by different parts of the UK Government, including the Foreign and Commonwealth Office (FCO), Overseas Territories Environment Programme (OTEP), and the Department for Environment, Food and Rural Affairs (DEFRA). In some senses, they blur into one another in my mind. By this time, I had been asked to replace John Topp as the government's science adviser for the territory, and across all these expeditions, I tried to create an integrated and coherent research programme of both scientific value and of use to BIOT as well. It may sound like a planned, multi-year programme today, but after each trip, we could never be sure that we could ever return!

One problem with creating an integrated research strategy for the biological workings of the archipelago was that it was made very clear, repeatedly, that I was to have nothing to do with fisheries; this being the turf of the contracted fisheries consultants. Fisheries that were extracting quite a lot of both targetted species and of by-catch species are an important ecological component of a marine ecosystem. Ecologically, that restriction lessened the coherence of policy by the BIOT Government. However, there was plenty to do in such an under-studied location, and a programme evolved by inviting scientists to join who were already senior in whatever aspect or subject that I thought needed studying next. The study of the corals was one that I have held to be central; they build the reefs after all. Coral cover, their biogeography, recruitment of new juveniles—the 'Next Generation' of corals if you will—their mortality, diseases, and other factors have all featured in what I hope has been a consistent study of the Chagos reefs conducted now by a growing number of leading scientists. For years, we had to ship in all equipment needed and ship it out again at the end of each expedition—a ludicrously expensive process, considering this would include air cylinders, air compressors, inflatable boats, and outboard engines. We were not permitted any storage space in Diego Garcia, and we never knew if we would be allowed back anyway.

The wastefulness of this became recognised by the government in the end. After we obtained funding for a series of three annual expeditions, the certainty of the later trips allowed us to obtain a place to store the equipment between its periods of use. Today, things have developed much further: through connections made via the Blue Foundation, the philanthropic Bertarelli Foundation has funded a large programme lasting several years, involving a vastly increased number of expeditions with equipment, and using chartered vessels as well as the BIOT ship. This is ongoing. By this stage, I had experienced more than enough of the interminable struggle of organising them and was delighted when others, notably a unit from the Zoological Society of London, took over all the central logistics.

However, in the first decade of the new millennium, I was still the main organiser of the expeditions. By then, we knew of the catastrophic consequences of the 1998 warming that had all but killed these reefs, and much of the later work, as well as several later chapters here, focusses on this.

Expeditions took place at very irregular intervals at first, but then they took place almost once each year. Once, in 2006, the authorities allowed me to arrange a 'double' expedition, which included more scientists than the total that had visited before, turning out to be very productive. The same programmes continued and were extended, and were joined by others focussing on, for example, offshore and deeper waters.

Alongside these thoroughly enjoyable though sometimes difficult expeditions, I visited Diego Garcia every year as BIOT Administration's scientific adviser. On several occasions, I could also join a trip to the northern atolls with a group of Royal Marines engaged in other duties to carry out a limited amount of work then too. Like John Topp had done, I continued that for a decade. I had become quite immersed in the archipelago and its wildlife.

2006 ONWARDS

Always, the aim was to be open, inclusive, as well as integrated in terms of the science. The quantity of work grew to something that was well beyond what any one person, funder, or organisation could handle alone. The total amount of work done is far less, of course, than that which emanates from a well-established research station in a western country like the USA or Australia. However, to someone who had tried to put such an unusual place on the map for years, this progress was very gratifying. The arrival of further private funding then helped stabilise and secure the science programme in a way never possible before. Other funders also began to join in too, and these still support several of the projects that we had mapped out some years previously, as well as greatly expanding into other aspects.

On each expedition, the general routine was to conduct two dives per day from our inflatable boats, launched from the BIOT vessel. Two dives were the most that could realistically be done for logistical and safety reasons. While on present-day diving holidays, especially on a live-aboard dive boat, a diver may do double that number, they would have access to a nearby decompression chamber in case of the 'bends', and we did not have one. They may also be using a safer gas mix called nitrox, and we did not have that either. So, two dives per day was our limit, which, with work associated with a scientific dive such as specimen processing, equipment set-up, and data entry, is usually enough anyway.

Island parties would land on an island for their bird or plant research. These dives and island visits were always rich in experiences: sharks, dolphins, vast clouds of birds above the smaller islands, and vast numbers of fish and vibrant corals underwater. The reefs were recovering quickly and very well after being nearly wiped out by the warming of 1998. We might find ourselves steering the inflatable through a school of over one hundred dolphins, Spinners mostly, but sometimes Bottlenose, whose schools are smaller though the animals are double the size. You need not slow down for fear of hitting one, you won't, because they were far more manoeuvrable that we were. Indeed, if you do slow down, they immediately lose interest in accompanying you, and the faster you go the more they like it. The delight is to see them underwater, but for that you must be quick. The trick is to hang on to a rope on the side of a boat and get dragged along, preferably with a camera. But there the problem begins: if the boat goes at more than about two knots or so—a boring speed for the dolphins—your mask gets dragged off your face so you can't see anything, your snorkel and nose fill with seawater, and your shoulder feels like your arm is being pulled out of its socket. The bubbles around you as you are dragged along obscure much of the view anyway. But, if you slow down sufficiently so you don't feel like you are being pulled apart, the dolphins immediately lose interest and disappear. Time and again, we would try this. When spinners jump, as they do often, you see why they got their name—they spin a twirl or two before splashing back. There may be a good scientific reason for this, such as shaking off parasites, but if so, why don't other species do so too? Perhaps they just have fun.

Some scientific discoveries were made fortuitously, which later were realised to be important. A good example concerns the discovery of the vast seagrass beds. In the 1970s, I had seen and recorded some on the northern Speakers Bank, far from the islanded atolls, but we had only ever seen the odd scrap of a couple of species on all our thousands of dives near islands or in the lagoons [12]. This seagrass was mainly the species *Thalassodendron ciliatum*, which is common in most areas around the Indian Ocean.

It had been a mystery why there was so little in this archipelago. It had been known to occur for 50 years [13], but why were there no large meadows of it? Then in 2005, with a party of Royal Marines and other Royal Navy personnel based in Diego Garcia, I had gone to some shoals in the lagoon of the Great Chagos Bank to look at what that might contain. It was too stormy to dive, and all I could do was hang over the side of the boat with a mask on, being held by the waistband of my shorts by a Royal Marine so I did not fall overboard in the heavy swell (Figure 6.4).

The seabed was covered with seagrass! That story was left for a couple of years until I could traverse that area again, when a dive was possible, and the extent of the seagrass beds on that small shoal was shown to be huge. Since then, further exploration far away from land has shown that seagrasses may even be the norm over vast expanses. *Thalassodendron* is the main food supply for the green turtle here—it is what the green turtles in and near this archipelago are living on. Satellite trackers that have since been attached onto several green turtles now show that the animals reside

FIGURE 6.4 Part of an enormous bed of the seagrass *Thalassodendron ciliatum*.

in offshore shallow areas for weeks at a time, and so later inspections of those areas have revealed vast expanses of that seagrass there too, at least three sites extending over 128 km and supporting high densities of fish [14]. Seagrass is not a minor component at all, just minor on reefs near to islands that we study repeatedly. They are strongly photosynthetic primary producers, and in terms of energy flows and carbon sequestering in the sunlit marine environment of the archipelago, they will be more important than the corals themselves in the vast regions away from land.

Throughout this time, most of my own work was spent on environmental issues in other parts of the world, including several disasters or erecently war-torn areas and ruined marine habitats. I was also chief editor of a major science journal covering marine environmental and pollution problems, which I mention because that work illustrated for me the widening gap in condition, 'quality' (however that is defined), and biological richness between Chagos and most of the rest of the world. As more scientists visited, publishing a continuous stream of results showing what Chagos is like, it became ever clearer what a remarkable place it was. Chagos holds many 'world records' in today's degrading oceans.

These continuously showed us why the reefs of Chagos are exceptional. We measured the rate of recovery from the wipe out of 1998. There was, for example, to 2006 or so at least, an almost complete absence of marine diseases [15] and a total absence of marine introduced species [16], both remarkable features today in our damaged oceans. We must be careful to distinguish this from the severe invasive species issues on the islands.

Later in this series of expeditions, genetic work was commenced to show the relationship of Chagos with other sites in the Indian Ocean. This showed that it is firmly connected ecologically to the western side of the ocean but also shows very clear linkages with the east: Chagos reefs are a thoroughfare, a stepping-stone, between east and west [17]. It has rather less connection with the Maldives, which are much nearer to the north, and this must be because the prevailing currents flow east or west at various times of each year, and so currents, carrying larvae, only very rarely flow northwards or southwards.

Reef fish studies were amongst the most striking and showed that this archipelago supported the greatest recorded biomass of reef fishes found anywhere [18]. This crucial work is amplified later. Together with modelling work by several others [19], this strongly suggests that the lack of human exploitation was the simple cause.

Further legislation established the Chagos marine reserve in 2010 as the world's largest fully protected area, and many of us have repeatedly said that the world needs a lot more of them. A 'Big Ocean Network' has developed, and now others amongst Britain's Overseas Territories are joining the group of large protected marine areas. Some exceed the size of Chagos, the whole becoming part of Britain's Blue Belt Programme—an initiative extending and expanding across many parts of the ocean [20]. But Chagos is the most fully protected.

REFERENCES

[1] Wilkinson C. 2004. *Status of Coral Reefs of the World: 2004*. Townsville, Australia, Australian Institute of Marine Science. **And**:
Souter D, Lindén O. 2005. Coral Reef Degradation in the Indian Ocean: Status Report 2005. Kalmar, Sweden, CORDIO.
[2] Anderson C, Sheppard CRC, Spalding M, Crosby R. 1997. Shortage of sharks at Chagos. *Shark News* 10: 1–3.
[3] Sheppard CRC. 1999. Changes in coral cover on reefs of Chagos over 18 years. In: Sheppard CRC, Seaward MRD (eds) *Ecology of the Chagos Archipelago*. Occasional Publications of the Linnean Society of London. No. 2, pp. 91–100.
[4] Sheppard CRC, Seaward MRD (eds). 1999. *Ecology of the Chagos Archipelago*. Occasional Publications of the Linnean Society of London. No. 2, 350 pp.
[5] Seaward MRD. 2000. The lichen flora of the Chagos Archipelago, including a comparison with other island and coastal tropical floras. *Tropical Bryology* 18: 185–198. **And:**
Seaward MRD. 1999. Cryptogamic flora of the Chagos Archipelago. In: Sheppard CRC, Seaward MRD (eds) *Ecology of the Chagos Archipelago*. Linnean Society, London, pp. 207–224.
[6] Topp JMW. 1988. An annotated check list of the flora of Diego Garcia, British Indian Ocean Territory. *Atoll Research Bulletin* 313: 21. **And:**
Topp JMW, Sheppard CRC. 1999. Higher plants of the Chagos Archipelago. In: Sheppard CRC, Seaward MRD (eds) *Ecology of the Chagos Archipelago*. London, Linnean Society, pp. 225–240.
[7] Symens P. 1999. Breeding seabirds of the Chagos Archipelago. In: Sheppard CRC, Seaward MRD (eds) *Ecology of the Chagos Archipelago*. London, Linnean Society, pp. 257–272.
[8] Emms C, Barnet LK. 1999. The insects of the Chagos Archipelago. In: Sheppard CRC, Seaward MRD (eds) *Ecology of the Chagos Archipelago*. London, Linnean Society, pp. 241–256.
[9] Reinicke GB, Van Ofwegen LP. 1999. Soft corals (Alceonacea: Octocorallia) from shallow water in the Chagos Archipelago: Species assemblages and their distribution. In: Sheppard CRC, Seaward MRD (eds) *Ecology of the Chagos Archipelago*. London, Linnean Society, pp. 67–90.
[10] Graham N, Spalding MD, Sheppard, CRC. 2010. Reef shark declines in remote atolls highlight the need for multi-faceted conservation action. *Aquatic Conservation: Marine and Freshwater Ecosystems* 20: 543–548.
[11] Price ARG, Harris A, McGowan A, Venkatachalam AJ, Sheppard CRC. 2009. Chagos feels the pinch: Assessment of holothurian (sea cucumber) abundance, illegal harvesting and conservation prospects in British Indian Ocean Territory. *Aquatic Conservation* 20: 117–126. **And:**
Price ARG, Evans LE, Rowlands N, Hawkins JP. 2013. Negligible recovery in Chagos holothurians (sea cucumbers). *Aquatic Conservation: Marine and Freshwater Ecosystems* 23: 811–819.
[12] Drew EA. 1980. Seagrasses in the Chagos Archipelago. *Aquatic Botany* 9: 179–184.
[13] Willis JC, Gardiner JS. 1931. Flora of the Chagos Archipelago. *Transactions Linnean Society London II, Zoology* 19: 305.
[14] Esteban N, Unsworth RKF, Gourlay JBQ, Hays G. 2018. The discovery of deep-water seagrass meadows in a pristine Indian Ocean wilderness revealed by tracking green turtles. *Marine Pollution Bulletin* 135: 99–105.
[15] Sheppard CRCet al. 2013. Chapter 18 Coral reefs of the Chagos Archipelago, Indian Ocean. In: Sheppard CRC (ed.) *Coral Reefs of the UK Overseas Territories*. Springer, Dordrecht. pp. 241–252.

[16] Tamelander J, Campbell M, Lundin CG. 2009. *Detecting Bioinvasions on Small Islands in the Indian Ocean – Project Completion Report*. IUCN Global Marine Programme 2009. Gland, Switzerland, IUCN, pp. 25.
[17] Sheppard CRCet al. 2013. Chapter 17 British Indian Ocean Territory (the Chagos Archipelago): Setting, connections and the marine protected area. In: Sheppard CRC (ed.) *Coral Reefs of the UK Overseas Territories*. Dordrecht, Springer, pp. 223–240. **And:**
Eble JA, Craig MT, Rocha L, Bowen BW. 2011. Not all offspring stay close to home: Trans-Pacific dispersal and gene flow in Indo-Pacific reef fishes. *Journal of Marine Biology* Article ID 518516, 12 pp. doi:10.1155/2011/518516.
[18] Graham NAJ, McClanahan TR. 2013. The last call for marine wilderness? *BioScience* 63: 397–402. **And**:
Graham NAG, Pratchett MS, McClanahan TR, Wilson SK. 2013. Chapter 19 The status of coral reef fish assemblages in the Chagos Archipelago, with implications for protected area management and climate change. In: Sheppard CRC (ed.) *Coral Reefs of the UK Overseas Territories*. Springer, pp. 253–270.
[19] Purkis SJ, Graham NAJ, Riegl BM. 2007. Predictability of reef fish diversity and abundance using remote sensing data in Diego Garcia (Chagos Archipelago). *Coral Reefs* 27: 167–178.
[20] https://www.gov.uk/government/publications/the-blue-belt-programme.

7 The First Ocean Heatwave

The first ocean heatwave occurred in 1998, or, more accurately, it was the first heatwave we are aware of because at least one seems to have happened earlier, during the scientific 'dark ages' when scientists were not allowed to visit. One of the first indications of how important Chagos would become in terms of marine science stemmed from this disastrous event that almost wiped it out. While more damaging heatwaves began in 2015, these were anticipated; the one in 1998 took everyone by surprise.

For years, it had been known, particularly through research in the Galapagos and Eastern Pacific [1], that a gradually warming ocean, overlaid with episodic pulses of very warm water, can trigger widespread coral bleaching. If this persists for an extended period, it can lead to the death of corals. The warming phenomenon is a part of the general climate change that we are currently experiencing.

Although the phenomenon of coral bleaching and mortality had been reported in several locations around the world, little was known about it in the Indian Ocean by the time we resumed research in 1996. In that year, our comprehensive collection of reef information proved especially fortuitous. Just two years later, in 1998, reports of widespread coral bleaching in the Indian Ocean started to surface, swiftly followed by reports of massive coral reef mortality. Therefore, our 1996 work became a fortuitous 'pre-disaster' record against which we could later measure quite accurately the magnitude of the effects of warming seawater. At the time, unfortunately, the mortality event caught us off guard, and in hindsight, we should have been more aware. The scientific literature did contain warnings, though it is worth noting that there might not have been anything anybody could do to prevent it.

Initial reports of issues with coral reefs in the Indian Ocean emerged from the southern parts of the East African coastline shortly after the warming water pulse passed over them. As the sun tracked northwards across the globe in the first half of the year, reports came in from points further north, including the Seychelles, the Maldives, and the Red Sea. By August, the most northern reefs of the Indian Ocean, in the Arabian Gulf, were very badly damaged too. During a visit to Qatar in the Arabian Gulf shortly afterward, some students from Qatar University showed me reefs that had been scientifically described as being especially rich 30 years earlier [2]. In two dives lasting one hour each, we could find not one single living coral. It was an ecological disaster, and the sight was heart-breaking. Had Chagos' reefs also been affected?

The obvious way to determine whether coral mortality was occurring on Chagos reefs, and to what extent, was to ask someone on-site. However, despite the nearby atolls of the Maldives and Seychelles displaying significant mortality on most shallow reefs, the response from British Indian Ocean Territory (BIOT) was that there was no bleaching on Chagos reefs.

DOI: 10.1201/9781003423300-7

We did not believe it. Satellite maps of ocean surface temperature available to us showed that the huge pool of warm water in the Indian Ocean covered the Chagos Archipelago too; it was situated right in the middle of it. Subsequently, we sent an acquaintance who was stationed in Diego Garcia a disposable underwater camera. They took a series of photographs, sent them to us, and sure enough, the images confirmed that massive bleaching and mortality had taken place, as expected. The observer in Chagos should not have missed it.

Based on those photographs and on evidence of the huge pool of warm water detected by satellite, I informed the BIOT Administration that their territory appeared to have experienced a massive mortality of reef life. I emphasised the need to explore more, considering the territory's dependence on live, healthy coral. I explained how growing corals aid in keeping coral islands above water and highlighted the severe consequences if they were now dead. This exchange went back and forth for nearly a year but eventually in 1999 I revisited, with a brief to explore the situation further. This visit was intended to be a swift snorkelling trip, covering several atolls, and I was accompanied by John Topp, the conservation adviser to BIOT. As it turned out, the bleaching and subsequent mortality of corals were amongst the worst and most extensive in the world.

The scene we saw almost everywhere in 1999 was heart-breaking. It is representative of similar events that are now becoming common everywhere, similar also to the later, more extensive warming eventof 2015–2016. It is worth examining this situation in more detail. Throughout our observations during the 1999 trip, which took place a year after the marine heatwave, we found that the corals were dead, and their skeletons were crumbling (Figure 7.1a and b).

There were no live corals at all over huge, shallow areas. As we were limited to snorkelling, we could see only the shallowest 20–30 m or so. However, wherever we looked, almost all the coral skeletons were grey, sedimented, and broken, with very few left alive in scattered places. By that time, relatively inexpensive digital cameras with underwater housings were available, and I had bought two (in case one flooded, as occasionally happens). I recall taking hundreds of pictures, all monotonously depressing. The limestone coral skeletons were often recognisable as corals, but many were being turned into amorphous and eroded rubble with no remaining structure.

(a) (b)

FIGURE 7.1 Two examples of corals killed by the warming water in Chagos: (a) branching staghorn corals and (b) table corals, both *Acropora* species. In the right photo, the greenish patches are still living, contrasting with the grey dead parts.

The primary cause of coral mortality is the expulsion of single-celled plants that live symbiotically with the coral tissues, leading to subsequent death of the corals. Each coral polyp contains millions of these tiny, single-celled algae called zooxanthellae. We know now that their photosynthetic mechanism breaks down under the combined effect of warmer water and bright light. The oxidative stress caused by the products of the damaged photosynthetic system causes the corals to expel the zooxanthellae. Both heat and light play crucial roles in causing this, and while they are distinct factors, 'warming' is the shorthand phrase commonly used to describe the process leading to the problem. When the coral expels the zooxanthellae, the coral can no longer benefit from the food products derived from the symbiotic association, resulting in literal starvation and death. That is the most common reason for coral mortality. However, if the temperature rises sufficiently, the excess heat can kill the coral and its algal cells directly and quickly, faster than the length of time that starvation would take.

Coral bleaching is the term used to describe the initial phase of this process. This is because most of the darker, brownish-green colour of a coral comes from its algal cells, and when these are expelled, the only tissue remaining is the thin layer of the animals, which is pretty much transparent. As corals lay down pure white limestone skeletons, the coral looks bleached at this point: hence the term 'coral bleaching'.

Following the coral bleaching, one of two things may occur. If the water cools relatively quickly, the coral may recover its population of coloured zooxanthellae and survive. Conversely, if the water stays excessively warm for too long, the coral dies. In this scenario, the dead coral tissue quickly dissolves, leaving a bare skeleton. Subsequently, a film of filamentous algae and many other micro-organisms quickly grow on the bare and exposed limestone skeleton, causing the skeleton to darken. From a distance, the coral no longer appears bleached. This bleached period may last only for a few days, or a couple of weeks in deeper, darker waters. This complcates tracking of these global phenomena by satellite, as the coral may recover and darken again, or if it dies, it also darkens again. Both outcomes may look roughly similar to an untrained eye or to a satellite sensor, but they result in utterly different consequences later.

Soft corals, relatives of corals, have been much less researched than corals, yet they occupy a lot of space on the reef too. In Chagos, they had been conspicuous, and on reefs facing the Southeast Trade winds, they had even provided most of the living coverage on the reef. Most shallow species have similar symbioses with algae and so these had also died.

However, due to their non-stony skeletons being composed of a soft gelatinous matrix containing many calcareous spicules, soft corals left no visible traces whatsoever. (There are some in parts of the tropics where these spicules are fused into dense concretions, but this does not happen in Chagos reefs.) In 1999, we saw that these areas of reefs had a substantial and abnormally high expanse of apparently uncolonised, bare rock. This was very unusual to see because any bare substrate usually quickly becomes colonised by seaweeds. The bare rock areas were where the high cover of soft corals had previously existed (Figure 7.2).

An explosion of seaweed did not occur on the Chagos reefs and this phenomenon became another very important line of research. The absence of fishing or pollution on these reefs meant that a huge abundance of grazing, herbivorous fish remained. While algae likely grew quickly on the bare reef, they were as quickly grazed.

FIGURE 7.2 Reef previously dominated by soft corals that died and disintegrated, leaving no skeletons and bare rock. Photo taken after the 2015 ocean heatwave.

Seaweeds can swamp a reef when too much fishing has taken place because fishing almost inevitably removes the herbivores, and this is made worse where nutrient enrichment derived from sewage has fertilised the seaweeds. However, on the Chagos reefs, there were almost no large seaweeds to be seen anywhere. The limestone substrate was occasionally bright white but more often had a dusty grey appearance, caused by a covering of very fine algae and other micro-organisms.

This lack of seaweed biomass was another indication of a 'Chagos difference'. The absence of nutrients from sewage or shoreline disturbance, coupled with the huge abundance of herbivores, meant that no explosion of macro-algae had taken place here. These enormously important factors permitted good coral recovery to take place later.

'THE REEFS ARE IN BLACK AND WHITE'

The scene that we faced in 1999 was appalling. I wrote the following for *Chagos News* after our visit [3].

"I snorkelled along the northern edge of Nelsons Island on the northern side of the Great Chagos Bank. The water was clear and calm, and on that part of the island the drop-off lies close to shore. I swam, with the conservation adviser and others from the fisheries patrol vessel, from the edge of the reef flat out to the drop-off. With a lot of surface diving, we could see clearly to 20 m deep, maybe more. But no corals or soft corals were left alive. The corals were all there, just dead, standing upright in their positions of growth. Instead of providing a colourful and varied scene, they were standing like tombstones, covered in a film of greyish fuzz. Whether we looked in the shallows where corals are mostly sturdy, digitate forms, or swam down to between eight and 10 m deep where the large table corals densely cover a strip along the top edge of the drop-off, all were dead. As the ship's chief engineer put it, it was like seeing the reef in black and white instead of in colour. A little further along there was a little coral, and my notes record a trace of soft coral too, but in a total of perhaps 45 minutes over what would have been a couple of acres of once vibrant reef, I saw less coral and soft coral than once would have fitted into a single one of my quadrats. I had been looking at similar scenes for a week by this stage: it was similar on the seaward sites of all five islanded atolls, but this island, called Nelsons, was the final, depressing stop on this tour of the northern atolls. I remembered what we called the coral gardens on the southern side of this isolated island—this had been one of the loveliest and, with dozens of sharks, one of the liveliest diving sites in the 1970s. At the coral gardens I recorded about 6% of the substrate left living, mostly soft coral in this case, with 1% of the stony corals left alive."

Due to this depressing result, quickly published [4], a proper diving survey was clearly needed, and permission for this was granted for early 2001. This time, with scuba diving equipment, the survey extended to 30 m depth or so, and quantitative data were collected on several aspects such as the degree of coral mortality in each atoll with depth, the degree to which the coral skeletons were being bioeroded into rubble, the abundance of new or juvenile corals, and some preliminary studies of the fish communities. Before visiting, a new satellite sea surface temperature data set had been analysed too. The sea here had indeed been warm in 1998.

Sea surface temperature had by then shown a mean or underlying rise of 0.65°C since 1950. This may not seem much, but, in fact, it is quite marked for the corals. In Chagos, at least, sea temperature rises slower than air temperature because of the much greater thermal inertia of the ocean. It must be remembered, though, that it is not only underlying temperatures rises that matter as much as the briefer periods of peak temperatures that are superimposed on top of the underlying rise, and their duration. Based on these data, I had concluded earlier that the 'critical' sea surface temperature associated with the massive coral mortality of 1998 had been about 29.9°C. At least, that was the temperature during the crucial weeks in 1998, though we had no way of telling whether a slightly lower temperature might have been sufficient to have killed the corals too. We know now, following a huge amount of research from many places, that it is not only peak temperature and its duration that are important but also details such as the rate of initial rise, the previous thermal history of that location, the types of the corals' symbiotic algae, as well as illumination, which in turn depends on surface roughness or winds. All these, and other factors, affect temperature over different time scales in what is a rather more complicated picture than we realised at first [5].

We found that coral and soft coral mortality in shallow water (up to 15 m depth) was high everywhere, but the depth to which mortality occurred correlated with latitude. Extensive or even near-total mortality occurred from the surface to about 15 m deep in northern atolls, but the heavily killed range extended to as much as 35 m deep in the southern atolls of Diego Garcia and Egmont. Below these apparently critical depths, northern reefs retained a much more normal and vibrant appearance and coral cover. The transition from severely affected to apparently normal conditions in northern reefs could be very abrupt, usually spanning only a few metres of depth. If the central and southern atolls did have any transition to a better condition, it occurred deeper than the 35 m we could observe in this survey.

After the later and more severe warming starting in 2015, the depth to which coral mortality extended no longer showed as much difference with latitude; it was by then severe everywhere to the maximum depths we surveyed (Figure 7.3).

Lagoons of all atolls showed a much more complicated picture after each ocean heatwave. In these lagoons, the amount of seabed with good coral cover was irregular but sometimes considerably more than anything on ocean-facing slopes. Many large corals, including the very susceptible table corals, had survived in lagoons, even in fairly shallow water. Some large boulder corals of *Porites* and others of the more massive groups had also pulled through apparently unscathed, though one or two species seemed to have disappeared completely and have not, in fact, been seen since, with the huge *Diploastraea* being one. Because living corals in deeper water in the north remained more abundant, we thought that the lagoons possibly can provide sites from which further recruitment can take place throughout the archipelago. At least, that was our hope and later this appeared to be borne out both by observations and then explained elegantly by computer models. However, later ocean heatwaves showed us that even deeper corals were killed too.

Reasons why corals in the lagoon were better able to survive were speculated upon at the time. The obvious initial thought was that lagoons are much shallower, so lagoon water can surely heat up more. If this had happened to a small degree most years, corals in lagoons and their symbiotic algae might have become acclimatised to periods of warmer temperature, conferring some sort of thermal resistance to them—in other words, they might have become more used to it.

Deeper reefs in the northern atolls also had the potential to serve as major areas of spawning for future recruitment of juveniles. The best coral survival occurred near lagoon passes, which have the strongest water exchange and the coolest water flows. Reef areas previously dominated by tough 'wave-breaker' species in shallow water had lost almost all their corals. The surfaces of these reefs appeared to have 'dropped' by nearly a metre in some parts due to the loss of these dense and tough thickets.

Our measurements of total coral cover in 2001 indicated no improvement over what we had observed by snorkelling in 1999. This was disappointing. Initially, I wondered whether these reefs were gone for good, as has since appeared to be the

FIGURE 7.3 (a and b) Ocean-facing coral slope at about 12 m depth, before and after the 2015 heatwave.

case in many other parts of the Indian Ocean. However, to brighten this view, results from another line of research found that, very importantly, numbers of juvenile corals were extremely high, especially on dead tables of *Acropora* [6]. The numbers of juveniles counted in very many quadrats were the highest so far reported anywhere to that date. With so much spawning going on, the future could even be bright, although it was hard to see that when all around us the reef remained pretty much dead for several years. However, such an abundance of juvenile corals did indicate hope for the future.

This work showed that young corals were mostly 'broadcast spawners'—species that release gametes into the water where fertilisation and dispersal take place. In contrast, species that brood their larvae before releasing them, as several do, were under-represented because generally, these are shallow water species whose adult populations had been the most severely affected. It was thought that the 'brooders' would therefore probably make a slower recovery, which might even change the composition of the shallow water coral community. Amongst the brooders is *Isopora palifera*, a very important species in high-energy conditions, and this large, sturdy coral used to be a major contributor to the 'breakwater' functioning of Chagos reefs. These corals, and this breakwater function was, for the time being at least, lost. Because of the nature of the different kinds of reproduction, it was thought that fast-growing species with high reproductive outputs would dominate the most severely affected reefs for at least the next decade. This turned out to be true, following the 1998 warming event, and these 'weed' species, as they are sometimes called, did indeed dominate again seven or eight years later; one or two are the attractive tabular species of *Acropora*. On subsequent visits over the following decade, I observed similarly high levels of juvenile corals almost everywhere, but it was not until several years later that we were able to start proper repeat measurements which could quantify it.

ERODING REEFS

After a coral dies its limestone skeleton lies exposed. This limestone is in the form of aragonite, laid down by coral polyps in various lattice patterns with varying degrees of solidity. Some are relatively soft or crumbly. It forms a perfect substrate for many species of bioeroding animals and plants, that is, species that can etch their way into a coral or tunnel into it. They do this for their own purposes of shelter and protection. When a coral is alive, its polyps will simply eat any larval organism that settles on it. But the coral polyps had gone now, leaving the limestone bare—an ideal surface for bioerosion. Bioeroders had most certainly not been wiped out by the warming water. Bioerosion was considerable [6], and sponges, worms, and algae were now a major cause of the disintegration of dead corals. Little of the resulting fragments and debris had been carried up onto the reef flats or beaches, and we guessed that most of it had been carried along-shore and then into very deep water, out of sight. Bioerosion also had a latitudinal pattern. Larger coral fragments and rubble occurred in the north. Sheltered lagoon sites had larger rubble fragments and a wider range of rubble sizes. The branches of many collected dead coral fragments were split to reveal just how porous they had become, three years after they had died. All of them were riddled like Swiss cheese, with the tunnels being the burrows of organisms. With this bioerosion comes substantial weakening of the whole structure. Three years after this and other mortalities, a common sight was branching corals with their skeletons still apparently intact and in place, seemingly reaching upwards to the light just as they do in life. Still, with most of these, the gentlest pressure would fracture or topple them. They were not likely to survive the next storm.

All sites studied showed that extensive breakdown of branching corals resulted in a very flat reef surface. Much of the reason for the rich biodiversity on a coral reef is its 3-D structure, but affected reefs soon become flat, 2-D structures.

Rates of breakdown far exceed the growth of new corals, and so the substrate becomes more planar still. We had no time at this early stage to measure the invertebrates that usually co-existed on a reef, but it was obvious that there was also a huge loss of crustaceans, molluscs, and echinoderms too. If you cut down a forest, the birds and monkeys will disappear too, and it looked like an analogous situation had occurred on the reef. I had seen that where the forest of corals had been lost elsewhere, as in the Arabian Gulf, for example, almost all the fish, starfish, molluscs, and all other groups had disappeared too.

But in this respect, a 'Chagos difference' was evident again. While it appeared that some invertebrate groups had been severely reduced, there were still huge numbers of other groups, notably fishes including grazing herbivores on these reefs.

At the time, in 2001, we wondered whether something was different here, which permitted such significant numbers of large fish to remain and prevent the area from being taken over by seaweeds, as had been reported from so many other places with human populations. We could not get to Chagos with scientists familiar with researching this aspect until several years later when studies of the fish and reef erosion and accretion began in earnest.

RUBBLE

Most of the reefs' surface for several years after a mass mortality became covered with coral rubble. This debris is unconsolidated and would be unsuitable for successful settlement by new coral larvae. Such mobile rubble acts like liquid sandpaper during every storm, so that any juvenile coral trying to settle and grow becomes scrubbed off when the rubble shifts and moves. While we could see large numbers of juvenile corals in suitable areas that were elevated a little above most of the substrate, such as on dead table corals before they collapsed, we thought that the reef would probably require the rubble to disappear from the reef before it would see substantial growth of juveniles.

In the shallowest water, skeletons of dead finger-shaped corals retained their shape for a few years, but deeper than these, most branching and massive forms lost all surface structure; it was then impossible to distinguish the identity of most coral colonies, and sometimes impossible even to distinguish them from much older, bare substrate. Below them, in the 'table coral' zone (5–15 m deep) where water movement is much less, many dead table skeletons remained intact in some sites, presumably because no storms had reached that depth yet to topple them over, while in others, erosion or storms had carried them away, leaving only their central stumps.

The 'dead' areas remained essentially bare. On Chagos reefs, they are not covered with green or brown macro-algae, as was starting to be reported from other parts of the world, though those algae species do occur there too [7]. Algae did cover 10% of one site in Blenheim reef, for an undetermined reason. Chagos lies in a particularly nutrient-poor part of the Indian Ocean, and there were still huge schools of grazing fish. Once algae do get a dominant foothold, however, reef demise appears to be irreversible, and considerable research has taken place in recent years on coral-algal dynamics on coral reef, to find the reasons why the progression of a coral reef to an algal-covered limestone plain seems to be a one-way process. It is a ratchet, unlike a wheel that can move equally backwards and forwards. Once coral yields to algae, then it will usually stay in that condition, as far as we know, for a very long time.

However, reef fish abundance and diversity, measured at 15 m depth in our 2001 survey, were seen to have remained high at all sites. Some species groups that depend entirely on corals as a source of either food or shelter, such as the polyp-eating butterflyfish in particular, had unsurprisingly diminished or vanished, while a small number of herbivores and detritivores had increased, probably because of increased food availability. These high fish numbers, we thought, were encouraging, and this subject needed further exploration.

Longer-term impacts were worrying, particularly those associated with the loss of reef complexity. In 2001, we predicted that coral recovery and an increase in reef structure and rugosity would need to happen rapidly to avert long-term disaster. Later, we saw that this indeed happened.

RECOVERY AND EROSION

There seemed to be no recovery at all for several years. Then, slowly at first, we started to see more encouraging signs.

By the mid-2000s, repeated requests and explanations to the government began to be effective and permitted more scientific expeditions to the archipelago. I designed what I hoped would be a more consistently recorded series of measurements of various things such as coral cover from the same places and depths. We did this as best we could in several different years, and we saw with relief that coral cover started increasing at all depths down to our self-imposed 25 m depth limit. I also retrieved my old results from 1978 and included these findings. Although those measurements were taken differently, the pattern showed a steady trend of recovery after a lag of several years. A decade after the wipe-out, corals achieved a cover value in shallow and mid-depths of about the same or greater than it had been in our first survey in this series in 1996 [8]. Figure 7.4 shows the total cover by corals from numerous sites over all years during which such measurements were made. Aligned above the cover graph is the El Niño Southern Oscillation index.

Between 1978 and 1996, where no measurements took place, the lines are shown dashed because it is unlikely that their slopes are smooth in reality. The pink vertical bars mark the most notable warming events. The two rightmost bars show good alignment with the measured widespread coral declines. The two leftmost coloured bars marked with '?' indicated where coral cover might likewise have declined in a stepped manner, without anyone knowing.

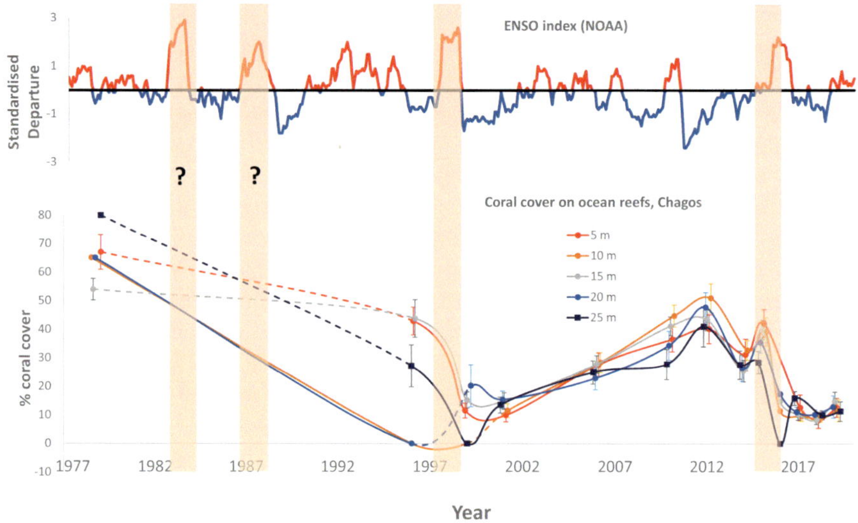

FIGURE 7.4 Coral cover values of all combined sites in the archipelago on ocean-facing slopes, with time. Each line is a different depth. (Error bars are standard errors.) For the Multivariate ENSO Index (top). Data are taken from https://www.esrl.noaa.gov/psd/enso/mei/table.html.

Recovery after 1998 was greatest in shallow water in some places, but generally, coral cover was similar at all depths. By 2012, coral cover had reached values similar to those before the 1998 event.

Then, in 2014, we observed a significant decline in coral cover again, though not as severe. In the intervening years, several events may have contributed to this. Firstly, all the tables that had started growing from around 2002 or so had now reached their maximum size. They were becoming senescent, or, to put it simply, they were at their natural end of life. However, other issues appeared to be increasing in importance as well. There had been several minor episodes (minor compared with 1998) of bleaching, not of the same overwhelming scale but sufficient to cause stress to the corals. Secondly, probably because of the warming that caused the bleaching, various diseases started to appear on the corals, diseases that we had not recorded earlier as being significant. In some areas, they were certainly spreading rapidly over the coral surfaces, killing the tissue with alarming rapidity in some places. Storms had occurred too, and dead and crumbling table corals are easily toppled. All these factors were leading to a loss of the dominant tables around 10 m depth, and, therefore, less overall coral.

In the early 2000s, further bleaching events occurred. Once or twice during my annual visits when there was no expedition, I went snorkelling in the lagoon or around the ocean reefs of Diego Garcia and observed extensive areas of snowy white, heavily bleached coral. However, observations the following year showed those corals to still be intact. Clearly, the bleaching did not last long enough or was not severe enough to kill the corals during these minor episodes.

It was possible that some acclimation to warmer water might have been taking place too. Basically, there are several different clades or species of symbiotic algae in corals. The ones preferred by corals generally are not the ones which are most tolerant to high water temperatures. There are more heat-resistant clades, but these are usually uncommon or rare in healthy corals because, in general terms, these are less efficient. As a result, they don't become abundant in their coral hosts unless there is some advantage to it.

However, in Chagos, these temperature-resistant clades have not been discovered so far despite considerable searching by colleagues [9]. Instead, they have found the presence and perhaps a gradual increase of a species which is resistant to high light intensities, known as Clade 'A'.

How can this be important given that the amount of sunlight striking the central Indian Ocean has not changed? The reason probably lies in the fact that a flat sea water surface allows considerably more light to pass than does a surface rippled by waves. Despite an increase in stormy periods, there has also been a rise in prolonged calm periods. During these calm periods, more light penetrates to the reefs.

We have no scientific measurements of this in Chagos. However, as an underwater photographer accustomed to the days before electronic cameras, when we adjusted camera apertures using *f* stops, I am confident that the light at any given depth can vary by one or two stops according to whether the surface is rough or glassy calm. (Each *f* stop change represents a doubling or halving of light.) During long, glassy calm periods in 1998, well over double the amount of light reached the corals, which proved excessive for their symbiotic algae. We possess numerous photographs where the top surface of a colony is dead, but the shaded sides and downward-facing surfaces remained alive and healthy (Figure 7.5). The only difference is the amount of light striking the different parts of such a colony.

FIGURE 7.5 Many examples can be seen of coral colonies that are killed on the top but have surviving polyps around the sides. It is assumed that water temperature is the same in both areas, but the top receives much more radiation from the sun, which kills polyps located there.

Some acclimations might be happening in Chagos too. If this is the case, our question changes to: will acclimation be enough to cope with gradually warming ocean water?

Predictions of sea temperature rise in shallow waters suggest an increase as the years go by, at an accelerating rate. How quickly this happens is all-important and the subject of much research work. This is crucial everywhere, land and sea, tropical and arctic, deep and shallow. The other important point is that it is not the average rise anyway which is the most important but rather the peak temperatures superimposed on the rising baseline, and peaks usually happen around March–April in this central Indian Ocean location. Researchers are finding that several factors provide some 'conditioning' to the corals, such as the past temperature history of an area, and the rate of increase of temperature into a warming period. These all appear to be important to whether the corals can survive any one warming episode.

Other changes should be measured if only we had the funds to do it. Coral cover increased following the collapse of 1998, but we don't know (except broadly) any changed identities of all corals that have recovered. Are they the same as those that dominated before the wipe-out? Would it matter if they were different anyway? A little of this was measured later.

Measuring coral cover is a relatively simple kind of measurement, and it is swift, permitting hundreds of quadrats to be measured every visit. However, they miss a lot of information. Visits were annual at most, lasting perhaps two weeks, with two dives of about one hour each day, so in contrast to terrestrial ecology measurements, sampling time underwater is extremely short. We simply did not have the time on-site or the resources to measure other aspects usually considered essential, such as the identity of the species forming the cover. The main species were recorded, but the numerous smaller, sometimes inconspicuous species that can be equally important were not. Cover measurements are quick and can be very informative, but their limitation must be understood. Inexperienced marine ecologists have sometimes claimed that a reef had recovered when they saw a recovery of total cover, but there may likely have been a profound change in what makes up that cover. As a terrestrial example, when a forest is cut down, the ground may be quickly replaced by a total cover of bracken; thus plant cover has recovered but it is obviously not the same ecosystem. So it is with a coral reefs too. But understanding cover can still provide much useful information. It was all we could do in the time allowed us and all that we could raise funds for.

REFERENCES

[1] Glynn P. 1984. Widespread coral mortality and the 1982-83 El Nino warming event. *Environmental Conservation* 11: 133–146.

[2] Kinsman DJJ. 1964. Reef coral tolerance of high temperatures and salinities. *Nature (London)* 202: 1280–1282.

[3] Sheppard CRC. 1999. Paradise lost. *Chagos News* 13: 2–4.

[4] Sheppard CRC. 1999. Coral decline and weather patterns over 20 years in the Chagos Archipelago, central Indian Ocean. *Ambio* 28: 472–478.

[5] Roche Rm Williams GJ, Turner JR. 2018. Towards developing a mechanistic understanding of coral reef resilience to thermal stress across multiple scales. *Current Climate Change Reports* 4: 51–64. https://doi.org/10.1007/s40641-018-0087-0.

[6] Sheppard CRC, Spalding M, Bradshaw C, Wilson S. 2002. Erosion vs. recovery of coral reefs after 1998 El Niño: Chagos reefs, Indian Ocean. *Ambio* 31: 40–48.
[7] Jolliffe AS, Basson PW. 1999. The subtidal distribution of macroalgae on the coral reefs of the Chagos Archipelago: A preliminary study. In: Sheppard CRC, Seaward MRD (eds) *Ecology of the Chagos Archipelago*. Linnean Society Occasional Publications No. 2. Otley, W. Yorkshire, Westbury Publishing, pp. 137–150.
[8] Sheppard CRC, Sheppard ALS. 2019. Chapter 11 British Indian Ocean Territory (Chagos Archipelago). In: Sheppard CRC (ed.) *World Seas: An Environmental Assessment*. Volume 3. Academic Press, London, San Diego, pp. 237–252.
[9] Yang S-Y, Keshavmurthy S, Obura D, Sheppard CRC, Visram S, Chen CAl. 2012. Diversity and distribution of *Symbiodinium* associated with seven common coral species in the Chagos Archipelago, central Indian Ocean. *PLoS ONE* 7(5): e35836. https://doi.org/10.1371/journal.pone.0035836.

8 Connections and the Major Reef Components

The biological complex that constitutes a coral reef is an interlocking network of many elements, none of which operates in isolation. Our work in the Chagos Archipelago has ecompassed most of the dominant biological groups found there, although not all. Since the earliest days, extensive surveys of various kinds have been prominent, along with several newer lines of investigation, ranging from molecular to landscape-scale ecology. Many of these studies have unveiled aspects of crucial importance. Recently, my own research has focussed on the recovery of reefs and corals following mortalities caused by warm waters, the monitoring sea temperatures, and their recovery from ocean heatwaves, now commonly referred to as such. The latter is discussed further in Chapter 10.

Most other major lines of research that have been conducted are important, but there are several gaping holes in what we were able to do. These gaps exist due to funding shortages, even though there are those who would dearly love to carry out the work. In earlier years, at least, there were also difficulties in obtaining permission to visit.

Some of the recent research derives from our increasing understanding of global collapse and from the knowledge that we now need to protect very large areas of the ocean so that they can serve as reservoirs of species and act as reference sites for areas that have suffered from overexploitation in the past. We have a good idea of what a healthy reef system looks like and how it functions. The knowledge gained can benefit the thousands of marine managers around the world who are trying to restore habitats in their own countries but are largely failing. Simply put, if they do not know what a reef that has not had direct human impacts should look like, then they won't know what to aim for or which impacts are the most important. In most countries, conventional forms of marine management are failing to arrest the decline of tropical marine habitats that support people and, in the case of coral reefs, provide so much in the form of food and protection from waves. This is a life and death matter to millions each year (I don't exaggerate [1]). The work in Chagos can also inform our government regarding its own environmental management. Sensible management cannot be done in the absence of scientific input.

STEPPING STONES ACROSS THE OCEAN

Substantial value derives from the role of Chagos reefs as a biological crossroads or stepping stone in the Indian Ocean [2]. It connects shallow habitats in the east and west, serving as a reservoir for species that are declining in the increasingly degraded Western Indian Ocean. Currents and proximity to other areas, many of which are badly damaged (meaning most of the rest of the ocean's coastline), are key factors.

 DOI: 10.1201/9781003423300-8

To the east, there is no shallow water until Cocos Keeling is reached, 2,750 km away, with Indonesia another 1,000 km further east. To the west, distances are much less, explaining why Chagos has been shown to be an outpost of the Western Indian Ocean more than it is a part of the East [3]. It is only just over 1,000 km to the commonly overlooked submerged banks of the 'Shoals of Capricorn', which form extensive shallow water between Chagos and the Seychelles. Chagos lies about 1,700 km from the maze of islands in the Western Indian Ocean: the Seychelles, the Comores, and others. Translating this into number of days of travel by tiny larvae carried in the water currents is more revealing. It takes 65 days to reach Cocos Keeling but only 25 days to the shallow submerged banks in the West and 35 days to the Seychelles (Figure 8.1). These westerly durations are not much of a barrier to the movement of species.

This goes a long way towards explaining the stronger biological connection between Chagos and the West rather than the East. These connections have now been demonstrated by both ecological and genetic methods.

Ocean currents passing across Chagos flow towards Southeast Asia between about January to April and reverse to flow westwards towards the archipelagos and African shores for most of the rest of the year. There are simultaneous east and west flows in the north and south, which have a boundary on occasion somewhere in the middle of the archipelago. This certainly helps to explain why Chagos is a centrally located biological stepping stone.

Several scientists have now used genetic methods to confirm that Chagos both acts as a stepping stone across the ocean and is a refuge for species in the Western Indian Ocean [4]. However, it also serves as a source of genetic diversity. For some species, it functions as a refuge, harbouring populations of species that are now under greater pressure in the increasingly degraded and populous western part of the Ocean.

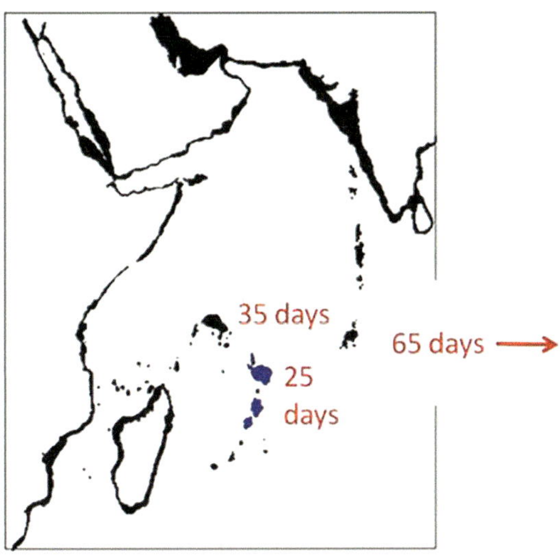

FIGURE 8.1 Time taken by larvae to travel to or from Chagos reefs. The black filled areas are shallow reef or limestone platforms. That beside the '35 days' label is the Seychelles Bank; that beside the '25 days' label is the shallow Saya de Malha Bank.

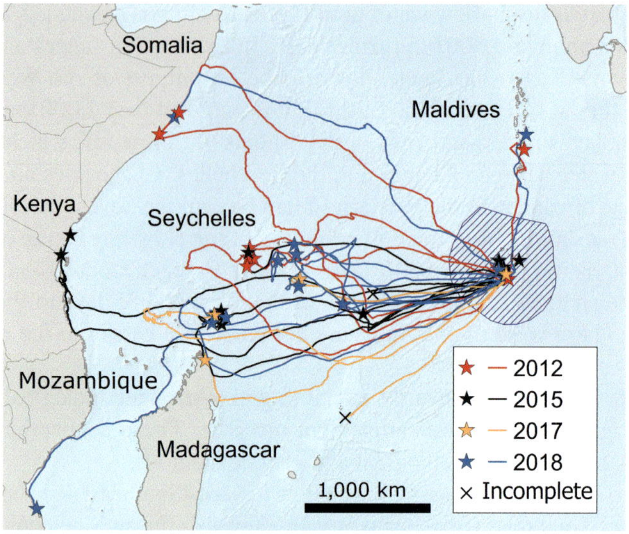

FIGURE 8.2 Satellite trackers have been attached to several Green turtles after nesting on beaches of Diego Garcia. They have been shown to forage as far as the coast of Africa.

Turtles, which are a particularly iconic species, provide a good example of this connectivity. For the Green turtles, several have had satellite transmitters attached to their shells after laying eggs on the beaches of Diego Garcia atoll, and their movement has been tracked between there and the rest of the Indian Ocean. Almost all travelled West to forage, and most travelled as far as the African coast (Figure 8.2). Fewer travelled north, going either to the Great Chagos Bank or the Maldives, but there seem to be no known linkages with the rookeries of Western Australia [5]. Turtles from Chagos beaches hold the gold medal in migration distances [6]. Turtles in Chagos and Seychelles are now known to form a single distinct genetic group.

For many fish species, Chagos also serves as a bridge between the eastern and Western Indian Ocean [7]. Regarding the globally endangered coconut crab, Chagos is a crucial refuge, as demonstrated earlier. Taken together, all emerging results confirm that Chagos is both a part of the Western Indian Ocean Province and establishes connections to the east as well. It might serve as a chokepoint for some; concerning corals, it has been termed 'the Chagos stricture', representing a relatively narrow conduit between the vast reef areas of the Western Indian Ocean and Southeast Asia [8].

Several people have expressed surprise, disappointment even, that there appear to be very few endemic species. Contrary to some people's expectation, this probably emphasises the importance of the place. If indeed it is a key stepping stone on the oceanic highway, it might be expected to have almost no endemic species at all; if it had many, then it would be at the end of a cul-de-sac rather than being a thoroughfare. High endemicity indicates a strong degree of separation from everywhere else because only isolation produces it. If there were many endemics in Chagos, then, although this would mean there are more species unique to it, it would not be so important in a global context. There is high value in the fact that it is a key part of this 'trans-oceanic highway' rather than being a less important backwater.

FIGURE 8.3 Banded coral shrimps, an example of the myriad small species that are mainly responsible for high diversity, and for nutrient and food recycling on reefs. Most species are even smaller.

SMALLER REEF CREATURES

We started new programmes examining the infauna: the tiny, mostly unnoticed, and cryptic forms of life, such as small crustaceans and worms. The diversity of these small species is greater by orders of magnitude (Figure 8.3) than that of the corals and fish that we do notice [9]. All form part of the ecosystem that keeps the reef healthy.

JUVENILE CORALS

Several colleagues, including previous doctoral students, have assisted in examining juvenile coral densities: the next generation of scientists looking at the next generation of reef builders, as it were. This required only the most basic of equipment (Figure 8.4) but produced important results. Here, "juveniles" means individuals that have recently settled and are only one polyp to a very few polyps old, and always less than 1 cm across. It is slow and tedious but needs only a Sherlock Holmes-type of magnifying glass. There is nothing hi-tech about it, but it does enable us to find and count juveniles among the debris, algae, and sponges that encrust any surface underwater. The ability to distinguish a single coral polyp from one of a soft coral or anything else is needed too, of course. We have tried to speed up this tedious process in several ways, notably by shining ultraviolet light on the scene, which causes coral tissues to fluoresce and, we hoped, stand out more clearly; this would be easier to do, but has given us non-reliable results. The eyeball was the best!

The large numbers of juveniles that we counted at depth intervals of 5 m down to 25 m initially set new records in the early part of this millennium, as with so many aspects of the biology of this place. However, this occurred before the marine heatwaves of 2015 and 2016 [10]. We know, of course, that most juveniles that settle on

FIGURE 8.4 Counting the density of juvenile corals. The equipment needed is only an engineers' ruler and a large ×5 magnifying glass (and the ability to distinguish tiny corals from juveniles of other groups).

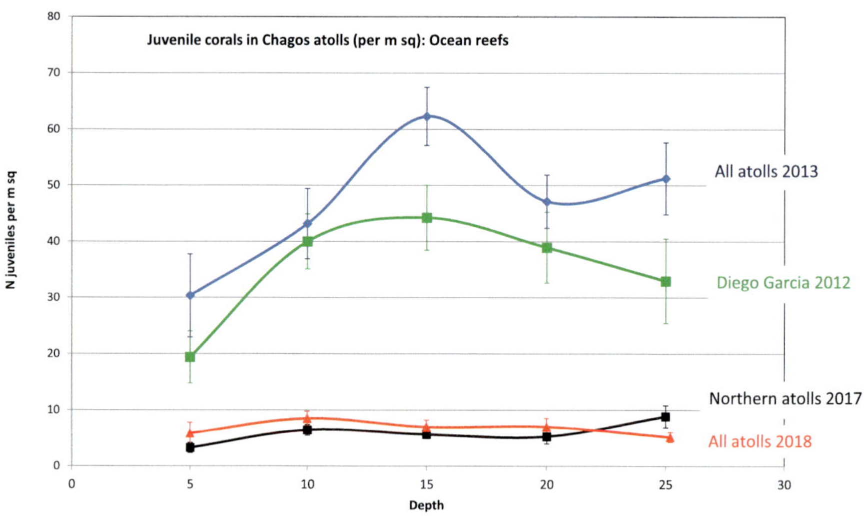

FIGURE 8.5 Numbers of juvenile corals on ocean facing reefs, measured in many replicate samples at five different depths. The top two lines show numbers a few years before the marine heatwaves of 2015 and 2016; bottom two lines shows densities shortly afterwards. Standard error bars are shown for each point.

the reefs and commence growth will not continue to grow into adults, just as the huge numbers of seedlings under a tree do not all grow into adult trees. Still, the fact that they were present was, at the time, enormously reassuring because, after all, if there are no juveniles, then there will not be a next generation at all (Figure 8.5 upper lines).

But after the heatwaves of 2015 and 2016, there was a severe collapse in numbers, even though there was by then far more dead limestone on which juveniles could settle. Perhaps there were simply too few adults to produce young (Figure 8.5 lower lines).

In several parts of the world, others also documented this collapse. However, in some areas, there was little to no recovery. For instance, following the wipe-out of 1998, coral cover on Chagos reefs recovered in less than a decade. In contrast, several reefs in the Seychelles either did not recover at all or did so very slowly (Figure 8.6) [11]. The factors hindering reef recovery may not necessarily be the same as those that caused the initial coral loss. While warming affected corals in both locations, pollution loads, fishing, and other pressures impeded recovery. This raises hope for future recovery in the Chagos reefs, provided that warming events do not recur too frequently.

This work recorded the density of juvenile corals directly on hard reef substrate. However, there were consistently higher densities observed on dead table corals as well. Coral planulae appeared to prefer settling on table coral tops, possibly because they actively select limestone to settle on. Figure 8.7 illustrates an example of specimens that were two years old after the warming event. Nevertheless, considering that these dead coral structures are prone to collapse and transform into rubble, it becomes a precarious location for settlement. Consequently, they will not contribute to the long-term coral growth of the reef.

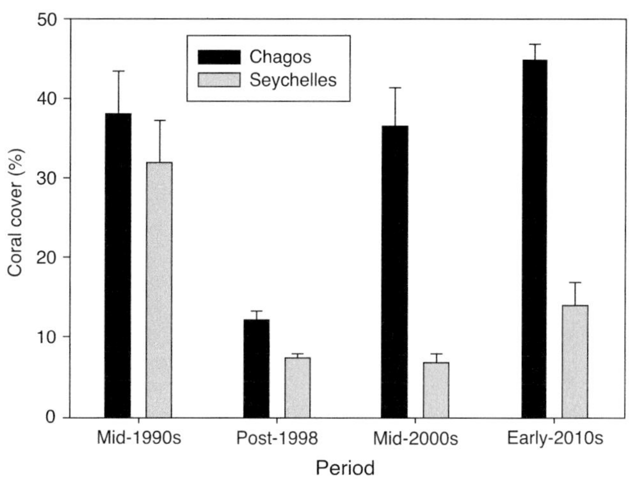

FIGURE 8.6 Reefs of the Chagos Archipelago compared with those from the Seychelles. In both areas, coral cover collapsed after the 1998 warming, but while it recovered in Chagos it recovered much less after 15 years in the Seychelles where there are other anthropogenic impacts. From Ateweberhan M, Feary DA, Keshavmurthy S, Chen A, Schleyer MH, Sheppard CRC. 2013. Climate change impacts on coral reefs: synergies with local effects, possibilities for acclimation, and management implications. *Marine Pollution Bulletin* 74: 526–539.

FIGURE 8.7 A common sight was large numbers of juveniles settled on table corals that had been killed in marine heatwaves. However, this substrate is precarious and due to disintegrate due to bioerosion, leaving the living corals amongst the rubble which will kill almost all of them.

A very useful classification has been made of reefs worldwide and in the Indian Ocean, grouping all reefs into four broad categories, from essentially dead and gone to healthy reefs [12]. In rough terms, only about a quarter of the world's reefs are now in a healthy state, and in the Indian Ocean, those of Chagos comprised about a quarter to half of the total quantity of reefs left in a healthy condition by 2010. It is an extraordinarily important place for this reason alone. The salutary lesson is that there has simply been a lack of people living there to degrade it and to prevent rapid recovery. Worldwide, reefs are degrading alongside the rise in the population of people, and the proportion of healthy reefs that still exist is diminishing at a rate of about 1% or 2% every year. As time goes on, therefore, if these present and gloomy trends continue, the value of Chagos increases proportionately year on year, provided they can remain unimpacted by the usual suite of human activities.

THE REEF FISH

The fish story is one of the most spectacular. The sensitivity of fish populations to depletion by fishing is now well known [13], and some groups of fish are more susceptible to depletion than others. However, climate change is exacerbating the loss of fish. If a warming event kills the corals, it also eradicates the habitats and food for those specialist forms of fish that need them, causing them to disappear as well. Several visiting colleagues have measured fish biomass, which is the quantity or weight of fish, in numerous locations [14]. They have employed the same method in many areas across the Indian Ocean, as have other colleagues in the Pacific as well.

The figures speak for themselves (Figure 8.8). The biomass of reef fish in the early part of this millennium was significantly higher in Chagos than anywhere else known in the Indian Ocean. It was 20 times greater than in the worst-off reefs, even

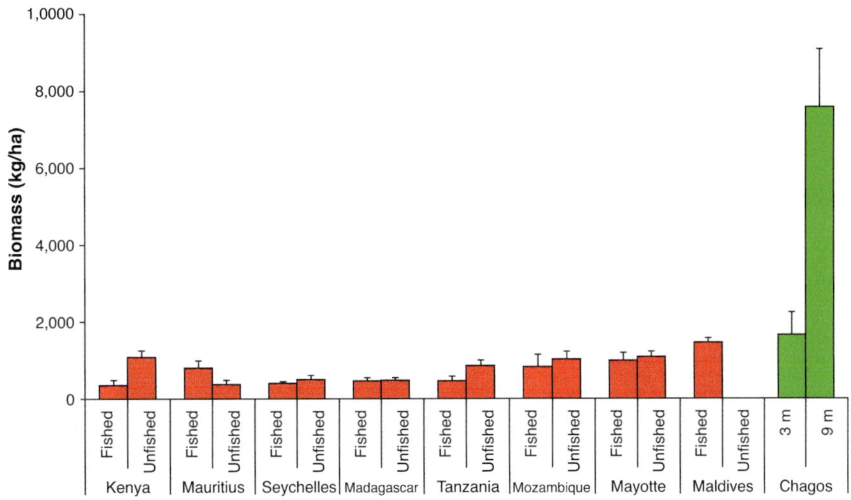

FIGURE 8.8 Biomass of reef fish from Chagos reefs and reefs of eight other countries, where fished and unfished sites are distinguished. Chagos reefs had, in the early part of the millennium, the highest biomass or weight of fishes from anywhere in the Indian Ocean, possibly the world. The red bars represent eight other countries, green bars represent reefs of Chagos, showing values ten times greater. Biomass even in the turbulent 3 m depth where fish are scarce is similar to all the other sites. Data courtesy of Prof Nick Graham.

in other countries' so-called protected areas. In one or two countries, the protection afforded to some reefs does allow fish abundance to be higher than in those country's fished areas, but not by very much. In most countries, however, none of the minimal protection has any noticeable effect whatsoever.

Even the results from Chagos reefs, in the turbulent 3 m depth where there are relatively few fish, are higher than in most other places. The data also revealed more detail about the trophic levels (TL) of the fish. Plants are at TL 1, herbivores are at TL 2, carnivores that eat those herbivores are at TL 3, higher carnivores that eat other carnivores are at TL 4, and so on. Many fish consume mixtures, resulting in fractions of TL; a fish may consume both herbivores and primary carnivores, etc. The biomass of higher trophic level fish in Chagos reefs is also enormous compared to all other Indian Ocean countries.

This illustrates what reefs could offer if they are not overexploited, and the vast scale of this phenomenon is interesting. It certainly surprises many people who remain unaware of just how important and productive a reef can be if left untouched. People have generally lost the folk memory of what things can be like if left alone—the 'shifting baseline syndrome' mentioned earlier—a memory that can only be regained from observing conditions they could see in the diminishing number of places like Chagos. The value of Chagos in this respect is extremely high. A key point here, however, is that these reefs at that time had nearly eight tons, sometimes more, of reef fish per hectare, or eight times the second best in this ocean and 20–50 times more than most exploited places. The country whose coral reefs appeared to

FIGURE 8.9 Many fish species remain unconcerned by divers on Chagos reefs as they have not learned to fear man. Many are persistently curious, like this red snapper. This does not happen on heavily fished reefs.

be in worst condition in this regard is Mauritius. This small country has severely overexploited its own reefs, perhaps unavoidably given the high population density. Its relatively high latitude also makes its corals particularly vulnerable to ocean heatwaves [15].

Fish patterns are not simple, however. The variability can be very high between atolls and different parts of atolls. Following the coral mortalities that result from ocean heatwaves, fish assemblages change greatly, varying with different proportions of remaining live and recently dead coral, for example. Key groups, such as a suite of grazer-detritivores like surgeonfish and parrotfishes, can vary in density over 40-fold between sites [16]. Overall, however, fish abundance is clear.

There was another observation about the fish as well: their 'flight distance' was much reduced. When diving on exploited reefs, fish tend to be shy and will scatter when a diver enters the water. (There are locations used by divers, in contrast, where fish are fed, in which case they may be attracted to a diver—an artefact.) Neither catching nor feeding occurs here, so fish can be extremely curious or may ignore you until approached very closely. Unlike in most places, they have never learned to fear us. To a large degree, this naivety toward humans also applies to many of the seabirds on the small islands too (Figure 8.9).

POACHING

Poaching is a global practice that undermines conservation efforts, and Chagos is a good example of this as well. We do not know when poaching started. There may have been very little before the expeditions in the 1970s because there was no sign of any poaching then: no evidence of boats at sea, nor of island encampments. But by 1996, we found evidence of a great deal; the 1980s and early 1990s clearly had been a free-for-all for poaching. There have been two major forms of poaching, one in which groups of people make these sometimes concealed camps from which they spread out to collect marine life from shore, targeting mainly sea cucumbers, coconut crabs, turtles, and probably some seabirds too—indeed, anything they find worthwhile. The poachers are later picked up by a returning boat. The other kind of poaching is wholly boat-based, where the poachers simply catch what they can, especially sharks.

Abandoned camps were found on almost every island we examined in 1996, as has been mentioned. Later, we discovered that most poachers at that time were Sri Lankans. It seemed likely that poaching started in the 1980s when news of the rich, unexploited marine resources of Chagos must have spread rapidly through the fishing villages strung along Sri Lanka's coast.

The camps were primarily for gleaning sea cucumbers (Figure 8.10) [17], but the last new camp we observed for this purpose was in 2006, by which time sea cucumbers had been pretty much depleted. These animals are highly sought after in East Asian markets. Alleged to be aphrodisiacs, they are important as cleaners and recyclers on the reef. We surveyed these areas on several occasions [18] and found simply that there were many more sea cucumbers around the waters of Diego Garcia, where the military base was located, and thus where there was no poaching. We quantified the severe depletion that had been taking place in northern atolls away from military eyes.

At the same time, Sri Lankan marine science colleagues made several visits to the fishing harbours in this country, where they inquired about the origins of sea cucumbers landed. They were often openly informed that the sea cucumbers came from Chagos. Following this, another Sri Lankan colleague obtained official import and export data for sea cucumbers from Sri Lanka, prompting us to scrutinise it as well. In Sri Lanka, consumption of sea cucumbers is minimal, if at all, but they are

FIGURE 8.10 A sea cucumber, a key 'cleaner' of sand and sediment on and near coral reefs. They are much sought after by several Asian countries as a 'medicine', or aphrodisiac.

recorded, processed, and re-exported. We converted recorded weight to shiploads and arrived at an estimate of approximately 200 shiploads entering Sri Lanka from the entire ocean each year, with an estimated one-third originating from the open and essentially unguarded waters of Chagos. Combining the remaining densities and the data from Sri Lanka, we concluded that, possibly, at least 60 Sri Lankan poaching boats might be returning from Chagos waters each year with their holds filled with sea cucumbers. While we couldn't definitively prove this number, it appeared to be a well-worked-out estimate.

The number of these animals on the reefs, collapsed and remained very low for many years. Now, sea cucumbers are increasing, and in some places, juveniles can be seen in densities similar to those observed in the 1970s and 1990s. The numbers will continue to rise, so vigilance is needed to ensure that these essential cleaners of reef and sandy habitats are not targeted again.

In later years, poaching mostly shifted to sharks. Shark numbers have collapsed in most parts of the world, and Chagos is no exception; here, several species are now known to have been caught in higher numbers and for longer durations than initially thought [19]. By 1996, the population had clearly crashed, and it is possible that by 2004, and certainly by 2012, numbers were slightly increasing [20], but there is a very long way to go before the large numbers of sharks seen in the 1970s will be regained.

The Sri Lankans, almost impoverished, endure an awful existence on the shark-poaching boats. On most captured boats, some sharks have started to rot, leading to revolting conditions. The stench on arrested boats that we visited is indescribable, and even a brief visit to the captured ships results in clothes and skin becoming permeated with the smell. Despite this, however, the arrested crew members I have met have mostly been a cheerful lot. Gone, hopefully, are the days when they thought the British would treat them like other regional countries do when they are caught, with a beating! Word had, at one stage, spread around the Sri Lankan fishing communities that when they are caught in Diego Garcia, they will get a comfortable, air-conditioned jail. They are given work for a modest daily allowance (but more than they are used to), they get clean clothes supplied, and they get shoes—something many of them don't have at all to start with. They are far from unhappy! The captain of the poaching ship, of course, is probably very unhappy; he will be facing the wrath of the ship owner who must pay the fine or lose his boat. Some of the owners are decidedly unpleasant, it seems; one Sri Lankan colleague, who emphatically did not want to be identified for his own safety, learned that at least one owner was also engaged in human trafficking when sea conditions were too bad to fish on the Chagos banks during the trade wind season.

From 1996, Sri Lankan poaching vessels were occasionally apprehended by the *Pacific Marlin*. The established procedure upon capture dictated that they be escorted to Diego Garcia, where their crews were detained (in a much more comfortable jail compared to their dire conditions on the small poaching ships). The catch is subsequently incinerated (Figure 8.11). The captain faced prosecution, the owner incurred fines, and these boats could occasionally be observed in the small boat harbour in Diego Garcia. The legal process of prosecution was highly tedious for the military, and costly. Although, in some instances, the crews were released to sail off in their boats once a fine was paid and their fishing equipment destroyed, on numerous occasions, the British government found itself burdened with an unwanted boat.

FIGURE 8.11 A captured haul of illegally caught sharks. These will be incinerated. Much data could have been gathered from the hundreds of illegal shark catches, but this seems never to have been done.

Owners, who refused to settle the bill and declined any further involvement with their arrested fishermen, posed a challenge. Consequently, the British Indian Ocean Territory (BIOT) Government was left with the significant expense of flying the fishermen back to Sri Lanka via Singapore. Subsequently, they had the often thoroughly decrepit boat to dispose of and the task of incinerating the sharks.

Other Sri Lankan colleagues surveyed several ports regularly and became friendly enough with local boat skippers. They estimated that the number of boats filled with sharks returning to Sri Lankan ports from Chagos waters specifically numbered several dozen each year. However, only about one dozen poachers in each recent year have been intercepted by the BIOT Patrol Vessel, usually much fewer. The single slow vessel, the *Pacific Marlin*, was doing its best, but those little fishing boats have almost no radar signature and could be spread anywhere over 650,000 km^2s of the BIOT marine reserve.

Capturing even a tenth is a substantial achievement from that perspective, but BIOT is apparently known in the ports of Sri Lanka as 'American Gala', with the word gala translating to 'rock' in Singhalese. That it became a widely known and favoured place for fishing due to its relative richness is not surprising, given the overfished state of much of the rest of the Indian Ocean. One of our own students, working in Sri Lanka on a different project, called in at a chart shop and asked whether they had any charts of Chagos. "Oh yes" replied the shop attendant, "We get asked for these quite a lot now". None of these sources wanted to be named or quoted.

In the 2013 season, when the *Marlin* caught only three shark poachers, a Greenpeace ship made just two traverses of BIOT waters and found eleven ships! That ship had a helicopter that made all the difference. More alarmingly, the helicopter also spotted a significant number of shark fins drying on the cabin tops of several poaching boats, providing the first evidence that the wasteful practice of shark finning was taking place [21]. We must then significantly increase our estimates of the numbers of sharks that were truly being caught, and this might well explain why shark numbers are not increasing much in BIOT waters. Possibly 90% of poachers were getting through, so monitoring and surveillance needed substantial improvement. Pressures are increasing all the time due the rapidly expanding numbers of people living in poverty in almost the entire Indian Ocean region. The temptation to poach in the protected seas of Chagos will become ever more severe. New and different methods of surveillance are being developed to address this problem.

COMMERCIAL OVERFISHING

Commercial overfishing is a global problem, and the Chagos story helps understand it. The tuna industry strongly opposed the idea of a fishing ban, and several of its representatives vehemently and aggressively conveyed this sentiment to me! Numerous reasons were put forward to convince me that catching tuna was beneficial, all of which seemed absurd and self-serving. Some companies expressed the opinion that BIOT shouldn't be too difficult a target to force a change, akin to how they dealt with third-world governments, perhaps!

Reasons for this opposition were perhaps the shock that someone was denying them the ability to pillage fish unfettered. The industry doesn't want any restrictions and rarely faces serious ones; fisheries around the world are collapsing as a result. Counter-intuitively perhaps, a fishing company's best way forward economically is to catch them all now. This was proven with the whaling industry many years ago but applies to tuna too. When a fish resource is gone, a multinational company simply finds somewhere else to put its money, like automobile spare parts, microchips, indeed anything. 'Sustainable fishing' is simply an oxymoron, not economic from their perspective, especially when some estimates show a large tuna ship can be paid for with very few years of catch. We don't ask gold miners to mine sustainably after all, so why expect it from protein miners? Thus, I was several times sought out at science conferences during my tenure as science advisor by sometimes abusive representatives of the commercial fishing industry. This hostility added to that from others who hated (not too strong a word) the government or military and who thought that research there of any kind was wrong, could sometimes make life rather unpleasant! More on this later.

Another issue with industrial fishing is the by-catch. A colleague compiled as much information as possible to document the high proportion of by-catch across all species being taken [22]. This appeared to be substantial. Furthermore, when fish like lancetfish, which have soft mouths and unpalatable flesh, were captured on long-lines, they would be jerked off the lines before being landed [23]. Since lancetfish were never actually brought onto the deck of the ship, they need not be counted as being by-catch. However, with their mouth torn off, they would almost certainly die anyway. The total tonnage of high trophic level biomass destroyed in such cases was comparable to that of tuna. Yet, the loss of a top-level carnivore will undoubtedly have ecological consequence as well.

ANCHORING ON THE CORALS — SHIPS BIG AND SMALL

Anywhere in the world, anchoring on coral reefs is highly damaging. The anchoring ship releases a length of chain several times longer than the depth of the water in which it is floating. As tidal currents change throughout the day, the ship swings, dragging the chain in a circle. Moorings should be used where possible—devices permanently embedded into the substrate, with a large buoy floating at the top, equipped with eyes to which a boat can attach. However, with anchoring, entire reefs can be destroyed, even by small yachts. I had been advocating for some time for the huge supply ships in Diego Garcia lagoon to use moorings instead of anchoring. In 2008, in collaboration with an American team, we investigated where in the lagoon the ships could go to cause the minimum amount of damage. Remember, corals are essential for maintaining the atoll.

Coincidentally, we were undertaking this work with the US Navy team when a sailing boat of the 'Chagossian People's Navy' entered the lagoon in Diego Garcia. The boat was crewed by two ex-skippers of Greenpeace, and it had been tracked throughout its journey as it entered the archipelago. This was not difficult to do, as they regularly posted their whereabouts and intentions on their webpage. The boat was intercepted by a group of Royal Marines as it entered the lagoon, and we listened to the unfolding drama on the VHF. Initially, there were several formal exchanges that requested, in a very proper and correct way, that the yacht turn around and please go away. The yacht, for its part, replied equally politely, stating that it declined to follow those instructions. Later, I learned (since this part was not radioed) that the sergeant in charge of the Royal Marine party went alongside the yacht and said something like, "Look, it's Saturday and we have a party tonight. Are you going to take yourself [or a synonym of that] out of here or are we going to board you and take you in?" The yacht declined to comply with the suggestion, so the next thing we saw was this rather gallant little sailing boat being escorted between the islands at the entrance to Diego Garcia and into the small boat basin. Adorning its sides were sheets saying, "US and UK imperialists go home" or words to that effect on one side, and on the other side "Chagos for the Chagossians". It was perhaps indicative of the feelings that were developing at the time.

None of the results from our lagoon survey were particularly surprising to us, nor to my American counterparts, who were equally eager to ensure minimum damage to the lagoon's corals. We utilised our findings to persuade the Americans to limit anchoring to areas with extensive sandy expanses in the lagoon. However, moorings would have even more preferable. We observed significant recovery of the previously damaged corals in subsequent years.

Coral growth is essential for eventual sand production, and shoreline erosion in parts of Diego Garcia has been substantial. My own observations and discussions with shoreline engineers earlier had made it clear that any loss of the sand supply would compromise the island's ability to sustain its shoreline. The calculations were unambigous. Our joint US/UK team estimated that the removal of sediment by tides through the only entrance in the north of the atoll was between a quarter of a million to 1.4 million tons per year, sand that mostly needed to be replaced by coral growth.

By relocating the ancoring location, we believed that the net loss would be significantly reduced, and hopefully, much shoreline erosion would have slowed (assuming no further rise in sea level, though that, of course, is unfortunately far from the case).

The anchoring issue also applied to visiting yachts in the northern atolls, even though the boats and chains involved are, of course, much smaller. After several discussions with BIOT Administration, the presently permitted anchoring areas were reduced to a few designated areas in the lagoons of those atolls, mostly those that were already preferred by the yachts. I was tasked with talking to a collection of about 20 boat owners and explaining BIOT's thinking about future anchoring and anchoring zones. Some yacht owners accepted this perfectly happily, though some did not. A few, especially those who thought that a yachting lifestyle was the ultimate in being eco-friendly (to use their own words), thought that their own activities were not causing any damage, even if the activities of every other yacht were. Some became belligerent. But at that time, we had a very enlightened and environmentally aware Administrator who implemented a system that both allowed the yacht visits to continue while greatly limiting the damage that they were causing. One component was a rise in visiting yacht fees, which did stop some visiting yachts from calling in. Still, by that time, a greater deterrence on visiting yacht numbers was Somali pirates, which were excluding much of the Western Indian Ocean from being a safe place. Most visiting boat owners, then and now, appreciate being able to pause in one of these two northern Chagos atolls as they criss-cross the Indian Ocean.

Most yachties, as they are called, do or would prefer to act responsibly. Most want to help protect the natural beauty of the place. But one thing they all appear to have in common is a belief that they could do little or no environmental damage and that they are eco-friendly, low-impact-living-off-the-land people. Many have said that they thought taking a few turtles and coconut crabs for their own consumption would surely not be a problem, is it? Well, yes, it is! The islands are tiny, the coconut crabs and turtles have recovered in many islands but not yet in others, so any number taken from the smaller islands does make a damaging difference. This belief that any resource use that we use individually will not make much difference is a worldwide issue. It is clearly seen in these small islands, but it underlies much of the world's environmental problems.

SEWAGE IN DIEGO GARCIA LAGOON

Sewage has long been recognised as a global issue for coral reefs. Similar to anchoring, many yachties seem unaware of the impact of their discharged sewage. When the number of boats is minimal, the discharged sewage may have little effect. However, considering that the most popular yacht anchorage location is in the confined and shallow area in the far southwest of Salomon lagoon, where greenish plankton blooms are sometimes visible, it clearly has a significant impact on local water quality. The problem lies in the fact that corals are adapted to living in water with very low nutrient levels, and sewage is abhorrent to them. Additionally, there is the potential for introducing pathogens in the sewage that could damage corals. This has already occured in the Caribbean, where pathogens associated with sewage seems to be the cause of some devastating diseases that have nearly wiped out the primary coral reef builders in shallow waters throughout that region. I certainly did not want to witness a similar event in the Chagos atolls, where, at that time, there was little evidence of coral disease as far as we could tell.

It is perhaps a universal human condition to suppose that one never causes such problems oneself.

In Diego Garcia, it was stipulated in BIOT law that discharging from ships in DG lagoon was also prohibited. On occasion over the years, requests were received for permission to discharge sewage into the lagoon, for example, during times of war when there was a huge surge in the population. The British always refused these requests, as there was a perfectly functioning sewage plant operating below capacity. Whenever sewage discharges were detected by the island's environmental team, it would be flagged up to me, as well as to their own authorities. However, in 2013, the Americans admitted to BIOT that some of their cargo ships had no holding tanks. The British Minister for Overseas Territories announced this to Parliament. Some journalists swiftly became excited by this news story, and so did the internet chatter. Headlines and internet blogs emerged along the lines of the US polluting the pristine waters of Diego Garcia, and so on. One belligerent American complained that the British were "pissing on their allies", an unfortunate choice of phrase in the circumstances, given that it was some American ships that were illegally discharging sewage into the British lagoon! Diego Garcia lagoon is one of the most enclosed, navigable lagoons in the Indian Ocean, possibly in the world, a factor that would concentrate any effects.

So, we conducted another survey, once again in collaboration with our American colleagues. The ships that were at fault were equipped with holding tanks, eliminating the need for them to discharge sewage into the lagoon.

This might be important in the longer term. Today, with seawater warming, corals throughout the archipelago are becoming increasingly stressed, as they are all over the world. We know that many of mankind's impacts act synergistically, so in such cases, the alleviation of any one impact will lessen the harmful effects of another. Such management can buy time. Diego Garcia needs its corals more than it needs anything else because it is built from them, and anything people can do to reduce stressors of any kind is highly desirable. This issue is gaining traction worldwide.

One final thought: To slow down the rate of death among the essential corals in DG lagoon and mitigate the erosion of its reefs, I suggested creating an entrance into the lagoon at the southeast end of the land rim. This would facilitate a significantly improved water exchange, particularly during the Southeast Trade winds season. Conducting an environmental study is imperative, and the turtles in that specific area especially may well preclude such a cut, but if it could be done it would likely expedite recovery of the corals and alleviate shoreline erosion. Objections were raised on the basis that this would constitute interference with nature, and indeed it would. But, we have already interfered in numerous ways with this atoll over the past two centuries, starting with the felling of hardwoods in the late 18th century, mostly yielding detrimental outcomes. Would one more intervention that yields positive results not be a prudent idea?

REFERENCES

[1] Sheppard CRC. 2014. Famines, food insecurity and coral reef 'Ponzi' fisheries. *Marine Pollution Bulletin* 84: 1–4.

[2] Sheppard CRC et al. 2012. Reefs and islands of the Chagos Archipelago, Indian Ocean: Why it is the world's largest no-take marine protected area. *Aquatic Conservation: Marine Freshwater Ecosystems* 22: 232–261.

[3] Obura D. 2012. The diversity and biogeography of western Indian Ocean reef-building corals. *PLoS ONE* 7(9): e45013. doi:10.1371/journal.pone.0045013 PLoS1.

[4] Sheppard CRC et al. 2013. Chapter 17 British Indian Ocean Territory (the Chagos Archipelago): Setting, connections and the marine protected area. In: Sheppard CRC (ed.) *Coral Reefs of the UK Overseas Territories*. Springer, Dordrecht, pp. 223–240. **And:**
Eble JA, Craig MT, Rocha L, Bowen BW. 2011. Not all offspring stay close to home: Trans-Pacific dispersal and gene flow in Indo-Pacific reef fishes. *Journal of Marine Biology*. Article ID 518516, 12 pp. https://doi.org/10.1155/2011/518516.

[5] Mortimer JA, Day M, Broderick D. *20th Annual Sea Turtles Symposium, 2000*. NOAA Technical Memorandum NMFS-SEFSC-477, pp. 47–49.

[6] Hays GC, Mortimer JA, Jerodiaconou D, Esteban N. 2014. Use of long-distance migration patterns of an endangered species to inform conservation planning for the world's largest marine protected area. *Conservation Biology* 28: 1636–1644.

[7] Eble JA, Craig MT, Rocha L, Bowen BW. 2011. Not all offspring stay close to home: Trans-Pacific dispersal and gene flow in Indo-Pacific reef fishes. *Journal Marine Biology* Article ID 518516, 12 pp. **And:**
Gaither MR, Toonen RJ, Robertson DR, Plane S, Bowen BW. 2010. Genetic evaluation of marine biogeographical barriers: perspectives from two widespread IndoPacific snappers (*Lutjanus kasmira* and *Lutjanus fulvus*). *Journal Biogeography* 37: 133–147.

[8] Veron J, Stafford-Smith M, DeVantier L, Turak E. 2015. Overview of distribution patterns of zooxanthellate Scleractinia. *Frontiers in Marine Science* 1, Article 91, pp. 1–19.

[9] Head CEI, Bonsall MB, Koldewey H, Pratchett MS, Speight M, Rogers AD. 2015. High prevalence of obligate coral-dwelling decapods on dead corals in the Chagos Archipelago, central Indian Ocean. *Coral Reefs* 34: 905–915. **And**:
Head C et al. 2018. Exceptional biodiversity of the cryptofaunal decapods in the Chagos Archipelago, central Indian Ocean. *Marine Pollution Bulletin* 135: 636–647.

[10] Sheppard CRC, Spalding M, Bradshaw C, Wilson S. 2002. Erosion vs. recovery of coral reefs after 1998 El Niño: Chagos reefs, Indian Ocean. *Ambio* 31: 40–48.

[11] Ateweberhan M et al. 2013. Climate change impacts on coral reefs: Synergies with local effects, possibilities for acclimation, and management implications. *Marine Pollution Bulletin* 74: 526–539.

[12] Wilkinson C, Salvat B. 2012. Coastal resource degradation in the tropics: Does the tragedy of the commons apply for coral reefs, mangrove forests and seagrass beds. *Marine Pollution Bulletin* 64: 1096–1105.

[13] Fenner D. 2012. Challenges for managing fisheries on diverse coral reefs. *Diversity* 4: 105–160.

[14] Graham NAJ, McClanahan TR. 2013. The last call for marine wilderness? *BioScience* 63: 397–402. **And:**
Graham NAG, Pratchett MS, McClanahan TR, Wilson SK. 2013. Chapter 19 The status of coral reef fish assemblages in the Chagos Archipelago, with implications for protected area management and climate change. In: Sheppard CRC (ed.) *Coral Reefs of the UK overseas Territories*. Springer, Dordrecht, pp. 253–270.

[15] McClanahan TR, Muthiga NA. 2020. Oceanic patterns of thermal stress and coral community degradation on the island of Mauritius. *Coral Reefs* 40: 53–74.
[16] Samoilys M, Roche R, Koldewey H, Turner J. 2018. Patterns in reef fish assemblages: Insights from the Chagos Archipelago. *PLoS ONE* 13: e0191448. https://doi.org/10.1371/journal.pone.0191448.
[17] Spalding MD. 2006. Illegal sea cucumber fisheries in the Chagos Archipelago. *SPC Beche-de-mer Information Bulletin* 23: 32–34.
[18] Price ARG, Harris A, McGowan A, Venkatachalam AJ, Sheppard CRC. 2009. Chagos feels the pinch: Assessment of holothurian (sea cucumber) abundance, illegal harvesting and conservation prospects in British Indian Ocean Territory. *Aquatic Conservation: Marine and Freshwater Ecosystems* 20: 117–126. **And:**
Price ARG, Evans LE, Rowlands N, Hawkins JP. 2013. Negligible recovery in Chagos holothurians (sea cucumbers). *Aquatic Conservation: Marine and Freshwater Ecosystems* 23: 811–819.
[19] Ferretti F, Curnick D, Kiu K, Romanov WV, Block BA. 2018. Shark baselines and the conservation role of remote coral reef ecosystems. *Science Advances* 4(3): eaaq0333. https://doi.org/10.1126/sciadv.aaq0333.
[20] Spalding MD. 2004. Partial recovery of sharks in the Chagos Archipelago. *Shark News, newsletter of the IUCN Shark Specialist Group* 15: 12–13.
[21] Greenpeace. 2013. Esperanza. *Indian Ocean Expedition 2013. Summary of Findings* 18 March–17 May 2013, 15 pp.
[22] Koldewey H et al. 2010. Potential benefits to fisheries and biodiversity of the Chagos Archipelago/British Indian Ocean Territory as a no-take marine reserve. *Marine Pollution Bulletin* 60: 1906–1916.
[23] Sheppard CRC, Spalding M. 2004. Chagos Conservation Management Plan for BIOT Administration. Chapter 5, Fisheries. Report for BIOT, 2004, pp. 19–24.33.

9 Creation of the BIOT Marine Reserve

It had become clear that Chagos serves a global purpose. We now know that we must strictly protect a substantial proportion of the world's marine habitats if any are to survive [1]. Most estimates suggest that one third of any habitat must be strictly protected for recovery to occur. That is a lot, and by 'protect', this means *really* protect, enough to prevent degradation and allow recovery. Merely declaring a marine reserve and not enforcing it, creating a 'paper park', does more harm than good because of the false comfort it provides. Furthermore, many so-called protected areas still permit various damaging activities to take place within them, following almost inevitable clamour from vested interests to exempt their activities. Fishing is a very ecosystem-distorting activity, and practitioners of this are particularly vociferous in their objections to protecting the habitats. Exemptions for them are commonly granted, making a mockery of any protection. Chagos and its expanse of reefs are huge and would go a significant way toward achieving the world's total area of properly protected reefs.

Another point is that, as noted earlier, an economics expert estimated [2] that the value of the Chagos area to the rest of the Indian Ocean region was in the hundreds of millions of dollars per year. This inadvertently places BIOT into the role of being one of the Indian Ocean's biggest donors, albeit unwittingly and perhaps unintentionally.

By about 2010, more than 200 scientists had been involved in one way or another with work on islands and reefs of Chagos. Half of them had directly participated in research expeditions, while others dealt with samples collected by the visiting scientists or conducted analyses of collected materials. The build-up of a consensus on the value of Chagos' reefs by some of the world's leading scientists was crucial if we were to achive full protection for this remarkable place, including the prohibition of the destructive industrial fishery. We needed a critical mass of opinion. With only a few of us, we could never have accomplished it.

The Pew Environment Group took the lead on this, and then an increasing number of other large marine organisations joined in. Pew has a programme to establish very large marine reserves around the world. Born out of a recognition of the need for preserving habitats and fish stocks in an environmentally declining global ocean, they constructed a grand plan to reverse the tide. To qualify for inclusion in what was to become the 'Big Ocean Network', a candidate site needed to meet three criteria: it needed to be big enough to make a difference to the oceans, it needed to be in good enough condition to be worth saving in the first place, and it needed to have governance or a government that could reasonably ensure its protection now and into the future [3]. BIOT fitted all three.

The 'Pew criteria' are important. There may be little point in preserving a place that is already a huge expanse of dead coral skeletons or that is heavily trawled mud.

DOI: 10.1201/9781003423300-9

There is no point in trying to preserve anything when it is situated next to towns filled with millions of hungry people. Likewise, there is no point in trying to achieve much with a corrupt or incompetent government, and there are too many of those. Most areas they have chosen are in the Pacific, and the Chagos Archipelago is the only such site in the entire Indian Ocean. There are none in the Caribbean, which is a salutary and alarming thought.

Pew hired some excellent staff and organised, along with the tiny Chagos Conservation Trust that had developed from the Friends of the Chagos, a group called the Chagos Environment Network (CEN). The CEN consisted of representatives from each of several leading NGOs and science societies, including the Royal Society, the Zoological Society, and the Linnean Society. (And, rather alarmingly, myself as the only individual.) Contacts in several other major organisations told me they would like to join as well, but the Chagossian story would make that unacceptable to some of their membership. The CEN advocated for Chagos to become a fully no-take protected area. With the powerful support we now had, we found that we were pushing at an open door. I was invited to brief the British Foreign Secretary, David Miliband, and was given a ten-minute slot to sell the idea. Also, present were two other Foreign Office Ministers and a couple of BIOT officials. According to his official report, he became "fired up" by the idea. My ten minutes extended to over 20 because of questions and discussion. Then the Foreign Secretary simply told the officials "Do it!"

Now, I don't think it is often done as easily as that! One view of this, as was voiced later by those with vested interests and who opposed the protection in the first place, was that the Foreign Secretary incautiously rode rough-shod over advice from his officials for political reasons. In contrast, another view is that he recognised the need and was simply avoiding bureaucratic inertia, which could have bogged the process down for years (as has happened with marine protected areas around the UK itself). That Foreign Secretary has since become engaged in other environmental and climate issues, so even if there was an element of trying to set this up just before his party lost the next election (which was imminent), as his detractors claim, he has shown that he has genuine interest and understanding too.

The creation of the marine reserve then occurred more swiftly and smoothly than we had thought possible. The accumulation of extensive research in what were now several hundred scientific documents by many individuals unquestionably showed that this was a particularly crucial location. We now possessed that critical mass, and the necessity for additional conservation was no longer doubted by anyone responsible. The need was only denied by fishing interests, the Mauritian government, which claimed the islands were theirs, and by some vitriolic critics of just about anything associated with BIOT or the military.

The government issued a consultation on the concept of a fully no-take marine reserve. Avazz brought it to people's attention. CEN responded too, stating that only the designation as a completely no-take MPA "guarantees full protection for the ecosystem and species of the Chagos Archipelago and its surrounding reefs, lagoons, and waters. Only [this] provides the complete protection needed to underpin the Chagos Protected Area's value as an important global reference site for a wide range of scientific ecological, oceanographic, and climate studies, as well as its continued benefits to humans into the future" [4].

This neatly summed it up, and the no-take marine protected area was swiftly proclaimed, extending to the 200 nautical mile boundary of the Territory. The Territory itself had been declared in the first place for military reasons, so some of the American military needed to be convinced that this would not affect their activities. Thus, Diego Garcia to 3 miles out was excised from the protected zone. That excision itself has attracted criticism too, inevitably, but in fact, Diego Garcia has several strict nature reserves of its own as well as a large Ramsar area, and already had much more effective protection than do most other marine protected areas in the Indian Ocean. It was claimed shrilly that the exclusion of Diego Garcia negated the MPA, though no grounds for that were ever given; the existence of towns in Queensland does not negate the Great Barrier Reef Marine Protected Area, for example.

The BIOT Marine Reserve thus became the largest strictly no-take marine reserve in the world for several years. It belongs to the 'Big Ocean Network', which is an information exchange network with other very large marine protected areas, all of which are in the Pacific. One or two others, mostly formed later, were larger but not fully no-take—activities such as fishing were exempted in several. The large conservation body IUCN has published a book on these giant marine reserves, with much information about how to manage them [5], which is a rather different process to managing a small or 'normal' MPA.

We had the backing of several eminent bodies from an early stage, although not all. After the MPA had been formed, several other NGOs wrote, in their own publicity or newsletters, about how important, indeed central, they had been to its successful creation all along! Following the establishment of the marine reserve, many changed their minds, including one or two who had declined to join CEN due to fears about their local membership's views. These bodies now claimed to have been important all along. Far from being irritated, I swiftly realised that this was the best endorsement of all and should simply be taken as flattery!

All this came about because of the preceding science that demonstrated the necessity for it. One crucial element of that was its capacity to provide information on how reef systems operate when they are unaffected by local human impacts. This is becoming more critical with each passing year. In the last count, the Chagos reefs and islands harboured hundreds of threatened species [6], and the place serves as a reservoir or refuge for most of them. We also have evidence, which is growing stronger as research continues, indicating that it may also function as a partial refuge for several migratory ocean species, such as certain tuna. Natural selection would ensure this in theory anyway, and there is evidence of protection for even wide-ranging tuna in large, protected areas in the Pacific [7]. Naturally, there is opposition from those who wish to exploit it, and we hope the government's resolve does not waver in the face of pressure from commercial sectors or other governments.

Some points cause worry, however. One concern is the money that governments can gain in the short term from tuna fishing licences, at least while fish stocks survive a fisheries onslaught. All scientists know the absurdity of this 'short-termism', and we hope that the UK and BIOT Governments will continue to resist it. This, for the moment, is likely, given numerous statements from them about the need for conservation and its newer Blue Belt programme of marine conservation around other UK Overseas Territories too. Another very important factor is that the International Court of Justice and the UN have given the opinion that the United Kingdom should give these islands to Mauritius as soon as possible. The UK government, at the end of 2022, stated they will now negotiate with Mauritius about sovereignty. The basis of the Mauritian claim seems to be that, although the UK took these from the French in about 1814, they were administered from Mauritius for much of the time since. The UK did not take this view, but as one of the judges said, it is the new perception of justice that is important. This perception is fuelled by the way the fate of the Chagossian people was handled.

Mauritius might not be as careful or able to afford the same level of caution regarding conservation matters, and it could potentially modify the conservation regime if it were to gain sovereignty. They certainly seem to have a strong desire for the fish! It is worth noting that the primary practical change resulting from the proclamation of the marine protected area was the prohibition of industrial fishing, an important measure. However, in all other aspects, it had been a protected area for 50 years previously due to its essential designation as a military exclusion zone. Incidentally, Mauritius still retains certain fishing rights, though it chooses not to exercise them.

DEEP WATER NOT YET EXPLORED

Work, still scarcely begun, ecompasses almost everything in the deep ocean beyond the central kernel of reefs and islands. It also includes studies on many of the major marine groups. Chagos has about 300 seamounts, which, unlike many in the rest of the world, have not been destroyed by huge ocean-going trawlers. It is likely that the now-protected seamounts will turn out to be extremely important biological assets. Between and around the seamounts is a vast area of abyssal depths, with an abyssal trench and huge plains, about which we know almost nothing. Investigating such areas incurs significant costs due to the specialised ships and equipment needed to work at such depths, ranging from several hundred metres to several kilometres deep. We can be sure that these areas contain immense biological wealth in their deep-sea organisms, as well as minerals, if only because we know they have never been trawled or exploited.

MORE CAVALRY FROM OVER THE HORIZON

For this offshore and deeper research, as well as for more detailed and extensive investigations, especially on large, charismatic, and migratory species, rescue has come from the Bertarelli Foundation. They have funded more scientists than ever before to carry out work in these areas. Scientists currently engaged in the work have already begun addressing offshore regions by tagging sharks, tuna, and turtles, deploying underwater acoustic arrays, employing eDNA techniques, and using other methods of measurement. It is highly instrument-focussed set of projects led by scientists from a wider range of countries, all of whom have started producing new results. The research now encompasses large predatory fish and their biology. However, basic monitoring has somewhat taken a back seat to these programmes.

Similar to the provision of ocean-going yachts in the earliest expeditions, funds needed for the work continue to come from generous private donors and foundations.

The biology of fish stocks that are commercially exploited elsewhere in the ocean is another under-researched area. Despite the licensed fishery, for years, only a bare minimum of data were collected during all that time to tell us about the biology of these animals, mainly tuna, but fisheries were outside my remit.

Occasional bits of information did appear from analyses of some collected data: the substantial by-catch of unwanted species, for example [8]. Sharks were at times part of the by-catch, but we know that they were also deliberately targeted, sometimes heavily, and particularly for their valuable fins. The fishing ban resulting from the marine reserve declaration prevented an unknown but significant amount of mortality of a wide range of non-targeted species. Marine systems are interconnected, and especially when some targeted species are secondary predators crucial for energy transfer through the entire ecosystem, it was crucial for the fishing ban be implemented. Perhaps the main failure of the previous fishing policy was that we still had little idea about the quantity of higher trophic level biomass being removed annually from the region. It must have been extremely high but was never recorded.

Funding for all this research and use of the BIOT Patrol Vessel to reach the islands had been problematic all along but is now being resolved by benefactors. Sometimes, the BIOT government seemed, for a long time, not to be aware (even if some of its officials were) of what a gem they have. However, a minimum of funding was usually found. In broad terms, one research trip of a couple of weeks might cost around a third of a million pounds or over half a million dollars. The BIOT government provided its ship for free, which is very valuable, but gave little else in material terms. Other UK government agencies commonly provided between £50,000 and £100,000 for each of the early expeditions, but the rest came from the resources of the institutes where the invited scientists worked or from grant providers funding the people who participated. By about 2010, probably more had been funded by each of at least three other countries than came from BIOT. The science done for BIOT has cost them a small fraction of its real cost. We often struggled to help the BIOT Administration get what they need. This is changing, partly because of the global increase in environmental awareness now that the ocean environment is better recognised as being in severe decline.

A final accolade for the Chagos project came a few years after the creation of the protected area. A body composed of the UK's research funding councils and relevant government departments highlighted the UK's achievements in development and conservation science by producing a 'Top 20' list of projects completed in the preceding five years. These projects were selected from total of about 7,000 projects, covering various disciplines such as science, sociology, and economics. We were in that 'Top 20' [9]. Furthermore, we were one of only a couple of marine science and conservation projects, the others addressed sociological, legal, financing issues, and, of course, terrestrial conservation and food security matters. We hope this success can endure into the future when resources become more depleted elsewhere and that the Archipelago will continue to provide the environmental services to mankind that it does today.

REFERENCES

[1] Toonen RJ and many otherset al. 2013. One size does not fit all: The emerging frontier in large-scale marine conservation. *Marine Pollution Bulletin* 77: 7–10.

[2] Gravestock P, Sheppard CRC. 2015. Valuing the ecosystem services of the Chagos: A review of challenges and estimates. *Marine Ecology Progress Series* 530: 255–270.

[3] Nelson J, Bradner H. 2010. The case for establishing ecosystem-scale marine reserves. *Marine Pollution Bulletin* 60: 635–637. **And:**
Lubchenco J, Palumbi SR, Gaines SD, Andelman S. 2003. Plugging a hole in the ocean: The emerging science of marine reserves. *Ecological Applications* 13(1): S3–S7.

[4] Pew Environment Group. 2010. http://www.globaloceanlegacy.org/.

[5] Lewis N, Day JC, Wilhelm A, Wagner D, Gaymer C, Parks J, Friedlande A, White S, Sheppard C, Spalding M, San Martin G, Skeat A, Taei S, Teroroko T, Evan, J. 2017. *Large-Scale Marine Protected Areas: Guidelines for Design and Management. Best Practice Protected Area Guidelines Series*, No. 26. IUCN, Gland, Switzerland, xxviii + 120 pp.

[6] Hayes G et al. 2020. A review of a decade of lessons from one of the world's largest MPAs: Conservation gains and key challenges. *Marine Biology* 167: 159. https://doi.org/10.1007/s00227-020-03776-w.

[7] Hernandez CM, Witting J, Willis C, Thorrold SR, Llopez JK, Rotjan RP. 2019. Evidence and patterns of tuna spawning inside a large no-take marine protected area. *Scientific Reports* 9: 10772. https://doi.org/10.1038/s41598-019-47161-0.

[8] Koldewey H et al. 2010. Potential benefits to fisheries and biodiversity of the Chagos Archipelago/British Indian Ocean Territory as a no-take marine reserve. *Marine Pollution Bulletin* 60: 1906–1916.

[9] https://www.ukcdr.org.uk/case-study/conserving-marine-environments/.

10 Climate Change Research

Today, climate change is one of the world's most signigicant scientific issues because it threatens the stability of the ecosystems that support us. Does it affect the Chagos ecosystem? We have witnessed what warming does to corals, but what other effects does it have, if any? Currently, warming is causing substantial damage to reefs in tropical oceans, but what else is being affected?

Climate is certainly changing in the Chagos Archipelago. Rainfall, an easily measured parameter, is observed to be increasing annually. Figure 10.1 (left) illustrates that annual rainfall has risen since 1950, from about 2,500 mm pear year to an average of a little over 3,000 mm per year. Figure 10.1 (right) depicts the seasonality of this change. Ordered from September, the months September to May now dispay increased rainfall, while the months of the Southeast Trade wind show a slight decrease in rainfall. These Trade wind months were already the driest. Interestingly, this overall annual rise is the reciprocal of the situation in East Africa, where rainfall is declining, leading to severe implications for local agriculture. In the Chagos, the effects of this on birds need to be investigated, as do the effects of rain on the temperature of beaches and the nesting success of turtles.

In the sea, despite geographical remoteness having once distanced Chagos from mankind's numerous assaults, reefs of the Chagos Archipelago suffered from warming water just as severely, and in some ways worse, than many other reefs around the world. Unfortunately, archipelagos like this were just as susceptible to marine heatwaves.

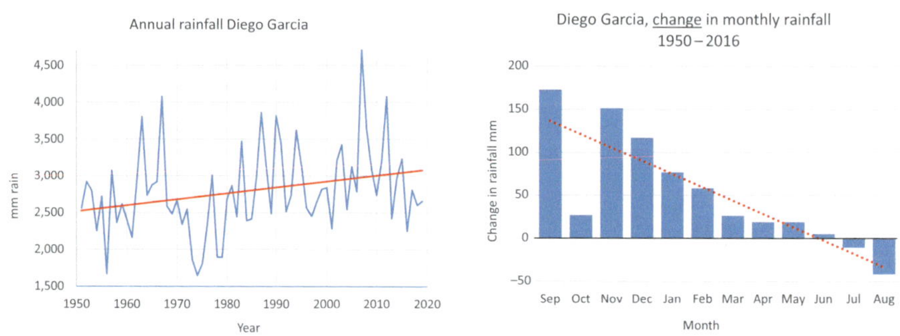

FIGURE 10.1 Rainfall in the Chagos Archipelago. Left: Annual averages, showing a significant rise since 1950. Right: The rainfall increase occurs during the months September through to May, while the remaining months when the Southeast Trade winds dominate show slightly reduced rainfall. Data from the US Government airport met station on the US Navy Facility, Diego Garcia, graphs by the author.

DOI: 10.1201/9781003423300-10

MEASURING WATER TEMPERATURES

Water temperatures can be measured in several ways: by satellite, which measures only the surface layer, by data loggers, capable of measuring it at any depth, and by estimates of past temperatures that can be accurately derived from cores taken from massive coral colonies. We have utilised all three methods. For long-term temperature trends, colleagues employed material from Chagos coral cores. If a core is drilled into a large boulder-shaped coral, and thin slices of the core are x-rayed, its growth rings—similar to the rings of a tree trunk—become visible. These rings are deposited annually, so a ring, for instance, 125 layers down from the surface was laid down 125 years ago. Geochemists then measure the ratios of different isotopes in that tiny layer. The various isotopes of oxygen in it correlate very closely with the temperature of the seawater that the coral inhabited at that time. Through this method, a temperature curve over hundreds of years before the present can be deduced. Furthermore, ocean salinity can be corelated with rainfall and computed as well. Chagos is situated in a region of high climate variability, and some of the signals obtained from this work have been crucial in understanding Indian Ocean climate change. This has resulted in a series of significant publications [1], from which many inferences were derived to better understand the ongoing climate change.

We also have a long series of two-hourly ocean temperature readings from data loggers in many parts of the archipelago, going back to early 2006 (Figure 10.2). These readings come from depths of 5, 15, and 25 m on lagoonal and ocean-facing reefs in all atolls. I hoped they would capture the next great warming event, which was already being predicted.

FIGURE 10.2 A temperature logger on a reef at 5 m depth. The logger is placed inside a plastic tube to protect it from browsing fish, and perhaps turtles. It is open at both ends so water freely mixes, and the whole is tied to a stake hammered into the reef.

They did achieve this, but initially recorded some minor warming events, including one that killed almost all the corals on the lagoon floor of Salomon atoll. Some unexpected results were also found: on ocean-facing reef slopes, ocean temperatures plunged by several degrees during certain seasons, in cycles with a periodicity of a few days [2]. The temperature plunges are the result of deeper, cooler water moving up the reef slope as the cold-water thermocline becomes shallower due to long 'internal waves'. This mostly happens when the surface waters have warmed to their highest temperatures of the year and might bring some respite to the corals, which could be why the reefs here recovered relatively quickly from bleaching damage. Lagoon slopes behave differently and do not show these temperature plunges; the cold water does not penetrate far into the lagoons.

These recorders then monitored the subsequent severe ocean heatwaves that occurred in 2015 and 2016, an even worse and more prolonged event than that of 1998, discussed in Chapter 7, with catastrophic effects every bit as severe. By then, due to the severity of these impacts, the aims of much of the work had expanded from describing what a rich reef system looked like and how it worked to aspects of recovery, consequences, and how this would affect the island shores as well as the reefs themselves.

More than a decade earlier I had calculated that the 'extinction point' of Chagos reefs might arrive by about the mid-2020s. This calculation was based on rates of recovery of both reef growth and coral growth (not the same thing but often conflated), as well as on the predicted increase in water temperature over time due to global climate change, and the increasing frequency of warm water episodes over time [3]. This work was later significantly amplified and refined by other studies [4], which confirmed those estimates. When I submited my initial paper on this to the journal *Nature* in 2003, I was certain that they would complain that the term 'extinction point' was overly dramatic, hysterical, and unscientific, at the very least. After all, some opponents to my Chagos conservation plans had used those terms against me. However, neither the journal nor the paper's several referees questioned it, and so it remained. I believe that, by this time, scientists had recognised the gravity of the situation.

The prolonged warming, starting in 2015, had peaks over two years. In both years, ocean heatwaves lasted for several weeks and were warmer than any we had seen before. The impacts on the corals and soft corals of the reefs were catastrophic. Some temperature loggers showed that 2016 was even worse than 2015, causing further mortality. They did not recover at all over the next three years, and my last visit was in 2019 before the COVID-19 pandemic closed it all down for a couple of years. During our 2019 visit, water remained over 30°C, sometimes 31°C, all the way down to 25 m depth. This had become a prolonged and lethal ocean heatwave.

What about the future? A decade is probably the fastest we might expect for a coral reef to regain its vibrant ecosystem and good ability to calcify, but what will happen when mass coral mortalities occur more frequently than this? Then, a more serious question arises: what will happen when they start occurring more frequently than every five years, which is roughly the average age most corals must attain before they can reproduce? These critical questions concern reefs everywhere and impact the human communities they now struggle to support.

MEASURING CORAL COVER

Coral cover is a widely used and simple indicator of coral reef health. It can be a valuable measure, for example, it correlates well with reef structural and habitat complexity, which is crucial for supporting a high diversity of life [5]. However, it is overly simplistic because it overlooks many aspects, such as identity of corals, associated calcareous algal growth, reef calcification, net reef growth, and several other key factors. Despite its limitations, simple coral cover has numerous applications. Most importantly, it is quick to measure compared to some more comprehensive methods. While better methods would involve identifying all the species comprising that cover, it's essential to remember that a whole year's sampling programme, which may require a ship for a couple of weeks, actually takes only approximately 28 hours of actual observation and measurement underwater—a relatively short duration. Although we can collect samples for later analyses and utilise extensive video footage, the methods we employ for direct observation likely yield the most information in the shortest time. I would like to conduct more detailed work on some of the 300 species present in the area, examining which species become more 'important' as other more conspicuous ones disappear. This information is crucial for the survival of a reef but demands considerably more time than available in this remote location. Establishing a local, permanently staffed research centre would be necessary for such comprehensive research efforts.

We know that the lethal temperatures for most corals was 29.5°C in 1998. Today, we can observe that the warmest pulses are now reaching 31°C. However, the effects are patchy over this large archipelago, and not every area responds in the same way at the same time. In Diego Garcia, I have witnessed several instances of sub-lethal episodes of coral bleaching where, a year later, the beds of formerly strongly bleached corals had regained their colour and appeared healthy again. In a contrasting example, in 2013, the lagoon floor corals deeper than about 10 m depth in Solomon Atoll were almost entirely killed over many square kilometres—a warm pulse had been recorded the year before. In this moderately enclosed lagoon, the floor had been dominated mainly by leafy coral species, and the vast expanses of now dead skeletons were becoming increasingly fragile. Fortuitously, we have a temperature logger in this region too, and subsequent years have shown even more prolonged temperature rises at 25 m depth in this location. Much of Salomon's lagoon floor remained dead when last seen in 2019, and perhaps as important, the deeper water in the area has become far more sedimented as the coral skeletons disintegrate.

MEASURING SEA LEVEL RISE

We now know that sea level is rising. Some climate change deniers still exist and can be found on several websites with tortuous explanations. I have also encountered several misinterpretations of the long-term Chagos data. Sadly, sea level is rising, and it has several components: overall oceanic levels that can now be measured by satellite, caused partly by melting polar ice and partly by the existing seawater expanding a little as it warms; by local land movements; and by local vagaries arising from atmospheric conditions. Even within one basin like the Indian Ocean, the spin of the Earth, vagaries of where continents lie, and regional differences in the force of gravity caused by different underlying rocks all cause local sea level differences. Another factor that still needs clarification is that the global ice caps exert an 'auto-gravity' that gravitationally pulls water towards that pole; as the ice melts and the meltwater spreads over the Earth, this gravitational attraction disappears, and with it, the previously attracted water. One unofficial estimate given to me suggests that the increased rise over the tropics may add another third to the presently predicted rise. Their summation will be detected by tide gauges, one of which (part of a global network) is in Diego Garcia. The data are available online, as they are from very many places. The gauge there is a suite of three sets of instruments: a pressure sensor, a radar, and a float sensor [6]. It is not just a stick in the sand! Sea level is rising significantly. The raw data is daily (hourly data is available too), but for various reasons, including averaging out tidal differences and other technical details, I usually chose to take the average in calendar months. In one month, there are two neap-spring cycles, so plotting average calendar months provides a pretty reasonable and widely used method.

From 1988, the sea level on ocean-facing reefs of Diego Garcia rose, on average, about 6 mm per year [7]. The rate has been accelerating. All the simple straight-line fits are highly statistically significant, and this pattern is observed at many sites around the tropical ocean. It is, of course, highly significant for low-lying inhabited coral islands throughout the tropics, as well as increasingly expensive to try and combat (Figures 10.3 and 10.4). On the two highest spring tides, there is sea water flooding in some areas already, with sharks swimming over grass [8], and rays seen swimming in a tidally flooded car park. Various organisations, including NASA, the World Bank, the IPCC, and others, have all warned the nearby Maldives that 80% of that country will be uninhabitable by 2050. The Maldives is on the same archipelagic chain.

FIGURE 10.3 A high spring tide in Diego Garcia brings water into the coastal vegetation. At such times, these shoreline trees and shrubs become inundated.

FIGURE 10.4 A broach of the shore on a spring tide in Chagos allows small sharks to swim over the grass where they were foraging for food. This shark was part of a group of six.

ISLAND EROSION

Many shores on several islands have shown considerable erosion due to the rising wave energy that strikes the reefs as sea level rises above the reefs protecting the beaches. The cost of shoreline 'hardening' in DG is now several million dollars per year, necessary to protect the infrastructure there [9]. All Chagos islands are low-lying and are built by coral, so what will happen when sea level rises further, and as rising temperatures kill the reef building corals? Earlier in 2014, some of us, led by distinguished US reef geologists, published a short rebuttal [10] in *Science* of some ill-considered and oversimplified results that asserted the growth of coral islands, such as those in Chagos, can keep up with the present rise in sea level. However, the average rise in reef growth around the world over thousands of years was only around 3.5 mm per year. We also made the point that this growth rate assumes good, healthy coral growth, but as shown above, warming means corals are not healthy at all. This average of 3.5 mm is derived from results ranging from 0.6 to 7.9 mm per year, and Chagos reefs lie, or at least did, towards the upper part of this range. Other colleagues have determined that because of the coral mortality, carbonate production by corals dropped, atleast for a while, by 77% as a result [11].

Other work we have been able to accomplish so far in DG used old aerial photos. A set was found that had been made into a mosaic of the entire atoll, presented to a retiring US Serviceman in the 1970s; this was retrieved, scanned, and compared with a modern high-resolution satellite image [12]. We observed considerable erosion of exposed shores but also a significant deposition of soft sediment in other areas of the lagoon. This accumulation compensates for the total area, but the net result is a loss of old, dark, organically rich soil with accompanying trees, replaced in terms of area by new soft sandy and muddy areas, which is not an equivalent replacement. A development of this work has shown that islands on reef flats may accumulate material on leeward sides as rapidly as it erodes on windward sides [13]. For a while, islands can adjust by migrating slowly over the reef flat in this way, but that cannot last forever.

One very important point here is the profile of most Chagos islands. Most of these islands have raised rims and depressions in the middle (Figure 10.5) [14].

Where the coastal areas of islands were low sand, the sand has been washed away (Figure 10.6a). However, sea level rise may show no significant erosion of the coastline for a while, up to the point when the island rim breaches. Rates of inundation of the land will be nonlinear with respect to sea level rise. This scenario is already observed in several islands, though the exact timing of when this occurred is not

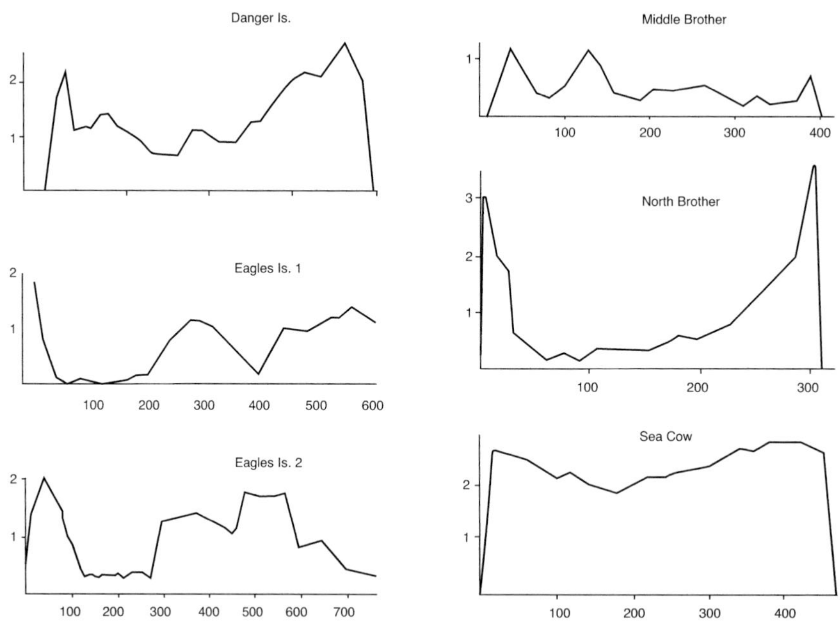

FIGURE 10.5 Cross-sectional profiles across several islands in Chagos (vertically exaggerated), showing depressions that approach or descend below high sea level. Data from military expedition personnel. All numbers are in metres.

(a) (b)

FIGURE 10.6 (a) Shoreline palms with recently eroded roots in intertidal areas. (b) A saline lake caused by incursion of the sea (Ile Anglais, Salomon Atoll).

known and predates modern times. One or two saline 'lakes' can be observed in aerial photos, where this breaching has occurred in years past (Figure 10.6b).

Everywhere, the most responsible predictions suggest that most atolls will be uninhabitable by the mid-21st century due to sea level rise [15]. Where shoreline defences are built on the inhabited atoll Diego Garcia, it is becoming extremely expensive, using rocks imported from Asia or Mauritius that are much harder than the soft Chagos limestone.

OTHER CLIMATE CHANGE FACTORS

Other climate change factors affecting reefs include an increase in the acidity of the water as atmospheric CO_2 continues to rise, much of which dissolves in seawater. We have never measured this in Chagos, and it needs to be researched. It is known from recent studies, such as those on Hawaii and the Great Barrier Reef, that this may become as important as warming over the longer term. In brief, rising acidification reduces the ability of corals to calcify and build their limestone skeletons. It also greatly affects calcareous red algae, including those that build the essential spur and groove structures and the algal ridges located at the seaward ends of the reef flats. Because these structures form the natural, major wave breaks protecting the shorelines, this greatly affects the viability of the islands behind them. Problems here could turn out to be the most important of all, and this still needs to be addressed.

Furthermore, in some of Earth's great extinctions in its long geological past, it is known that ocean acidity dropped significantly to values below those where corals can calcify. This is bad enough, but what's even worse is that we know from the fossil record that several hundreds of thousands of years needed to pass before ocean pH rose again to levels where reefs could return. Another even more salutary point is that there is a time lag during which atmospheric CO_2 levels reach equilibrium with that of CO_2 dissolved in seawater [16]. This time lag is about three decades, meaning that even if we can stop atmospheric CO_2 from rising any further right now, ocean acidity will continue to increase for many years.

Our atmospheric CO_2 concentration continues to rise. We know that the 'equilibrium levels' in the atmosphere of about 350 parts per million CO_2 is the maximum threshold above which corals will cease to grow. The Earth passed this point in 1989 and is now about 420 ppm.

There are other elements that also need addressing. Diseases are another factor that may be increasing in Chagos. They are certainly becoming more prevalent now, and a rise in temperature leads to increased diseases. This is particularly evident in Caribbean reefs, for example. Some minimal work on this was started in Chagos, but it has had to be discontinued for a while [17].

REFERENCES

[1] Pfeiffer M, Timm O, Dullo W-C, Garbe-Schonberg D. 2006. Paired coral Sr/Ca and _18O records from the Chagos Archipelago: Late twentieth century warming affects rainfall variability in the tropical Indian Ocean. *Geological Society of America* 34: 1069–1072. **And:**
PfeifferM, Dullo WC, Eisenhauer A. 2004. Variability of the intertropical convergence zone recorded in coral isotopic records from the central Indian Ocean (Chagos Archipelago). *Quaternary Research* 61: 245–255. **And:**
Pfeiffer M, Dullo W-C, Zinke J, Garbe- Schonberg D. 2008. Three monthly coral Sr/Ca records from the Chagos Archipelago covering the period of 1950–1995 A.D.: Reproducibility and implications for quantitative reconstructions of sea surface temperature variations. *International Journal of Earth Science (Geology Rundsch)* 98: 53–66. https://doi.org/10.1007/s00531-008-0326-z. **And:**
Leupold M, Pfeiffer M, Garbe-Schönberg D, Sheppard CRC. 2020. Reef-scale-dependent response of massive porites corals from the central Indian Ocean to prolonged thermal stress: Evidence from coral Sr/Ca measurements. *Geochemistry Geophysics Geosystems* 20: 1468–1484. https://doi.org/10.1029/2018GC007796.

[2] Sheppard CRC. 2009. Large temperature plunges recorded by data loggers at different depths on an Indian Ocean atoll: Comparison with satellite data and relevance to coral refuges. *Coral Reefs* 28: 399–403.

[3] Sheppard CRC. 2003. Predicted recurrences of mass coral mortality in the Indian Ocean. *Nature* 425: 294–297.

[4] Van Hooidonk R, Maynard J, Tamelander J, Gove J, Ahmadia G, Raymundo L, Williams G, Heron SF, Planes S. 2016. Local-scale projections of coral reef futures and implications of the Paris agreement. *Science Reports* 6: 39666. https://doi.org/10.1038/srep39666.

[5] Graham NAJ, McClanahan TR, MacNeil MA, Wilson SK, Polunin NVC et al. 2008. Climate warming, marine protected areas and the ocean-scale integrity of coral reef ecosystems. *PLoS One* 3(8): e3039. https://doi.org/10.1371/journal.pone.0003039.

[6] http://uhslc.soest.hawaii.edu/data/ (Diego Garcia is site number 104).

[7] Sheppard CRC, Sheppard ALS. 2019. Chapter 11 British Indian Ocean Territory (Chagos Archipelago). In: Sheppard CRC (ed.) *World Seas: An Environmental Assessment*, Volume 3. Academic Press, London, San Diego, pp. 237–252.

[8] Sheppard CRC. 2012. Sharks on the Lawn. The reality of rising sea-level on Indian Ocean Islands. *Ocean Challenge* 19: 17.

[9] Schwarzkopf J. 2012. Ships and anchors in Diego Garcia. *Chagos News* 40: 18–20.

[10] Hubbard D et al. 2014. Island outlook: Warm and swampy. *Science* 345: 146.

[11] Lange ID, Perry CT. 2019. Bleaching impacts on carbonate production in the Chagos Archipelago: influence of functional coral groups on carbonate budget trajectories. *Coral Reefs* 38: 619–624.

[12] Purkis SJ, Gardiner R, Johnston MW, Sheppard CRC. 2016. A half-century of coastline change in Diego Garcia – The largest atoll island in the Chagos. *Geomorphology* 261: 282–298.
[13] Wu M, Duvat VKE, Purkis SJ. 2021. Multi-decadal atoll-island dynamics in the Indian Ocean Chagos Archipelago. *Global and Planetary Change* 202: 103519. https://doi.org/10.1016/j.gloplacha.2021.103519.
[14] Sheppard CRC. 2002. Island elevations, reef condition and sea level rise in atolls of Chagos, British Indian Ocean Territory. *Cordio* 3: 202–211.
[15] Storlazzi CD et al. 2018. Most atolls will be uninhabitable by the mid-21st century because of sea-level rise exacerbating wave-driven flooding. *Science Advances* 4: eaap9741.
[16] Veron JEN et al. 2009. The coral reef crisis: The critical importance of <350 ppm CO_2. *Marine Pollution Bulletin* 58: 1428–1436.
[17] Sheppard CRC et al. 2013. Chapter 18 Coral reefs of the Chagos Archipelago, Indian Ocean. In: Sheppard CRC (ed.) *Coral Reefs of the UK Overseas Territories*. Springer, Dordrecht, pp. 241–252.

11 The World's Conservation Conundrum in One Archipelago

Decades ago, Cousteau lamented how parts of the Red Sea were deteriorating. I worked the full length of the Red Sea in the 1980s, marvelled at it, and wondered what on Earth he was talking about. I can never know exactly because, for all his huge achievements, Cousteau did not record the sort of data that we would need to tell. There are similar stories from many places, but these days the steady deterioration has been measured and documented carefully in most of them. I do know that most younger reef scientists today have never seen a near-pristine reef.

Going back a few centuries, the logs of some sailing ships related how they had been stopped in their tracks because the water was thick with turtles. Many stories tell of the sea "boiling" over several square miles from the huge densities of marine life. We assumed those writers were exaggerating—perhaps an old man's rose-tinted memories. This Shifting Baseline Syndrome [1] is something that seems to be hard-wired into us. Today, we have measured and quantified many aspects of climate change, so the debate has turned to why people appear unable to arrest the trend or, more pessimistically but pragmatically, how to live with the new equilibrium that the Earth is heading towards.

Another assumption that also seems to be hard-wired, probably because we so badly want it to be true, is that we could live in harmony with nature. If we could, then we might have less reason to worry, but if we can, why aren't we? There are now many examples of societies that have exploited their natural environment to their own severe detriment [2]. Unfortunately, decline is now so extensive globally that merely arresting the decline is not enough—we need to reverse it too, given the importance of all habitats, including reefs, to humans.

Many people have commented on what is needed to try to reverse this [3] and it is helpful to know why this is so difficult to achieve. Several answers can come from the story of the Chagos Archipelago because it is one that highlights some of the reasons why it is so challenging to protect reefs and the ocean in our increasingly resource-hungry world. While the world is too vast for us to grasp completely, many issues of the Chagos Archipelago are conceptually similar but smaller in scope, helping make global issues easier to understand. Not only are its reef systems and islands well studied, but the archipelago shows us what unexploited reefs would look like when left alone.

This has led to the present, horribly difficult problem whereby, as our population rises and expectations of standards of living increase, ever more vigorous exploitation

 DOI: 10.1201/9781003423300-11

FIGURE 11.1 Typical, vibrant deeper ocean-facing reef slope in the Chagos Archipelago at 30 m depth, taken before the 2015 warming.

is required to support us. It is like Alice's 'Red Queen' who had to run just to stay in the same place. The five decades without human occupation meant that Chagos' reefs avoided this, so that their condition contrasts starkly with reefs elsewhere, or used to, at least. But pressures to exploit it are many and increasing, and I have seen the resulting saga play out for years. It has been a fascinating, exasperating, often sad story, rich in lessons for reef science and conservation (Figure 11.1).

The Chagos Archipelago displays many superlatives: its huge reef fish biomass illustrates what humanity is currently missing and could regain with better control of human extraction. Its enormous populations of coconut crabs, its significance as a stepping-stone for species in the Indian Ocean, its crucial role as a refuge, its remarkably rapid recovery of coral cover after a bleaching event, high seabird densities on those few islands that were not razed for coconut plantations and colonised by rats, and the absence of marine pollution in sediments or biota [4], all demonstrate the existing potential. Scientists increasingly wish to observe how a 'real reef' works, and therein lies one of its crucial values today—a reference site without local interference—against which marine habitats elsewhere in the oceans can be compared. Even in the militarised Diego Garcia, the population is not dependent on local resources because it imports all its food and energy. Its own ecological footprint lies thousands of miles away.

Recreational fishing continues in parts of Diego Garcia, one of the few examples of resource exploitation that currently takes place. This situation also imparts a lesson. Only a few kilograms of fish are taken per hectare each year, or along each 100 m of reef. However, this appears to be sufficient to have significantly reduced this atoll's reef fish biomass compared to that measured on the uninhabited atolls of this group. Yet, the remaining amount is still as high as in the best-protected marine reserves almost everywhere else! The point here is that we can sustainably maintain only an extremely small population that depends on fishing because reef fishing tends to use up capital (spawning stock) until the fishery collapses in a 'Ponzi'-like effect [5]. Many studies support this [6]. Even moderate recreational fishing can substantially reduce fish biomass and alter its trophic balance [7]. It has been known for years, after all, that the concept of 'sustainability' still needs to be invented as a practical measure concerning reef fishing [8], and Chagos adds detail to that.

Offshore or blue-water fishing highlights another challenge in marine conservation. There has been no legal pelagic fishing in the no-take marine reserve since its creation in 2010, thus eliminating the risk not only for the tuna on migratory passages and those whose movement largely occurs within the MPA but also for reducing the previously substantial by-catch [9]. However, opposition to any fishing ban has been strong.

CONSERVATION AND DENIERS IN A CHANGING LANDSCAPE

Another global lesson gained from Chagos concerns territory and politics. Although many scientific publications have built up strong support for it, and a government consultation showed that the British public overwhelmingly supported the creation of the MPA, the issue is political because Mauritius claims the archipelago. The Chagossian issue has not been resolved, and various parts of the UN in 2012 told the UK that it should 'decolonise' and give the place to Mauritius. Several resettlement proposals, claiming to be cheap and sustainable, have been made, but conservation bodies have highlighted flaws in all of them, especially where they vastly underestimated the costs and ignored scientific evidence. One extreme example I saw was that a commercial runway could be built on one of the northern atolls for just $2 million if done by volunteer church groups—the airport built in another remote UK Territory in St Helena, which is inhabited, was well over $350 million. The alternative for access would be to use the military runway on Diego Garcia (DG) or limit all transport to travel by sea. The author of another feasibility study later more or less distanced himself from it in correspondence with me. Criticising such ideas has not been well-received by those who are wanting resettlement, of course, who therefore have accused the now numerous bodies collaborating on research there and individual scientists of being somehow anti-Chagossian. I know none that are.

Pointing out facts, however, is the first step in any responsible science. Some interested parties and observers, seem not to grasp this. Too many assume that scientific evidence is merely another 'stakeholder input', but of course, it is not. Not every stakeholder can claim equal validity because natural laws, sadly for some, will always trump a man-made law or idea. Our role in science has been, in part, to discover what those natural laws are and what they imply for the entire ecosystem.

Ownership of the area is an issue with important potential consequences for conservation. Abandoning attempts at conservation and starting heavy fishing would, of course, bring in several lines of revenue, but only over the short term. This is because it seems that you cannot sustain even a very modest fishery, if only because of that 'Ponzi effect'. Another common feature worldwide is that a conservation 'win' is only a win until a corrupt or vested interest overturns it for immediate and short-term revenue.

With regional demands on marine resources increasing in the area even faster than human populations, the future survival of reefs in Chagos cannot be guaranteed if exploited. The irony that the region's political and military importance has played a significant role in maintaining the better condition of Chagos reefs today generates much angst.

Another common issue faced by conservation efforts worldwide is the denial of the existence of climate change problems. Human psychology plays a role here, as explored in several books [10]. Various websites maintained by deniers assert that ocean temperatures are not rising significantly, sea-level rise is not a concern, and fish populations have not decreased, among other claims. If these assertions are repeated frequently and emphatically enough, some individuals come to believe them, especially if accepting them offers a path of least resistance, a stance often adopted by governments. Authorities may commonly employ a simple procrastination approach, arguing that no action should be taken yet due to 'uncertainty', insiting that more data are needed before any steps are taken.

Some deniers may believe in their own nonsense, but most opponents have vested interests, and in the case of the Chagos, simply dislike the military or its presence there. Aside from such opponents, there is undoubtedly a far larger number of people who simply don't like hearing bad news due to the human aversion to uncomfortable facts. Perhaps this is hard-wired too.

COSTS AND VALUES OF CONSERVATION IN CHAGOS

There is also the question of calculating the scientific and economic benefit of setting aside this large system. What benefits are there for the entire ocean and its people? What benefits exist for reef managers who can learn what to aim for from it, and what is its value as a reservoir, sink, and source of species? Valuing this in dollar terms is tricky and contentious. Many dislike the concept of viewing nature as a dollar resource in the first place. However, economists, not scientists, rule the world, so I believe it is worth doing. The increasing rarity of reefs is important, and one reason why estimated reef values are soaring. A famous work in 1997 costed the global benefit derived from reefs as $8,000 per hectare per year. However, by 2014, recognising their importance in storm protection, erosion protection, and recreation, and considering their fast decline in number, values were revised to around $352,000 per hectare per year [11]. It was using these and similar values that provide a 'price' of Chagos as many millions of dollars per year [12].

So, the government and society (which part of society?) must judge how to help Chagossians in those places where they remain impoverished. Some still advocate that we can have settlements alongside local extractive industries, maintain a sustainable lifestyle, and avoid degradation, but much evidence from many places suggests that realistically, we cannot. Reef deterioration could be avoided if a new community is supported from outside in the manner of those employed in DG, but not, unpalatable though it may be, if the new residents were to remain unsubsidised. It is a salutary point for anyone who feels that, with the global population high and rising fast, we can live within a tropical ecosystem without degrading it.

FIGURE 11.2 Most islands are tiny. Apart from Diego Garcia, only one or two in each atoll were large enough to support a permanent village in plantation days.

In any case, any resettlement plan must include a component for evacuation in just a few years' time. Ignoring this would be irresponsible. It was mentioned earlier that, in the very similar and nearby Maldives, much more research has shown that most of their islands will be uninhabitable in just 25 years or so. So it is with the Chagos islands too; they are on the same atoll chain (Figure 11.2).

HOSTILITY ABOUT WORKING IN CHAGOS

I long regretted that the British Indian Ocean Territory (BIOT) Government never countered vitriolic comments and accusations alleging, for example, that DG was a toxic mess. It isn't. The list of potential pollutants that are regularly measured there is published [13]. In addition, pollution measurements have been taken of many substances at various places in all the atolls, which have shown that this archipelago, including DG, has the cleanest seas on the planet in terms of metals and organic contaminants. It is cleaner than the Sargasso Sea and Antarctica [14], both commonly held to be the nearest thing to pristine marine environments still left today.

The governments did little to counter the accusations that DG was a toxic wasteland or radioactive disaster. Examples became quite ludicrous as several interested parties insisted that the lagoon was badly contaminated by nuclear leaks. It was not. Nor did the government counter allegations that alleged leaking stockpiles of Agent Orange were poisoning people. As often as rumours or false information came to my attention, in my role as science adviser to BIOT, I would show results to BIOT Administration, demonstrating these to be nonsense. However, people hostile to BIOT or its military would only shift to another alleged environmental problem or disaster. It became a little wearing, especially when the accusations suggested that I was colluding with BIOT in denying that DG was a radioactive dump of toxic chemicals. Once, a Freedom of Information request was made for my bank accounts, searching apparently for alleged payments for fabricating my story to fit assumed Government requirements. The demand was refused, but that did not stop a journalist from telling me that he had heard I was accepting bribes and would I like to comment. Some people could be as unpleasant as they were ill-informed.

I believe the Chagossian story has not been a public relations success for the British Government. This issue has garnered most of the media attention surrounding the Chagos Archipelago. On various occasions, journalists have abruptly ended phone calls with me or my colleagues in a fit of abusive anger when we declined to confirm one or another gross distortion for their 'human interest story'.

There is enough truth in the entire Chagossian story to provoke indignation in any casual reader. Much of the authentic narrative can be found in the voluminous legal judgements issued during the first two decades of the 21st century. Numerous judgements offer comprehensive reviews of the events, as does the meticulously researched book on Chagos history by Nigel Wenban Smith and Marina Carter [15], covering the period from the earliest days to the end of the plantation era and the establishment of BIOT. Subsequent history, including court judgements, is presented in short, easy-to-read, and accurate accounts by Ted Morris [16], available on both on the CCT website and the latter's zany, entertaining website [17].

One important point is: would Mauritian ownership of the archipelago help the Chagossians to return anyway? The principle of self-determination has been central to many of their arguments [18]. However, several groups of former residents and their descendants have told the press [19] that while they want to return, they also want self-determination, not government from Mauritius either. They dislike the Mauritian government and do not trust it. Some Chagossians working in shops or tending to the grounds in DG have told me that the process of recruiting or selecting people to go to work on the island actively discriminates against those of Chagossian heritage. One told me the first thing they would do after returning would be to 'raise the Union Jack'! If resettlement happens on any Chagos islands under Mauritian rule, would Chagossians be the selected people when many of them have said they want self-determination, potentially causing another problem for Mauritius?

Another facet of this complex story is that if the islands were part of Mauritian territory all along, then the movement of the people from one part of it to mainland Mauritius would not have been exile from their country in the first place. One can pick and choose an argument!

As a scientist, I personally believe a return would not be sustainable, having lived through several feasibility surveys on the issue. The same arguments that apply to the nearby Maldives apply here too. A subsistence lifestyle would be possible, of course, for perhaps 20 years. External support would be immensely costly, requiring the construction of education, health, housing, and more. There is not even a pier or harbour to offload needed materials. On the other hand, the emotive aspects are very strong: as one sociologist said to me: it isn't the truth of the past that is important; it is how the people want it to have been that matters. This is understandable, of course, especially to those now elderly, people who remember fragments of their childhood on the islands. Any future resettlement plan should include a plan and costing for evacuation if it is to be in any way responsible, for that is what will be needed. But never, even during my tenure as the government's science adviser for the place, was I involved in resettlement questions or asked for my opinion on it by the Government. My role was as an ecologist. This impinged on the question of resettlement, of course.

How could returning Chagossians make a living on the islands now? The American military base on DG poses problems for certain money-making activities for people newly settled there, including some that involve leasing islands to third parties. Mauritius is already giving or leasing islands elsewhere, such as the construction by India of a facility with a 3.5 km runway on another of its far-flung islands, Agelega. A lucrative scheme would surely be to rent one island in the northern atolls to China, sit back, watch the radio antennae being raised and the money rolling in! However, the present military has already considered that and doesn't much like the idea [20].

Other activities have been proposed. Tourism would struggle to get established. Seaweed farming is one activity proposed by some consultants, but masses of it already grow around the Indian Ocean's rim, where resorts are paying people to scrape it off beaches and burn it. Selling any seems unlikely. Likewise, the sale of hardwood timber has been suggested, but there is almost none left, and what remains needs to be conserved for other reasons. Also proposed had been farming of sea-cucumbers, these alleged aphrodisiacs being a kind of Viagra in several Asian cultures. But there are too few left to farm, with shiploads having been taken illegally to Sri Lanka when the early Fishery Protection Vessel was not looking. These animals are recovering slowly and will become a desired resource again in a couple of years. That leaves only fishing.

THE MILITARY ERA AND MODERN ENVIRONMENTAL AND COMMERCIAL PROBLEMS

Globally, reef conservation is failing, preventing reefs from realising their potentially enormous benefits to people. It has been stated: "...most of the causes of decline are due to local human activity... we can anticipate that climate change and ocean acidification are going to become ever more important as causes of reef decline, meaning that ... causes of reef decline will be less easily remedied by local actions than they are at present." [21]. Resources from Chagos will become increasingly sought after. If solutions are challenging now, they will become even more difficult and expensive if left unaddressed.

Long-term thinking was evident from the beginning of BIOT's existence, as seen in the fact that the US lease on DG was initially for 50 years with a renewal for 20 years thereafter. This perceived need has not changed; an article in a Harvard review emphasises that DG is "set to play a disproportionately important role" [22], as do reports issued by a group of retired Admirals and Generals [23]. The Americans intended to be in the Indian Ocean for the long term, and this was one location they expected would be available for many decades without local politics getting in the way. With the enormous and accelerating buildup by China in the Indian Ocean region today, it seems likely that the facility in DG will be wanted for a while yet. Conservation happened to be a collateral benefit of this requirement.

Legal cases have abounded, many with some vitriol. One in 2016 was a case heard by the UK's Supreme Court, no less, which encompassed me and my own alleged past wrongdoings [24]. While it is a common logical fallacy to attack a person when you cannot attack their science, it is not pleasant! In one part of the case, the lawyers for the complainants claimed that my scientific advice over about a decade was wrong, incompetent, and deliberately misleading the Government because of my clear interest in conservation. I had been receiving much abuse and slander leading up to that case in public fora. It was very clear to me that a lawyer may try and 'prove' something, whether it is true or not, which is not at all the scientific approach. So, although my involvement was just one part of a larger issue, it was with trepidation that I obtained the Supreme Court's ruling on whether my science advice was severely faulty and nonsensical, as alleged. I searched the long ruling for my name and found it was flagged many times. Yikes!! In the event, I could not have been more pleased and relieved. The President of the Court was resoundingly clear in exonerating myself and in dismissing the accusations about incompetence and bias. Fortunately for me, that ended the ongoing abuse that had been levelled at me. However, it did not stop the legal actions against the British and BIOT Governments.

I have been criticised for delving into politics and, equally, for not delving into politics. This is not uncommon for conservation scientists. When I first wrote about the Chagossian eviction in an article in the British *Geographic Magazine* as far back as 1980 [25], the lack of any reaction whatsoever from the later vocal western supporters was notable. Only 20 years later did opposition from westerners gather pace.

It is astonishing to me that a resolution has not been found regarding this problem. Perhaps it cannot be resolved while people with other axes to grind or vested interests to pursue are using Chagossians as pawns. This is one of the saddest aspects of it all. While the ability to participate in and lead much of the science over many years has been a rewarding honour, my own odyssey has sometimes been affected by

FIGURE 11.3 A juvenile booby photographed by a survey drone. The shallow lagoon is below the drone, contrasting in colour with the deep blue of the far greater depths in the north.

the sorry Chagossian story and what, to my mind, have been despicable attempts to misuse Chagossians for political ends. I think the story of the Chagos islands, with its resource demands, politics, and territory and conservation issues, continues to be the story of the world in microcosm (Figure 11.3).

REFERENCES

[1] Pauly D. 1995. Anecdotes and the shifting baseline syndrome. *Trends in Ecology & Environment* 10: 430. **And:**
Sheppard CRC. 1995. The shifting baseline syndrome. *Marine Pollution Bulletin* 30: 766–767.

[2] Jared Diamond J. 2005. *Collapse: How Societies Choose to Fail or Survive.* Penguin Books, London. ISBN 978-0-241-95868-1.

[3] Sale PF et al. 2014. Transforming management of tropical coastal seas to cope with challenges of the 21st century. *Marine Pollution Bulletin* 85: 8–23. https://doi.org/10.1016/j.marpolbul.2014.06.005.

[4] Sheppard CRC (ed.). 2013. *Coral Reefs of the United Kingdom Overseas territories.* Chapters 17–21. Springer, Dordrecht, 323 pp. **And:**
Everaarts JM, Booij K, Fischer CV, Mass YEM, Nieuwenhuize J. 1999. Assessment of the environmental health of the Chagos Archipelago. In: Sheppard CRC, Seaward MRD (eds) *Ecology of the Chagos Archipelago.* Linnean Society of London, Westbury Publishing, London, pp. 305–326.

[5] Sheppard CRC. 2014. Famines, food insecurity and coral reef 'Ponzi' fisheries. *Marine Pollution Bulletin* 84: 1–4.

[6] Fenner D. 2014. Fishing down the largest coral reef fish species. *Marine Pollution Bulletin* 84: 9–16.

[7] Graham NAG, Pratchett MS, McClanahan TR, Wilson SK. 2013. Chapter 19 The status of coral reef fish assemblages in the Chagos Archipelago, with implications for protected area management and climate change. In: Sheppard CRC (ed.) *Coral Reefs of the UK Overseas Territories.* Springer. Dordrecht, pp. 253–270. **And:**
Graham NAJ, McClanahan TR. 2013. The last call for marine wilderness? *BioScience* 63: 397–402.

[8] Pauly D, Christensen V, Guénette S, Pitcher TJ, Sumaila UR, Walters CJ, Watson R, Zeller D. 2002. Towards sustainability in world fisheries. *Nature* 418: 689–895.

[9] Koldewey H et al. 2010. Potential benefits to fisheries and biodiversity of the Chagos Archipelago/British Indian Ocean Territory as a no-take marine reserve. *Marine Pollution Bulletin* 60: 1906–1916.

[10] Sale PF. 2021. *Majestic Realms under the Sea: Coral Reefs.* Yale University Press, New Haven, London, p. 269.

[11] Costanza R et al. 2014. Changes in the global value of ecosystem services. *Global Environmental Change* 26: 152–158.

[12] Gravestock P, Sheppard CRC. 2015. Valuing the ecosystem services of the Chagos: A review of challenges and estimates. *Marine Ecology Progress Series* 530: 255–270.

[13] Readman JW et al. 2013. Chapter 21 Contaminants, pollution and potential anthropogenic impacts in Chagos/BIOT. In: Sheppard (ed.) *Coral Reefs of the United Kingdom Overseas Territories.* Springer, Germany, pp. 283–298. **And:**
Guitart C, Sheppard ALS, Frickers T, Price ARG, Readman JW. 2007. Negligible risks to corals from antifouling booster biocides and triazine herbicides in coastal waters of the Chagos Archipelago. *Marine Pollution Bulletin* 54: 226–246.

[14] Readman JW, Tolosa I, Bartocci J, Cattini C, Price ARG, Jolliffe A. 1999. Contaminant levels and the use of molecular organic markers to characterize the coastal environment of the Chagos Archipelago. In: Sheppard CRC, Seaward MRD (eds) *Ecology of the Chagos Archipelago*. Linnean Society, London, pp. 297–304.
[15] Wenban Smith N, Carter M. 2016. *Chagos: A History. Exploration, Exploitation, Expulsion*. Chagos Conservation Trust, London, pp. 550.
[16] Morris TA. 2013. *A Brief History of the Ilois Experience*. Second item down in http://www.zianet.com/tedmorris/dg/links.html#history.
[17] Morris TA. *Go to Diego Garcia. Do Not Pass Go. Do Not Collect $200*. http://www.zianet.com/tedmorris/dg/.
[18] Sands P. 2022. The Last Colony: A Tale of Exile, Justice and Britain's Colonial Legacy. Weidenfeld and Nicolson London. **And:**
Mandarin F. 2015. Chapter 20 Living memories: A worker's view of the 1950s. In: Wenban Smith N, Carter M (eds) *Chagos: A History. Exploration, Exploitation, Expulsion*. Chagos Conservation Trust, London, pp. 550.
[19] http://www.seychellesnewsagency.com/articles/16412/Publicity+stunt+or+not+Chagossians+in+Seychelles+question+Mauritian+government%27s+recent+expedition. **And:** Boffey D. 2023. Chagos Islanders demand say as UK-Mauritius sovereignty talks begin. *The Guardian Newspaper, UK*, 2 January 2023.
[20] https://www.dailymail.co.uk/news/article-12106789/White-House-raises-concerns-plans-Britain-hand-aircraft-carrier-island.html.
[21] Sale PF. 2014. Addressing the decline of coral reefs. *Reef Encounter* 40: 15–17. **And:** ale PF. 2015. Coral reef conservation and political will. *Environmental Conservation* 42: 97–101.
[22] Erickson A, Ladwig W, Mikolay J. 2013. Diego Garcia: Anchoring America's future presence in the Indo-Pacific. *Harvard Asia Quarterly* 15.2: 20–28.
[23] CNA Military Advisory Board. 2014. National Security and the Accelerating Risks of Climate Change. CNA Corporation, Alexandria, VA, 45 pp.
[24] Neuberger L, Hale L, Mance L, Kerr L, Clarke L. 2016. *29 June 2016 Judgement on Application of Bancoult v. Secretary of State for FCO*. The Supreme Court, London.
[25] Sheppard CRC. 1980. New life on forsaken Chagos Isles. *Geographic Magazine* 52: 825–829.

12 What of the Future?

A POOR PROGNOSIS?

Seawater temperature is rising more rapidly now, and every few years, a marine heat wave reaches temperatures that, two decades ago, caused massive mortality. How long can this continue, and how long can acclimation to it continue for those tiny animals that build the reefs and islands? In 2019, every dive we undertook showed water temperatures of over 30°C–31°C, right down to our maximum working depth of 25 m. Is this destruction simply, as some have suggested, road-kill as the Earth travels the road from the Holocene epoch, which lasted since the ice ages, to the Anthropocene epoch that we have now entered? Is it just collateral damage in mankind's progress?

Healthy and growing reefs depend on physical characteristics of the oceans remaining relatively constant and constrained within narrow bounds. These physical characteristics are changing faster than marine species can adapt. What can we do about global reef deterioration? There are a couple of possible responses that we must resist strongly. One is simply to shrug off the problem in a resigned way. Another response seriously suggested to me is to exploit the system rapidly in a manner I call the MAWBID school of thought (Might As Well Because It's Doomed). The latter has been a not uncommon form of approach in some resource-extraction industries, even if practised unconsciously.

We must avoid fatalistic syndromes. Caution, science, and the application of sense can now buy several more years for these reefs, but not too many. Few places have reefs as resilient to recovery as those in Chagos because, although they may be killed more frequently now, most places seem to have factors that prevent recovery afterward. Many world records have been found here, and future research should capitalise on these aspects. The example it sets and the information it provides can be used to benefit the countless people who are trying to restore their own damaged reefs and who otherwise would have a poor idea of what to aim for. It is well worth treating Chagos with great care to ensure it remains in this state, for there is almost nowhere else left in the Indian Ocean like it.

The terms 'management', even 'sustainable management', are common nowadays. However, applying these terms to reefs or islands is misleading hubris. We may like to think we can manage a reef, but we cannot yet properly manage some small parts of it or any one species on it. What we can manage is human activity and its impact on them, which is quite different. If we effectively manage that, a reef and its components can rebound with greater resilience when given a chance. With good governance, we should be able to sustain Chagos reefs and maintain them as a reservoir for many years into the future. Who knows what methods we might have at our disposal then?

The Chagos reefs are down right now, but not out.

DOI: 10.1201/9781003423300-12

I used to be an optimist after witnessing, for example, the rapid recovery of the coral cover following the 1998 wipe-out. A movement called 'Ocean optimism' emerged from the desire not to discourage people [1]; it was thought that discouragement would steer people away from addressing the problems. The opposing viewpoint argues that this fosters complacency, as evident in many governments. I believe we need to alert people in authority because only that seems to prompt the necessary action. Perhaps we need to jolt apathetic politicians into action. If there is an optimistic way out, why should governments or industrialists bother to change anything? The more recent heatwaves of 2015 and 2016 set the situation back to what some of us termed 'ground zero' and triggered more alarm than before. Predictions of climate change were, after all, proving to be true.

Recent estimates suggest that a critical level of coral cover on a reef for the reef to grow is around 10% or so [2]. After the 2016 ocean heatwave, much of the shallow areas showed cover less than that. Indeed, 10% was about the average on Chagos reefs, meaning half the places we visited showed much less—zero, in fact, to the nearest round number. At most sites, it was hard to find even a few percent of living corals, and there were even fewer soft corals. This disastrous scene extended in 2019 down to about 15 m depth in many places, after which coral cover became more like a badly damaged coral reef, but a reef at least. Sometimes there might be a band in the 2–3 m depth range where there were still massive *Porites*, but otherwise, corals and soft corals had largely disappeared [3].

Following the mortality of adults, juvenile coral numbers collapsed, which is unsurprising given the state their parents were in. Curiously, most juveniles were growing on the dead and disintegrating *Acropora* tables. This seemed a foolish choice and survival strategy in the circumstances, but then, this was an unprecedented set of conditions in coral evolutionary terms in which stable conditions have existed for thousands of years. We had noted the same settlement onto disintegrating tables after the 1998 warming too.

Some species groups were completely absent. Almost none of the branching forms *Stylophora*, *Seriatopora*, or *Pocillopora* were found in the top 15 m zone, nor any of the stubby-finger *Acroporas* such as *A. humilis* and *A. digitifera*. Skeletons of all these were now covered by calcareous red algae. The shallow part of the reef was formerly the main habitat for these, so the likelihood of a strong and swift recovery was poor. Sadly too, the iconic Chagos brain coral, *Ctenella chagius*, which is largely endemic to the archipelago, had all but vanished. Its numbers are a small fraction of 1% of its former abundance. As it is a fairly shallow species, its recovery will be slow if it happens at all. If not, a local extinction might also become a global one. The reduction of any animal population by a third is usually enough to declare a terrestrial species as 'Endangered', so how should we describe this vastly greater reduction of almost all of them?

Several years ago, we produced a highly illustrated catalogue of the corals that existed on Chagos reefs; the total tally was about 300 species [4]. We do not know which ones have been permanently lost from the archipelago, but most have been significantly reduced.

In Chagos now, "It looks like the wheels are falling off" (to borrow a colleague's phrase). Furthermore, positive feedback loops, often referred to as vicious circles

FIGURE 12.1 A black or dark purple sheet of the encrusting sponge *Cliona*, which is a bioerosive sponge, at 5 m depth. In several shallow areas it occupies much more of the reef that do corals. The pale dots over its surface are exhalent pores.

or tipping points, seem to be setting in, wherein fewer corals can produce fewer juveniles. In several places now, there is also less suitable substrate for juveniles to settle on [5]. This is because sheets of the encrusting and coral-eroding sponge called *Cliona* have occupied much of the substrate in some shallow areas, and these occupy far more substrate than the corals do on several reefs exposed to strong waves. Any coral larva attempting to settle would find sponge on the surface, not the bare coral rock that they need. An example of this is shown in Figure 12.1, and in Figure 7.2, divers are decompressing in the shallows after a dive, with one sheet of this sponge visible to the right.

At every high spring tide, a little bit more of many of these islands seems to be washed away. True, sediments deposited on other parts of the islands help restore the area of sand above water, but this remains suitable only for nesting terns for many years, not for large trees or people. Few people have had the good fortune to watch over several decades and notice the difference. It is the high tides that count here, of course, not the average sea level, and during equinox high spring tides, the results can be spectacular: the ocean washes over increasing areas of land, sharks can forage over the grass, and rays forage over a car park in Diego Garcia beside a sign that tells us not to get in the water! [6]

Presidents of other countries that also consist of atolls have stated that they anticipate their nations to be deserted by 2050. These countries hope to relocate, possibly by acquiring land in other nations [7]. They have no alternative. Naturally, there are significant sociological questions surrounding such extensive population relocations. The last time this occurred on a large scale (the establishment of a new nation where others already lived, such as Israel) it was not exactly trouble-free. It is clear that sociology and politics are lagging far behind the scientific aspects.

Given this apparently inevitable gloomy prognosis for the islands and their reefs, why do I, and others, continue to do research there and develop proposals for restoring some of the islands? I don't know if there is a logical answer, except to say that, like probably most people, I never entirely lose hope. After all, we all know we will be dead one day but would still see a doctor tomorrow if we needed to. Why?

Given present human inertia, the prognosis is not good, so has all the work been worth it for me personally? A resounding "yes"! Again: why? Large areas of dead reefs and eroded islands will be the inevitable result of warming and sea level rise. There can be very few branches of science whose practitioners hope that the outcomes of their lifetime's research might be wrong or become irrelevant, but that is increasingly the case for scientists researching climate change and its effects on most natural habitats, not only coral reefs.

WHY JUSTIFY IT?

We know that strictly protected or no-take marine reserves are the primary means to ensure the survival of large, highly fecund adults of many species, thereby ensuring the existence of the next generation of the species. Criticisms have been raised about many marine reserves [8], but the arguments are usually dismissed briefly and robustly [9]. One might ask why scientists with conservation leanings, or even a government, need to justify themselves to extractive, poorly regulated industries in the first place. I think they don't, although they do so to counter erroneous information. It should also be questioned whether over-extractive activities should have any stakeholder rights anyway, in British Indian Ocean Territory (BIOT) or elsewhere. It is now well understood that even small marine areas benefitting from *effective* protection can provide substantial benefits to both humans and natural systems [10]. Nuances may be debated, but the overall benefit is established. Reef areas that are properly protected: "...can be a useful tool ... for maintaining coral cover... the benefits of MPAs appear to increase with the number of years since MPA establishment" [11], and with proximity to human populations [12].

None of this is surprising. What is surprising, or perhaps alarming, is the size of the problem: for years, we have believed that about a third of any marine habitat needs to be strictly protected if the oceans are to recover. It would have been less if proper protection had been put in place years ago, but it wasn't. The corollary is that even more will become necessary if society delays further. This, perhaps, is one of the main values of the Chagos protected area: it can be, and was, set aside as a giant no-take area as it fits the Pew criteria for being one. It is also well worth repeating that simply declaring a marine protected area and then not enforcing it, or allowing exceptions for various stakeholders who can then extract from it, is not sufficient; such protected areas abound and are commonly called 'paper parks'. They may allow a government to proudly boast of an achievement or fulfil a declaration, but they don't really succeed in achieving anything.

POLITICS AND THE FUTURE

The public view generally matters greatly to politicians, more than the science. However, correct scientific input and evidence should never be viewed as just one more negotiable or expendable stakeholder input. Ecosystems may be easily destroyed, especially coral reefs whose ability to adapt to multiple stresses is poor [13]. Resource extraction from the world's reefs already far exceeds sustainability [14], leading to the global degradation noted. It would be easy to destroy the value of BIOT's reefs if 'sustainable extraction' were to be attempted there too, and nobody can show why Chagos reefs might avoid this fate if exploited.

At the time of writing, negotiations are being held with the Mauritian Government reagrding the transfer of sovereignty to Mauritius. A conservation plan for the territory has been prepared by the Mauritian Government and its agencies [15], which used a modelling method requiring good input data to operate. However, the plan studiously ignored almost all the research results described here. Presumably, this was a political decision, given that almost all the publications listed in the Endnotes to the chapters in this book are publicly available. Unsurprisingly, the plan comes up with some unusual suggestions, allocating bird-rich islets that were never settled for two centuries as being suitable for resettlement use. Meanwhile, it suggests the second-largest island, abandoned in the 1930s and currently a derelict coconut monoculture overrun with rats, as requiring strict protection. Importantly, it also removes the fishing prohibition on over half a million square kilometres of offshore areas. The Indian Ocean would suffer a considerable reduction in the amount of proper protection it now has.

Coral reefs have been considered to provide 99 benefits to mankind in nine major categories [16], some commercial or monetary, and many non-monetary. BIOT's reefs will no doubt progressively suffer damage from climate change, along with all reefs, due to the rising CO_2 levels [17]. At the same time, our dependence on natural resources is non-negotiable, regardless of the wishes of several parties.

IN THE END...

My personal research adventure in this archipelago has extended over more than 20 visits to these islands, spanning nearly half a century, with my wife Anne serving as my scientific colleague. She photographs and writes about it in her own right [18]. It has been truly delightful. Headaches from those who have caused grief have been trivial compared to the joy of trying to do something constructive in such a remarkable place. We have introduced many students to the area, as well as senior scientists. They are now carrying on the work for global benefit, for many more years to come. This is made possible thanks to substantial new funding from private sources.

In public lectures and presentations, I offer an optimistic outcome: common sense will prevail. It surely has to! Privately, I am not so sure, given the extent of opposition to conservation in general, including with my own country. Is it honest to continue being hopeful in the face of gloomy data? It has become desperately important for the peoples of the Indian Ocean region that more oceanic decline does not affect the Chagos Archipelago, but environmental tipping points are approaching.

I am not the only one facing the predicament of whether to sound optimistic or otherwise. Scientists are supposed to report on the evidence, unpalatable or otherwise. The laws of nature will always transcend man-made laws in the end, an often-unwelcome truth. However, coral reefs face an existential threat: they simply won't be around in a few decades if present warming trends continue. They will be something much more impoverished. Younger scientists, especially those who go to

FIGURE 12.2 Western Peros Banhos atoll, looking seawards.

the Chagos Archipelago after studying, for example, Asian or Caribbean reefs, are generally optimistic compared to older ones who were around when those other reefs were in far better condition. Is it something to do with the ageing process itself? I have more than one colleague who has shed tears underwater on reef areas that once were sites of superlative richness but had become no more than boneyards, yet where, at the same site, a young colleague seeing it for the first time suggested it looked pretty good! That is really why environmental scientists collect numbers to show what the story really was and what it has become, unencumbered by any personal bias, so we can compare then and now.

I believe that still there is time, but only just. For a long time now, it has been more of a political, sociological, and governmental problem than a scientific one. In a global context, the costs of doing nothing will far exceed the costs needed now to mitigate many of the problems. Much reef research now merely adds more decimal places of accuracy to the post-mortem of reefs, and I believe that we have no more time for this. This is really the value of the Chagos Archipelago; it has shown what the 'best condition' is or could be.

We have perhaps a decade or less to succeed in driving societal change. We can do it, we must, but we must avoid platitudes and more delay (Figure 12.2).

REFERENCES

[1] http://www.oceanoptimism.org/.

[2] Perry CT, Morgan KM. 2017. Bleaching drives collapse in reef carbonate budgets and reef growth potential on southern Maldives reefs. *Scientific Reports* 7: 40581. https://doi.org/10.1038/srep40581. **And:**
Perry CT et al. 2018. Loss of coral reef growth capacity to track future increases in sea level. *Nature* 558: 396–400. https://doi.org/10.1038/s41586-018-0194-z.

[3] Sheppard CRC. 2017. The wheels are falling off. *Reef Encounter* 32: 58–60.

[4] Sheppard CRC, Sheppard ALS, Fenner D. 2014. *Corals of Chagos*. https://chagosinformationportal.org/corals.
[5] Sheppard CRC, Sheppard ALS, Fenner D. 2020. Coral mass mortalities in the Chagos Archipelago over 40 years: Regional species and assemblage extinctions and indications of positive feedbacks. *Marine Pollution Bulletin* 154: 111075.
[6] Sheppard CRC. 2012. Sharks on the lawn. The reality of rising sea-level on Indian Ocean Islands. *Ocean Challenge* 19: 17.
[7] His Excellency Anotr Tong Te Beretitenti (President of Republic of Kiribati). 2013. Foreword. In: Stone GS, Obura D (eds) *Underwater Eden*. University of Chicago Press, Chicago and London, pp. vii–xi.
[8] Kaplan DM et al. 2013. The true challenge of giant marine reserves. *Science* 340: 810–811.
[9] Pala C. 2013. The true challenge of giant marine reserves – Response. *Science* 340: 811. **And:** O'Leary BC et al. 2018. Addressing criticisms of large-scale marine protected areas. *BioScience* 68: 359–370.
[10] Angulo-Valdés J, Hatcher BG. 2010. A new typology of benefits derived from marine protected areas. *Marine Policy* 34: 635–644. **And:**
Lester SE et al. 2009. Biological effects within no-take marine reserves: A global synthesis. *Marine Ecology Progress Series* 384: 33–46. **And:**
Lubchenko J et al. 2003. Plugging a hole in the ocean: The emerging science of marine reserves. *Ecological Applications. Supplement* 13: S3–S7.
[11] Selig and Bruno. 2010. A global analysis of the effectiveness of marine protected areas in preventing coral loss. *PLoS ONE* 4(2): e9278. https://doi.org/10.1371/journal.pone.0009278.
[12] Williams IF et al. 2011. Differences in reef fish assemblages between populated and remote reefs spanning multiple archipelagos across the Central and Western Pacific. *Journal of Marine Biology* Article ID 826234, 14 p. https://doi.org/10.1155/2011/826234.
[13] Ateweberhan M et al. 2013. Climate change impacts on coral reefs: Synergies with local effects, possibilities for acclimation, and management implications. *Marine Pollution Bulletin* 74: 526–539.
[14] Newton et al. 2007. Current and future sustainability of island coral reef fisheries. *Current Biology* 17: 655–658.
[15] Badall R et al. 2021. *Creation of the Chagos Archipelago Marine Protected Area*. Prime Minister's Office, Department for Continental Shelf, Maritime Zones Administration & Exploration. Report, May 2022, pp. 74.
[16] Angulo-Valdés J, Hatcher BG. 2010. A new typology of benefits derived from marine protected areas. *Marine Policy* 34: 635–644.
[17] Kennedy EV et al. 2013. Avoiding coral reef functional collapse requires local and global action. *Current Biology* 10: 912–918.
[18] Sheppard ALS. 2015. *Coral Reefs: Secret Cities of the Sea*. London, Natural History Museum, 112 pp.

Index

Note: **Bold** page numbers refer to tables; *italic* page numbers refer to figures.

For Product Safety Concerns and Information please contact our
EU representative GPSR@taylorandfrancis.com Taylor & Francis
Verlag GmbH, Kaufingerstraße 24, 80331 München, Germany

Admirals in Court

Admirals in Court

Discipline, Honour and Naval Justice, 1778–1814

John Morrow

BLOOMSBURY ACADEMIC
LONDON • NEW YORK • OXFORD • NEW DELHI • SYDNEY

BLOOMSBURY ACADEMIC
Bloomsbury Publishing Plc, 50 Bedford Square, London, WC1B 3DP, UK
Bloomsbury Publishing Inc, 1385 Broadway, New York, NY 10018, USA
Bloomsbury Publishing Ireland, 29 Earlsfort Terrace, Dublin 2, D02 AY28, Ireland

First published in Great Britain 2025

A catalogue record for this book is available from the British Library.

A catalog record for this book is available from the Library of Congress.

ISBN: HB: 978-1-3504-6727-9
ePDF: 978-1-3504-6728-6
eBook: 978-1-3504-6729-3

Typeset by Deanta Global Publishing Services, Chennai, India

For product safety related questions contact productsafety@bloomsbury.com.

To find out more about our authors and books visit www.bloomsbury.com and sign up for our newsletters.

To Peter Morrow and Peter Mahoney, and in memory of Peter Holding, 1950–2021

Contents

Preface

This book explores British flag officers' experiences of the naval justice system in the late Georgian period. It examines the events that led them to be summoned for, and in some cases request, courts martial, their trials and the immediate aftermath and longer term impact on admirals' careers and reputations. Courts martial were used by the Admiralty Board and less directly by governments to uphold discipline and punish wrong-doing (which included failures in key duties) and maintain the aggressive and dynamic culture of the Royal Navy. They also provided individuals with a (admittedly high risk) means of vindicating their conduct and upholding their professional reputation and honour in the face of criticism in the press, the upper echelons of the service and the wider elite. The case studies of nine courts martial which form the core of the book are set within the broader judicial, service culture and political contexts of naval justice.

My major debt in researching this book is to the University of Auckland Library and its staff. As with earlier projects, the value of the library's extensive physical and electronic resources has been enhanced by excellent, courteous services from its collection management and inter loan staff. I particularly want to record my thanks to Hester Mountifield, the Associate Director Collections and Digital, for her invaluable assistance over a number of years.

My work in UK archives and libraries has benefitted from the courteous professionalism of staff at the Caird Library, National Maritime Museum, Greenwich, the Essex County Records Office in Chelmsford and the National Archives at Kew. Staff at the Beinecke Rare Books and Manuscript Library, Yale University, New Haven, Rice University Library, Houston, the Bedfordshire and Luton Records Office, and the National Library of Wales have responded promptly and helpfully to requests for copies of materials held by their institutions. I have also utilized manuscripts held in the British Library, the Cambridge County Archives, Devon Heritage Centre, Hyde Parker Papers, Melford Hall, Suffolk, the National Library of Scotland and the National War Museum of Scotland that I consulted when working on an earlier study. I am most grateful to these institutions and to the late Sir Richard Hyde Parker for facilitating access to this material. The quotations from the Ashton Hall Papers in chapter ten are reproduced with the permission of the National Library of Wales.

My friend and former colleague Professor Jonathan Scott showed a most encouraging early interest in this project and gave me the benefit of his advice on the proposal and on initial chapter drafts. Professor Warren Swain of the Faculty of Law, University of Auckland provided invaluable guidance on aspects of legal history relevant to naval courts martial. Robert Burnham and Ron McGuigan have assisted with advice and references on the British Army. Richard Hiscocks, the editor of the More than Nelson web site, helped me trace some biographical information on Sir John Duckworth; Alison Jordan, the Warden of St Mary's Church, Chigwell, Essex, kindly clarified an obscure reference in the Harvey Papers. As in the past, I have enjoyed generous hospitality from Peter and Rachel Morrow in Suffolk and Peter Mahoney and Issy Ryder in Hampshire when undertaking research in England.

I am grateful to Bloomsbury's readers for their insightful reports on the proposal and the completed manuscript. It is a particular pleasure to record my appreciation of my editor Maddie Smith. She showed a keen interest in the project from the beginning and has offered invaluable advice along the way.

As always, my wife Diana has been a great source of warm encouragement and practical help. Her initial interest galvanized me to embark on the project and she cheerfully assumed full responsibility for an exuberant puppy when I took a research trip to England. Di has read many versions of proposals and draft chapters and set aside time from her own writing to read the entire manuscript. I have benefitted hugely from her incisive commentary and sharp eye but as is always the case recognize that any lurking errors are entirely my responsibility.

John Morrow
Devonport
New Zealand
12 November 2024

Introduction

Admirals in the late Georgian Royal Navy had extensive experience of courts martial. Some officers had the misfortune to be summoned for trial in earlier stages of their careers, most likely when a ship to which they belonged was lost in battle or wrecked. They would also have been called as witnesses and sat as post captains on trials on foreign and home stations. A fair number of them presided over courts martial or served with other flag officers on particularly important cases. The confidentiality of these deliberations means that we know virtually nothing of their opinions of the hearings on which they sat, although a number of them complained of how trying and arduous they found this duty. Aspects of these earlier experiences would, no doubt, have been in the minds of the admirals who are the subjects of this study. In the years 1778–1815, the Board summoned nine flag officers to courts martial and several others applied unsuccessfully to be tried in vindication of their conduct and honour.

This book provides accounts of the genesis and progress of these officers' courts martial, explores their significance for the leadership responsibilities of British admirals in the period and discusses their impact on the lives and careers of the officers concerned. The accused in all these cases were hitherto successful senior naval officers whose *amour propre* gave a distinctive, entitled edge to conflicts with their superiors and subordinates. The highly competitive and highly politicized environment of flag command meant that courts martial had important implications for admirals' sense of personal and professional self-worth, their professional and public reputations and prospects.

Courts martial were a central element in the Royal Navy's disciplinary armoury, but for flag officers they also provided a means through which they could seek to preserve their personal honour and professional reputations in the face of perceived mistreatment by the Admiralty Board or senior colleagues, or innuendo or open criticism from within the service and among opinion-formers in the broader public sphere. Although this study focuses on the nine trials held on late Georgian flag officers, it also considers cases where officers sought unsuccessfully to be summoned to answer for their conduct before a court martial or, in one case a 'court of inquiry', a more comprehensive investigation without the power to punish misconduct but which could vindicate an aggrieved officer or identify grounds for charging him. There was a considerable risk attached to these moves. Critical reputational issues were at stake, and flag officers might find, as Earl St Vincent warned, that 'the sound of a Court Martial, has the same pestilential effect, as a suspicion of female chastity'.[1] If questions of cowardice or disobedience in the face of the enemy were involved (as for Vice Admiral Sir Hugh Palliser in 1778, Vice Admiral Sir Robert Calder in 1805 and Admiral Lord Gambier in 1809), they hazarded their lives against honour and professional standing.

By requesting a court martial, admirals placed themselves in the hands of the first lord and risked further reputational damage if circumstances and personal and political agendas frustrated their wishes.

Flag officers' trials were the central element in a broader court martial experience. Whether they were brought to trial or not, their careers, sense of personal and professional well-being, standing in the service and sense of honour (which included the perceived reactions of members of their 'honour group', the collective reference point for their sense of honour) were all affected by that experience. It began when a precipitating event aroused the Admiralty Board's suspicions of misconduct or it was brought to its attention by an aggrieved party within the service. These developments invariably came to the attention of service colleagues and opinion-forming elites beyond the service and were often the subject of speculation in the press. Public notice raised the stakes for officers directly concerned, the first lords of the admiralty and the governments to which they belonged. It placed pressure on first lords to investigate conduct and lay charges and prompted flag officers to consider requesting a court martial if they were not summoned by the Board.

Admirals faced courts martial for failures in leadership defined by the legally sanctioned Articles of War and the printed instructions and regulations that supported them. Those charged with breaching these rules had to endure the preliminaries to their trial and the court hearing and contend with its outcome and subsequent implications. The aftermath included the immediate reactions of the accused's family, friends and unsympathetic colleagues and the impact of precipitating events, the charge, trial and verdict on their career prospects and professional reputation. The court martial experience was most traumatic for those found guilty and only marginally less so for those whose acquittal included a note of censure. Even those who received unqualified 'honourable' acquittals resented what they perceived as the Board's poor or vindictive judgement in putting them through an expensive and humiliating process which, if St Vincent was right, might leave an indelible stain on their honour.

As a major state institution headed by a cabinet minister and consuming a large share of the government's budget, the late Georgian Royal Navy was integrated closely with the political culture of the United Kingdom, government agencies in London, the parliament at Westminster and networks of political interest that extended over the three kingdoms. The absence of large stable political parties able to deliver parliamentary majorities and furnish deep cadres of able and willing aspirants for high office meant that governments' responses to naval affairs were often affected by a sense of their vulnerability in the face of hostile press commentary and internal tensions and rivalries.[2] When the country was embroiled in prolonged multi-theatre wars in which the Royal Navy played a key strategic role, these structural features had significant implications for the Board's approach to disciplining senior officers.

In this context, the failure of fleet and squadron commanders to live up to their responsibilities had unavoidable political implications. Admiral Keppel's and Vice Admiral Sir Hugh Palliser's trials were affected by intense partisanship arising from sharp divisions in the upper echelons of the service. While this degree of politicization was unusual, the agendas and personalities of first lords, the stability of the ministries to which they belonged, the perpetual need for governments to demonstrate the soundness of their naval administration and their keenness to profit politically from the successes of senior naval commanders and distance themselves from their failures, all had a bearing on how the Admiralty Board responded to reports of flag officers' misconduct and speculation on it in the service and among the elite. Even when leading figures in the navy were not involved in politically framed debate on their colleagues' conduct, performance issues played a central role in the politics of intra-service relations. The alleged failure of those who had hitherto been successful in the intense competitive struggle for advancement among commissioned officers was likely to leave its mark on flag officers' networks of 'friends' and dependents within the service and beyond and provide sardonic comfort to unfriendly rivals.

The publicity attracted by flag officers' trials reflected their political significance. Keppel's and Palliser's trials in early 1779 were extraordinary in this respect. The events leading to them, the preliminaries, the trials and their aftermath were the subject of highly divisive speculation in the service, extensive, highly partisan press coverage and long debates in parliament. A wave of nationwide demonstrations and pro-Keppel, anti-Palliser and anti-government rioting in Portsmouth and London greeted Keppel's acquittal. These reactions were a consequence of the highly partisan context of these officers' trials and widespread opposition to the American War. While public reactions to other flag officers' courts martial did not reach these heights of indignant excitement or plumb the depths of vindictive disorder, they still attracted significant public interest.

The press published daily accounts of flag officers' trials and often provided their readers with information on the accused's demeanour in the courtroom and on receiving the judges' verdict. In addition, it was common for consolidated accounts of courts martial proceedings to be published as pamphlets shortly after the conclusion of a trial; enterprising publishers sometimes issued separate versions of flag officers' statements of defence. Some of these publications were based on official 'minutes', that is, the transcript of the hearing made by the judge advocate and sent in daily instalments by overnight 'express' mail to the Admiralty Board. Others, however, were based on verbatim reports 'taken down' by shorthand writers during the trial and published on the authority of the accused to publicize an acquittal or otherwise justify his conduct. Unofficial trial transcripts included sharp exchanges on points ruled inadmissible by the court and excluded from the official record that gave insights into points of contention that would otherwise only be known to those in court or their friends. Rival publications of trial transcripts and multiple editions of some of them suggest significant public interest in flag officers' courts martial and underline the extent to which they were celebrity events.

When flag officers faced courts martial, they were charged with conduct that ran contrary to obligations specified in the thirty-six 'Articles of War' and in printed *Regulations and Instructions* issued under the authority of the Lords Commissioners of the Admiralty (the 'Board'). The first thirty-five articles of war addressed specific obligations, and the thirty-sixth covered other offences 'not mentioned in this Act'. All the articles were legally enshrined provisions, and offences against them were criminal. Despite their common source and shared underpinning penological assumptions, they were qualitatively different from the codes that specified crimes and punishments for the civilian population. The Articles of War and related regulations upheld what contemporaries called the 'discipline of the service' by identifying offences and authorizing the punishment of wrongdoing. In some cases, however, they also specified officers' duties, albeit by reference to punishing failures to perform them. In this broader sense, the 'discipline of the service' referred to properly ordering and applying its resources, personnel and activities. As we shall see, the prescriptive or 'directive' force of the Articles of War and the regulations and instructions were particularly significant for the leadership responsibilities of flag officers.[3]

The nine admirals who faced court martials comprised approximately 4 per cent of the flag officers' cadre in this period. However, since only around half of those who held this rank were ever employed on flag commands and thus eligible to be summoned for court martial, a charge rate of around 9 per cent gives a truer picture of their incidence. When account is taken of the admirals who appealed unsuccessfully to secure public exoneration, the proportion of flag officers caught up in the court martial experience increases to approximately 11 per cent. By contrast, only approximately 1 per cent of army generals faced courts martial during the American and French Wars.[4]

In this period, flag officers' trials could result in execution by a firing squad, being 'dismissed the service', made ineligible for promotion or advancement in seniority and condemned in the eyes of their colleagues in the service and the wider public by more or less damning reprimands. In the intensely competitive environment generated by a sharp wartime increase in the numbers of flag officers relative to opportunities for employment, reprimands or even equivocation in the wording of verdicts were likely to be career-limiting. The growing importance of ideas of honour among commissioned officers in the second half of the eighteenth century exacerbated the harmful impact of any note of censure from a court. Honour and the considerations of merit that played a variable role in promotion and employment decisions stood in a symbiotic relationship to flag officers' professional and public reputations and hence to the factors that could either enhance or undermine their prospects of attaining wealth and royal honours from distinguished naval service.[5]

Flag officers' courts martial were usually longer than most other naval trials and were also more elaborate, at times involving extensive lists of witnesses. Provisions for adjournment removed time constraints applying in criminal courts onshore.[6] In naval courts martial, judges, accusers and the accused were at liberty to question witnesses at length and the court could recall them if necessary. The defence statements of men from the lower deck were often brief, confined mainly to acknowledging guilt and seeking, by reference to previous good service, to mitigate the severity of the penalty. That was not the case for flag officers.[7] One admiral (who pretty much admitted his offending) adopted this approach, but others took full advantage of the opportunity to provide detailed rebuttals of charges and the evidence of prosecution witnesses. Flag officers invariably had assistance from legal counsel when writing their defence statements and they usually read them to the court on the accused's behalf. However, legal counsel played no other formal role in court martial proceedings. Consequently, although few service members could afford legal representation, their trials were conducted under the same procedures and practices as flag officers' and underwritten by principles common across the naval justice system.

Although most contemporary commentary on late Georgian admirals' courts martial was produced by partisans in the public controversies surrounding them, some trials also attracted the attention of contemporary or near contemporary authors of biographical memoirs of senior naval officers. However, these works are not necessarily free from partisanship and were more concerned with reevaluating verdicts than considering flag officers' court martial experiences in the broader context of the system of naval justice.[8] The single exception appears in James Ralfe's *Historical Memoirs*, where, in light of the verdicts handed down on Sir John Duckworth and Vice Admiral Stirling, the author remarks on the 'strange and anomalous' nature of naval courts martial.[9]

In line with the recent trends towards the social aspects of naval history, modern historians have tended to focus on the impact of the naval system of justice on seamen and private marines. John Byrn's *Crime and Punishment in the Royal Navy* provides an overview of the naval justice system and examines the nature and levels of punishment, captains' summary adjudication and reactions to offending in the service. Byrn also provides interesting data (drawn from the Leeward Islands station in the French Wars) on offending and on punishments handed down by captains as well as those determined by courts martial.[10] After publishing *Crime and Punishment*, Byrn edited an extensive selection of transcripts of naval courts martial that help to convey a qualitative view of how trials were conducted.[11] Byrn's data from the Leeward Islands is complemented by Thomas Malcomson's quantitative research on crime and punishment on the North American station in the War of 1812. This work is particularly useful in facilitating comparisons between charging and conviction rates for commissioned officers and other members of the service.[12]

Byrn's and Malcomson's characterization of the naval justice system draw on comparisons with criminal courts in England, and both writers discuss the commitment to ideas of exemplary deterrence punishment which underpinned sentencing in both naval and civilian courts. However, the most extensive and well-informed comparisons between naval and criminal justice (albeit in the mid rather than the late eighteenth century) appear in Markus Eder's *Crime and Punishment in the Royal Navy of the Seven Years' War, 1755–1763*.[13] N. A. M. Rodger's *The Wooden World* (which is also set in the Seven Years' War) and *The Command of the Sea* (which extends through to the end of the French Wars) provide extensive analysis of disciplinary and punitive attitudes and practices, primarily with reference to the relationship between commissioned officers and men from the lower deck.

While there is thus a growing body of scholarship on important aspects of the late Georgian system of naval justice, there are only very limited treatments of flag officers' court martial experiences and the perceived leadership failures that triggered them. In *The Wooden World*, N. A. M. Rodger provides an account of a court martial (that of Rear Admiral Byng in 1757) which had an important ongoing role in setting expectations of flag officers' leadership in battle.[14] Peter Smith's *Sailors in the Dock* considers two late Georgian cases discussed in this book, and particular flag officers' trials are usually referred to in biographical studies of major figures.[15] Unsurprisingly given the scope and focus of these works, however, they do not set these invariably painful episodes within the framework of naval justice or compare their subjects' experiences with those of other flag officers facing trial. Family memoirs of Admirals Keppel and Gambier and the nineteenth-century biography of Palliser include significant detail on their trials but are generally defensive rather than analytical; that on Vice Admiral Cornwallis is far more even handed.[16] For the most part, however, surprisingly little systematic attention has been paid to records of flag officers' trials, even though these are critical in understanding the cases made against them and their court room responses. There are no detailed studies of flag officers' courts martial as distinctive phenomena or comparative treatments of their experiences as objects of naval justice in the context of prevailing leadership expectations of high naval command. There are, however, some insightful comments on broader leadership issues and their relationship to failures in political and administrative oversight in Richard Harding's essay on the mid-eighteenth-century navy and Ruddock Mackay's and Michael Duffy's discussion of naval leadership in *Hawke, Nelson and British Naval Leadership, 1747–1805*.[17]

This study seeks to provide a comprehensive and systematic treatment of flag officers' courts martial by reference to the following questions: How and why did flag officers' courts martial occur? What roles did the personalities and political dispositions of other flag officers and first lords of the Admiralty play in the management of charges, trials and outcomes? How important was context in explaining charges and outcomes? How did flag officers' experience of the naval justice system differ from that of other members of the service? What role did issues of reputation and honour play in defining flag officers' court martial experiences?

The book opens with an examination of the legal and procedural basis of naval trials in the period and then considers aspects of the service culture which had a bearing on the initiation of flag officers' courts martial and their impact on those involved. Courts martial sat at the end of a continuum of formal and informal controls that owed their effectiveness to the highly competitive environment in which ambitious senior commissioned naval officers operated. Flag officers' awareness that failures of duty compromised their honour as heads of the corps of naval gentlemen at arms and affected their pursuit of career-related ambitions – appointments, glory, royal honours, pensions and sinecures – sharpened the punitive outcomes of unfavourable trials and unsuccessful attempts at self-accusation.

The first two chapters provide the regulatory and cultural framework for the case studies presented in Chapters 3 to 12. Three of these studies consider aspects of the 'Keppel-Palliser affair' of 1778–81. They examine the events that led Lord Sandwich's board to charge Admiral Keppel in late 1778 at the instigation of Vice Admiral Sir Hugh Palliser and the Admiral's dramatic trial in early 1779, Palliser's motivation for taking the unpopular and risky step of charging his superior officer, his own trial and acquittal, and the implications of Palliser's acquittal both for him and his commander-in-chief. Flag officers' courts martial in the French Wars are considered in subsequent chapters. These studies examine the courts martial experiences of Vice Admiral Cornwallis (1796), Vice Admiral Sir William Parker (1802), Vice Admiral Sir John Duckworth (1805), Vice Admiral Sir Robert Calder (1805), Rear Admiral Sir Eliab Harvey (1809), Admiral Lord Gambier (1809) and Vice Admiral Charles Stirling (1814). They explore the context of each case, the careers, roles and motives of the principal actors, their perceptions of contemporary professional and public opinion, the outcomes of each case, contemporary reactions to them and their subsequent implications for those involved. The concluding chapters of the book address general interpretative issues arising from the case studies and data on intra- and inter-service charging and conviction rates. They consider the role of politics in generating flag officers' distinctive experience of naval justice and the importance of duty and honour in defining that experience. They also offer some comparative observations on significant variations between the charging and conviction rates for flag officers and those on the lower deck, on the one hand, and their peers in the upper ranks of the British army, on the other.

1

Framework and Procedures

The courts that tried flag officers were part of a system of formal adjudication that applied to all members of the Royal Navy, from the humblest boy seamen to its highest-ranking and ennobled admirals. Although soldiers and sailors were subject to courts martial, each service had distinctive judicial systems. The naval justice system addressed breaches of its basic code, the Articles of War, by men 'on service' in ships, port facilities and specified harbours and estuaries. Commissioned officers (including admirals) were only liable to be summoned for offences committed when 'employed', that is, on full pay. These specifications explain why the unfortunate and possibly insane superannuated Rear Admiral Bradley was tried at the Winchester Assizes in 1813 for a fraud involving seamen's mail committed on the Isle of Wight. Although Bradley could not face a court martial, the Board punished him for dishonouring his rank and the service by removing him from the superannuated rear admirals' list and thus depriving him of half pay.[1]

The first part of this chapter identifies the main features of the late Georgian naval justice system and compares aspects of it with the British army's judicial framework. It examines the legislative and regulatory basis of naval courts martial, the range of offences for which flag officers were tried, the inquisitorial function of courts and their dual responsibility for determining guilt and sentencing, the role of judge advocates and provisions for moderating sentences by appeal to the King in Council and to parliament. The second part of the chapter outlines the main procedural features of the system, including processes for calling courts martial, the treatment of those summoned for trial, the trial process and the determination of sentences.

The framework: Legislation, Articles of War and the *Regulations and Instructions*

The legislative and regulatory framework for naval courts martial was established in the reign of Charles II. These laws were repealed and superseded by an act of 1757 (22 Geo. II. C.23), which was further 'altered, amended, and new modelled' in 1779 by the Naval Courts Martial Act (19 Geo. III. C. 17).[2] Thirty-six Articles of War were supplemented by the Admiralty Board's *Regulations and Instructions* of 1757, issued in an extensively amended form in January 1806. The coverage of courts martial in the 1757 edition was very light, but the revised version contained a great deal of detail on matters not covered in the acts of 1757 and 1779. While specifying flag officers' general obligation to obey their superiors, the *Regulations* and Articles of War made few references to flag officers' offending. As noted below, however, some articles aligned closely with their responsibilities.

N. A. M. Rodger thought that the Royal Navy's reliance on the Articles of War and *The Regulations and Instructions* 'largely' left the service without a 'developed legal code' to guide captains in their day-to-day disciplinary responsibilities.[3] While this is undoubtedly true, it is far from clear that closer engagement with the 'ordinary law of land' would have addressed the problem. Eighteenth-century criminal courts administered a large body of 'ineffective, severe, unsystematic obscure laws' that defied codification or even, until the mid-eighteen twenties, significant consolidation or revision.[4] In any case, codification seems incompatible with a penal regime where punishments reflected captains' and courts' assessments of the deterrent necessary in the circumstances.

Before the legislation was 'new modelled' in 1779, courts martial had no discretion to impose 'other punishment' for ten of the twenty-five offences that carried death sentences. This group included two sets of offences under articles twelve and thirteen – 'withdrawing or keeping back from fight' and 'forbearing to pursue an enemy' – that applied primarily to those commanding ships and fleets. In 1757 the lack of discretion resulted in a court condemning Rear Admiral John Byng to death while appealing for clemency on the grounds that its hands were tied. Byng was executed despite this plea and the refusal of a naval commissioner of the Admiralty to sign the death warrant. Moral and judicial hand-wringing over this outcome did not lead to an amendment to the legislation and, as a result, Admiral Keppel faced a mandatory death sentence when charged with these offences in January–early February 1779. Debate arising from his case prompted the 1779 amendment which allowed for discretion for offences framed by these articles.

John Byrn and Thomas Malcomson suggest that the naval justice system was intended primarily to uphold the authority of the officer corps in much the same way that civilian criminal law upheld the hegemony of the dominant class in England.[5] Legal historians have challenged this characterization of criminal law by showing that most eighteenth-century trials dealt with offences against the persons and property of those outside the social and political elite. Criminal law thus played a role in protecting the legitimate interests of community members rather than merely being a class instrument.[6] One can usefully apply this insight to naval justice.

While authority was a central focus of naval discipline, it was not an end in itself and only five of the thirty-six articles addressed it. Articles condemning 'delaying or discouraging any service'; 'mutinous assembly'; 'stirring up disturbance'; 'striking a senior officer . . . disobedience'; and 'mutiny, desertion, disobedience on shore' dealt directly with challenges to superiors, while that concerning 'desertion and entertaining deserters' did so indirectly by punishing those who sought to remove themselves from their superiors' control. In addition, the first article specified the religious duties underwriting the theological basis of the eighteenth-century Anglican church-state. These clauses all relate in various ways to upholding authority within the service. As with civilian law, however, the naval system maintained the conditions of 'communal living' and ensured the ship's safe operation.[7] Articles prohibiting drunkenness, murder, theft, quarrelling and sodomy may all be seen in that light and were thus, like authority itself, deemed necessary for the effective 'government' or 'discipline' of the service.

However, while these articles were prohibitive, others also implied positive duties. Rodger's characterization of the Articles of War as a 'haphazard collection of regulations and admonishments largely concerned with court martial offences by officers' captures their unevenness and gestures to their prescriptive functions.[8] The positive injunctions of some articles were reinforced in the broad-ranging statement of responsibilities in the revised *Regulations and Instructions:*

> Every Flag Officer, Captain, and Commander . . . Is to obey every Order of his Superiors, and discharge every part of his duty, with the utmost zeal and alacrity. . . . He is, on all occasions, to promote the good of the public service, in all its branches and so to conduct himself, in every situation, as to be an example of morality, regularity, and good Order, to all who may be subject to his Command.[9]

While this instruction bound all officers, flag officers' position at the head of a strongly hierarchical institution meant the weight of responsibility fell particularly heavily on them. The Articles of War construed serious failures in criminal terms. Still, even where charges were not preferred or not upheld in court, perceptions that flag officers had not performed at the expected level resulted in nuanced punitive outcomes touching on their honour and reputation that differed markedly from the guilty/not guilty verdicts of criminal courts.

In some respects, however, late Georgian naval courts martial intersected with other English legal institutions and practices and were thought by an informed contemporary to embody the principles and spirit of English law.[10] Naval courts were required to follow criminal courts' practices when its regulations were silent, including such important matters as the rules of evidence. Moreover, both systems relied on deterrent punishment to uphold their respective bodies of law. The suggestion that late Georgian naval and criminal courts specified punishments 'to fit the crime' is misleading.[11] Sentences of transportation for stealing goods worth less than a shilling, capital sentences for burglary, dozens of lashes for drunkenness, disobedience or uncleanliness are inexplicable in these terms. Deterrent punishments discouraged offending by making an example of an offender that terrified others into not offending. As the historian John Beattie aptly put it, 'let some suffer horribly in public so that many will be deterred from crime'.[12] Recent scholarly work has corrected stereotypes about the 'brutality' of naval discipline, pointing out that the wanton mistreatment of men on the lower deck was likely to be counterproductive and was resisted by the victims and widely condemned by more rational and humane naval disciplinarians. During the French Wars, there was a growing tendency for some senior officers to question the navy's reliance on corporal punishment and explore alternatives to it.[13]

Nevertheless, prevailing views of the potential for offending among a large and heterogeneous body of men, the conditions of recruitment, the hardships of service at sea and heightened perceptions of the implications of lower deck disorder for the navy's effectiveness meant the navy often inflicted harsher physical penalties on malefactors than criminal courts where judges stipulated that whippings ended when 'blood came'.[14] Moreover, the alternative range of 'pains and penalties' utilized in the criminal justice system over the eighteenth century – transportation, houses of correction and imprisonment with hard labour – could not be adopted in the war time navy.[15] It is not necessary, however, to assume that all members of the lower deck were kept to their duty by the fear of severe punishment, just that this was the case for some proportion of them. As a very experienced, and from all appearances a relatively humane, army deputy judge advocate put it, naval justice relied on the use of example, 'for restraining by the sight and the fear of punishment, those who abstain from crimes only out of fear ... .'[16]

While the criminal and naval justice systems employed common penological assumptions, there were significant differences in how they conducted trials. In the first place, naval courts martial were empowered to enquire into matters relevant to the charge and to try the person or persons implicated in them. An exchange in Admiral Lord Gambier's trial in 1809 exemplified this obligation. When the court insisted on calling further witnesses and Gambier declared that he was 'very desirous that every inquiry should be made in the fullest', a court member retorted sharply, 'We have no doubt of its being your wish but it is our absolute duty'.[17] The inquisitorial role of courts martial was distinct from that of 'commissions' or 'courts' of inquiry. The Board convened these bodies to investigate alleged failings of senior personnel, and while they had no juridical powers, their reports could identify *prima facie* grounds for a court martial.[18]

Secondly, and as a direct result of the scope of naval courts martial, the members of courts were judges of fact as well as of justice; that is, they were responsible for determining whether the accused was guilty as charged and then, within the constraints of the Articles of War, imposing a penalty. Judges in naval courts thus played the roles assigned to both jurors and judges in other British courts. In addition, their inquisitorial functions were similar to those of investigating magistrates in some continental European legal systems. This feature meant that the marked shift towards adversary trials in eighteenth-century criminal courts did not occur in the naval justice system.[19]

Naval courts martial bore some similarity to nineteenth-century professional tribunals that investigated and sanctioned their members' conduct.[20] These tribunals, however, invoked a principle of trial by peers which was inconsistent with a system of law framed for a strongly hierarchical institution, some of the provisions of which directly upheld relationships of obedience and subordination. The principle might also be problematic in light of the role of members of courts martial as judges of law as well as fact: ordinary seamen's education and subordinate situations would be incompatible with the 'dignity and solemnity of a court'.[21] Although the two leading contemporary professional commentators on courts martial defended the narrow basis of their deliberative membership, this was a matter of critical comment from other writers.[22] Where flag officers were concerned, however, the analogy with professional tribunals is apposite. Their judges were peers and senior officers from the same professional and social milieu with similar standing and experience of the ethos and expectations of the service. They also possessed the technical expertise necessary to understand fleet commanders' active service challenges and options.

Naval judges' capacity to bring expert knowledge to their deliberations makes it very likely that they acted as 'self-informing jurors'.[23] Their knowledge of technical issues was certainly apparent in their questioning of witnesses. Although the confidentiality of courts' deliberations makes it impossible to gauge the impact of that expertise on the outcome of trials, it is inconceivable that men of their status, used to occupying positions of authority, would rely entirely on the testimony of witnesses. In modern courts, juror expertise has resulted in retrials because it was not subject to cross-examination before the accused.[24] No such prohibition applied in naval courts or, indeed, some other eighteenth and early nineteenth-century judicial institutions. Judges hearing mercantile cases could establish 'special juries' of merchants to decide on technical matters, and in some criminal trials, juries of 'matrons' were used to determine whether condemned women were entitled to delay and eventual remission of their sentences by 'pleading their bellies'.[25]

Finally, members of flag officers' courts martial subscribed to the same code of gentlemanly and professional honour as those they judged and would be aware of the impact of courts martial on their colleagues' standing as officers and gentlemen. As we shall see, questions of honour played a significant role in flag officers' reactions to the court martial experience. It also affected the conduct of trials. As a contemporary authority on naval justice put it, a naval court martial was 'a tribunal which naturally respects the characters even of those it may be compelled to impeach'.[26] The equitable treatment of the accused in naval trials will be discussed later. At this stage, it can be noted that the fact that judges were flag officers' peers facilitated a degree of cohort respect and consideration; they were also part of a shared culture that extended beyond service settings to social and ceremonial occasions on shore. Unless a court martial resulted in the dismissal of a flag officer from the service, the accused and his court were likely to come into contact during their duties and resume relationships of collaboration, command and obedience arising from them. They may even occasionally find themselves dining together in the great cabins of warships, exchanging bows across the assembly rooms at Bath and Cheltenham and standing in line to pay their dutiful respects to the King and Queen at royal levees and drawing rooms in London.

The regulations specified the appointment of 'judge advocates' to naval courts martial to ensure the judicial integrity of a system in which wide-ranging responsibilities rested on the splendidly epauletted shoulders of judges with a deep knowledge of the service but no legal training or judicial experience outside of it. Presidents appointed judge advocates by issuing warrants to them, probably acting in important cases on the advice of the Board or its solicitor.[27] In addition to preparing documents for the use of the court (often with the assistance of the Solicitor to the Admiralty) and summoning witnesses, these officials advised presidents on procedural matters and points of legal contention that occurred during a trial.[28] Where a commissioned officer instigated a charge, it was usual for the 'accuser' to lead the prosecution. If the charge originated from the Board's initiative, courts usually took the lead, but if the Board deemed the nature, potential difficulty and risk of a case warranted it, it assigned the prosecutor's role to the judge advocate or Admiralty solicitor.[29]

On foreign stations, an admiral's secretary or purser might perform judge advocates' functions, but they were never assigned (as in the army) to a commissioned officer.[30] These arrangements were criticized because these officials lacked professional expertise and might be subject to undue influence from senior officers.[31] On home stations, however, particularly in high-profile and potentially contentious trials, judge advocates were drawn from a professional cadre headed by the judge advocate to the fleet, who could delegate his authority to deputies with legal knowledge and experience of naval and other courts. The criminal courts were particularly relevant since they provided a model on matters where legislation and printed instructions provided no direction.[32] It is unclear whether George Jackson, the judge advocate in Keppel's, Palliser's and Cornwallis' trials, had formal legal training. Still, he had an extensive background in the upper reaches of public service and more than held his own during an extremely hostile examination before the House of Lords in early 1779.[33] Moses Greetham, Jnr, the judge advocate in the other trials considered here, studied at Gray's Inn and was admitted as a solicitor. His experience of naval justice went back to the early 1770s–1780s, and while serving on close to three hundred courts martial he developed an extensive legal practice in Portsmouth.[34]

Naval courts comprised no more than fourteen and no fewer than five judges drawn from commissioned officers down to the rank of master and commander on the station where the trial was held. The court had the power to excuse judges from further participation on the grounds of ill-health, but the number of judges could not fall below five. In flag officers' trials, the Board's views on what constituted a 'respectable court' ensured an appropriate representation of admirals, if necessary, by ordering some of them to hoist their flags on the station.

The Board's role in constituting a court was delicate, if not ambiguous. It appointed presidents but had no direct control over the number of judges sitting and could not intervene directly in their selection: eligible officers had a right and an obligation to sit based on seniority. But while the Admiralty Board could not pick and choose from among those eligible to sit, it could determine their availability by ordering ships to leave or join the station and flag officers to strike or hoist their flags. It was thus able, subject to the operational practicalities of the situation (and presumably also the need to avoid the appearance of packing a court), to influence the membership of a particular court. As with many other areas within the Board's control, however, it used this power after carefully judged calculations of expediency, interest and decency that sometimes left it exposed to charges of undue influence in high-profile cases involving flag officers.

Unlike army courts martial which operated at regimental, garrison and 'general' levels, Royal Navy courts martial formed a unified system supplemented by summary justice dispensed by captains of ships. The vast majority of cases captains dealt with involved those below the rank of warrant officer, but for some offences, such as drunkenness, warrant and commissioned officers could be punished by their commanding officer.[35] In the army system, 'general courts martial' reviewed decisions made at regimental and garrison trials, but this option was not available for naval courts martial. They did not review captains' summary punishments, and the adjudication of claims against the decisions of naval courts took place beyond the ambit of the navy's justice system and, indeed, the Admiralty Board. Thus, when Captain Isaac Coffin was sentenced erroneously to be dismissed from his ship for false mustering, the law lords' ruling that only courts martial could determine sentences quashed the Board's attempt to correct the court's mistake by ordering him to be cashiered as the Articles of War specified.[36]

The King reviewed army sentences handed down in Great Britain and sentences of death passed on naval personnel in home waters.[37] In other respects, however, naval courts martial were largely autonomous. They could refer procedural questions to the Board but, as noted earlier, it could not intervene in sentencing. That did not mean, however, that the findings of courts martial were final; that would have been contrary to the general principles of English law within which they operated. Their decisions were subject to three forms of review.

First, individuals could appeal to sovereigns to amend penalties inflicted on them. These pleas were heard in the Privy Council, a body which, among other duties, advised monarchs on exercising their 'prerogative', that is, powers not subject to parliamentary or judicial control. The Privy Council sought the advice of the Admiralty Board when considering 'humble petitions' for modifying the penalties inflicted by naval courts martial. In some cases (including that of Rear Admiral Sir Eliab Harvey discussed later), first lords advised sovereigns of intended appeals to test how they were likely to receive them. An act of 1797 (37 Geo. III. cap. 140) affirmed the King's prerogative of 'pardoning and remitting punishment'. However, the Crown also possessed the power of summary dismissal following a not guilty verdict by a court martial.[38]

Secondly, the conduct of naval judges was subject to the jurisdiction of the Court of the King's Bench and the Court of Common Pleas. Actions in these courts focused on the liability of individual judges 'for any wanton abuse of power or illegal proceedings'.[39] A notable case occurred in 1743 when a lieutenant of marines won damages of £1000 against the president of a court martial and subsequently secured the other court members' arrest. When they sent a remonstrance to the Admiralty Board challenging the court's right to make this order, the Lord Chief Justice forced the naval judges to recant and compound with the officer concerned. These proceedings were against individual judges' roles in particular judgements and did not consider the Board's involvement in laying charges.

The third route for reviewing courts martial lay through parliament's powers to frame recommendations to the sovereign to issue directions to the Admiralty Board on charges, sentences arising from a court martial and on bringing other officers to trial.[40] Although parliament's powers were extensive, the need to proceed through the various stages – examining minutes, calling for papers and framing and moving resolutions – by majority votes in the House of Commons meant that the ministry and the Admiralty Board had a crucial role in determining how far initiatives progressed. After 1745, no parliamentary resolutions on naval courts martial were laid before the King. However, the legislature's right to review these trials gave flag officers' friends and senior naval officers in both houses of parliament opportunities to air cases in which they were interested. Foreshadowing and moving motions on naval courts martial were particularly likely in highly politicized trials such as Admiral Keppel's and Vice-Admiral Palliser's in 1779 and Lord Gambier's in 1809.[41]

Procedures and practice

All the courts martial considered in this study were held in Portsmouth. Although in some cases the incidents that sparked them occurred on 'foreign' stations rather than within the scope of the Channel, North Sea, Scottish and Irish commands, the officers concerned all returned to England before they were charged. The printed regulations are silent on whether flag officers could be court-martialled on foreign stations, but for several reasons that would not have been practical. Commanders-in-chief were empowered to authorize trials of officers and men on their stations but could not, for obvious reasons, charge themselves. When they wished to charge a subordinate flag officer they applied to the Board to recall him to face trial at home.

Although there appears to be no statutory requirement for flag officers' trials to be at Portsmouth, and admirals Richard Lestock and Thomas Mathews were court-martialled at Chatham and Deptford in 1746, Portsmouth's size made it easier to bring together courts of sufficient seniority and 'respectability'. Ease of access to the Admiralty Board may well have been a consideration because it expected to receive daily transcriptions of the minutes of flag officers' trials; these were sent by overnight express mail from Portsmouth but would have taken several days from Plymouth. The same was true of any communications with the Board on procedural questions that the president of a court and the judge advocate could not resolve.

Flag officers' courts martial originated in an Admiralty order summoning them to trial and indicating a timeframe subject to the availability of witnesses (some of whom would be at sea, sometimes on foreign stations) and the accused's preparation requirements. Although the court martial system was standing, the Board authorized each trial by a warrant issued to the president.[42] In some cases, the Board acted entirely on its initiative following reports that had come to it in the ordinary course of business or as the result of its authoritative 'requests' for further information on a matter of concern. It might also issue a summons in response to a request from a superior or subordinate of the person charged, or from an officer who wished to vindicate his conduct in the face of adverse commentary in the press and innuendo circulating within the service and polite society.

In common with all those ordered to face a court martial, flag officers were arrested and referred to formally as 'the prisoner'. Other officers might be confined to their cabins if their captain so ordered and ordinary members of the ship's company were routinely confined below deck. Flag officers' treatment at this stage of the proceedings was different. Having been arrested by the provost martial, he released them on giving their word of honour to appear when ordered. They usually returned to their homes, sought their family and friends' advice and moral support, and consulted legal advisers on how best to prepare for the ordeal ahead. However, as in the case of lesser naval mortals, the provost martial took them into court in his custody to symbolize their status as prisoners. If flag officers were members of parliament, the ministry notified the House of Commons or the House of Lords of their arrest.

The legislation specified that courts martial were to be held on board ship. Admiral Keppel's trial ashore was an exception to this practice that had to be authorized by an act of parliament. Before the Naval Courts Martial Act of March 1779, judges were obliged to remain on board the ship until a trial concluded. After enduring thirty-six days of seclusion (albeit onshore rather than in far more restricted accommodation on a man-of-war) Keppel's judges wrote to the Admiralty Board complaining of the 'severe hardship' of their 'long confinement' and claiming that it was not 'useful to the public, or consistent with the character of officers who are called to sit as judges'.[43] When the House of Commons debated the matter, a member argued that as judges were under oath and the seclusion requirement did not extend to the judge advocate, it was a slight on their honour. Henceforth, judges were able to live ashore. Flag officers lived ashore during their trial, but a comment in a press report indicates that they were assigned a cabin for their use in the ship where the court sat.[44]

The criminal character of the proceedings was signalled by the requirement that the provost marshal stand close to the accused throughout the trial and its solemn dignity by the Board's stipulation that members of the court must wear full dress uniforms, elaborately decorated with embroidery until 1795 and with copious gold lace thereafter.[45] The accused wore more austerely decorated but still very fine 'undress' to mark his status as a prisoner.[46] After the provost marshal brought the prisoner into the courtroom, the judges and judge advocate were sworn in and the latter read the charge and related documentation into the record. Judges were under oath to 'duly administer justice, according to the articles and order established . . . without partiality, favour, or affection' and they and the judge advocate also swore not to 'upon any account, at any time whatsoever, disclose, or discover the vote, opinion of any particular members of this court martial, unless thereunto required by act of parliament'. The author of one set of 'rules' for courts martials claimed that this specification extended to secrecy on the overall vote of a court and hence to a prohibition against judge advocates inserting the word 'unanimous' in the wording of a sentence.[47] With one exception, this rule is reflected in the practice of the courts examined in this study. These prohibitions do not seem to have applied to earlier trials; the published sentence on Admiral Thomas Mathews in 1746, for example, noted unanimous resolutions on particular charges and recorded the number of votes ('Yes', 'No', 'Dubious') on others.[48]

Officers having a personal interest in the subject of the trial (taken to include those who had sat on an earlier inquiry whose findings gave rise to a court martial) were precluded from being judges. As we shall see, however, this prohibition did not include those who had close professional and personal attachments to the accused.[49] Challenges to the membership of a naval court martial were rare in the period, and none were made by flag officers. However, there was an inconclusive discussion in a cleared court of the propriety of Admiral Keppel's witnesses and judges sitting on Palliser's court.[50] Although the written regulations were silent on how challenges should be made and adjudicated, contemporary authorities thought courts should hear them because they were subject to legal and parliamentary scrutiny on the justice and impartiality of their proceedings. The situation in civilian criminal courts was quite different because there was a presumption that judges who had sworn to administer law impartially were incapable of bias.[51] It seems possible that an unstated version of this presumption occurred in flag officers' trials. Even when public questioning of the 'constitution' of flag officers' courts arose from suspicions of undue leniency towards the accused, there was usually a professed delicacy in phrasing objections. As we shall see, however, members of parliament speaking under privilege were less guarded.

Following the judge advocate's reading of the charge, witnesses were ordered to leave the court until called to be sworn and give testimony. Unlike those facing trial in other criminal courts, in naval courts martial the accused did not plead in response to the charge. Indeed, the complex and tentative wording of charges authorizing an inquiry and a judicial determination would have made that difficult, if not impossible.[52] The court first heard the witnesses for the prosecution, that is, those called by the prosecutor or the court to give evidence in support of, or at least in elucidation of, the charge. These witnesses were examined by the prosecutor (the accuser or the judge advocate) and subject to cross-examination by the accused. They could also be examined at will by the court and the judge advocate, who could insist (in conformity with the court's obligation to conduct as full an inquiry as possible) on calling and recalling witnesses even though the prosecutor or accused considered their case was closed. When the examination of prosecution witnesses was complete, the court invited the accused to deliver his statement of defence. In trials of men from the lower deck, these statements were often very brief, but flag officers usually offered elaborate defences and invariably had the assistance of counsel in composing them.

Unless (as was frequently the case) counsel read the defence, barristers played an uncharacteristically mute role in naval courts martial. During the trial, they were permitted to sit near the accused and advise him on the framing of questions on matters of fact to put to witnesses, but they were not allowed to make statements to the court or examine or cross-examine witnesses. A contemporary authority justified these restrictions on the grounds that the cause should be determined on its merits and judges should not be exposed to flights of lawyerly rhetoric.[53] They were also consistent with the idea that lawyers were expert in the law but only the accused and other witnesses could inform the court of the facts.[54] The naval justice system thus avoided the emerging tendency in the criminal courts for lawyers to dominate trials.[55] In naval courts, the judges were not lawyers, judge advocates did not need to be lawyers, and barristers were kept very much in the background.

While the judge advocates who officiated at flag officers' trials were legally competent, they were of a different status in the profession than their army equivalents. Sir Charles Morgan, the long-serving judge advocate general to the army, was an MP, privy councillor and king's counsel, and he held several lucrative sinecures secured through the support of George III. The Honourable Richard Ryder, the son of a peer, an MP, a leading member of the bar and a former lord commissioner of the Treasury, succeeded Morgan.[56] The background of these officials might explain a feature of the courts martial of senior army officers that differed significantly from the naval practice. Although counsel was not prominent in the trials of general officers in the period, judge advocates played a distinctly lawyerly role in them. This tendency was marked particularly in the court martial of Lieutenant General Sir John Whitelocke in 1808. Ryder made a substantial opening address to Whitelocke's court, sparred with the accused and some of the judges during the hearing, and gave an extensive summary and rebuttal for the prosecution following the accused's statement of defence.[57] When judge advocates led the prosecution and even when the Admiralty solicitor took this role, they restricted themselves to leading the questioning of witnesses.

Naval courts heard defence statements without interruption and included them in the minutes. The accused was then entitled to call witnesses to give sworn testimony on questions put by him. Defence witnesses were subject to cross-examination on their evidence (not on 'new or extraneous matter') by the prosecution and questioning by the court and judge advocate.[58] When defence witnesses' examinations concluded, the president adjourned the proceedings and cleared the courtroom so its members could deliberate in private. The first stage of this process involved the judge advocate's recital of the minutes he had taken during the trial. He was also responsible for drawing up a list of questions to guide the judges' discussion and drafting a sentence when they had come to a view on the case. In both naval and army courts martial, outcomes were determined by a majority vote, with members voting in reverse order of seniority, supposedly to prevent superiors from swaying the votes of more junior officers. Since the voting was not by secret ballot, this provision against undue influence was not likely to be particularly effective: superiors knew how their inferiors had voted and during the court's deliberation junior officers probably acquired a pretty accurate sense of their seniors' views.

The court voted first on whether the case was proven and, if necessary, deliberated and voted on penalties. Contemporary authorities differ on whether naval courts martial followed the army in excluding those in the minority on the first vote from participating in determining a penalty. One contemporary authority thought it absurd for those who had voted 'not guilty' to be involved in deciding a penalty; the other saw this procedure as reflecting the tendency of English law to favour the accused by giving those who had voted for acquittal an opportunity to argue in favour of punishments mitigating the more severe penalties proposed by those who voted guilty.[59] The veil of secrecy in which courts' deliberations were shrouded makes it impossible to evaluate these discrepant claims. Still, the fact that the first one was advanced by a writer who had been present at nearly three hundred court martial deliberations lends credence to his position. At the end of the day, however, a majority determined both questions. If judges' initial votes on the question of guilt were evenly split and further deliberation had not produced a majority, the charge was 'not proven' and the prisoner was acquitted. Unless the court arrived at a single set of alternative penalties, this procedure could not be applied, which might explain the length of some deliberations. As we shall see, in addition to declaring a verdict, naval courts martial might also gild the lily of acquittal by issuing declaratory riders on the accused's merits and the accuser's poor judgement and tawdry motivation. These riders conveyed an implied reprimand to the Board for allowing the charge to proceed. The published sentences on Vice Admiral Lestock and Admiral Thomas Mathews included detailed rationales of their courts' findings. This practice was also followed in army generals' trials in the French Wars.[60] However, by the end of the century, naval courts martial restricted themselves to very brief non-explanatory sentencing statements. This practice reduced the scope for post-trial litigation but makes it difficult for historians to understand the court's findings.[61]

With one possible exception (discussed in a later chapter), there is no indication that the judges and judge advocates involved in late Georgian trials of flag officers failed to honour their oath not to disclose sentencing deliberations.[62] When the army's courts martial regulations were reviewed in 1749, there was sharp debate on the propriety of secrecy requirements in military courts, with some critics claiming that they were contrary to the principles of English law and likely to encourage malpractice by preventing access to information on which claims for redress could be made.[63] Be that as it may, the oath of secrecy made considerable sense in the context of peer trials of flag officers. If the disclosure of preferences and voting were permitted, it would have opened the way for recriminations by superiors and embarrassment, ill-will and conflict among colleagues who were likely to come into regular contact during naval business and related social engagements. References to the principles applying in other courts are not compelling because judges in civilian courts were highly unlikely to interact socially or professionally with those on whom they passed sentence.

Conclusion

The courts that late Georgian flag officers faced were part of a long-established, well-defined and regulated unitary system of criminal justice applied to all service members. There were links with civilian criminal courts in the sense that procedural matters not specified in the legislative and regulatory framework were to be determined by the practice of the criminal courts. However, there were also significant differences in approach, some of which were a consequence of the ethos and requirements of the service. The most significant difference between naval law and that applied in criminal courts ashore is that the former specified offending in both prohibitive and prescriptive terms. The prescriptive force of naval law was particularly significant for the court martial experiences of flag officers because it gave rise to a conception of criminality that embraced acts of omission and commission. Some of the charges flag officers faced arose directly from their failures to perform their duties with sufficient skill, commitment and vigour. However, even when charged with breaking a rule rather than failing in an obligation, the expectation that they would demonstrate exemplary leadership compounded their offending.

The membership of courts reflected the hierarchical principles upon which the Royal Navy was based, with judges drawn from the senior ranks of the service and flag officers' courts being notable for the participation of other flag officers. As a result, admirals' courts martial were essentially trials by peers and, as in trials in the House of Lords, courts were careful of the dignity and honour of those who stood before them. Unlike trials in the criminal courts, judges and the accused were on the same social and professional footing; this gave them a common basis of understanding and respect. It also carried the risk that familiarity would foster prejudice. Nevertheless, judges' professional expertise helped them appreciate the technical issues often at stake in the trials of senior naval officers and equipped them to play active roles as self-informed jurors in their investigatory, deliberative and judicial functions.

The distinctive structural and procedural features of naval courts martial provided the framework for a system of naval justice that applied to all members of the service.

As far as flag officers were concerned, however, courts martial stood at the end of a continuum of formal and informal disciplinary tools that criminalized leadership failures and reinforced legal sanctions by perceptions that those who failed in their duty weakened their claim to the honorific status of gentlemen at arms. The implications of the professional cultural dimensions of the naval justice system for flag officers will be considered in the next chapter.

2

Discipline, Criminality and Honour

Navy personnel could only be summoned to a court martial for offences committed on active service. In a situation where up to 85 per cent of flag officers were living ashore on half pay and more than half of those who became admirals were never employed, those with mediocre records as post captains and limited interest were never likely to come near a court martial unless needed as judges.[1] Flag officers who faced courts martial were thus likely to be better performed than many of their colleagues, have stronger connections with other senior figures in the service, members of the Admiralty Board, influential politicians, the social elite and, in some cases, members of the royal family. While some flag officers' aristocratic pedigree assisted their careers, others gained royal honours (peerages, baronetcies, knighthoods) through distinguished service.[2] Of the nine flag officers court-martialled during the American and French Wars, one had been made a peer, two were 'honourables', younger sons of hereditary peers, one inherited a baronetcy, three recently had that dignity conferred upon them, one was a knight of the Order of the Bath and only one was plain 'Mr'. The professional and social standing of successful flag officers meant that when courts martial loomed, they were likely to be noticed within the service and among the broader elite. These considerations raised the stakes for those involved by sharpening the threats to their professional reputations and honour.

This chapter will locate courts martial within the range of implicit and explicit disciplinary controls to which flag officers were subject. Only the Board was authorized to order admirals to stand trial, but there were three distinct pathways through which their misconduct became the subject of criminal charges: at the instigation of the Board; at the request of an accuser who might be a superior or subordinate in the service; or by 'self-charging', that is, at the request of an officer who believed that hostile speculation in the service and beyond compromised his reputation. The chapter concludes with a preliminary account of the role of prevailing conceptions of honour in flag officers' court martial experience.

The continuum of control: Reprimands, recalls and courts martial

Admirals who were professionally, physically or psychologically unfit for active service and those who preferred to live ashore on half pay had to respond to the Board's forceful 'requests' for financial information on earlier service and might occasionally be summoned to sit on courts martial, report on technical innovations or attend ceremonials.[3] It was the custom for many of these officers to make formal offers to serve from time to time but nothing seems to have hung on this courtesy, and for the most part, their interactions with the Board were confined to the formalities necessary to claim their half pay. Ambitious flag officers were in an entirely different position. They could only pursue their ambitions through active service and that necessarily drew them into a highly competitive environment where they were exposed to the scrutiny of their peers and the sharp disciplinary gaze of superiors.[4] Commanders-in-chief and subordinate flag officers on active service were acutely aware that perceptions of weak leadership, poor discipline in ships under their command, operational blunders and turbulent relations with superiors and subordinates posed a threat to prospects of future employment and the honorific and material rewards that might follow from it.

Contemporary statements on flag officers' duties referred to their need to model effective and honourable leadership, to 'shew themselves good Examples of Honour and Virtue', 'to animate his officers by the force of his example, and promote a sense of emulation in those who are under his command ... '.[5] These qualities were prominent in the careers of Lords Hawke and Nelson and the flag officers St Vincent held up as models of activity, commitment and decisiveness: Lord Collingwood, Admiral Cornwallis, Lord Keith and Sir James Saumarez.[6] Flag officers' awareness of the need to live up to the expectations of the Board and their senior colleagues is apparent in the constant appeals for assurance which punctuate their correspondence and the note of desperation that creeps in when they fear it might not be forthcoming. When they faced courts martial, flag officers acknowledged the principle that rank is an 'aggravation' of an offence by appealing to the implausibility of men of their standing being guilty of the misconduct alleged against them.[7]

When the Board was dissatisfied with a flag officer's performance on active service, it had a range of sanctions available, beginning with carefully calibrated written statements of oblique and direct disapproval. These unwelcome communications passed in ascending order of severity, from tart expressions of 'surprise' that implied a reprimand, carpingly worded orders construed in the same light and unequivocal statements of disapprobation and censure. As we shall see, the Board's reaction to perceived failure was context specific. In serious cases, a flag officer's appointment might be terminated by a reprimand that presaged a court martial.

In mid-1795, Lord Bridport, who had been standing in for Lord Howe in command of the Channel Fleet and hoped to succeed him, complained to Lord Spencer of recent promotions in the fleet and the unreasonable length of his last cruise. Spencer responded that he was 'very much mortified to find . . . that the Promotion which His Majesty has been pleased to authorize me to make . . . has proved so little satisfactory to your Lordship'. He also reminded Bridport that the length of deployments was a matter for the Board: 'His Majesty's Servants will endeavour to decide on it in the manner that shall appear to them to be most for the benefit of the King's Service'.[8] As a commander-in-chief of the Mediterranean and Channel fleets, St Vincent had been remorseless in putting down presumptuous flag officers and captains. He continued in the same vein when he became first lord. When Rear Admiral Sir James Saumarez, an officer whom he respected, protested being superseded by a senior flag officer, St Vincent warned: 'I cannot sufficiently express my surprise at the contents of your public and private letters upon the subject . . . and I persuade myself that you will, long before this can reach you, have seen the great impropriety of your public letter.'[9] In early December 1812, at a very difficult stage in the naval war against the United States, Lord Melville told Admiral Sir John Warren, the commander-in-chief in North America, that he was 'surprised' that he had not already set up an effective blockade of United States ports. Melville's Board subsequently professed itself 'exceedingly perplexed' by Warren's tardiness in reporting on the disposition of the more than seventy vessels on a command that extended from Newfoundland to Jamaica.[10]

These informal reprimands sometimes took the form of 'private' letters from first lords rather than formal 'public' communications from the Board. Even in these cases, they were likely to disturb the *amour propre* of recipients, cast a shadow over their prospects and threaten their sense of professional self-worth. Vice Admiral Sir Hyde Parker could have been in no doubt about the first lord's meaning when he advised, 'as a private friend, that any delay in your sailing would do you irreparable injury'.[11] Alleged failures in duty could also be construed as compromising a flag officer's honour, and where interpersonal disputes or questions of financial impropriety were involved, sensitivities on that score heightened. In 1806, when Lord Howick headed the Board, William Marsden, the Admiralty Secretary, was instructed to raise concerns with Vice Admiral Sir Alexander Cochrane regarding the quality of prizes he had purchased on the Navy's behalf. As there was some criticism in the service of the Cochrane family's avarice and commanders-in-chief benefited directly from prizes bought into the navy, Marsden's letter stung Cochrane into raising this matter with Howick's successor, Thomas Grenville. While dismissing such claims as products of 'private pique' Cochrane said that coming from Marsden, 'they convey a direct censure . . . that hurt my feelings more than I can well express'.[12] Nothing came of this matter, but Cochrane was no doubt aware that reprimands were the thin end of a short wedge that could give rise to orders of recall.

It was a widely recognized convention that flag appointments lasted about three years. Unless early recall was due to major shifts in strategic priorities and explained in those terms, flag officers took it as a sign of official disapproval or ingratitude. In the late Georgian period, several admirals suffered this fate. Lord Spencer dismissed Admiral Lord Hood from the Mediterranean command in 1795 and removed him from the Admiralty Board after he expressed public resentment at the inadequacies of the fleet assigned to him and claimed that it risked compromising his honour, making him 'the instrument of disgrace to the nation'.[13] Lord Spencer told the king that 'discipline and subordination . . . would be entirely at an end, if public and official representations of this kind were allowed to pass unnoticed'.[14] Although a few of Hood's close friends were outraged by this decision, other senior officers were less sympathetic and thought he had forced the first lord's hand and deserved punishment.[15] Rather than loudly protesting this decision, Hood determined to keep a low profile. He did not press for an inquiry or a court martial, being keen to avoid collateral damage to his brother, Admiral Lord Bridport, and to fatally compromise any chance of retirement preferment.[16] Hood's discretion on this occasion was just enough to induce Spencer to adhere to an earlier undertaking to appoint him governor of Greenwich Hospital when the post became vacant.[17] More than a year later, however, Hood still bitterly resented Lord Spencer's 'indifference and inattention' to him and all his connection.[18]

Other flag recalls were more consequential. Thus, in 1796 when Lord Spencer recalled Sir John Laforey from the Leeward Islands command because of doubts over his energy and temperament, Laforey's friend Sir Charles Middleton tried to dissuade the first lord against taking a step that lowered Laforey in the eyes of his colleagues. This dispute resulted in Middleton's resignation from the board.[19] In the summer of 1797, Lord Spencer acceded to St Vincent's ultimatum to recall a junior flag officer, Sir Charles Thompson, for his failure to obey a critical signal during the Battle of St Vincent and for protesting the commander-in-chief's decision to execute mutineers on a Sunday.[20] Although Thompson had significant interest through a family tie with the Duke of Beaufort and was esteemed professionally by Rear Admiral William Young, a long-serving naval commissioner on the Admiralty Board, he remained unemployed until the following year.[21]

As we shall see, the Board recalled Vice Admiral Sir William Parker from the North American command for allegedly ignoring its orders and engaging in sharp practice; when it seemed prepared to leave him in a fog of unresolved accusation, Parker successfully appealed to be court-martialled. His namesake, Vice Admiral Sir Hyde Parker, was less fortunate. He was ordered home from the Baltic but not summoned to a court martial and was unsuccessful in his attempt to secure a court of enquiry.[22] Several years later, the volatile Vice Admiral Sir George Berkeley was recalled from North America for issuing orders that encouraged one of his captains to fire a broadside into a United States man-of-war, killing some of its crew and coming close to provoking a war between Britain and her former colonies. Berkeley, who was capable and very well connected, was not otherwise punished for his role in this affair.[23] Finally, as we shall see in a later chapter, a concerted campaign against Vice Admiral Charles Stirling's alleged misuse of his position as commander-in-chief at Jamaica played a role in a summary recall in 1813 and subsequent court martial.

The Admiralty Board took the initiative in recalling these officers, but in other instances, it was taken by commanders-in-chief. In 1795, Sir John Laforey got rid of his second-in-command (the troublesome Rear Admiral Charles Thompson) by sending him home from the Leeward Islands with a convoy and asking the Board to order a court martial on his conduct.[24] When a court martial presided over by Rear Admiral Richard Bligh acquitted two people caught up in the notoriously brutal mutiny on HMS *Hermione*, Sir Hyde Parker roundly abused his second-in-command and wrote an angry letter to Lord Spencer demanding his recall. He told the first lord that the verdicts were entirely due to Bligh's 'supine' performance as president and accused him of 'lacking the Energy for Enforcing Discipline by the terror of Exemplary Punishment in this melancholy crisis'.[25] Lord Spencer declined Parker's demand that Bligh be recalled, ignored the resignation ultimatum that accompanied it and reprimanded him for inappropriate treatment of his second-in-command.[26] Parker's mishandling of Bligh almost certainly contributed to his own recall. However, the fact that he had held the post beyond the normal three years made it unnecessary to offer any explanation except regret at his poor treatment of Bligh and a pointed reference to the amount of prize money he had made on the station.[27]

In 1799, St Vincent exceeded his authority by sending Vice Admiral Sir John Orde home from the Mediterranean without requesting a court martial on him. Having learnt a painful lesson when Lord Spencer rebuked him for doing so, he appealed unsuccessfully to have Sir William Parker (whom he regarded as Orde's dupe) recalled.[28]

Even where a recall was not freighted with disciplinary implications or personal animosity, it could provoke claims of reputational damage. As we shall see, Vice Admiral Sir John Duckworth protested intemperately when the Board recalled him from the Jamaica command. The first lord, Lord Melville, was clearly offended by the tone of his communications and reminded Duckworth sharply that his recall was consistent with the conventions governing the length of flag commands.[29] Duckworth accused the Board of ingratitude for past services. The same claim was made by Sir Alexander Cochrane when he was relieved of the Leeward Islands command on becoming governor of Guadalupe. Having earlier sought the governorship of Martinique, he was angered to find that his appointment to Guadalupe came at the cost of his naval command. The first lord held his ground when Cochrane complained bitterly about the financial cost of being 'ousted' and the Board's implied lack of recognition of his achievements in capturing several French and Danish West Indian territories. Charles Yorke told Cochrane that the standard convention precluded naval and civil commands.[30] In other cases, Yorke went to some pains to advise flag officers of their impending recall and to consult their 'convenience' over the timing.[31] Yorke's delicacy in these matters testifies to admirals' sensitivities to perceptions of implied rebukes and reputation-sapping speculations, as well as his determination to remove grounds for offence.

Initiating courts martial

During the controversies over Admiral Keppel's and Vice Admiral Sir Hugh Palliser's courts martial in early 1779, it was confirmed the Admiralty Board had discretion over whether it would accept charges laid by officers against one another or by an officer against himself. The first lord at the time, the Earl of Sandwich, later said he would be prepared to authorize a court martial where there was an accusation and a *prima facie* case to answer.[32] This specification was primarily formal and, while it left room for discretion, it did not refer to the contextual considerations that invariably played a role in the Board's decision-making. Even without the intrusion of the extreme political partisanship that played such a significant role in the Keppel-Palliser affair, the Board's discretion would usually take account of political and operational considerations, intra-service relations and the particular circumstances of the alleged offending. These considerations are prominent in the case studies discussed in the following chapters.

Courts martial only took place when the Admiralty Board ordered them. In some cases, they occurred wholly on the Board's initiative. When the Board received information that provided grounds for serious concern with a flag officer's conduct, it charged them directly. The Board's suspicions may have arisen from commanders-in-chiefs' despatches and prompted it to seek further details from those directly involved. It was sometimes spurred into action by reports and speculation in the British press and in service circles. In Keppel's and Vice Admiral Sir Robert Calder's cases, the local press reprinted senior enemy officers' self-justificatory reports from foreign newspapers.

The most straightforward examples of Board-instigated trials were those ordered on Vice Admirals Cornwallis and Stirling and Rear Admiral Harvey. Cornwallis was charged on the basis of his despatches and other correspondence with the Board, while Stirling's charge arose from matters reported to the Board by his superior officer that originated in a letter of complaint from a Naval Board official. The Admiralty Board took the initiative in charging Harvey after receiving his superior officer's (Lord Gambier) account of his misconduct and notice that he would lay an accusation if the Board did not act. Gambier subsequently requested a court martial to clear his name in the face of press rumours and a threat by a subordinate to expose his shortcomings in parliament. In the event, the Board laid the charge itself.

In other cases, the pathways to court were more tortuous. Vice Admiral Palliser wished to respond to rumours of his disobedience in battle by being called to trial at his request. When the first lord declined to do so, Palliser sought to salvage his reputation and honour by accusing Admiral Keppel of failing to reengage an enemy fleet when he had the opportunity to do so. Evidence of Palliser's alleged misconduct produced in Keppel's trial then provided the basis on which the Board charged the accuser. Vice Admiral Duckworth was also charged at the instigation of an accusing officer. Duckworth had already complained to the Board about this officer's disobedience to his orders when commander-in-chief at Jamaica but stopped short of requesting a court martial on him. As soon as Duckworth returned to England, however, the Board accepted Captain Wood's charge that Duckworth had mistreated him grossly and transported goods to England on his flagship in contravention of the Articles of War.

The other two flag officers who faced courts martial in the American and French Wars were charged at their request. Vice Admiral Sir William Parker requested a court martial when the Board recalled him from his North American command for disobeying orders but did not summon him for trial. Sir Robert Calder was also charged at his own request in the face of criticism in the press and the service over his alleged failure to reengage an enemy fleet. Unbeknownst to him, however, the Board had decided to charge him if he did not request a trial. These officers felt compelled to request courts martial because they were trapped in a limbo of reputation-destroying accusation and were prepared to undergo the risky ordeal of a trial as the only way to secure public vindication.

Flag officers and the 'sound of a court martial'

Flag officers who stood trial were exposed to the full range of the court martial experience. Having been involved in the events that led to the Board laying charges against them, they were often helplessly indignant observers of hurtful speculation in the press and the service. They then underwent the ordeal of a trial by their peers and had to contend with any recriminations and disappointments that resulted from their sentencing and its ongoing impact on their personal and professional lives. Several officers, however, were touched by what St Vincent called the 'sound of a court martial' without having the opportunity to have their conduct vindicated by laying charges against a senior colleague or standing trial themselves.

As we have seen, St Vincent incurred Lord Spencer's Board's displeasure by ordering Vice Admiral Sir John Orde home. This decision culminated in a prolonged conflict during which St Vincent accused his subordinate of gross insubordination and undermining his attempts to improve discipline within the fleet. Orde claimed that his commander-in-chief was usurping the rights of subordinate flag officers and subjecting him to public humiliation.[33] Orde's circulation of his correspondence with St Vincent fanned the flames of their dispute. The latter dismissed this material as a tissue of 'misrepresentations, partial statements, and gross falsehoods'; it was an attempt at character assassination: '[H]e has taken down every conversation he hears, and uses it, as an Italian does a stiletto.'[34] St Vincent, no doubt mindful of his own advice on these matters, had not asked the Board to charge Orde and was probably happy to inflict on him the embarrassment of an early recall. Orde responded by asking Lord Spencer to court-martial St Vincent, and when he declined, construed the dispute as a matter of personal honour and issued a challenge. Duelling was illegal, but St Vincent refused to meet him on the grounds that he was too ill to fight and was not, in any case, personally responsible for public measures.[35] Spencer presumably believed that a court martial was not warranted because, however regrettable, St Vincent's conduct towards Orde did not provide the basis for a clear charge. Sympathy in the service and the strength of his family connections – his older half-brother served in Pitt's administration and was raised to the peerage as Lord Bolton in 1797 – increased the risk of the case becoming an embarrassing *cause célèbre*. Spencer was probably also keen to avoid exposing St Vincent's harsh treatment of Orde to public view. He was a highly valued, if very self-willed and tricky senior flag officer, and his enemies in the service would have enjoyed the spectacle of a trial, whatever its outcome.

In his calmer moments, Hyde Parker must have realized there was no prospect that Lord Spencer would charge Rear Admiral Bligh for presiding over a court martial that found on the evidence rather than his commander-in-chief's vengeful prejudices. However, he also tried to persuade the Board to charge Bligh for failing to act on information about valuable enemy ships off Cape Correntes in February 1799. The Board would not entertain this idea, but when Parker's claims became a subject of gossip, Bligh hoped 'their Lordships would not allow his character to be whispered away'.[36] In September 1800, when Hyde Parker was back in England, Bligh asked Lord Spencer's Board to hold a court martial into his conduct off Cape Correntes or charge Sir Hyde Parker 'for having acted in a manner unbecoming the Character of an Officer by having made a false representation of my conduct to their Lordships'.[37] The Board granted Bligh's request, but in the event, the case did not go ahead.[38] There were problems in securing witnesses of such a distant event, and it seems likely that the case was subsumed by St Vincent's approach to a far higher-profile affair arising from Hyde Parker's conduct off Copenhagen in the spring of 1801.[39]

Lord Spencer appointed Hyde Parker commander-in-chief of the North Sea fleet, with Lord Nelson as his second in command. When St Vincent became first lord, preparations were underway to send the fleet on an expedition against the Danes. In his new role, St Vincent attempted to instil in commanders-in-chief the severe ethos of operational efficiency he had enforced in his Mediterranean and Channel commands. Consequently, when he suspected that Parker's personal affairs were impeding the fleet's departure from Yarmouth, St Vincent warned of the dangers of further delay and directed Parker to play an aggressive and vigorous role in bringing his fleet to action against the Danes and forcing them to come to terms. The military objectives were achieved through Nelson's initiative in bringing his division quickly into action under heavy fire and ignoring a recall signal from the commander-in-chief.[40] Parker's report on the battle obscured the relative contributions of the flag officers involved and put the first lord in the embarrassing position of sending unwarranted 'hearty' congratulations and fulsome praise on Parker's 'bold design and daring execution' and arranging for a vote of thanks in parliament.[41] There were also questions about Hyde Parker's diplomatic follow-up to the action. Once St Vincent had more complete information on the battle, he ordered Parker's recall, offering the humiliating choice of coming home in a sloop or limping back to England in a badly damaged, awkwardly sailing ship-of-the-line.

Sir Hyde Parker's sudden and unexpected recall, the fact that the other two flag officers on the station were unwell and keen to go home, and the Board's pointed failure to provide a ship appropriate for an officer of his rank, signalled quite clearly to other members of the service that he was being ordered home under a black cloud of unofficial disapprobation. Parker himself claimed that his recall had cost him a peerage.[42] Initially, however, he seemed resigned to his fate, finding consolation in the idea that his 'professional character stands as high as ever' among his 'brother officers'. Sir Harry Parker, the head of the family, did not see things that way. He told his younger brother that the Board's treatment impugned his honour and that he should seek to vindicate it by requesting a court of inquiry.[43] The Board's response – 'on due consideration of the circumstances' their lordships 'do not think it proper to institute an inquiry into your conduct' – did not explain the decision but made it clear that there was no official avenue of vindication open to Parker. St Vincent no doubt wished to avoid a wide-ranging inquiry. He was also keen to drive home the idea that flag officers should follow Nelson's example rather than Parker's, by leaving him perpetually under the shadow of an ignominious recall. Parker was reduced to printing the correspondence and other documents as a pamphlet and circulating it to his friends in the hope that they would see that he had done his duty.[44] Two years later, he made an inquiry to the Board on cases where other flag officers had been recalled but nothing further came of this initiative.[45]

Flag officers were prepared to press for courts martial and risk a humiliating rebuff by first lords, or unfavourable verdicts, because unanswered rumours of misconduct compromised their standing as 'gentlemen at arms'. Questions of honour may have been at stake in some civilian trials of members of the upper classes, but they were central to the court martial experience of flag officers. They played a crucial role in encouraging admirals to seek vindicatory courts martial, in their responses to being charged involuntarily and their reactions to sentencing. For these reasons, a contemporary authority on naval courts martial described them as 'courts of honour' as well as courts of justice.[46]

Courts of honour

Honour and duty have been described as 'twin concepts' but eighteenth-century commissioned naval officers were seen as 'gentlemen at arms' whose honour was defined by the duties they owed to the service, the state and the Crown.[47] Commissioned rank in the Royal Navy was one of the 'posts of honour' discussed in a series of periodical articles published originally in the mid eighteenth-century. These posts, which were bestowed on the meritorious and 'executed with fidelity and courage', were distinguished from those filled on 'private, personal, and corrupt' considerations by venal politicians. A later work, significantly entitled *Enquiry into the Duties of Men in the Higher and Middle Classes of Society*, included a chapter on naval officers which stressed their obligation to strive to excel in performing their duties rather than merely going through the motions.[48]

These accounts reflected the emergence of a unitary professional ethos that focused on commitment and performance and ideas of honour that related to it. As Sara Cuato neatly puts it, 'professional honour' overlaid, 'sometimes eventually replacing . . . ideals of nobility'.[49] While the 'interest' of their families and friends aided the promotion prospects of those from noble and gentry backgrounds, merit and professional regard played an increasingly important role in appointments to the higher reaches of the service. Indeed, the careers of the most successful admirals of the French Wars demonstrate that distinguished service was a route for ennoblement: Lords St Vincent, Nelson, Collingwood and Duncan came from middle-class backgrounds and were made peers following spectacular victories at sea. Alexander Hood and his brother Samuel were made Irish and then British peers for their contributions during the American and French Wars. Richard Howe, who had already made his mark as a post captain before inheriting an Irish peerage in 1758, was made an English baron at the end of the American War and an earl in 1788. He declined a marquisate after his victory on 1 June 1794 because he lacked the fortune to support this elevated rank but accepted a place in the highly prestigious Order of the Garter. The strong connection between duty and honour created a virtuous circle through motivating exemplary performance and fostering a strong spirit of emulation within the service. The link between honour and duty and the specification of the latter in the Articles of War and the *Regulations and Instructions* helped tie honour to broader notions of the public good. Since respect for rank was a feature of the naval honour system, members of flag officers' 'honour group' were likely to look with unsympathetic eyes on those who dishonoured their rank by failing in the duties of their station.[50] Moreover, since a shared commitment to honour contributed to flag officers' sense of solidarity, suspicion of failures of duty and its confirmation through an unfavourable court martial verdict meant that the personal toll on those concerned was likely to weigh heavily upon their self-worth and professional and social standing.[51]

The Royal Navy's critical role in national defence and the protection of strategic and trading interests overseas meant the connection between duty and honour gained strength and validity from the emerging sense of patriotic national identity to which ideas of nobility had become attached.[52] Functionless baronets like Jane Austen's Sir Walter Elliot resented the social respect paid to the naval elite, but to their chagrin, it was legitimized by royal honours and by flag officers' participation in the King's levees and the Queen's 'drawing rooms'. The press noted flag officers' presence at these courtly rituals, and it is perhaps significant that those who had been subject to the trauma of a court martial seemed to make an honour-absolving attendance at the royal court one of their first ports of call when the ordeal was over. Be that as it may, flag officers' presence at court demonstrated that the nation's elite now incorporated 'men of action' as well as 'men of rank' and that despite their lack of social polish, the military achievements of the former put them on an honorific par with the latter.[53]

A gentleman's refusal to face or make a challenge to vindicate his name carried the taint of cowardice, but for flag officers, this fatally dishonouring imputation arose from the duty specified in the tenth, twelfth and thirteenth articles of war to 'prepare for fight' and to pursue, engage, capture and destroy the enemy. Insulting behaviour that warranted the issue of a challenge in private life had its naval equivalent in articles of war addressing disrespect to superiors, quarrelling with peers and tyrannizing over subordinates (XXII, XXIII, XXXIII). Although eighteenth-century conceptions of interest meant that the line between corruption and acceptable personal material advantage was fluid, widely accepted notions of honesty applied in personal dealings. In some ways, the duties of senior naval officers in this area were more straightforward than for civil office holders. The misuse of public resources for personal advantage was prohibited in specific terms in the Articles of War (XVII, XVIII, XXIV) and, as we shall see, dishonest motivation aggravated other offences such as the misuse of power and failures to follow orders. A number of the cases considered in later chapters concerned obedience to superiors, and since this was related closely to the perceived disciplinary requirements of a particularly hazardous fighting service, there was no personal equivalent of this duty.

As will become apparent in the cases considered in the following chapters, flag officers' reactions to various stages of the court martial experience demonstrated their perception of its implications for their status at the head of the corps of naval gentlemen of arms. They also reflected the extent to which the risk of dishonour depended on the judgement of other senior members of the service and related political and social elites. Flag officers' requests to be charged brought the wider concern with honour into particularly sharp relief. St Vincent's *bon mot* only applied to those who sought to court-martial others; for those whose conduct was the subject of hostile chatter in the service and the press, the damage had already been done. Consequently, they faced the difficult option of living under a cloud of unresolved suspicion or seeking a trial, hoping an acquittal would dissipate it. However, a successful application to face trial exposed them to the risk that they would be condemned rather than acquitted or that their vindication would not be as clear and fulsome as hoped. If a request was unsuccessful, the context of public and service criticism which promoted it might well compound the ignominy under which the officer concerned already laboured. Given these risks, flag officers' willingness to seek a court martial testified to how dearly they held their honour.

Conclusion

This chapter has provided an account of the broader service culture in which flag officers' courts martial were located. These trials were the apex of a system of naval justice backed by the full force of statute law that made findings of criminality on a par with those of criminal courts ashore. In common with these courts, naval courts martial were empowered to hand down both capital and corporal punishments. They also, however, issued sanctions that were distinctive to the culture of the service and owed their effectiveness to it. When trials resulted in sentences of dismissal or debarment from further employment, they terminated flag officers' careers and ended any prospect of gaining the honorific and financial rewards regularly bestowed on senior officers who distinguished themselves in the line of duty. When a guilty verdict resulted in a formal reprimand, flag officers were likely to be disadvantaged in the sharp competition for significant flag appointments. A 'not guilty' verdict accompanied by a note of censure might have the same effect. In all these cases, however, the formal outcomes of courts martial were compounded by informal sanctions resulting from their impact on flag officers' sense of professional self-worth, their standing in the service and elite society. These damaging consequences resulted from a conception of commissioned officers as naval gentlemen at arms and a professionalized idea of honour resting on a zealous commitment to duty. It was assumed that the claims of honour were particularly demanding for those at the head of a strongly hierarchical service.

This chapter has addressed two implications of the alignment of honour and duty. First, it meant that a common thread ran through the range of disciplinary tools the Admiralty Board applied to flag officers. Thus, even when a series of reprimands did not result in a recall and a recall was not the prelude to being charged, they signalled reservations about a flag officer's performance that compromised his honour. Secondly, when reservations about performance were canvassed in the press, gained traction within the service and became a concern of the Admiralty Board, flag officers were prepared to run the risk of facing a court martial to vindicate their honour and requested the Board to charge them.

The series of case studies presented in the following chapters treat flag officers' trials in a broad context, including reactions to the incidents leading to their being charged and the implications of their trials and outcomes. However, flag officers' trials were more than a traumatic personal episode in their professional lives. Courts martial were a central element in a naval system of justice designed to uphold the 'discipline of the service' in both its narrower and broader senses by punishing infractions of codes that specified the duties required of all members of the service. Those at the head of the service had the primary responsibility for maintaining the system of authority on which the good of the service depended and for exemplifying the commitment to duty to which this authority was a necessary means.

3

The Keppel-Palliser Affair

In the early months of 1779 two admirals were court-martialled in Portsmouth for their conduct in an inconclusive action against a French fleet a hundred miles west of Ushant on 27 July 1778. These trials were unusually long (the first ran for thirty-one days and the second for twenty-one days), widely publicized and intensely politicized.[1] Although the fleet returned to Plymouth immediately after the battle, the Board did not order Admiral Augustus Keppel's court martial until early December. Following his honourable acquittal in February 1779, the Admiralty Board ordered a court martial on his accuser, Vice Admiral Sir Hugh Palliser, Keppel's third in command and also one of the naval lord commissioners. Keppel's court asserted in a rider to its verdict that Palliser's accusations were 'false and malicious'. Although evidence from Keppel's trial provided the basis of the charges of disobedience against Palliser, he too was exonerated fully, but the verdict included an observation that Palliser's detractors construed as a reprimand. Keppel's political allies made sporadic attacks on Palliser in parliament over the next two years, and the affair had an ongoing impact on intra-service relations throughout the rest of the American War and into the 1790s.

The prolonged bitterness engendered by these trials resulted from what the Duke of Grafton termed the 'unnatural civil war' between Britain and its North American colonies.[2] Some senior naval officers identified openly with the parliamentary opposition's relentless pursuit of Lord North's government, its attacks on Lord Sandwich's performance as first lord of the Admiralty and promotion of Keppel as a model successor.[3] As the affair gathered momentum over the late summer and autumn of 1778 it polarized opinion within the upper ranks of the Royal Navy and the broader elite. The split within the service is impossible to quantify and may well have shifted as the affair unfolded. Even before Palliser charged Keppel, however, nearly two-thirds of the captains and admirals in the Channel Fleet were thought to be firmly committed or inclined to one or the other of the protagonists with the balance of opinion very much in Keppel's favour.[4] After the charge, twelve flag officers (out of a total of thirty-two) signed a letter to the King protesting his treatment at the hands of the Admiralty Board. Divided loyalties extended down into the lower deck. Shore leave was cancelled before Keppel's trial for fear of riots and disturbances by rival ships' crews, and the commander-in-chief at Portsmouth advised Sandwich of the need for similar precautions before Palliser's court convened: 'should [the ships'] companies meet it would be fatal to many of them as there is such an inveteracy towards each other.'[5]

Augustus Keppel was the second son of the Earl of Albemarle, head of a family with roots in the Dutch nobility now deeply embedded in the high Whig aristocracy. In 1765–6, he was a lord of the admiralty in the Earl of Rockingham's short-lived administration. More recently, his political allies were seeking to capitalize on the war's unpopularity to regain power and save the country from alleged ministerial tyranny. Keppel was a protégé of Admiral Lord Anson, having been a midshipman on his horrendous South Pacific expedition (1740–4). It was a measure both of Keppel's commitment and energy and his patron's estimation of his merits that Anson regularly appointed him to commodore's roles in his mid-twenties. Keppel's letters to the first lord are full of warmth and enthusiasm, nicely balancing signs of ambition with well-measured appreciation of his patron's support. After extensive successful service in the Seven Years' War, Keppel spent fourteen years on half pay, often in poor health. He suffered from rheumatism and gout during his Channel command and was also subject to periodic returns of malaria contracted in the course of Anson's voyage.

The action off Ushant, 27–28 July 1778

The Keppel-Palliser affair originated from the second of three cruises the 'grand fleet' made in the summer and early autumn of 1778. During the first sortie, intelligence on the unexpected strength of the French fleet prompted Keppel's return to Plymouth to augment his squadron and improve its manning and provisioning. The second cruise ended with an inconclusive action with an evenly matched French fleet. The French seemed disinclined to come to battle but were finally forced to do so late in the morning of 27 July. Very early that day, Keppel's first captain, Rear Admiral Campbell, closed a gap that had opened up overnight by ordering six of Palliser's ships to 'chase' the enemy. Because of a shift in the wind, this move forced the French fleet to engage but left Palliser's division with limited support in the line of battle and meant the British fleet was in a relatively loose formation. Palliser showed commendable courage during the action. He ordered his flagship to back its mizzen as it passed down the enemy line, thus allowing more time to attack the French ships. As a result, *Formidable* sustained considerable damage to its sails, rigging and spars. Keppel initially intended to renew the attack immediately but after a preliminary evolution to facilitate that, he turned away to protect damaged ships that were in danger of being cut off and taken.

Keppel regathered his own centre division and the red division of Sir Robert Harland, his second-in-command, and towards evening ordered ships in Palliser's division – some distance away and preoccupied with repairing damage – into their station in the line of battle. However, action was not joined that day, and when dawn broke on the 28th, most of the French fleet was over the horizon. After ordering a chase of the ships in sight, Keppel decided that a prolonged pursuit would be futile and risk his fleet on a lee shore at Ushant. He therefore recalled the chasing ships and took his fleet back to Plymouth to refit.

Early rumblings

At this stage, the action was generally seen as a modest victory because the French had retired leaving the British fleet in control of the Channel. Before the fleet sailed again, however, sections of the press raised questions about Keppel's energy and resolve in the aftermath of the action. The moderately pro-ministerial *Morning Post* referred cautiously (without complete information) to his delay in re-engaging. On the same day, the staunchly anti-opposition *Morning Chronicle* claimed that Keppel's public letter to Sandwich was 'universally reprobated among the seamen, as a communication totally unworthy of a British commander'. It then gave an unvarnished account of his performance that foreshadowed the charge laid against him: 'we cannot help owning we find it difficult to reconcile the conduct of Admiral Keppel with what we have ever been led to consider as the first rule to a British officer, viz *to fight the French whenever he can*.'[6] In terms of later rhetorical developments, it is significant that even at this stage an opposition newspaper developed a narrative to counter pro-ministry claims by referring to 'Keppel's victory at sea, as 'tis called at Court (when not a French ship was taken, or destroyed)'.[7]

These matters were canvassed in the press over the next few weeks, along with claims of a ministerial plot to discredit Keppel and conspiratorial references to secret orders that he was to spar with but not seriously engage the enemy.[8] At the same time, rumours of tensions between Keppel and Palliser began to circulate, including a wildly inaccurate but symbolically prescient report of a duel between the two officers that had a wide enough general circulation to prompt pro-ministerial newspapers to deny it.[9] Although there is no evidence of significant, open disagreement between Keppel and Palliser at this stage, Palliser's role as Sandwich's right-hand man on the Board and the doubts encouraged in Keppel's anxious mind by conspiracy theories may have generated friction between the two men as they grappled with the challenges of refitting the fleet. Sir Samuel Hood, the naval commissioner at Portsmouth, reported that the master of a coastal trader had talked of sharp differences between the flag officers at Plymouth.[10] Be that as it may, Keppel and Palliser seem to have worked well enough together on the last, frustratingly fruitless cruise of the year. Causes of serious, and as it turned out unsalvageable, disagreement only emerged when the fleet returned to Portsmouth in late October 1778.

The affair begins

Although Keppel and Palliser initially maintained a public veneer of collegiality, both officers subsequently claimed to harbour strong reservations about each other's performance on the 27th of July. Keppel maintained that he conveyed his concerns in an oral message to Sandwich said to have been delivered by the officer carrying his despatch on the action.[11] When Palliser was shown an anonymous item published in the anti-ministerial *General Advertiser and Morning Intelligencer* on 15 October, the two men's positions hardened.[12] The author asserted that while Palliser was really to blame for Keppel's limited success on 27 July because he ignored his commander-in-chief's signals, 'the noble *Whig Admiral*' was subject to treacherous misrepresentation orchestrated by Lord Sandwich to 'rise his minion the V. Admiral upon the other's ashes'.[13] The *General Advertiser* letter played a critical role in the affair by projecting any hidden disagreements between Keppel and Palliser into the public domain, pitching the two flag officers in intractable opposition and framing the dispute in starkly partisan terms.

As long as the press and the public thought the action a limited British victory, both Palliser and Keppel could bask in the warm if not brilliant glow of their fleet's performance.[14] However, the *General Advertiser* report and a related pro-Keppel pamphlet discredited this reassuring narrative by presenting the action as an opportunity lost through Palliser's treacherous disobedience.[15] In doing so, they painted both Palliser and Keppel into a corner by making it impossible for Keppel to absolve Palliser without incriminating himself.[16] Moreover, by identifying Palliser as the villain of the piece, opposition politicians could now present Keppel as a brilliant but mistreated commander and utilize him as an icon in the latest rounds of internecine warfare between the ministry and the Rockingham Whigs.

Before this scenario began to play out, moves were made to contain the damaging implications of the *General Advertiser*'s deliberately incendiary report. In early November, Palliser tried unsuccessfully to persuade Keppel to put his name to a statement confirming the vice admiral's conduct was 'in every respect proper and becoming a good officer' and that he had no intention of renewing the action on 27 July.[17] In making this claim, Palliser could refer to a despatch that Keppel wrote shortly after the action but subsequently disavowed.[18] Keppel refused to sign Palliser's document because it was 'untrue' and told Captain John Jervis (the future Earl St Vincent) that when Palliser came to his London house to discuss it, he was 'quite rude' and left the room abruptly.[19]

Immediately after this meeting, Palliser published a narrative of the battle in the pro-ministerial *Morning Post* that included thinly veiled criticisms of Keppel's fleet management before and after the action.[20] Keppel criticized Palliser roundly for stooping to defend himself in the 'common press' and told Jervis that 'the matter must not end with the Morning Post'. It was subsequently taken up by Keppel's friends in parliament and it seems highly likely that he had a hand in orchestrating this attack. Since Keppel alerted Jervis of his suspicion that his 'warm friends' would be sent to other stations, it also seems that he thought a court martial was in the offing and the ministry planned to limit the range of witnesses called.[21] The King told Palliser in early November that Keppel declined to discuss the action with him because it was *sub judicia*.[22] Lady Pembroke, the non-partisan wife of a violently anti-Palliser courtier, reported that Keppel had considered charging Palliser, but once the affair was in train he always disavowed any intention of doing so.[23]

When parliament opened in late November, however, Lord Sandwich still harboured some hopes that the affair would peter out. He rejected Vice Admiral the Earl of Bristol's demand for a wide-ranging inquiry into the ministry's alleged misconduct of the war and the 'untrophied return of our fleets into port everywhere'. Sandwich told the House of Lords that inquiries of this kind

> into the conduct of men in high stations, and superior commands, imply some foundation of censure. . . . I dare suppose that the two gentlemen alluded to by the noble lord . . . performed their duty gallantly and ably; and if they, in the issue of the day, fell short of the public expectation, it is only to be attributed to those accidents to which the naval service is more subject than any other; and which it was impossible for the utmost skill, zeal and bravery, to remedy or prevent.[24]

Understandably, Sandwich wished to avoid a wide-ranging and fraught inquiry. Still, the line he took on this occasion was consistent with what he later described as his settled practice of being 'always averse to bringing [inquiries] forward, except in very flagrant cases or when a charge is formally exhibited'.[25] Ironically, Bristol's speech marked the beginning of a process that frustrated the first lord's sanguine hopes and led Palliser to abandon any idea that the affair could be left to rest.

The Honourable Temple Luttrell, a vociferous parliamentary critic of Sandwich, precipitated this development in a debate on the navy estimates. Luttrell was a very crude tool – the parliamentary historian John Brooke characterized his speeches as 'a foundation of cant, taken from Burke, decorated with threats and abuse' – but his intervention was helpful for opposition members who wished to use the fallout from 27 July in their remorseless pursuit of Sandwich and North.[26] It set the scene for what William Cobbett characterized as an 'altercation' between Keppel and Palliser.

Keppel distinguished Palliser's courage from his obedience and ran a line that was prominent in his subsequent interventions. While declaring that he 'laid no blame anywhere', he attributed his fleet's failure to re-engage the enemy to his third-in-command's failure to respond to his signals. He was also critical of Palliser's resort to publishing a defence in the press. Although Keppel declined to go into 'particulars' in the House, he stated that he was willing to answer in the 'proper place' and confirmed an earlier-stated determination not to serve at sea with Palliser.[27] Palliser treated this declaration as a challenge. Within a week, he applied to the Board for his commander-in-chief to be brought to court martial on a charge which evoked memories of Byng's trial and execution.[28]

Keppel's awareness of what was at stake no doubt underwrote his initial response to the Board's decision: 'to so very extraordinary a Proceeding I can for the present only say, that I must take some Time for Consideration before I can return any other Answer, than that I have received your Letter.' Later the same day, Keppel recovered sufficiently to express indignation at the Board's decision and resume his campaign against Palliser. He 'desired' the Secretary of the Board to 'represent to the Lords Commissioners my utter Astonishment at the Countenance their Lordships have so far given to this Proceeding, as to resolve . . . to order a Court Martial against the Commander in Chief of the Fleet, on an Attack from an inferior Officer, under all the very peculiar Circumstances in which Sir *Hugh Palliser* now stands'.[29] Characteristically, Keppel showed no sign of giving any countenance to the role that his refusal to charge Palliser played in precipitating his own court martial.

Palliser's charge provoked a stream of highly wrought anti-Sandwich and anti-Palliser criticism in parliament and the press. The *General Advertiser* published a letter from 'A Plain Dealer' that took both the first lord and the vice admiral to task in its canvas of the certainty of a packed court 'appointed very judiciously by [Palliser's] *patron*, *colleagues*, and *party* which is nearly tantamount to his *own appointment*; and . . . making him both *Judge* and *Plaintiff in his own cause*'. 'A SAILOR' decried Palliser as 'an accuser, who labours himself under the public blame of criminal backwardness and disobedience . . . [making] the desperate attempt of drawing innocence into ruin to palliate his guilt'. Palliser was later dubbed 'Sir H-Jackal'.[30]

In parliament, criticism of the Board's acceptance of Palliser's charge provoked ministerial speakers to unwisely deny its discretion. In its absolute form, this claim was untenable and by the end of the debate opposition speakers were able to identify inconsistencies that implied the Board had some discretion. These exchanges were significant at this stage of the affair because they bolstered the opposition's claim that Palliser was Sandwich's tool in a plot to destroy Keppel.[31] Despite Palliser's repeated assertions to the contrary, the opposition and even some more disinterested observers believed he had acted in concert with Sandwich to bring Keppel to court martial.[32] Palliser's position on this point has never been refuted and, indeed, as N. A. M. Rodger points out, his request posed an impossible dilemma for Lord Sandwich. The first lord was fully aware of the political controversy that would ensue and its damaging impact on a fractured service culture. He was acutely aware also of the claims arising from Palliser's position as the aggrieved party, their close professional relationship, his long and distinguished service, and the implications of the opposition's politicization of the dispute between the two officers and their supporters in the navy. The 'affair was out of control, and there was very little Sandwich could do but ride out the storm.'[33] Of course, the first lord could not admit this publicly, so when challenged by the Earl of Coventry on the inconsistency of the decision to court-martial Keppel and his earlier 'no fault' argument, Sandwich reiterated his lack of discretion and 'lamented' the necessity for 'a duty arising from his membership of the Board, although against his inclinations as a peer and a minister'.[34]

Vice Admiral Lord Bolton addressed a memorial to the King eight days before Keppel's trial, restating parliamentary and press criticisms of Palliser and the Board. It was signed by twelve flag officers, headed by Admiral Lord Hawke, the admiral of the fleet, and including Vice Admiral Sir Robert Harland, Keppel's second in command. The admirals 'represented' to the King's 'wisdom and justice' the dangers of ordering courts martial on senior officers at subordinates' request on 'concealed charges' and 'recriminatory accusations' after a long delay. They warned particularly of the 'mischief and scandal' of a subordinate in 'high civil office' compromising naval discipline by attempting to 'corrupt the public judgement by publications of libels on their superior Officers in a common news-paper'. The King assured Bolton that the admirals' representations 'should receive his most serious attentions' but Lord Bristol's anticipation that the memorandum would 'overset' both the Board and the ministry was wildly misplaced.[35] The King thought the document 'extraordinary', noted that the memorial ended without a request and was unmoved by what he took to be its main point: an expression of 'great wrath at Sir Hugh Palliser and the Admiralty'.[36] Despite the lack of substantive regal response, however, the memorial was significant in the history of the affair in demonstrating solidarity with Keppel among senior naval officers and protesting actions by Palliser and Lord Sandwich deemed unjust and destructive of the discipline of the service.

Trial preparations

After Lord Hawke declined the court's presidency on the grounds of strategic ill-health, the King and Lord Sandwich canvassed the names of other senior flag officers before settling on Admiral Sir Thomas Pye, the commander-in-chief at Portsmouth.[37] The Board agreed to Keppel's request to include as many flag officers as possible on account of the accuser's and accused's rank and seniority. Vice Admiral John Montagu, who played a prominent and notorious role on the court, was in some ways an accidental inclusion. Having returned for the winter from commanding at Newfoundland, his flagship was at Spithead when the charge was laid. The flag officers serving at Portsmouth were supplemented by those at the Nore, Downs and Plymouth when Keppel was charged.[38] The court was made up initially of six flag officers with the balance of the judges being the eight most senior eligible post-captains on the station.

The Board accommodated Keppel's request that it retain key witnesses at Portsmouth and recall others from distant stations. Successful efforts were also made to secure the return on parole of two prisoners of war in France.[39] Keppel's concern over the availability of witnesses was understandable, but one aspect of his handling of this matter was highly questionable. When Palliser asked George Jackson for a list of Keppel's witnesses, the judge advocate advised him that he would have to put the request to Keppel. He refused in a tone of petulant hauteur he frequently adopted in the affair. Keppel told Jackson he was 'determined to avoid any degree of Intercourse with that Gentleman: I therefore beg to decline saying anything on the Subject'.[40] As a result, neither the accuser nor the accused received a copy of their protagonist's witness list. This disadvantage fell more heavily on Palliser since he had a case to prove.

Within a few days of the Board's summons, one of Keppel's keenest supporters, Vice Admiral Hugh Pigot, introduced a bill for the trial to be held ashore. He claimed that prolonged confinement in the close-packed fug of a flagship's great cabin and many mid-winter passages across Portsmouth Harbour would impose undue hardship on a person of Keppel's age and state of health.[41] The ministry resisted attempts to name the members of the court in the bill but took the view that there was nothing to be gained in preventing its passage into law.[42] The unprecedented decision to hold the trial ashore had a critical bearing on the proceedings. The Board canvassed the Military Academy in the dockyard as a venue, but in the event the governor of Portsmouth's house (adjacent to what became the Garrison Church) was chosen because of the extent of its accommodation and ease of access.

The change in venue benefited Keppel's health and was also highly convenient. He lived during the trial in a rented house on the nearby High Street with his three legal counsel; witnesses from his flagship lodged in a neighbouring property. Keppel and his friends were also no doubt aware that if the court had convened on a flagship, space for spectators would have been very limited. In the debate in the House of Commons, the Solicitor General's attempt to move an amendment granting the court the right to exclude 'strangers' at its discretion was opposed as being 'contrary to the first principle of English law'.[43] In the event, the trial venue enabled partisan behaviour that was extraordinary by any standards and set naval judicial decorum entirely by the board.[44] Keppel's warmest friends revelled in the toxic partisan atmosphere of the court, but others who were sympathetic to his cause saw the move ashore as a degradation and were critical of those who had left London to take part in it. Frederick Robinson told his brother (at this stage ambassador in Lisbon) that 'all reasonable people are agreed in disapproving of those who are gone [to Portsmouth] as supporters of Admiral Keppel, prejudging his cause, and giving the appearance of a popular contested election to a most solemn trial'. The reasonable people included Lady Pembroke, who, although no admirer of the ministers, thought the leaders of the opposition 'behav'd very foolishly' in attending the trial.[45]

Keppel's trial: Charge, prosecution and defence

The trial began with a signal to admirals and captains at Portsmouth and Spithead to come on board Sir Thomas Pye's flagship, HMS *Britannia*. After the judges were sworn in, the trial was adjourned to the hall of the Governor's House, where the judge advocate read the charge. Keppel was to be tried for 'misconduct and neglect of duty . . . in sundry instances'. The statement of charge identified four instances when Keppel's handling of his fleet was neglectful of his responsibilities to do the 'utmost in his Power to take, sink, burn, or destroy the French Fleet'.[46] He was also charged with failing to sustain a chase of the French ships on 28 July. If proven, the charge would have been fatal to Keppel's professional reputation, his standing in the fashionable world and his honour. It would also, however, endanger his life because the Articles of War mandated death sentences for three of the instances named in it.

At the start of the second day, HMS *Robust*'s master's refusal to swear to his logbook's originality because he had amended it on his captain's orders provoked a sensation in court and was frequently referred to as an emblem of pro-ministerial skulduggery. In truth, however, this matter was not material because the court never tested the validity of the amendments and objections were made subsequently to several logbooks, including that of Keppel's flagship HMS *Victory*. Nevertheless, the timing of the revelation damaged Palliser's credibility because Alexander Hood, *Robust*'s captain, was a member of his division and was identified politically with Lord Sandwich.

After the best part of a day wrangling over logbooks, the court spent the next eighteen days examining and cross-examining thirty-one witnesses called by the prosecution. Keppel, and perhaps some of the witnesses favourable to him, benefited from the advice of two long-established members of the London bar and Thomas Erskine, an up-and-coming barrister and future Lord Chancellor. Erskine read Keppel's extensive statement of defence. This document seems to have been a joint product of Keppel's legal team, with Erskine (who had served briefly at sea) playing a leading role and some input from Captain John Jervis.[47] The defence dealt with four matters: the distinctive responsibilities of commanders-in-chief and their discretion in meeting them; the circumstances of Keppel's appointment and his approach to it; his objections to being brought to trial and to Palliser's alleged motives in doing so; finally, he addressed each instance of the charge in preparation for his examination of defence witnesses.

In response to claims of alleged deficiencies in fleet management, Keppel argued that as a commander-in-chief acting under the orders of the Admiralty Board, the ministry and the King to ensure the safety of the kingdom, he was not constrained by the limited and specific professional responsibilities which applied to subordinate officers. Moreover, he claimed a distinctive political mandate with instructions from the Secretary of State as well as the Admiralty Board.[48] Keppel argued that the widely recognized duty of 'every sea officer to do his utmost to take, sink, burn, and destroy the Enemy's Ships wherever he meets them' must be set within the context of this discretion; depending on the circumstances, it might become the duty of a commander-in-chief to 'postpone or totally omit' an engagement with enemy forces.[49] That was not altogether the case on 27–28 July, but since the limited engagement with the French fleet had driven it back to port, Keppel claimed to have fulfilled his duty in terms of 'the great end of national defence'.[50]

In addition to arguing for the strategic discretion of commanders-in-chief, Keppel also claimed a discretion arising from their commanding perspective and the physical position from which their tactical decisions were taken. In ignoring both these considerations, Palliser had, Keppel argued, 'conceived very mistaken Notions of what my Duty was; and on that bad Foundation he has laid the whole Matter of his Charge'.[51] Keppel also criticized Palliser for his delay in expressing dissatisfaction with his conduct (a claim which surely cut both ways) and for bringing him to trial on 'recriminatory' grounds, that is, to protect his own honour and reputation. Keppel concluded the lengthy introductory part of his defence by referring (in terms later reflected in the court's rider to its verdict) to Palliser's 'malicious Calumnies'.[52] Although these matters did not affect the charge directly, Keppel canvassed them in order to present himself as a model of honour and public virtue. References to the circumstances of his appointment, to his admirably patriotic restraint in the face of lukewarm support from the Board and abuse in the pro-ministry press, were part of this campaign: 'If I gave no just Cause of Doubt about my real character before my Appointment I gave as little Cause of Uneasiness afterwards.'[53]

In addressing the specific instances detailed in Palliser's charge, Keppel defended himself against claims that he mismanaged the fleet on the morning of 27 July by arguing that he used his discretion when deciding to attack the French in an unusual, but not, he was at pains to add, a confused formation. He did so in order to take advantage of a wind shift that provided an opportunity to bring a reluctant opponent to action. Keppel explained his subsequent actions by his determination to renew the engagement later that day, plans that were frustrated by Palliser's repeated failure to keep his ships in their proper station, to respond to signals and an oral instruction conveyed by HMS *Fox*. Finally, Keppel justified his decision not to pursue the French fleet on the grounds that the balance of risks and probabilities did not warrant jeopardizing the overarching objectives specified in his instructions. Given the circumstances, pursuit would be futile and the looming lee shore at Ushant posed a significant risk to the fleet.

Keppel called thirty-four witnesses. His examination focused on the positioning of Palliser's division, its commander's response to signals and messages from the admiral's flagship, the timing of messages carried by two frigates, HMS *Milford* and HMS *Fox*, the latter conveying Keppel's intention to reengage with the French fleet in the late afternoon of 27 July, and the viability of pursuing the French towards Brest the next day.[54] Rear Admiral Campbell's answers to questions about Palliser's responsiveness to signals and orders that testified emphatically to his 'direct disobedience' supported the accusations that Keppel had made before the trial and detailed in his defence.[55]

Keppel's trial: Naval justice, service loyalty and political partisanship

There is no surviving record of the attendees at Keppel's trial, but contemporaries remarked on the intense interest it generated among the populace and Keppel's well-wishers from London society and opposition circles.[56] The presence in court of large numbers of people who were not subject to naval discipline, the sense of elite entitlement felt by many of them and the taste for riotous fun of others went some way to explaining the lack of judicial decorum which marked the trial. Observers reported audience participation more fitting to a theatre than a court. Edmund Burke revelled in the partisan atmosphere of the trial: 'When any thing appears very honourable to Keppel out of the mere professional Jargon and which borders on Sentiment, the audience cannot be restrained from shewing their Sympathy by clapping.' A witness's emotionally charged judgemental testimony was greeted with tears by half of the audience and applause from the rest.[57] The noise level in the court might explain why the judge advocate sometimes repeated questions put to witnesses and their answers. At the end of the trial, Jackson told Lord Sandwich that he would generally have taken the herculean task of producing a daily draft of the minutes in his stride but had found working in 'so rare a noise, and such incessant interruptions' exceedingly distracting and fatiguing.[58]

When Jackson reported the hissing that greeted the sensational revelation of changes to *Robust's* log, he noted that it went unchecked.[59] This episode was emblematic of Admiral Pye's consistent failure to control his court. Horace Walpole pointed out his shortcomings: he was 'an old dotard' and 'took little part' in the proceedings.[60] Significantly, Pye appears to have issued no warnings to attendees and only withdrew the judges when they needed to confer. It is inconceivable that a court sitting in the great cabin of a man-of-war, attended almost entirely by naval personnel, would have countenanced behaviour tolerated in the governor's house.

The partisan ambiance of the court was a tonic to Keppel. The private and public accolades of his supporters no doubt reinforced his perception that in defending his life and honour against the calumnies orchestrated by Lord Sandwich, he was also playing a noble role in a more significant cause which he and his political allies identified with the safety of the state. Lord Abingdon told Lord Rockingham that Keppel's acquittal was more important than a victory over the French would have been, construing 'solid national advantage' in strictly party terms.[61] This partisan sense of professional, moral and political rectitude, which became a standard trope of the Foxite Whigs over the next half century, was apparent in Keppel's reaction to being charged and in statements made before the court and in parliament.[62] It may also have encouraged him to take a high-handed line with witnesses whose testimony did not reinforce these perceptions. After the master of HMS *Ramillies* expressed scepticism of the dangers of chasing the French fleet on 28 July, Keppel subjected him to a lofty put down: 'I shall not condescend to measure my Conduct as Commander in Chief of the Fleet, by the Opinion of a Master of a Ship.' The master of HMS *America* received similar treatment: 'I am not one of the elder brethren of the Trinity House, and therefore I shall not ask this man any questions.' When Keppel became a younger brethren in 1767 he seemed to have harboured some hope at this time of being elected an elder brethren. This remark indicated his ongoing resentment at Palliser having gained that distinction (no doubt with Sandwich's support) in 1773.[63] It was typical of Pye's management of the trial that the court failed to uphold the professional dignity of those testifying under oath or the senior officer who led the prosecution.

On other occasions, the more openly partisan judges took audacious advantage of Pye's reluctance or inability to preside effectively. Horace Walpole thought that Vice Admiral Arbuthnot clearly took Keppel's part, but he was really only a secondary player to Vice Admiral John Montagu. Montagu's motivation remains unclear. Unlike Arbuthnot, who had served under Keppel's command, Montagu was not connected with him. He did not oppose the American War and did not decline to serve in it. A contemporary biographer attributed Montagu's clashes with Palliser and some witnesses to a concern to uphold the 'honour' of the court, but Montagu's courtroom contributions and his involvement in post-trial celebrations suggest other motivations more closely connected to Keppel's fate.[64] His conduct in the trial may well have been determined by his professional concerns, including views on the unfairness of a commander-in-chief being brought to trial by a subordinate flag officer for recriminatory reasons. If that was the case, he seemed determined to compensate for alleged injustice by treating witnesses in a way that observers as diverse as Horace Walpole and the King thought outrageous. Neither the official minutes nor shorthand transcripts indicate that Pye attempted to curb Montagu's excesses.

Montagu made strenuous efforts to lead and, if necessary, bully witnesses into offering their opinions and judgements rather than testifying on matters of fact. This strategy had the effect of co-opting witnesses into judges and thus producing a weight of judgemental opinion in favour of Keppel's acquittal. Montagu first employed this approach on the third day of the trial at the conclusion of a prolonged examination of Samuel Marshall, captain of the frigate *Arethusa*. When he was asked 'Do you from your own Observation or Knowledge know of any Act of the Commander in Chief, Admiral *Keppel*, behaving or conducting himself unbecoming a Flag Officer?' Palliser objected that as a 'matter of Opinion' the question was 'perfectly irregular'. He nevertheless offered to withdraw his objection if he was allowed to ask such questions. The court agreed to this proposal.[65]

For a court to sanction an impropriety because it was to be reciprocated looks pretty odd, especially as witnesses' testimony was the factual basis for the court's judicial opinions. Understandably, this trade-off became a source of difficulty if witnesses thought it inconsistent with their obligation to testify under oath. When Sir William Burnaby, another frigate captain, was asked by Montagu whether 'to your Knowledge Admiral Keppel negligently performed the Duty imposed on him?' he declined to answer on the grounds that he 'did not think himself competent to the Question'. He explained that 'it appears to me, that it comes before this Court to judge from the Facts given in Evidence'. Although courts martial had the power to imprison witnesses who prevaricated – and Burnaby's reply would have met that test if the question was proper – Pye's court let the matter drop.[66] Subsequently, Captain Alexander Hood, under intense pressure because of revelations about alterations to his ship's logbook, declined to answer a similar question on the grounds that it raised a matter for the judges to decide. The court upbraided Hood but did not attempt to induce him to answer by threatening sanctions.[67]

During a particularly torrid cross-examination, Captain John Bazely, Palliser's flag captain, withstood pressure from Montagu to offer a judgement on whether Keppel's conduct 'tarnished the honour' of the service.[68] These exchanges did not deter Montagu from his favoured line of questioning. Captain Samuel Goodall declined to be drawn into making judgements, stressing that they were the court's responsibility and offering a warning about establishing a precedent which devolved this duty to a series of witnesses: 'it appears to me to be rendering my Evidence nugatory – and I think it an Assumption upon the court, in whom Judgement upon that Evidence rests alone, and not with me.'[69]

Matters came to a head when Lord Mulgrave was called. He was a lord of the Admiralty, had served in Palliser's division on 27 July, and defended the ministry's handling of aspects of the affair in parliament. Having already declined to answer Palliser's 'questions of opinion or conjecture', he maintained this position when Montagu rolled out his stock question on Keppel's negligence. Mulgrave told the court that he was under oath to answer truthfully to all questions, not to express his opinions or offer judgements: 'The Court are to judge of the Facts before them. . . . The Facts I can speak to as a Matter of Knowledge – as to Opinions, I cannot.' Montagu retorted that Mulgrave entirely misunderstood the question, denied that he was being asked for his opinion and tried to demonstrate that by rephrasing his question in the language of factual testimony: 'From your Lordship's Knowledge or Observations of the Transactions of these two days, did Admiral Keppel negligently perform the Duty imposed on him?' Mulgrave declined to be drawn and restated the basis of his position:

> It is for the Court to decide . . . and not for me. I have answered the Facts, and if I am to be urged more by the Count, it is not the Admiral accused but it is me that they are trying, because I am to form an Opinion, how the Fleet was to be conducted, and not the man who commanded it. I think it is not my Duty, as a Witness, to do that; if it is pressed by One Member of the Court, I must desire to have the sense of the Court, that they will consider the Oath that they have taken – that I have taken – and take into their Minds, whether the Opinion of an Individual ought to influence their Judgement in a Trial of this Importance?[70]

The court construed Mulgrave's claim as a censure and when he denied that was so it retired to consider the matter. It decided that Mulgrave's language and the 'warmth' of his expressions were 'improper'. On the substantive question, however, the court determined that if Mulgrave thought the question '*to lead to a Matter of Opinion, you are at Liberty to answer to it or not*'. Ironically, Pye presented this as a settled rule of the court when the next witness was questioned on a matter of opinion by Palliser.[71]

The court's uneasy and entirely unsatisfactory compromise epitomized Pye's failures as president. He initially allowed an alleged impropriety to continue, provided that the prosecution could avail itself of it and permitted a member of the court to attempt to bully witnesses into answering. When they refused, the matter was either allowed to drop or the questioner reprimanded them without the court resorting to, or even threatening, the sanctions for prevarication. Having failed to uphold its authority, the court settled on a solution halfway through the trial that weakened it further. Its stance also skewed the weight of 'evidence' (now made up of facts, opinions and random judgements) towards the views of those willing to respond positively to an invitation to offer a judgement. Given Montagu's line of questioning and some witnesses' scruples over answering him under oath, the court's indulgence favoured the accused: only those keen to respond in the affirmative would answer. Unsurprisingly, they tended to do so in statements akin to laudatory character references.

If some of the judges' handling of witnesses compromised the proceedings' impartiality, so did their indulgence towards Keppel and their failure to extend any of this judicial leeway to Palliser. They allowed Keppel great latitude in breaking in on the questioning of witnesses and occasionally answering for them. He was also allowed to make statements almost at will. Thus when Palliser had finished questioning *Robust's* master, Keppel treated the witness as unworthy of his attention and was allowed to make a long peroration attacking Hood.[72] The court refused Palliser permission to call witnesses on this issue on the grounds that Hood was not on trial. This reasoning was replete with unintended irony since by this stage it had become clear that Keppel, some witnesses and members of the court were levelling accusations against Palliser. This line of questioning, which first appeared in a very hostile examination of Captain Bazely, concentrated on discrediting Palliser rather than eliciting information on Keppel's conduct.[73]

By far the most egregious instance of the courts' partisan mismanagement of the proceedings occurred when it prevented Palliser from summarizing his case after he had finished examining his witnesses. During this exchange (which the judge advocate expunged from the official minutes), Montagu assured Palliser that they would hear him when the prisoner concluded his evidence.[74] However, after Erskine read the prisoner's defence, the court allowed Keppel to review the evidence and vilify his accuser. As he put it, the aim was 'to place the conduct of my accuser in its proper view'.[75] Keppel's attempt to shift the focus of the trial onto Palliser gained momentum as it moved to its conclusion, helped by claims made by Captain Jervis and Rear Admiral Campbell. When Palliser attempted to question Campbell, Montagu shut him down, and Keppel was permitted to interject. At the conclusion of Keppel's evidence, the court refused, despite Montagu's earlier assurance, to hear Palliser and moved immediately to consider its verdict.[76]

Palliser later argued that as the court had not disowned Montagu's assurance, it should have stood.[77] He also claimed that he would have withdrawn from the trial if he had not received this assurance. This threat was not necessarily an empty *post hoc* gesture. At an earlier stage, the King was sufficiently concerned about Montagu's blatant partisanship (he described his final question to Captain Marshall as 'very extraordinary') to write to Lord Sandwich about the risk arising from Admiral Buckle's withdrawal from the trial through illness. This development meant Montagu became the second most senior court member and would automatically assume its presidency if Admiral Pye fell ill. In that case, not particularly unlikely given Pye's age and the health hazards of mid-winter English weather, the King believed that Sandwich would abort the proceedings.[78] He was not alone in canvassing this possibility. Horace Walpole was ill-disposed to Palliser and regarded him as a tool of the ministry in this affair. Nevertheless, he thought that he should have refused to proceed in the face of the partiality and prejudice that infused the trial.[79]

Palliser's request to sum up for the prosecution was entirely in keeping with the practice of a wide range of English courts and army courts martial, but if it was not unprecedented in naval courts martial, it was unusual. In the circumstances, however, the request seems eminently reasonable. The trial was unusually long and complex, involving many witnesses and a serious and sustained defence. Moreover, as Palliser rightly observed, although Keppel, witnesses and some court members presented him as an object of accusation, the court prevented him from presenting any defence.

The verdict showed that Palliser's concerns were well-founded. After more than a day of deliberation, the court acquitted Keppel with full honour on all charges and condemned Palliser's accusations as 'unfounded and malicious'. By honourably acquitting Keppel, the court signalled that there was no shadow over his performance and thus responded to the admirals' pre-trial memorandum, which advised the king that even if a court martial acquitted an officer, his honour and reputation might still suffer. The condemnatory rider endorsed Keppel's pre-trial claims that the Board's decision to charge him was unjust and a slight to his honour and dignity. It was thus as much a reproach to Sandwich as it was to Palliser.

It is a paradox of Keppel's trial that the range of procedural injustices and disruptive improprieties disfiguring it did not compromise the soundness of the overall verdict. Neither the bear-garden atmosphere created by Keppel's supporters, the laxity of the court's president, nor the bias in some of its procedures disguised the fact that Palliser's case was not proven. His handling of the prosecution did not help his cause, and he seemed particularly ineffective in questioning key witnesses from among officers on Keppel's flagship. However, even with better preparation of his case and more effective handling of the information available, it seems highly unlikely that Palliser would have persuaded a far more impartial and orderly court to convict Keppel of a capital crime.

The aftermath

The drama of Keppel's trial was eclipsed by the celebrations and retaliations that followed it. He proceeded from the Governor's House with members of the court, sixty naval colleagues and political friends to a 'very elegant entertainment' in his honour at the Fountain Inn in Portsmouth High Street; the toasts included one to the prospect that 'every prosecution be tried by a Court as independent as the present'.[80] On Keppel's return to London, highly excited members of the populace pulled his carriage through the streets, and the Common Council feted him with the freedom of the city. Private houses and public buildings were illuminated, and there were wildly enthusiastic and sometimes riotously destructive demonstrations throughout the country. The local standing of Palliser's Portsmouth landlord protected the house he had rented there, but his possessions were burnt in the street.[81] Pro-Keppel mobs showed far less restraint in London. They sacked his accuser's house, pillaging and burning his furniture. Forewarned by events in Portsmouth, Palliser attempted to find safety in his official accommodation in the Admiralty Building in London but was only able to do so because a military patrol prevented a mob from seizing him on the streets.[82] *Hoi polloi* were not alone in perpetrating vengeful celebrations. There are reports of drunken young Whig lords among the London rioters, and Charles James Fox was rumoured to have been out on the streets too.[83] The Duke of Alcaster, who was arrested during the night, was the half-brother of Lieutenant Albermarle Bertie, a key witness in the trial.[84]

The scale and intensity of these demonstrations were manifestations of a convergence of 'extra-parliamentary' political activism and anti-government campaigns mounted by the Whig opposition in parliament. Keppel had an extensive professional following in the navy and political allies among the Rockingham Whigs, but his status as a public idol was a consequence of the alignment between his cause, the agenda of the Whig opposition and the political agency of radical anti-government forces among the wider population.[85] Once elevated to that status, he became the focus of publications, prints, pub sign iconography (the 'Keppel's Head'), and commercially motivated memorabilia, including ceramics from Josiah Wedgwood's company.

Even though Keppel's fighting achievements were exceedingly modest, the celebrations greeting his acquittal matched those sparked by Admiral Vernon's notable victories almost forty years before. The opposition identified him with a heroic image of admirals as 'seaborne defenders of king, constitution, and country' and presented the acquittal as vindicating his professional and personal character. It was also a triumphant assertion of true patriotism and constitutional propriety in the face of a corrupt and oppressive ministerial machine's threats to public and private liberty.[86] These themes were presented in poetic effusions published in newspapers and broadsheets. William Hayley's pamphlet-length *Epistle for Admiral Keppel* castigated Palliser for his role in bringing his superior to trial after having frustrated his plans to force the French into a decisive action:

> . . . the Muse disdains to think
> A naval son of England e'er could sink
> To sell his fame, and as a hireling rend
> The unsuspecting bosom of a friend.
> . . .
> Thy warlike signal call'd a tardy train;
> And disobedience join'd with an envious night,
> To rob thy valour of the promis'd fight.[87]

The anonymous author of a broadside ballad urged 'Britannia' to smile on 'Admiral Keppel . . . / Thy darling son; / With laurels crown his head'.[88] Another admirer thought the trial added to Keppel's already golden lustre:

Illustrious Keppel! Who canst well abide
The Test, like Gold, when in the Furnace try'd;
And like that polish'd undiminsih'd Ore,
Unsully'd shine, much brighter than before.[89]

Members of parliament were as unrestrained in their praise and expressions of relief as balladeers and poets. Isaac Barré, whose seat at Calne was in the gift of the opposition politician Lord Shelburne, claimed the public response to the verdict meant it was not just a vindication of Keppel but a 'great national deliverance'. In the Lords, Lord Rockingham praised his political ally as one 'whom he esteemed to be the pride and ornament of his country; of consummate skill and experience in his profession, and one of its best bulwarks in the hour of danger'. Keppel responded in due form: 'I can only say, that the warmest gratitude for this great honour and favour will make me ever desirous of meriting it by the most strenuous endeavours to serve my country.'[90]

In the short term, these endeavours included joining the parliamentary opposition's attacks on Sandwich. Keppel also assailed the first lord in a letter to the King. Having repeated earlier claims about his silently dutiful approach to his command, he advised the King that he wished to add his name to the signatories of the flag officers' memorandum. He 'humbly' implored the sovereign's permission not to go again to sea: 'Under Men on Whom I have learnt from Experience I cannot depend for the Support which is necessary for every Commander.'[91] Charles Jenkinson, the secretary-at-war, told the King that Keppel 'wishes to be able to say that He was turn'd out & would reduce your Majesty to the Dilemma either of dismissing Him or your Ministers'.[92] Jenkinson thought the 'manly' course would be to dismiss Keppel but noted the political risk. Within two weeks, however, the Board tested Keppel's resolve by asking him to confirm whether he would continue to command the 'western' squadron in the coming season. He responded by making a general complaint about his past treatment. Keppel declared his ongoing respect for the Board as a formal entity but declared he would not be 'secure in' his 'honour' serving under its present membership. Understandably, the Board treated this statement as a refusal to serve and ordered Keppel to strike his flag. He received this direction 'with satisfaction' because it relieved him of further correspondence with the Board. In a parting shot, Keppel upbraided the Board through its secretary for the terms in which it had conveyed this otherwise welcome news: 'there is so much offence conceived in the expression of your letter, written by the Lords' directions, that nothing less than the deference due from me to the Board of Admiralty would prevent my replying in terms that would not be pleasing to their Lordships.'[93]

Conclusion

Keppel's removal from his command resulted from his willingness to politicize his professional relationships and concerns rather than (as his supporters claimed) the government's vindictive reaction to his acquittal. His behaviour most recently involved a decision to remain in London to speak in favour of Charles Fox's latest motion attacking Sandwich's management of naval resources.[94] Such conduct was utterly unacceptable to the ministry and the king and resulted in their interest being used to oust Keppel from his parliamentary seat at Windsor. It also, however, compromised his support within the navy. Thus Rear Admiral Campbell, a midshipman with Keppel on Anson's voyage and a key witness in the admiral's court martial, was reported as having told the first lord that he 'condemns Admiral Keppel greatly for mixing Politicks with his profession; acknowledges that Government cannot go on if Military people are to point out who shall or shall not be the Kings ministers; & is very ready to serve whenever Your Majesty thinks proper to command him'.[95] It also seems likely, as N. A. M. Rodger suggests, that the hero-worship of Keppel (which he did nothing to discourage) would also have disgusted some sections of naval opinion.[96] John Stevenson, a junior naval officer who supported Palliser, nevertheless brought a due sense of perspective to these matters when he later observed that Keppel had been lauded by both houses of parliament in very similar terms to those greeting Rodney's significant and unequivocal victory at the Battle of the Saintes: 'so much honour has been conferred, where so little seems to have been done to deserve it.'[97] Lady Pembroke thought Keppel should have been embarrassed at his supporters' behaviour on his acquittal but saw no sign of that. '[A]fter the tryal, they walked with him in procession thro' the streets, & before him was play'd "See the Conquering Hero comes", all of which if he is a sensible man must have distress'd him terribly & made him feel small, for tho' he had done as well as he could yet there was nothing very great done.'[98]

While Keppel's post-trial political commitments dulled the lustre of his name in some quarters and ensured that he never saw active service again, they strengthened his claim for preferment when the opposition's campaign against Lord North finally bore fruit in 1782. Keppel succeeded Sandwich as first lord of the admiralty and became a viscount in the peerage of Great Britain. In the meantime, however, he underwent the mortification of being a highly reluctant witness in Palliser's court martial and seeing his protagonist acquitted of charges that his disobedience had been responsible for the shortcomings of the engagement off Ushant.

4

The Palliser-Keppel Affair

The historical literature has tended to look far more closely at Keppel's trial than Palliser's and has not considered his perspective on the affair.[1] This chapter aims to redress the balance by re-examining Palliser's decision to challenge Admiral Keppel's account of the action off Ushant and lay a charge against him. It also examines evidence produced in his own trial that raises questions about Keppel's conduct on 27 July and has important implications for the aftermath of the trials and the reputations of the officers concerned.

Sir Hugh Palliser's antecedents and attachments were very different from Keppel's. He came from a relatively obscure background and lacked his commanding officer's wealth, public profile and popularity in the service. Palliser made his way up to flag rank through distinguished service at sea and demonstrated his administrative talents as a reforming naval governor of Newfoundland and at the head of the Navy Board. Unlike Keppel, Palliser was a Tory and as his career progressed, he worked increasingly closely with Lord Sandwich, the first lord of the Admiralty. N. A. M. Rodger describes him as 'an outstanding officer' and Sandwich's 'chief asset' in forging effective relations with the Navy Board.[2] Palliser, who was interested in explorations and surveying, picked out James Cook when serving as an able seaman under his command and provided ongoing support for him.

When he was appointed comptroller of the Royal Navy in 1773, Palliser was exposed to the politically infused elite snobbery that was to provide a powerful undercurrent in his spectacular public conflict with Keppel:

> I discovered (and not the first time) a formed design by an envious artful few to put a bar to my ambitious pursuits in his Majesty's service in the military line by procuring a determination that might be construed into a declaration by Admiralty that accepting employment in this branch of the naval service for the benefit of the income as I *was uncivilly told in your Lordship's presence*, should take way my pretensions and render me unworthy of a place amongst them![3]

Sandwich assured Palliser that the King endorsed his rejection of this bid to exclude him from flag promotions. He became rear admiral while head of the Navy Board and subsequently became a lord commissioner of the Admiralty and a baronet. In late 1775, when Sandwich appointed his valued associate to the sought-after sinecure of lieutenant-general of Marines, he faced a wave of criticism from senior naval officers, including Keppel. This squabble over precedence and profit does not seem to have poisoned relationships between the two flag officers at the time but became a source of retrospective aggravation among Keppel's supporters once the affair got under way.[4] There were also tensions between Palliser and some flag officers and captains in late 1777 and early 1778. Admiral Lord Shuldham assailed Palliser 'in great heat' over the supersession of one of his followers and led a protest of senior officers in which Admiral Keppel took part.[5]

While Palliser lacked Keppel's popularity within the service, many colleagues respected his courage and commitment and, except in the febrile minds of Sandwich's implacable enemies, he only became a pariah during his conflict with Keppel. His correspondence with Lord Sandwich suggests a depth of respect that went beyond self-interest or conventional patron-client deference. Palliser was said on occasion to display a 'warmth of temper' but did not have a reputation for irascibility.[6] His reactions, like those of Keppel, may have been affected by poor underlying health. Palliser was wounded severely by an accidental discharge of firearms below decks and was not expected to survive. In the event, permanent injuries to one of his legs caused constant severe pain and constrained him to fitful sleep in a chair.

Historians, although fully aware of the highly charged partisan atmosphere of the affair, have tended to deal with Palliser's role in terms paralleling those of contemporary detractors.[7] J. H. Broomfield, the author of an accomplished essay on the affair, thought Palliser's decision to publish a rejection of the *General Advertiser*'s claims was 'rather foolish' and his charge against Keppel 'the hasty action of an angry man'; it was 'very rash'.[8] Palliser was unduly sensitive to an anonymous item in the press and most unwisely became the self-interested accuser of a popular senior naval figure. N. A. M. Rodger thought Palliser's best-worst option was to clear his name by demanding a court martial on his conduct rather than ineptly seeking exoneration by charging Keppel.[9] In these accounts, Palliser is seen as the author of his own misfortunes and the affair as a disastrous termination of his career.

While there is some truth in these assessments, the picture that emerges from reconsidering the key aspects of the affair, including the often-neglected details and implications of Palliser's trial, suggests a lighter shade on Palliser's side and some threatening storm clouds on Keppel's. In what follows, I will re-examine Palliser's decisions to respond to the *General Advertiser* article and to charge his commander-in-chief. Given Keppel's strategy of accusing without charging and his parliamentary friends' support for it, Palliser had no choice but to respond in these ways. Although Keppel's acquittal was a triumph, the Board's immediate determination to try Palliser prompted anxiety among his antagonist's supporters, manifest in their attempts to prevent him from coming to trial and Keppel's ongoing refusal to lay charges. It is suggested here that there were some grounds for these concerns since Palliser's acquittal tarnished Keppel's triumph and raised awkward questions about some of the evidence that had vindicated Keppel by assigning blame to his subordinate.

Palliser's response to Keppel's campaign of 'insinuation': Refutation and recrimination

In light of criticisms of Palliser's alleged overreaction to the *General Advertiser* publication, it is interesting to note that he assured Sandwich he would not 'do anything rashly'.[10] Three days later he referred to 'an easy quiet route' or 'a more direct way of coming at the point and matters of fact, but which may be productive of many things disagreeable to others which had better be avoided if possible'.[11] He hoped initially to secure Keppel's agreement to correct the statement of blame made in the *General Advertiser*, but when the admiral and his staff rebuffed him, Palliser moved to plan B; that involved publishing an alternative account of the action in the pro-ministerial *Morning Post*.

Having taken this step, Palliser seemed prepared to let the matter rest. Although this expectation seriously misread Keppel's and his political friends' intentions and their probable reaction to the implied criticisms of his commander-in-chief in the *Morning Post* article, Palliser was not alone in taking this position. There were many members of the naval officer corps whose professional interests and patriotic sense were not filtered through the lens of partisan attachments and who wished to see a swift end to a dispute that threatened the operational efficiency of the wartime service. By the very nature of things, these voices are largely absent from the historical record but were probably represented by the mild-mannered and thoughtful Captain Robert Walsingham. He had fought at the battle off Ushant, was a witness at Keppel's trial and, while aligned politically with him, was a warm personal friend of Lord Sandwich. Walsingham did not think any blame attached to either Keppel or Palliser. A few days after Palliser's statement appeared in the *Morning Post*, he still hoped that the dispute could be settled.[12] As noted in the previous chapter, Sandwich echoed Walsingham's general position in response to Lord Bristol's demand for an enquiry.[13] A few days later, however, any prospect of reconciliation was blasted by Keppel's and Palliser's altercation in the House of Commons. When it became clear that Keppel was determined to persist with his strategy of 'insinuation', Palliser embarked on the radical and risky step of calling for a court martial on his commander-in-chief to clear his own name. This resort to 'recrimination' was condemned by Keppel, his friends and more disinterested contemporaries.

Palliser's signed contribution to the *Morning Post* almost certainly spurred the parliamentary opposition (including Keppel) to go on the offensive as soon as the opening of parliament gave them a platform. It seems highly likely, however, that private gossip, overlapping political and service networks, and the *General Advertiser* piece would have provided sufficient oxygen to a story which fitted neatly with the opposition's narrative of ministerial incompetence, corruption and Machiavellian scapegoating. Palliser's resort to the *Morning Post* was entirely understandable in this context.

The *General Advertiser* piece allowed Keppel and his supporters to expose Palliser to damaging imputations without bringing him to trial. Palliser's rejoinder allowed him to present an account of the events of 27 July that left his professional reputation and sense of honour unsullied. Many contemporaries of Palliser's class and rank would not hesitate to issue or accept a challenge when questions of personal honour were at stake and would certainly not see the risk of duelling as a reason for not doing so. For much the same reasons, Palliser could not, as some of Keppel's supporters disingenuously and insultingly suggested, ignore the claims made in the *General Advertiser*.[14] These accusations were not merely the despised products of the 'popular prints'; they also had currency in the circles in which men like Horace Walpole moved. The fact that they had received Keppel's implied *imprimatur* also made them highly damaging among Palliser's colleagues in the service.

The King, a closely engaged and in many respects shrewd observer of elite politics and naval affairs, thought that Palliser was justified in taking this step. He told Sandwich, 'This must make an eternal breach between the two admirals, and occasion much ill-humour among those concerned in that day; but Palliser could not avoid the step he has been drove to without the greatest blame.'[15] When Keppel criticized Palliser for putting his name to the *Morning Post* piece, he responded that this was more 'manly' than relying on anonymous, third-party denigration to protect one's reputation.[16] He offered a striking contrast between the honourableness of his approach and that of his protagonist: 'all the art and policy were on the side of the admiral; all openness, and, if we are to judge by events, all the unguardedness, were on mine. But I do not envy the hon. admiral such a superiority.'[17]

If Palliser's intervention in the *Morning Post* made sense in his peculiarly intractable circumstances, so did his decision to ask the Board to court martial Keppel when he attacked him in parliament but showed no signs of charging him. The Board could not charge Keppel because there was no official intimation that he had done anything wrong.[18] Historians' suggestion that Palliser should have sought a court martial on himself is only compelling if there was an indication that Sandwich would agree to it. However, there is no evidence of that and no surviving record of Palliser discussing this matter with either the first lord or other members of the Board. Palliser's very able speech of defence in the House of Commons in late 1780 gives insight into his position. It provided a clear statement of the dilemma posed by Keppel's passive accusation strategy and explained why he thought the only channel of exoneration lay through a trial on his commander-in-chief:

> Had the admiral avowed accusation when he was thus urged to do it, I could have had an immediate trial, without being exposed to the odium of first appearing as an accuser. But the admiral would neither exculpate nor accuse me; knowing that the Admiralty would not grant me a trial without a charge of some kind or another; or that if I had been granted one without any charge under the then circumstances, it would have been called a sham trial. By this manoeuvre I was driven to the fatal alternative, either of becoming an accuser of a man too great to be questioned without the utmost hazard, or of submitting to the injurious imputation of being deemed the cause of our doing so little in the action, when, if there was blame, I thought that it must belong to him.[19]

Although Keppel's trial proved to be a humiliating non-contest, it does not follow that Palliser made a gross misjudgement in requesting a court martial on him. He could not have known the circumstances in which the trial would take place when he laid the charge and, as noted in the previous chapter, he did a poor job of prosecuting the case. Moreover, Sandwich would not agree to Palliser's request to try him without a charge from Keppel. This decision probably had less to do with Palliser's interests than with Sandwich's wish to avoid the perpetual embarrassment of what his enemies would dismiss as a sham trial. In light of the verdict and the rider handed down by Keppel's court, however, both the King and Sandwich thought it necessary for Palliser to be court-martialled; the evidence produced at the trial provided a basis for the charge. Keppel's trial thus cleared the way for what Palliser had always wanted and removed a political barrier to Sandwich agreeing to it.

This process was exceedingly painful for Palliser, but his options in laying a charge were as limited as Sandwich's in accepting it. If anything, the condemnatory rider probably hardened both Palliser's and Sandwich's resolve, the former for his honour and reputation, the latter because a trial vindicating Palliser might help justify the highly unpopular decision to try his superior officer. If the court condemned Palliser, Sandwich could at least have claimed to have done his duty by responding appropriately to information arising during Keppel's trial. The term 'misjudgement' implies a choice between viable alternatives and it is clear that Palliser did not see himself having such a choice. Given a concern for honour and reputation that was at least as valid as Keppel's, and given that it was clear from an early stage that Keppel was determined to vindicate himself by condemning Palliser to a limbo of unresolved incrimination, the decision to bring Keppel to trial was as reasonable as the double-bind circumstances allowed. As Palliser said, 'what he had done was purely the vindication of his own honour and character.'[20] Moderate contemporary opinion may have condemned Palliser's action as unreasonable, even 'mad', but in so doing, it (and some historians) has discounted the implications of Keppel's strategy for Palliser's honour and professional reputation.[21]

While it is understandable (though hardly admirable) for Keppel to have prioritized his reputation and honour over Palliser's, it is curious that historians have followed suit. N. A. M. Rodger thinks Keppel was guilty of allowing himself to be used to destroy Palliser's career for political purposes but is also critical of Palliser for adopting a course of action that threatened Keppel's life: 'From vindicating his own honour, it seemed, Palliser has passed to attempting his commander-in-chief's life.'[22] However, as Keppel's accusations finally (if indirectly) resulted in Palliser being brought to court martial to face capital charges, one could also say he placed not only his honour but also the prospect of political advantage over the life of his fellow flag officer.

Keppel's friends' efforts to derail a trial supported his refusal to press charges. After Keppel declared that he 'forgave' Palliser and that there was thus no need for him to stand trial, Charles James Fox proposed removing Palliser from the navy into inglorious but well-pensioned retirement as an appropriate, even humane, end to the affair.[23] Palliser's honour was to be degraded permanently to uphold Keppel's. Two of Keppel's supporters in the House of Lords opposed a court martial on Palliser because it would serve as a ministerial weapon against Keppel. The Duke of Richmond claimed that any trial would necessarily be a 'mock trial' providing the Board with 'new grounds for aspersing Mr Keppel'. The Earl of Bristol and Lord Pembroke made a similar point. Having rehearsed opposition views that Keppel was the target of the Admiralty Board's machinations, Bristol warned that if Sir Hugh were acquitted, the conclusion Sandwich and his friends would draw was that 'if any fault was committed, it could not be fairly imputed to the vice-admiral of the blue'.[24] Bristol did not spell out a corollary of this conclusion: if Palliser was not at fault then Keppel might be. It was, however, implicit in Lady Pembroke's shrewd observation that Keppel's acquittal made Palliser's trial inevitable because 'his disobedience made part of the defence' of his admiral.[25] Of course, Palliser might be found guilty of disobedience, but from

Bristol's perspective there was always a possibility that a court set up under Sandwich's malign direction would acquit him. As things stood, there was in any case no reason for Keppel to run even a moderate risk. His purposes were very well served by his own acquittal, the court's impugnment of Palliser's honour and honesty, and his ongoing availability as a stalking horse for the opposition to deploy against Sandwich and Lord North. In the event, parliamentary attempts to abort the trial failed and Keppel's allies in the House of Lords were reduced to finding what satisfaction they could in calling the judge advocate to the bar of the House and subjecting him to an ill-tempered two-hour examination on his approach to the trial.[26]

The trial

When Keppel's acquittal seemed inevitable, Palliser told Sandwich that he would be seeking a court martial on himself.[27] In the event, however, the Board took matters into its own hands. Sandwich thought that a trial held at the instigation of the Board would be less liable to misrepresentation as a mock trial than one in which Palliser charged himself.[28] He also thought it necessary for Palliser to resign both his seat at the Board and his lieutenant-generalcy. Having tried for a month to persuade Keppel to lay charges, the Board finally decided to use evidence from Keppel's trial as the initial basis to investigate and try Palliser. Despite Palliser's request to face a specific charge of disobedience, the Board's instruction to Vice Admiral George Darby, the court's president, referred to 'several matters . . . given in evidence respecting the conduct and behaviour of . . . Sir Hugh Palliser . . . which demand strict examination and that he be tried for same'.[29] It was, however, widely understood that the 'matters' involved allegations of disobedience and that meant Palliser was on trial for his life, even though the article under which his charge fell ('XI. Obedience to orders in battle') did not impose a mandatory death sentence.

In the course of his unsuccessful attempts to persuade Lord Sandwich to hold a court martial at his request, Palliser explained that he was concerned that if a trial took place at the Board's instigation he would face a barrage of hostile witnesses who had already effectively testified against him in Keppel's trial.[30] This concern was well-founded. Although charges were not stated at the beginning of the trial, the evidence produced in response to the court's questioning tended to confirm the impressions that had arisen in the earlier trial. The King was aware of this and so too was Palliser. George III warned Lord Sandwich of 'the impressions the very uniform and clear answers of the gentlemen produced on the court martial cannot fail to have made on the minds of impartial men'. Palliser sent the first lord an anguished plea that he and his friends 'not . . . abandon me before I have made my defence'.[31]

Whether by luck or good judgement, this plea was prescient and the King was given grounds for revising his view of Palliser's position. His defence, which was read when the court finished examining prosecution witnesses, had a marked impact on the subsequent direction of the trial. The absence of a statement of charge by the court allowed Palliser to identify charges emerging from the witnesses' testimony and respond to them in a way that had not been permitted at the earlier trial. Palliser specified three charges and made a preliminary response to them before seeking support for his rebuttals from defence witnesses.

The first charge was that he had failed to respond to signals from the admiral's flagship immediately following the action and throughout the afternoon.[32] Sufficient doubt was raised in testimony about the visibility or applicability of the flagship's signals to weaken claims that Palliser had disobeyed Keppel's orders. The second charge concerned Palliser's alleged failure to lead his division into its place in the line of battle during the afternoon of the 27th and to obey signals and repeated signals to this effect. Palliser's response to this charge relied partly on evidence of the damage suffered by the ships in his division and partly on the withdrawal of the line of battle signal during the latter part of the afternoon. Evidence from *Formidable's* officers on the extent of the damage to sails, hull, rigging and spars – 'a perfect wreck', as Captain John Bazely put it – was supported by the testimony of Captain Sir William Burnaby of the frigate *Milford*.[33] Significantly, witnesses at Keppel's trial depreciated the damage suffered by *Formidable* even though their commander-in-chief had expressed surprise in correspondence with Sandwich at the crippling effect – 'beyond any degree I ever saw' – of enemy fire on his ships' masts and rigging.[34]

Evidence that Keppel's flagship did not regulate its speed to enable badly damaged ships to keep pace with her challenged claims that Palliser's division failed to obey orders to take its station in *Victory's* wake. In cross-examination, witnesses from *Victory* acknowledged that the speeds noted in the ship's logbook were notional rather than a record of castings of the log line. Helpfully for Palliser's case, the sailing master's claim that *Victory* had 'lay to' for several hours in the afternoon (thus allowing slower vessels to catch up) was contradicted by testimony from Keppel's first captain, Rear Admiral Campbell.[35] Captain Marshall's (HMS *Arethusa*) testimony that the flag was hauled down a little after 3.00 pm and not hoisted again until shortly after 6.00 pm that evening supported Palliser's claim that he did not ignore the line of battle signal.

The final charge was potentially the most damaging because the disobedience alleged was blatant, and failure to obey was tied directly to the frustration of Keppel's plans to reengage the French fleet before the close of day. This charge hinged on the transmission of signals from the admiral's flagship and Palliser's response to a message sent by the frigate *Fox*. *Formidable*'s gunner's written record of gunpowder expended in firing a round to draw attention to signals, and testimony of officers from other ships, cast doubt on claims that Palliser failed to repeat a critical signal to the ships of his division.[36] However, the most significant new evidence in Palliser's favour concerned the *Fox* episode.

There were two issues at stake here: the content of the message and the time of its delivery. These matters were critical because they directly affected whether Palliser was told that Keppel wanted him to take his station so the attack could commence and whether the message was delivered in a time frame that was consistent with that intention. The court also heard that if the British fleet was to engage before dark – Keppel regarded a night time attack as too risky – it would need to do so by 7.00 pm at the latest. Rear Admiral Campbell testified that Keppel intended to renew the attack at 5.00 pm and that he would have done so if Palliser had 'led down his division' to its place in the fleet. Keppel's flag captain, Jonathan Faulkner, gave 6.00 pm or 'shortly thereafter' as the latest time for the fleet to be gathered to renew the action.[37] Keppel and his officers testified to his extreme frustration ('much uneasiness, disappointment, and displeasure') at Palliser's failure to respond to orders for organizing the fleet for an attack.

Evidence on the content of the message sent by *Fox* was inconclusive. Witnesses from the *Victory* and *Fox* testified that Palliser was told that Keppel was waiting for his division to join the fleet so that an attack could begin; those from the *Formidable* claimed that he was merely told to join the fleet with no mention made of the intended attack.[38] There was general agreement on Palliser's response – to the effect that he perfectly understood the order – but as that was consistent with either the short or long form of the message, it was of no consequence in determining the matter at hand. Significantly, there were no independent witnesses to support the claims of either side.

There was also sharply conflicting evidence on the timing of *Fox's* message. *Formidable's* officers were clear and consistent in their testimony that the frigate did not heave to off *Formidable's* stern until around 7.00 pm. Thus Captain John Bazely testified that *Fox* arrived 'rather before sunset', that is, a little before 7.30 pm. He also testified that the signals ordering ships to join the admiral – timed at 6.10 pm – were repeated before *Fox* came down and that Palliser was 'very eager' to obey the signal as soon as *Formidable* could do so.[39] This timing corresponds with Palliser's *Morning Post* account and meant that the message was delivered when an attack on that day was no longer possible. The *Formidables'* testimony conflicted with the equally emphatic statements of the officers on *Victory*, the captain of *Fox* and one of his lieutenants.[40] They all placed *Fox*'s arrival off the stern of Palliser's flagship at around five o'clock, in good time for Keppel to gather the fleet for an attack before dark.[41] Statements of the timing of *Fox's* summons to the *Victory*, the transmission of the message to her captain and calculations of the time it took the vessel to reach the *Formidable* supported these accounts.

Bazely was ridiculed in parliament by Keppel's friends, but midway through Palliser's trial, his evidence was corroborated by Captain Marshall. He testified that the signal calling *Fox* to the flagship was hoisted at 5.32 pm, a shift in timing that was critical to Palliser's defence and potentially fatal to Keppel's claims that he intended to re-engage the French on the 27th.[42] Three things lent credence to Marshall's testimony. In the first place, he was not identified with Palliser (as Bazely and his officers were), and Keppel had praised evidence given by him in the House of Commons. These considerations meant that Marshall had good standing as a witness and that Palliser could boost his credibility by referring to Keppel's praise.

Secondly, unlike the other witnesses who testified on the timing of *Fox's* mission, Marshall's evidence was backed up by a contemporaneous timed written record (made by the purser) of all the signals hoisted on the flagship and repeated on *Arethusa*. Although Marshall had handed a copy of this record to Sir Thomas Pye at the earlier trial and it was read to the court by the judge advocate, its contents were not otherwise available to Palliser on that occasion and the court ignored it.[43] The document contained a great deal of detail and George Jackson may have intoned it at a speed which made it hard to hear over the background noise in the courtroom in the governor's house. For whatever reason, Palliser did not refer to *Arethusa's* purser's record in Keppel's trial. That was highly unfortunate because it was very precise on the time *Fox* was summoned to the flagship and thus provided a firm basis for calculating when Keppel's message was delivered to Palliser. Taking account of the distance between *Fox's* station, the flagship and *Formidable*, Marshall's evidence was that *Fox* received the message around 6.00 pm and delivered it around 7.00 pm.[44] This timing was generally consistent with Bazely's and his officers' testimony but seriously at odds with that of officers from *Victory* and *Fox*.

Thirdly, Marshall's timing was consistent with the evidence of two officers from HMS *America*, another ship in Palliser's division, who saw the *Fox* coming down under the stern of *Formidable*.[45] It also gained circumstantial strength from the timing of a general signal for ships to join the fleet and a slightly later series of signals addressed to particular ships in Palliser's division. These signals, which Formidable repeated, were hoisted at 6.10 pm, a few minutes after *Fox* (on Marshall's timing) came under the lee of *Victory* to receive the message for Palliser, and at 6.33 pm. The generally agreed timing of these signals sits far better with Marshall's and Bazely's accounts than with those of *Victory's* officers. Their timing leaves an awkward delay of almost an hour between the delivery of *Fox's* message and the hoisting of closely related signals. However, signals hoisted between 6.10 pm and 6.33 pm were entirely consistent with Bazely's and Marshall's timing of *Fox's* message.

It is surprising that except for the disputed testimony of the oral message sent by *Fox*, Keppel and his staff made no effort to convey the commander-in-chief's intentions and frustrations to Palliser. Given the peremptory command style common among Georgian flag officers, it seems extraordinary that Keppel would not have sent Palliser a (perhaps softened) version of directives routinely issued by St Vincent, Keith and even Nelson and Collingwood. Nor did the management of Keppel's flagship give indications of an imminent determination to gather his fleet to attack the French. As noted above, *Victory's* sailing speed distanced her from parts of the fleet. Finally, on Marshall's timing of *Fox*'s despatch, Keppel did not give directions to his errant third in command until the last feasible time for a re-engagement on 27 July had passed.[46]

In short, the picture of fleet management that emerges during the late afternoon of 27 July is incompatible with a narrative of the careful planning and execution of a renewed attack on the French Fleet. *Victory* outsailed ships she wished to gather around her in battle formation, did not keep the line of battle signal hoisted, neglected to order ships in Palliser's division to take their station until very late in the day and sent a critical message to him after the fail-safe time for an attack. These events speak of uncertainty, indecision and perhaps even confusion, not the execution of a determined course of action.

In early May 1779, after a trial of twenty-one days, Palliser was acquitted of 'misconduct or misbehaviour'. The press reported that the verdict was greeted with 'three shouts of acclamation' by 'the whole audience' in the courtroom, that crews of the ships attached to Palliser's cause 'instantly' returned these cheers, and that he went ashore to ringing bells and cheering well-wishers. There was even a report of illuminations 'throughout Portsmouth and the Commons'.[47] These celebratory demonstrations were in striking contrast to Palliser's treatment after Keppel's acquittal and were no doubt heartening to him. However, while the Court found his conduct exemplary in many respects, it noted that he had failed to inform his commander-in-chief of the seriously damaged state of his flagship, HMS *Formidable*. Keppel's friends made much of this qualification without acknowledging that he and his staff had made no efforts to ascertain the fleet's condition after the initial engagement.

The implications of Palliser's acquittal

Because courts' deliberations were confidential and only judge advocates were permitted to record them, we lack reliable information on how the court reached Palliser's verdict and the impact of the conflicting testimony given by officers from *America, Arethusa* and *Formidable* on one hand and *Victory* and *Fox* on the other.[48] Plausible contemporary hearsay suggests sharply divided opinions between some (unknown) judges on some (unknown) points. Palliser's judges conferred for two and a half days, and a London newspaper reported that the last half day had seen 'very warm debate'. On a later account, the court cleared the quarterdeck of HMS *Sandwich* to prevent raised voices from being overheard. It reported a verdict based on a vote of 7/5.[49] The highly partisan Lord Pembroke was told of an even closer split: '5 . . . for shooting him, 2 for breaking him, & 5 for acquitting' with Rear Admiral Digby persuading one of the 'breaking ones' to become an acquitter.[50] These claims cannot be evaluated, but given the implications of Palliser's acquittal, the pro-Keppel weight of voluble public opinion and fractured relationships within the service, long deliberation ending in a tight verdict would not be surprising. There was probably also vigorous debate over whether to qualify the verdict. Even so, Palliser's acquittal indicates that a majority of his judges thought that the testimony given at his trial cast significant doubts on critical evidence given at Keppel's.

N. A. M. Rodger's suggestion that 'at worst' Keppel had done nothing 'during the battle' to 'justify any accusation beyond incompetence' may accurately reflect the situation until the fleet's return from its autumn cruise. However, imputed incompetence that fell short of the criminal reach of the Articles of War would be highly damaging to the professional reputation and prospects of a flag officer and doubly so to a man who had been endowed with an aura of military greatness by his political friends and seemed increasingly comfortable basking in its heroic glow. In addition, Keppel and his supporters sought to discredit Palliser's performance by casting aspersions on him which were not supported by the evidence presented at his trial. These developments had potentially significant implications for the campaign that Keppel and his friends had waged against Palliser and for the reputational and honorific value of his acquittal. That depended, however, on the soundness of Palliser's trial. Two matters must be considered here: the court's membership and its conduct.

During a parliamentary debate after Palliser's acquittal, Charles James Fox spoke with characteristic indignation of the scandalous improprieties of the court's 'constitution'. His most substantial support for this assertion was the presence on the court of Captain George Walters, Palliser's nephew and heir apparent.[51] His appointment might appear to involve a blatant conflict of interest, but that was not as clear-cut at the time as it may seem to later observers. The legislation referred to officers 'who were personally interested in the matter to be tried', not their relationship to the prisoner, and all judges swore to act 'without partiality, favour or affection'.[52] Another member of the court, Captain Adam Duncan, who had also been a judge at Keppel's trial and served under him at every rank from midshipman to post captain, was likely to have been as attached to his cause as Walters was to his uncle's. In light of Duncan's performance in Keppel's trial, Lord Sandwich sought to deploy him to another station. However, 'Keppel's Duncan' (as a later first lord affectionately dubbed him) resisted this attempt on the grounds that his ship was not yet in a fit state to go to sea.[53] There may thus have been some truth in Commodore George Johnstone's rejoinder to Fox that the objections to Walters' presence on the court were 'far-fetched' and 'the hon. gentlemen who had recourse to it, were extremely hard set'.[54]

Walters' participation was certainly not due to Sandwich's machinations. It may have been discouraged by Palliser on the grounds of appearance and because he thought that a less obviously compromised judge would be more beneficial to his cause. When the first lord wrote to the president asking why Walters was to be a judge, Vice Admiral Darby told him that he had insisted on ending his leave early and his eligibility and seniority entitled him to sit. However, Pye also told Sandwich that after it was too late, Walters changed his mind and 'strongly expressed a desire not to sit'.[55] Walters' reluctance may explain why he played an entirely silent role in the public part of proceedings. It also seems likely that if he had attempted to exert undue influence on the court's deliberations it would have been exposed and negated by Duncan and Captain John Colpoys who were far more significant officers than Walters. The trial transcript indicates that Colpoys was keen to ensure that the court was cleared promptly when procedural questions arose and thus to avoid some of the open wrangling that marred Keppel's trial. If one assumes that Walters voted in favour of his uncle it would almost certainly be offset by Duncan's vote against him and was not likely to have been critical to the outcome. Even if another one of the court's votes had gone against Palliser, the resulting tie would, after further deliberation, have resulted in his acquittal.[56]

Fox named two other captains, Samuel Goodall and Mark Robinson, when criticizing the constitution of Palliser's court. These officers had served in Palliser's division on 27th July and were witnesses at Keppel's trial. Claims that they were ineligible by virtue of 'being personally interested in the matter to be tried' did not stand up because the framing of the trial made it clear that Palliser's conduct was at issue, not his captains.[57] That Goodall resisted intense pressure when Montagu sought to force him to offer a judgement on Keppel's conduct and gave compelling arguments for doing so attested to good sense and courage of conviction rather than venality. Beyond the circle of Keppel's ardent followers, Goodall, a friend and correspondent of Nelson, was held in high repute in the service and very well regarded by the King. An assessment of captains and admirals Sandwich sent to the King before the Board charged Keppel, judged him 'an exceedingly good officer & worthy man. Not eager on either side'.[58] The same assessment was made of Captain Robinson. Captain Joseph Peyton, a defence witness in Keppel's trial and one of Palliser's judges, had written to Lord Sandwich deploring the partisanship of other witnesses and saying that he had deliberately avoided their triumphal social celebrations. He got on badly with Keppel, but that does not necessarily indicate bias in Palliser's favour. None of these officers showed partisan tendencies in the trial.[59] Thus by the standards of Keppel's court, the judges in Palliser's trial do not seem to have been exceptional in their attachments to the accused and cannot be said to have constituted a packed court.[60]

Palliser's trial certainly avoided the contemporary opprobrium incurred by Keppel's. While two of the flag officers on Keppel's court had been singled out by Horace Walpole for their improprieties, those on Palliser's were unexceptional in their impartiality and professionalism. Vice Admiral George Darby took the presidency reluctantly, but as a well-regarded senior officer who was not associated with any party, he was a good choice for a difficult job. He was very popular in the fleet when he commanded at sea after the trial.[61] The minutes and shorthand transcript indicate that he was an effective president; he certainly avoided the well-merited censure that Walpole levelled at Vice Admiral Pye. When Darby gave evidence for the prosecution at Keppel's trial, even such a partisan as Edmund Burke commended his character: 'his Evidence is decisive in our Admiral's favour though he conducts himself with as much reserve as can be without injury to Truth, which I am persuaded he has too much honour to pervert.'[62] Robert Digby, a very recently promoted rear admiral, sat with Darby. Although he was a friend of Palliser's (which may explain the role attributed to him by Lord Pembroke) and had been appointed to a flagship so he would be eligible to take a place on the court, there is no indication that his relationship with Palliser overrode his sense of judicial responsibility. Before Keppel was charged, Sandwich's informant praised Digby's non-partisan position in the dispute and during Palliser's trial Digby's interventions were as measured as Darby's.[63] The King thought well of him and entrusted his son to his charge when he went to sea as a midshipman in mid 1779.[64] Finally, Palliser's court was not subject to a domineering senior figure like Vice Admiral Montagu or the distracting, intimidating presence of an entitled, promiscuous, vocal and participatory audience.

These considerations help to explain a restoration of the controlled tones of judicious earnestness typical of naval courts martial and also the prominence of the judges in the proceedings. Compared with the earlier trial, Palliser's judges subjected witnesses to thoughtful, measured and intensive questioning on relevant matters of fact. More than half of the questions came from court members, while just under a quarter came from the judge advocate and in cross-questioning by Palliser as the prisoner.[65] By contrast, except for interventions by Montagu, the proceedings in Keppel's trial were dominated by the main protagonists.

Conclusion

Despite the protestations of some of Keppel's parliamentary allies, there are no compelling reasons for writing off Palliser's trial as a sham. Indeed, the court conducted the trial with far greater propriety than Keppel's, and while the verdict may have been tight and arrived at after heated discussions among the judges, that does not necessarily mean it was unsound. The court's verdict is explicable in light of two pieces of crucial evidence that challenged the decision of Keppel's court to exonerate him and execrate Palliser.

The evidence on the timing of *Fox*'s mission and the line of battle signal cast significant doubt on Keppel's claim that he could not reengage with the French fleet on the 27th because of Palliser's disobedience. Witnesses at Keppel's trial gave evidence on these points, but it came from those who were openly attached to Palliser and was ridiculed by partisans in the press and parliament and implicitly discounted by Keppel's judges. In Palliser's trial, however, independent witnesses backed by contemporaneous documentation supported earlier evidence on these points. Moreover, unlike in Keppel's trial, Palliser was able in his defence to summarize the case against him, raise questions about its soundness and point to the significance of the new evidence. In other words, he could present a sufficiently compelling argument to the court to persuade a majority of its members that the charge of disobedience had not been proved. It also challenged the conspiracy narratives which imputed the alleged disobedience to a government plot to discredit Keppel.

Keppel's and Palliser's trials were, in a sense, mirror images and, in the absence of appeal processes within the courts martial or judicial system – as opposed to parliamentary inquiries – the latter provided the basis for testing the earlier verdict. The implications of this possibility for the post-trial life of the Keppel-Palliser affair will be considered in the next chapter.

5

A Tale of Two Acquittals

The Keppel and Palliser trials were unusual because they concerned the same series of events, relied on a similar range of witnesses and closely related but not identical bodies of evidence. At first sight, however, the verdicts appear contradictory. Keppel's court affirmed his intention to do everything possible to engage with and destroy the enemy fleet and implicitly supported the inference that his efforts had been frustrated by Palliser's disobedience; Palliser's cleared him of disobedience and any wilful responsibility for the fleet's failure to reengage. The verdicts thus appeared to confirm Lord Sandwich's intuition that the disappointing outcome was due to accidental occurrences that were liable to frustrate fleet commanders' best-laid and most nobly executed plans. More than a decade later, a careful analysis by Richard Beatson, a naval historian, suggested that a very inadequate signalling system may have been to blame.[1] The deep antagonisms generated since the publication of the *General Advertiser* piece would have made these explanations very bitter drafts for either of the protagonists to swallow. In any case, some of the evidence at Palliser's trial opened up a range of problems for Keppel and his supporters. It made it more difficult to present Keppel as a heroic leader who had been deprived of the victory he deserved by the treachery of his subordinate and gave new life to the spectre that someone other than the vice admiral of the blue was responsible for the disappointments of 27 July. It also raised the possibility that, as in the earlier highly publicized trial of Vice Admiral Lestock, some of the evidence on which his acquittal rested was false.[2] It will be suggested in this chapter that because Keppel's parliamentary allies continued to use Palliser as a stalking horse in their pursuit of Lord Sandwich and he was able to respond from his seat in the House of Commons, the paradoxically incompatible verdicts had important implications for Keppel's and Palliser's post-affair reputations.[3]

Charged memories, hearsay and collusion

Captain Marshall's evidence on critical signals and the timing of the order relayed to Palliser raise important questions about the testimony of witnesses from HMS *Victory* and HMS *Fox*. The uniform testimony of officers from these ships meant that any innocent errors arising from faulty memory, poorly synchronized time pieces or an erroneous sense of the passage of time must have been identical and that defies the bounds of possibility. Nor were the discrepancies within the range of a reasonable margin of error. To the contrary, they covered the difference between afternoon light and the approach of sunset. If a mistake is ruled out, however, it seems that evidence that contributed to Keppel's juridical acquittal and reputational exoneration was tainted by collusion and was thus false testimony.

The circumstances of service life and the management of courts martial meant that the integrity of proceedings rested heavily on participants' sense of decency and honour and the binding power of testifying under oath. Although witnesses were excluded from the courtroom after the judges were sworn in, no steps were taken to prevent their intermingling outside the court. This risk might not matter in run-of-the-mill proceedings which were over within a day, but the length of Keppel's and Palliser's trials increased the risk of collusion, either with corrupt intent or through witnesses 'charging their memories' in apparently innocent discussions with others. It seems inevitable that these conversations took place. Keppel's officers lived together close to his rented house in the High Street in Portsmouth, officers from *Formidable* shared accommodation in the town during Keppel's trial, and cross examination of one witness revealed discussions involving Palliser, his officers and his legal advisers before he testified.[4]

Captain Windsor and Lieutenant Bertie of HMS *Fox* may have been inadvertent swearers of false testimony. On 10 September 1778, Windsor commanded *Fox* in a prolonged and unequal battle with a much larger French frigate. There were many casualties; the enemy reduced the ship to a virtual wreck, and Windsor (who was among the seriously wounded) surrendered to the French. He and his surviving crew members, including Lieutenant Bertie, were landed at Brest and imprisoned. Over the Christmas of 1778, when preparations for the trial were underway, Keppel told Sandwich that he wished to call Windsor and Bertie as witnesses.[5] With the assistance of the admiral's brother, Lieutenant General William Keppel, the British authorities secured the release of the captain and his lieutenant on parole. They arrived at Gosport in early January and were immediately engaged in the trial.

Other witnesses, including Keppel himself, Rear Admiral Campbell, Sir Robert Harland (Keppel's second in command) and Captain John Jervis, complained of the difficulty of 'charging their memory' on events that occurred months before. This challenge was much more significant for Windsor and Bertie. They had suffered the trauma of an unsuccessful action, the capture of their ship, imprisonment and, in Windsor's case, serious injury. The previous summer's events must have seemed even more remote to them than to their grumbling superiors. It would not, therefore, be surprising if Windsor and Bertie reviewed their recollection of the events of the 27th when Keppel's trial was in the offing and looked to Keppel's friends, or even to his counsel, to 'charge their memories' on some points of detail. The position of *Victory*'s officers was very different. Once a court martial seemed likely, they had plenty of opportunities to establish a common narrative on the relative boat speed of *Victory* and *Formidable*, the timing and visibility of signals, Keppel's intention to reengage and the timing and purpose of *Fox*'s message. Ironically, Palliser's account in the *Morning Post* indicated most of the critical areas of future contention.

The officers from *Fox* and *Victory* may have thought that in providing evidence based on a tacitly agreed narrative, they were not in breach of their oath since they believed the narrative was true. That is not the same, however, as giving evidence on matters of observed fact and when substituted for it was inconsistent with a witness's oath: they were swearing to hearsay that they could not know to be true experientially. In the highly charged environment where these events were played out, collusion may have seemed a necessary safeguard even if Keppel's conduct had been all he and his friends claimed. It would have been imperative if he or his officers had contributed to the failure to renew the action late on 27 July. Is there any indication that this might have been the case?

In the first place, the evidence on handling the *Victory* did not support claims about Keppel's urgent wish to reform his fleet to renew the attack; nor did the substantiated testimony on the timing of the *Fox*'s message. Secondly, Keppel's contemporaneous written statements show him contemplating an attack on the 28th of July, not the 27th.[6] Thirdly, Captain Marshall's evidence supported claims by *Formidable's* officers that the 'line of battle' signal was not hoisted on *Victory* between 3.00 pm and 6.00 pm on the 27th, and there was thus no indication that a renewed attack was imminent. Finally, there is also the matter of Keppel's surprising passivity in the late afternoon. In light of his reported frustrations with Palliser's alleged misbehaviour, it is curious that Marshall, who was called on board *Victory* for an hour in mid-afternoon, was not given a message or any orders. Moreover, although he discussed the fleet's 'disposition' with some of *Victory*'s officers he did not recall any mention of Keppel's plans or Palliser's hindrance of them.[7] Finally, until the despatch of the *Fox*, Keppel did not attempt to convey his intentions to Palliser or to direct his conduct in a way that would be expected of a commanding officer in such circumstances.

Keppel's dilemma: What does England expect?

Marshall's evidence and Keppel's handling of his fleet point to the difficulties he faced after the initial action. Ironically, these difficulties resulted from the elevation of high-level strategic considerations above opportunities to 'sink, burn and otherwise destroy the enemy' enunciated in Keppel's defence'.[8] This doctrine required Keppel and his staff to decide whether to reengage the French on 27 July or to wait, as his initial written records suggest, until the next day.[9] The determining consideration would have been the balance of risks in the context of his instructions. Even without any difficulties arising from Palliser's conduct, the lack of good intelligence on French damage exposed Keppel to a potentially superior enemy force. He could have mitigated this risk by repairing his ships, preventing the enemy's escape and launching a strong attack early on 28 July. Even so, this strategy was vulnerable to the possibility that the French would then be out of reach and a consequent failure to capitalize on what might prove in retrospect to be the only window of opportunity.

There are indications that Keppel and his staff were grappling with this dilemma during the afternoon of 27 July and that incoherent fleet management, demonstrated particularly by Marshall's testimony on the lowering of the line of battle signal and the timing of the message sent by the *Fox*, suggests a lack of certainty about how to act in the face of it. In the event, reengagement was deferred (whether by accident, design, missed opportunity or Palliser's wilful tardiness) until the morning of 28 July. That day dawned with the French fleet disappearing over the horizon towards its safe haven at Brest. But while that sight was highly unwelcome, it did not necessarily mean that Keppel had failed in his mission. This outcome was compatible with a victorious narrative of French flight and Keppel presented it in this light in his report to Sandwich: 'That I have beat the French there cannot be a doubt.'[10] It was also consistent with Keppel's understanding that his primary duty was to protect the trade and the coast rather than to 'attack, take, burn and destroy' the enemy at any and every opportunity. Unfortunately for Keppel and Palliser, however, extreme political tensions quickly cast the events of 27 and 28 July in terms of avoidable disappointment and criminal culpability.

There may be a further set of considerations that had a bearing on the apparent lack of effective agency and direction on the *Victory*. Horace Walpole (no friend of Sandwich or Palliser) reported that the admiral had suffered a 'stroke of a palsy' on the afternoon of 27 July which manifested itself afterwards in 'indistinct' speech.[11] If Walpole was relying on something more than uninformed gossip, these afflictions may help to explain the lack of correspondence between Keppel's reiterated intention of reengaging on 27 July, the management of the fleet and his failure to communicate his plans effectively. Walpole's report gains some credence from glimpses of Keppel's situation on the day. In evidence at Palliser's trial, he referred to the physical and mental demands of the previous days. The expectations of the Board, the service and the public made naval high command stressful in any circumstances and particularly when combat situations were preceded by days and nights of anxious pursuit and positioning. Flag officers often embarked on actions after prolonged periods of intense psychological strain and sleep deprivation that were likely to affect their decision-making on the day and their subsequent recollection of events. Keppel told Palliser's court that on the afternoon of the 27th he was 'worn out' and so stressed – 'I lost my patience to a degree of indiscretion' – that he could not recollect the 'particular terms' of *Fox*'s message and advised that it rely on the evidence of Campbell and Windsor.[12] He also referred to the difficulties and, in some cases, the impossibility of 'charging his memory' and told the court that he was aware of the inadequacy of his evidence.[13]

If Keppel was significantly incapacitated, the position of Rear Admiral Campbell and his senior officers would have been challenging. Walpole mentioned Keppel's indistinct speech; other post-stroke symptoms include erratic and sometimes aggressive reactions to advice and attempts at assistance, extreme lassitude and lapses in concentration and coherent communication. These afflictions would severely hinder fleet management in a pre-battle situation and make it difficult for a senior colleague such as Campbell to be an effective stand-in. Assuming the rights of a more senior officer was a risky move for the officer or officers concerned. They needed to avoid any hint of forcing their superior's hand and to cover themselves by acting on the advice of a surgeon. The situation was particularly fraught when a commanding officer's incapacity was incomplete, intermittent and not necessarily apparent to himself.

This possibility makes sense of the tension between Keppel's alleged intentions, fleet management and communication on the afternoon of 27 July and may also explain the subsequent conduct of his officers. It does not require that Keppel himself was a party to collusion, except in the sense that Campbell's and Faulkner's advice may have furnished his stroke-afflicted memory. It is perhaps significant that both Campbell and Keppel swore to evidence that *Fox* and another frigate, HMS *Milford*, were called to *Victory* simultaneously, even though that was entirely inconsistent with *Arethusa*'s signal record and the recollection of the *Milford*'s captain.[14] The vagueness of Keppel's testimony at critical times may have been due to his unwillingness to swear to the memories of others. He was an extremely reluctant witness and tried unsuccessfully to be excused from testifying. This stance was consistent with Keppel's wish to have nothing to do with charging Palliser, but it might also have been due to an awareness of his own limitations as a witness.

There was one transaction on the night of 27–28 July of which Keppel could know nothing. In Keppel's trial, Rear Admiral Campbell testified that those on HMS *Victory* did not see that the enemy fleet had escaped until daylight on July 28. When asked whether frigates had been stationed between the fleets to watch the enemy's movements, he gave the surprising reply that such a precaution was unnecessary because Palliser's disinclination to respond to signals meant that Keppel would not have risked a chase at night with a depleted force.[15] Later accounts of this episode indicate that Campbell was responsible for this decision. He gave a highly emotional testimonial to Keppel at the first trial, and on the night of 27 July his solicitude may have prompted a decision that inadvertently assisted the French fleet's withdrawal.[16] After Keppel's death, a correspondent to the *Morning Post* recounted Commodore George Johnstone's criticism of the arrangements put in place to watch the French fleet on the night of 27–28th and Campbell's decision to let Keppel sleep on when the enemy fired many signal rockets an hour before midnight. Johnstone was a volatile and undisciplined ministerial speaker with an unsavoury reputation as a duellist. He was not, however, afraid to speak the truth as he saw it. There is some support for his account of Keppel's somnolent role from an unusual quarter.[17] A week after the article on Johnstone appeared, a correspondent to the same newspaper recounted a speech made at a grand Whig celebratory dinner at the Shakespeare Tavern in London. The 'noble lord' who proposed a toast to Keppel allowed that although the admiral was sometimes 'caught napping . . . it was only when the exhausted spirits of Nature yielded to the fatigues of duty'. The French fleet thus escaped by taking advantage of a 'sleepy night'.[18]

Reactions to Palliser's acquittal

In the months following Palliser's acquittal, the high tide of political and public interest in the affair ebbed. The newspaper that played a critical role in setting the direction of the affair continued its campaign, but its interventions were fitful and short-lived. Two days after the verdict, the *General Advertiser* described both trials as 'the prostitution of Courts Martial' and abused Captain Bazely without acknowledging that witnesses whose independence was unquestioned had supported his evidence. Three days later, it printed a snide report of Palliser's recent attendance at the King's levee. He 'received no other mark of his Sovereign's notice, than a *gracious nod*, after which he retired, probably like Sir John Falstaff, *he may be sent for in private*'.[19] At the month's end, a correspondent summoned Jonathan Swift's lines to the Earl of Oxford in the Tower of London to vilify Palliser and warn the King against ever employing him: 'who with traitors would his safety trust?'[20] This piece seems to have been the limit of the *General Advertiser*'s involvement in the affair. Thomas O'Beirne's *Considerations on the Principles of Naval Justice*, a robust pro-Keppel polemic, enlarged on opposition claims about the constitution of Palliser's court and continued its pursuit of George Jackson.[21] For the most part, however, public and professional audiences were better served after the second trial by publications from Palliser's side.

The official minutes and shorthand transcriptions of the trial were advertised in the press, and judging by the number of editions called for, they enjoyed substantial circulation.[22] Although *Thoughts on the Conduct of Admiral Keppel* was written by a supporter of Palliser, its successive editions reflected a careful reading of the records of both trials and provided relatively even-handed comments on them and Keppel's behaviour throughout the affair. The author highlighted the implications for Keppel's position of non-partisan testimony on *Victory's* sailing speed, the timing of *Fox*'s run to *Formidable*, the lowering of the line of battle signal on Keppel's flagship and Palliser's transmission of signals from *Victory*.[23] The author of a pamphlet comparing Hawke, Keppel and Palliser was highly critical of Keppel's presumption in declaring himself unwilling to serve under Sandwich's administration, accusing him of challenging the fundamental principle of subordination out of 'party prejudice and animosity'. Keppel's stance posed a threat to the effectiveness of the navy as a bulwark of the cause of constitutional liberty to which he and his political friends were stridently committed.[24]

Before Palliser's trial, the volume of parliamentary debate on the affair very much favoured his protagonist, but within a year or so, the balance had been redressed. A few days after the trial, Charles James Fox foreshadowed a motion for the minutes to be laid before the house. At this stage, there had been no formal statement of the verdict, so Fox could capitalize on inaccurate versions circulating in the press. He declared the sentence absurd and grossly partial: it 'convicted the vice-admiral of the principal fact alleged, and nevertheless openly permitted the offender to escape with impunity'.[25] Opposition speakers also raised questions about the composition of the court and particularly Captain Walters' membership. In response, Lord North and Commodore Johnstone reminded the House that the judges had sworn to act justly and impartially. Tellingly, however, the debate was dominated by claims about the scandalous weakness of Sandwich's administration, evidenced by discontent in the fleet and a few examples of officers who were unwilling to serve. Fox's motion was defeated by a large majority, thus stopping any plans that he might have had to move for a parliamentary inquiry into Palliser's trial and its outcome. In the following year, however, Sandwich's decision to compensate Palliser by appointing him governor of Greenwich Hospital gave the opposition a fresh opportunity to utilize Palliser in attacks on Sandwich.

In the the Common's debate on the King's speech from the throne in late 1780, Fox described Palliser's appointment as an 'insult ... upon the navy ... [an] object of universal detestation .... The cause of it being given to Sir Hugh ... was not his conduct on board the Formidable, but his subsequent behaviour . . . his attempts to ruin the reputation of that gallant officer' Keppel. The gallant officer joined the fray, accusing Palliser of being responsible for all the dissensions in the Navy, although like Fox, the focus of his attention was on Sandwich's failings.[26] On this occasion, the opposition's claims went pretty much unanswered, but in a later debate on Navy estimates, when Fox said that Palliser had been 'convicted' of 'false and malicious accusation', Lord North, the prime minister, replied (quite correctly) that the court had not found Palliser guilty of that offence. To the contrary, the court 'had exceeded the line of their jurisdiction, and had condemned a man unheard, who had no opportunity of trial, no opportunity of entering upon his defence'. The prime minister went on to make a spirited defence of Palliser, referring in highly favourable terms to his acquittal and the Greenwich Hospital appointment.[27]

More significantly, Fox's gratuitous reference to Palliser allowed him to offer an extended defence of his role in the affair. Since Palliser wrote out this speech, he clearly expected the matter to be raised sooner or later.[28] Palliser highlighted the evidence that justified his acquittal and claimed that it had had a significant impact on his 'former detractors'.[29] He also pointed out that his situation was now virtually identical to Keppel's and chastised the admiral's supporters for failing to acknowledge that: 'We have both been accusers; we have both been accused; we have both been tried; we have both been acquitted. In any one of these points, what can the hon' admiral's friends object to me, without detracting from his own fame, from his merits, his importance, at least in an equal degree?'[30] Palliser, however, avoided pointing to any implications that evidence at his trial might have for Keppel's vindication, adopting an essentially defensive stance to limit the impact of the dispute on 'the public service' and castigating Keppel's supporters in parliament for keeping the issue alive.[31] Keppel's failure to respond effectively to Palliser's speech left unanswered questions about the terms of his own acquittal that could be inferred from it. Early in 1781 they were aired by a naval officer who was far less reticent than Palliser.

Fox again provided the opening for partisans to discuss the trials in parliament. On 1 February 1781 he moved a motion condemning Palliser's appointment to the governorship of Greenwich Hospital. In his speech, Fox continued to play fast and loose with the riders to the courts' verdicts, claiming that his judges had found Palliser guilty of criminal neglect.[32] Lord North rejected this misrepresentation and made a telling point against the repeated criticism of Palliser's 'recrimination' of Keppel: 'Either it must be admitted that the commander in chief accused first, or it can never be said that the vice admiral recriminated.'[33] However, the most powerful contribution to the debate came from the redoubtable Commodore Johnstone, whose speech showed a close knowledge of the details of the trials.

Johnstone opened his speech with the characteristic declaration that he 'would say what he thought'. This stance gave him licence to criticize Palliser for his poor political judgement in bringing Keppel to trial while extolling his bravery and using this and his record to recommend his future employment. Johnstone was highly critical of Keppel's failure to tell the first lord of his reservations on Palliser's performance on the 27th of July, characterizing it as a dereliction of his duty: 'If the vice-admiral . . . had been to blame, he ought to have been stigmatized, not praised. If once commanders overlooked disobedience of orders, there was an end of discipline.'[34] Johnstone's speech tended to dispel the image of entirely blameless virtue propagated by Keppel's supporters and to show that he and Palliser were not without faults in the affair. He thus questioned Keppel's passivity in the face of Palliser's alleged persistent disobedience and was critical of his failure to take measures to guard against the French slipping away unseen on the night of 27–28 July.[35]

When a service colleague reprised Johnstone's speech in response to an adulatory obituary notice of Keppel, he described it as having 'turned the House of Commons, and I may say the nation, from their delirium'.[36] This claim was probably exaggerated, but the debate to which Johnstone contributed undoubtedly marked the end of the affair as a *cause célèbre*. Keppel's response to Johnstone was feeble and merely allowed Palliser to reiterate his earlier claim about how eager Keppel and his friends had been to prevent him addressing the court 'from apprehension that if they had been heard, the court perhaps could not have totally acquitted Mr Keppel or have passed a sentence of malice' upon his accuser. Later in his speech, Palliser pointed to the connection between the 'fair trial' he enjoyed, the acquittal verdict it handed down, and the 'many disagreeable truths' that 'come out in the course of it'.[37] This debate also marked the stage where Keppel's professional reputation and the imperatives of opposition politics had begun to diverge. The Opposition might seek to use Palliser's acquittal to attack Sandwich, but in so doing they exposed Keppel to risks arising from some of the evidence given during his subordinate's trial. He was doubtless relieved that Fox's maladroit motion was the last such debated by parliament.

Keppel's waning star

It is curious that while Keppel was memorialized on English pub signs and in the Whig pantheon erected on Lord Rockingham's estate, he has had no enduring fame as a naval icon. There were no widespread commemorations on his death and a report of a monument in Westminster Abbey proved unfounded.[38] The press reported on his wealth and a legacy of £1000 per annum for Charles James Fox, but obituary accounts of Keppel's naval achievements focused on his career up until the end of the Seven Years' War and drew a veil over the events of 1778–9.[39] When the trials were mentioned in Palliser's obituary notices a decade later, he and his commander-in-chief were both portrayed as victims of 'party violence'.[40] Given the partisan background to the affair, it is ironic that one of Keppel's nephews criticized Edmund Burke's panegyric on Keppel in the *Letter to a Noble Lord* (1796) for wrongly disassociating him from Fox, misrepresenting the character and depth of his political commitments in suggesting that he, like Burke, would have supported the present government.[41] Even in death, Keppel was a token of political partisanship. In other respects, however, the widespread interest in Keppel barely survived beyond the acquittal of his adversary. A range of considerations may account for his eclipse.

In the first place, the public interest aroused by Keppel's trial and the outburst of fevered acclamation that greeted his acquittal was due to his role in the opposition's resistance to the allegedly corrupt tyranny of Lord North's administration. The

Rockingham Whigs were able to play up Keppel's service reputation because of his alleged victimization by Lord Sandwich and his minions. As one of the Pembroke family's correspondents shrewdly observed, Palliser's accusation played a significant role in boosting Keppel's popularity.[42] However, the inference that sympathizers drew from Keppel's acquittal – that if Palliser had not disobeyed his signals, he would have renewed the engagement with the French fleet – did not turn the action into a splendid victory. At most, it relieved Keppel of responsibility for not having seized the opportunity and left him with credit for commanding a fleet in a limited, short-lived and inconclusive action. Thus, Keppel's record as a flag officer was modest even on the most favourable account. By the end of 1779, Lady Pembroke reported that 'it was the opinion of all & seamen too, that Keppel might have made more for us of the 27th than he did, but the moment there was a Court Martial there was an end to knowing any true opinion, for it became a Party affair '.[43] Keppel's less sympathetic contemporaries were quick to make invidious comparisons between his achievements and those of Lord Rodney. Rodney's action occurred after Keppel (now first lord) had decided to recall him, a gift to his political enemies that James Gillray exploited in a print titled 'Rodney Triumphant – Admiral Lee Shore in the Dumps'.

Keppel emerged as a celebrity figure in 1778–9 due to a fleeting combination of factors. First, his limited professional achievements as a commander-in-chief were obscured by the fervid partisan atmosphere that developed over the midwinter of 1778–9. Secondly, his popularity in the service made it easy for his supporters to portray him as a victim of politically motivated injustice. Thirdly, his status as a victim meant that his cause was taken up by anti-ministerial forces 'out of doors', including those on the fringe of formal politics who operated in the popular public sphere. Keppel's celebrity status thus depended upon the momentary alignment of elite, professional and popular forces and was always likely to be short-lived. Within days of his acquittal, Keppel and his political friends already thought it necessary to distance themselves from the more exuberant demonstrations of the ordinary people of London.

Moreover, attempts to paint his modest achievements in heroic colours, and the increasing lack of restraint he showed in making party-political capital out of the affair so qualified the support he enjoyed from within the service that by the early autumn of 1779 Lords Mulgrave and Sandwich could refer sanguinely to 'the remains of Keppel's party'. At the same time, Keppel's extreme politicization of service issues alienated independent members of parliament.[44] Opposition attempts to build Keppel into a hero had an earlier counterpart in the role assigned to Admiral Vernon in the 1741 election campaign but lacked the substantive achievements upon which to build sustained support.[45] Finally, Keppel's popularity had been underwritten by the opposition's campaign against Lord Sandwich's naval administration and its harmful impact on the pursuit of the war. By 1780, Rodney's relief of Gibraltar and subsequent defeat of a Spanish squadron off Cape St Vincent gave the ministry some respite and lowered the temperature of support for Keppel.[46] John Stevenson ('Nautilus'), the naval pamphleteer, was Palliser's admirer but there was much truth in his summary of the situation: 'Many . . . are now ashamed of the late popular *delusion*; and future generations will read the account of our *Keppel-phrenzy*, I presume, with a mixture of wonder and unbelief.'[47]

Evidence at Palliser's trial may also have given cooler and less interested heads beyond the service cause for thought and encouraged them to see Keppel's performance during the affair in a less than heroic light. Within a month of Palliser's acquittal, the rabidly pro-Keppel Lord Pembroke was indignantly warning his son not to believe reports that Keppel's 'vogue' was ending and Palliser's defence worth considering.[48] Insinuating criminal wrongdoing while declining to prefer a charge, and doing so for partisan reasons, was not glorious, and it is difficult to believe that Palliser's cogent post-trial statements on these matters did not have an impact on non-partisan opinion within the service and beyond. It is possible also that when the heat of partisan outrage cooled, Keppel's pronouncements and behaviour may have tempered enthusiasm for him. His determination to report directly to the King on the action and his vague and perfunctory despatch to Lord Sandwich attracted criticism in the press and was noted with concern by the first lord. The King, however, perhaps thinking back to the beginning of his reign and his cosy constitutionally suspect relationship with Lord Bute, the 'minister behind the curtain', approved of Keppel's conduct, ignored Lord Sandwich's complaints about being kept in the dark and told him that the admiral's control of communications was 'an additional proof of his prudence, which can alone be equalled by his resolution in action'.[49] Two years later, the King had changed his tune. In early December 1780, he was highly critical of Keppel's 'illiberal altercation' with Palliser in the House of Commons, noting acidly to the prime minister that he and Lord Howe were 'as usual trying to shew their own significance which they certainly have not Oratory to convince the House of, particularly when their conduct this War cannot justify the Assertion'.[50]

In his defence, Keppel appealed to the sensitivities of senior flag officers by claiming a special discretion for them and throughout the affair made slighting references to Palliser's status as his subordinate. Julia Banister has noted that while Keppel's witnesses were almost all admirals and post captains, Palliser relied heavily on sailing masters to give testimony on issues such as the danger of the lee shore at Ushant.[51] This choice reflected Palliser's appreciation of these officers' professional responsibilities in navigation; it signalled an awareness of significant expertise beyond the charmed circle of the service's conventional elite that had earlier led him to sponsor the rise of able seaman James Cook to the quarterdeck. By contrast, Keppel went out of his way to put masters in their place when their evidence ran counter to his own and dismissed them as unworthy of cross-examination.

As noted earlier, one of Keppel's warmest supporters in the service was disillusioned by the relentless partisanship. Any reservations on that score must have hardened when Keppel brought this mindset to the first lordship.[52] His declared intention of evicting Palliser from the governorship of Greenwich Hospital – a gratuitously vindictive measure that was deplored both by the King and by Lord Lansdowne, a senior cabinet colleague – was a clear manifestation of his ruthless pursuit of party advantage. In short, age, adversity and ill health may thus have conspired with political ambition and vanity to undermine the public profile which carried Keppel through his trial. The charm and good nature that helped him build a significant following in the navy may have begun to wear thin under the strain of a frustrating and exhausting spell as commander-in-chief, the intense anxiety engendered by his court martial and the coarsening effect of parliamentary infighting. When he took office as first lord in 1782, Keppel became fair game. A satirical order of service for 27 July 'as a day of fasting and humiliation' intoned that 'When the fighting man turneth away, and flyeth from his enemy, he shall save his bone whole, and be made a Viscount'.[53]

Pain and rehabilitation: Palliser's post-trial career

The perspective on Palliser's trial reflected in Daniel Baugh's suggestion that Palliser's court found 'his conduct to be no better or worse than Keppel publicly said it was' and that the verdict did him 'little good' is hard to sustain in light of the evidence produced at his trial and its aftermath.[54] Despite the obloquy heaped on Palliser's head over the winter of 1778–9 and the best efforts of Keppel's friends thereafter, Palliser's reputation was rehabilitated to some extent over the last fifteen years of his life.[55] The waning of Keppel's star, the sobering impact of evidence given in his own trial and his restraint set the groundwork for this process. In his vindicatory speech in the House of Commons, Palliser declared that he had no intention of depriving Keppel of any of the benefits of his acquittal and kept to this undertaking. Thus, while he remarked indignantly on 'false' testimony on the timing of *Fox*'s message he did not dwell on its implications for the earlier trial or offer any comment on the conduct of the witnesses who gave it. These matters could have no bearing on his acquittal, but airing them in parliament might have afforded Palliser some retaliatory satisfaction. His restraint may have reflected a genuine concern to avoid raising issues that would impact adversely on the morale of the service at a critical juncture in the war. This consideration would undoubtedly have been uppermost in Lord Sandwich's and the King's minds and Palliser was aware that he could not purposefully prolong the affair without the first lord's political support.[56]

In the months following his acquittal, Palliser was despondent about what he described as the 'general wreck of my fortune and honourable employments'. He faced legal costs of £3000, and unlike Keppel, whose counsel had returned 'presents' of this value that he sent to them, Palliser did not have a private fortune and had lost all forms of professional remuneration except his half pay.[57] The affair's impact on his morale and its perceived impact on his professional standing was even more alarming than the financial cost. Although he made an offer of service to Lord Sandwich at the beginning of July – 'lest it should hereafter be said by ill-natured people that I did not desire to be employed at a time like this' – when a group of West Indian merchants canvassed his appointment to the Leeward Islands command, this unexpected sign of confidence was depressing rather than consoling. He told Lord Sandwich that 'it was a matter I cannot say anything to, that my situation is very singularly critical and dangerous, and my health precarious, that from the treatment I have met with from all quarters I feel myself degraded'.[58] However remote this prospect and one arising in a later canvas of Palliser's name as a potential commander-in-chief in the East Indies, it must at least have provided some assurance of continued professional regard to set against the abuse he had endured during the affair.[59]

Although Sandwich declined Palliser's request to restore him to the Admiralty Board and the lieutenant generalcy of Marines and did not support his hope to succeed

Rodney as Rear Admiral of England, the appointment to the Greenwich governorship involved the first lord in some political cost.[60] This position was less well remunerated than the Marines but attracted significant side benefits, including accommodation in the governor's suite at Greenwich. It was also likely to be more secure than other appointments. Fox and Keppel would have moved with lightning speed to eject Palliser from the Board and the Marines when they came to power in 1782. As it was, nothing came of their belated sabre rattling over the governorship.

In appointing Palliser to this office, Sandwich conferred a lifetime financial benefit that went some way to relieving the impact of the severe financial penalties arising from his conflict with Keppel. The first lord also took a series of steps that bolstered Palliser's sense of professional self-esteem and sent an important signal to service members not blinded by partisan prejudice. Within a few days of his acquittal, the ministry directed the Board of Works to make good the damage inflicted on his house in Pall Mall. This step was seen in the press as signalling the 'countenance and support' Palliser still enjoyed from the government.[61] Sandwich ensured his return as MP for his family seat and continued to consult him on service matters. In 1782, a highly demanding successor at the head of the Navy Board commended Palliser's report on timber stocks at Deptford. He also provided Sandwich with detailed advice on naval operations in the Channel in 1781 and in 1782 wrote an extensive report on the fleet's condition to assist him in a hostile parliamentary inquiry launched when Keppel became first lord.[62] The appreciation of Palliser's professional expertise outlived him. In 1793 he sent a paper on invasion strategies to Prime Minister William Pitt which was reviewed in 1798 by Henry Dundas, the secretary for war, and Lord Spencer, the first lord of the admiralty. Dundas agreed with the line that Palliser had taken and referred to the paper as coming from 'that great and valuable officer, after a life of long and useful experience'.[63]

Keppel had sneered at Palliser's membership of the Court of Trinity House, but his ongoing involvement as an Elder assisted his rehabilitation and provided further opportunities for working with Sandwich.[64] Finally, although Palliser's prolonged exposure to the trials and tribulations of naval courts martial was extraordinarily testing, his disappointments did not blunt his loyalty to Lord Sandwich or weaken his gratitude for the first lord's support. After he left office, Palliser sought permission to signal his appreciation by placing a portrait of Sandwich in a prominent place in Greenwich Hospital.[65]

It seems very likely that Sandwich's post-trial support played a role in the King's subsequent treatment of Palliser. His confidence had been badly shaken by his poor showing during Keppel's trial, and he remained gloomy about his prospects in the early stages of the second trial.[66] These episodes, however, are not relevant in assessing his attitude *after* Palliser's acquittal.[67] Despite some misgivings about the likely political reaction, the King did not resist Sandwich's decision to appoint Palliser to the governorship and was critical of plans to remove him from the post. The fact that he and other members of the royal family made friendly official visits to Greenwich Hospital during Palliser's governorship suggests more than distant forbearance.[68]

Collateral damage

In the wake of the Keppel-Palliser affair, close associates and innocent and marginal figures within and beyond the service suffered collateral damage. Lieutenant General William Keppel, the admiral's brother, was the first high-profile victim. He resigned all his appointments and emoluments as soon as Keppel was charged.[69] Between the trials, George Jackson, the judge advocate, was shamefully manhandled by Keppel's allies in the House of Lords.[70] When Keppel became first lord in 1782, Jackson was dismissed from his second secretaryship of the Admiralty Board, an office in which he was said to have performed admirably.[71] Following revelations of the changes to HMS *Robust*'s logbook, Captain Alexander Hood's London house was sacked by some of Keppel's more unruly admirers. He subsequently got on the wrong side of Lord Sandwich and the King when he resigned his command in protest at the first lord's well-meaning attempt to remove him from the glare of adverse publicity by sending him to North America.[72] Keppel was so disgusted with Commodore Johnstone's speech in the House of Commons in early 1781 that he withdrew a request for him to take one of his followers as a midshipman; the hard-boiled Commodore obliged by discharging the unfortunate individual. This young man suffered momentary disappointment but Keppel's interest probably meant he soon found a place in another ship.[73]

Captain John Bazely's son Henry faced a more humiliating ordeal a few years later. He was a midshipman on a ship on which Commodore the Honourable Leveson-Gower temporarily hoisted his flag. As a captain, Leveson-Gower had been a witness at Keppel's trial and subsequently declined to serve. When Bazely was a guest at his table, the alleged sins of the father were visited on the head of the son. 'The name flashing across the Commodore's recollection, he burst into a violent strain of abuse, and he had the indelicacy, the meanness to provoke the poor boy to tears by harsh, ungenerous, and false reflections on his father's character.'[74] Leveson-Gower was notorious for the strength of his prejudices but other junior officers almost certainly suffered from their association with the leading players in the affair. Competition for promotion and employment was so intense that partisans' prejudices against an officer's connections could be indulged in the silent form of support withheld. In Henry Bazely's case, however, his mistreatment at Leveson-Gower's ungentlemanly hands did not presage a blighted career. He was a very able and personable officer who became a post captain during the French Wars.

There were some humble victims beyond the service too. No doubt many of Keppel's plebeian supporters in Portsmouth and London suffered bruises or worse in their clashes with the forces of law and order. They would undoubtedly have rough-handled anyone who declared for Palliser. Those found guilty of rioting while celebrating Keppel's acquittal included the printer of the *General Advertiser and Morning Intelligencer*, the newspaper which played a critical precipitating role in the affair. At the end of 1780, the *London Evening Post* reported that he was serving a sentence in Newgate Prison for rioting and announced a subscription for the benefit of his family.[75] Those who suffered on Palliser's side included a partially disabled former shipmate who had been one of his servants in Portsmouth and valiantly resisted attempts to destroy the contents of his rented house. Palliser had given this man his 'particular thanks' but when his employment with the vice admiral ceased he found other opportunities blocked because of that connection.[76] Finally, Captain Walters' career was probably too closely identified with his uncle's interest to withstand his departure from the Board. His last command was in early 1779 and he died in 1789, several years before the wars with France opened up new prospects of employment or at least flag promotion on half pay. Walters and his family appear to have lived with Palliser at Greenwich.

Conclusion

Keppel's and Palliser's trials were more dramatic than other courts martial considered in this study and aroused far more excitement in the navy, parliament and 'out of doors'. The bitter antagonism that marked this affair owed much to the fractures in parliament and the service arising from the sharply divisive issue of Britain's armed conflict with its North American colonies. Protagonists' capacity to join their political associates in the House of Commons in rhetorical re-litigation of their trials and court martial experience heightened its dramatic bitterness.

The fissures within the service arising from the affair lingered until the opening years of the French Wars. Lord Howe's victory on 1 June 1794 provided a unifying focus that finally laid them to rest.[77] Howe's personal thanks to Captain John Bazely for his role in the action symbolized the reconciliation process.[78] Many of Howe's captains were resentful that their contributions were not recognized appropriately, but Howe did not allow the events of the late 1770s to obscure his view of Bazely's merits. St Vincent continued to see the hand of the 'Hood faction' behind the discipline-sapping machinations of his enemies in the new century, but that was indicative of his domineering temperament and his relish for confrontation, not of serious ongoing antagonisms within the Navy.[79]

The Keppel-Palliser affair had an impact on three aspects of navy courts martial. First, as noted in an earlier chapter, the experience of Keppel's judges prompted an amendment that ended the practice of confining judges for the duration of a trial. Secondly, another amendment made after Keppel's trial and before Palliser's removed the mandatory death penalty in the thirteenth article of war; this had been a cause of anguish during the Byng affair and raised the judicial and rhetorical stakes of the early stages of the dispute between Keppel and Palliser.[80] Finally, these officers' reluctance to report officially on their opponent's alleged shortcomings may have had an impact on the Admiralty Board's radically revised and enlarged *Regulations and Instructions* of 1806. Officers were now instructed explicitly on their responsibility for 'censuring, punishing, or reporting to his Superior . . . those whose misconduct deserve it'. Commanders-in-chief were enjoined never to suffer 'neglect or in any one to pass unnoticed' and to report on conduct in action 'without partiality or affection'.[81] Had these regulations been in force in 1778, Keppel would not have had the option of formally ignoring Palliser's misconduct and impeding the Board's investigation of it.

In the wake of the affair, Lord Sandwich expressed concern at the Board's limited capacity to act effectively against recalcitrant senior officers. He complained of the 'state of our political system, and the weakness which I perceive in government, who,

I think, can bring no inquiry into the misconduct of their generals or admirals to a fair and impartial decision'.[82] As the toxic partisan atmosphere dissipated, these fears proved to be largely unfounded. As we shall see in the following chapters, however, the relationship between first lords and flag officers, the discretion of commanders-in-chief, intra-service solidarity and contextual considerations continued to play significant roles in determining whether flag officers faced courts martial and how they fared as a result of them.

6

The Limits of Discretion

Vice Admiral William Cornwallis and Lord Spencer, 1796

Captain the Honourable William Cornwallis was among a large group of senior naval officers who deplored the Earl of Sandwich's decision to court martial Admiral Keppel. A decade and a half later Cornwallis, now a vice admiral and commander-in-chief of the Leeward Islands, found himself in a similar situation when Lord Spencer's Board ordered him to be tried for not following its instructions and disobeying a direct order. Although the court returned a largely favourable mixed verdict, Cornwallis' resentment at being charged removed him from active service for five years. Before his trial, Cornwallis and senior colleagues were at loggerheads with their political masters over whether soldiers should be subject to naval discipline when serving on ships, but this dispute was not a weapon in a partisan attack on the first lord and the government. To the contrary, Cornwallis' family's connections aligned with the ministry rather than pitching him in opposition to it. Although he was an MP for forty-one years, Cornwallis never spoke in the House of Commons and was averse to intruding partisan political concerns into professional life. That did not mean, however, that he was an easy officer to manage. In the wake of Keppel's trial, Cornwallis responded to what he saw as Lord Sandwich's failure to find him a suitable command by accusing him of bad faith and threatening to give up his current employment: 'I must conclude that these expressions that your Lordship honoured me with were mere matter of civility and that your Lordship had no real intention of doing me a service.' This correspondence did not openly evoke political considerations and Cornwallis promptly offered a half apology 'if improper expressions . . . had given you offence' but it demonstrates his capacity for ill-judged interactions with his superiors.[1]

William Cornwallis was the second son of the first Earl Cornwallis, the head of a family whose ancestors had been baronets in Elizabeth's reign and whose place in the English peerage went back to the mid seventeenth century.[2] The Cornwallises were entrenched among the Whig aristocracy after the Glorious Revolution, but in the mid-1780s, William's older brother Charles, a soldier and a statesman, became an admiring supporter of the Tory prime minister William Pitt. He had inherited the earldom in

1762 and was raised to the marquisate in 1788 on being appointed governor-general of Bengal. At the time of the court martial he held cabinet rank as Master General of Ordnance. His younger brother joined the navy at the age of eleven in 1755, and having seen significant action as a midshipman during the Seven Years' War, his service record and family interest enabled him to progress rapidly to post rank. He was thus well-placed to gain active service appointments in the American War and was employed throughout that conflict. Following a successful command of the East Indies squadron during his brother's governorship, William Cornwallis was promoted to rear admiral in 1794 and became a vice admiral the following year. His service as a subordinate flag officer in Lord Bridport's Channel Fleet included a fighting retreat in the face of a significantly superior French squadron that won him the admiration of his professional colleagues and the plaudits of politicians and the press. Lord Spencer subsequently appointed him to command the naval forces in a large-scale expedition to the West Indies.

Cornwallis lacked Keppel's charisma but service colleagues admired his courage, professional excellence and leadership. His capacity for personal kindness formed the basis of warm friendships with Nelson, Lord Hood and St Vincent. Although Cornwallis was as jealous of his honour as Keppel, he was entirely free of the vanity which Keppel displayed in the Keppel-Palliser affair. Following his famous rear-guard action, he firmly resisted pressure from Lord Spencer to accept the King's enthusiastic offer of a coveted knighthood of the Bath. He apparently thought that only victories merited honours and did not see his sense of professional value and personal dignity as reliant upon them. Royal honours were 'very well in their way, but . . . [w]orth makes the man and want of it the fellow'.[3]

On his arrival in India, the diarist William Hickey recorded the jarring effect of Cornwallis' 'roughness of address and manners' on the sensibilities of the merchant and legal elite of Calcutta. Since Hickey was told that Cornwallis' prickly demeanour was 'assumed' it probably reflected his contempt for the nabobs' self-importance, self-indulgence and self-interest.[4] Cornwallis' intransigent reaction to his court martial and its aftermath showed that this lack of balance in personal relations became entrenched as he got older. He had apologized to Sandwich but showed no signs of doing so to Lord Spencer.

The context of Cornwallis' court martial: Dundas' West Indian strategy

Cornwallis' appointment to the West Indian command was a critical element in advancing a regional strategy developed by Henry Dundas, Secretary of State for the Home Department and Colonies and then Secretary of State for War.[5] When war with France broke out in 1793, Dundas prioritized seizing its West Indian colonies and ensuring the defence of British possessions in the area. The French West Indian trade in sugar, coffee and cotton produced large amounts of revenue and played a crucial role in sustaining the state's maritime workforce. British conquests in the islands would divert revenue to its war effort, deprive the French of a nursery of seamen for its navy and serve as bargaining counters to protect the country's European interests in peace negotiations. When Lord Spencer took his seat at the head of the Admiralty Board in mid-December 1794, he immediately assumed responsibility for the naval aspects of a major combined service operation in the West Indies.

Given that operations of this kind relied on effective collaboration between the army and the navy, it was particularly unfortunate that the ministry launched it against the backdrop of the unsettled dispute with the army. When the army commander-in-chief, the (royal) Duke of York, issued clarificatory regulations, it provoked a protest of flag officers at Portsmouth that would have been condemned as mutinous if made by men from the lower deck. In the short term, the flexibility of the expeditionary force commander (Lieutenant General Ralph Abercromby) and a concerted effort by the Admiralty Board to replace soldiers with marines defused the dispute. These measures did not, however, address the fundamental question of the authority of naval captains over army personnel. Nor did they alleviate some senior flag officers' resentment at a perceived bias towards the army within the ministry or convince them that Lord Spencer had been wholeheartedly committed to counteracting it. His initial handling of the appointment of a new naval commander-in-chief to the Leeward Islands station did nothing to relieve these concerns.

Spencer and Dundas believed that the senior flag officer on the station would not be suitable for the new role. Vice Admiral Sir John Laforey, experienced but elderly and in indifferent health, had been reprimanded recently by Spencer for being insufficiently energetic.[6] It is likely also that an ongoing dispute with his second-in-command and strained relations with local elites indicated that his temper was ill-suited to the challenges of inter-service collaboration. That was undoubtedly Dundas' view, and he made it clear to Spencer that he thought Laforey should be superseded and replaced by Rear Admiral Hugh Christian. Dundas' preference for Christian was due to his experience working effectively with the army as chair of the Transport Board. In the event, naval sensitivities to Christian's lack of seniority and suspicion of his close relationship with the army led Spencer to recall Laforey and give the overall command to a more senior officer. Spencer's decision to supersede Laforey angered Sir Charles Middleton, the senior naval commissioner, and led to his ill-tempered resignation from the Board. His appointment of Cornwallis in Laforey's place caused considerable difficulties for his relationships with Dundas, Abercromby, Christian and Cornwallis himself.

In November 1795, Cornwallis had told Spencer that the dispute with the army was of such importance that it might result in an officer declining to serve. This stance recalled the line some opponents of Lord North's administration took during the American War. When Cornwallis was appointed commander-in-chief in late January 1796, he again raised the question, noting that Abercromby's accommodation relied on the personal disposition of the parties involved and might not survive a change of key personnel.[7] In a letter sent to Spencer shortly before he sailed, Cornwallis told him that he would not have accepted the command if he had known of the situation and expressed a 'sincere desire' to be relieved. Spencer sidestepped this request by stressing the Board's confidence in him and asked Rear Admiral Young, one of the naval commissioners, to arrange for a colleague in Portsmouth to talk with Cornwallis. Sir Roger Curtis reported that he was still very agitated on the 'military question' and had not accepted Spencer's assurances. Cornwallis wanted definitive instructions 'and was in expectation of receiving information before he sailed'.[8]

Cornwallis' reservations on the army discipline question and other concerns over the quality of some of the ships and captains placed under his command must have tried the first lord's patience, especially as he raised them when Spencer was fending off challenges to his appointment from Abercromby and Christian. Spencer would not entertain any interference from Abercromby and had a very tense interview with Christian over his objections to the Board placing a senior officer above him. Although Spencer doubted whether Christian should go to the West Indies after raising these difficulties, he determined not to relieve him.[9]

The Board ordered Cornwallis to take a convoy to the West Indies and assume his duties there. There were some delays due to bad weather and the need to pay the men, but the convoy finally cleared St Helen's on the last day of February, accompanied by a small squadron commanded (under Admiralty orders) by Sir Charles Cotton. The fleet almost immediately encountered rough weather in which Cornwallis' flagship, the *Royal Sovereign*, was badly damaged in a collision. He continued to convoy the troopships until they were clear of the Channel and then, having handed over to Cotton, returned to Spithead so his flagship could be repaired.

When Cornwallis arrived at Spithead in mid-March, he received news of his appointment to the valuable sinecure of rear-admiral of England. In a separate communication, however, the Board disapproved of Cornwallis' decision to return home rather than shifting his flag to Cotton's *Minotaur* and continuing to the West Indies in that ship. When it ordered him to sail immediately in the frigate HMS *Astraea*, Cornwallis remonstrated to Spencer that he was 'not able' to sail in this ship because of his precarious state of health. He was also concerned that *Astraea* was not fitted out for West Indian service, was not an appropriate flagship and could not accommodate his trusted followers. Spencer brushed these objections aside, telling Cornwallis that his response was tantamount to relinquishing his appointment and thus jeopardizing his future employment.[10] Having initially instructed him to continue flying his flag in the *Royal Sovereign*, the Board ordered Cornwallis to be court-martialled. This decision, which aroused significant resentment in the service and adverse commentary in the press, must be understood in the context of Britain's West Indian strategy and Spencer's difficulties over the army issue.

The expedition placed a massive strain upon the government's logistical, military and financial resources and pushed the machinery of the state beyond its capacities.[11] Dundas' timelines had already begun to slip badly and threatened to compromise the imperative of completing the campaigning season before the onset of heavy summer rains and sickly climatic conditions. All government agencies supporting the navy and the army felt the burden of logistical overload, but its political weight and much of the high-level management fell on Dundas' already heavily loaded shoulders.[12] In light of his absorption in complex arrangements to source ordnance, medical supplies, provisions, troops, transports and a large naval force, it is not surprising that the Secretary of State showed little patience with what he saw as Spencer's prevarications and the issues of naval 'etiquette' invoked to justify them. Having finally appointed Cornwallis over Abercromby's objections (with which Dundas sympathized) and ordered him to sail immediately with a large convoy, Cornwallis' return to Spithead and refusal to sail in *Astraea* placed Spencer in a very difficult situation. There is no record of Dundas' reaction to Cornwallis' noncompliant conduct, but his sharp impatience with Spencer and the Board and his personal and political stake in the expedition make it very likely that he placed pressure on the first lord to act. Cornwallis' role in the admirals' protest probably made it less rather than more likely that the first lord would overlook his latest transgressions.

The Marquis Cornwallis attempted to avert what was threatening to become a highly damaging episode in his brother's career and a source of pain and embarrassment to himself. He was deeply worried at the prospect of a court martial and sceptical of his brother's justifications for his conduct.[13] He thought the real issue was Cornwallis' determination not to sail without his highly favoured flag captain, Captain John Whitby, and was alarmed at his brother's claim that the Board's order to sail on *Astraea* 'could not have been in earnest, . . . but has been intended to affront me, and put me on shore': 'After all that has passed, can such suspicions be combatted by any rational argument?'[14] The Marquis wished to persuade his brother to offer concessions to the first lord and begged Spencer to stay his hand until he had had the chance to visit him: 'I am convinced that you will make allowance for my feelings on the present distressing occasion, and forgive my endeavouring . . . to avert the evils of a Court Martial.'[15] In the event, 'adequate concessions' were not forthcoming and William Cornwallis was summoned to trial nine days later. His truculently fatalistic response to his elder brother's overtures reflected a state of mind that made the trial outcome more damaging than it might have been. Cornwallis told the Marquis that the court martial might as well come on as not: 'I really think whatever my fate may be, that it would be for the good of the service, and of course the country, to have the matter canvassed, that it may be ascertained to what stretch an officer in my situation is liable to be degraded and insulted.'[16]

The trial

On the morning of Cornwallis' court martial Lord Howe led the judges across Portsmouth Harbour to HMS *Orion* in a string of barges with each officer's flag flying in the bow of their boat.[17] This unusual ceremony probably demonstrated the court's solidarity with a colleague who had upheld the honour of the service in the dispute with the army and had now, in its view, been made a scapegoat. The two-day trial contrasted sharply with the marathons endured by Keppel and Palliser. The witnesses' testimony and the accused's defence were completed by early afternoon of the first day, and the court then deliberated for 'several hours'. After Cornwallis declined to provide additional evidence in his defence, the judges spent 'some hours' in further deliberation the next morning.[18]

If the trial was unusually short, the court was unusually, indeed uniquely, well-stocked with admirals. Cornwallis' fears that Lord Spencer would remove flag officers from the station proved groundless. The secretary of the Board told him that while the needs of the service might require the departure of 'one or more' flag officers before the court convened, the Board 'are equally desirous with you that a Court, as respectable as possible, should be assembled on this Occasion' and that 'there will remain at Portsmouth a greater Number of Flag Officers than has ever sat upon the Trial of a Flag Officer'.[19] Earl Howe, the Admiral of the Fleet, was joined by nine other admirals (including Sir Roger Curtis) and three post captains. There were three future admirals of the fleet among the judges, two officers who succeeded Howe as commanders of the Channel fleet and five other flag officers who regularly held commands at sea.[20] The number and quality of flag officers on the court signalled the significance of the trial for the service as well as for the accused. Curtis' membership was potentially significant in light of his knowledge of Cornwallis' attitude towards his command as he left Portsmouth.

Unlike Palliser's trial, Cornwallis' began with a clearly framed charge. The Board spelt out the details in its letter of direction to the president. The court martial was to

> inquire into the Conduct of the said Vice Admiral . . . in returning to Spithead . . . and to try him for the same; to try him for Disobedience of our Order . . . in not proceeding to Barbadoes [*sic*] as expeditiously as possible . . . and also to try him for Disobedience . . . by declining to proceed to Barbadoes in the *Astraea*, as . . . directed.[21]

As in other courts martial, the statement of charge was accompanied by supporting correspondence between the accused and the Board. In terms of Lord Spencer's attitude towards the prosecution, it is significant that he did not produce the letter in which Cornwallis indicated he wished to resign the command. Had he done so it would have shed potentially damaging light on Cornwallis' actions at sea and on his return to Spithead.

While Palliser's judges were very active in examining witnesses, Cornwallis' highly distinguished court was notable for its implacable reticence. It asked only eleven questions of prosecution witnesses and three questions of witnesses called by the accused. The court called Captain Sir Charles Cotton and Edward Tippet, the Master Shipwright of Portsmouth Dockyard. Its questioning of these witnesses was minimal and there was no cross-examination by the accused. Cotton produced his Admiralty orders and Cornwallis' order to accompany his convoy and was asked by the court whether he showed the former to Cornwallis. Tippet testified to the damage to *Royal Sovereign*, its unserviceability and the impossibility of making good this damage in the West Indies.[22] These questions concerned matters of fact arising from Cornwallis' journal and his correspondence with the Board. The question put to Cotton related to Cornwallis' professed reluctance to interfere with his command by shifting his flag into HMS *Minotaur* and thus preventing the squadron from fulfilling its Admiralty orders; that posed to Tippet bore on the justifiability of Cornwallis' decision to return to England to repair the *Royal Sovereign*.

Cornwallis called only three witnesses, and he questioned them very briefly. His flag captain, John Whitby, testified to Cornwallis' 'readiness' to carry out his orders to proceed to the West Indies, to explore options to repair the *Royal Sovereign* without returning to Portsmouth and the state of his commander-in-chief's health. The master of the *Royal Sovereign* confirmed Whitby's testimony on repair options and the vice admiral's keenness to fulfil his orders; the surgeon testified very briefly to the precarious state of Cornwallis' health by confirming 'violent attacks' of a bowel complaint and 'fits' of gout.[23]

These factual matters played a justificatory role in Cornwallis' extensive statement of defence, a document that effectively comprised the substance of the trial. It occupied eight pages of the printed minutes; the evidence of prosecution and defence witnesses ran to three and a half pages and was supported by seven pages of correspondence and five pages extracted from Cornwallis' journal. Thomas Erskine, now firmly established as a leading figure at the London bar, read the statement on his client's behalf. Given his role in composing Keppel's defence, it seems reasonable to assume that he would have assisted Cornwallis in explaining and justifying his actions.[24]

Whatever role Erskine might have played in framing Cornwallis' defence, its opening statements carry the authentic ring of a distinguished flag officer devoted to his profession and fully aware of senior officers' reactions to recent challenges to the rights of the service. Cornwallis told the court that if the charges against him were well-founded, they would 'at once deprive me of the Comfort I have enjoyed in the Reflection of having assiduously and zealously, if not successfully, devoted my whole Life to the Duties of my Profession, and the service of my Country'. He then referred to his 'anxiety' that 'the Defence . . . which I have thus humbly to lay before you should be very distinctly understood, is greatly increased by the Regard I must feel for the Dignity and Independence of the Navy' and warned of the implications of an adverse verdict for the professional 'honour' and 'character' of members of the court.[25] These sentiments are entirely consistent with what we know of Cornwallis' personal and professional commitments and also accord with values to which the court members adhered.

The doctrine of discretion Cornwallis used to justify his return to Spithead was presented in a similar light. He justified his actions as a particular exemplification of a long-standing principle of the service:

> By the Customs of the Service . . . superior Officers have never been held responsible in their Lives and Stations, or in their Characters, which are dearer than both, for mere Differences of Judgement . . . more especially when the Act or Transaction to be judged of has been followed by no disastrous Consequences, nor has drawn after it any Inconvenience to the Public.[26]

The discretion that Cornwallis claimed was not absolute; it was conditioned by flag officers' overarching duty and the consequences of their actions, and hence the particular context in which they exercised it. He thus told the court that if his conduct

> appears to you to have been criminally weak and ignorant, it may be censured or punished at your Discretion, but unless you are prepared to pronounce against me this disqualifying and mortifying Judgement, I am persuaded that you will not

> reduce the Condition and Character of a superior Officer to a perilous and servile Dependence upon the Shades and Varieties of Judgement.[27]

Cornwallis argued that he acted in conformity with his instructions in prioritizing the safe despatch of the convoy and no ill consequences followed from his decision to return to England in the *Royal Sovereign*. He claimed that since the ships in Cotton's squadron were not fitted out for West Indian service, he could not have used one as his flagship on the Leeward Island station. That being so, his discretionary judgement was that delays arising from repair of the *Royal Sovereign* would be more than offset by the advantage to the service (rather than to his personal convenience) of arriving on the station in a properly fitted-out ship accompanied by trusted staff to support him in the fulfilment of his responsibilities.

Cornwallis accompanied these claims with the far less plausible argument that he had not received any intimation of the urgency of taking over from Sir John Laforey 'until after I had taken the Measure which has been disapproved of and returned back again into Port'.[28] This line of defence smacks of lawyerly ingenuity and may have reflected one of Erskine's contributions to Cornwallis' defence. It is true that the Board did not spell out the urgent need to replace Laforey in Cornwallis' instructions. Still, it clearly expected him to take over the command as soon as he arrived on the station: 'you are to take under your Command such of His Majesty's Ships and Vessels as you may find on that Station, and carry into Execution the Instructions which you will receive herewith, as well as such standing or unexecuted Orders as may be delivered to you by Admiral Sir John Laforey'.[29] The wording of this order followed the standard form and could reasonably be taken to convey the Board's usual determination to brook no delays.

Moreover, during Cornwallis' last-minute wrangling with Spencer, the first lord referred to 'the Service on which you are so urgently called to proceed'. He received sailing orders to the same effect.[30] It was thus disingenuous of Cornwallis to tell the Secretary of the Board that he did not think it required his 'immediate presence' in the West Indies 'particularly as there is an Officer there of higher rank than myself, who probably, for any Thing I am acquainted with, might have staid some Time after my Arrival'.[31] This embellishment was inconsistent with Cornwallis' instructions and relied upon the implausible assumption that he was entirely ignorant of the background to his appointment. That included the sharply differing views over whether Laforey should be recalled in favour of Rear Admiral Christian, the acceptability of such an appointment within the upper ranks of the service and the need for the expedition to achieve its objectives before the onset of the 'sickly season'.

Given all these considerations, the first lord must have been embarrassed to learn of Cornwallis' return to Spithead and deeply irritated by the reasons he gave for it. That the Board did not immediately reprimand him did not necessarily mean his conduct was unobjectionable.[32] Cornwallis assumed quite wrongly that the Board had no discretion over issuing reprimands or laying charges and that in this case it could have justifiably argued that its order to sail immediately in *Astraea* demonstrated the importance it placed on him replacing Laforey in the West Indian command. While Cornwallis was correct in saying, 'Had I sailed again in the *Astraea*, I could not surely then have been arraigned for my return in the *Royal Sovereign*', he was wrong to assume that this matter might not be an object of charge in other circumstances.[33] His refusal to leave in *Astraea* created a situation where the Board, having discretion on whether questionable conduct should be subject to courts martial, decided to lay charges for both alleged failures of duty.

Cornwallis' defence against the *Astraea* charge was in two parts. He argued that a winter Atlantic crossing in such a small vessel would undermine his fragile health and thus compromise his performance as commander-in-chief. It would also restrict the number and range of staff and followers he could take with him and deprive him of the support necessary for his comfort and effectiveness. Arguments along these lines would not usually justify disobedience to a direct instruction, so Cornwallis' defence offered the novel suggestion that the order was not really an order and that he had not in any case refused to obey it. He claimed that an instruction for a vice admiral and commander-in-chief to sail in a frigate was a mark of the Board's displeasure rather than a serious proposition. Presented in this light, Cornwallis' response was not an act of disobedience but a reasoned statement of objection (a 'representation') proposing an alternative that was in the best interests of the service.[34]

In justifying this position, Cornwallis referred to the widely recognized rights of all those in high office: 'When a Communication is made, accompanied with a Reason for declining the Execution of an Order, the Reason has always been taken to be a Submission of its Validity to the Power which is to decide upon it ... . Upon this Principle I acted, and upon this Principle I rest my Defence.'[35] Whatever the value of this statement in an exercise in jurisprudence, it was open to the objection that Captain the Honourable Thomas Pakenham made on the flag officers' protest against the Admiralty Board's promulgation of the Duke of York's instructions: 'it is as great an outrage against naval discipline and the plain intention and obvious construction of the Articles of War, as if it had happened among any inferior officers or men in his Majesty's navy.'[36]

Spencer's handling of some exchanges that preceded Cornwallis' court martial showed signs of the uncertainty in his approach to earlier episodes in naval preparations for the second West Indian expedition. Given the questions over Cornwallis' return to Spithead, the timing of the message appointing him rear admiral of England was unfortunate, to say the least. Moreover, as Cornwallis noted in his defence, Spencer had written that he had given '*very* satisfactory Reasons' for returning to England on the *Royal Sovereign* and had initially seen his disinclination to sail on *Astraea* as a statement of resignation rather than an act of disobedience.[37]

These lapses did not have any bearing on whether Cornwallis acted wrongly in not transferring his flag to one of Cotton's ships or had been disobedient in declining to sail in the *Astraea*. They were, however, significant in terms of Spencer's management of Cornwallis and had at least some rhetorical force in the undertow of complaint at being called to court-martial that ran through Cornwallis' defence. Thus, while he used the idea of commanders-in-chief's discretion to defend his decision to return in the *Royal Sovereign*, he sometimes suggested that this discretion meant that he should not have been made answerable before a court martial for acting on it. Cornwallis argued,

> If the Opinion I thus formed, under all these Circumstances, was not the best which might have been adopted by an unerring Judgement, I deeply lament it, and cheerfully submit to have it corrected by the Judgement of the Court. Yet for the Honour and Advantage of the Service, I feel an Interest beyond myself, in claiming for a Flag Officer, charged with a high Command, the Exercise of a reasonable Discretion in Service, if to your Justice it shall appear that I acted to the best of an honest Judgement.[38]

He also complained, however, that 'It seems therefore hard, that an Officer should be subjected to a Court Martial for not having exercised a Discretion for the Exercise of which he must have been subject to a Court Martial also.'[39]

Cornwallis returned to this point in thinly veiled criticisms of the Board in the concluding section of his defence. He reiterated that a commander-in-chief must 'proceed upon his own Views and Opinions' and observed that 'officers witnesses to his proceedings' had not criticized his conduct. In calling him to court martial the Board risked undermining 'that Firmness and confidence, which is essentially necessary to high Command', compromising his character – it 'suffers from rash Question, as well as from Condemnation' – ungratefully ignoring a lifetime commitment to the service and betraying an entirely unwarranted lack of trust. Cornwallis' defence concluded with a heartfelt appeal to the court: 'I feel more than I can express upon this Subject, and I speak myself to those who cannot but feel along with me. My own Conscience acquits me of all Blame, and if your Judgement shall fortunately confirm it, my Satisfaction will be complete.'[40]

The court's response to this appeal was almost certainly not as clear-cut as Cornwallis hoped. It found that

> Misconduct is imputable to the Vice Admiral for not having proceeded to the West Indies either in the *Mars* or *Minotaur* . . . but, in Consideration of the Circumstances of the Case, they do acquit him of any further Censure on that Account: The Court is also of Opinion, that the Charge of Disobedience of the Order of the Lords Commissioners of the Admiralty . . . by declining to proceed to Bardadoes [*sic*] in the *Astraea*, is not proved; they therefore acquit him thereof; and he is hereby acquitted accordingly.[41]

The *Times* reported that the windows and doors of the captain's cabin were locked while the court deliberated, and perhaps for that reason, there were no press accounts of leaks to fuel speculation on voting.[42] However, the fact that the court took such a long time deliberating on a short hearing and asked Cornwallis on the second day if he had anything further to offer in his defence suggests considerable debate on the outcome. There is no indication of the role that Lord Howe played in the court's deliberations, but as far as one can decipher from his opaque statement on the charges in advance of the trial, he seems to have thought that Cornwallis was guilty on the *Astraea* charge. There appeared to be 'strong ground for disapprobation' and Cornwallis' letter of refusal 'contains all the requisite proofs thereto'.[43] If these were Howe's views, they were not reflected in the verdict, nor is there any indication of the role that Sir Roger Curtis' inside knowledge played in it.

While the court regarded Cornwallis' decision to return in the *Royal Sovereign* as 'censurable' misconduct, the fact that it believed its statement to that effect was an appropriate response might mean that it thought Cornwallis' claims to discretion allowed for distinctions between marginal errors in judgement on a non-critical matter on the one hand, and 'criminally weak and ignorance' conduct on the other. Since this notion of discretion did not apply to the second charge, the court's 'not proven' verdict could only be justified on the dangerous grounds that commanders-in-chief had the right to wrangle with superiors over whether or not to obey particular orders. In this case, however, the verdict probably had less to do with the facts of the case than with signalling an endorsement of Cornwallis' deep resentment at being charged and flag officers' displeasure with Spencer's failure to protect the service from perceived slights to it. It was thus an expression of service solidarity in the guise of a judicial verdict. By contrast, the first part of the verdict dealt with a relatively straightforward matter of professional judgement on operational instructions unrelated to inter-service rivalry and political favouritism.

As the *Times* reported that Cornwallis was 'very cheerful and quite collected during the whole of the trial' and 'appeared both from his behaviour and his language to have no doubt of being honourably acquitted', he was probably surprised by the court's verdict.[44] The crew of the *Royal Sovereign* came up on deck and gave three cheers when they heard the verdict, but their flag officer's reaction was far more restrained.[45] The press reported Cornwallis as listening 'without any emotion', then making a 'slight bow to the court' before retiring with Erskine and other 'friends'.[46] Three days later, the proprietors of the Fountain Inn in Portsmouth again benefited from a post-court martial celebration. On this occasion, the officers of the *Royal Sovereign* gave what the *Morning Post* described as a 'most elegant entertainment' to Cornwallis and 'other officers' of distinction. Toasts to the vice admiral and Erskine were drunk 'with enthusiasm'. The toast to Cornwallis was accompanied by a rendition of 'See the Conquering Hero Comes', perhaps with the Lords Commissioners of the Admiralty as well as the French in mind.[47]

Aftermath: Cornwallis' reaction

Cornwallis' slight bow to the court maintained the external appearance of 'great composure and firmness' which marked his conduct throughout the trial but is unlikely to have portrayed his inner feelings.[48] As we have seen, he had refused to make concessions to avoid a court martial and made it quite clear the Board's treatment of him and its decision to bring him to trial angered him. The experience of the trial and the element of equivocation in the court's findings would have done nothing to lighten his mood. Sir John Barrow, Lord Howe's biographer, later claimed that the court acquitted Cornwallis of disobedience on the first charge, but that does not accord with the language of the verdict or contemporary reactions to it. In a letter to the *Morning Post*, the radical pamphleteer Joseph Cawthorne derided the verdict as an '*Iricism*': Cornwallis was guilty and not guilty at the same time.[49] A similar point was made by the Whig orator and dramatist Richard Sheridan in a witty aside in a debate on a motion for an inquiry into the conduct of the war. Sheridan criticized the ministry for resisting the motion, pointing out that it was keen enough to investigate the conduct of a 'gallant admiral' and suggesting that the verdict should encourage it to take its chances before parliament: 'the sentence of that court was truly extraordinary – that he was right and wrong; that he deserved censure and credit for his conduct. Perhaps if the House went into the inquiry, a similar judgement might be passed on ministers.'[50]

Pride and service solidarity probably made Cornwallis reluctant to comment publicly on his trial, but Erskine's client probably shared his 'chagrin and disgust on the proceedings'.[51] The misconduct finding must have been a blow to Cornwallis' professional pride and compared with Keppel's verdict, and even Palliser's, the court's language was not fulsome. There was no reference to an honourable acquittal, and the Scottish verdict of 'not proven' said more about the passivity of the judges than the virtues of the accused. The unsubstantial nature of the court's enquiry meant that the prosecution effectively rested on the statement of charge, and the acquittal did not emerge from a close or prolonged examination of witnesses.

The court's approach may have reflected its members' objection to Cornwallis being brought to trial, but it limited the scope for public exoneration, which had made Keppel's court martial a triumph. It also resulted in proceedings so bland and brief that there was very little for the press to get its teeth into. The *Morning Post*, which described the trial as 'very important in the principle as it regards the discretion of British officers in High Command', published an item criticizing Lord Spencer for his 'precipitate conduct with regard to Admiral Cornwallis' and advised him that he 'can never expect popularity in the Navy, if in every sudden fit of spleen he brings an Officer of such acknowledged gallantry and skill to a Court Martial'.[52] With this exception, the press gave only limited coverage of the case. Several papers published transcripts of the hearings, Cornwallis' defence, and some details of the proceedings. The *Times* provided sympathetic commentary on the trial, held the press for the verdict and reprinted it the next day.[53]

In the week of the trial, Samuel Grenville advised Lord Spencer that he expected the parliamentary opposition to 'take some advantage' of the affair, but nothing substantial came of that.[54] Apart from Sheridan's jocular, opportunistic reference, the trial only received one further brief mention in parliament. In the course of a 'state of the nation' debate in the House of Lords, Lord Lansdowne 'lamented the interruption which the service had sustained by the Court Martial' and urged the Board to take the steps necessary to re-appoint Cornwallis to a major command.[55] Two weeks earlier, Lansdowne had written an encouraging letter to Cornwallis on the same theme: 'very few things would give me more concern than that this country should be deprived of the service . . . of one of the first officers of Europe'.[56]

It has been claimed that Cornwallis contemplated raising his own case in the House of Commons if he could secure Pitt's support.[57] There is no evidence of that and it seems highly unlikely. Cornwallis never spoke in parliament, and if it is hard to imagine that he would break his silence to plead on his own account, it is even more implausible he would have made Pitt's support a condition for doing so. That would have set the prime minister at odds with the first lord of the admiralty and the secretary of state, and put him in the same camp as the ministry's inveterate opponents. If the account of

Cornwallis' intentions is accurate, it merely shows the damage inflicted on his powers of judgement by the strains of the previous months.

Before the trial, Cornwallis was inclined to blame 'the Board' but in its aftermath he came to think that Lord Spencer was the prime mover.[58] This shift may have been due to accounts of Spencer's role behind the scenes or to the tendency toward paranoia which reoccurred at the end of Cornwallis' Channel command. On this occasion, he reacted angrily to Marquis Cornwallis' attempts to help him salvage his career. The Marquis was on good terms with Spencer, and there is no indication that he was sceptical of the first lord's private assurance that he was satisfied with the trial's outcome and that the court martial was a 'necessity . . . my public duty imposed on me'.[59] He was alarmed by his brother's vilification of Spencer's 'most violent and arbitrary proceedings', the 'cruel persecution' and the 'unmerited attack which he commenced against me'.[60] It is significant that a decade later, Marquis Cornwallis still thought that his brother's actions were very unwise and had posed a grave threat to his professional future.[61]

The outcome of Cornwallis' trial provided mute testimony of some senior flag officers' views on Spencer's handling of the case, but contemporary and later opinion is mixed. Lord Howe's views before the trial have already been noted, and Nelson, although a close friend of Cornwallis, also expressed some reservations. He told Collingwood that it could not be right for him to have 'deserted his command' and suspected that 'some ill-treatment of the Admiralty after he sailed . . . induced him to return'.[62] None of the evidence given at Cornwallis' trial confirmed this suspicion. William Dillon recalled the 'extraordinary feeling' generated among the officer class in Portsmouth during the trial. He also noted that 'many' opinions circulated on the affair and offered his view that Spencer 'acted with proper spirit'.[63] Andrew Lambert set his treatment of Cornwallis' court martial in the context of criticisms of Spencer's handling of the dispute with the army, the replacement of Sir Charles Middleton at the Board by the 'significantly more compliant' Sir James Gambier and his (politically motivated) dismissal of Lord Hood from the Mediterranean command.[64] Cornwallis' family biographer and the author of the definitive study of the West Indian strategy are far more sympathetic to Spencer.[65] So too is Michael Lewis. He outlines the difficulty of Spencer's position, hedged in as he was by impatient cabinet colleagues such as Dundas, his regard for Marquis Cornwallis, his appreciation of Vice Admiral Cornwallis' merits and reputation in the service, the unsettled temper of many senior flag officers and disciplinary requirements. Spencer's handling of the matter demonstrated the 'judicious exercise . . . of compromise'.[66] Lewis does not explain what was involved in the compromise. Still, Spencer may be given credit for insisting that disciplinary norms were signalled by ordering the court martial, minimizing the risk of an unhelpful guilty verdict by facilitating the appointment of a court that was very sensitive to the rights of the navy, and withholding Cornwallis' resignation letter from the documents laid before the court.

If this was Spencer's plan, it was a very cunning one and worked out well. The public and parliamentary reaction was minimal and short-lived, and the upper ranks of the service soon settled down. The fleet mutinies in the spring of 1797 may have been salutary in alerting flag officers to the dangers of challenging their superiors. Lewis described Cornwallis' court martial as the 'last gust of the Army v Navy breeze'; if so, no comparable *cause célèbre* occurred during the French Wars to provoke further concerted action by flag officers.[67] Spencer had sometimes appeared indecisive in his first year in office and fallen into difficulties by finessing situations rather than coming to firm resolutions. At the same time, however, he had shown that he was not to be trifled with by veteran administrative street fighters like Sir Charles Middleton or superior commanders-in-chief like Lord Hood and William Cornwallis.

It is sometimes suggested that Cornwallis resigned his command, but that was not the case. The Admiralty order to strike his flag and go onshore was printed in the unofficial version of the trial proceedings announced in the press on 18 April, and Cornwallis later told his brother that he felt 'considerable satisfaction in reflecting that I am not the instrument of my own retirement'.[68] He also refused to make the conventional gesture of declaring himself available for consideration for future employment: he did not deem that a 'general offer of his services' was necessary in the circumstances.[69] The Marquis Cornwallis responded to this declaration in placatory terms – he 'lamented with the most heartfelt concern that the country has been deprived of your services, at a time when they were so much wanted' – and encouraged his brother to take all steps consistent with his honour to resolve the situation. Cornwallis' brother's role in the ministry and his high sense of public duty made the vice admiral's failure to respond politically embarrassing and strained their relationship.[70] Spencer may have read it as an indication that Cornwallis would reject any overtures from his Board. The first lord was becoming used to dealing with demanding and entitled admirals and, while acutely aware of how few officers had the expertise and temperament to undertake major commands, he was very unlikely to expend pride and patronage on those who were likely to rebuff him.

Cornwallis remained ashore on half pay for the better part of five years, missing the major fleet actions St Vincent and Nelson commanded. The impasse over his employment was not resolved until Spencer left the Board in early 1801. Admiral Earl St Vincent, who had long admired Cornwallis and was now first lord, immediately appointed him as his successor commanding the Channel Fleet.[71] This appointment allowed Cornwallis to show his mettle during prolonged service on the most demanding command.[72] It also allowed him to continue to patronize Captain John Whitby. As indicated earlier, Cornwallis' solicitousness for Whitby's career may have played a role in the events that resulted in his court martial.[73] He was replaced as captain of *Royal Sovereign* two months after Cornwallis lost his command and did not return to active service until more than three years after the trial. He appears to have owed his appointment as a frigate captain in 1799 to Nelson's and St Vincent's regard for his service patron. This command provided Whitby with opportunities to gain experience he lacked and to prepare himself to reassume his career as Cornwallis' flag captain of the mighty 110-gun *Ville de Paris* in the Channel fleet.[74]

Conclusion

The issue of whether the Board should order a flag officer to be court-martialled played a central role in Cornwallis' case as it had in the Keppel-Palliser affair. Though every bit as outraged as Keppel, Cornwallis' coolly dignified and proudly reserved courtroom demeanour meant that his public reactions were marked by constrained seething rather than histrionics. Nevertheless, at critical stages of his transactions with Lord Spencer, Cornwallis' responses made a court martial unavoidable. They also exacerbated the effect of its outcome on his state of mind, his relationship with a close family member and on the next stage of his career. While there was considerable sympathy for Cornwallis within the service and disenchantment with the first lord of the admiralty, this reflected in part the effect of unresolved conflict over Lord Spencer's failure to uphold the perceived rights of senior naval officers and was thus a matter of service rather than party politics.

If the court's approach reflected these sympathies, their role in the outcome of Cornwallis' trial was mixed. In the absence of formal explanatory commentary on the court's verdict or even plausible hearsay on its deliberations, it is impossible to recover the reasoning that underwrote them. However, external signs indicate considerable debate on the verdict, reflecting a divergence of views among court members. That the court reconvened briefly after half a day of deliberation to ask Cornwallis whether he had anything more to offer in his defence suggests that at least some judges were searching for evidence that aligned with their sympathies. When the terms of the verdict are considered in light of the wording of the charges, the testimony of witnesses and Cornwallis' defence, it seems that although the court wished to express its general support for Cornwallis, it had reservations about the way he exercised his discretion when he had the opportunity of proceeding to the West Indies in a ship of the line. As the president and another senior court member had served on the Admiralty Board, the court may also have been sensitive to the risk of setting a precedent that seemed to allow commanders-in-chief to disregard the letter and spirit of their instructions when other viable options were available.

The dispute with the army created tensions between Lord Spencer and senior members of the service that bore directly on how he responded to Cornwallis' actions. First lords usually managed intemperate and difficult flag officers without recourse to formal disciplinary procedures, but the broader context of the West Indian strategy and the need for Spencer to establish his authority in the face of challenges from flag officers, board members and ministerial colleagues precluded that. These considerations exacerbated Spencer's difficulties in dealing with Cornwallis, making it seem essential for him to order Cornwallis' court martial and possible for him to see this as a duty he owed to the service and his office rather than an episode in a personalized professional dispute. Ironically, the general terms – if not the overwrought language – of Cornwallis' fate-laden statement of his willingness to stand trial could equally well have been used by Lord Spencer to justify charging him: 'it would be for the good of the service, and of course the country, to have the matter canvassed . . ..'[75] Seen in this light, Spencer's satisfaction at the outcome of the trial was perfectly sincere. It was only Cornwallis' unwarranted assumption that the first lord acted in bad faith, and stubborn refusal to recognize the constraints under which he laboured, that removed him at a critical stage in his career from the professional sphere to which his life had been committed and in which he enjoyed the esteem of his colleagues.

7

A Hostage to Enmity

Vice Admiral Sir William Parker and Earl St Vincent

Vice Admiral Sir William Parker faced a court martial at his own request in late 1801 after Earl St Vincent's Admiralty Board recalled him from the North American command but did not charge him. It claimed Parker deployed two ships to the West Indies in the autumn of 1800 in direct contravention of the Board's orders and suspected him of doing so with a view to taking prizes within the limits of the Leeward Islands and Jamaica stations. Parker would have benefited from a commander-in-chief's share of their prizes and one of the captains was his son-in-law. During these incursions, both vessels ran aground and one was initially thought to be so severely damaged as to be unfit for future service.

The author of the *ODNB* entry on Parker describes the offences as being 'technical' but that is not an adequate characterization. Since the Board believed that Parker had deliberately ignored its orders and done so to enrich himself and two of his captains, the charge of disobedience was a substantive one and conviction would have been highly damaging to Parker's honour, professional respectability and prospects in the service. His alleged disobedience fell within the twenty-second article of war ('disobey any lawful command of any of his superior officers') and, if shown to be motivated by personal gain, was also encompassed by the thirty-third article's reference to 'scandalous' behaviour 'unbecoming an officer'.

Parker's court martial was the culmination of clashes with St Vincent dating back to 1798 when he was a subordinate flag officer in the Mediterranean fleet. Until then, he had enjoyed a solidly, rather than spectacularly, successful career. Parker's father had some modest interest arising from his involvement in the politics of Queenborough, a small port town in Kent, close to the large naval station at Sheerness. It returned two members to parliament with the representation determined by the Admiralty (which employed most of the voters) and the Ordnance Board. Parker's father was mayor in 1776 and was thus a member of a very tight corporation that controlled the borough.[1] These connections aligned the Parkers with Tory administrations led by Lord North and William Pitt; St Vincent's political allegiances were to the Whigs.

William Parker entered the navy at about fourteen, having first received training in service-related mathematics at a school in Portsmouth. He was known for his skills in navigation and surveying and worked with James Cook charting Newfoundland.

Parker's rise in the service was not meteoric; he was promoted to lieutenant after ten years as a captain's servant and midshipman and served another seven years before being made master and commander. He became a post captain a year later following his father's mayoralty and was regularly employed in that rank during and after the American War. His peacetime appointments included a term as commodore and commander-in-chief in the Leeward Islands. Parker was commanding HMS *Audacious* at the outbreak of the French War and played a widely commended role in one of the preliminary skirmishes leading to the Battle of the Glorious First of June, 1794. He subsequently enjoyed the distinction of being the lowest-ranked post captain raised to rear admiral in the extensive promotion of early July, which meant the Board decided to set the range of seniority on the post captains' list to include him.

It was thus not surprising that Parker was soon employed at flag rank, initially as commander-in-chief at Jamaica and subsequently as Sir John Jervis' third in command of the Mediterranean fleet. His division contributed significantly to the British victory off Cape St Vincent in mid-February 1797. After the action, Jervis (about to become the Earl St Vincent) named Parker specifically in praising his flag officers' roles in the victory and supporting their elevation to the dignity of baronetcy.[2] Shortly thereafter, however, a sharp deterioration in the two flag officers' relationship led to a permanent breach that was probably a significant factor in the Board's response to the events that led to Parker's court martial.

The pre-history of Parker's court martial

The proximate cause of St Vincent's and Parker's initial dispute was the Board's decision to deploy Sir Horatio Nelson on a separate service that destroyed a French fleet in Aboukir Bay on the Egyptian coast. Parker had earlier (and with some justice) taken umbrage at Nelson's failure to give due credit to other ships' contributions to his spectacular capture of two Spanish men-of-war at the Battle of Cape St Vincent.[3] When he complained to St Vincent about the favour shown to a junior and younger officer, the commander-in-chief emphasized Lord Spencer's role in Nelson's appointment and encouraged Parker to direct his complaints to him. The terms in which Parker did so displayed a sense of grievance that quickly tainted his relationship with his overbearing commander-in-chief. In his letter to Spencer, Parker adopted the overwrought tone and the breathless, sometimes ungrammatical prose that were a marked feature of both his correspondence and the statement of defence he presented to the court martial:

> I have been, my Lord, many years in the service, and in employ, and met general, approbation, therefore but little prepared to expect an injury of this sort. . . . I was happy to be employed, my Lord, in any situation, holding it my duty to be so while the nation was engaged in war; but could not thereby expect to be subject to the degradation I suffer indeed, after so many years' service with a reputation unexceptional, to be stripped of it as I am in the instance of this appointment, my feelings are more hurt than I can describe, or any event likely to occur can bring me to recover or reconsider.[4]

Although St Vincent gave sardonic countenance to Parker's aggrieved representations, he soon began to suspect him of underhand insubordination which challenged his authority as commander-in-chief. These suspicions were connected to the pre-existing dispute between St Vincent and another subordinate flag officer, Vice Admiral Sir John Orde, discussed in Chapter 2.

St Vincent, who was facing severe challenges in the operational aspects of his command and incidents of mutiny on the lower deck, was increasingly high-handed with subordinate flag officers and captains. These disciplinary challenges, which seemed particularly ominous as they followed in the wake of the large-scale mutinies at Spithead and the Nore in the spring of 1797, sharpened his already authoritarian sensitivities to behaviour that challenged his authority and good discipline in the fleet. In late 1798 Cuthbert Collingwood, at this time a senior captain, was relieved when a spell of leave removed him from the 'disagreeable' atmosphere created by St Vincent's clashes with his subordinate flag officers and his bullying behaviour towards his captains: 'having no very material service to execute' he 'carried trifles with a high hand, took dislikes and prejudices most capriciously'.[5] St Vincent claimed that Orde – a character 'fraught with the most malignant policy' – had 'worked on' Parker – 'a very weak man' – and encouraged him to criticize his commander-in-chief's orders that marines were to be berthed apart to prevent the rest of the crew from tainting them with its mutinous tendences.[6] As was often the case, St Vincent reacted to these perceived affronts to his authority by abusing the officer responsible. St Vincent construed Parker's complaints to Lord Spencer as further, open challenges to himself.[7] Having suffered the indignity of what he saw as an unjustified reprimand for exceeding his authority by sending Orde home, St Vincent demanded that the first lord relieve him of another troublesome subordinate.[8]

St Vincent's rough handling of Orde probably made Spencer and the Board less likely to accede to his demands to remove Parker, especially as his complaints were personal and general rather than framed by breaches of orders and regulations. In the event, Parker remained with the Mediterranean fleet until St Vincent was elevated to the Channel command and replaced by Lord Keith. In parting shots, St Vincent warned Keith of Parker's malignancy and sent a savagely upbraiding letter he had withheld while Parker was still under his command.[9] The spiteful closing salutation proclaimed that 'I am no longer bound to conceal the opinion I formed of your conduct towards Sir, your obedient humble servant, St Vincent.'[10] At about this time, Parker won a legal case against St Vincent over subordinate flag officers' shares of 'freight', that is, the fee paid for carrying bullion on naval ships.[11] St Vincent made a point of treating disputes over prize money as a matter of service principle, not personal animosity, but given his contempt for Parker, Lord Eldon's ruling very likely helped confirm St Vincent's dislike of him.

By this stage, Parker was beyond the reach of St Vincent's savage animosity and had sufficient interest and professional standing to secure an appointment to the North American command. It was, however, entirely in keeping with his sense of assertive entitlement that he wrangled with Spencer over the timing of his departure for Halifax, seeking to delay it to arrange his personal affairs and gather followers with whom to share the fruits of his new command. At one point, Parker bid for the Newfoundland command and governorship, presumably because this appointment enabled flag officers to spend the winter months in England.[12]

Parker finally arrived at Halifax in late 1800. Unfortunately for him, Spencer left the Admiralty Board shortly after that and was succeeded by St Vincent. The new first lord remodelled the Board to make room for two of his most loyal subordinates, Captains Sir Thomas Troubridge and John Markham. These changes were not necessarily fatal to Parker's prospects because first lords could not recall commanders-in-chief on a whim, and the King and some senior members of the service would have known of St Vincent's earlier transactions with Parker. In the event, however, he did not have to wait long before Parker furnished grounds for terminating his command.

St Vincent's chance arose when two ships from Parker's squadron went aground while deployed to the West Indies. HMS *America* was so severely damaged that she was thought to be no longer fit for service; HMS *Cleopatra* was only salvaged after prolonged, costly and risky efforts. The responsibility for these accidents lay in the first instance with the vessels' commanders. At this time, the *America* was thought to be a total loss and in line with usual practice, the captain (Joseph Bingham, Parker's son-in-law), his officers and crew faced a court martial. Although they were acquitted, the report on the trial drew the Board's attention to Parker's deployment of these vessels and prompted his recall.

Parker's recall

At a meeting on 25 April 1801, the Board accepted Parker's exoneration of the captain and crew of *America* but formed the view that he had acted with 'great indiscretion' in sending a ship of the line to carry out a task – the transportation of a small number of army deserters and malefactors to the base at Martinique – that could easily be assigned to a frigate. Worse still, Parker's very detailed orders led the Board to suspect that the real reason for these deployments was to provide the captains (and the flag officer under whom they served) with an 'advantageous cruise' on another flag officer's station. The Board condemned these 'extraordinary proceedings', made 'more reprehensible' by an earlier order instructing flag officers to warn their captains against encroaching on neighbouring stations. Before Parker left Spithead to take up his North American command, the Board ordered him to make inquiries when he arrived at his station and 'give positive injunction to the several Captains under your Command, not to go to the West Indies excepting in cases of absolute necessity'.[13] After the Board considered the documentary evidence, it decided that Parker should be recalled.[14]

Although St Vincent did not attend the Board meeting when it discussed the wreck of the *America*, he 'referred' the matter to it for consideration and recommendation and probably discussed it with Markham and Troubridge.[15] These staunch service allies would almost certainly have been aware of the first lord's contemptuous view of Parker's personal and professional merits. Troubridge had been a highly favoured protégé when St Vincent commanded the Mediterranean fleet and Markham served under him in the West Indies and the Mediterranean and Channel fleets. The first lord's absence from the discussion on the 25th of April and his attendance at Board meetings on days either side of it make it likely that he absented himself to avoid claims of predetermination, relying on Markham and Troubridge to come up with a recommendation that he was only too willing to accept.

The Board duly recalled Parker, but he found on arrival in England that he was not to be court-martialled. That non-decision may have resulted from the Board's view that the recall was a sufficient punishment for the offence. Still, it is equally likely that St Vincent wished to achieve the humiliating effect of insinuation without a charge he had used against Sir Hyde Parker. Sir William wrote to the Board from Spithead on 7 August requesting a court martial, 'having been recalled from my Station upon Charges stated to me in a Minute of the Board . . . very prejudicial to my Reputation, and I feel conscious unmerited'.[16] There is no indication that St Vincent resisted this request. As opposition began to mount to the first lord's campaign to reform dockyard administration and purge perceived abuses from the service, he may well have thought that it was impolitic to repeat the stonewalling that had frustrated Hyde Parker's pursuit of public exoneration and led to parliamentary questions.[17] The Board, however, only acceded to Parker's request after reviewing his journals and other papers relating to the army's application to transport its personnel and merchants' solicitation of convoy protection by *Cleopatra*. As we shall see, St Vincent's reaction to Parker's trial indicated that he had expected him to be found guilty.[18]

Parker's trial

The court was not convened for four months, possibly because Parker wished to ensure that it included a respectable number of flag officers and witnesses from foreign stations. There was some sympathetic advanced notice of the case in the anti-ministerial press. It blandly noted Captain Bingham's relationship with Parker, suggesting that if his ship had not come to grief there would probably have been no complaint and no 'insinuation' of 'making prizes'.[19] When the matter finally came to court, the Board extended the range of the charge to include Parker's deployment of HMS *Cleopatra* on a convoy to Jamaica. The prosecution prepared an elaborate written statement of its case, but the trial itself was relatively brief, beginning on the morning of the 13th November and probably concluding on the afternoon of the 14th.

The court, convened on HMS *Gladiator* in Portsmouth harbour, was presided over by Admiral Sir Thomas Pasley, second in command of the station. Pasley was a veteran of the victory on the Glorious First of June and had lost an arm in that action. The other flag officers – Admiral Skeffington Lutwidge, Vice Admiral Alexander Graeme and Rear Admirals John Holloway and Thomas Totty – were respectable workhorses rather than the major figures who dominated Cornwallis' court. Lutwidge and Graeme were ordered to hoist their flags at Portsmouth so they could serve on the court martial.[20] The eight captains included Charles Stirling, who was later tried on charges touching on his financial integrity. One flag officer was keen to avoid the trial and managed to do so. Cuthbert Collingwood, Parker's brother-in-law, was relieved to be safely out of the way serving off the Irish coast.[21]

Since Parker was tried at his own request, there was no prosecutor. The court collectively took the lead, with the judge advocate's formal role restricted to reading correspondence into the record and delivering Parker's statement of defence. He and the Board's solicitor prepared the paperwork that made up the substance of the case for the prosecution. Unusually, the circumstances of this case meant that the prosecution called no witnesses. The proceedings opened with a lengthy statement of charge that canvassed the orders issued to Parker by the Board and quoted extensively from those he had given to the captains of *America* and *Cleopatra*. Parker's highly detailed instructions to his captains were held to be 'directly contrary to and in disobedience of their Lordships said Order and Command'.[22] The charge covered parts of Parker's orders which permitted these ships to 'cruise' against the enemy at various points in the West Indies as they made their way back to Halifax 'instead of directing the Commanders of the said ships, after they should have executed the Services, which had furnished him with the pretence for sending them to the West Indies, to return, by the most expeditious route, to Stations within the limits of his Command'.[23] Although the charge did not directly attribute venal motives for these detachments, they were signalled in the words 'furnished' and 'pretence' and referred to in the accompanying documentation. Even if (as seemed doubtful) members of the court had not heard of the Board's views on the matter through service gossip, it played a prominent role in Parker's defence and was referred to explicitly in the verdict.

The charge made it clear that the Board believed that Parker's offending was exacerbated by its disastrous consequences. He had deployed ships away from their proper station, leaving the coast insecure, allowing a French frigate to get safely into Norfolk, Virginia, and exposing a ship of the line and a frigate to unnecessary risk, which materialized on the Formigas shoal on the coast of Jamaica and off the island of Abaco in the Bahamas. These points were relevant to the charge because the applicable article of war specified 'death, or *such other punishment . . . according to the nature and degree of the offence*'.[24] If Parker had been found guilty, the circumstances may have justified his dismissal rather than a reprimand.

At the conclusion of the lengthy statement of charge that comprised the case for the prosecution, relevant correspondence was read into the record by the judge advocate. He then read Parker's defence and further correspondence relating to it, following which three witnesses were questioned by Parker and cross-examined by 'the court'. As the manuscript minutes are the only complete record of this trial, there is no indication which particular judges posed questions on behalf of their colleagues. The procedure adopted in this case gave the trial an oddly unbalanced appearance, but in the circumstances, that seemed unavoidable. The statement of charge and the documentation included in it reported on the preliminary investigation of the case by the judge advocate and Admiralty solicitor and identified the instances of criminality allegedly arising from it. There were very few witnesses to the transactions that led to the groundings, and as Parker called them, they were not available to be summoned by the prosecution.

As was common in the courts martial of flag officers, Parker's defence touched on the circumstances in which the charge had arisen to highlight its implications for his honour and professional reputation. Since Parker had sought a court martial, he felt it necessary to explain to the court and readers of trial reports why he risked public disgrace to avoid the certainty of private contempt. He told the court that the terms and manner of his recall were

> so injuriously degrading to my reputation and distressing to me under all the Circumstances of my Situation, I was led upon my arrival in England to desire that my Conduct might be investigated . . . at a Court Martial . . . . I conceived I owed it to my Reputation and necessarily to be expected of me to retain my Credit in the Service.[25]

Parker sought to counter stigma arising from being court-martialled by reminding the court that the Board drove him to request a trial by compounding the injustice of his recall by leaving him in limbo: 'I expected if I was thought wrong, to have been made sensible of it in a different manner, for I felt myself as much entitled to the Countenance and Protection . . . and to be heard upon the Occasion as any other officer in a similar situation.'[26]

In his direct responses to the charge, Parker focused on the claim that he had directly disobeyed the Board's order on deployments, on the bearing of his orders to the captains of the *America* and *Cleopatra* and on the Board's inference that he had been motivated by the prospect of enriching himself and these favoured officers. In the first place, he denied that the deployment of *America* and *Cleopatra* contravened the order the Board had given him before he left England. He argued that this order was addressed to the captains of ships to prevent them from cruising off their station on 'frivolous occasions'. He did not believe that it was intended to prohibit commanders-in-chief on the North American station from sending vessels to the West Indies when they thought the public good required it, and argued that the urgency of requests from the army and the legitimacy of the case for a convoy justified him in doing so on these occasions.[27] Parker understood the Admiralty's instruction 'as a kind of Order or Warrant to me to send them there when necessary and proper to do so'.[28] Moreover, he claimed that it was not uncommon for ships to be deployed from the North American to the West Indian stations in winter because the severity of the Halifax climate made it highly desirable to remove them when legitimate opportunities arose. Parker justified the use of *America* for the mission to Martinique by referring to the availability and condition of other ships on his station. He attributed the failure of his squadron to keep the French frigate out of Norfolk to the deployment of other vessels, arguing that he could not foresee this risk when he ordered *America* to Martinique.[29]

Parker's second line of defence focused on the orders he had given his captains, particularly the references to 'cruising'. He denied that he had deployed *America* and *Cleopatra* for the 'especial purpose of cruising'. Rather, his orders permitted the captains to cruise where he anticipated they would be delayed waiting for weather and tidal conditions necessary for their passage back to the North American station. Parker identified an error in part of his orders which gave a misleading impression of his intentions and claimed that his captains would have realized this from the lengthy discussions he had with them about the best courses to steer to make timely returns to their stations in North American waters. Although his orders were very detailed and apparently prescriptive, Parker claimed that the commanders of *America* and *Cleopatra* fully understood from their discussions with him that they had discretion in determining the routes they should take to ensure they were back on station by the specified date.[30] Parker was unaware that the Board had defined the limits of his station with any exactness and argued it was common for essential duties such as convoys to take ships beyond their home commands. In making this point, Parker referred to his earlier experiences in the Leeward Islands and Jamaica.[31]

The final element in Parker's defence addressed the allegation that the real reason for the deployment of *America* and *Cleopatra* was to provide their captains and commander-in-chief with opportunities for poaching prizes on other officers' stations. This accusation touched on Parker's integrity and if proven would have left an indelible stain on his honour and professional reputation. For its part, the Board was keen to discourage practices that created friction between flag officers, threatened to disrupt the working of prize courts by disputes over jurisdiction and also encroached on its prerogatives in appointing flag officers to stations in the expectation this would allow them to benefit from prizes available on them. The rich pickings usually made on West Indian commands were commonly seen as compensation for the health hazards faced by those serving there. Parker responded to the Board's imputation of venality with a statement of a career-long record of rectitude designed to demonstrate the implausibility of accusations of impropriety. He declared that 'in every situation in which I have been placed, I am conscious I have conducted myself to the best of my Judgement, for the advantage of His Majesty's Service and of the Object of my appointment'. He reminded the court that he had been regularly employed as a captain and a flag officer and enjoyed a high reputation in the service.[32]

Following the reading of his defence and documents relating to it, Parker called three witnesses in the expectation that they would give testimony under oath supporting his rebuttal of the charges. Captain Israel Pellew of *Cleopatra*, who was on passage from Halifax, was not called, presumably to avoid further delay. Captain Oakes Hardy was not a party to the events that resulted in Parker's court martial but he had escorted a convoy from Halifax to the West Indies the previous year and was able to testify that, in his experience, the best route corresponded with Parker's orders to his captains. Hardy also gave evidence on the ill-defined limits of the North America station.[33] He was supported on this point by Captain Bingham's testimony that, to the best of his knowledge, the Admiralty Board had never set limits to the Leeward Islands and Jamaica stations and that previous commanders – Lord Hugh Seymour and Sir John Duckworth – had set them by 'private agreement'.[34]

Bingham's most significant contribution to his father-in-law's defence lay in testimony supporting Parker's claims that he meant his detailed instructions to be subject to discretion and that his captains understood them in these terms. The meetings he had on board Parker's flagship before *America*'s deployment were discussions of the commander-in-chief's understanding of navigational possibilities rather than briefings on pre-determined orders. In one case, he attributed a discrepancy between his written and oral instructions to a mistaken transcription and explained that he had assumed this was so because Parker would not have changed his written instructions without 'explaining' it to Bingham in a meeting.[35] In response to one of only two questions put to Parker's witnesses by the court, Bingham affirmed his understanding that his orders 'were discretional' and that Parker's instruction that he was not to cruise in places where he saw a ship 'that in your Opinion more probably belonged to that station than you did' was a constraint on the limits of cruising rather than a precaution against being seen doing so.[36] He also swore to an instruction arising in his discussions with Parker (but not appearing in the written orders) that cruising would only be justified where local intelligence warranted it.[37]

Parker's final witness was his secretary, the Reverend Souter, whose evidence concerned his commanders-in-chief's understanding of the implications of the order issued by the Admiralty following Seymour's reports of incursions onto his station by ships of the North American command. In response to a heavily loaded question, Souter testified that if he had thought this order forbade commanders-in-chief from sending ships to the West Indies on 'necessary services', he would have reminded Parker of it when the deployment of *America* and *Cleopatra* were in contemplation.[38] Souter echoed Parker's view (using very similar language) when testifying that the Board's order prohibited captains from Halifax going to the West Indies on 'slight or frivolous occasions'. He claimed that if Parker had thought the rider applied to commanders-in-chief, he would have clarified his discretion on deployments with the Admiralty Board before he left England. Finally, Souter testified that Parker never used the West Indies as a rendezvous for his ships and had always been chary of convoy requests, only acceding to them when exceptional circumstances applied. He had never ordered his ships to cruise 'beyond those which he considered to be the limits of his Station'.[39]

The outcome and its aftermath

Neither the official minutes nor the press reports indicate how long the court deliberated on its verdict, but as the trial did not extend into a third day, it cannot have done so for more than a few hours. Its somewhat breathless conclusion was that Parker was

> justified in sending ships to the West Indies and that the Vice Admiral was indiscreet, in having given such detailed Instructions to their Captains, for their Return within the limits of their Station, but the general Character of the Vice Admiral was such, as to preclude the Idea that he had been guided by any Motive unconnected with the Good of His Majesty's Service, and do therefore adjudge him to be acquitted.[40]

This verdict was, in effect, a qualified acquittal that lacked the words of praise adopted by Palliser's judges. Its delivery was, however, accompanied by official and private gestures that must have provided some compensation for the mortifications that Parker had suffered at the hands of St Vincent's Board. The press reported that Sir Thomas Pasley 'complimented him in the handsomest manner' as he returned his sword to him, that he received 'eager congratulations of many friends' and that the bells of Portsmouth rang when news of the acquittal reached the town.[41] This mark of local support may have reflected the goodwill engendered by Lady Parker's popularity as a hostess when the family lived in Portsmouth. It could also have been a gesture of defiance in the face of St Vincent's campaign to abolish alleged abuses in managing royal dockyards.[42]

The restrained language of the verdict may well have reflected the nature of the charges and the unusual procedural features of the trial. In the event, the bearing of both the captains' written orders and the variable guidance they had received during their pre-deployment discussions with Parker presented the court with a series of hypotheticals because the grounding of *America* and *Cleopatra* meant they never got to the places where they were authorized to cruise. As a result, the significance of written orders and oral instructions came to rest on untestable assumptions about what Parker meant and what his captains came to understand by them.

The accounts of Parker's discussions with Bingham and Pellew make interesting, if somewhat curious, reading. The commander-in-chief appears to have engaged his captains in an open-ended seminar on the navigational and climatic challenges of the eastern coast of North America and the Caribbean. Like any fair-minded tutor, Parker had his views on addressing these challenges but was unwilling to force them on his pupils. These transactions may well have reflected Parker's enduring interest in scientific seamanship. Still, they exposed his captains to the risk of acting on their discretion in the face of written instructions authorizing them to cruise on the stations of other flag officers.

Even though the court faced some unusual evidential challenges, it failed to pursue lines of inquiry that were relevant to the case. Its passivity in the face of remarkably uniform testimony from witnesses who were closely connected with the accused, and with whom there had been plenty of time to discuss events, was surprising. Nor did the judges test Parker's justification for deploying vessels to the West Indies. This matter was critical because if Parker's rationale did not stand up – and the Board certainly thought that was the case – it weakened his claims about the meaning of the Board's order and its suspicion of illegitimate prize hunting became far more plausible. Unexplored aspects of Parker's order which bear on these matters included the frequent references to cruising in his written orders, the unexplained instructions to *Cleopatra* to stay beyond signal distance of Port Royal, leave her convoy off the coast of Jamaica and avoid contact when watering on the island, and the injunction not to cruise where ships more closely connected with the station were present. These matters were relevant to the Board's suspicions and if the court had enquired into them it may have gained information on Parker's motivation to strengthen a purely circumstantial inference or weaken suspicions of impropriety. In failing to do so, the court's verdict relied entirely upon assumptions about Parker's character derived from their knowledge of his record and his references to it.

Despite the accolades he received at the conclusion of his trial, Parker was reported as being unhappy at the court's finding of indiscretion.[43] This response says more about Parker's self-righteousness than any weakness in the case against him. His use of both written orders and oral instructions was a potential source of confusion, and as the former authorized his captains to cruise on other flag officers' stations, Parker was fortunate in having this clear breach of the Board's orders covered by the veil of indiscretion. However, even this relatively benign finding would have been unwelcomed by a conscientious officer and particularly unwelcome to someone of his awkwardly entitled disposition. Nevertheless, in the absence of evidence of Parker's corrupt motivation in ordering the deployment of *America* and *Cleopatra*, the Board's suspicion on that score remained a matter of conjecture. Since that was the primary basis of its decision to recall Parker, his acquittal seems justified. At the same time, however, he was fortunate that his judges made no serious attempt to investigate matters relevant to the charges more thoroughly.

St Vincent was no doubt frustrated at not being able to prevent Parker from going to trial and greatly irritated by the verdict. His reaction was apparent from a covering letter to the King accompanying the minutes of the court martial and the Admiralty documentation. The first lord did not think the reason for the charge required further explanation but could not 'help observing that of all sentences which have come to his knowledge, no one ever appeared so extraordinary as the present, indeed even the ordinary forms of pronouncing whether the charges were or were not proved, have not been observed'.[44] As far as the trials of late Georgian flag officers were concerned, St Vincent's complaints do not stand up. The verdicts handed down on the admirals considered in this study do not follow any discernible common form and are often expressed in oblique terms which are more reflective of contextual considerations than a concern for judicial punctilio. By these standards, the verdict on Parker was relatively direct. In determining that he was justified in deploying *America* and *Cleopatra* to the West Indies, it addressed implicitly the issue of whether Parker was in breach of the Admiralty's order to his captains and whether he was blameable for the unforeseen consequences of removing ships from his station and exposing them to the navigational hazards of the waters around Jamaica and the Bahamas. The second part of the verdict made it perfectly clear that the court did not believe the deployment had been motivated by venal considerations.

The first lord's reference to the 'extraordinary' sentence of the court might well have been a guarded expression of his views on the shortcomings of the judges' handling of the trial. That he was likely to have been blinded by prejudice against Parker did not alter the fact that Pasley and his colleagues had given the accused a remarkably easy ride. St Vincent's widely known vendettas with senior officers in the Mediterranean fleet in the late 1790s were almost certainly a major consideration in explaining that. Indeed, the conduct of Parker's court suggests that other senior officers endorsed Collingwood's views on St Vincent's gratuitous mistreatment of his subordinates and that in the face of the first lord's ongoing pursuit of Parker they were prepared to give him the benefit of the doubt.

St Vincent would have known the King was aware of the feuds played out in the Mediterranean and would have harboured no illusions that he would countenance a parliamentary inquiry into the sentence. Having expressed his displeasure at the conduct of the court and thus implicitly affirming the Board's decision to recall him, St Vincent knew better than to force the issue. While he remained the head of the Admiralty Board, he was singularly well-placed to frustrate Parker's service-related ambitions and, given the intense competition for employment among flag officers, would have had no difficulty in doing so. In the short term, St Vincent could wait on events. Parker's court martial took place six weeks after the British government signed preliminary articles of peace with France, and in common with other wealthy naval officers, he was unlikely to seek peacetime employment. The longer-term career impact of Parker's court martial was never tested. Just over a year after his trial, he died at his house in London following a fit of what contemporaries termed 'apoplexy'.

Conclusion

Whatever their political differences, Keppel's professional relationship with the Earl of Sandwich only descended into intractable enmity when he was charged. By contrast, St Vincent's impatient contempt for Parker was of long standing. Thus, while different sorts of political considerations heavily influenced the Keppel-Palliser affair and Cornwallis' courts martial, Parker's trial resulted from a situation where sharp personal and professional animosity gave a first lord's use of his disciplinary powers the unseemly appearance of score-settling. There is no record of the court's views on this issue, but it may have had a bearing on the marked lack of agency it demonstrated during Parker's trial. Although judges had broad discretionary scope for intervening in the examination of witnesses and recalling them when necessary, the court showed no signs of pressing witnesses on their understanding of Parker's intentions that were relevant to the charges made against him.

While partisan loyalties do not appear to have played a role in St Vincent's pursuit of Sir William Parker, it may have been affected by his political agenda as first lord. As in Sir Hyde Parker's case, a senior flag officer's alleged leadership failings gave a recently appointed first lord the opportunity to underline aspects of this agenda. Sir Hyde had singularly failed to demonstrate the energy and zeal St Vincent expected of fleet commanders, and he silently but effectively punished him for it. The charges laid against Sir William highlighted St Vincent's insistence on obedience at all levels of the service, and in imputing venal motives for his disobedience, they attacked one of the many instances of the corruption he was determined to root out.

It seems likely, however, that St Vincent and his Board overplayed their hand in imputing Parker's alleged disobedience to corrupt motives. Given the limited range of witnesses and the absence of supporting documentation, it would have been difficult to prove this part of the charge and senior officers' suspicion of St Vincent would have been heightened by the court's sensitivity to questions of honour raised by it. The fulsome references to Parker's 'character' in his judges' verdict showed how keenly aware they were of the reputational and honorific implications of deliberate disobedience prompted by avarice and nepotism. While the court's finding of 'indiscretion' was a black mark against Parker's professional judgement and signalled a failure to live up to the Board's expectations, his court spared him from a finding that would have had a direct and highly damaging bearing on his honour, honesty and reputation.

8

Vice Admiral Duckworth's Excess Baggage

In late April 1805, a day after Vice Admiral Sir John Duckworth set foot in England upon being recalled from Jamaica, he was summoned to face a court martial on two charges laid by Captain James Athol Wood, late commander of the frigate HMS *Acasta*. These offences (oppressive treatment of Wood and carrying 'goods and merchandise' on a King's ship) did not carry capital penalties but would, if proven, have besmirched Duckworth's honour, seriously damaged his professional reputation and put an end to a lucrative career in flag command. Duckworth's sense of deep grievance at being recalled as Spain joined the war added fuel to the outrage triggered by Wood's audacity in laying charges against him and the Board's ill-considered and ungrateful endorsement of them.[1]

Duckworth's rise in the service had been steady rather than spectacular, but distinguished conduct as a post captain during the American War and the early stages of the French Wars ensured employment when he became a rear admiral in February 1799.[2] As a subordinate flag officer in the Mediterranean, Duckworth won large sums of prize money, including a share of a single treasure-laden convoy said to be worth £75,000 (*c.* £7.7m in today's terms).[3] Earl St Vincent advanced Duckworth's career and clearly valued his professional attributes. He did not, however, accord him the warm respect that marked his interactions with other successful flag officers such as Cornwallis, Lord Nelson and Sir James Saumarez. Thus, when he recommended Duckworth's appointment as a commodore to work with a notoriously difficult senior army officer, he did so in distinctly unflattering terms. He told Lord Spencer that Duckworth was suited to this role because he possessed 'a large share of forbearance, which he acquired under the high hand of Captain Fielding'.[4] As first lord, St Vincent took full advantage of this forbearance by being exceedingly demanding in placing his nominees in Duckworth's ships on the Jamaica station. He also put Duckworth very firmly in his place when, following the Treaty of Amiens, he asked to be relieved of an expensive peace-time command.[5]

The unedifying features of Duckworth's relationship with St Vincent reflected character traits that affected his interactions with various political, social and professional superiors. A capacity for knuckling under and a penchant for addressing secretaries of state, first lords and noble patrons with the obsequiousness of Jane Austen's Mr. Collins was combined with a sense of entitlement that fuelled a steady stream of pained grievances. During his time in Jamaica, Duckworth frequently invoked the 'poignancy' of his 'feelings' in plaintively assertive correspondence on honours withheld unjustly, the expense of peacetime command, failures to be relieved of it and the inequities of being recalled so soon after the recommencement of war. These pleas and others on questions of patronage and interest were addressed to St Vincent as a commander-in-chief and first lord, his successors at the head of the Board, other senior politicians, the prince regent and his most influential patron, the Duke of Northumberland. Duckworth's correspondence with Lord Spencer on being offered a baronetcy (rather than a knighthood of the Bath) following a successful joint services operation in the West Indies in mid-1801 is a fair sample of his passive-aggressive epistolary style:

> You cannot I am sure be surprised when I express the Poignancy of my Feelings … at the different return I *again* receive for my Exertions compared with those of my colleagues … [S]uch a lukewarm attention my Lord implies rather Censure than compliment … I will not sacrifice my Profession by accepting any secondary consideration but have its Rights unimpaired and drop into oblivion with a heart conscious of Rectitude.[6]

Duckworth's ambition, avarice, sense of entitlement and personal foibles all played a role in triggering his court martial and influencing his reaction to this wounding experience.

Captain Wood's career up to this point had been very successful. He fought with distinction in the American War and, having played a role in assisting prisoners of war when he was on parole in Paris, was commended to Lord Melville, the first lord. He was promoted on his return to England and subsequently appointed to the *Acasta*, a crack frigate. He also attracted the favourable notice of both St Vincent and Cornwallis.[7] Later unsubstantiated accusations by one of Duckworth's followers of a harsh and unbending application of service discipline did not harm his subsequent career.[8]

Captains and cargoes at Port Royal: The genesis of Duckworth's court martial

The dispute that led to Duckworth's court martial emerged in February 1805 at Port Royal, Jamaica. It originated from the Admiralty Board's decision in late October 1804 to order his recall and appoint Rear Admiral Richard Dacres, his second in command, to replace him.[9] Duckworth did not receive his recall until early February but had been informed of it towards the end of January in a private letter. This unwelcome news, and the indication that he was being recalled as a matter of course without any other explanation than reference to the time served on the station, sparked a volley of hurt and outraged correspondence. On 26 January he told St Vincent that it is

> not without a large Portion of Chagrine [sic] that I inform your Lordship of my having received communication *through* private Letter that the Lords commissioners of the Admiralty signed a Commission in October for Rear Admiral Dacres to succeed me as Commander in Chief. I understand the Pretext [being] my having served three years, to make out which your Lordship will

be aware that Peace and *War* Service must be blended; thus I am thrown out of Credit & Emoluments of the Spanish War.[10]

The following day, Duckworth responded to a Christmas greeting from Vice Admiral Sir John Colpoys, a member of the Admiralty Board, that 'Alas! It is a Season of Chargrine [*sic*], and I had almost said Disgrace' and consoled himself that the 'Poignancy of that harsh measure' was only softened by his sense of rectitude in the service of King and country.[11]

Once he had received the despatches carried by *Acasta*, Duckworth complained directly to Lord Melville that 'this strong mark of disapprobation was unmerited'. Conveniently forgetting the time that would necessarily elapse before he left the station, Duckworth pointed out that he had only served two years and nine months when Dacres' commission was issued, adding for good measure that he never solicited the appointment and had tried to give it up. Several days later he told the secretary of the Board that 'It is impossible for me to convey to their Lordships . . . the poignancy of my feelings at this harsh measure', but once at sea, he reiterated his complaints in a further letter.[12] Lady Nugent, the wife of the governor of Jamaica, wrote that Duckworth wept when telling her of his recall; given his reaction to this affront, his tears seem as likely to be provoked by spleen as by sentiment.[13]

Lord Melville responded sharply to Duckworth's rebukes, disclaiming any 'harsh' and 'unjust' treatment and saying that he had consulted the naval commissioners over the Jamaica 'arrangements' and plans for employing Duckworth on his return.[14] These responses did nothing to alleviate the poignancy of Duckworth's feelings. However, despite his subsequent (unwarranted) claims that recalls without cause were unprecedented, he does not appear to have had any substantive basis for complaint. Duckworth implicitly recognized that a period of three years was the usual term and taking account of his earlier wartime appointment on the Leeward Islands station, his claims about being deprived of opportunities for profitable and honourable employment do not ring true. Accounts sent by his agent from 1803 to 1805 show prize receipts of £31,000 in this period.[15]

Once Duckworth received wind of his recall, he took two steps to maximize his advantages on quitting his station. On the basis of the Board's order to proceed 'to England in such ship as you shall judge most proper', he decided to shift his flag into HMS *Acasta*, the frigate to which the Admiralty Board had appointed Wood.[16] HMS *Hercule*, a man-of-war commanded by Duckworth's flag captain Richard Dunn, would usually have carried the commander-in-chief home, an arrangement in keeping with his highly tuned sense of rank and dignity. Duckworth thought, however, that *Hercule*'s removal at this stage would alarm the principal residents of Jamaica.[17] This decision was entirely proper and need not have given rise to conflict with Wood. However, Duckworth also resolved to remove Wood from his command and appoint Dunn in his place. Dunn was a follower of Duckworth and had been his flag captain on the Leeward Islands station.[18]

Duckworth presented the exchange as being to Wood's advantage because the *Hercule* was a bigger ship and a more significant command than a frigate. Wood, quite understandably, did not see things in that light. Some post-captains preferred frigates because they provided more scope for quasi-independent operations and prize earnings than ships of the line. The arrangement which Duckworth forced on Wood carried several other disadvantages. It condemned him to service on a notoriously unhealthy station and precluded the prospect of 'freight money' from commissions to carry specie home. In the event, *Acasta* carried silver dollars valued at approximately £115,000; this shipment would yield from *c.* £1000–2000 in freight money, with the usual division being a third to the flag officer and the rest to the ship's captain.[19] Moreover, it soon became apparent that any advantages of a removal into *Hercule* would be very short-lived. Dacres had already informed Duckworth that he would appoint one of his followers into the flagship and move Wood into HMS *Theseus*. This ship had been so severely damaged in a hurricane that it was presently unfit for service. Wood was thus deprived of a command headed for England and left to superintend an extensive refit that would require him to live ashore in Jamaica for a considerable time, without even the consolation of prize money to set against the risks of the sickly season on the island.

Even before he knew of Dacres' intentions, Wood declined the move into *Hercule*, pleading ill-health and insisting that once clear of Jamaica he would be fit to take the *Acasta* back to England. Since Duckworth would not alter his plans, Wood asked initially for a medical survey as a preliminary to travelling home on the packet ship. The survey, which did not occur until after the packet had sailed, referred to a combination of physical ailments, the effect of prolonged confinement in his cabin and Wood's great 'anxiety of mind'; it recommended his removal to a 'Northern Climate'.[20] In the meantime, Wood's resolve hardened. He declined a commission to command *Hercule* and insisted he would remain on board *Acasta*, ignoring Duckworth's warning 'against such an un-officer-like and hasty step'.[21]

Although Duckworth's staff arranged for Wood to have a small cabin below, he resented deeply the loss of status and the inconvenience resulting from his displacement. Duckworth declined his plea to share the 'great cabin' because he had already promised accommodation to two West Indian notables. There were also squabbles and misunderstandings over sending livestock and provisions ashore and the stowage of Wood's personal effects. Having declined Duckworth's offer to dine in the great cabin as his guest, Wood was forbidden to accept invitations from the wardroom, presumably because that would imply a deliberate slight to the vice admiral. These interactions were managed by Captain Dunn and Duckworth's staff, and there was no doubt scope for misunderstanding and maladroit handling of an overwrought, demanding, unwanted passenger. However, Duckworth's decision to supersede Wood and the embarrassing transactions that resulted from it led Wood to believe that he had behaved, in the words of the thirty-third article of war, in a 'scandalous, infamous, cruel, oppressive . . . manner, unbecoming an officer'.

The second part of Wood's charge was discrete but was linked in his mind by the thought that he had been evicted from the *Acasta* to facilitate the shipment of a cargo contrary to the eighteenth article of war. Wood's letter of charge claimed that Duckworth 'did in the most shameful and scandalous manner load, receive on board, and suffered to be received on board . . . an immense quantity of Goods and Merchandize, other than for the good of the ship'. This cargo, which even Duckworth's witnesses estimated to weigh forty tons and may have been significantly more, was packed into *Acasta's* hold, bread room, gun room, spirit room, storerooms and hold. It was said to take up so much space between decks that some crew members were displaced from their usual berths.[22] The shipment included 200 dozen bottles of wine, 92 dozen bottles of porter and small beer, 5 dozen bottles of spirits, casks containing 1,450 gallons of Madeira and 145 gallons of rum, 11 mahogany logs and numerous cases of new furniture, 14 dozen cocoa nuts, 200 pounds of arrowroot, 24 quarts of castor oil and a number of turtles.[23] In the days before *Acasta* sailed from Port Royal, Wood looked on from the deck of his recent command as seamen on the station laboured to transfer Duckworth's spectacular excess baggage from *Hercule* and the 'Admiral's Pen', Duckworth's residence ashore in Kingston.

Duckworth's trial

The preliminaries to Duckworth's court martial were brief and overlaid by decisions on related matters that were only conveyed to interested parties when *Acasta* arrived at Spithead. Before he left Jamaica, Duckworth had written to the Board complaining that Wood's conduct bordered on mutiny. The Board's response (dated five days before Duckworth's return) ignored this claim and announced that it 'thought proper to reappoint Captain Wood . . . upon the return of the ship to England'.[24] This decision was a potential setback for Duckworth (and for Dunn), but the Board did not give effect to its resolution because Wood wrote on 19 April asking it to lay charges against his superior officer. Duckworth was summoned on the 20th, and the trial began on HMS *Gladiator* in Portsmouth Harbour on 25 April. The Board's very constrained discretion in declining to summon senior officers meant that its acceptance of Wood's charge must have been a formality.

Far from being rushed into court, Duckworth was keen to be tried as quickly as possible and urged the Board to avoid delays in bringing the court together.[25] His eagerness may have been due to the realization that as the displacement of Wood and the extent of the cargo shipped on *Acasta* would soon be common knowledge, it was essential to clear his name as quickly as possible. But while the Board accommodated Duckworth over the timing of the trial, it resolutely declined his attempts to persuade it to order the Admiralty solicitor to defend him and to meet the costs out of the public purse.[26] In addition to being keen to save the cost of engaging counsel, Duckworth no doubt also wished to limit the reputational damage of being called to trial by having the Board openly in his corner. The fact that Wood provided a writ to the Customs and Excise drawing attention to goods about to be unloaded from *Acasta* also played a role in Duckworth's attempt to mitigate the indignity of being charged.[27]

The haste with which the court was assembled had a bearing on its threadbare composition, the availability of witnesses and the prosecutor's and the accused's opportunities to prepare for the trial. In contrast to other admirals' courts in the period, Duckworth's included only three flag officers. The president was Admiral George Montagu, the commander-in-chief at Portsmouth. He was a mediocre officer patronized with condescension by St Vincent but had considerable experience presiding over courts martial. Montagu's senior colleagues were Rear Admiral Sir Isaac Coffin, a maverick flag officer whose zeal extended from the quarterdeck to the reform of dockyards, and Vice Admiral Sir Erasmus Gower, who had just completed his first year as governor and commander-in-chief of the naval squadron at St John's, Newfoundland. Ten post captains under Montagu's command formed the bulk of the court.

Wood's limited scope for preparation was highlighted in a belated request for the court to adjourn so he could obtain copies of Duckworth's correspondence with the Board, information on the replacement of captains acting under its orders and the number and condition of other frigates on the Jamaica station. The court refused Wood's request on the grounds that it did not want to delay proceedings and that the accuser should have requested this information when he charged Duckworth. Whatever the merits of the first point, the second was hardly reasonable. Wood could not know at that stage what documents might be necessary to make his case, and the tight timeframe prevented him from making applications to the Board in his hurried preparation for the trial. The court's eagerness to bring the proceedings to a close may have reflected the president's penchant for judicial urgency. In a trial later in the year, he insisted on the accused giving his defence on Christmas day.[28]

Since Wood had preferred charges against Duckworth, he was the prosecutor. As had been the case when Palliser prosecuted Keppel, Wood was not very effective in the role. The main result of his extensive questioning of Dr Primrose Blair, Fleet physician at Jamaica, was testimony on his own fragile mental health and tendencies to hypochondria. Blair's evidence demonstrated the effect of Duckworth's actions on Wood but did not address their legitimacy or reasonableness or support the critical accusation that Duckworth's displacement of him had been oppressive or disrespectful. Wood did not even attempt to pursue Blair on his prevaricating responses to questions on whether he had been 'turned out' of his quarters in the great cabin or whether Duckworth had forbidden his officers to invite Wood to dine with them.[29] Neither the prosecutor nor the court took up promising lines of inquiry on the reasonableness of Duckworth's determination to supersede Wood, his challenge that he 'seek redress' from the Admiralty Board if he 'did not like it' and the implications of Rear Admiral Dacres' determination to appoint his flag captain to *Hercule*.[30] When questioning George Morley (Duckworth's steward), Wood established that the furniture from the 'Admiral's Pen' was not used on board but did not ask that question about other items in Duckworth's cargo.[31]

The two most interesting witnesses called by Wood were Thomas Headlam, Duckworth's secretary, and Captain Dunn. Headlam's testimony seemed implausible and indicated collusion between witnesses before the trial. Although he had been involved in managing Duckworth's prize claims since 1801 and later produced a copy of the advertisement for freight, Headlam denied all direct knowledge of arrangements for securing and assigning freight for *Acasta's* return voyage. He acknowledged, however, that the advertisement was posted before Dunn superseded Wood and that this was the first case he knew where a captain had been removed from his command after advertising for freight.[32] Headlam's testimony on *Acasta's* cargo was even more surprising than his evidence on freight. He claimed not to have noticed the ship being loaded with tons of excess baggage or its presence on board during the voyage home. In a statement that pointed to collusion between at least two witnesses, he testified that he only had 'knowledge' of the cargo when he saw the list drawn up by Duckworth's steward, just before the beginning of the trial.[33]

Dunn's position was beset with potentially conflicting interests. The forbearance Duckworth had shown earlier in his career was generally reckoned to be essential for captains who had to manage their ship under the direct eye of active admirals, and Dunn's relationship with Duckworth was very close. He was a major beneficiary of the freight secured at Port Royal and of an arrangement which saw him commanding a homebound ship after many years in the West Indies. Dunn also had a share in some of the cargo taken on board by Duckworth. He was the beneficial owner of 370 gallons of Madeira listed by George Morey and some of the mahogany; he also owned sixty gallons of rum not listed in the manifest.[34]

Although Dunn acknowledged a distinction between things that were 'for the use of the ship' and those shipped on behalf of other people or as presents, neither Wood nor the court pursued that matter. The prosecutor then muddied the water by follow-up questions that hinged on whether part of the cargo was 'merchandize', that is, goods for sale.[35] Dunn was adamant that none of the cargo was 'goods' in that sense but made evasive responses to questions about the resources needed to bring Duckworth's baggage on board and whether the cargo interfered with berthing and storing arrangements. His response on the first of these points was not consistent with the volume of cargo, and his claim on the second – 'there was not a man in the ship but was berthed' – was contradicted by later testimony that some men were displaced from their berths by Duckworth's baggage. Contrary to regulations on the security of the ship's spirits, Dunn ordered the removal of these supplies to accommodate the freight and Duckworth's liquor. A later witness testified that other items of Duckworth's cargo caused inconvenience to the ship's company and additional work in getting access to provisions.[36]

Duckworth's defence opened and closed with attacks on his accuser and, as in Keppel's trial, alerted the judges to the 'malicious' basis of the charge.[37] Other parts of the defence showed signs of the haste in which he wrote it. Duckworth declared that he had 'resolved' to return to England in whatever ship brought out his despatches 'in case the Admiralty did not allow me to go home in the *Hercule*.'[38] He then changed tack and said that the poor state of the *Theseus* prevented him from deciding until the arrival of his despatches. When the order of recall left the mode of return to his discretion, he decided that it was in the interests of the service that *Hercule* remain on the station and that he return in *Acasta*. This account did not come to grips with Wood's attempts to persuade the court that Duckworth had made this choice because, although other frigates were available on the station and some of them needed to return home to refit, *Acasta* had a markedly superior capacity for carrying cargo. Moreover, while Duckworth dwelt at length on Wood's refusal to accept the commission to command *Hercule* and to leave *Acasta* when ordered to do so, he did not address the implications of Dacres' determination to place his flag captain in command of the ship into which Wood was supposedly being removed.

In a curious passage that aroused the ire of Wood's brother when he raised the matter in parliament, Duckworth claimed that he owed it to 'the honour of my Flag and my own character' not to expose himself to the risk of accidents 'by crossing the Atlantic in a Ship commanded by a Stranger'. Duckworth combined this argument with a more general claim about senior officers' followers that was likely to appeal to members of the court and echoed part of Cornwallis' defence: 'Judge then the necessity of having a Captain and some Officers acquainted with my ideas of service: for I will venture to say, there is not an Officer of this Court, tho' not advanced to the rank of an Admiral, who has not found the inconvenience of being appointed to a Ship with Officers unknown to him.'[39]

Duckworth dealt only briefly with what he described as 'the illiberal and disgraceful epithet which the Prosecutor made use of, namely – defrauding him of his freight, and of the Agent advertising for it, while he was on board the *Acasta*'.[40] He did not address the question of Wood's right to share in the freight nor deny that Wood was still captain of the *Acasta* when the advertisement solicited freight. He attributed this unusual timing to the merchants' pressing requests for him to notify them of his intentions and his duty to facilitate their wishes.

The final part of Duckworth's defence addressed his excessive baggage. As noted earlier, Wood's handling of this charge shifted between whether the cargo was for 'the use of the ship' and whether all or part of it was 'goods and merchandise'. Duckworth's defence focused wisely on the latter point. He insisted that the cargo was made up of stores and furniture from the Admiral's pen, presents for friends and presentation to the King and liquor and other goods shipped home on behalf of other officers.[41] Duckworth vehemently rejected Wood's claim that some goods were intended for sale. He thought the mere suggestion was an affront to his honour and sought to rebut it by testimonial statements on his character that his counsel read to the court. Duckworth also made a ponderous appeal to his status as a knight of the Bath. He asked the court 'whether it is probable, that, after bearing on my person, the honourable pledge of my Sovereign's approbation, and receiving testimonials from various quarters honourable to myself, I would lightly trifle with a reputation, which it has ever been my ambition to acquire and maintain?'[42] Duckworth refuted the validity of the customs writ that Wood had sworn against him by pointing to arrangements he had made for clearing his baggage with customs at Cowes, Portsmouth and Plymouth.[43] These matters were not part of the charge but had a bearing on appeals to his honour and probity in countering it.

Duckworth's defence concluded with an open attack on his accuser. He scoffed at claims that he had insulted Wood's honour by inferring that a man who had shown 'the character of a common informer' had no honour to lose. Duckworth emphasized this point by retailing hearsay of Wood boasting in 'an unguarded moment' of having got the better of customs officers by smuggling wine ashore at Portsmouth and then contriving to have them reprimanded for an illegitimate search by moving the contraband. 'Such have been the avowed actions of a man who has charged me, without being able to substantiate a single proof, with infamous and fraudulent conduct; but who has asserted, in his letter to the Admiralty . . . that his character is dearer to him than life.'[44]

Defence witnesses offered opinions and judgement on the outlandish claim that an officer so well-known for his high sense of honour would seek to enrich himself by shipping merchandise on *Acasta*. In a more factual vein, Dr Blair attested that there was nothing 'tending to oppression' in Duckworth's conduct or communications with Wood and that he always treated him with 'the respect due to an officer of his rank'.[45] Captain Dunn testified that Duckworth told them to adopt the 'mildest manner' when he and Rear Admiral Dacres were sent to 'advise' Wood to 'consider the consequences of' refusing to receive a commission to command *Hercule* and questioning Duckworth's authority to make that appointment because he had been recalled.[46] Evidence on Duckworth's moderation and consideration were accompanied by references to the stubborn impropriety of Wood's conduct.

Early in the afternoon on the third day, the court was cleared, and after a brief deliberation, Duckworth was 'fully and honourably acquitted' and the president returned his sword to him. Wood's charges were condemned as 'gross, scandalous, malicious, shameful, and highly subversive of the discipline and good government of his Majesty's service'.[47] The president's repeated references to the court's unanimity on Duckworth's future employment may have signalled how its members voted on the substantive questions.[48] Immediately after his acquittal, the naval commissioner, Sir Charles Saxon, entertained Duckworth and 'a large party of friends' at a dinner in his official residence. There are no reports of wider public rejoicing at Duckworth's acquittal, but there were, no doubt, many private expressions of relief by captains and flag officers who generated excess baggage in the expectation that it would be carried home on king's ships.

Aftermath

Duckworth refrained from criticizing the Board directly in his defence, but his references to malicious charges involved oblique references to its lack of consideration for his honour and past services. Once the trial was over, any sense of constraint quickly gave way before his highly developed aggrieved entitlement. He immediately sought the Board's permission to publish the minutes of his trial – 'that the Public may know that I am neither oppressive or [*sic*] Fraudulent or Scandalous' – and chastised it for allowing him to be charged.[49] Duckworth was in the happy position of being able to complain bitterly to a first lord who apparently had no role in his recall or charge. Lord Melville headed the Board when he was recalled and he was summoned before Lord Barham had replaced him. Even so, there was scope for characteristically maladroit airing of grievances and ambitions. Vice Admiral James Gambier, Barham's highly favoured nephew in the service and under strapper in naval administration, was a member of Melville's board and the first lord had relied on his uncle for unofficial advice.[50]

The day after Barham took office, Duckworth wrote complaining of being recalled without cause and replaced by a junior officer, the outrage of being charged at Wood's instigation and the humiliation of being the subject of entirely unnecessary attention from the customs and excise service. A week later, after what the press reported as 'a very long' interview with the Admiralty Board, Duckworth expanded on his grievances. By recalling him 'without being charged with error' the 'late admiralty' had treated him in a manner such as 'never before occurred with a commander-in-chief when in time of war'.[51] Duckworth framed his complaints as part of a package of alleged mistreatment to persuade the first lord to support his ongoing pursuit of an Irish peerage. He had now convinced himself that a peerage was warranted to show that his unjust recall, court martial and customs embarrassments had not lowered him in the eyes of the great and the good. 'Some hereditary mark of his Majesty's favour' would 'convince the public of my rectitude.'[52]

In late May 1805, Duckworth made a similar case in a long letter to Prime Minister William Pitt.[53] These appeals were unsuccessful, and fresh salt was rubbed into Duckworth's wounded ego when the government dashed his expectations for hereditary recognition following a successful action against a French squadron off St Domingo in February 1806. It offered him instead the 'degrading' compensation of a pension of £1000 per annum. The man who had crammed a frigate with material comforts scorned this 'dirty lucre' but could not avoid receiving the pension without insulting the king. Despite further applications advanced through the Duke of Northumberland, the Earl of Westmorland, Lord Mulgrave and the Duke of Portland, the highest hereditary honour Duckworth secured was a baronetcy after the successful completion of his term as commander-in-chief and governor of Newfoundland in 1813.[54] St Vincent supported a nomination for this honour in 1801, but Duckworth had a peerage in sight then and perhaps to keep that hope alive wrangled for a (non-hereditary but highly honorific) knighthood of the Bath.[55]

Six months after the court martial, Duckworth narrowly missed what must surely have been his best chance of securing a peerage. Unfortunately, however, although appointed to a subordinate flag officer's command in Nelson's Mediterranean fleet, he was in Plymouth when it defeated the enemy off Cape Trafalgar. There was some bad luck involved in this matter but the tragically poor timing was mainly due to his inflated sense of entitlement. Duckworth delayed his departure to wrangle with the Board to secure what he regarded as a suitable flagship and await the return of Captain Dunn and other followers, including members of his band, from *Acasta*. He seemed particularly anxious to recover an awning from one of the ship's boats to add to his comfort and dignity in the Mediterranean.[56] Given Duckworth's record, there is every reason to suppose that he would have served with distinction at Trafalgar and in the difficult salvage operations that followed. His delay in joining the Mediterranean fleet may thus have been crucial in terms of his honorific and service ambitions. Involvement in the greatest naval victory of the war would also have removed any taints from his court martial. When Duckworth was on his way to join the fleet in early November his flagship, HMS *Superb*, intercepted (and delayed) HMS *Pickle* as she dashed to England with Collingwood's despatches on the victory and Nelson's death. The poignancy of his feelings on this occasion can scarcely be imagined.

Even so, and despite Duckworth's claims that his unjust recall and summons had cast a cloud over decades of devoted and distinguished service, he was regularly employed thereafter even though his performance was mixed and he had a penchant for leading squadrons in chases off station and exceeding his orders. Following service under Collingwood in the Mediterranean, during which he commanded a squadron in a successful action off St Domingo, and as a subordinate flag officer in the Channel fleet, Duckworth was governor of Newfoundland and commander-in-chief of the squadron based at St John's from 1810 to 1812. He was an energetic and engaged governor who enhanced a recent tradition of effective naval government of the settlement and paid much appreciated attention to planning the island's defences on the outbreak of the War of 1812.[57] Although he continued to lobby for major active service roles during and after his term in Newfoundland, Duckworth had to settle for the peacetime command at Plymouth. He died in post in 1817.

Duckworth's acquittal and the sound of a court martial

Duckworth's recall and court martial fuelled his sense of grievance, but it is far from clear that they damaged his subsequent career. Advancing seniority and a steep rise in the number of flag officers through successive wartime promotions meant that many admirals' expectations were not realized. It is also notable that Duckworth never attracted the level of elite respect shown to distinguished contemporaries. A comparison with Sir James Saumarez is instructive on this issue. Saumarez's pursuit of a peerage paralleled Duckworth's and was not concluded until 1832, long after Duckworth's death. Despite the similarities in frustrated ambitions, Saumarez's colleagues did not subject him to the grudging praise and limited respect that greeted Duckworth's achievements. Thus, while St Vincent spoke warmly of Saumarez, his support for Duckworth was invariably enveloped in an air of exasperated condescension. Lord Barham had employed Duckworth shortly after the court martial and Duckworth regarded him as a friend. Barham, however, worked behind the scenes to minimize the significance of the action off St Domingo and endorsed the convenient but ungenerous administrative fiction that Duckworth's claims were limited because he was under Lord Collingwood's orders. Barham also credited Rear Admiral Sir Alexander Cochrane with a critical initiative with which his senior officer had merely 'complied'.[58] Since Cochrane had written warmly of his gratitude 'for the permission he gave me to accompany him to Leeward',[59] Barham's put down was so entirely gratuitous that it must have sprung from prejudice, but he may have been able to ignore Duckworth's claims because of the tarnishing effect of the recent court martial.[60]

In a series of memoirs of naval officers published a decade after Duckworth's death, James Ralfe remarked pointedly on the dubious outcome of the trial and hinted at perjury by some of Duckworth's witnesses. He also suggested that while Duckworth was admired warmly by some colleagues in the service, others held him in scant regard:

> By some we are solicited to believe, that he was open-hearted, just, and generous . . . But others . . . who appear equally entitled to credit, represent him as mean, selfish, sensual; one who would curry favour by abject and contemptible means, and who was incapable of giving vent to one generous sentiment, or performing a worthy action, but from interested motives.[61]

Duckworth's friends reacted sharply to this passage in Ralfe's essay, but that was consistent with his account of divergent views on the admiral's character.[62] Legal and parliamentary challenges to the verdict, the Board's favourable treatment of Captain

Wood and the detailed evidence produced in the trial may have helped to prompt the damaging views of Duckworth's morals and merits to which Ralfe referred.

Wood issued a notice of a civil action immediately after the trial but set this option aside when he sought redress through official channels.[63] The process began with a 'Memorial' to the Admiralty Board which stated that he would

> consider himself unworthy of the commission which he has the honour to bear in his majesty's service, as well as wanting in that respect which he owes to the lords commissioners of the admiralty, were he not, with the greatest deference and respect, to state to their lordships, that so far from the charges which he preferred against vice-admiral Duckworth having been either gross, unfounded, malicious, or scandalous, your memorialist trusts he shall be able to satisfy your lordships, that such charges have been as fully substantiated as it was possible for them to be, under all those unfavourable circumstances, under which your memorialist was placed.[64]

The memorial, which made a far more compelling statement of Wood's charge than he had managed as Duckworth's accuser, concluded with five legal opinions on a hypothetical case on the eighteenth article of war. It included details of the cargo but was anonymized and gave the 'officer of the navy' the benefit of not being 'fully aware' of the eighteenth article and being able to prove that the goods were for gifting, not for sale. The opinions, by barristers of Lincoln's Inn, including the solicitor general and Thomas Erskine, who became Lord Chancellor in the following year, were as unanimous as lawyers can be in opining that the officer would have breached the eighteenth article of war. They also observed that the act gave no discretion to the court to moderate the specified penalties of dismissal and permanent debarment from naval service.[65] These opinions did not show conclusively that the court's verdict was wrong, but they at least pointed to areas of substantive doubt that undermined its damaging rider against Wood.

Wood's memorial prepared the ground for a parliamentary motion to produce the minutes as the first step in a review of the trial and its outcome. The motion was put forward by Colonel Mark Wood MP, Captain Wood's brother. He foreshadowed it on 24 May 1805 but advised the House on the 31st of a further delay to accommodate a minister 'who wished to have time to consider the propriety of the motion'. He finally spoke to his motion on the 7th of June, having circulated copies of Captain Wood's memorial to members of the House earlier that day.[66] Colonel Wood's speech raised several issues bearing on the soundness of the court's verdict. He deliberately eschewed presenting the case solely in terms of redress for his brother and framed it around more general issues. The injustices suffered by Captain Wood were 'immediately connected with the violation of an act of parliament, the foundation and key-stone of our naval discipline and glory; ... the violation of this law is sanctioned by the late naval court martial, and a door thereby thrown open to the greatest abuses in the naval service of this country'.[67]

Colonel Wood acknowledged that Duckworth had the right to go home in *Acasta*, although he pointed out that many other frigates could be used for that service and that keeping *Acasta* 'under the walls of Port Royal idle one month until the yellow fever commenced its havoc' was not for the good of the service.[68] He also drew attention to *Acasta*'s extensive carrying capacity and questioned Duckworth's right to displace her captain, attributing this measure to the benefit of placing the vessel under the command of an officer who would not object to the volume of cargo he wished to pack into it. Captain Wood's displacement was wrong and deprived him of his rightful share of freight and a worthwhile alternative to the command to which the Board had appointed him. Duckworth deviously claimed to be placing him in a more advantageous command when he already knew that Rear Admiral Dacres had other plans for HMS *Hercule*. Colonel Wood dismissed Duckworth's claim about not trusting himself to a stranger on the voyage home as a 'scandalous libel' on every captain in the navy except Captain Dunn. The court's implicit endorsement of this claim signalled 'that a commission from the admiralty is no protection . . . against the whim, or caprice, or revenge, of a commander-in-chief on a foreign station, who may shift them from the finest frigate in the service into any old hulk bearing a pendant'.[69]

In addressing the alleged breach of the eighteenth article of war, Colonel Wood pointed to the terms of the act, the admissions made during the trial that the excess baggage was not for the use of the ship and the legal opinions attached to his brother's memorial. He claimed that as the commanding officer of the *Acasta*, Captain Dunn was liable to answer to a court martial for *Acasta*'s cargo and for breaching naval regulations by risking the secure and safe storage of the ship's spirits. There was also a potentially damaging question about the origin of some of Duckworth's cargo. In the trial, it was established that furniture from the Admiral's pen was not for the 'use of the ship', but there was more to the matter than this. It was not even part of the pen's fixtures and fittings, having been made by naval personnel overseen by a man styled the 'admiral's joiner' to furnish the admiral's grand house near Exeter. Finally, Wood pointed to precedents for courts martial to be examined in parliament and declared 'partial, arbitrary and illegal'.[70]

Colonel Wood's motion that the court's proceedings, Wood's memorial, the legal opinions and the customs returns on *Acasta*'s cargo be laid on the table of the House was opposed by William Dickinson, a civil lord of the Admiralty. Dickinson's response was a dismissal rather than a rebuttal but was nevertheless significant because it showed there was no government support for the motion and that it would therefore fail. He claimed that the proceedings were already so well known that 'no reflection could possibly with justice be cast' upon Duckworth. Conveniently ignoring the implications of Palliser's acquittal, Dickinson asserted that the censure of Captain Wood was justified and supported by the precedent of the rider to Keppel's verdict. However, the real reason for the government's refusal to allow its supporters to vote for Colonel Wood's motion was that he 'saw no advantage likely to arise to the public from the house interfering with the sentence'.[71] This rationale was political rather than judicial.

Most of the other responses to Wood's speech took the form of testimonials to Duckworth's character, which, as far as the excessive baggage issue was concerned, were not to the point: the case put to legal counsel did not rely on the cargo being 'merchandize'. Two speakers defended Duckworth (and incidentally, the court) on the grounds that it was common for captains to carry personal effects home. Rear Admiral

Markham, until quite lately a member of the board, raised a laugh in the house with his statement that 'With respect to the law opinion . . . not an officer in navy but might be superseded on such an opinion; for hardly one of them was free from the sin of transgression as to the 18th article of war'. Markham told the house that he had asked 'naval friends' to bring wine for him from 'wine stations'.[72]

Colonel Wood's motion was defeated without a division in what was probably a very thin house. Two months later, there was a further fleeting attempt to gain parliamentary redress for his brother. At the very end of the session, Richard Sheridan wished to present a petition from Wood but was interrupted by the speaker, who had a message on another topic from the House of Lords. The parliamentary session closed after the Commons considered the Lords' message. Sheridan did not intervene on Wood's behalf again, and his petition disappeared without trace.[73] In 1808, Colonel Wood made a further unsuccessful attempt to call Duckworth to parliamentary account, this time for his lacklustre role in a bungled assault against Turkish forces in the Dardanelles.[74]

Although William Dickinson dismissed Wood's case rather than addressing it, Duckworth's acquittal appears unexceptional from a purely legal point of view. Proven perjury would have compromised it, but Colonel Wood's and James Ralfe's claims remained mere assertions. The Board's reinstatement of Wood implied a silent rebuke for Duckworth and its rejection of his claims that the captain's conduct bordered on mutiny. However, in the absence of evidence of the Board's intentions, all that can be said is that it absolved Wood of significant blame without suggesting that there was anything more than a *prima facie* case that Duckworth had breached the thirty-third article of war. Wood's career indicated that first lords did not place any weight on the disparaging rider issued by Duckworth's court. He was employed in significant roles throughout the war, knighted in 1810, became a knight of the Bath in 1815 and gained flag rank in 1821.

That Wood was seriously, even traumatically, disturbed by his removal from his command did not mean that Duckworth was criminally wrong in ordering it. Moreover, much of Wood's resulting angst was due to his reaction rather than Duckworth's and his officers' oppressive treatment. Once Duckworth decided to replace Wood, the other steps he ordered were necessary consequences and were not shown to have been taken to degrade him. Wood presumably construed this part of his charge as mistreatment because the prevailing regulations were silent on the commander-in-chief's rights to supersede those appointed to a particular ship. Shortly after the trial, Barham's and Gambier's revisions to the *Regulations and Instructions* implicitly supported Duckworth's court's view on this matter. The new regulations included a clause on the appointment powers of commanders-in-chief on foreign stations that made the supersession of a captain of a flagship an exception to the general rule that commanders-in-chief could not replace captains without their consent.[75]

There was also a degree of uncertainty about applying the eighteenth article of war because statute, custom and practice were not aligned. The law prohibited the shipping of 'goods and merchandize . . . other than for the sole use of the ship'. The Board's instruction to Sir Hyde Parker as commander-in-chief at Jamaica in mid-1800 to order captains not to 'bring merchandize of any description to England' suggests sustained official sensitivity on the issue, but in practice it was shrouded in ambiguity.[76] Wood's legal opinions treated the 'use of the ship' proviso as an overriding condition not affected by the cargo's nature, source or destination. In the course of the trial, however, Duckworth resisted the charge on the grounds that the cargo was personal property not intended for sale. The court implicitly accepted this approach when it framed its questioning in terms of cargo for 'private use' and 'things as come under the eighteenth article of war'.[77] This distinction is foreign to the article in question and was not in the minds of Wood's legal counsel. It may well, however, have reflected a belief that the eighteenth article was framed to prevent officers from using King's ships for trade. In addition, as Markham's jocular and self-serving observation made clear, it was grounded in customary practice as an extension of the entirely reasonable assumption that those returning from foreign stations were entitled, if room allowed, to bring home their personal effects. As Duckworth said in his defence, these effects were likely to be considerable in the case of flag officers. This point and perhaps also the recognition that gifting was part of the exchange culture of Georgian patronage networks lay behind a qualification to the strict enforcement of the letter of the eighteenth article suggested by one of Wood's counsel. His opinion prioritized the 'use of the ship' proviso but also noted that the volume of baggage was a consideration in the application of the act and that it was appropriate to make 'liberal' allowances on that score.[78]

Conclusion

Even if the court's verdict was legally defensible, aspects of the case were potentially damaging to Duckworth's honour and professional standing. Regardless of subsequent regulatory developments, Duckworth's argument about the reasonableness of admirals selecting their flag captains was strained to the limit when applied to a single passage in a vessel that he would never have accepted as a flagship on a substantive, prolonged command. Arguably, Duckworth's determination to load down the *Acasta* with his personal effects also involved a degree of unprincipled, if not illegal, overreach that was exposed during his trial and circulated more widely by his sponsorship of the publication of the proceedings. His excess baggage far exceeded the 'liberal' allowance of Wood's counsel's opinion and was far beyond customary practice measured by Markham's references to captains bringing home 'a pipe or two' of wine. Moreover, the volume and nature of the cargo suggest that Duckworth was actually accumulating goods to be shipped home, rather than seeking a reasonable accommodation for his extensive personal effects. That was most clearly the case with the furniture from the admiral's pen and the bulky mahogany logs and slabs which displaced water casks from the ship's hold. Colonel Wood suggested that the proper thing for Duckworth to have done with the furniture would have been to leave it at the pen for his successor. That would have been especially appropriate for joinery manufactured by labour paid for and victualled by the navy but would have removed the motive to have it made.

Late Georgians were not squeamish about becoming rich, and naval officers were no exception to this cultural norm. Flag officers vied for commands that would bring them wealth and honour, congratulating their friends on 'lucky' terms on lucrative stations and windfall riches gained in battle or the seizure of treasure ships and convoys. However, there was an ambivalence in commissioned officers' attitudes towards prize wealth, and this was more marked among senior officers.[79] Prioritizing prize hunting over operational objectives was generally condemned, and even where there was no suspicion of that, attitudinal limits to acquisitiveness exposed officers to the wry contempt of some of their colleagues. There are no surviving accounts of Collingwood's, Nelson's or Saumarez's reaction to Duckworth's court martial, but it seems unlikely that they would take Markham's indulgent view of his excess baggage.

The extraordinary bulk of Duckworth's private cargo must also have prompted questions in some people's minds about his attitudes towards wealth. Indeed, some items on Duckworth's inventory invoke the pathetic avarice of modern householders who strip light bulbs from houses they are vacating. The 'pen' was not only emptied of liquor, preserved fruits, spices and furnishings but also bottled water. As a post captain between the wars, Duckworth had been poor, and while his second marriage and the fortunes of the French Wars removed the reality of poverty, they might not have banished the spectre. At the beginning of his service in Jamaica, he had been exercised over recovering outlay on furniture and fittings at the pen from a successor.[80] The excess baggage he shipped at the end of his commission was of a piece with the attitude that underlay that concern and extended into the management of his property and relations with some members of his family. Despite his wealth, Duckworth complained bitterly that relatively modest sums spent on repairs to his country house left him 'drained at every pore'.[81] In his private papers there is an unsettling self-righteous letter detailing and justifying his refusal to loan his widowed sister £500 after the death of her 'infernal' husband had left her in straitened circumstances. Duckworth was subsequently outraged at not being the beneficiary of her will and instructed his lawyer to recover two bonds worth £75 from her estate.[82] Among some members of the lower deck Duckworth was said to bear the unflattering sobriquet 'greedy Tommy' and a warrant officer who served under him in the Leeward Islands was scathing at his naked regard for his own interests, his irascibility to his subordinates, sycophancy to social superiors and casual disregard for the welfare of those on the lower deck: 'Tommy, Tommy, if you are not paid off for it in this world, you may be in the next.'[83]

Even the cargo that Duckworth identified as gifts was not necessarily beyond reproach. Presents to powerful 'friends' such as the Duke of Northumberland and Lord and Lady Spencer were part of the exchange relationships which were integral to the patronage network, but excessive gifting might smack of unseemly ostentation and subservience that attracted the contempt of some third parties, if not of the recipients. Lady Nugent's accounts of Duckworth's socializing in Jamaica suggest overreach, and one wonders whether Lord and Lady Spencer were any more appreciative of Duckworth's lavish gifts of turtles, French liquor and pots of ginger than the herrings and painting of a Dutch pilot that Admiral Lord Duncan sent them from his North Sea command.[84]

Thus, whatever the legality of Duckworth's handling of Captain Wood and his excessive baggage, his court martial exposed his conduct to the public at large, may have lowered him in the eyes of some of his colleagues and imposed a blot on his honour despite his acquittal and the court's undeserved vilification of Captain Wood. That Duckworth sought to give a wide circulation to the findings suggests a lack of confidence in his claims to unimpeached virtue and a lack of awareness about how aspects of these transactions were likely to be perceived by others; so too did his attempt to seek the reassurance of royal honours. If so, the judgement on Cromwell's roundheads in *1066 and All That* may also apply to Duckworth's court martial experience: he was 'right but repulsive'.[85]

9

Discretion and Misjudgement

Vice Admiral Sir Robert Calder

When Admiral Keppel was tried for his life in 1779, he called Lieutenant Robert Calder as a witness. Two and a half decades later, Vice Admiral Sir Robert Calder Bart faced a court martial on a similar charge. It arose from an action on 22 July 1805 against a slightly superior combined French and Spanish squadron off Cape Finisterre. Earlier in the month, the Board ordered Calder's ships (augmented by those that had been blockading Rochefort) to cruise off Cape Finisterre to intercept an enemy fleet heading from Antigua. Unbeknownst to Calder, it had decided that his squadron should inflict as much damage on the enemy as possible to discourage future sorties.[1]

The engagement was a confused affair during which much of the enemy fleet was partly hidden in thick fog banks. Although Calder's squadron captured two ships of the line and caused significant damage to others, it also suffered; two ships could not be restored to fighting condition without being refitted in port. The enemy remained in sight for the next two days but Calder did not attempt to reengage with them. He later claimed that he was concerned about the condition of his ship and prizes and did not want to risk an unsuccessful action that would leave British shipping and the coast of England exposed to powerful squadrons coming out of Ferrol and Rochefort.

Calder had forty-seven years of service in the Royal Navy when he was court-martialled. Having been commissioned as a lieutenant in 1762, probably with the assistance of interest arising from his father's connections with the court and the Earl of Bute, he spent seventeen years in that rank before being made master and commander in 1779 and post-captain a year later.[2] Although Calder was unemployed after the American war, the timing of this promotion meant he had good seniority at the outbreak of the French Wars and was well-placed to benefit as the frequency and volume of flag promotions increased rapidly. He was Lord Howe's flag captain at the Glorious First of June 1794 and Sir John Jervis' captain-of-the-fleet at the Battle of Cape St Vincent in 1797. On St Vincent's recommendation, he was knighted after that action and made a baronet in 1798. Calder became a rear admiral in 1799 and vice admiral in 1804. In 1796, St Vincent had commended him to Lord Spencer as a captain 'whose zeal cannot be outdone' but it is perhaps a sign of his limited regard that he later referred sardonically to Calder's assiduous execution of orders based on erroneous information: 'the energy and precision with which you pursued the wrong scent . . . never will be exceeded.'[3] Less unforgiving contemporaries expressed reservations about the judgement and good sense Calder displayed in his reaction to the events that led to his court martial.

Shifting expectations: Public and private responses to Sir Robert Calder's action

Following the disengagement of the British and enemy squadrons, Calder drafted a public letter to the Board and also wrote a private letter to Lord Barham, the first lord. In some ways, these were triumphalist communications, but the letter to Barham conveyed an undertow of uncertainty that subsequently came to dominate their correspondence. Calder told Barham, 'I hope your Lordship and my Royal Master will think I have done all that it was possible to have done.' Although Calder received the 'approbation' of the Board, his bid for 'royal bounty' for himself, 'royal honour' for Captain Charles Stirling, his second in command, and promotion for a string of junior officers was disregarded.[4] The first lord's response almost certainly reflected the Board's growing unease about the aftermath of the action. The government was conscious of its weakness in the face of recriminations on the ongoing impact of St Vincent's programme of dockyard reform and William Pitt's efforts to exploit them to regain office. The naval dimensions of this tussle were particularly significant given public fear of a French invasion.[5]

When Calder recommended his officers for the first lord's attention, he expressed concern that his public letter had not been published in full in the *London Gazette* and thought this omission encouraged 'the Papers and the World to bestow on me many remarks and publish a great deal of nonsense'. He was resigned to these barbs but nevertheless looked to Barham for moral support.[6] A month later, his realization that claims about lost opportunities were gaining traction within the service began to undermine his confidence: 'I never dreamt that any prejudices could [have] gone forth so as to have in any manner affected my character as an Officer or as a Man in not having brought the Enemy to action on the succeeding day, after the Victory I had obtained over them.' As this questioning came from a 'quarter not to be doubted', Calder felt it necessary to ask Barham and the Board 'to cause an Inquiry to be made into my conduct' on the 23 July and any related matters.[7] One of Calder's causes for concern was that Lieutenant James Nicholson, who had carried his despatches to Cornwallis and then to England, was reported in the press as having told eager auditors in a London coffee house that the commander-in-chief intended to renew the engagement as soon as possible. Calder told Barham this report was 'erroneous in almost every particular' but it was, nevertheless, highly embarrassing because it ran directly counter to Calder's account of his intentions.[8]

The Board's approval of Calder's conduct on 22 July was made with the expectation that he would renew the action. In a communication dated 1 August addressed to Cornwallis for transmission to Calder, it hoped that 'the advantage obtained will be improved to the utmost' of Calder's 'power'.[9] The Board's expectation on this score mirrored those canvassed in the press and Lieutenant Nicholson's account of Calder's intentions. It is significant in relation to later developments that some press reports praised Lord Nelson for driving the enemy squadron into Calder's path and speculated hyperbolically on his future exploits.[10] Thus *Cobbett's Weekly Political Register* combined cool congratulations to Calder with regrets that Nelson 'did not come up with the enemy'.[11] Within a few days, however, matters seemed less clear-cut. On 5 August, when the press reported that Calder had lost sight of the enemy, questions were raised about his intentions and the implications if he had let an opportunity slip. Joseph Farington, the diarist, reported dissatisfaction in the city of London with Calder's performance, and the *Morning Chronicle* opined that if Calder 'had it in his power, on the 24th and 25th, to renew the battle, and did not do so, he has been guilty of a breach of duty, and has suffered the enemy to escape'. While acknowledging that the lack of firm information made it difficult to determine the circumstances of the fleets after the initial action, it suggested that Calder 'is placed in a most disagreeable predicament, by the opinions delivered on the respective situations of the two fleets after the battle, and indeed by the opinion imputed to himself'.[12] In mid-August, when Nelson thanked Sir Thomas Fremantle for sending him a packet of newspapers, he was 'bewildered by news of Calder's victory and expressions of disappointment in the press'.[13]

On 10 August *Cobbett's Weekly Political Register* claimed to discern a shift against Calder in 'ministerial prints and circles'. This development can be traced to a piece in the *Morning Post* a few days before, which used its reports of 'public opinion' to run with the fox and hunt with the hounds: 'as far as public opinion has yet manifest itself . . . there certainly appears more symptom of disappointment than applause'.[14] By the twentieth of the month, the *Post* had clearly sided against Calder: 'we cannot but lament that many points of his conduct are far from manifesting that degree of presence of mind, of promptitude, and decision, which the situation in which he was placed so imperiously called for.' The publication of reports from the French and Spanish commanders increased the pressure on Lord Barham and his colleagues and, with more of a time lag, on Calder. They were greeted initially with a degree of scepticism, but it was noted that details attributed by the *Moniteur* to the French commander, Admiral Villeneuve, only diverged from British statements when it moved beyond the 22nd. Villeneuve claimed Calder frustrated his determined attempts to renew the battle: it was 'impossible to bring our squadron to action'.[15] The Spanish commander reported that the English 'manoeuvred to avoid a second encounter'.[16]

In early September, private and public rumours were circulating that the Board would recall Calder.[17] These reports were well-founded. When Nelson left London on 13 September 1805, he received orders to take over Calder's and Collingwood's squadrons and an oral message telling Calder that the Board thought he should be court-martialled. Having already raised this matter, Calder welcomed Barham's message and promptly followed his advice to write formally to the secretary of the Board requesting a court martial.

Calder's exchanges with the Board reflected contemporary perceptions of courts martial as mechanisms for protecting the honour and reputations of senior naval officers labouring under unwarranted public criticism. Given the role of the press in creating an environment of expectation and condemnation that made courts martial a political and reputational necessity, it is ironic that the commentary arising from Calder's action included a succinct statement of the challenge confronting Barham and his Board. A *Morning Chronicle* correspondent critical of the government's deployment of its naval forces wrote that 'it behoves us to be thankful for the victory we obtained with such an inferior force, and Sir Robert Calder should either have some mark of honour conferred upon him, or a Court Martial. It is universally thought by his own squadron, that he did his duty, and that more could not have been done considering all the circumstances'.[18]

Since Nelson told Barham that 'it will give your Lordship pleasure to find, as it has me, that an inquiry is what the Vice-Admiral wishes', there do not seem to be any grounds for the suggestion that Calder had to insist on a court martial over Nelson's objections. Rather, the latter's reference to a 'very distressing scene' with Calder was due to Nelson's concern that he had misread the attitude of the Board and underestimated the gravity of the situation.[19] Calder was desperate to get to England to clear his name, giving Nelson the impression that he was very sanguine about his prospects. The day before he left the fleet, Calder told Nelson, 'My heart is broken. . . . I hope and trust I shall not be kept here until Vice Admiral J. T. Duckworth arrives.'[20] Nelson, who was in an excellent position to gauge the atmosphere of official, political and public expectation during his recent visit to London, thought Calder's haste and optimism were dangerously misplaced and tried to impress on him the benefits of facing a court martial *after* participating in a generally anticipated, large-scale action.

When Calder left the fleet, Nelson told Collingwood that he was relieved that he had gone but also hoped he would 'end his inquiry well. I endeavoured to give him all the caution in my power respecting the cry against him; but he seemed *too wise*'. Nelson thought Calder's trial was likely to be 'of a very serious nature' and he was concerned that he intended to rest his defence on strategic considerations rather than the impossibility of getting the enemy to engage: 'keep to that, *prove* it and his character is retrieved.'[21] But if Calder's approach to his trial was hasty and his judgement questionable, there does not appear to be any firm basis for the suggestion that his preference for going home indicated that he was not 'emotionally attracted to battle' and in the grip of a 'narrow concern for his own welfare'.[22] One of Calder's captains, Edward Codrington, commented on the impact of Vice Admiral Collingwood's prohibition on ship visiting on such a sociable man as Calder.[23] This remark highlighted the effect of prolonged isolation on Calder's state of mind as his affairs moved towards a crisis. Left to his own devices and isolated from those whose overriding anxiety was that short-term deployments would rob them of the opportunity to meet the enemy, the volume and strength of the rumours assumed such proportions that the need to seek vindication dwarfed all other considerations. Calder certainly never lacked courage, and Nelson and his colleagues were confident that he would have acquitted himself well in a major action.[24] It seems far more likely that his eagerness to be gone reflected a combination of embarrassment at his position in the fleet and an impatience to clear his name in what he expected would be an open and shut court case.

During the passage home, Calder recovered his spirits and would have been buoyed by the reception that greeted him at Portsmouth on 9 November. The *Hampshire and*

Portsmouth Telegraph (a paper that was consistently sympathetic to him, perhaps because of his local connections) took 'great pleasure in stating' that Sir Robert 'looks remarkably well. He was greeted by the ringing of bells and was received with flattering attention. A large party waited on him immediately after his landing'.[25] The encouraging effect of this welcome was probably short-lived. His arrival in England a few days after the news of Trafalgar may have sharpened his appreciation of the significance of Nelson's warning about the 'cry' raised at his performance off Finisterre and the magnitude of the opportunity missed.[26]

Calder's court martial

The Admiralty Board took the first formal step in Calder's court martial on 15 November 1805, nine days after it had received the news of Nelson's victory. Admiral George Montagu, commander-in-chief at Portsmouth, was 'directed' and 'required' to assemble the court and preside over a trial

> for enquiring into the whole of the said Vice Admiral's conduct and proceedings on the said 23d of July last, and into his subsequent conduct and proceedings until he finally lost sight of the enemy's ships. And to try him for not having done his utmost to renew the said engagement, and to take or destroy every ship of the enemy, which was his duty to engage.[27]

As the wording of this charge made specific, if oblique, reference to an article of war (XIII) that carried a capital sentence, the Board decided that the deputy judge advocate of the fleet should lead the prosecution and the Admiralty solicitor, Charles Bicknell, should travel to Portsmouth to assist him.

The flag officers on the court were solid rather than stellar performers at that rank. Montagu, who had hastened Duckworth's trial to a speedy conclusion, was joined by Vice Admiral John Holloway, his subordinate flag officer at Portsmouth who had also sat on Duckworth's court. The other four admirals, Vice Admirals Bartholomew Rowley and Edward Thornborough and Rear Admirals Sir Isaac Coffin and John Sutton, were all employed regularly at flag rank; Sutton was the least distinguished of them, but his spells in subordinate positions on home stations provided significant experience of high-profile courts martial. Seven captains supplemented the admirals including Duckworth's putative victim, James Athol Wood.

When Calder requested Lord Barham to authorize a court martial, he gave an extravagant and entirely unrealistic indication of the number of ships that would need to return to England to provide an appropriate panel of witnesses.[28] After discussions with Nelson about the requirements of the service, he agreed that three captains would accompany Calder and stand as witnesses. They included Charles Stirling (promoted to flag rank before the trial), thus depriving that unfortunate officer of a role in a major fleet action. In the event, the timing of Nelson's funeral meant that all the officers present at the action off Cape Finisterre who survived Trafalgar could testify at his trial.

The prosecution called Stirling, three men who had commanded ships of the line in Calder's action and six masters. Perhaps in response to the confusion over logbooks in Keppel's trial, five masters were merely asked whether the logbook was of their ship and accurate to the best of their knowledge.[29] Calder called nine captains and the signal lieutenant and chaplain of the *Prince of Wales* as defence witnesses.

The prosecution's examination of its witnesses was brief and far from incisive. Stirling's testimony that Calder's primary objective was to protect the 'crippled ships' of his squadron and the prizes was supported by three other witnesses, as were his related remarks on the inability of the squadron to have 'fetched' the enemy 'if they had chosen to avoid them'.[30] This last point was part of a more general account that Calder had a settled intention to avoid risking his fleet and its prizes because of the damage it had suffered and the threats posed by the Rochefort and Ferrol squadrons. Stirling testified that when his squadron withdrew from the blockade of Rochefort to join Calder's fleet, the enemy ships were in a state of advanced readiness to put to sea and the prospect of them doing so was high.[31] In response to a question from the judge advocate whether 'the Vice-Admiral, according to your remarks and observations, [did] everything that might have been done to renew the action, and to take and destroy every ship which it was his duty to engage?' Stirling effectively anticipated Calder's defence by explaining that his commander-in-chief did not see this as a primary objective in the circumstances.[32]

The evidence of two further witnesses, Rear Admiral George Martin, a captain in the action, and Captain Henry Inman of HMS *Temple*, was generally consistent with Stirling's testimony, but that of Henry Craddock, master of the *Glory*, and Captain Phillip Durham appeared to pose a threat to Calder. Craddock challenged a plank in Calder's case by testifying that the prevailing wind would have made it impossible for the enemy squadron to come out of Ferrol. Surprisingly, Calder did not choose to cross-examine this officer, but after Martin had given his evidence, he asked the court to recall him, presumably because he had further information on weather conditions. The court would not allow Calder to cross-examine Craddock but, consistent with its obligation to secure as much information as possible, put the question itself. In response, Craddock acknowledged that for a time on one of the days in question, variations in the prevailing winds made it possible for the enemy squadron to get out of Ferrol.[33] This amendment supported Calder's claims of a perceived threat from the Ferrol squadron.

Captain Durham's evidence was more problematic, but subsequent developments partly nullified its impact. In response to the prosecutor's question, Durham testified that having been ordered to keep the enemy in sight on 24 July Calder directed him to withdraw. Durham also testified that he had seen no significant damage to the British fleet, except to the *Windsor Castle*.[34] Calder's agitated response to the invitation to cross-examine Durham – 'I can ask Captain Durham no question whatever. It is impossible' – no doubt reflected his view of how damaging this evidence might be.[35] However, when he came to examine his witnesses, Calder had recovered his temper and was better prepared to blunt the impact of Durham's testimony. The incident on the 24th subsequently turned out to be the result of a misreading of the flagship's signals on Durham's ship, and Calder's witnesses testified consistently on the damage suffered by his squadron on 22 July.

Although there was a nearly six-week gap between the Board charging Calder and his case coming to trial, he was surprised when the prosecution finished its case in less than a day and the court called for his defence. After an adjournment that extended from the late afternoon of 23 December until 10.15 on the morning of 25 December, Calder's 'friend Mr Gaselee' read his statement of defence. At this time Gaselee, who came from a prominent Portsmouth family and was a barrister on the western circuit, was well advanced in a career which saw him become a KC, a knight and a high court judge.[36] The barrister and his client, and possibly other friends, used Christmas Eve to produce a largely effective response to the substantive points raised by the prosecution. Unfortunately, however, the defence also provided two attitudinal hostages to fortune. If these were the work of Calder rather than Gaselee, they spoke to failures of judgement which played a significant role in the court martial and its aftermath. In contrast to Cornwallis' exceptionally restrained account of his achievements in the service, Calder made much of his 'decisive victory' and offered a passive-aggressive criticism of the Admiralty Board for having framed the charge to exclude consideration of his conduct on 22 July and thus deprive him of bragging rights in court.[37] More damning still were comparisons he drew between his victory and those of Lord Howe and the Earl St Vincent.

Calder had mentioned these parallels in a letter to Vice Admiral Sir Charles Cotton in late August as a means of vindicating his conduct to his 'friends'. His intention to use them in court may have contributed to Nelson's unease at his approach to the challenge he faced.[38] When Calder raised them in his defence, he acknowledged these comparisons were beside the point but seemed oblivious to their impact on members of the court who admired Howe and St Vincent. On this occasion, Calder damned them with impertinent faint praise as 'two very great and gallant Officers, who, after having obtained most brilliant Victories over the Enemy, did not think themselves justified in bringing them a second time to action, although they were in sight of them fully as long as I was'.[39]

These gaucheries aside, Calder's defence provided a generally clear and effective vindication of his conduct that was very well supported by the testimony of defence witnesses. Calder did not argue that physical circumstances or, as Keppel had claimed, a senior subordinate's disobedience prevented him from re-engaging the enemy fleet. Rather, he maintained that the circumstances of 23–24 July meant that it was his duty *not* to renew the action. In taking this position, it was necessary to show (presumably with the assistance of Mr Gaselee) that the duty specified in the Articles of War did not apply in his case and was, indeed, not of universal application. 'I am ready to admit, that it is so much the duty of an Officer to engage the enemy wherever he meets with them, that it is incumbent upon him to explain satisfactorily why he does not, but, in making that explanation, it is not necessary for him to prove the physical impossibility of doing so'.[40]

Calder defended his conduct by an appeal to a principle of discretion that was very similar in form, if not in application, to those advanced by Keppel and Cornwallis: 'the discretion of the Commander, to be exercised according to the best of his judgement, and subject to that responsibility which attaches to all persons in situations of command'.[41] In the closing stages of his defence, Calder summarized the circumstances that justified his departure from the strictures of the twelfth and thirteenth articles of war:

> To 14 sail of the line, without any frigates, the enemy had to oppose 18 sail of the line and 7 frigates, besides other vessels. Against such a force I could not hope to succeed without sustaining considerable damage, I had no friendly port near me, and in that situation had the Ferrol and Rochefort squadrons fallen in with me, I must have become an easy prey to them. Had they taken a different course and sailed for Ireland or England, there was no squadron to arrest their progress. Had I been defeated, although many of the enemy's ships must have been disabled in the conflict, I should have lost the advantage I had obtained over them, the enemy would have acquired spirit, their remaining squadrons would have been unmolested, and it is impossible to foresee what might, in that case, have been the consequence.[42]

The details of Calder's defence – the condition of his ships, the lack of information on the damage sustained by the combined squadron, the need to protect his crippled ships and prizes and the risk posed by the Ferrol and Rochefort squadrons – gave substance to his overarching justification and were supported by the testimony of defence witnesses. They gave evidence that the enemy never chased or tried to force an action on 23 July, that Calder ensured that his squadron was placed between the enemy and the crippled ships and between the enemy and the coast around Ferrol, that if the ships from the combined squadron had got within signalling distance of the telegraph stations on the coast, enemy forces would have been mobilized against him, and that while the ships of Calder's squadron had sustained considerable damage, he had no information on the condition of those in the combined squadron. After four witnesses provided uniform testimony on these matters, 'the Court', presumably Admiral Montagu, decided it was unnecessary to pursue them with other witnesses because 'these points are sufficiently established'.[43] The captains of frigates towing the prizes and crippled ships then gave evidence that sea conditions prevented the removal of crews and prisoners from prizes and hence the destruction of these vessels, thus addressing the suspicion that Calder was more interested in prize money than in ridding himself of encumbrances to pursuing the enemy.[44]

Captain William Cuming of *Prince of Wales*, Calder's flag captain, was the only witness explicitly asked to testify to the psychological basis of Calder's decision-making. He gave an emphatic 'most certainly not' to Calder's question, 'As you were near my person during the time of the action of the 22nd, was any part of my conduct to be attributed to fear, or want of zeal for his Majesty's service?'[45] Finally, Calder's chaplain, who assisted when the Vice Admiral's secretary was unwell, gave evidence supporting Calder's account of his intentions at the time, referring particularly to his belief that a renewal of the action was highly imprudent, the probability of the Rochefort squadron being at sea and the likelihood of that at Ferrol 'getting out'.[46]

When Calder laid out his doctrine of discretion, he allowed for the possibility (also canvassed by Cornwallis) that the court might, having 'considered all the circumstances that at that time presented themselves to my consideration, and the various objects to which my attention was necessarily directed, tell me I have acted erroneously' and trusted 'they will not do so'. Press reports of his demeanour during the trial suggest that this statement of optimistic expectation was not a desperate rhetorical flourish. In the event, however, his confidence was misplaced. After deliberating for six hours, the court exonerated Calder of the fatal taints of 'Cowardice or Disaffection' but gave a backhanded and highly unwelcome endorsement of his earlier acknowledgement of the implications of the discretion of commanders-in-chief. Its verdict was that he was guilty because of 'Error in Judgement, and is highly Censurable, and doth adjudge him to be severely reprimanded'.[47] Since the court appeared to accept the evidence on the particular matters that contributed to Calder's decision not to reengage, its verdict implied that in matters of judgement, the whole may be greater than the sum of its parts. Thus, while Calder's concern with protecting the crippled ships and his belief that his squadron had suffered significant damage on the 22 July and that the Ferrol and Rochefort squadrons posed a risk may have been reasonable in themselves, they did not justify his decision not to attempt to reengage with the combined squadron to inflict maximum damage upon it.

Aftermath

After Calder's trial, the *Morning Chronicle* reported that the court had taken the unusual step of prohibiting the publication of the proceedings as the trial progressed, perhaps to avoid witnesses being prompted by testimony reported in the press. It noted, however, that it had allowed press representatives to take a daily record of the proceedings provided they did not publish them until the trial ended.[48] In the event, there was significant reporting after the court delivered its verdict, and the *Hampshire and Portsmouth Telegraph* issued a complete transcription of the proceedings authorized by Calder.[49] Those acquitted often took this step as a vindicatory celebration, but Calder may already have agreed to it before the trial. He may also have seen the publication as a way of giving wide circulation to his defence and demonstrating disapproval at being found guilty in the face of the evidence produced at his trial.

There were variations in the press detail on how Calder conducted himself on hearing the verdict, with some newspapers concluding their reports with his stunned immediate reaction (the vice admiral 'scarcely lifted his head, which was apparently bowed down by the weight of the sentence pronounced upon him'[50]) and others extending their accounts to include reference to his subsequent reaction. A report in the *Caledonian Mercury* included interesting references to an 'uncommonly crowded' court and the sympathy for Calder expressed by members of the audience.[51] Unsurprisingly, the *Hampshire and Portsmouth Telegraph* printed the most extensive account of Calder's post-trial behaviour. Its publisher had an incentive to keep interest alive until the full minutes were issued, and the newspaper had been markedly sympathetic to Calder and optimistic about a favourable outcome in the run-up to the court martial.[52] Given that the *Telegraph* was a local publication and was making a complete record of the trial, there are grounds for regarding its account as more comprehensive than those of more distant publications that almost certainly relied on second-hand reports.

The *Telegraph* noted that while the prosecution was making its case, Calder's 'firm' conduct 'seemed to proceed from a clear consciousness that he had done his duty to the country in declining to pursue the enemy on the 24 July, and that his evidence would completely vindicate his judgement'. Mr Gaselee's reading of passages in Calder's defence referring to his lifetime commitment to King and country reduced the vice admiral to tears that did not disgrace his manhood: 'no doubt they flowed from a wounded heart, mixed with some indignation at what to him seemed injustice in his country.' The *Telegraph* echoed the *Mercury*'s reference to the audience's sympathy when the judge advocate read the sentence. It also noted that having withdrawn to his cabin for a few minutes, Calder 'regained his fortitude' and at least some of his social graces. He made his way to his barge through crowds of sympathetic and 'uncovered' bystanders and 'bowed with much attention and regard for the disinterested feelings of the spectators . . . We are happy to conclude by saying – *though he feels the blow, he feels it like a man*'. The demonstrations of sympathetic regard continued the following day when Montagu, Sir Charles Saxton (the naval commissioner at Portsmouth), Sir John Carter (the mayor and sometime MP), aldermen and 'many distinguished people' waited on Calder at his lodgings.[53]

These expressions of sympathy raise questions about the view that Calder's verdict was affected by the harsh light thrown on his performance by Nelson's victory off Cape Trafalgar.[54] Trafalgar, and a subsequent action in which Rear Admiral Strachan captured four ships of the line that had escaped into the Atlantic, cast a large shadow over Calder's achievements. They may also, however, have relieved the ministry and the Admiralty Board of the pressure of vocal public anxiety which had fuelled the rising 'cry' against Calder.[55] The public reaction was restrained compared with the howls of public outrage that greeted news of Rear Admiral Byng's lacklustre performance and the invasion threat had receded; by the time Calder came to trial, the government had relatively little at stake in the outcome.[56] Indeed, there are some indications that the Board may have been willing to attempt to mitigate the risks posed by its earlier decision to summon Calder to court martial.

On 1 January 1806, the *Morning Chronicle* published an affidavit sworn by Commander James Nicholson before the Lord Mayor of London. In his defence, Calder repeated his earlier dismissals of the account attributed to Nicholson in the press and noted that he had not been called as a witness. In his affidavit, Nicholson swore that in a private meeting on the evening of 24 July, Calder 'ordered me to tell the Commander in Chief . . . that he was determined to bring the enemy to action the next morning' even if that exposed the 'crippled ships' and the frigates to an increased risk of being taken by the enemy. There is no way of determining the accuracy of this statement, but if it were true, it would entirely disrupt Calder's narrative of a settled determination not to reengage. Nicholson, who knew he would be promoted for carrying home despatches on a successful action, had no reason to fabricate to Calder's disadvantage. Moreover, as Calder's language to Cornwallis was ambiguous in referring to future attempts to mop up the enemy's ships, a combination of extreme fatigue on his part and excitement on Nicholson's might have led to innocent miscommunication.

Be that as it may, the second half of Nicholson's affidavit dealt with a curious conversation that had occurred only a few days before. Nicholson swore that the

Admiralty Board ordered him to travel to Portsmouth for Calder's trial and on his arrival in the town was told by the judge advocate that the vice admiral wished to see him. When Nicholson went to Calder's lodgings, however, Charles Bicknell advised that Calder would not see him until the trial was over but had asked Bicknell to convey his 'astonishment' at the press statements attributed to him. Although Nicholson stuck by his guns – 'I had made no report but what was ordered to make by Sir R. Calder' – he indicated to Bicknell that he would be a reluctant witness: 'having every reason to believe, from what he had told me, that he was favourably inclined towards Sir R. Calder, I was glad to have an opportunity of saying to him what I must have declared had my evidence been called, in hopes it might be dispensed with.' The prosecution did not call Nicholson but Calder traduced his 'reputation as an officer and a gentleman' during the trial by unchallenged imputations on his honesty.[57]

If Nicholson's account of these matters is accurate, it raises crucial questions about the background of Calder's trial. While it is odd that a judge advocate should facilitate a private meeting between a witness and the accused, Charles Bicknell's role as Calder's friend and spokesperson is extraordinary. As the Admiralty's solicitor, Bicknell played a significant role in determining the prosecution's approach to the trial and travelled to Portsmouth at the direction of the Board. As a professional man who relied primarily, if not entirely, on the Board for his livelihood, it is inconceivable that Bicknell would have favoured Calder in the face of Lord Barham's determination to prosecute the case vigorously. In other words, Bicknell's meeting with Nicholson suggests that the Board wished to offer a purely token effort. The half-hearted case made by the prosecution is consistent with this, and as we have seen, there were problems with the only evidence that posed a threat to Calder. It may also be significant that, in the trial, Bicknell intervened to prompt Calder to re-examine Captain Durham on the misreading of signals on his ship.[58]

Bicknell's actions suggest the Board wished to eliminate the risk that Calder would be found guilty of a capital charge. Given ongoing sympathy for him in the service (discussed in more detail below), this verdict would have seemed vindictive, unnecessary and almost certainly divisive. It would also risk recalling the controversy aroused by Rear Admiral Byng's condemnation nearly half a century before. Alternatively, the Board may now have believed that the case against Calder was not strong and that no ill-consequence would follow from his acquittal. If this were so, it would have been mildly but not greatly concerned with the outcome and almost certainly relieved that in the atmosphere of mournful celebration that enveloped Nelson's funeral, it ceased to be an item of primary public interest. The authoritative invitations to this event went out in the last week of December and the funeral took place a week after Nicholson's affidavit was first published. It was reprinted in a Scottish newspaper as mourners were gathering in London, but after that, the affidavit and the officer who swore to it seem to have sunk without a trace. The Board never promoted James Nicholson beyond the rank which Calder had secured for him and never seems to have employed him at sea again.

While critics within the service may have had a role in the cry in the press against Calder, there was also sympathy for him. Collingwood was genuinely regretful that Calder had not delayed his return to England until after the anticipated decisive battle.

Just before the court martial, he told Admiral Sir Thomas Pasley that he was 'sorry that Calder was not of the party that he might have settled his account with M. Villeneuve'. Captain Thomas Hardy reported that one of the last things said by Nelson before the battle began was 'what would poor Sir Robert Calder give to be with us now?'[59] While other officers pointed to shortcomings in Calder's judgement they praised his collegiality. Captain Thomas Freemantle thought that Calder was 'not wise' but 'so fair to serve with and so accommodating, that I am much interested in him getting off with credit'.[60] Edward Codrington had been critical of the Board's 'vindictive' order for Calder to return to England in a frigate, and after the trial, he described the sentence as 'one of the severest . . . I ever heard of' and claimed that the Admiralty had 'wantonly ruined' Calder's character.[61]

Once Calder had come to terms with the shock of the verdict, expressions of sympathy from service colleagues may have reinforced his confidence in the justness of his cause and kept alive the smouldering resentment at what he saw as the injustice of his treatment by public opinion and the court. There are indications these reservations were shared more widely. In early 1806, the highly eccentric Duke of Norfolk's ruminations in the House of Lords on whether Calder's contributions on 22 July warranted inclusion in a vote of thanks implicitly questioned the implications of his court martial. Towards the end of the year, the far more level-headed first lord, Thomas Grenville, gave some consideration to appointing Calder to a subordinate flag officer's role in the Channel Fleet but found informed opinion against it on grounds which reflected to some degree the findings of the court: Calder's 'indecisiveness' was 'almost as bad for command as downright fear'.[62] In the following year, Lord Mulgrave offered Calder a subordinate role which he, in yet another demonstration of poor judgement, declined as inappropriate for an officer of his rank and experience.

Calder remained on half pay until Charles Yorke became first lord in May 1810. Earlier that year, Yorke had spoken in the House of Commons to defend Lord Gambier's acquittal on a similar charge to that faced by Calder. He may have recalled the earlier trial and now believed that Calder's court had treated him harshly. A month after taking office, Yorke appointed him to the port admiral's command at Plymouth. Calder later claimed he was encouraged to see this appointment as a stepping stone to something better. After two articles in the *Naval Chronicle* criticized his condemnation, he sent an ill-judged and ungracious letter to the first lord. Calder reminded Yorke of his wish for employment 'in the great line of the Service to which I have always been accustomed' and claimed that he had 'acceded' to his request to take the Plymouth command in the expectation that it was an initial advance on a more substantial restitution payment. 'I am now induced to hope the time is not far distant when I may have the offer of a Command more suitable to my wishes, as well as more honourable & profitable than the very obscure and laborious one I now have.' He concluded with a gesture of flattery spiced with emotional blackmail: 'I leave myself in the hands of a man who knows how to feel for those who have been so unjustly & cruelly persecuted.'[63] Yorke responded by reminding Calder that he owed his present appointment to the first lord's sense that he 'had been harshly treated on a former occasion' and shutting down any prospect of the kind of appointment for which he was angling: 'merits & services will always meet with due consideration from me' but 'existing arrangements' allowed no prospect of satisfying Calder's expectations.[64]

In a half-apologetic reply to the first lord, Calder sought to justify himself by evoking a Duckworthesque poignancy of feelings at being passed over for the Mediterranean command in favour of a 'junior officer'.[65] This correspondence demonstrated a remarkable lack of realism and proportion. In recent years, several distinguished or very well-connected flag officers, including Sir Thomas Pasley, Sir John Colpoys and Sir William Young, held the appointment that Calder scorned. Sir Edward Pellew, the 'junior officer', now commander-in-chief in the Mediterranean, had been made a rear admiral five years after Calder but had a distinguished early career commanding squadrons of frigates and had since been appointed to two independent flag commands.

In addition to making unsuccessful direct bids to first lords, Calder utilized the wider patronage network. He had rehearsed his views on the Plymouth command to Thomas Coutts, the immensely wealthy London banker whose money helped accommodate the Prince of Wales's wildly extravagant lifestyle. He was also the father-in-law of the Marquis of Bute, a political ally of the Prince, with whom Calder's family had a long-standing connection.[66] In early 1812, Calder thanked Coutts and Lord and Lady Bute for their good wishes for securing a more agreeable appointment, naming the Channel command as 'the height of my ambition & wish'. Now that the Prince of Wales had become prince regent, Calder hoped Coutts would remind 'his Royal Highness of his former favourable opinion of me and my most cruel and harsh treatment'.[67] Calder's friends' appeals to the prince regent were no more successful than Duckworth's. When Sir Charles Cotton died in post in command of the Channel Fleet, the Board moved with indecent haste to appoint Lord Keith, an officer whose taste for prize money and power had not been dulled by a long, successful and highly lucrative career in flag command. Keith had close long-standing personal connections with the Prince Regent.[68]

By the time Calder was relieved of what he termed 'the slavery of a Port Admiral' in late 1813, he seems to have become slightly more reconciled to his lot. In early 1814, he told Coutts that he was settled at home in rural Hampshire, 'domesticating very fast after the bustle of Plymouth'. He was making arrangements to place his mentally fragile wife in the care of 'friends' but also looking forward to resuming his outings with the local hunt. While putting a brave face on things, however, – '*Mais n'import je me trouve bien malgree tous cela*' – the indignity of being forced to uphold his reputation and honour through a court martial and the pain of the perceived injustice of the outcome still rankled deeply. On visiting London at the termination of his command, Calder reported that he had been received graciously by the Prince and at the Admiralty but observed to Coutts 'this you will say is all very well and flattering but will not make me any fatter, or heal my wounds'.[69]

Conclusion

Calder's action could be seen as a more significant victory than Keppel's in that he captured two enemy ships and achieved the key strategic objective of preventing the enemy fleet from entering the Channel.[70] His cautiously calculating approach to fleet command may also have foreshadowed a turn away from the highly aggressive tactics employed successfully and to great acclaim on several occasions in the French Wars. His action has been compared favourably with those in March and July 1795, which earned Vice Admiral William Hotham an Irish peerage.[71] Even before the galvanizing example of Trafalgar, however, Calder's leadership off Finisterre prompted critical public comment and his decision-making seemed to have fallen short of the Board's expectations. It is significant that although it formally acceded to Calder's request for a court martial, Lord Barham had already made it clear that a trial was necessary. This move, which owed something to the public reaction to Calder's performance, suggested that the imperative of the twelfth article of war could not be traded off against particular operational objectives.

The possibility that Calder was guilty of cowardice struck at the heart of ideas of honour common to officers and gentlemen. The court's finding of serious misjudgement spared him that fate. Nevertheless, it stigmatized Calder by imputing failures of leadership and duty that were professionally damaging and compromised his standing as a gentleman at arms. These failures were particularly significant because they occurred in a fleet action. The opportunity to command a fleet in battle with a matched enemy force was the acme of flag officers' ambitions, one that eluded otherwise distinguished admirals such as Cornwallis and Collingwood. Less than 10 per cent of flag officers commanded large-scale fleet actions in the French Wars.[72] Calder's misjudgement thus threw away a chance for which many of his colleagues would have given a great deal. These opportunities were, however, always freighted with risk. As Captain Edward Codrington put it, 'How few there are who even at the close of a long life of hard service have had . . . an opportunity of distinguishing themselves; and how few of those have been favoured with an opportunity and done their utmost have escaped public apprehension.'[73]

Finally, Calder's case demonstrates the full range of considerations that played a role in flag officers' court martial experience. The reaction to his performance off Cape Finisterre reflected the interplay of strategic and political pressures, flag officers' sensitivity to their honour and its vindication and the role of the press, elite and service opinion in bringing matters to a head. Calder's personal foibles also played a role in the prelude to his trial, his approach to it and his behaviour in its aftermath.

10

Trouble in Basque Roads

Rear Admiral Sir Eliab Harvey and Admiral Lord James Gambier

The courts martial considered in this and the following chapters arose during Admiral Lord Gambier's command of the Channel Fleet in the early months of 1809. In the first trial, Gambier's second-in-command, Rear Admiral Sir Eliab Harvey, was tried for gross insubordination. Two months later, Gambier requested a court martial to defend himself against imputations (from Captain Lord Cochrane) of failing to inflict maximum damage on the enemy. While Harvey was found guilty and Gambier was honourably acquitted, their trials gave significant publicity to unflattering views on the latter's merits as a commander-in-chief. Harvey's abuse of his senior officer involved unmistakable references to Gambier's lack of the decisive thrusting spirit necessary for naval high command – qualities epitomized by Nelson, under whom Harvey had served with great distinction at Trafalgar. While this matter was not put to the test in Harvey's court martial – that focused on the breach of discipline in his verbal onslaught on his commanding officer – it was the central issue in Gambier's trial.

These courts martial involved a clash between senior officers from very different backgrounds, with strikingly different temperaments and strongly contrasting leadership styles. Cochrane, who had more in common socially and professionally with Harvey than with Gambier, played the role of a lightning rod in the events that precipitated both trials and was a source of disruptive thunderbolts in Gambier's court martial experience. During his long career, Cochrane rose to the heights of popular acclaim and plunged to the depths of official disgrace. In Basque Roads he played important direct and indirect roles in visiting some of this drama on other senior officers.

The events that gave rise to these trials occurred when Gambier's fleet was stationed in Basque Roads in the Bay of Biscay, watching a large French squadron moored close inshore in Aix Roads. Shortly after Cochrane joined the fleet on Admiralty orders to lead a flotilla of fireships to make an initial attack on the French, Harvey went on board Gambier's flagship and assailed him with disrespectful, highly insulting language. He accused his commanding officer of ignoring an initiative he had proposed and conniving with the Admiralty Board to bring Cochrane in over the heads of his colleagues. Harvey also disparaged Gambier's fleet management and fitness for high command. His conduct towards Gambier clearly breached the nineteenth article of war's prohibition of 'contempt to superior officers'; indeed, if it had included active disobedience as well as oral abuse, it would have been mutinous. On receiving Gambier's allegations against Harvey, the Board ordered his recall and summoned him to face a court martial. His trial resulted in an unequivocal finding of guilt and his dismissal from the service. Although the penalty was subsequently set aside on appeal to the Privy Council, the conviction was not and ended what had been a notable career.

Harvey's family interest assisted his rapid movement through the ranks of lieutenant (1779), master and commander (1782) to post captain in 1783. He was involved in several successful actions in the French Wars and played a highly distinguished role as commander of HMS *Temeraire* at the Battle of Trafalgar. *Temeraire* engaged enemy ships on either side and captured them both despite suffering significant casualties and great damage. In a letter written to his wife on the day of the battle, Harvey described it as 'this most glorious action . . . if not *the most* decided action[s] ever fought'. Harvey wearied some of his fellow captains with accounts of his ship's role, but Vice Admiral Collingwood, Nelson's second in command and not a man given to flights of fancy, singled out *Temeraire*'s contribution in his despatch to the Board: 'I cannot resist the Pleasure I have in making it known to their Lordships.'[1]

Having been made a rear admiral in the post-Trafalgar promotion, Harvey was employed in the Channel Fleet under an even more demanding judge than Collingwood. The Earl St Vincent commended Harvey's 'ability', 'zeal' and 'perseverance' and noted the 'esteem and regard' he had for him.[2] In early 1809, Harvey was appointed as a subordinate flag officer in Gambier's Channel Fleet, and in early April, he was second in command of the squadron deployed in Basque Roads. Harvey's well-earned reputation as a courageous fighting officer matched his equally well-merited reputation for personal recklessness. When one of his fellow flag officers heard an incomplete account of the altercation that triggered his court martial, he was said to have guessed the offender's name from the nature of the offence.[3]

Eliab Harvey came from a long-established family in the English baronetcy with estates in Dorset, Essex, Northamptonshire and Suffolk and significant electoral interest in the Essex borough of Maldon and the county of Essex; Sir Eliab represented both constituencies in the House of Commons. He was a second son but came into the estate, the title and the electoral interest while still a midshipman. On doing so, he soon gave compelling evidence of a capacity for highly impulsive behaviour that turned up trumps at Trafalgar but then upset what may have been a promising career in flag command.

Midshipman Harvey's trustees provided a handsome allowance of £2000 per annum (compared with an admiral's pay of a little over 60 per cent of that figure), but his taste for high stakes gambling quickly outran it. One night at the Cocoa Club in London, Harvey faced a loss of the staggering sum of £100,000 (£22.5m in 2024 terms) to a professional gamester, Mr O'Birne. Either in response to Harvey's appeal or on O'Birne's initiative, the two agreed to decide on the toss of a coin to settle for £10,000 or for O'Birne to take the entire estate. The midshipman's luck momentarily turned and saved an estate worth close to £5000 per annum in rents alone. It is unclear whether this experience cured Harvey's taste for gambling, but if not he must have indulged it after that with uncharacteristic restraint. Despite providing handsome marriage portions for his four daughters, he died a wealthy man, maintaining the splendid house and grounds at Roll Park in Essex and extending an impressive collection of paintings.[4]

Rear Admiral Harvey speaks his mind

Even before Lord Cochrane joined the fleet, Harvey launched the first stage of his assault on Lord Gambier. In a dutiful, bureaucratically efficient reaction to the Board's instructions, Gambier circulated his captains, asking for one officer and twenty seamen from each ship to volunteer for the dangerous fireship mission. Harvey responded by giving a rousing address to his ship's company and then reporting to Gambier that he, all the officers of the *Tonnant* and the vast majority of its crew volunteered to undertake the initial attack. As Harvey could not serve under an officer of Cochrane's rank, this move put Gambier in the embarrassing position of declining the offer as inconsistent with the Board's instructions.[5] Worse was to follow.

In a meeting in the great cabin of Gambier's flagship (HMS *Caledonia*) on 2 April, Harvey responded with a 'high tone and disrespectful manner' when told the Admiralty Board had instructed Gambier that Cochrane should command the squadron of fireships. He threatened to strike his flag and resign his commission, berated Gambier in a 'vehement and insulting manner' for neglecting his 'former services' when a member of the Board and accused him of covertly arranging Cochrane's appointment despite Harvey's earlier (unacknowledged) presentation of a plan of attack on the French squadron in Aix Roads. Harvey threatened to request a court martial on Gambier to expose what he described as his 'misconduct and bad management of the Fleet'. Gambier later testified that Harvey assailed him with insulting gestures and language and 'anger and heat in his countenance'.[6]

After berating Gambier in the relative privacy of his cabin, Harvey compounded his offending by moving to the captain-of-the-fleet's quarters and regaling the first captain and Lord Cochrane with the commanders-in-chief's shortcomings. He addressed these officers 'with great vehemence and rapidity of expression', subjecting them to a rant on Gambier's unfitness for flag command, saying he had never seen a fleet so 'ill-conducted' and criticizing him for 'amusing himself' with routine tasks such as mustering crews when he should have been scoping operational options for attacking the French.[7] Harvey continued his tirade on *Caledonia*'s quarterdeck in the presence of thirty officers and men, proclaiming against Gambier's 'methodistical and jesuitical Conduct and . . . his vindictive temper'. Harvey reinforced his contemptuous allusion to Gambier's well-known evangelical attachments by references to hypocritical 'canting methodism' that took financial advantage of the gullibility of 'poor widows'.[8] He reiterated these views in front of officers and crew members when he returned to his flagship later in the day.[9]

Gambier acted promptly to these affronts to his personal dignity and professional authority. On 4 April he reported that Harvey's behaviour was 'so contemptuous and insulting as to amount even to Mutiny' and told the Board that if it did not order a court martial on him he reserved the right to apply for one. In a follow-up letter written on the same day, Gambier drew the Board's attention to the implications of Harvey's abuse. He had 'spoken of him, his character and his conduct at different times in an un-officer like and contemptuous manner tending to subvert the discipline of the Fleet, much to the prejudice of the public service.'[10] The Board immediately authorized Harvey's court martial and directed Sir Roger Curtis to preside over it. Harvey was ordered home and struck his flag at Plymouth on 17 April.[11] By that time, however, the affair was common knowledge. On 14 April the government gave notice in the House of Commons that Harvey had been detained in custody by the provost martial to be released on giving his word of honour to appear when called. This notification was necessary because he was an MP.[12]

Details of various aspects of the affair quickly spread into the provincial press. The *Norfolk Chronicle* confirmed that 'Admiral Harvey had been sent home . . . under arrest, for having accused his superior officer, Admiral Gambier, with being a religious Hypocrite'.[13] Two days later, the *Caledonian Mercury* gave Scottish readers a detailed account of the dispute and Harvey's abusive treatment of his commanding officer. This report traced the affair to the ethos of the navy and hoped it would soon be settled.

> We are extremely sorry for any occurrence of this nature in the fleet, which, nevertheless, proceeds from a feeling most characteristic of the general spirit of the British navy, namely, a jealousy of honour, an ardent desire to be in the midst of danger, which has, perhaps, in the present instance, broken out into a little irregular fit of spleen, but which, we still hope, will involve none of the parties concerned in any serious consequences.[14]

The *Bath Chronicle* allowed that Harvey's language towards Gambier was 'very disrespectful' but also expressed some sympathy for him: 'Admiral Harvey is a *fighting* man, and we should be sorry his zeal in this instance had outrun his prudence.'[15]

Lady Harvey, a better judge of her husband's prudence and temper than the press, was far from optimistic. In the wake of Trafalgar, her letters captured the family's excitement about Harvey's role in the battle and pride in his promotion to flag rank: he was now 'the *Admiral*'. Understandably, her reaction to news from Basque Roads was entirely different. Her reports to their eldest daughter were full of uncertainty and foreboding and infused with an unstated sense that 'your father has really done it this time'. She told her daughter that she was consulting her mighty relatives, the Buckinghams, about Harvey's situation: 'I fear it will end unpleasantly for yr Father[;] the expressions he used towards Lord Gambier are highly censurable.' After Harvey arrived in London, however, there were hopes of settling the matter: 'Admiral Bentinck is in Conference with yr Father . . . and I hope will endeavour to reconcile matters before a Court Martial takes place if *he can*.'[16] William Bentinck came from a very well-connected family and was related to the Duke of Portland, the prime minister. His discussions with Harvey may have induced the latter to apologize to Gambier. In the event, Gambier declined to settle the matter privately on the grounds that the dispute was not merely a personal one because the honour, discipline and good of the public service were also at stake. Harvey was tried by a court martial on-board HMS *Gladiator* in Portsmouth Harbour from 22 to 23 May 1809.

Harvey's trial

Harvey's court was heavily stacked with nine flag officers, with four post captains making up the balance. The president, Admiral Sir Roger Curtis, who had sat on Cornwallis' court martial, was Lord Howe's first captain on the Glorious First of June. He was regularly employed in subordinate flag commands following his elevation to rear admiral in July 1794 and was commander-in-chief at the Cape of Good Hope in the closing years of the French Wars. He was not employed in active service in the early years of the Napoleonic Wars but became port admiral at Portsmouth in early 1809. Other flag officers on the court included Vice Admiral John Holloway, who was between seasons of residence at his command and governorship of Newfoundland, and Sir John Duckworth. Curtis' appointment was unexceptional in procedural terms, but he was a lifelong friend of Gambier, took a cautious approach to high command and had a submissive attitude to superiors. Detractors accused him of fawning on Lord Howe, and James Gillray published a cartoon entitled 'What a Cur'tis!', which portrayed him as a dog licking Howe's shoes. There is, however, no indication of concern on Harvey's part about the membership of the court and no discussion in the press on that question. In truth, Curtis' appointment as president and the entire composition of the court were matters of little consequence since the case against Harvey was overwhelming and partly endorsed by the accused.

The Board's minute to Curtis pointed out that the public nature of Harvey's misconduct – 'insulting and contemptuous language to Admiral Lord Gambier' – Harvey's seniority and its occurrence while preparations were underway for a major operation compounded his offending. It tended to 'subvert due confidence and discipline and to militate so much against the proceedings of the public service'.[17] Although Gambier had complained to the Board, it laid the charge so he was not the accuser and could thus be called as a witness. The Board ordered Charles Bicknell, the Solicitor to the Admiralty, to be the prosecutor. In contrast with Calder's trial, there is no indication of the prosecution being willing to pull any punches. Harvey's legal 'friend' was Mr Serjeant Best, a successful barrister and judicial officeholder with an indifferent reputation for legal acumen. Best's maverick tendencies ran in different, less honourable, but safer lines to Harvey's. He had a reputation for political and career opportunism and libertinism.[18]

The trial was relatively brief and very straightforward. The prosecution case focused on establishing the facts of Harvey's interactions with his commander-in-chief and the public repetition of his accusations against Gambier. Gambier testified to details of the abusive language and 'insulting manner' that Harvey used in their private discussion and stressed that he had not provoked him. His responses to the various passages of Harvey's tirade were 'calm', avoiding 'anything that might give him the least offence, or increase his irritation'.[19] When Harvey cross-examined him on the proffered apology he 'offered to make any apology to your Lordship that a man of Honour could make for the expression that escaped me' – Gambier told the court that he would have been happy to accept the apology 'had it been consistent with my duty to my Country, to my Profession as a naval officer and what I owe to the character that I hold in my public capacity of commander-in-chief of the Fleet, for I must state that I bear no personal Enmity or Resentment to Admiral Harvey for his Conduct'.[20] The last phrase suggests a triumph of Christian forbearance over the notions of personal honour that underwrote contemporary justifications of duelling, while the rest of the explanation rested on an idea of professional and public honour attached to office holders that was distinct from the personal honour of a gentleman. Gambier and his friends related this idea to their belief that evangelical officers' military achievements demonstrated that piety and heroic public service were compatible.[21] Harvey's later claim that his apology to Gambier was 'satisfactory to his feeling' was thus beside the point.[22]

Sir Henry Neale (Gambier's first captain) and Lord Cochrane gave evidence on Harvey's rant to them, and the flag captain of HMS *Caledonia*, Captain William Bedford, testified to his abusive remarks in front of thirty officers and men on the quarterdeck. Since Bedford was closely associated with Gambier's evangelical endeavours, Harvey's allegations of religious hypocrisy were particularly unfortunate. The court, however, was less concerned with religious sensitivities than with the size and nature of Harvey's audience. Bedford testified that Harvey's highly disrespectful comments were audible to all those on the quarterdeck and pointed out that accounts of them were promptly transmitted by the 'public papers'. Finally, officers from Harvey's flagship testified that he had aired claims about Gambier's unfitness for command in the hearing of other members of the ship's company.[23]

Harvey addressed the question of the dissemination of his expostulations in his defence. While claiming that the 'evidence . . . falls short of proving the charges', he acknowledged, 'I should, however, not be acting a fair and candid part were I to deny that a conduct which I cannot justify, has been established against me; and I now offer my most humble apology to the Court for it.'[24] Harvey denied, however, that the prosecution had established that his highly disrespectful remarks to and about Gambier were heard widely and harmful to discipline: 'I spoke only to persons of rank and station in the Fleet, on whose mind my words could have no injurious affect.' He claimed that the prosecution had not proved that his words had been 'disseminated amongst the inferior orders of the Navy' and noted that it had not called any seamen or petty officers as witnesses.

The final part of Harvey's defence reflected the view of the ethos of the service that had already been aired in the press. 'Excess of zeal and impatience of restraint when an opportunity of enterprise presents itself, although faults are such as the most eminent naval commanders have not been free from.' He argued that these traits were 'all that can be found blameable in my conduct'. Harvey concluded by denying he intended to 'thwart' his superior officer, referring to his record of 'entire submission', appealing to the court members' knowledge of his character and reading letters from Collingwood and St Vincent as testimonials.[25]

Given Harvey's candid confession of his misconduct and the weight of evidence on that score, his attempt to cast doubts on its dissemination and bearing was the only avenue open if he was to escape with a reprimand. Mr Serjeant Best no doubt bent his legal mind to enable Harvey to make the best of a very bad job, but this part of the defence flew in the face of Captain Bedford's evidence and ignored the publicity given to Harvey's tirade in the press. It also relied on judges suspending their experience of the transmission of unofficial information through ships and fleets. In this case, the lack of enthusiasm on the lower deck for Gambier's attempts to suppress swearing, drunkenness and fornication, and the popularity engendered by Harvey's courage and combination of paternalism and 'damn your eyes' gentlemanly conduct, is likely to have made accounts of his abuse of Gambier a ripe topic for lower deck gossip and delight. Naval views on the need to act decisively to make an example of those who challenged their superiors meant Harvey's language and sentiments threatened discipline. Even his appeal to 'zeal and impatience of restraint' involved the implication that Gambier was deficient in these qualities. Finally, in challenging Gambier's right to command, Harvey questioned implicitly the judgement of those who appointed him.

The court martial ended after Harvey's defence. He called no witnesses, and it is, indeed, hard to see how he could have done so. That the court deliberated for two hours on such slender proceedings might indicate that at least some of its members thought there was room for manoeuvre to mitigate the penalty.[26] In the event, its verdict was that Harvey was guilty as charged and dismissed him from the service.

Aftermath

The press reported that the court was very full on both days. There was considerable sympathy for Harvey in the service, and he received the court's verdict 'firmly'.[27] He then went ashore, walked to his lodgings and left shortly after for his London house in Clifford Street, Mayfair. The trial had implicitly upheld the honour of Gambier's office and the service, and close colleagues duly celebrated his vindication with an 'elegant' and presumably temperate 'entertainment' on board HMS *Caledonia* at Spithead.[28]

Given Lady Harvey's alarm when news of the altercation reached her, she cannot have been surprised by the verdict. She is also likely to have had a clear view of its impact on her husband. Later in the year, she told her eldest daughter that a promised present of a turtle had arrived but that Harvey was in such poor health and spirits that she doubted whether the planned feast upon it would go ahead.[29] His eldest son, Captain Edward Harvey, who was serving with the army in Spain, had heard of the likelihood of a court martial, but news of the outcome did not reach him until late August. He had not received newspapers with details of the trial and so could remain confident that the verdict had been a mistake and that his father would be reinstated. Uncertainty over the court martial had added significantly to the stress of active service in a highly demanding campaign. Captain Harvey told Charles Lloyd, his brother-in-law, that he had 'been exceptionally anxious about my father's business, it has been a disagreeable and unfortunate affair, but I cannot conceive that there can be the smallest degree of blame attached to my father, and I cannot doubt but he will be reinstated if it has not already taken place'.[30] The captain's touching faith in his father's innocence was misplaced, but his confidence in his reinstatement was well-founded, if a little premature.

Harvey was restored to his place on the list of rear admirals by the Privy Council on 21 March 1810.[31] The Navy Privy Council reports show that its role in settling appeals from commissioned officers of the Royal Navy applied to untitled lieutenants as well as to rear admiral baronets. Nevertheless, when Harvey told his son-in-law that his restoration owed 'more to my good friends than any Merit of my own', he was acknowledging that interest played a role in the processes through which appeals were advanced to the Council.[32] There does not appear to be any documentary evidence of how Harvey's friends approached their task or who they were. The Duke of Buckingham and Chandos and Rear Admiral William Bentinck were almost certainly among them. Earl St Vincent may also have been in Harvey's corner. As a former first lord and senior distinguished admiral, his voice might carry some weight. He was a near neighbour in Essex, and his professional respect for Harvey and dislike of Lord Gambier may have been enough to overcome any disciplinary scruples about the rear admiral's conduct.

Although the details of the mobilization of interest remain a matter of speculation, the process to which Harvey's friends applied it is well documented. In early March 1810, Lord Mulgrave, the first lord of the admiralty, wrote to the King that it had been 'intimated' to him that Harvey intended to petition the Crown for reinstatement. He explained that Lord Gambier wished the case to be considered and that both the professional lords of the admiralty thought that there would be no risk to the discipline of the service provided that 'the justice and propriety of the sentence of the court martial should be fully asserted in the report which it would be for the Admiralty to make upon your Majesty's gracious reference from the Council'. Furthermore, they stipulated that Harvey's 'distinguish'd gallantry' in the Battle of Trafalgar should be the entire grounds for a decision in his favour. Mulgrave successfully sought an assurance that the King would not object to Harvey's petition being forwarded by the Board to 'your Majesty in Council'.[33]

Following Mulgrave's exchange with the King, Harvey (already primed to act) presented a 'Humble memorial' to 'The King's Most Excellent Majesty in Council'. In this document, he offered a full *mea culpa* in terms of the conditions in Mulgrave's letter to the King and based his appeal on his record of thirty-six years of 'honourable employment'. This document almost certainly reflected private advice from Mulgrave or the naval commissioners. Harvey acknowledged that he was 'unfortunately betrayed into the use of intemperate expressions towards . . . Lord Gambier, which your Petitioner is now sensible were inconsistent with good Order, and the maintenance of Naval Discipline'. The petition did not refer to the mitigating considerations that had been advanced in Harvey's defence but stressed that his previous record had been free of any taint of 'insubordination' and was marked by 'zeal and fidelity' that had 'given satisfaction to the many distinguished officers whom it had been his good fortune to serve under'.[34]

The Privy Council considered Harvey's appeal two days after he submitted it and instructed the Admiralty Board to 'consider . . . and Report their opinion thereupon to His Majesty at this Board'. The Admiralty Board reported back four days later in terms virtually identical to those used in Mulgrave's letter to the King. In supporting the petition, the Board reiterated that it did so 'without impeachment of the justice and propriety of the sentence' and in 'consideration of his long and meritorious Services'. The Privy Council's determination repeated these phrases. The Board recommended that Harvey be restored to his 'former rank' but an annotation on the Privy Council's documentation clarified that he would be 'restored to his place on the list according to his former rank'.[35] This specification meant that Harvey became a vice admiral in the next promotion round at the end of July 1810.

Harvey's reinstatement was reported in the press in early April 1810, and the news quickly reached his eldest daughter's family.[36] Charles Lloyd sent welcome news of its reception by his neighbours among the gentry of the Welsh marches. Rear Admiral Harvey (as he had now become again) wrote to tell Lloyd that it 'is very flattering to me to hear so Numerous and Respectable attendance as were at Shrewsbury during your Assizes have thought my restoration to my former rank in the Navy worthy of their attention'.[37] An account by Admiral Sir William Hotham suggests that Harvey appreciated Lord Gambier's attitude towards his appeal for reinstatement. When chairing a club dinner shortly afterwards, he proposed a toast to Gambier and spoke with 'many kind and manly expressions as to the unfortunate difference that had taken place between them'.[38]

Although Harvey benefited from promotions that saw him become an admiral of the blue in 1819 and was made a KCB in the remodelled Order of the Bath in 1815 and a GCB in 1825, he was never employed again. As his name is not prominent among the multitude of half-pay flag officers who offered their services to the Board, it may be that another, hidden, condition of his reinstatement was that he would neither seek nor be offered employment. Harvey was embittered by the early end to his career and that, combined with the grief he suffered as the result of his eldest son's death in action in Spain in 1812 and his second son's death through illness in 1825, exacerbated his tendency for erratic behaviour. The year 1818 seems to have been very challenging. There were reports of violence against his wife and an unmarried daughter, destructive rampages through his garden targeting French plants – beans and young vines – and an incident where he verbally abused the local vicar, Mr Thomas Layton, in front of a group of farm labourers and amused them by inviting the gentleman to kiss his arse.[39]

These brain fades were, however, merely regrettable episodes in a more regular existence as a wealthy member of the English gentry. Harvey could be solicitous towards his family as well as abusive. He was particularly closely attached to his eldest daughter, Mrs Louisa Lloyd. When her son, William Lloyd, was seriously ill in London in the spring of 1821, Harvey visited his bedside, sent him books and reported to the boy's mother on his condition and the care he was receiving.[40] After the double blow of this boy's death and Harvey's second son in 1825, he contemplated making Louisa's surviving son Edward his heir; since he would also inherit his father's estate, this grandson would have been very wealthy. However, Harvey abandoned this arrangement in an outburst of temper following a 'trifling disagreement'. During the last years of his life (he died in early 1830) Harvey caused unease in his family with what Louisa called his 'desultory manner of talking of his affairs' before deciding very late in the day to divide his landed property and his collection of paintings among his daughters. The three youngest were also to receive £10,000, while Louisa, his favourite and the oldest of his surviving children, was to get £15,000.[41] This arrangement upset the younger daughters, and Louisa was concerned about the breakup of the estate: 'thereby destroying forever the Old family of Harvey in the County of Essex – the very place where my Brothers and all the family are buried will in that case be sold to strangers'.[42] As part of the settlement between the sisters, Louisa eventually secured

Roll Park. In a process that inadvertently echoed Sir Eliab's taste for games of chance, the various portions of the landed property were surveyed, consolidated into parcels and then allocated by lot.[43]

In his enforced retirement, Harvey continued to perform the role of a prosperous member of the gentry. He served as a magistrate, filled the office of Verderer of Waltham Forest, which had long been in the family, and was one of the two MPs for the county of Essex (1802–12, 1820–30). Harvey regularly attended parliament and voted as an independent Tory. Thus, in 1821, he was in the majority against the continuation of the malt tax, and in 1827, he opposed a measure reducing protection for corn producers; these votes reflected Harvey's attachment to the interests of farmers and landholders. In 1821 and again in 1824, he voted with the minority (and in alignment with the sentiments of Church and King Tories) against measures to relieve Roman Catholics of civil disabilities.[44] Harvey presented a petition to the House in favour of the abolition of colonial slavery in 1826, but it is unclear if he favoured this cause or saw it as his duty to act on behalf of local opinion as expressed by a meeting in Chelmsford.[45] Harvey may have vandalized French plantings, but prime dogs and livestock roused him to flights of bucolic affection. He described a sow as 'beautiful and as near perfection as I would wish', and on hearing a favourite dog was in pup he enthused 'I cannot but love her and her Progeny.'[46]

Harvey's funeral in late February 1830 was very much a county affair reflecting local attachments and interests. There is no mention in press reports of naval dignitaries in the 'mournful pageant' in which the lord lieutenant of Essex led the nobility and gentry of the neighbourhood and twenty-eight tenants on horseback. Obituary notices skated over Harvey's shortcomings as a parent and husband, giving prominence to his 'liberality' as a landlord. Some of those who followed his coffin in 1830 would have benefited from Harvey's willingness to forego several thousand pounds in income when he made a ten shilling an acre reduction in rents during the post-war agricultural depression.[47]

Conclusion

Harvey's very one-sided dispute with Gambier was unusual in that it has left an official record of open oral abuse of one flag officer by another. It was far more common for clashes between commanders-in-chief and their subordinates to be played out at a distance through written correspondence. Typically, the protagonists communicated in tones of icy, disdainful civility, occasionally punctured by sharp sarcastic barbs. These exchanges were self-regulated by the knowledge that they were likely to be forwarded to the Admiralty Board in the hope of securing its support for disciplining a difficult subordinate or its protection against exercises of unreasonable and unwarranted superiority. This pattern was apparent in St Vincent's numerous disputes with flag officers under his command and acrimonious transactions between Vice Admiral Sir John Laforey, Lord Keith and Vice Admiral Sir Hyde Parker and their senior subordinates.[48] The veil of formal privacy that screened these disputes was entirely lacking in Harvey's interactions with Gambier and his senior officers. Publicity broadened the audience for his tirades and thus gave rise to concerns about their implications for discipline and due subordination in the service. Because Harvey was free of constraints that arose in written communications, he used language that hastened the dissemination of details of the incident and thus exacerbated its damaging effects.

Given there was no doubt about Harvey's conduct and the court's verdict made it clear that it did not accept that knowledge of the dispute was confined to a few senior officers, the penalty imposed on him seemed almost a matter of course. His court martial was thus unique among those held on flag officers in this period in resulting in an unequivocal finding of guilty as charged and dismissal from the service. It was also unique in having the penalty remitted by the King in Council. Unlike earlier cases involving Palliser and Duckworth, there was no attempt to revisit the court's decision through a parliamentary inquiry into the conduct or finding of the court martial. In these cases, a parliamentary recommendation to the King to set aside a verdict would have to show that it was unsound. By contrast, Harvey's appeal to the Privy Council recognized explicitly the 'justice and propriety' of the court's sentence. The insistence that the original verdict was to stand was an interesting use of the monarch's prerogative since a judgement of 1788 determined that a royal pardon 'can take off the whole of the punishment' and 'entirely absolve him from the crime'.[49] The Crown did not apply this ruling to Harvey's appeal; its response was framed explicitly to sustain the court's judgement on the dangerous disciplinary implications of gross insubordination. The weight placed on Harvey's prior service, particularly his role at Trafalgar, mitigated the impact of the penalty in the same way that commutation of a sentence of death spared the offender without impeaching the 'justice and propriety' of the original sentence. In Harvey's case, the character of his past services was sufficiently unusual to avoid setting precedents for future decisions which, in any case, remained a matter of complete discretion. A few years earlier, a similar caveat was attached to a pardon granted on the court's recommendation to a major general cashiered for duelling. The King granted the pardon but decreed that the commander-in-chief should notify the sentence in 'General Orders . . . for the sake of example'.[50]

A range of considerations may explain why the Crown applied discretion in Harvey's favour in 1810. References to popularity and sympathy are insufficient to warrant mitigating the sentence in what was, after all, a very clear-cut case. There is no evidence of 'misgivings' about the fairness of the verdict; the evidence presented in court was unequivocal, there were no procedural irregularities, and in his petition Harvey accepted full responsibility for his offending.[51] However, sympathy for Harvey and appreciation of his gallantry at Trafalgar may have helped make Lord Mulgrave receptive to Harvey's plea for reinstatement. Paradoxically, Harvey's well-known volatility may have made his language seem more excusable than if it had come from a cooler, more obviously calculating head.

The contempt shown by Harvey for Gambier's evangelical attachments may have given satisfaction to those who scoffed at the mission of 'blue light' officers in the navy, and his denigration of Gambier's leadership qualities would have struck a chord with those who saw his appointments and honours as triumphs of interest and administrative seat-warming over demonstrated merit.[52] Gambier's extended terms as a lord commissioner of the Admiralty gave plenty of scope for arousing resentment among those who felt neglected (like Harvey) or thwarted (like St Vincent).[53] The maladroit handling of arrangements arising from Gambier's appointment to command the naval forces in the assault on Copenhagen in 1807 provoked significant resentment among senior figures in the service.[54]

If popularity and sympathy served at least to remove impediments to the Board's support for Harvey's case, it seems clear that interest played a critical role in bringing it to the attention of Mulgrave and his colleagues. Harvey said as much in his letter to Charles Lloyd, and Mulgrave's careful clearing of the ground and the implicit agreement on the nature and basis of the approach confirm his generous acknowledgement of his 'friends'. Mulgrave's letter to the King was masterful in specifying the conditions of an appeal and referring to the views of the naval commissioners upon it. Mulgrave's account of his consultations with Vice Admiral William Domett and Captain Robert Moorsom would have reassured the King. They had both been on the Board when Harvey was charged and convicted and were well-respected officers. The decision to support a case on the conditions specified indicates that the Board's view was that Harvey's ongoing punishment was not necessary for the good of the service. His dismissal had served an exemplary deterrent function, and the terms of reinstatement reiterated that while recognizing Harvey's outstanding service record. At the same time, however, it seems likely that the circumstances of the charge and Harvey's initial reaction in his statement of defence raised questions about his temper and judgement which, since they resulted in de facto exclusion from active service, continued to perform an exemplary, disciplinary role.

Finally, matters of timing are also likely to have played a role in the Board's support for Harvey's case. Gambier had come through his trial with flying colours and thus relieved the pressure of Harvey's and Cochrane's damaging claims about his fitness to command and their implied criticism of the Board's judgement in appointing him. Mulgrave did not resign the first lordship until the end of April 1810, but for several months before that he had made it clear to the prime minister that he was exhausted by the burdens of the office and wished to be relieved of them as soon as possible.[55] He may thus have thought that the time was ripe to respond effectively to Harvey's friends and to any qualms that the Board had about prolonging his punishment.

11

More Trouble in Basque Roads

Admiral Lord Gambier and Captain Lord Cochrane

Two months after Harvey's trial, Lord Gambier was back in court, answering a charge laid by the Admiralty Board at his request. It arose from the action against a French squadron in Aix Roads which had taken place a few days after Harvey's oral assault on his commander-in-chief. Although frigates and fireships from the British fleet succeeded in inflicting significant damage on the French forces, accounts in the English press questioned whether Gambier had made the most of his opportunities. The Board was prepared to ignore these murmurings and to support parliamentary votes of thanks to Lord Gambier, but in late May 1809 Captain Lord Cochrane announced that he would oppose a vote in the House of Commons. In response to this move, Gambier successfully requested the Board to charge him with the offences for which it court-martialled Admiral Keppel: 'withdrawing or keeping back from fight', not doing 'his utmost to take or destroy every ship which it shall be his duty to engage'.

James Gambier's father was lieutenant governor of the Bahamas, and his uncle was a vice admiral, but he was brought up in the family of another naval uncle, Captain Charles Middleton. Middleton was comptroller of the Navy from 1776 to 1793, a naval commissioner of the Admiralty from 1794 to 1796, and, as Lord Barham, first lord of the admiralty, 1805–6.[1] Gambier's career owed much to Barham's support and that of other well-connected relatives, including Henry Dundas, later Lord Melville, Secretary of State and first lord of the admiralty, and the Pitts, the family of a first lord of the admiralty and a long-serving prime minister. Gambier followed Middleton in his attachment to evangelical Anglicanism, becoming a leading member of a loosely knit group of naval officers committed to bringing Christian faith and practice to bear in the service.[2] He also followed Middleton, often with his direct support, in forging a career as a naval administrator. Gambier's experience in flag command was very limited. He had spent eight and three-quarter years on the Admiralty Board, three years as commander-in-chief and governor of Newfoundland – a posting with administrative and political rather than operational responsibilities – and a year as a subordinate flag officer in the Channel fleet.

While on the Board, Gambier was appointed to a six-month command of the naval squadron responsible for seizing the Danish fleet and supporting the army by bombarding Copenhagen. The attack on Copenhagen achieved its objective of preventing the Danish ships from falling into French hands and was most welcome to the government of the day.[3] However, the operation involved a pre-emptive strike on the land and sea forces of a neutral power that resulted in close to a thousand civilian casualties and extensive damage to private property. Although one of Gambier's critics opined that the fleet had 'little else to do than look on', he earned prize money of £150,000 and was made a peer.[4] This honour, which matched that given to Vice Admiral Sir Cuthbert Collingwood after Trafalgar, may have resulted from the government's wish to act equitably after rewarding the army commander by raising him from the Scottish to the UK peerage.[5] Lord Mulgrave, a civilian first lord from 1807 to 1810, ignored the claims of other more experienced officers when appointing his fellow commissioner to the Baltic command. He was a close friend of Gambier, relied heavily on him at the Board and again favoured him with the command of the Channel fleet.

In March 1809, Lord Gambier's squadron was in Basque Roads, blockading a French squadron moored under shore batteries in an inner anchorage, Aix Roads. In early April, he was joined by Lord Cochrane, whom the Admiralty Board had appointed to lead a flotilla of fireships and vessels packed with explosives in an initial attack on the French ships.[6] Cochrane, the elder son of a ninth earl in the Scottish peerage, had a well-earned reputation for daring actions at sea and attacks on ports and defence facilities on enemy coasts. He was also, however, a very difficult officer to manage. He harboured a growing list of grievances against the Admiralty and former superior officers over appointments and recognition. An ever-increasing band of detractors in the upper reaches of the navy suspected him of being indecently concerned with prize money. He was also associated with radical opposition figures in parliament and 'out of doors' and was one of the MPs for the volatile Westminster constituency.

Gambier had written to the Board proposing the use of fireships, but by the time Cochrane arrived he did not seem sanguine about such an attack.[7] When Cochrane led his force in on the night of 11 April, it did little direct damage to the enemy ships but broke the boom protecting them and caused panic that resulted in collisions and groundings. Early the following day, Cochrane signalled his commanding officer on the state of the enemy ships and told him that half the British fleet could destroy them. Although Gambier moved his ships nearer to the enemy and sent in bomb vessels with Cochrane's frigate *Impérieuse*, he did not, despite hectoring signals from his subordinate, commit other ships until later in the day. When Cochrane was trying to organize an attack the next day, there were again delays, and Gambier sent him contradictory instructions, one of which suggested he withdraw. On 14 April Cochrane was recalled to the fleet and ordered to take home the officer from the flagship who had not taken part in the action but was carrying Gambier's despatches to the Board.

Gambier's action in Basque Roads: Accolades and recriminations

On 22 April 1809, the *Morning Post* announced the 'Glorious Intelligence' of the 'Destruction of [the] French Fleet at Basque Roads'.[8] Two days later, it reported that this 'glorious enterprise' had been celebrated by 'a partial illumination, which for the most part was of a very brilliant description'. The victory was particularly valuable 'as giving additional force to the proven truth that nothing can resist the energy and daring of our brave tars . . . that neither their batteries nor their shoals can give safety to their fleets in the presence of a British squadron'.[9] These sentiments, if not the language, were entirely consistent with the initial ministerial reaction to Gambier's despatch. The Board referred twice to 'the brilliant success of the force under your command' and took advantage of the destruction and containment of the French ships to redeploy some of Gambier's squadron off L'Orient. He was ordered to return home to appear in Rear Admiral Harvey's trial.[10] Over the days following, further communications from Basque Roads recorded reductions in the size and viability of the French fleet by small vessels from the British squadron, fires, storm and grounding damage, and the effective decommissioning of ships of the line that were no longer fit for purpose.[11] At the same time, however, a counter-narrative of lost opportunities emerged in the British press.

The first widely publicized sign of disenchantment appeared in *The Times* on April 25. Having noted 'our joy' at the news of the destruction of French vessels in Basque Roads, the correspondent had 'been given to understand, that there are some people more conversant in these things, whose satisfaction is not quite so complete as was our own'. The action appeared to be 'not so fatal to the enemy as it might have been'. These views were associated openly with Lord Cochrane. While the correspondent allowed that Cochrane's 'heroic ardour' may have run ahead of realistic possibilities, he nevertheless suggested that an investigation was necessary. Two days later, a piece tellingly entitled 'Lord Cochrane's Victory' praised the captain, attacked Gambier for criticizing his appointment and damned the ministry with faint praise for having *'for once'* entrusted a critical mission to an energetic junior officer. The pro-ministerial *Morning Post* reported the circulation of claims that 'more might have been accomplished' and sought to refute them. The *Times* printed a letter from 'Eye Witness' extolling the fleet's achievements and depreciating claims about a 'lack of cordiality' between Gambier and Cochrane but also referring to the circulation of adverse commentary on these matters.[12] These reports prompted the Admiralty Board to ask Gambier for a fuller account of events in Basque Roads and secure additional details from his captains. Gambier responded at length after his return to London.

Notes of discord in the press and elite and service gossip occurred too late to repress the artistic, entrepreneurial and patriotic impulses of the proprietors of the Royal Amphitheatre at Westminster Bridge. Their 'new Nautical Spectacle consisting of Recitative, Songs, duets, Glees and Choruses, with Appropriate Action & forming a true and lively Portraiture of the late Proceedings and Glorious Event . . . in Basque Roads' opened in early May.[13] This spectacle, applauded by critics from both the ministerial and anti-ministerial press, attracted large audiences – early in its run, it had received 'most enthusiastic applause from admiring thousands' – and did not close until early June.[14] By that time, however, Cochrane had deflected the Board's written request for information explaining why he intended to oppose a parliamentary vote of thanks to Gambier and made it clear to Lord Mulgrave that he would adopt a version of what amounted to Keppel's strategy of insinuation without charging. Gambier was informed of this development and secured the Board's agreement to summon him to face a court martial.[15]

The prelude to Gambier's trial

The trial was delayed initially by the need to recall witnesses and by preparations in Portsmouth to launch a massive expedition against enemy forces in the Scheldt estuary below Antwerp. The delay gave fresh scope for commentary and speculation in the press and the service. As soon as the court martial became public knowledge, the *Caledonian Mercury* reported from London that the 'occasion has already produced much dissatisfaction among our naval officers'.[16] William Cobbett, an ally of Cochrane's radical political friends, gave a satirical endorsement of Lord Gambier's request for a trial: he 'certainly is the best judge of whether he *ought to be tried*, or not; all that I can say upon the subject is, that I most sincerely wish *he may have his due*'.[17] Having earlier announced that Gambier and his friends would live in Government House at Portsmouth during the trial and that he had paid to refurbish rooms there for the occasion, the local newspaper advanced the view that the court martial would not take place because there was 'no person whatever to prefer any charges against his Lordship'.[18] The pro-ministerial *Morning Post* refuted this claim and reported correctly that as there was 'no voluntary Prosecutor' Gambier would be tried 'at the Prosecution of the Crown'.[19]

This approach accorded with that taken in other cases where flag officers were tried at their request, as well as those where the impetus for a court martial originated with the Board. It differed from the cases of Keppel and Duckworth where accusers of flag officers became their prosecutors. When the Crown was the prosecutor, decisions on who would conduct the prosecution varied. In Palliser's trial the role was assumed by the court itself, but it was more common for the judge advocate to lead the prosecution with the support of the Admiralty solicitor. This arrangement was potentially problematic as this official was also charged with advising the court on legal and procedural questions. The Board avoided these difficulties by ordering the Admiralty solicitor to lead the prosecution. It had instructed Charles Bicknell to travel to Portsmouth to assist the judge advocate in 'selecting and preparing evidence' for the prosecution, but when the trial opened he was the named prosecutor.[20] This arrangement may have been made in anticipation of difficulties arising from Lord Cochrane's role as the primary witness for the prosecution.

Although the composition of Gambier's court was a subject of criticism after the court martial, there was no pre-trial press commentary on this matter and no record of representations to the Board by Gambier or Cochrane. Sir Roger Curtis again presided and was joined by six other flag officers, three of whom had connections to the accused. Admiral William Young was, like Curtis, a friend of Gambier and had been his colleague on the Board from 1795 to 1801. Rear Admiral John Sutton was Young's subordinate in the Plymouth command. Vice Admiral Sir Henry Stanhope had been Gambier's second-in-command at Copenhagen. His standing as a biblical scholar and translator of the Hebrew Old Testament into English is likely to have appealed to Gambier. Another judge, Sir John Duckworth, had served under Gambier in an unsuccessful blockade of Brest that preceded the British fleet's deployment to Basque Roads. Duckworth, Stanhope and Sutton were judges on Sir Eliab Harvey's court martial. Two other vice admirals, Billy Douglas, commanding at Great Yarmouth, George Campbell, and four post captains joined these men. These officers do not appear to have had any notable links with Gambier. One of the post captains, Richard Dunn, had been Duckworth's long-term flag captain and a rather dubious witness at his court martial.

Gambier's trial

The Board's statement of charge was focused initially on Gambier's alleged failure to respond promptly to Cochrane's signal that the grounded French ships could be destroyed if half of the squadron was committed to the operation. This part of the charge alleged 'neglect or delay taking effectual measures for destroying' the enemy. It thus made Gambier liable for the capital offence for which both Keppel and Calder had stood trial. The charge included Gambier's 'whole conduct' commanding the squadron in Basque Roads, from 12 to 29 April, but the prosecution focused primarily on the days up to Cochrane's departure for England on the 15 April.[21] The fundamental question was whether Gambier had taken appropriate advantage of opportunities to destroy the enemy fleet.

In the first part of the trial, this question was pursued through the lengthy and somewhat unruly examination of Cochrane and the more straightforward elucidation of the testimony of a range of other witnesses from the fleet. The prosecution called nine witnesses, and then, following Gambier's statement of defence, twenty-two witnesses were called by the accused and the court, some of them being recalled. Only one of the post captains commanding in Basque Roads was not called to testify; the procession of other witnesses included the master of the fleet and a number of his colleagues. This feature of the witnesses' profile, mirroring that of Keppel's and Palliser's trials, reflected the extent to which the charge stood or fell on technical issues.

As in Keppel's trial, Gambier's began with a dispute over the veracity and currency of logbooks that were 'produced' and hence sworn to by the officers responsible for them. While examining Mr John Sparling, master of Cochrane's ship *Impérieuse*, the court noted 'material' additions to the ship's log, including records of winds and tides.[22] Sparling insisted that he had first-hand knowledge of events in his log and made additions from notes taken at the time. However, he immediately qualified this account by saying he committed them to memory and wrote them up afterwards.[23] In cross-examination, Gambier questioned Sparling about a visit made to HMS *Indefatigable* in Plymouth Sound, during which he had examined and sought to copy material from that ship's log. In response to close questioning by the president and Rear Admiral Stanhope, Sparling testified that he asked to see *Indefatigable*'s log wholly for his interest and denied that Cochrane knew anything of the matter.[24] While the court was careful to note that it was not impugning Sparling's word, it seems clear that it was not convinced that his logbook was a contemporary record of what he had seen. The same air of scepticism hung over the log produced by the master's mate of HMS *Beagle*. The court found it hard to believe that a record completed day by day was entirely free of 'blots and blurs' and corrected mistakes.[25]

After the log and signal books had been produced, the prosecution called Lord Cochrane for a very long and intensive examination marked by clashes with the prosecutor, the judge advocate and members of the court.[26] Some of these disputes concerned procedural questions, but some were a consequence of Cochrane's repeated attempts to respond to questions with a narrative of events highlighting Gambier's failures.[27] The case that emerged from Cochrane's testimony hinged on Gambier's alleged delay in sending ships into Aix Roads on the morning of 12th April to complete the destruction of the French fleet, the premature recall of ships that Gambier eventually sent in and his failure to effectively utilize frigates and smaller vessels on subsequent days. It was apparent from Cochrane's often oblique and rambling evidence that he believed Gambier had singularly failed to take advantage of the opportunities available and had ignored his forceful directions on the most effective response. In his view, the outcome of Gambier's 'neglect' was that the British fleet was forced to settle for a partial destruction of the French forces rather than their complete annihilation.

Lord Cochrane's accusations against Gambier relied upon claims about the conditions under which ships of the line could gain safe access to, and egress from, Aix Roads in particular winds and stages of the tide; the vulnerability of British forces to fire from French ships moored there and from shore-based fortifications protecting the anchorage; and the depth of water and room for manoeuvre available at different states of the tide. Some of these matters raised questions about the accuracy of available charts, the implications of soundings made by boats from the British fleet, calculations of the rise and fall of tides in the area, and the relative worth of conflicting information on these matters that Cochrane claimed from previous experience on that coast and Gambier obtained from local pilots and the masters of the ships under his command. These sources also held radically differing views of the strength of land-based fortifications and their threat to British vessels under conditions likely to prevail during attacks.

Charles Bicknell seemed to think that his examination of Lord Cochrane provided a sufficient statement of the case for the prosecution and proposed bringing it to a close when he finished questioning him on his advice that Gambier send a squadron of frigates into Aix Roads under the command of Rear Admiral Robert Stopford. On Cochrane's withdrawal, Bicknell only thought it necessary to ask a 'general question' of some of Gambier's officers. This question – whether 'you know of any neglect or unnecessary delay on the part of the commander-in-chief in taking effectual measures for the destruction of the enemy's ships' – was a fact-focused formulation of the general question put to witnesses in Keppel's trial.[28] Stopford's response to Bicknell's general question was emphatic and carefully phrased:

> Under all the circumstances of the case, viewed in every point which I am capable of, and giving to the Commander-in-Chief the free use and exercise of that discretion which every Commander-in-Chief must possess, in the execution of those measures for which he alone is responsible, I do not think there was any

delay or deficiency on the part of the Commander-in-chief, in executing the service entrusted to his Lordship's care.[29]

Given that Cochrane had advised Gambier that Stopford's 'zeal for the service' made him an ideal choice to command the frigates and small vessels sent into Aix Roads, Stopford's rejection of the charge was likely to carry weight. Nevertheless, the court thought that Bicknell's move to close the prosecution was premature and arranged for the further examination, and in some cases the re-examination, of several witnesses.[30] It was quite proper for the court to take this line although in the event the additional evidence given for the prosecution did nothing to support Cochrane's claims about the viability of excursions into Aix Roads by large ships.[31] Before finally deciding that the case for the prosecution was closed, the court deliberated for half an hour. It then invited Gambier to make his defence.

Gambier's defence opened with an attack on Cochrane for having made 'insinuations' that have 'compromised, not only my own honour, but also that of the brave officers and men serving under my command'. He claimed that it was without precedent that the commander of a fleet whose service had been approved by the Board and thought worthy of the thanks of both houses of parliament should be obliged 'from a sense of what is due to his own character and honour, as well as to the profession to which he belongs, to appeal to a naval tribunal against the loose and indirect accusations of an officer, so much his inferior in rank'.[32] Gambier rejected the priority that Cochrane had given to his responsibilities as a member of parliament and warned him of the grave miscalculation he had made in doing so:

> Whether Lord Cochrane supposed he might, with impunity, endeavour to lower me in the opinion of my country, and of my sovereign . . . I know not, but if these were his ideas, I assure myself the result will prove to him, that they were founded in error, for I will never permit any man to proceed as Lord Cochrane has done, without availing myself of the means which the laws of my country afford, to shew the futility and injustice of such an attack.[33]

In issuing this challenge, Gambier was buoyed by the weight of prosecution evidence undermining the claims made during Cochrane's testimony. He argued that this evidence showed that his handling of the ships under his command had effectively secured the neutralization of the threat posed by the French squadron without incurring the 'wanton destruction' of many of his ships and the deaths of 'valuable seamen'. '[N]ot a single additional ship of the enemy's would have been destroyed by a more early adoption of those measures, which it is imputed to me I delayed or neglected.'[34] Gambier supported this claim by referencing evidence on the strength of fortifications on the Isle D'Aix and the threat they posed to vessels operating in confined and often shoal waters in the prevailing winds and tides. The reliability of charts and masters' and pilots' information was a significant set of considerations and Gambier had to act on the basis of information available to him at the time.[35] The grounding of Stopford's frigates in a subsequent attack on ships in the mouth of the Charente River and their reliance on a 'providential' shift in the wind to get clear showed that attacks by ships-of-the-line were not feasible and challenged the navigational information upon which Cochrane's approach to the operation and the charge relied.[36]

Having delivered his defence, Gambier examined witnesses whose testimony he thought would support it. He initially called eleven witnesses from among the captains and commissioned and warrant officers of the fleet, but when he proposed bringing the case for the defence to an end, the court called eleven more witnesses. They testified to the strength and effectiveness of the shore batteries, the accuracy of charts and the navigational hazards of Aix Roads.[37] During this testimony, it became apparent that Lord Cochrane's estimations of the feasibility of more extensive operations against French ships rested on the assumption that three or four ships-of-the-line would be lost.[38] With the exceptions noted below, the witnesses' testimony was remarkably consistent.

The two dissenting voices were Captain George Seymour of the frigate HMS *Pallas* and Captain William Broughton of the ship-of-the-line *HMS Illustrious.* Seymour seemed to support Cochrane's claims about the depth of water in various parts of Aix Roads, but on closer examination, his views on this matter were shown to be based on information that came to hand later. In any case, Seymour would not be drawn on the question of whether Gambier should have committed ships-of-the-line at an earlier stage on 12 April and acknowledged that his testimony only showed there was enough water for the ships to stay afloat, not that other conditions for effective action were satisfied.[39]

Broughton's evidence initially seemed more damaging. He supported Cochrane's claims about the poor state of shore-based fortifications and the viability of ships-of-the-line going into Aix Roads on the morning of 12 April. However, his information on the fortifications dated from 1 April, and he equivocated on whether or not the batteries possessed furnaces for producing red-hot shot. Moreover, Broughton's view on the timing in response to Cochrane's signal rested on the question-begging assumptions that ships of the line could come close enough to the batteries to silence them without sustaining significant damage and the French would not put up a stiff resistance.[40]

After deliberating for between three and four hours, the court acquitted Lord Gambier in fulsome terms that were presented in the published version of the minutes in a plethora of capital letters: his conduct between 17 March and 29 April was 'marked by ZEAL, JUDGEMENT, ABILITY, and an anxious Attention to the Welfare of His Majesty's service, and both adjudge him to be MOST HONOURABLY ACQUITTED....' Sir Roger Curtis returned Gambier's sword with the court's expectation that he would continue to use it 'for the honour and advantage of your country, and to your own personal honour' and his sense of the 'high gratification I have upon this occasion'.[41]

Aftermath

The public reaction to Gambier's acquittal was muted. The run-up to his trial was reported widely in the London and provincial press, and they circulated more or less full accounts of the daily proceedings.[42] These sources did not report that Gambier's acquittal was greeted with cheers by bystanders or the crews of ships moored nearby, nor did those who orchestrated the ringing of church bells in Sir William Parker's honour stir themselves. The sole reference to a public celebration appeared in the *Hampshire and Portsmouth Telegraph*. It reported that seamen of Gambier's flagship, HMS *Caledonia*, illuminated their ship at Spithead in honour of the commander-in-chief's acquittal.[43] A gesture of this kind must have been gratifying to Gambier but probably owed as much to the authoritative agency of his officers as to the spontaneous feelings of the lower deck.

The *Telegraph* was silent on whether Gambier was present to appreciate the *Caledonians'* efforts in his honour, but one assumes that he spent a least a couple of days in Portsmouth before returning to London. He was certainly back in the capital and within easy reach of the Admiralty within four days of his trial. The *Morning Chronicle* reported somewhat euphemistically that he attended a 'private levee' with the King at the Queen's House on the 9th of August 'on his return from the sea'.[44] Over the next few weeks, he received letters of condolatory congratulation from well-placed friends. William Wilberforce, the leader of an evangelical group in the House of Commons, thought he was justified in encroaching on the sabbath to 'return thanks for your having been enabled to preserve that dignified calmness throughout the long and vexatious trial of temper to which you were subjected, and to exhibit a true specimen of Christian heroism' far superior to Cochrane's 'heroism of dauntless bravery in the hour of battle'.[45]

In contrast to Wilberforce's serene self-righteousness, William Morton Pitt, Gambier's closest cousin among the Pitts, adopted a tone of aggrieved, entitled worldliness. He told Gambier that he had 'been extremely ill-treated, your reputation hazarded, your purse put to enormous charge . . . and an insult is then at last offered to you, in proposing a red riband, placing you on that list after Lord Cochrane!' Morton Pitt urged Gambier to reject this insulting offer and rally the great and well-connected (the Duke of Portland, Spencer Perceval, the prime minister) to approach the King to amend his patent of nobility to at least ensure that the title could pass to a nephew or other close relation. This measure was presented as the minimum necessary to signify unequivocal royal approval of his achievements commanding in Basque Roads and to compensate for the financial sacrifices in prize earnings arising from his extended service at the Admiralty Board.[46] In common with Gambier's nineteenth-century family memorialist, Morton Pitt conveniently discounted the value of Gambier's relatively easily gained prize money and plunder from the Copenhagen expedition. He also criticized the Admiralty Board unfairly for bringing his cousin to court martial. Cochrane's strategy of blaming without charging forced Gambier to seek a court martial but that was not the Board's fault. Naval sympathizers did not make this mistake. Admirals Hammond and Gore and Ambrose Serle, a long-serving transport commissioner appointed when Sir Charles Middleton dominated the Naval Board, offered congratulations emphasizing the benefits Gambier derived from his court martial and triumphant acquittal.[47]

The comfort and self-affirmation that Gambier received from this consolatory and congratulatory correspondence no doubt helped shield him from barbs thrown by those who took a more sceptical view of his performance in Basque Roads. These reactions were delayed by the timing of the acquittal. The verdict was handed down after parliament had gone into recess, London was emptying at the close of the season and the disastrous unfolding of the Scheldt expedition overshadowed the action in Basque Roads.[48] However, William Cobbett warned that the court martial 'must not be passed over in that silence, in which some persons were anxious to see it buried'. The 'most curious evidence' presented in it should be laid before the public for its scrutiny.[49] In the event, Cobbett and his allies kept their power dry until parliament was in session.

Two days after parliament opened, the ministry moved to have Gambier's sentence laid before the House of Lords. This step was a necessary preliminary to the vote of thanks since the last time Lord Gambier's name appeared in the Lord's Journal was to notify the House of his arrest and pending court martial.[50] Lord Mulgrave subsequently moved a vote of thanks for Gambier's 'zeal, judgement, ability, and attention to his Majesty's naval service'.[51] Although the House endorsed this rather cool praise without a dissenting vote, the debate was decidedly mixed.

Lord Holland drew on a free thinker's wry knowledge of arcane religious rituals to liken the government's deferral of the original vote to the medieval Roman Catholic practice of subjecting a prospective saint's character and reputation to the vindictive attention of a 'devil's advocate'. Holland would not oppose the motion but was keen not to spare the Admiralty Board. Nor was Lord Melville, a former first lord. He referred to the delicacy of the situation produced by the Board's appointment of Lord Cochrane and neatly highlighted the diverse perspectives of the two principal actors: 'The object of Lord Cochrane of course was glory; the duty of Lord Gambier as the Commander-in-Chief, undoubtedly was to take care that the fleet was not exposed to unnecessary danger, and that no more ships were hazarded than were requisite.' Melville, conveniently forgetting one of the lessons of the Keppel-Palliser affair and Cochrane's resort to insinuation, claimed that while it was natural for Gambier to ask for an inquiry, it was wrong for the Board to grant it. He regarded the principle of courts martial on demand as harmful to the service; there should be a prosecutor or at least a 'real charge'.[52]

Two other speakers questioned whether a vote of thanks was warranted. The Earl of Darnley, making a point that must have occurred to a fair number of people within and beyond the service, thought that equating Basque Roads with Camperdown, the Nile and Trafalgar would be the 'height of presumption'. He attributed the motion to an attempt to 'throw a false lustre' on the ministry. Lord Grenville claimed that the court martial had forced those who might not otherwise have supported a vote of thanks to now do so to avoid casting unjust blame on Lord Gambier.[53] Having secured an unopposed vote, the ministry did not feel obliged to lend credence to these objections. The Lord Chancellor's presentation speech made a virtue of the delay and the transactions that had taken place during it: 'the time which has intervened has tended only to prove more strongly the character which you have always maintained, and the justness of your title to the distinguished honour now conferred upon you'.[54]

Lord Cochrane led an extensive debate on the trial in the House of Commons. When the government gave notice of the congratulatory motion, Cochrane sought to have the minutes of the court martial laid before the House to question its proceedings. He claimed that there was 'nothing more partial than the conduct of the court martial' and that an examination of the minutes was necessary to determine if Gambier deserved a vote of thanks. If the minutes were produced and he failed to prove 'all he asserted', Cochrane would resign his KB and his seat in the House.[55] Several speakers, including Sir Francis Burdett, his fellow MP in the large, promiscuous and frequently radical borough of Westminster, supported Cochrane's motion. Burdett referred to the House's right to investigate court martial sentences in extraordinary cases. Charles Yorke, a senior figure in the House, rejected these arguments. Yorke accused Cochrane of using the occasion as a stalking horse for his own opinion.[56] Gambier's friend William Wilberforce regarded Cochrane's motion as a slur on the members of the court in a case where there was no doubt. Lord Newark added that it was also a slur on the witnesses and claimed (who knows on what basis) that there was united opposition in the service to Cochrane's approach. Both Yorke and Charles Wynn thought the overwhelming basis of the evidence against Cochrane's 'insinuations' weakened any case for a parliamentary inquiry. Two senior naval officers also spoke against Cochrane's motion. Captain John Poo Beresford, a witness at the trial, said that Cochrane's claims were a libel on the court. Beresford told the House that the judges 'were officers of as high honour and character as the noble lord'. His subsequent reference to Cochrane having 'formed his charts and log-books in favour of the evidence to be adduced before the Court Martial' made it clear that he thought the court's honour and character was higher than Cochrane's.[57] Vice Admiral Sir John Orde, no stranger to bitter disputes between senior naval officers, objected that support for the motion would mean that Gambier was to be tried again.[58] George Ponsonby (leader of the opposition and also a lawyer) raised doubts on that score and made the interesting point that trying someone a second time for the same offence was contrary to the principles of English justice. Its use in courts martial threatened to undermine the system of military law by removing confidence in courts composed of leading members of the profession.[59]

Cochrane's motion for an inquiry was lost 161 to 19. The margin on the motion for a vote of thanks was far more favourable to his cause but the debate was cursory. Spencer Perceval, the prime minister, referred to Gambier's 'eminent services' but only spoke of the 'late glorious and successful attack' when referring more generally to the fleet he commanded.[60] Cochrane introduced some venom into the occasion by questioning Gambier's courage and judgement and insultingly comparing his claim to a vote of thanks with that of Sir Hyde Parker following the first Battle of Copenhagen. He asked whether his merit 'consisted in the anxiety which he evinced for the service by himself remaining in the outer harbour' and warned the House that it 'has posterity to answer for thus prostituting the Thanks of Parliament'.[61] Neither Sir Francis Burdett nor William Windham thought there was evidence of a level of performance to warrant a vote of thanks.[62] Other members shared these reservations. Unusually for a motion of this kind, 39 members voted against it and 161 in favour. While there was never any danger that the motion would succeed, the voting indicated that reservations about the affair extended significantly beyond Cochrane and his allies.

Even while parliament debated the votes of thanks, the toxic fallout of disasters unfolding in the Scheldt estuary overshadowed disputes over Basque Roads in parliament and the press. Surprisingly, the redeployment of large ships from the Channel fleet did not lead the Admiralty Board to adjust the arrangements for commanding it. Despite the press rumour that Admiral William Young would replace Gambier, he remained commander-in-chief until August 1811. It was perhaps even more surprising, although in keeping with his career record, that Gambier retained his command while living ashore. He never saw active service again but was appointed in 1814 as the British commissioner responsible for negotiating peace with the United States.

Conclusion

Lord Cochrane's presence in parliament provided ample scope to revisit a trial which he claimed he never wanted and wrongly rejected his criticisms of his commander-in-chief. Given the close links between Gambier and members of his court and Cochrane's barely concealed resentment at alleged ill-usage at the hands of several first lords, these charges were unsurprising. However, as with Palliser's court, personal and professional connections do not seem to have given rise to discernible partiality by Gambier's judges. Criticisms of Curtis and Young's highly active approach to their responsibilities fail to take account of the challenges they faced in dealing with Lord Cochrane; their close examination of witnesses did not seem to amount to bullying or harassment to the accused's advantage.[63]

The case involved a great deal of highly contentious technical data, and it is understandable that questions on winds, the rise and fall of tides, soundings and sea room in Aix Roads should fall to sea officers on the court rather than the Admiralty solicitor. In addition, Cochrane's approach to the proceedings meant the court faced ongoing problems in getting him to respond to questions and refrain from using them as a pretext for developing lengthy narratives vilifying Gambier. The court rightly felt it necessary to check Cochrane when he launched long, ill-directed digressions that he sometimes justified as working towards answering questions that it had not put to him.[64] The published minutes graphically illustrate the disproportion between the length of the questions put to Cochrane and his replies. They also show the number of occasions on which the court thought it necessary to upbraid Cochrane for his disrespectful attitude towards the prosecutor and to address points of order provoked or raised by him. A comment in Cochrane's autobiography published half a century later helps explain but hardly justifies his conduct during the trial. When he complained that the court would not allow him to cross-examine other witnesses, it was clear that he had wilfully misunderstood his role. Having declined laying a charge against Gambier, he presumed the right to act as the accuser and prosecutor.[65]

The trial appears to have been conducted with due propriety. Cochrane complained bitterly when the court ordered witnesses to withdraw during Gambier's defence, but the judge advocate did not challenge the president's claim that it was a common practice. As we have seen, there was significant risk of collusion in elite courts martial and Curtis' directive seems appropriate when witnesses (like Cochrane) who had already testified were likely to be recalled later in the trial. It is significant that when an earlier court attempted to control the circulation of records of the proceedings while the trial was in train, the president had been particularly concerned about access to the statement of defence.[66] In Gambier's trial, the court and judge advocate paid careful attention to what counted as evidence, and officers of the court challenged both the judges and Gambier on that issue. Finally, as discussed earlier in this chapter, the court made it clear that it intended to hear all the available evidence and would not accept Bicknell's or Gambier's proposals to curtail the examination of witnesses.

Cochrane's later claims about excluding potentially hostile witnesses do not stand up to scrutiny. Of those commanding ships in Basque Roads, only one officer, Captain Maitland of the *Emerald*, was not called, and it seems unlikely that his testimony would have counteracted that of the string of witnesses whose evidence supported Gambier's account of the risks and opportunities facing him. The two witnesses whose testimony seemed most likely to threaten Gambier's safety proved on closer examination to have been relying on assumptions that were by no means self-evident and served to confirm the lack of consensus on critical navigational and operational questions that underwrote judgements on whether Gambier had been sufficiently zealous in the performance of his duties. These considerations suggest that while Gambier's performance as commander-in-chief was not brilliant, it was not shown to be negligent, and the verdict of his court was thus not unsound.[67]

By 1811, Lord Gambier had reached the stage where realistic expectations of further high commands had probably ended, so the court martial did not affect his prospects of active service appointments. It is very likely, however, that it may have lowered his standing in the service. That was certainly the case for the King. In July 1807, he had accepted Mulgrave's roseate assurance that the expedition against the Danes was in the hands of a man of 'tried talents & zeal for your Majesty's service'. Nine months later, the King responded enthusiastically to Gambier's appointment to the Channel command: his 'gallantry & abilities have been tried and will do credit to any command entrusted to him'. Two years later, his view had changed. When Spencer Perceval (a religious fellow traveller) proposed Gambier as one of the prospects to succeed Lord Mulgrave as the head of the Admiralty Board, he met with a very cool royal response. The King told him that although he had a 'high opinion of Lord Gambier's honourable character and of his courage, he conceives that his appointment to the Admiralty would not be a popular one with the Navy in which his professional abilities are not held in the highest estimation'.[68] Gambier's long spell managing promotions at the Admiralty Board provided plenty of scope for offending service colleagues and their patrons. Members of the service may also have thought that when compared with Collingwood, he was over-rewarded for his role at Copenhagen. That was certainly the view of some figures in the political elite. The Earl of Malmesbury, a veteran ambassador, was highly critical of Gambier's lack of diplomatic initiative – he and the military commander 'did not go a step beyond their orders – like unwilling servants' – and the former secretary of state William Windham pointed out that as Copenhagen was not a military target, Gambier could not 'value a peerage given him on that occasion because he had distinguished himself brilliantly as a captain in the year 1794'.[69] The Prince Regent and Second Lord Melville do not seem to have valued Gambier's services particularly highly. Having declined a knighthood of the Bath in 1809, he was nominated for that honour in 1815. It now stood, however, in the second class of the new order and placed him below the sixteen flag officers (among whom were Cornwallis and Duckworth) made Grand Knights' Crosses (GCB).[70]

12

Vice Admiral Charles Stirling's Misadventures in the West Indies

Following a two-day court martial in early May 1814, Vice Admiral Charles Stirling was found guilty 'in part' of breaching the seventeenth article of war's prohibition against 'demanding' or 'exacting' 'money or other reward from any merchant or master for convoying any ships or vessels entrusted to their care'. Although offences under this article could attract a death sentence, Stirling's court availed itself of the 'or other punishment' provision to sentence him to remain permanently on half pay without further promotion. Because the offence involved corruption, the conviction was the most reputationally damaging one suffered by a late Georgian Royal Navy flag officer.

Charles Stirling had built his career on service interest (his father was a post captain) and on his own merits. Given the context of his court martial, it is perhaps significant that although Stirling came from a Scottish family, there is no indication that he enjoyed the support of the Dundas connection or any other civilian patron. Well-regarded service in the American War saw him rise from lieutenant to post captain and enjoy regular employment in the French Wars. In July 1801, he commanded HMS *Pompeé* in Rear Admiral Saumarez's action off Algeciras. When this ship paid off in early 1802, the entire crew declared their willingness to serve under him on his next command.[1] In July 1805, Stirling wished for an appointment in the West Indies, referring to some officers' reluctance to serve in a deadly climate and the fact that he had 'had a seasoning' during earlier service in the region and very recent employment as the Navy Board's commissioner at Port Royal.[2] In the event, he was posted to command a squadron in Cornwallis' Channel fleet blockading Rochefort and redeployed to Sir Roger Calder's squadron off Cape Finisterre. Calder commended Stirling for his role in the inconclusive action and brought him home to testify at his trial. Stirling was promoted rear admiral in November 1805. Following his first flag command on the South American station, he received a vote of thanks from both houses of parliament for his efforts in a difficult campaign.[3] After serving as commander-in-chief at the Cape of Good Hope, he was finally posted to the West Indies as commander-in-chief at Jamaica in 1811. When the Board incorporated the West Indian stations into Admiral Sir John Warren's North American command during the War of 1812, Stirling became a subordinate flag officer reporting to the commander-in-chief at Halifax. This development and the Board's direction of Warren played a significant role in the events that led to Stirling's court martial. So, too, did his extremely difficult relationship with

Captain Isaac Wolley, the Commissioner at Port Royal, and with some mercantile interests in Jamaica.

Context: The Jamaican command in the War of 1812

The decision to absorb the Jamaica station into an extended North American command had important implications for Stirling's role. It almost certainly affected his remuneration and allowances and deprived him of the substantial prize earnings and patronage usually associated with the Jamaica command. As a commander-in-chief, Stirling was entitled to an eighth of the prize money made on the station. Though the British seizure of enemy colonies in the region made it less lucrative than it had been in the past, he earned approximately £4000 in the year he was commander-in-chief.[4] As a subordinate flag officer, however, he was obliged to share prize money with Warren and all the other junior flag officers. Although he gained a share in their earnings, it was unlikely to compensate for this loss. Warren left England heavily freighted by patronage 'requests' from the first lord and one of his first acts on taking up his command was to remind Stirling where he now stood in the chain of interest. He told him to send a list of vacancies he would fill from the Admiralty's list, his flagship and 'those under my patronage in the squadron'. Warren would take account of Stirling's recommendations 'when circumstances conveniently admit'.[5]

Apart from status, prizes and patronage, the change in reporting line drew Stirling into tensions between Warren and the first lord in London. One of the consequences of the war was that ships of the United States' navy and privateers operating from its ports posed a significant threat to British merchant shipping in the region and hence to the cargoes of planters and merchants. These interests formed a powerful lobby in British politics that pressured the Admiralty Board in London to secure convoy protection.[6] The Board transmitted this pressure to commanders-in-chief and thence to their subordinates.

Sir John Warren's relationship with the Board exacerbated the military and political sensitivities of wartime convoy protection and resource management. He was a very able and experienced officer but in poor health when he was sent to North America, initially to use his diplomatic skills to avert war and then to pursue it with the utmost vigour. The Board accompanied its ungracious and grudging responses to his request for more suitable ships with increasingly directive and critical comments on his energy, deployments, reporting and discipline within the squadrons under his command. At the beginning of December 1812, Warren received a hectoring letter from Melville on maintaining a 'vigorous blockade' of the Chesapeake and Delaware and criticizing his lax management of a subordinate flag officer.[7] Communications such as these prompted aggressive responses from Warren. When a squadron of United States ships under Commodore Rodgers managed to evade the blockade, Warren complained to the Board of the number and condition of the vessels available to him, the condition of the crews and the heavy demands of convoy protection on the extended command. He also noted pointedly the large number of ships available to Lord Howe in 1778 when he was responsible only for the North American parts of the command.[8]

These interactions fostered an environment of pressure, mistrust and affront which conditioned the Board's and Warren's reactions to recriminations surrounding the conduct of navy business in Jamaica. In addition, Stirling thought the effective downgrading of his command emboldened those in Jamaica who wished to discredit him and prevented him from dealing effectively with them. He later claimed that only a sense of duty discouraged him from seeking to be relieved from what had become a highly unsatisfactory appointment.[9] His tenure was likely to be short-lived in any case. As a relatively senior vice admiral and former commander-in-chief on three stations, Stirling was too senior for his current subordinate role. It is significant that when the Board recalled him without any explanation in mid-April 1813, it replaced him with a junior rear admiral.

Acrimony on the Jamaica station: Vice Admiral Stirling, Commissioner Wolley and the West Indian merchants

Stirling's difficult relationship with Captain Wolley and other influential figures in Jamaica was thus played out against the tension-laden background of the American War and the Board's dissatisfaction with Warren's performance. His earlier experience in Wolley's post contributed to these difficulties and so too did his staunch commitment to public economy. Like St Vincent, Stirling thought dockyard administration needed to undergo significant reform, but unlike the former first lord, he believed it could be achieved through a graduated transition from customary practice to the rational management of resources.[10]

Nevertheless, when Stirling applied his reforming ideas during his commissionership, they led to tensions with vested interests in Jamaica and with the commander-in-chief, Sir John Duckworth. Duckworth had acted as naval commissioner before Stirling's arrival and seemed reluctant to give up the reins. Stirling complained to the Navy Board (to whom he reported) of Duckworth's assumption of authority over him, tactfully stating that it did not interfere with the management of the dockyard at the moment because of his respect for Duckworth's capacity and their good personal relationship; he noted, however, that Duckworth's pretensions were a dangerous precedent for a less able commander-in-chief.[11] He subsequently complained of irregularities in managing ships on the station and the misuse of forest timber by the military.[12] While there is no reason to suppose that Stirling's vigilance was misplaced, it was likely to make for fractious relationships with merchants and suppliers and with local officials and captains whose attitude towards public expenditure differed from his.

These antagonisms focused on Stirling's relationship with Captain Wolley. The main bone of contention was conflicting views on the best way to secure specie to pay the expenses of the dockyard at Port Royal and other West Indian ports for whom Wolley acted. Wolley's approach relied upon advertising at Kingston and ensuring tenders were taken up promptly by paying a 5 per cent premium on government bills. Stirling argued that this strategy discounted these bills unnecessarily because trade between Jamaica and Spanish colonies in South America provided a substantial supply of specie that merchants were pleased to trade for undiscounted bills to avoid the cost and risk of shipping bullion back to London. Disagreement on this point was not merely a technical dispute on public finance. It had a significant bearing on operational priorities on the station and serious ramifications for the commander-in-chief's relationship with his captains, local trading and commercial interests and their allies in London.

When Wolley and Stirling aired these matters in early September 1812, their correspondence spawned suspicions and increasingly open accusations of corruption.[13] Stirling claimed that Wolley's approach favoured 'money holders' in Jamaica but did not cast aspersions on Wolley himself.[14] The commissioner, however, complained that the commander-in-chief benefited from freight on specie sent to England and that these shipments made it more difficult to raise funds through tenders in Jamaica. This claim later provided Wolley with a basis for accusing Stirling of encouraging these shipments to provide freight payments for a nephew going home in command of a sloop.[15] Over the next few months, Wolley raised other issues with the Navy Board. When Stirling was short of suitable vessels, he hired a private ship and shifted crew members, provisions and deck stores into it. Stirling had reported this arrangement to the Admiralty Board, but Wolley saw it as a corrupt misuse of government resources. The Board directed its staff to 'enquire minutely' into Wolley's claim but did not find anything incriminating.[16] The commissioner also complained of Stirling's exploitation of an emergency shipment of flour to the island to secure a share of freight, of the timing of an advertisement for freight by Stirling's agent which interfered with one of his tenders and the percentage of freight that Stirling took from his captains.[17] Freight shares were a general issue of contention only settled by an English court after Stirling left Jamaica but before he was court-martialled. Stirling later claimed that captains took advantage of the downgrading of his command to question his rights, sometimes agreeing to recognize them but not paying him the sums due when they cleared the station.[18] Be that as it may, this cause of dispute may well have heightened tensions arising from Stirling's declared intention of eliminating abuses.

Finally, and most important for his future career, Stirling's time in Jamaica was bedevilled by the challenge of meeting merchants' expectations of adequate convoy protection. This was a perennial issue for fleet and station commanders. It was exacerbated by the war with the United States, by the Admiralty Board's sensitivity to criticism of its deployments and by periodic alarms raised by merchant interests in the colonies and London.[19] In late January 1813, Stirling reported local concerns about his capacity to meet convoy requirements after receiving a memorial from local merchants stressing the importance of the trade in British manufactured goods with the Spanish Main. A month later, he met with merchants over convoy arrangements to England but questions of timing made agreement difficult.[20]

Stirling responded at length to complaints about protecting the trade from Jamaica that the Board forwarded to him and copied to Warren.[21] He pointed out there was no evidence of convoyed British ships being captured and attributed complaints to ill-disposed individuals in Jamaica. They were 'agitated by men, who appeared to attend more to private pique, than the public good, and therefore they took advantage of apprehension entertained from an expected swarm of American Privateers, to agitate the Public mind, with grievances, which have not been realized'.[22] It was indicative of the factional basis of complaints against Stirling that a few months after being assailed for failing to provide adequate convoy protection, he received an offer of plate worth £500 from merchants trading to the Spanish Main in recognition of his support of that trade. It is an equally significant sign of his sensitivity to the Board's view of his efforts and perhaps also of his acquisitive restraint, that he declined this and other departing gifts 'until I know whether my conduct has been approved by my Lords Commissioners of the Admiralty'.[23] It takes a stretch of the imagination to conceive of Duckworth passing up such an offer.

Although Stirling did not know it at that stage, his difficulties over convoys and freight and his antagonistic relationships with Wolley gave credence to an allegation of corruption that ended his career and blighted the rest of his life. Wolley, who stated publicly that he intended to ruin Stirling, wrote to Warren in February 1813 accusing him of authorizing a convoy to Honduras at the request of two merchants on the promise of a payment.[24] These ships were to be convoyed by HMS *Sappho*, a sloop under the command of Captain Hayes O'Grady. Warren forwarded Wolley's letter to the Board and informed Stirling of this misconduct claim in the spring of 1813. He did not provide any details but Stirling knew that Wolley was involved. He told his commander-in-chief that he could not 'conceive it possible for enmity to be carried to such an extent . . . .'[25] Several months later Warren forwarded Wolley's letter to Stirling with a demand for an explanation, but it arrived in Jamaica after his recall.

The Board ordered Stirling to return home before it received Wolley's accusation about the *Sappho* convoy, so that was not the cause of his recall. It seems very likely that the stream of irritating reports it had been receiving from Jamaica encouraged the Board to treat the downgrading of his command as a sufficient reason to terminate it. Stirling did not protest his recall and replacement by William Brown, a relatively junior rear admiral. Brown benefited from the interest of the powerful Duke of Rutland and was sufficiently prominent among Lord Melville's priorities for flag appointments to have already enjoyed employment as commander-in-chief of the Channel Islands squadron. Unfortunately, he was not as well seasoned for the West Indies as Stirling and died of yellow fever within a year of taking up his command there.

The *Sappho* Incident

The charge against Stirling arose from his order for HMS *Sappho* to convoy two merchant vessels to Honduras and perform other duties in the area before escorting ships bound for England as far as Bermuda. At first glance, this was a straightforward deployment and Stirling notified the Admiralty on 1 February 1813. Three weeks later, however, Wolley wrote to Warren to say that Stirling had accepted a fee under the guise of advanced payment for freight on the merchant vessels' return voyage, a transaction in breach of the regulations. It was, in any case, fraudulent because no freight was carried from Jamaica and there was no intention of shipping it from Honduras. Wolley claimed that Stirling frequently connived with perpetrators of similar frauds that blighted the Royal Navy's reputation in Jamaica but provided no other examples; this incident was the only one 'within my actual knowledge because of information received'.[26] Mr Bogle, Stirling's distant relative and agent, managed the matter at his house in the vice admiral's presence. Wolley claimed that Stirling's order for O'Grady not to discuss the freight with his fellow captains proved that he was a knowing party to a corrupt transaction.

When O'Grady found no freight at Honduras and two local merchants told him there was never an intention of shipping it, he claimed to have become suspicious. Although he wrote to Stirling three times during his voyage, he did not mention his qualms about the transactions. However, after Stirling left Jamaica in early July, O'Grady wrote to his agent instructing him to return the freight payment to the merchants and implicated Stirling in the improper transaction: 'the sum of money which you received for me . . . was obtained by the Admiral and his Agent contrary to the rules of the service'.[27] Early in the new year, O'Grady arranged for the two merchants' clerks to provide affidavits sworn before the mayor of Kingston, effectively clearing him of any knowing participation in a fraudulent transaction and implicating Stirling as an active party to it.[28]

Stirling was unaware of the details of Wolley's most recent claims when he left Jamaica, so he could not gather material from local sources to support his side of the story. Although Brown did not indicate serious trouble brewing in London, Stirling's caution over receiving gifts from the merchant community suggests that he was sensitive to the reputational impact of Wolley's earlier complaints and merchant claims of inadequate convoy protection. These matters aside, there is no indication that Stirling had any inkling that he would be court-martialled or took any steps to prepare for it by drafting exculpatory reports to the Board on the passage home. Like other flag officers, he spent his time at sea dealing dutifully with the Board's onerous accountability requirements, providing detailed reporting on those receiving hospital treatment in Jamaica, on surveys of dubious stores, unfit personnel and the state of vessels on the station when he relinquished his command.[29]

Stirling's trial

Whatever peace of mind Stirling enjoyed during a summer passage across the Atlantic was shattered in early September 1813 when the Board told him that he was to be court-martialled on information supplied by Captain Wolley. However, it was not until 11 April 1814 that the Board received a report from the Admiralty solicitor who, having 'examined' Captain O'Grady, believed there was a case to answer; on the following day, it instructed him to draft a charge.[30] Stirling was charged on 21 April 1814 and brought to trial in Portsmouth on 9 May. Wolley's letter to Warren amounted to an information laid against Stirling that the board thought was sufficient to trigger a trial but could not serve as an evidential basis for one. Nor could Wolley stand as a witness since his knowledge of the alleged transaction was second-hand, that is, hearsay. In any case, his declared animus towards Stirling would also have posed a risk to the prosecution. The Board's solicitor, Charles Bricknell, struggled to identify eligible witnesses, but Wolley's arrival in London later in the year on his way to the naval commissionership in Malta appeared to provide a way forward. In early November 1813, Wolley was told (by 'members of the Admiralty Board') that he should assist Bicknell in identifying witnesses. Wolley understood that the Board had not yet determined the focus for a court martial and sent Bicknell a long letter repeating the incidents he had reported to the Navy Board earlier in the year and identifying witnesses of each alleged offence. He also summarized complaints on Stirling's 'general mode of conducting the freight and convoy business'.[31]

Stirling later claimed that he had expected to face several charges based on Wolley's information and for the commissioner to give evidence against him. He was thus surprised to find that he was to face a single charge and that Wolley was not to be involved in the trial.[32] Of those who might testify on the *Sappho* incident, Wolley named the merchants directly concerned who were then in London and Mr Bogle. He thought the latter would be 'an unwilling evidence' although it seems equally likely that the Spanish merchants would be most reluctant to have their affairs exposed under oath.[33] In any case, Bicknell thought better of these suggestions and Captain O'Grady (who had not been named by Wolley) was the only witness called for the prosecution.

Stirling's court martial was held on board HMS *Gladiator*, the scene of many of the naval-legal trials of strength considered in this study. It was short by the standards of flag officers' courts martial, extending over only two days. The president was Vice Admiral Sir Richard Bickerton, whose career included a five-year term on the Admiralty Board. He was the senior naval commissioner when the Board appointed Stirling to the Jamaica command. Two vice admirals, five rear admirals and five captains sat on the court. The admirals had good service records as post captains, but except for the most junior of the rear admirals, Sir Thomas Byam Martin, they were not flag officers of particular note. Four of them had been brought to Portsmouth from neighbouring stations to strengthen flag representation on the court.

After the opening formalities, the court considered two objections that Stirling made on the advice of his counsel and in deference to his professional reputation.[34] He challenged the admissibility of the merchants' clerks' affidavits. They had not sworn them in court, were thus immune from perjury charges and could not be questioned by the accused. Stirling also objected to being tried by court martial for an offence committed on shore. The court declined to accept either of these objections, and Stirling later regretted making them. But while he was undoubtedly drawing a very long bow with the second claim, his objections to the affidavits were supported by statutory requirements. The court's response that as they were mentioned 'in their Lordships' order they should be read as forming part of the charge' was evasive and otherwise unsatisfactory.[35] These documents were not necessary to the charge, and although they were not produced as evidence, they hung over the trial, had to be addressed by the defence and may have had an impact on the attitudes of the judges. An opinion later secured by Stirling's counsel declined to criticize the court but was highly sceptical of the status of these documents. He insisted, however, that since the court declared them admissible, they were to be regarded as legal evidence unless a crown law officer overturned its decision.[36]

As the Board had instigated the charge, the judge advocate was the prosecutor, but members of the court also played a significant role in questioning the only witness called. Although Captain O'Grady had linked Stirling to the illegal pre-payment of freight in his letter to his agent, he did not maintain this position when testifying under oath. When questioned on the conversation at Bogle's house, he said that while he *believed* that Stirling had heard what his agent told O'Grady about the payment, he could not swear to it. O'Grady subsequently testified that he had no knowledge of either Stirling or his agent making a 'bargain' with the merchants.[37] He also told the court that Stirling had ordered him to convoy all vessels at Port Royal bound for the west of Jamaica and Havana. As a result, a brig that had arrived in port at the last minute sailed in convoy with the Spanish merchants' two schooners.[38] Finally, while Wolley made much of Stirling's stipulation that O'Grady should not discuss the freight with other captains, O'Grady acknowledged that such discretion was often a security caution to conceal specie shipments from predators' informants and was employed even where there was no question of the legitimacy of a transaction.[39]

Given the seriousness of the charge, it is surprising that the prosecution called only one witness and that its case was so brief. Despite the delay caused by the court's *in-camera* consideration of Stirling's initial objections and the reading of documents into the record, the prosecution's case was concluded by 2.00 pm. The hearing was then adjourned until 9.00 am on Monday 11 May, when the court invited Stirling to present his defence. He and his counsel thus had Saturday afternoon and Sunday to finalize the lengthy statement read by Sergeant Blosset.

In some respects, Stirling's defence was an impressive document. While disclaiming any intention of reflecting on Wolley's general conduct and allowing for his 'zeal for the service', he nevertheless referred to the disputes between them and the 'hostile and vindictive spirit' of his letter to Warren.[40] He argued that Wolley did not show in the 'numerous imaginary instances' to which he referred, or in Stirling's particular case, that he knew the freight was not to be shipped. O'Grady's sworn evidence did not support the claim about his superior's complicity in the letter to his agent. Stirling insisted that freight negotiations were a matter for O'Grady and Bogle; he was not involved.[41]

The lack of evidence for Wolley's claims compounded the weakness of circumstantial considerations alleged against Stirling. O'Grady admitted that confidentiality over specie shipments was not unusual, and in addition, Stirling explained that he wished to avoid arousing jealousy among O'Grady's fellow captains. This precaution was understandable in light of the ill-feeling caused by Stirling's insistence on his share of freights. Stirling also pointed to the public nature of all the transactions involving his agent and offered a sharp corrective to Wolley's claim about the benefit he would receive from the freight. He had mentioned a sum of close to £250 but omitted to recognize that Stirling's obligation to share with other junior flag officers on the extended station would have reduced his benefit to £16, that is, approximately four days' flag pay.[42]

Finally, Stirling's defence addressed O'Grady's account of his suspicions about the transaction and his response. O'Grady said he was concerned when no specie was put on board his vessel at Port Royal but later testified that merchants never shipped it from Jamaica to the Spanish Main. When he discovered that the merchants had no intention of shipping specie at Havana, he did not attempt to convey his concerns to Stirling. His first recorded response to discovering a fraudulent transaction was the instruction for his agent to repay the freight paid to his account.[43] He subsequently arranged for the affidavit from the merchants' representatives, which cleared his name and implicated Stirling, even though he later told the court that the individuals concerned were notoriously untrustworthy.[44]

These arguments made a compelling case that there was no sworn proof of Stirling's involvement in a fraudulent transaction, and they also showed how little incentive he had to risk his honour and career by engaging in one. Stirling's defence also provided an effective rebuttal of circumstantial considerations that may have supported evidence of his guilt. At the same time, however, it contained material on his approach to protecting trade between Jamaica and the Spanish Main that left a hostage to fortune when the court deliberated on its verdict.

The key points were Stirling's frank acknowledgement that in light of his perceived duty to facilitate trade with the Spanish Main and his views on the benefits of this trade in ensuring a regular flow of specie into Jamaica, it was appropriate for him to take promises of return shipments of specie into account when allocating convoy protection.[45] Although this strategy assisted the sale of British manufactures in Spanish colonies and also provided cash to meet the needs of the dockyard operations at Port Royal, it was vulnerable to misrepresentations about return specie shipments by those hoping to secure convoys from the commander in Jamaica. Stirling candidly recognized this vulnerability when he noted that it was impossible to be sure that those who proffered return specie shipments were acting 'sincerely'.[46] He explained that in the past, pre-payments of freight had been used in Jamaica to mitigate this risk, but as Stirling denied any knowledge of an advanced payment, he did not feel the need to defend the practice in his trial. He later insisted, however, that he was aware it was contrary to the regulations and had alienated local trading and service interests by refusing to countenance it during his command. As proof of his sensitivity on this point, Stirling said that when he had heard a rumour of a pre-payment, he tackled Bogle and was assured that it was false.[47]

In closing his defence, Stirling professed astonishment that when he found himself charged with such a 'heinous offence' the only evidence produced was Captain O'Grady's. He set this testimony against his service record on 'stations, where purity, integrity, and honesty, were at least as essential as personal bravery, and professional skill'. This record had been called into question by the 'personal dislike, misrepresentation, and unfounded aspersion' he had faced in Jamaica, but Stirling assured the court that 'neither on this nor any other occasion, am I conscious of having wilfully deviated in the slightest degree, from the path of honour and of my duty'.[48] He later claimed that the *Sappho* freight was a last-minute arrangement, with the merchants taking advantage of a cruise he had already planned and notified to the Board. Significantly, however, Stirling did not provide this information at his trial.[49]

Nevertheless, the deficiencies of O'Grady's testimony and the effectiveness of Stirling's defence in highlighting them were sufficient to persuade the court that he was not guilty as charged. However, it found him 'guilty in part' and imposed a sentence that ended his active service career and any prospect of promotion while on half pay. As was customary, the court did not elaborate on its findings or sentence, leaving the accused and the world at large to ponder what it meant. Although the sentence seems harsh when compared with that handed down to Calder for a grave error of judgement in a combat situation, it was not commensurate with a finding that Stirling had been a knowing party to a corrupt transaction; that would have warranted dismissal. As indicated earlier, however, Stirling's concern with facilitating specie shipments led him to adopt a strategy vulnerable to fraud. It also offered unauthorized incentives for providing convoy protection which, since they involved a clear if indirect benefit to flag officers, exposed the service to the reputational damage that Wolley had denounced in his letter to Warren. Although Wolley's claims appear to have been greatly exaggerated and fuelled by personal and professional animus, the dangers to which he pointed were real and clearly sufficient to induce the court to hand down a verdict which stopped short of condemning Stirling for corrupt practice but probably reflected a finding that he had shown very poor judgement in going beyond his instructions and acceptable practice in prioritizing convoy protection. Stirling was, in effect, a victim of his commitment to a programme of reform in dockyard administration which included an obsessive concern with lowering government funding costs by boosting specie flow into Jamaica.

The court's findings against Stirling sit awkwardly with the seventeenth article of war's focus on the personal advantage of those who 'demand or exact any money or other reward from any merchant or master for convoying any ships or vessels entrusted to their care ... .' Arguably, however, they were within the spirit of the article and certainly corresponded with the Board's expectations that flag officers would not introduce extraneous considerations into the assignment of convoys. This expectation was particularly significant in light of Warren's stretched resources, a heightened perception of the threat posed by US privateers and the Board's exposure to West Indian interests' lobbying. It is significant that even before Warren heard of the *Sappho* convoy, he warned Stirling that convoys to the Spanish Main were not a priority for the Admiralty Board.[50] From this perspective, Stirling's sentence sharpened the minds of flag officers on their management of convoys, particularly where there was an actual or perceived background of corrupt practice.

Stirling's counsel thought there was substantial prejudice against him 'at Portsmouth', which presumably referred to members of the service, including those who came into social contact with the judges.[51] Although Sergeant Blosset thought the Board should move the trial elsewhere, no attempt was made to do so, probably because Stirling would have regarded it as a sign of moral weakness and implied guilt. Understandably, those who saw themselves as having honourably forsworn private advantage from an arduous and tedious duty, especially if they also sided with Stirling's captains on the freight-share issue, would have deplored the conduct alleged against him. It is significant that when Stirling arrived back in England, the press reported that his flagship carried $3m of freight.[52] This amount would have yielded Stirling a sum that was wildly out of kilter with a verified statement of his earnings later submitted to the Board. Still, the report itself was indicative of suspicions within the service and an absence of sympathy that may have hardened Stirling's judges' resolve when they decided on his sentence. In that respect, the finding against him contrasts strongly with decisions made by Keppel's, Cornwallis', Parker's, Duckworth's and even Calder's courts.

Aftermath

A month after the trial, the Board instructed its solicitor to consult an earlier legal opinion bearing on the legality of the sentence. This step was, however, primarily a technical exercise that had nothing to do with substantive qualms about either the verdict or the penalty. It concerned a court's right to specify that an officer remain on half pay for the rest of his life; the reference point was a similar finding against a marine officer in 1803.[53] The opinion was that this part of the sentence should be treated as a recommendation to the Board since the matter lay beyond the court's competence. The Board decided this opinion applied to Stirling's case and accepted the court's recommendation.[54]

As we have seen, some flag officers were keen to lay their court martial minutes before the public in pamphlet form. Stirling sought access to the Board's copy of the minutes and was permitted to copy them on the condition that he paid the clerk for the job.[55] He did not, however, produce a printed copy for seven years and did not publish it.[56] Stirling's trial was not raised in the House of Commons, and he took no steps to publicize it in the wake of the court martial. Nor did he attempt (as Harvey had done) to approach the Privy Council to moderate the penalty. The reason for that became apparent in 1826 when Stirling published a preface and annotated 'notes and observations' to a pamphlet reprinted from the highly favourable 'historical memoir' that had earlier appeared in James Ralfe's *Naval Biography of Great Britain*. Stirling told his readers that he felt forced to assume the unlikely guise of an author out of dire necessity: 'I must either force my Case on the attention of the people, or I must continue in that mortifying and penal retirement to which I have been condemned.' He complained that otherwise well-disposed advisors had not come to grips with the issue or listened to his justification.[57]

Stirling's frustration with those who sought to console him on the grounds that he had merely 'yielded to a bad custom, which others had been allowed to practice with immunity' was understandable because this mode of absolution did nothing to restore his sense of honour.[58] However, he was equally dismissive of other explanations for his conviction that seemed closer to the mark. Some of Stirling's friends assured him his offence involved 'no moral turpitude' and that 'my character remains untarnished'. They advised him to submit quietly 'to the misfortunes in which a combination of untoward circumstances, and not my guilt, has implicated me'. To the extent that this advice reflected an awareness that Stirling's conviction and the sentence was affected by the distinctive political and operational challenges of the American War, it was apposite. By the same token, however, Stirling's refusal to give it credence says much for his state of hurt intransigence in the wake of his trial. He rejected any solace from having been a victim of circumstances and insisted on seeing his conviction in terms of a reading of the seventeenth article of war that focused exclusively on personal corruption: 'The offence, whatever opinion there might be about its moral turpitude, was contrary to the rules of the service; and if I ever sanctioned it, I am willing to allow I deserve my fate.' Stirling claimed that the failure to believe his protestations of innocence further damaged his 'personal character'.[59]

This perspective underwrote the only attempt Stirling made to have his case reconsidered. His counsel sought legal advice in 1816, which raised questions about the admissibility of the merchants' affidavits and the bearing of Captain O'Grady's evidence on the charge, but at that stage the matter does not seem to have been pursued.[60] Over the next two years, however, Stirling became aware of a shift in local opinion in his favour. Rear Admiral John Douglas, the commander-in-chief from 1816-17, told him that Jamaican opinion now recognized that the fraudulent transaction was Bogle's work and that Stirling had known nothing of it.[61] In 1818, he received another indirect signal of support from the West Indies. Rear Admiral Sir Home Popham, whom Stirling had relieved of the Buenos Aires command in late 1806, made a special recommendation to the Board to promote Stirling's nephew James to post captain.[62] These welcome developments were not sufficient to overcome Stirling's despairing state of mind – 'hitherto so depressed, and my feelings so much agitated . . . by incurring the bare suspicion of improper conduct, and . . . by that suspicion being confirmed by the sentence of a Court Martial' – but in 1821 he appears to have raised his case with the Admiralty Board.[63] A clerk in the Admiralty office sent a copy of the sentence and other papers to the Secretary of the Board in June 1821, who passed it to Rear Admiral Sir Henry Hotham, one of the naval commissioners. Hotham was on the Board when it promoted James Stirling and may have had some knowledge of the affair during service on the North American station during the war of 1812.[64]

In July 1821, Stirling submitted a lengthy statement to the Board, canvassing the main points of his defence. It emphasized his consistent refusal to countenance the practice of which he was accused, drew the Board's attention to the impact of the delay in charging him on his preparation for the trial, provided verified details of his modest prize and freight earnings and also reported on Douglas' letter. Stirling wished the Board to set the sentence aside because the evidence produced at the trial did not support his conviction. The Board, however, acknowledged receipt of Stirling's statement of his case without taking any further public action. A letter from Stirling to Hotham in March 1822 demonstrating that he had 'shewed a more than ordinary inattention to my own interest' indicated that he still harboured hopes of an inquiry into his sentence.[65]

As we have seen, courts martial were very often painful and humiliating occasions for flag officers, even when they escaped unfavourable verdicts on their conduct. In Stirling's case, however, the opacity of the court's verdict conspired with his sense of impugned honour and his obtuseness to ensure that the aftermath of his trial was long, drawn out and painful. Twelve years later he still felt himself 'a victim to the prejudice that has obscured my character, blighted my prospects, and embittered my life'.[66]

Conclusion

The republication of Ralfe's memoir in 1826 appears to have been the last shot in Stirling's campaign for exoneration. If, as suggested earlier, these attempts at vindication rested on a misunderstanding of the basis of the verdict and Stirling's refusal to listen to those who attempted to dispel it, they were bound to fail. While it is just conceivable that the Board would have supported an appeal to the Privy Council to modify the penalty, it is inconceivable that it would have countenanced moves to overturn the verdict or sanction a parliamentary inquiry into the court martial. The two key figures involved in Stirling's recall and laying a charge against him, J. W. Croker, the highly influential Secretary of the Board, and the second Lord Melville, the first lord, were still in office in 1821. Neither man was of a particularly forgiving disposition, and the lack of any parliamentary discussion of the verdict in 1814 demonstrated Stirling's incapacity to marshal significant political interest to soften their sensibilities. If seen in the context of challenges on the North American station in 1812–14, and a broad interpretation of the seventeenth article of war, the court's finding was defensible, if harsh.

James Ralfe treated the verdict on Stirling as an example of 'strange and anomalous trials by courts-martial' and pointedly compared it with 'acquittals taking place where guilt was apparent, as in the case of Admiral Duckworth'.[67] As suggested in an earlier chapter, however, Duckworth seems to have been guilty of behaving badly rather than of criminal misconduct and, given the circumstances of Stirling's misguided rather than venal offending, an exemplary punishment for the misuse of convoy resources was consistent with the 'good of the service'. In later years, the Board saw no need to revisit it when Stirling's appeals focused on reversing the verdict rather than moderating the punishment. Indeed, to the extent that Stirling's questions about the bearing of O'Grady's evidence on the charge and the evidential status of the affidavits opened up areas of legal risk, Croker and Melville could justifiably claim in response to Hotham's sympathetic concerns that it was not in the good of the service to revisit the case.

13

Politics, Honour and Justice in Flag Officers' Courts Martial

This chapter discusses three central themes that emerge from the detailed examination of flag officers' courts martial experiences. It looks first at the role that different political pressures played in decisions to bring admirals to trial and their implications for the character of naval justice in the late Georgian period. It then considers the impact of ideas of honour and duty on the experiences of flag officers called to trial and the idea of naval justice entailed by it. The final section of the chapter utilizes flag officers' court martial experiences to identify key characteristics of the late Georgian system of naval justice, compares admirals' charge and conviction rates with those of other members of the service and offers some explanations for them.

Politics and naval justice

By the late eighteenth century, the Board required flag officers to demonstrate a high level of commitment to the wide range of logistical and managerial responsibilities necessary to keep fleets at sea, pay close attention to discipline at all levels, be responsive to its instructions and pursue the enemy remorselessly when opportunities occurred. Significant failures attracted the Board's critical attention and were likely to be discussed by senior service colleagues. If they occurred in operational situations, political and service sources fed information to the press, which also reported on reactions in parliament. Public expectations fuelled by Britain's naval dominance and the highly competitive ethos of the service, meant that shortcomings in combat could be as damaging politically as clear failure. Admiral Keppel, Sir Robert Calder and Lord Gambier were court-martialled on these grounds, but the Board only charged them after several months of controversy in the press, service and elite circles. Keppel's and Calder's cases were affected by the impact of widespread invasion fears on embattled ministers. Gambier was charged with the same offence as Keppel and Calder, but the political context was somewhat different. In this case, an unstable ministry led by an ailing prime minister had been weakened and demoralized by a prolonged scandal involving the army's commander-in-chief, and there was acute uncertainty over developments in the war in the Iberian Peninsula and the implications of Napoleon's successful campaign against Britain's Austrian ally.[1] The ministry initially saw Gambier's partial destruction of a French squadron as a godsend, but when the press circulated rumours of his failure to strike a knockout blow and one of his officers threatened to air them in parliament, the Board agreed to Gambier's request for a court martial.

Lord Spencer's board's decision to court-martial Vice Admiral Cornwallis occurred in a context where a forceful senior cabinet colleague was keen to demonstrate his determination to brook no delays in embarking on a critical stage of the government's West Indian strategy. Spencer probably also wished to dispel any impression of weakness and hesitation on that issue and in an unresolved dispute between the government, the army and senior naval officers. Given these considerations, Spencer had little choice but to charge Cornwallis. The same applied to Lord Mulgrave's decision to order a court martial on Gambier, although in this case the first lord bore some responsibility for the developments that led to the trial.

Gambier's appointment to command the Channel Fleet testified to the power of interest and political favouritism over experience and demonstrated merit. Having appointed his former colleague to a command for which he was ill-prepared by experience and probably also by temperament, Mulgrave ineptly attempted to compensate by inserting the predictably volatile Lord Cochrane into Gambier's operational planning and execution. Given this toxic combination of political, professional and personal sensitivities, the Board then edged the participants closer to open acrimony and the courtroom by exaggerating Gambier's achievements. These accolades vindicated Gambier's appointment and enhanced a weak ministry's profile but provoked Cochrane to move from bad-mouthing Gambier among his friends to issuing an all-too-credible threat to disparage him publicly. Once Gambier got wind of this – presumably from Lord Mulgrave – it was inevitable that he would demand a court martial and also unavoidable, given the circumstances and the Board's limited room for exercising discretion, that it would order one.

While Earl St Vincent's personal animus against Sir William Parker played a role in precipitating his court martial, it was related to two sets of objectives he hoped to pursue from his recently acquired seat at the head of the Admiralty Board. Recalling Parker for disobedience gave exemplary prominence to the obsession with discipline that marked St Vincent's Mediterranean and Channel commands and which he saw as a *leitmotif* of his naval career: 'Obedience has ever been the maxim of my professional life – I regard obedience as the Pole Star of the Service.'[2] In addition, however, the implication that Parker's venality promoted his disobedience allowed St Vincent to signal the root-and-branch attention to corruption, which he saw as a primary objective of his naval administration.

Allegations of financial impropriety were central to the Board's summons to Vice Admiral Stirling, but it also reflected the government's long-standing commitment to trade protection and its sensitivity to the demands of trading interests. Political and operational vulnerabilities arising from United States' privateers and the lacklustre performance of the Royal Navy in the early stages of the conflict sharpened the government's reaction. Stirling's recall and court martial were preceded by the Board's prolonged campaign of carping criticism of his commander-in-chief's energy and deployments.[3]

Flag officers' courts martial were affected by the low politics of parties jockeying for power and settling scores, as well as the high politics of wartime strategy. Those in power naturally sought to glory in the fighting achievements of admirals at sea but equally obviously wished to limit political damage arising from significant failures of senior naval leadership. These factors were most clearly at play in the Keppel-Palliser affair. The Rockingham Whigs' concerted attempt to use the government's conduct of the American War to bring down Lord North's administration had a determining impact on the atmosphere of Keppel's and Palliser's trials and the behaviour of principal actors. The entrenched partisan attitudes reflected in performative parliamentary debates made their way into the upper echelons of the navy, threatening to undermine its operational efficiency in the face of significant challenges from French and Spanish maritime power.

Although no subsequent court martial generated the factional political heat of the Keppel-Palliser affair, there was a distinctly partisan edge to Lord Cochrane's challenge to Lord Gambier. Cochrane's flamboyant personality and highly aggressive leadership style, a great asset when commanding small squadrons in daring episodes of littoral warfare, were ill-suited to working harmoniously with a staid senior officer. In addition, however, Gambier was a close political friend of the first lord in a Tory administration, while Cochrane was associated with radical government critics. A long catalogue of perceived personal injustices at the hands of the senior naval establishment were subjoined to these professional and political antagonisms to fuel a press campaign against Gambier, culminating in Cochrane's declaration that he would oppose a parliamentary vote of thanks.

Cochrane's post-trial resort to parliament was one of several examples of the interpenetration of politics and naval justice apparent in flag officers' courts martial experiences. His parliamentary interventions, like Keppel's allies' proposed motions on Palliser's trial and Colonel Wood's attempts to exonerate his brother, questioned an acquittal by inferring that the ministry had somehow protected the accused from the consequences of criminal failures of duty. It was also possible, however, for parliamentarians to intervene on behalf of flag officers alleged to be the victims of unjust judicial processes and/or politically motivated decision-making. The vote of thanks to Keppel may be seen in this light, as were stillborn suggestions of a parliamentary motion on Cornwallis' behalf in the House of Commons, gestures of parliamentary support for Sir Hyde Parker's right to an inquiry and Sir Robert Calder's vindication. Even though the ministry's control of the House of Commons prevented motions from progressing, parliament's right to review the conduct and outcomes of courts martial gave government critics opportunities to extract political mileage from them. Ministry speakers responded in kind. They defended Gambier (and themselves) when Lord Cochrane tried to press home his attack after the trial; a civil commissioner of the Admiralty and members of the service defended Duckworth's acquittal in the House of Commons. When leading actors had seats in parliament, they intervened directly in debates on their cases. Keppel was to the fore in parliamentary sallies against Palliser and Lord Sandwich, and Palliser became increasingly effective in debates instigated by Keppel's supporters. Cochrane's membership of the House of Commons put him in a prime position to embarrass the ministry's attempt to secure reflective glory from Gambier's action.

Political considerations played a role in decisions to ensure that flag officers' courts included a 'respectable' number of their fellow admirals. This term implied significant peer representation to uphold the dignity of the accused. It may also have reflected the Board's interest in courts with sufficient experience and confidence to convict flag officers where necessary. That was clearly the case with Keppel's and Cornwallis' trials and may also have applied to Calder's and Stirling's. The heavy partisan atmosphere of the Keppel-Palliser affair affected Keppel's trial, and flag officers' suspicions of the motives of first lords may well have explained the lack of enquiring spirit shown by Cornwallis' and Sir William Parker's judges. Their approach contrasted markedly with the punctilious zeal demonstrated by Gambier's court, but that may well have reflected its determination to head off claims of a ministerial job. For the most part, however, the well-maintained secrecy of judges' deliberations means that it is impossible to do anything other than speculate on the impact of political considerations on the outcomes of flag officers' courts martial. Judges were bound by oath to perform their duties justly and impartially, and even in the heat of parliamentary debate and under the cover of parliamentary privilege, only the most highly partisan political actors impugned judges' honour by questioning their judicial honesty.

Finally, courts martial processes were often affected by the politics of intra-service relationships. Although these connections were not insulated from other political forces, they were distinct in that they primarily concerned the interactions of senior naval officers on important professional matters. Keppel's popularity in the service and widely held suspicions of ministerial skulduggery meant that his supporters presented the Keppel-Palliser affair as a defence of the service and the constitution. Cornwallis' colleagues' view of his treatment by Lord Spencer was affected by intra-service solidarity provoked by the ministry's handling of the dispute with the army. Questions of solidarity also probably affected the outcomes of Parker's and Duckworth's trials. Whatever the impact of Trafalgar on Calder's court martial, speculation in the service on how Nelson would have behaved off Finisterre contributed to the pre-trial idea that Calder had 'not done enough'. Finally, the intense feeling against Stirling among officers in Portsmouth presumably reflected a widespread endorsement of Commissioner Wolley's claim that his handling of convoy business had damaged the Navy's reputation. It may also have been due to post captains' resentment at flag officers' claims to a share of freight payments and Stirling's prominent role in that controversy.

Honour, ambition and naval justice

St Vincent's analogy of 'the sound of a court martial' and 'a suspicion of female chastity' which 'when once wounded may never be recovered' highlighted the role of honour in processes of naval justice.[4] Because contemporaries saw naval trials as 'courts of honour' and 'courts of justice', those they touched were highly sensitive to allegations of misconduct. As we have seen, flag officers gave vent to feelings of hurt and degradation when they believed they were unjustly summoned for trial, when they felt obliged to request a court martial and when the Board declined to grant them one. Even the most fulsome 'honourable' acquittals and riders disparaging the honesty of accusers did not necessarily assuage the wounded feelings of those brought to trial or make them feel secure in their honour. For those who received verdicts of qualified acquittal, 'guilty in part' or 'guilty as charged', the feelings of pain and humiliation were likely to be proportionally more intense. In a strictly hierarchical service culture, dishonouring claims of dereliction of duty were likely to be felt most strongly and articulated forcefully by those in its upper reaches. The Admiralty Board was thus able to achieve the deterrent effect that severe physical punishment had on members of the lower deck by availing itself of the intense fear of public shame and private mortification that flag officers suffered from facing, or failing to face, courts martial.

In several admirals' trials, alleged failures to engage, pursue and destroy the enemy involved imputations of cowardice. Cowardly conduct by flag officers was particularly reprehensible because it flew in the face of their obligations to ensure, by example and through disciplinary measures, an appropriately aggressive vigour in the face of the enemy. These failures were radically incompatible with the raison d'être of armed naval service conveyed most forcefully by Rear Admiral Byng's condemnation. Witnesses' testimonies to Keppel's and Gambier's keenness to engage were sufficient to dispel insinuations of cowardice, but it is significant that in Calder's trial, where he admitted the possibility of reengaging, he secured testimony from his flag captain to counter suspicions of tell-tale signs of personal anxiety and fear. The verdict absolved Calder of the taint of cowardice, but its finding that he was guilty of a serious error of judgement made it clear that he had failed in his duty and thus compromised his honour as a 'gentleman-at-arms'. Rear Admiral Byng's case had shown that flag officers' determination was as crucial as their courage, and as we have seen, Thomas Grenville regarded Calder's 'indecisiveness' as debilitating as cowardice.[5] The courts martial experiences of Cornwallis, Parker, Duckworth and Stirling make it clear that questions of honour were not confined to combat situations.[6]

The impact of flag officers' courts martial on their subsequent careers compounded the direct reputational damage of their trials. Ambition was a 'constituent' of naval honour or, perhaps more accurately, a motivation closely aligned with it.[7] Flag officers' laudable ambitions focused on successful command in a fleet action, distinguished fulfilment of other significant active service duties, enrichment through prize earnings and public rewards and recognition by the award of royal honours, pensions and sinecure appointments. However, the sine qua non for realizing all these ambitions was appointment to a command on a strategically significant station and that might be placed at risk when flag officers became embroiled in courts martial.

A sentence of dismissal obviously ended any prospects in the service, but penalties that fell short of that might also be fatally career-limiting. The intra-service fissures laid bare in the Keppel-Palliser affair were probably sufficient to shut off any prospect of further active service employment for these flag officers. Cornwallis suffered self-inflicted career damage and Sir William Parker was removed from the scene by death. Harvey's restoration of rank seems to have precluded future service, and Stirling's condemnation to half pay certainly did. Despite his acquittal, Duckworth's court martial may have revealed aspects of his character that played an adverse role in his subsequent career. The King's unenthusiastic reaction to the prospect of Lord Gambier as a first lord probably reflected service opinion that emerged from the exposure of his performance at Basque Roads.

Thus, to the extent that flag officers' court martial experiences hindered their subsequent careers, it also blighted their successful pursuit of the prime objects of admirals' ambitions and the honour and recognition arising from them. Palliser remained a baronet and had to be content with the governorship of Greenwich Hospital. Keppel became a viscount but that was purely a matter of party politics. Duckworth never gained the peerage to which he thought he was entitled and felt dishonoured by the pension of £1000 per annum awarded to him after his victory off St Domingo. Lord Gambier remained on the lowest rank of the United Kingdom peerage, and Stirling's court martial almost certainly deprived him of a knighthood in the remodelled Order of the Bath.

Flag officers' reactions to being charged suggest that they feared that the honour of a gentleman at arms did not admit of degrees: once tainted, it was compromised indelibly. One of the potential costs of bearing this stigma was the impact on the sense of collective identity that flag officers enjoyed as members of a distinctive honour group within the service.[8] Successful flag officers were long-serving and deeply embedded members of their profession and trial by court martial, or a disgrace that lingered in the absence of a trial, was likely to be particularly traumatic. Being dishonoured meant they felt excluded from the circle of honour to which their previous service had inducted them and on which their social consequence and psychological well-being largely depended. This dire possibility explains the fulsome assurance given by court presidents when handing down honourable acquittals to relieved flag officers and issuing damning riders to their accusers. It was also reflected in the processions of senior officers accompanying their colleague, *honoris redivivus,* to post-trial celebrations. These displays contrast with the truly poignant image of Sir Eliab Harvey walking back to his lodgings in Portsmouth with his legal 'friend' and the air of desolate isolation that hangs over Vice Admiral Stirling's later life. His friends' attempts to minimize the implications of his conviction only served to sharpen the pain of alienation.

When flag officers were summoned for trial, their friends' and families' concerns for their well-being, professional prospects and honour compounded the stress arising from the court martial experience. The highly wrought reactions to Admiral Keppel's court martial among his friends and political allies are unusually well documented, but there are also indications of less overtly performative responses from flag officers' closest connections. Keppel's mother, the septuagenarian dowager countess of Albemarle, was reported as being 'very miserable and full of apprehension' as his trial approached and, as we have seen, the Marquis Cornwallis was alarmed at the prospect of his brother's trial.[9] Sir Robert Calder's pending court martial upset his wife's fragile mental equilibrium, and Sir Eliab Harvey's taxed the fortitude of Lady Harvey. News of Harvey's conviction compounded the stress faced by his eldest son on active service in the Peninsular War. Captain Edward Harvey's anxious reaction to his father's condemnation contrasts sharply with the sense of relief that infuses the congratulatory correspondence that Lord Gambier received from friends and relations on his acquittal.[10]

These personal and familial considerations help explain the high emotional tone that marked flag officers' reactions to their courts martial. Keppel reduced himself and his supporters to tears, and even Sir Hugh Palliser, a far more phlegmatic figure, made little attempt to hide the emotional toll the two trials had taken upon him. He made heartfelt appeals for Lord Sandwich's sympathy and support and defended himself in the House of Commons with references to the 'manliness' of his conduct in the face of potentially humiliating adversity.[11] Cornwallis' public demeanour was very controlled, but his correspondence with Lord Spencer and his brother was no less emotionally charged than Palliser's.[12] Parker's reaction to his initial treatment by the Board included frank, indignant statements of major injury to his honour and professional standing. Still, these were restrained compared to Duckworth's frequent declarations of the 'poignancy' of 'feelings' prompted by indignation at being charged, his resentment of his accuser's base motivation in doing so and bitter frustration at the first lords' disinclination to provide compensatory recognition and rewards.[13] The volume and frequency of Calder's public expressions of poignant feelings did not come close to Duckworth's but were, nevertheless, prominent in his correspondence with colleagues, first lords and patrons and in statements made in his trial.[14] Finally, while Stirling's sense of entitlement hardly registered against those of Duckworth and Calder, his perception of the Board's unjust treatment provoked highly charged references to his honour that he reiterated during his unsuccessful attempts to secure redress.[15]

Flag officers' courts martial and naval justice

Although systematic data on comparative intra-service charging and conviction rates is not available, it is possible to arrive at approximations of the relative impact of the naval system of justice on the main divisions within the hierarchy: flag officers, other commissioned officers, warrant officers and seamen and marines. If the relevant population of flag officers is restricted to those employed in the period, the charge rate is close to 9 per cent. Identifying a conviction rate for this group is complicated by the verdicts handed down on Palliser, Cornwallis and Parker. These officers were all acquitted, but their courts added riders to their verdicts that carried notes of qualifying censure. Depending on how these qualified acquittals are viewed, the conviction rate of those charged is either 33 or 66 per cent, giving rates of either 3 or 6 per cent of eligible flag officers. Data from Thomas Malcomson's study of the North American station (including the West Indies) during the War of 1812 suggests that flag officers were more likely to be charged and convicted or subject to a qualified acquittal than other commissioned officers. However, the charge/conviction figures for warrant officers were 6 and 94 per cent and for seamen and marines 1 and 80 per cent. The extraordinarily high conviction rate for warrant officers seems related to the easily proven nature of the charges of drunkenness and insubordination they usually faced, while the extraordinarily low court martial charging rate for seamen and marines is due to the statistically overwhelming tendency for them to be tried summarily by their captains. Bryn's and Malcomson's figures on summary punishments suggest overall charging and punishment rates for seamen and marines ranging from 10 to 25 per cent of the relevant population.[16]

These data are far from robust but undoubtedly good enough to indicate that the punitive weight of naval justice sat far more heavily on those on the lower deck than the flag officers at the head of the service. However, two sets of considerations have a bearing on these figures. The first concerns the highly significant differences in conditions of service at different points in the naval hierarchy and the impact of service sub-cultures on the likelihood of offending. Although the proportion of pressed men in the service was not as high as once thought, forced recruitment still accounted for about 25 per cent of a diverse lower deck workforce.[17] Whether pressed or not, men from the lower deck were liable for continuous wartime service and did not enjoy formal shore-leave provisions. Although warrant and petty officers trained them to fulfil their particular shipboard duties, the low ratio of commissioned officers to seamen (*c.* 88:1, excluding captains) and high turnover rates of both officers and men from ship to ship militated against the systemization of discipline through the effective, service-wide inculcation of behavioural norms and the surveillance necessary to promote self-imposed conformity.[18] While it is highly likely that many men serving on the lower deck were not only deterred from offending out of fear, it is equally possible that in all ships there were a greater or lesser number of men for whom fear was the only effective deterrent. These features of the disciplinary sub-culture of the lower deck explain the Georgian navy's reliance on savage exemplary punishment to keep disorder in check and maintain the disciplinary requirements of an effective fighting force.[19] As with deterrent punishments generally, this approach was likely to produce a self-reinforcing reliance on severe forms of physical punishment and their application to men whose commitment to the norms of the service varied significantly. Given these considerations, the hardships of life at sea and hence temptations to drunkenness, alcohol-prompted misconduct and desertion, relatively high rates of charging and conviction were to be expected; in a very real sense, the system seemed hardwired for them.

The position of commissioned officers, particularly those who rose to flag rank, was radically different. They were all volunteers pursuing careers that they hoped would bring long-term financial rewards, public recognition and, in many cases, an enhancement of their social status and consequence. Moreover, while officers were subject to the unavoidable hardships and dangers of sea service and combat, their style of life bore some resemblance to that of their social equals ashore and, far from being prisoners of the service, they were free to resign their commissions and live ashore if they wished. Indeed, the huge oversupply of commissioned officers of all ranks made forced unemployment as likely as employment at sea.[20]

If the conditions of service pressed less hard on these men, so too did its discipline. This outcome resulted from their sub-culture rather than pervasive elite self-indulgence. Those wishing to pursue a career as a sea officer were subject to extensive training and inculcated into the norms of the service and the duties of their station. These norms included ideas about the close relationship between duty and honour that gave their commitment to the requirements of the service a prudential, symbolic and moral basis. Consequently, they understood their authority rested on the overarching disciplinary structure of the service and that misconduct in superiors undermined the legitimacy of the chain of command. The *Regulations and Instructions* formalized these expectations.[21] It is significant that when two particularly thoughtful flag officers discussed the conditions for establishing 'steady regular discipline without violence', they focused on close and constant attention to 'every movement, almost to every look of the men' and the need for officers to constantly model 'regular discipline' in front of their men.[22]

Employed flag officers were a highly selective subset of the service, even more firmly inculcated into its norms than more junior commissioned officers. They also occupied positions in the service where realistic motives and opportunities for offending were comparatively limited. Of the twenty-five named offences that men from the lower deck could conceivably commit, a number of them (physical violence, fighting, disobedience, contempt, desertion, mutinous activity, striking an officer) were almost their special preserve and accounted for the overwhelming majority of charges and convictions.[23] Admirals could conceivably be charged with swearing, drunkenness and sodomy but those inclined to such behaviour would have been unlikely to have survived long enough to gain flag rank. The offences for which flag officers were tried during the American and French Wars covered the full range to which they were plausibly exposed: not engaging, holding back, disobedience, illegal shipment of goods, receiving payment for convoy, conduct unbecoming and quarrelling.

While these considerations affected charge rates, they do not explain the vast differences in conviction rates between admirals and those from the lower deck. There is no evidence to support the apparent explanation that flag officers received more favourable treatment in the court martial process than those from the lower deck. The sole formal advantage conferred by their rank was that flag officers were not subject to confinement before trial. A contemporary authority maintained that ordinary sailors as well as commissioned officers benefited from the navy's courts martial procedures and practices, a judgement supported by J. D. Byrn's sample of lower deck court transcripts and N. A. M. Rodger's qualitative analysis of mid-eighteenth-century trial records.[24] All those facing courts martial were provided with 'friends of the court' to assist them, and presidents knew they had a duty to ensure that courts and prosecutors treated the accused fairly. Men from the lower deck also benefited from the absence of the time constraints which were a feature of civilian criminal courts of the period and, as noted in an earlier chapter, naval trials were far more orderly than many of those held ashore. Moreover, the status of the judges in courts martial militated against intimidatory behaviour that partisans directed at civilian juries.[25] Ironically, his aristocratic airs and graces notwithstanding, Keppel's court came closest to replicating the hurly-burly of the more disorderly trials of working-class felons at the Old Bailey.

These observations apply only to the treatment of men from the lower deck in courts martial, proceedings that account for a very small portion of the punishments inflicted on them. In the absence of studies of summary processes – as opposed to data on the character, incidence and level of punishment resulting from them – it is not possible to do more than note the likelihood that hundreds of captains of widely different temperaments facing markedly different disciplinary challenges were likely to adopt a variety of approaches to exercising their summary jurisdiction.[26] In the absence of evidence to the contrary, however, there is no reason to assume that vindictive savagery was the norm. As Rodger points out, feelings of humanity, religious conviction and prudential considerations would all count against that.[27]

Available figures for lower deck convictions show that most were for a narrow range of personal behavioural infractions of the Articles of War: desertion, drunkenness, contempt, mutiny, disobedience, fighting, uncleanliness, theft.[28] Lower deck trials focused on relatively straightforward investigations of matters of fact, and in many cases there was virtually no attempt to offer a rebuttal by the accused; statements of defence often consisted of apologies to the court and their officers, references to previous good conduct and the presentation of testimonials in support of these claims. By contrast, the charges faced by most flag officers often required highly technical investigations to establish evidence of offending. Even when that was not the case, they usually involved elaborate statements of defence. These features of admirals' trials reflected the complex context of their offending and the difficulty of finding an evidential basis for charges where motivation was often an issue. Only Stirling's and Harvey's cases came close to replicating the straightforward reliance on establishing matters of fact that characterized lower deck trials.

The lack of systematic service-wide data or modelling of offenders from the main rank divisions of the service, and the distorting effect of large numbers of summary punishments imposed on members of the lower deck, mean that it is impossible to arrive at an empirically based explanation of comparative trial and conviction rates. Nevertheless, flag officers' motivations and opportunities for offending must explain at least part of the gap between their charging and conviction rates and those of other service members. Their more complex cases also made clear-cut convictions less likely and encouraged courts to add damaging notes of censure to acquittals. These sentences provided a means of signalling shortcomings in judgement and leadership when prosecutors did not prove criminality. The expectation that flag officers would exemplify outstanding conduct and commitment and prompt a sense of emulation through their example, set a high bar in their courts martial. In line with the rationale of deterrent justifications of punishment, flag officers the Board brought to trial faced the prospect of becoming a cautionary example to their colleagues by being punished or publicly exposed for their shortcomings.

The most glaring inequity in the naval justice system concerned the nature of the punishments handed down to those at different ends of the hierarchy. The Articles of War were even-handed in prescribing death sentences for a range of offences and imposing them on flag officers as well as ordinary seamen. However, once parliament removed the mandatory death sentences for not engaging and pursuing, the prospect of capital punishment loomed larger for types of offending (mutiny, striking an officer) likely to be committed by men from the lower deck. Nevertheless, the most marked inequities and the ones most likely to materialize concerned the widespread utilization of corporal punishment for lower deck offenders and its complete absence for commissioned officers. Navy practice on this point reflected assumptions about social class and sensitivity that spared gentlemen ashore from being sentenced to be whipped. The assumption here was that the public humiliation of a whipping made the punishment excessive, presumably in terms of the requirements of effective deterrence.

However, John Beattie's research indicates that those who did not claim to be gentlemen dreaded the prospect of being publicly beaten like a dog, and Markus Eder suggests that summary sentencing to run the gauntlet for theft inflicted humiliation on offenders as well as physical pain.[29]

As we have seen, the non-capital punishments applied to flag officers took the forms of dismissal, formal debarment from future employment and reprimands. These sanctions were, however, supported by the punitive effect of reputational damage arising from notes of censure attached to acquittals and to some degree from the entire court martial experience. The formal and informal sanctions applied to flag officers had a deterrent effect without invoking the prospect of physical terror. Flag officers were punished through economic and 'symbolic' sanctions which affirmed the legitimacy of the discipline of the service upon which their status relied. The former included the indirect financial penalties suffered by those whose prospects were blighted by reprimands, recalls and courts martial, while the latter almost certainly involved forms of 'emotional stigmatization' associated with physical punishments.[30]

Conclusion

The previous section of this chapter has discussed features of flag officers' courts martial that distinguish them from the discipline applied to other members of the late Georgian Royal Navy. The concluding section provides a general evaluation of the fairness of the treatment of the nine officers who were court-martialled. It will focus on charging, the conduct of trials and their outcomes.

Although all flag officers called to courts martial were subject to significant psychological, social and financial penalties, there is no indication that late Georgian first lords abused their power by laying trumped-up charges. Naval courts martial combined investigative and judicial responsibilities, and it is arguable that there were prima facie grounds for laying charges in all the instances considered here. In making this point, it is essential to recall that the Articles of War and *Regulations and Instructions* contained both prescriptive and prohibitive specifications and that the former encompassed positive duties central to flag officers' responsibilities. As their fulfilment of these responsibilities was often context-specific and a matter of degree, there was significant latitude in deciding whether an admiral's conduct in a given situation warranted closer investigation. Furthermore, because naval justice was grounded in penological principles that treated punishment as a selective and exemplary function, it also required context-specific judgements on whether to lay a charge or rely on extrajudicial disciplinary tools. Paradoxically, in the instances most deeply mired in political antagonisms and personal animus (Keppel, Palliser, Parker and Gambier) first lords were obliged to lay charges against their better judgement.

As noted earlier, naval courts martial were exemplary by the standards of the time in their orderly conduct and in adopting measures to ensure that participants got a fair hearing. Keppel's court was a notable exception, and while the partisan aspects of his trial did not affect the verdict, they probably made it easier for the judges to issue a rider that effectively condemned Palliser. Flag officers' judges demonstrated varying amounts of investigative energy during their trials, which was to some extent related to the number of prosecution witnesses called at the instigation of the judge advocate and the Admiralty solicitor. It is likely also, however, that it reflected preconceptions that the judges brought to their role. In his essay on Charles Stirling, James Ralfe noted that while judges swore to act impartially, they were also likely to have 'prejudices' that affected their behaviour in court. If these preconceptions were unconscious biases, they were compatible with a sincere intention to impartiality but might still compromise judicial behaviour and judgements. Judges in civil courts were equally likely to carry prejudices into their courtrooms but lacked the professional and/or personal links that commonly existed between flag officers and their judges. The secrecy that shrouded naval courts' deliberations means that it is impossible to assess the impact of judges' preconceptions in particular instances. However, as noted below, no particularly egregious cases of injustice are apparent in the outcomes of flag officers' trials.

The naval courts martial were subject to two further structural anomalies. First, the framing of the charges faced by flag officers varied significantly in specificity and their stated relationship with the Articles of War. However, while some participants and observers commented on this matter, it does not seem to have been a source of practical difficulties for courts or the accused. They seemed well able to identify the main instances of a charge from the questions put to prosecution witnesses and their testimony. In any case, variations in the framing of charges seem unavoidable in overtly investigative judicial processes. Secondly, Keppel's and Duckworth's trials highlighted weaknesses in assigning the prosecutor's role to accusers. This approach may have worked reasonably well in straightforward cases of limited duration and was widely used in early eighteenth-century civilian courts. However, Palliser's performance as Keppel's accuser and Captain Wood's as Duckworth's, suggested that officers without experience in legal interrogation were likely to make a poor job of it and thus inadvertently assist those they had accused.

The outcomes of flag officers' courts martial are opaquer than those of general officers in the British army because naval courts martial did not explain their verdicts and sentences. Presumably because sentences of general courts martial were subject to confirmation by the commander-in-chief at the Horse Guards, army courts offered elaborate accounts of their sentencing decisions. But while naval courts' reasoning was hidden, the cases discussed here do not support James Ralfe's general claims about their 'anomalous' outcomes. To the contrary, verdicts on flag officers in the late Georgian period seem unexceptional in light of the evidence produced during their trials. Ralfe was offended particularly by Duckworth's acquittal and Stirling's partial conviction. Still, the former was explicable in light of custom and practice and evidence of Duckworth's intentions; the latter was a consequence of Stirling's breach of regulations, albeit in misguided good faith. As noted earlier, Stirling's sentence reflected contextual considerations that could form a legitimate element in exemplary punishments. Evidence produced at Palliser's trial may have had adverse implications for Keppel's sentence, but it was not brought forward at the earlier trial. Although Cornwallis' court treated him leniently, Lord Spencer's reaction to the outcome suggests that the trial had served its exemplary purposes. Parker's guilt was unclear, and witnesses for the prosecution did not support Cochrane's claims about Gambier's conduct. Finally, when

Calder's verdict is set in the context of the prescriptive force of the relevant articles of war, it was consistent with the evidence. The court presumably believed that his decision not to engage fell short of prevailing expectations of the duties of commanders-in-chief. Criticism of the verdict by reference to subsequent expectations is anachronistic and beside the point in evaluating the outcome of Calder's court martial.

Leaving aside the overwrought reactions of parliamentary partisans, the contemporary criticism of courts martial processes and outcomes seems remarkably restrained. Those closely connected with the service may have been critical of the Board's charging decisions but refrained from impugning judges' honesty. Commentary on verdicts referred (as in Calder's case) to a court treating an officer 'hardly' or 'harshly' rather than being flagrantly unjust. That is, it recognizes that verdicts and sentences were often a matter of degree and that a judgement may be questionable without being demonstrably unsound. Comparisons with other cases, as in Ralfe's remarks on Duckworth's and Stirling's fate, or those provoked in Calder's favour after Gambier's acquittal, are understandable but ignore the requirements that court's judge on evidence produced before them and recognize the role of deterrence in sentencing. It is interesting that although Rear Admiral Lord Gardner thought (presumably in light of Gambier's verdict) that Calder had been 'hardly dealt by' he also remarked on the 'confidence the people have in the justice of sentence by Naval Courts Martial – that they are seldom questioned, – and if the case appears hard, opinions soon subside'.[31]

Conclusion

The Admiralty Board was the formal prime mover in all flag officers' courts martial since it ordered trials, appointed court presidents and summoned the accused to appear before them. When cowardice and disobedience in battle were at issue, the Board had little choice but to lay charges and thus reiterate the highly effective deterrent sentence passed on Rear Admiral Byng.[1] Neither the severest reprimand nor the most humiliating recall was sufficient for that purpose. However, where other allegations raised the possibility of a charge or when flag officers asked to be court-martialled, the Board's response depended on various considerations.

Only four admirals were charged between 1700 and 1775, but nine suffered this fate in the next forty years over an identical period of armed conflict. The relatively high number of charges laid during the French wars is understandable given the greatly increased size of the Royal Navy, the scope of its activities and the number of flag officers on active service. It was also consistent with a general tightening of discipline and heightened expectations of committed and highly professional leadership that emerged during these wars. That is, the sharp increase in central control of fleets, dockyards and victualing from the mid-1790s also made itself felt in the Admiralty's handling of its most senior officers.[2] Lord Sandwich's successors did not repeat his complaint about the political difficulties of disciplining senior naval officers. Ironically, the two flag officers' courts martial on his watch were deemed necessary because of politically related pressures which he could not resist. When first lords did not face these pressures, they were free – as when accepting Captain Wood's charges against Sir John Duckworth and Lord Gambier's against Sir Eliab Harvey – to apply Sandwich's rubric when considering officers' requests to charge their colleagues.

Although these cases met the formal requirements for laying charges, other factors no doubt came into play. Wood's brother was a wealthy MP with close connections to the ministry, and this, together with a strong sense of grievance encouraged by the Board's apparent disinclination to support Duckworth's claims against Captain Wood, made it very likely that the admiral's conduct would become a matter of critical public comment. In these circumstances, the Board's decision to accept Wood's charge addressed several risks. In a subsequent case, Gambier's close relationship with the first lord and the uncomfortable implications of Harvey's claims about his fitness to command aggravated misconduct so blatantly contrary to service discipline that Lord Mulgrave could not ignore it.

Even though Cornwallis' misdeeds fell within the scope of Lord Sandwich's rubric and did not entail a capital charge, a first lord might have dealt with it by removing him from his command and condemning him to live ashore on half pay. This option was probably not open to Lord Spencer in early 1795. As we have seen, he responded to strategic considerations and the perceived need to exert his authority in the wake of the recent admirals' protest. If that had not been so, however, Cornwallis' high reputation in the service and the strength of his connection with the ministry made it virtually impossible for the Board to cast him aside without the benefit of due process. His widely admired capabilities would have made it imprudent to do so.

In the closing years of the war, the Board again found it necessary to court-martial a flag officer as a warning to his colleagues and to convince vital political interests of its attention to them. The fears promoted by privateer action in the War of 1812 conspired with fractious relationships between the commander-in-chief of the North American station and the Board, and Vice Admiral Stirling's aberrant views of convoying priorities, to lend credence to one of the claims made by a vindictive colleague in Jamaica. As there is some indication that Stirling's alleged misconduct alienated colleagues in the service, the Board's decision to charge him must have been pretty much a matter of course.

When flag officers asked the Board to charge them in the face of criticism in the service and wider public, it was aware that issues of justice, professional reputation and honour were at stake for the officer concerned. These matters were not purely personal since, as Sir William Parker's claim for the Board's protection showed, first lords and the naval members of the Board had responsibility for those it had appointed to active commands and served under its direction. They would also be aware that successful flag officers were part of patronage networks and they or their 'friends' could mobilize political interest to support their appeals to the Board. These considerations were part of a more complex decision-making environment. Lord Sandwich was a ministerial patron of Sir Hugh Palliser and was personally well disposed towards him, but until Keppel was acquitted and Palliser vilified in the court's rider, he did not think a trial necessary or desirable and could resist it because there was no accuser. Lord Spencer rebuked Sir Hyde Parker for mistreating Rear Admiral Bligh and was receptive to the plea that his reputation was in danger of being 'whispered away' through the agency of Parker and his friends. After the first Battle of Copenhagen, however, Parker probably overplayed his hand by demanding that his recall be subjected to an enquiry since that widened the net and would have provided an opportunity for his friends to damage St Vincent. There was no political pressure on St Vincent to recall Sir William Parker, but political considerations probably led him to accede to Parker's request for a court martial when the first lord preferred to leave him dangling. Ironically, St Vincent's criticism of the verdict suggests that he did think there was a case to answer. Calder's treatment was unusual in that the Board agreed to his request to be tried after it had already determined that a court martial had become necessary. Finally, while Lord Mulgrave was mindful of the damaging reputational effects of Lord Cochrane's campaign against Lord Gambier, he was no doubt also aware that a court martial provided an opportunity to vindicate the appointment of a close political associate and salvage credit for the ministry for his action.

The Board's (or probably in most instances, first lords') decisions to summon flag officers to face courts martial thus involved a complex range of factors concerning the nature of the alleged offending, reactions to it in the service and elite opinion, and a raft of contextual considerations that came into play in different ways in different cases.

Ministries that were otherwise vulnerable were likely to be highly responsive to widely circulated claims about the operational failings of fleet commanders, particularly when they were close associates of first lords and key strategic objectives were at stake. The fate of a flag officer whose conduct might in other circumstances have resulted in a court martial provides a useful counterfactual to the cases discussed earlier in this chapter.

In late 1796 and early 1797, Rear Admiral Man, a subordinate flag officer in Admiral Sir John Jervis' Mediterranean fleet, ignored the orders of Sir Hyde Parker, his immediate superior, and took his squadron back to Spithead rather than re-joining the main fleet.[3] Although Lord Spencer expressed regret that Man had not had the foresight to link up with his commander-in-chief, he took no formal action against him; indeed, he later availed himself of Man's well-earned reputation for good sense and professional competence by appointing him to the Admiralty Board. Man's case mirrored that of Cornwallis to some extent, and Spencer may have already thought that the earlier trial had underlined his determination that flag officers obey their superiors.

In addition, however, several other considerations may explain why Man's major indiscretion was allowed to pass virtually unnoticed. First, since mid-1796 his correspondence with Spencer and Jervis made it clear that he was undergoing a mental breakdown. Although Jervis was aware of Man's fragile mental state, he was largely unsympathetic. Spencer, however, accepted Man's request to be relieved and had been taking steps to find a replacement. Secondly, although Spencer thought Man's premature return most unfortunate, he excused it as a reasonable act of discretion prompted by the realization that Hyde Parker's original instructions were no longer relevant and Jervis' order to re-join the fleet had not reached him. Thirdly, since Man consulted his captains on his plan to return to England and they had unanimously endorsed it, a court martial would have inevitably drawn in a number of other officers whom Jervis suspected of being desperate to get back to England. Finally, Man's conduct did not have any ill consequences for the first lord or the operational effectiveness of Jervis' fleet, and the latter did not request a court martial. Spencer was not facing the intra-ministerial pressures that played a role in his decision to court-martial Cornwallis and had begun to fill his role with growing confidence. Moreover, while Man's lack of initiative irritated Jervis and weakened the forces available to him, he nevertheless managed to conduct a highly successful action against a combined French and Spanish fleet. Within six weeks of Man's crestfallen return, the euphoria of the victory off Cape St Vincent, Nelson's heroics in the course of it and Jervis' elevation to the peerage as Earl St Vincent entirely obscured any earlier failings on the rear admiral's part.

Throughout the American and French Wars, those in the upper echelon of the Royal Navy were far more likely to be called to trial than general officers in the army. Even though there were four times more generals than flag officers, only five of the former faced courts martial in the period.[4] These marked discrepancies in upper echelon charge rates may have been partly due to the conditions under which flag officers operated. Naval command often involved individualized responsibilities that exposed senior officers to the scrutiny of their colleagues and superiors. By contrast, many generals were subsumed in large-scale combat and administrative machines.

Significant differences in the chain of command in the two services may also have affected charge rates. The contextual considerations that played a role in naval court martial decisions – the situation of a ministry at a given point in time, the jockeying of ministers and the impact of widespread publicity on its decision-making at critical strategic moments – bore in a direct, unmediated form on first lords who were usually politicians rather than members of the service. By contrast, the army was presided over by a commander-in-chief who, by the late 1790s, had displaced civilians and politicians from decision-making roles on army discipline and all but the most senior appointments and promotions.[5] There was no equivalent of this office in the navy. Admirals of the Fleet were largely ceremonial figures without distinctive powers or responsibilities and with no capacity to authorize in-service non-judicial responses to misconduct. Where army cases went to trial, the commander-in-chief had an independent role in confirming and modifying sentences that first lords lacked. He could also seek the King's permission for letters of reprimand to be notified publicly to the entire army. For most of the French Wars, the Duke of York commanded the British army from 'the Horse Guards', an office responsible for most of the matters dealt with by 'the Admiralty'. The Duke was a career soldier, the King's favourite son and a highly effective and engaged military administrator. The close and generally cordial relationship between the Duke and his royal father probably allowed for informal exchanges on army disciplinary matters.[6]

These structural differences may have affected how the two services dealt with high-level transgressions. First lords were flag officers' superiors but not part of the military command structure of the navy and were subject to a range of pressures in managing disciplinary issues. By contrast, the Army commander-in-chief was at the apex of the military chain of command and could ensure that many performance failures were dealt with by the 'Horse Guards'. That is, they were managed administratively rather than being the subject of judicial proceedings. Thus, when Major-General Lightburne seriously blotted his copybook while serving in the Peninsula campaign in 1808, misconduct that was unspecified but 'outrageous' and may have included incapacitating drunkenness in a combat situation, did not lead to a court martial. General Sir Arthur Wellesley told the Duke's military secretary – a key figure in the Horse Guards' hierarchy – that he 'could not' court-martial Lightburne, presumably because a trial would have been an embarrassing divisive distraction. He appealed to 'God and the Horse Guards to deliver me from General Lightburne'.[7] The Horse Guards solved the problem, with or without divine assistance, by recalling Lightburne and never employing him again.

In 1808, public outrage at the Convention of Cintra prompted a court of inquiry into an armistice permitting a defeated French army to leave Portugal on British ships with its arms and personal baggage, including plunder from earlier actions. The ministry may have taken this approach to facilitate a wide-ranging investigation of where responsibility lay rather than narrow the scope to particular charges against named individuals.[8] After being forced to come to a determination by the Duke of York, the seven-member court (appointed by him without consultation with the Secretary for War) approved the convention by a bare majority. By this time, however, the heat had gone out of the affair, public attention had shifted to other military disasters in the peninsula and nothing was to be gained by a court martial. Two senior generals had already suffered public exposure of their inadequacies, and in the wake of the inquiry, the senior commander was admonished in a public letter expressing the King's 'disapprobation' of some of his decisions.[9]

In early 1809, the disastrous large-scale inter-service joint service operation in the Scheldt estuary prompted bitter interservice recriminations that gave the opposition the opportunity to embarrass the government through a parliamentary enquiry.[10] The army commander, the Earl of Chatham, head of the Pitt family and a long-serving, if notably lethargic, cabinet minister, showed far more energy defending himself and blaming his naval colleague than he had during a woefully ill-managed campaign. The *Times* called for him to be court-martialled, but Chatham took the precaution of sending an exculpatory report to the King, with whom he was on good terms. The ministry was heavily invested in promoting the expedition, and independent MPs' suspicions of the opposition's motives were sufficient to ensure the defeat of hostile motions. The inquiry exposed Chatham's lack of energetic leadership, but he resigned his cabinet post of Master General of Ordnance before it concluded. The naval commander was offered a minor command, which he declined, and was never employed again. The interplay of political forces that sometimes made courts martial unavoidable in this case prevented them.

Four of the summons issued to senior army personnel arose in similar circumstances to those that triggered admirals' courts martial. In early 1783, Lieutenant General James Murray faced twenty-nine charges laid by his second in command following an unsuccessful defence of Minorca and more than two years of highly antagonistic exchanges between the two officers.[11] A letter of complaint from Rear Admiral Hallowell to the naval commander-in-chief of the Mediterranean was said by the judge advocate to make a court martial on Lieutenant General Sir John Murray for his 'deplorable proceedings' in a joint operation in Spain in 1813, 'almost a matter of necessity'.[12] Two other generals were charged with misconduct in the War of 1812. The more senior of these officers, suspected in some quarters of using his position as governor-general to pin the blame on an unpopular subordinate, was subsequently summoned to face a charge framed by the senior naval officer on the station.[13] He died before the case came to trial. In 1808, Lieutenant General Sir John Whitelocke was court-martialled following the complete failure of an expeditionary force sent to recapture Buenos Aires in 1806. Whitelocke's trial was unusual in that his incompetence was almost beyond question, and the prosecution presented the case to uphold the credibility of the officers and men whose lives and reputations had suffered from it.[14]

Major General N. C. Burton was the only general officer tried for a non-combat offence. His case was similar to Sir Eliab Harvey's in that it involved personal misconduct with broader disciplinary implications. The court cashiered Burton for duelling (both illegal and contrary to army regulations) in January 1804, but the Crown accepted its recommendation for a pardon in consideration of Burton's otherwise distinguished record. However, in a move that mirrored Harvey's treatment, the Duke of York insisted that the original sentence was notified in General Orders to the whole army 'for the sake of example'.[15]

Leadership failures in wartime were likely to be especially troubling to first lords for both operational and political reasons. It is thus no accident that the four eighteenth-century flag officers' trials before the Keppel-Palliser affair all arose from battle situations and that no admirals were charged between the American and French Wars. With the onset of a prolonged general peace in 1815, flag officers' courts martial became a thing of the past. Very few admirals were on active service, so there were far fewer occasions for them to run afoul of the limited number of articles of war which applied to officers in their position. If they did offend, the Board was far less likely to see the need to run the risk of making a public example of them. Even in peacetime, however, other members of the service continued to be court-martialled. Ships were still lost, and plenty of scope remained for the desertions, insubordination, drunkenness and uncleanliness that were grist to the judicial mill for those below flag rank.

Notes

Introduction

1 BL Add Ms 31, 167, f140, 10 Aug 1800.
2 See Christopher D. Hall, *British Strategy in the Napoleonic War 1803–15* (Manchester: Manchester University Press, 1992), 53–73, for the implications of political structures and practice for the framing and execution of strategy.
3 Herein, 10–11.
4 See herein, 199–200. Rear Admiral Richard Bligh was acquitted by a court martial in 1795 but that was for 'loss of ship' in 1794 when he was still a post captain. His trial is not discussed here but he is mentioned briefly in connection with his attempt to clear himself of later claims of dereliction of duty on flag command.
5 Herein, 24–5, 31–2.
6 John H. Langbein, *The Origins of Adversary Criminal Trial* (Oxford: Oxford University Press, 2003), 16–18.
7 John D. Byrn, ed., *Naval Courts Martial* (Aldershot: Ashgate/Navy Record Society, 2009) prints a number of such defences, but as his sampling excluded transcripts of more than ten pages, the selection cannot be treated as representative.
8 See the references to the works of William James, Robert Beatson and James Ralfe, herein, 188–93.
9 Herein, 181.
10 John D. Byrn, Jr., *Crime and Punishment in the Royal Navy. Discipline on the Leeward Islands Station, 1784–1812* (Aldershot: Scholar Press, 1989), *passim*; see herein, 189, 191.
11 Byrn, *Naval Courts Martial.*
12 Thomas Malcomson, *Order and Disorder in the British Navy, 1793–1815. Control, Resistance, Flogging and Hanging* (Woodbridge: The Boydell Press, 2016), *passim*, see herein, 189.
13 Markus Eder, *Crime and Punishment in the Royal Navy of the Seven Years' War, 1755–1763* (Aldershot: Ashgate, 2004).
14 N. A. M. Rodger, *The Wooden World. An Anatomy of the Georgian Navy* (London: Collins, 1986), 205–51, 247–9.
15 Peter C. Smith, *Sailors in the Dock. Naval Courts Martial Down the Centuries* (Stroud: The History Press, 2011), 111–28. In addition to *Oxford Dictionary of National Biography's (ODNB* hereafter) entries on the flag officers considered in this study, there are more detailed essays on some of them in two collections edited by Peter Le Fevre and Richard Harding. The More Than Nelson website provides a growing list of officer biographics, some on figures who do not appear in the *ODNB.*
16 Herein, 95.
17 Richard Harding, 'Neglect or Treason: Leadership Failure in the Mid-Eighteenth-Century Royal Navy', in *Naval Leadership and Management, 1650–1950. Essays in Honour of Michael Duffy*, ed. Helen Doe and Richard Harding (Woodbridge: The Boydell Press, 2021), 53–54; Ruddock Mackay and Michael Duffy, *Hawke, Nelson and British Naval Leadership, 1747–1805* (Woodbridge: The Boydell Press, 2009), 89–121.

Chapter 1

1 NA ADM 2/1094, f 208; *Hampshire Telegraph and Sussex Chronicle*, 22 Aug 1814. Bradley was condemned to death at the Winchester Assizes; the sentence was commuted to life transportation and he was then pardoned by the prince regent, having entered a recognizance to leave the country and never return; *Morning Post*, 17 Aug 1814, *Salisbury and Winchester Journal*, 3, 24, 31 Oct 1814.

2 These acts and the relevant chapters of the *Regulations and Instructions* are conveniently reprinted in John D. Byrn, ed., *Naval Courts Martial, 1793–1815* (Aldershot: Ashgate/Navy Records Society, 2009), 4–27. The introduction to this volume includes an account of the naval courts martial system; see also Byrn, *Crime and Punishment in the Royal Navy. Discipline on the Leeward Island Station 1784–1812* (Cambridge: Scholar Press, 1989), 9–63. Markus Eder, *Crime and Punishment in the Royal Navy of the Seven Years' War, 1755–63* (Aldershot: Ashgate, 2004), deals with the mid-eighteenth century and includes suggestive comparative analysis of civilian courts. The two contemporary authorities (Delafons and McArthur) are referred to herein notes to chapter 1 and 2.

3 N. A. M. Rodger, *The Wooden World. An Anatomy of the Georgian Navy* (London: Collins 1986), 218.

4 J. Cornish et al., *The Oxford History of the Laws of England 1820–1914* (Oxford: Oxford University Press, 2010), XIII: 187, 191–3.

5 Bryn, *Crime and Punishment*, 123; Thomas Malcomson, *Order and Disorder in the British Navy, 1793–1815: Control, Resistance, Flogging and Hanging* (Woodbridge: The Boydell Press, 2016), 8–9.

6 J. H. Langbein, 'Albion's Fatal Flaw', *Past and Present* 98 (1983): 105, 119.

7 Richard Blake, *Evangelicals in the Royal Navy 1775–1815: Blue Lights and Psalm Singers* (Woodbridge: The Boydell Press, 2008), 157; Rodger, *The Wooden World*, 226–9.

8 Rodger, *The Wooden World*, 218.

9 *Regulations and Instructions Relating to His Majesty's Service at Sea* (London: Admiralty, 1806), Section 1, chap. 1, VI, 3.

10 John McArthur, *Principles and Practice of Naval and Military Courts Martial, with an Appendix Illustrative of the Subject*, 4th edn., 2 vols (London: J. Butterworth, 1813), I: 13, 227, 268, II: 312–13.

11 Byrn, *Crime and Punishment*, xxvii.

12 J. M. Beattie, *Crime and the Courts in England 1660–1800* (Oxford: Oxford University Press, 1986), 490.

13 N. A. M. Rodger, *The Command of the Ocean: A Naval History of Britain, 1649–1815* (London: Penguin Press, 2005), 89–92.

14 Ibid., 462–3.

15 Ibid., 468ff, 524 for these developments.

16 Stephen Payne Adye, *A Treatise on Courts Martial; Also an Essay on Military Punishments and Rewards*, 8th edn (London: Vernon, Hood and Sharpe, 1810), 215–16. Eder considers the function of naval law in light of suggestions that criminal law ashore may have included retributive elements and concludes that deterrence was 'central to . . . navy law'; see *Crime and Punishment*, 5, 154.

17 W. B. Gurney, *Minutes of a Court Martial Holden . . . on the Trial of the Right Honourable Lord James Gambier* (Portsmouth: Mottley, Harrison, and Miller, 1809), 205.

18 John Delafons, *A Treatise on Naval Courts Martial* (London: s.n., 1805), 48, 57.
19 See John Langbein, *The Origins of the Adversary Criminal Trial* (Oxford: Oxford University Press, 2003), *passim.*
20 Russell G. Smith, *Medical Discipline: The Professional Conduct Jurisdiction of the General Medical Council, 1858–1990* (Oxford: Clarendon Press, 1994).
21 McArthur, *Principles and Practice,* I, 141.
22 See Eder, *Crime and Punishment*, 154.
23 See James Oldham, *The Varied Life of the Self-Informing Jury* (London: Selden Society, 2005), *passim.*
24 Ibid., 3–4.
25 Ibid., 27–9, 31–4, 39–43.
26 Delafons, *A Treatise*, 167.
27 McArthur, *Principles and Practices*, I, Appendix XXV, 440, for a blank warrant form.
28 Ibid., I, 279–80.
29 Ibid., 285.
30 Delafons, *A Treatise*, 155.
31 Eder, *Crime and Punishment*, 152. It is ironic that both the contemporary experts (Delafons and McArthur) had learnt their trade as admirals' secretaries employed as judge advocates. They both developed legal expertise and also had experience of the parts of courts' deliberations that were hidden from the public.
32 McArthur, *Principles and Practice,* I, 280.
33 See herein, 58.
34 Moses Greetham is not in the *ODNB*, but there are a few details of his career in 'The Greetham Family' on the History in Portsmouth website: historyinportsmouth.co.uk/people/greetham.htm.
35 See Patrick Schmidt, 'Disobedient Officers in the Royal Navy, about 1680–1720', *Mariner's Mirror* 108, no. 2 (2022): 167 for the summary punishment of officers.
36 NMM GRE/7, 'Rules for Naval Courts Martial', unpaginated ms; Delafons, *A Treatise*, 120–1.
37 See McArthur, *Principles and Practice*, I: 131–2, 136 and A. N. Gilbert, 'Military and Civilian Justice', *Journal of British Studies* 17, no. 2 (1978): 62–3 for the army.
38 McArthur, *Principles and Practice*, I: 111–12.
39 Ibid., I, 268.
40 Ibid., 452–3.
41 See herein, 57, 62–4, 164–5.
42 Delafons, *A Treatise*, 31–2.
43 McArthur, *Principles and Practice*, I, Appendix XXIII: 435–6, 11 Feb 1779.
44 See herein, 138.
45 Byrne, *Crime and Punishment*, 56.
46 Dudley Jarrett, *British Naval Dress* (London: J. M. Dent and Sons, 1960), 49–51.
47 NMM GRE/7.
48 *Resolutions of the Court-Martial . . . Against Thomas Mathews* (London: sn, 1746?).
49 McArthur, *Principles and Practice*, I: 226 and see herein, 62–4, 158–9.
50 Delafons, *A Treatise*, 137–8.
51 McArthur, *Principles and Practice*, I: 272–4; Delafons, *A Treatise*, 120–2.
52 Delafons, *A Treatise*, 170, notes the absence of pleas but does not explain it.
53 McArthur, *Principles and Practice*, II: 45–6.
54 See Langbein, *The Origins*, 26, 33–4.
55 Ibid., 253ff.

56 *ODNB.*
57 W. B. Gurney, *Proceedings of a General Court Martial . . . For the Trial of Lieut. Gen. Whitelocke*, 2 vols (London: Longman, Hurst, Rees and Orme, 1808), I: 3–10 , II: 677–9, 793–828.
58 McArthur, *Principles and Practice*, II: 183.
59 Delafons, *A Treatise*, 269–70; cf McArthur, *Principles and Practice*, II: 312–13.
60 *The Sentence Pronounc'd by the Court-Martial on Vice Admiral Lestock* (London: M. Cooper, 1746); *Resolutions of the Court-Martial, Upon the Several Articles of Charge against Thomas Mathews, Esq.', n.p., s.n.*; see herein, 19, 201–2 for army trials.
61 Delafons, *A Treatise*, 276–7.
62 Herein, 62.
63 McArthur, *Principles and Practice*, I: 307.

Chapter 2

1 See John Morrow, *British Flag Officers in the French Wars, 1793–1815. Admirals' Lives* (London: Bloomsbury Academic, 2018), 127–47, 165–76.
2 Ibid., 190–7.
3 Ibid., 240–5.
4 Ibid., 176–84.
5 William Falconer, *Universal Dictionary of the Marine*, 6th edn (London: T. Cadell, 1789); not paginated, entry 'Admirals' in alphabetical sequence; William Mountaine, *The Seaman's Vade-Mecum and Defensive War by Sea*, 5th edn (London: Mount and Page, 1793), 65. There is a long extract from Falconer's entry in Ruddock Mackay and Michael Duffy, *Hawke, Nelson and British Naval Leadership, 1747–1805* (Woodbridge: The Boydell Press, 2009), 91–3.
6 See Mackay and Duffy, *Hawke, Nelson*, 90–7.
7 *The Proceedings of a General Court Martial . . . on Major General Burton* (London: R. Faulder, 1804), 10.
8 BL Add Ms 35196, f77, 19 July 1795.
9 D. Bonner-Smith, ed., *The Letters of Lord St Vincent, 1801–1804*, 2 vols (London: Navy Records Society, 1922–7), I: 211, 2/10/1801.
10 NMM WAR/82, f18, 3 Dec 1812, f29v, 30 Dec 1812.
11 Bonner-Smith, *St Vincent's Letters*, I: 86, 11 March 1801.
12 NLS Cochrane Papers MS2296, ff36-7, 1 Dec 1806.
13 Roger Morriss, ed., *The Channel Fleet and the Blockade of Brest, 1793–1801* (London: Navy Records Society, 2001), 61, 28 April 1795.
14 Arthur Aspinall, ed., *The Later Correspondence of George III*, 5 vols (Cambridge: Cambridge University Press, 1962–70), II: 341, 4 May 1795.
15 See Dorothy Hood, *The Admirals Hood* (London: Hutchinson & Co, 1934), 152–5 for Hood's friends' reaction and Morriss, *Channel Fleet*, 62, 3 May 1795, and J. S. Corbett, ed., *Private Papers of George, 2nd Earl Spencer*, 2 vols (London: Navy Records Society, 1913-14), I: 31–2, 3 May 1795, for more critical comments. Among modern historians, Andrew Lambert sees Hood's sacking as a politically motivated attempt to shift blame from the Board; *Admirals: The Naval Commanders Who Made Britain Great* (London: Faber and Faber, 2012), 180, while Michael Duffy describes the dispute as 'unfortunate', 'Lord Hood, 1724–1816', in *Precursors of Nelson: British*

Admirals of the Eighteenth Century, ed. Peter Le Fevre and Richard Harding (London: Chatham, 2000), 271.
16 BL Add MSS 35200; Devon Heritage Centre, 152M/c1795/ON3, 8 May 1795.
17 Morriss, *Channel Fleet*, 148, 20 March 1796.
18 'Extracts from the Papers of Samuel, First Viscount Hood', in *Naval Miscellany*, I, ed. J. K. Laughton (London: Navy Records Society, 1901), 246–7, 2 August 1796.
19 See herein, 85.
20 Corbett, *Spencer Papers*, II: 409, 1 July 1797, 411, 9 July 1797; M. A. J. Palmer, 'Sir John's Victory', *Mariner's Mirror* 77, no. 1 (1991): 40–1.
21 Sir Lewis Namier and John Broke, *The House of Commons, 1754–1790*, 3 vols (London: HMSO, 1964), I: 281, II: 86; *ODNB*; NMM WYN/104, 18 March 1799, 19 March 1799.
22 Herein, 30.
23 Spencer C. Tucker and Frank T. Reuter, *Injured Honor: The Chesapeake-Leopard Affair, June 22, 1807* (Annapolis: Naval Institute Press, 1996), 115; see also Julian Gwyn, *Frigates and Foremasts. The North American Squadron in Nova Scotia Waters, 1745–1815* (Vancouver: University of British Columbia Press, 2003), 121–4.
24 NMM THO/2e, 10, 11 July 1795. See herein, 26 for subsequent developments in this case.
25 NA ADM, 1/248, f25, 28 May 1798; Dudley Pope, *The Black Ship* (London: Secker and Warburg, 1988), 260–1.
26 H. W. Richmond ed., *The Private Papers of George, second Earl Spencer, First Lord of the Admiralty, 1794–1801*, 2 vols (London: Navy Records Society, 1924), III: 286, 11 May 1800.
27 Ibid., 285, 10 April 1800.
28 BL ADD Ms 31167, f25v, 27 March 1799. See herein, 29, 101 for Orde.
29 Herein, 112–13.
30 NMM YOR/3 f10, 14 Dec 1810, f13, 18 April 1811. Newfoundland was an exception to this rule.
31 NMM YOR/3 f 72, 26 Feb 1811, f83, 20 March 1812, YOR/4, f6, 6 Aug 1811.
32 Herein, 39.
33 Edward Pelham Brenton, *Life and Correspondence of John, Earl of St Vincent, G.C.B., Admiral of the Fleet*, 2 vols (London: Henry Colburn, 1838), I: 373–5, 396. Denis Orde's *Nelson's Mediterranean Command* 2nd ed.(Barnsley: Penn & Sword Maritime, 2014) is (despite the title) a detailed defensive account of his ancestor's career. For a scholarly treatment of Orde, see Kathrin Orth, 'Sir John Ord, 1751–1824', in *British Admirals in the Napoleonic Wars*, ed. Peter Le Fevre and Richard Harding (London: Chatham, 2005), 67–90.
34 Sir John Orde, *Copy of Correspondence &c Between . . . The Admiralty . . . Earl of St Vincent . . . Earl Spencer . . . and . . . Sir J. Orde* (London: R. Faulder, 1802); BL Add Ms 31167, 17 February 1799.
35 Corbett, *Spencer Papers*, II: 473, 24–6, 28 Sept 1798; Richmond, *Spencer Papers*, III: 6, 7 October 1799; Mark Barton, 'Duelling in the Royal Navy', *Mariner's Mirror* 100, no. 3 (2014): 288.
36 Melford Hall, Hyde Parker Papers, F 75/3, 15 March 1800, F75/9, 10 June 1800.
37 NA ADM 2/1090, ff232-3, 23 Sept 1800.
38 Melford Hall, Hyde Parker Papers, F94/1, 25 Sept 1800.
39 Ibid., F75/15, 24 September 1800. There is no record of Bligh's trial in the court martial series in the National Archives or in the press.

40 Peter Le Fevre provides a detailed account of the background to the action in ' "Little Merit will be given to me": Admiral Sir Hyde Parker (1739–1807) and the Diplomatic Build up to the Battle', in *Battle of Copenhagen: 200 Years*, ed. Stephen Howard (Shelton: The 1805 Club, 2003), 1–29.
41 Bonner-Smith, *St Vincent's Letters*, I: 89–90, 17 April 1801.
42 Melford Hall, Hyde Parker Papers, F42/2, nd, F75/27, 22 May 1801.
43 Ibid., F75/27, 28, 22 May 1801.
44 Ibid., F86/2, *Hyde Parker's Defence* (1801), 9, 1.
45 NA ADM 2/1091, f 90, 4 February 1803.
46 John Delafons, *A Treatise on Naval Courts Martial* (London: s.n., 1805), 167.
47 Geoffrey Best, *Honour Among Men and Nations: Transformations of an Idea* (Toronto: University of Toronto Press, 1982) 9; N. A. M. Rodger, 'Honour and Duty at Sea, 1660–1815', *Historical Research* 75 (2002): 443, 447. Cf Evan Wilson who, while appearing to endorse Rodger's position, restricts the 'confluence of honour and duty' to behaviour in combat; Evan Wilson, *A Social History of British Naval Officers 1775–1815* (Woodbridge: The Boydell Press, 2017), 200, n. 71, 201–2.
48 John Hildrop, *An Essay on Honour in Nine Letters* (Elizabeth-Town, MD: sn, 1791), 2–3; this work was published originally in England in the 1750s. Thomas Gisborne, *Essays on the Duties of Men in the Higher and Middle Classes in Society in Great Britain* (London: B. and J. White, 1794); this book went through a number of editions.
49 Sara Cuato, 'Mercenary Gentlemen? The Transnational Service of Foreign Quarterdeck Officers in the Royal Navy of the American and French Wars, 1775–1815', *Historical Research* 94, no. 226 (2021): 808.
50 On honour groups in military settings, see James Bowman, *Honour: A History* (New York: Encounter Books, 2006), 4–5. Caroline Cox's treatment of the relationship between rank and honour in George Washington's army deals with the challenges facing officers in a situation where rank was not necessarily derived from family social status and thus provides a parallel with the late Georgian Royal Navy; see Caroline Cox, *A Proper Sense of Honor. Service and Sacrifice in George Washington's Army* (Chapel Hill: University of North Carolina Press, 2004), 38–40.
51 See Best, *Honour among Men and Nations*, 10–11 on honour and solidarity in military settings.
52 See Linda Colley, *Britons: Forging the Nation*, 1707–1837 [1992] (London: Pimlico, 2003), 167–8.
53 Ibid., 177, for royal levees.

Chapter 3

1 See Julia Banister, *Masculinity, Militarism and Eighteenth-Century Culture, 1689–1815* (Cambridge: Cambridge University Press, 2018), 151–84; Daniel A. Baugh, ' "Too Much Mixed in This Affair": The Impact of Ministerial Politics in the Eighteenth-Century Royal Navy', in *New Interpretations in Naval History. Selected Papers Presented at the Fourteenth Naval History Symposium 23-25 September 1999*, ed. Randy Carol Balano and Craig L. Symonds (Annapolis: Naval Institute Press, 2001), 38–41; J. H. Broomfield, 'The Keppel-Palliser Affair, 1778–1779', *Mariner's Mirror* 47 (1961): 195–207; N. A. M. Rodger, *The Insatiable Earl. A Life of John Montagu, 4th Earl of*

Sandwich (London: Harper Collins, 1993), 238–55; Nicholas Rogers, *Crowds, Culture, and Politics in Georgian Britain* (Oxford: Oxford University Press, 1998), 122–51.

2 Quoted Thomas Keppel, *The Life of Augustus Viscount Keppel, Admiral of the White, and First Lord of the Admiralty in 1782–3*, 2 vols (London: Henry Colburn, 1842), II: 11, 18 Nov. 1777.

3 William Cobbett, *Parliamentary History of England*, 36 vols (London: R. Bagshaw, 1806–20), XIX: 967, 23 Mar. 1778; for the naval focus of opposition in the American War, see Clive Wilkinson, *The British Navy and the State in the 18th Century* (Woodbridge: The Boydell Press, 2004), 174, 183, 187–9, 203–4.

4 J. Fortescue, ed., *The Correspondence of George the Third from 1760 to December 1783*, 6 vols (London: Macmillan, 1927–8), IV: 225–7, Nov 1778; twelve officers were reckoned neutral with the partisan/supporter count running 5/11 to 1/5 in Keppel's favour.

5 *Public Advertiser*, 2 January 1779; G. R. Barnes and J. H. Owens, ed., *The Private Papers of John, Earl of Sandwich, First Lord of the Admiralty, 1771–82*, 4 vols (London: Navy Records Society, 1932), II: 243, 31 March 1779.

6 *Lloyd's Evening Post*, 3–5 Aug 1778; *Morning Post*, 6 August 1778; *Morning Chronicle*, 6 Aug 1778.

7 *General Advertiser and Morning Intelligencer*, 6 Aug 1778.

8 *St James Chronicle*, 20 Aug 1778.

9 Horace Walpole, *Journal of the Reign of King George the Third*, ed. Dr. Doran, 2 vols (London: Richard Bentley, 1859), II: 290; *Morning Post*, 25 Aug 1778, *St James' Chronicle*, 22–25 Aug 1778.

10 D. Hannay, ed., *Letters Written by Sir Samuel Hood (Viscount Hood) in 1781–2* (London: Navy Records Society, 1895), 2, 4 Aug 1778.

11 Keppel, *Life*, II: 50, 166.

12 Rodger, *The Insatiable Earl*, 246, tentatively attributes this piece to Keppel's nephew, Lieutenant the Honourable George Berkeley, a member of a leading aristocratic family with strong affiliations to the Whig opposition; he had served on Keppel's flagship and was promoted to master and commander shortly after the action. Rogers (*Crowds, Culture, and Politics*, 126) supports this attribution from a report in the London *Public Advertiser* of 5 January 1779 but does not note that on the next day the printer disavowed the attribution on the 'fullest and most Respectable authority'. However, Palliser regarded Berkeley as the author (see NMM, 'Sandwich', 6), and other officers treated him as a prime mover (see Fortescue, *Correspondence*, IV: 225–6).

13 *General Advertiser and Morning Intelligencer*, 15 Oct 1778, 1–2.

14 *Public Advertiser*, 3, 6, 7, 10, 13 Aug 1778; Cobbett, *Parliamentary History*, XX: 68, 11 Dec 1778.

15 *An Address to the Lords of Admiralty, on Their Conduct Towards Admiral Keppel* (London: J. Almon, 1779), 23–6.

16 *Morning Chronicle*, 7 Aug 1778.

17 Cited Robert M. Hunt, *The Life of Sir Hugh Palliser, Bart, Admiral of the White and Governor of Greenwich Hospital* (London: Chapman and Hall, 1844), 234.

18 Ibid., 189; Keppel, *Life*, II: 48; Barnes and Owens, *Sandwich Papers*, II: 128, 132, 29, 31 July 1778.

19 Keppel, *Life*, II: 82.

20 *Morning Post*, 5 Nov 1778.

21 Keppel, *Life*, II: 82–3.

22 Barnes and Owens, *Sandwich Papers*, II: 208, 6 Nov 1778.
23 Lord Herbert, *Henry, Elizabeth and George (1734–80), Letters and Diaries of Henry, Tenth Earl of Pembroke and his Circle* (London: Jonathan Cape, 1939), 134, 13 Dec. 1778.
24 Cobbett, *Parliamentary History*, XIX: 1297–8, 28 Nov 1778.
25 Barnes and Owens, *Sandwich Papers*, IV: 298–9, 31 December 1781.
26 https://www.historyofparliamentonline.org/volume/1754-1790/member/luttrell-hon-henry-lawes-1737-1821.
27 Cobbett, *Parliamentary History*, XIX: 1382–3, 2 Dec 1778.
28 Barnes and Owens, *Sandwich Papers*, II: 193, 9 Dec 1778. See Margarette Lincoln, *Representing the Royal* Navy: *British Sea Power, 1750–1815* (Aldershot: Ashgate, 2002), 53, 56 for these parallels and their political implications.
29 George Jackson, *Minutes of the Proceedings ... Keppel* (London: W. Strahan and T. Cadell, 1779), appendices IV and V, 170, 10 Dec 1778.
30 *General Advertiser*, 17, 18, 24 Dec 1778.
31 Cobbett, *Parliamentary History*, XX: 58ff, 64–5, 11 Dec 1778; *An Address to the Lords of Admiralty*, 6–8, 26–7.
32 Cobbett, *Parliamentary History*, XX: 65, 11 Dec 1778 for Palliser's denial.
33 Rodger, *The Insatiable Earl*, 248.
34 Cobbett, *Parliamentary History*, XX: 97–9, 18 Dec 1778.
35 *Public Advertiser*, 4 Jan 1779.
36 Fortescue, *Correspondence*, IV: 254, 1 Jan 1779; Barnes and Owens, *Sandwich Papers*, II: 212–13, 31 Dec 1778.
37 Barnes and Owens, *Sandwich Papers*, II: 210, 10 Dec 1778.
38 Jackson, *Minutes . . . Keppel*, appendix XXXIII: 178, 4 January 1779.
39 Ibid., VIII: 171, 12 Dec 1778.
40 Ibid., XXXIX: 179, 6 Jan 1779.
41 Cobbett, *Parliamentary History*, XX: 92, 17 Dec 1778.
42 Ibid., 106, 18 Dec 1778.
43 Ibid., 93, 17 Dec 1788.
44 John A. Delafons, *A Treatise on Naval Courts Martial* (London: s.n., 1805), 233–4, 237 on orderly and respectful courts martial as the naval norm.
45 Bedfordshire and Luton Records Office L30/14/333/170,15 Jan 1779; Herbert, *Letters and Diaries*, 149, 18 Feb 1779.
46 Jackson, *Minutes*, 3.
47 Keppel, *Life*, II: 129n.
48 See Lincoln, *Representing the Royal Navy*, 55, for Keppel's claim to discretion on political grounds.
49 Cobbett, *Parliamentary History*, XX: 104.
50 Ibid.
51 Ibid., 103.
52 Ibid., 109
53 Ibid., 105.
54 Jackson, *Minutes*, 121–9, 131, 136–7, 140.
55 Ibid., 126.
56 See Keppel, *Life*, II:100 for a comprehensive list of elite attendees.
57 John A. Woods ed., *The Correspondence of Edmund Burke* (Cambridge: Cambridge University Press, 1963), IV: 37–8, 12 Jan 1779.
58 Barnes and Owens, *Sandwich* Papers, II: 224–5, 5 Feb 1779; 227, 10 Feb 1779.
59 Ibid., 216, note, 8 Jan 1779.

60 Walpole, *Journal*, II: 329.
61 Quoted Keppel, *Life*, II: 188–9.
62 See Leslie Mitchell, *Holland House* (London: Duckworth, 1980), 43–9.
63 Jackson, *Minutes*, 95, 99; 'Sir Hugh Palliser', John Charnock, *Biographia Navalis*, 6 vols (London: R. Faulder, 1794–8), V: 495; Keppel, *Life*, I: 396–7; Hunt, *Palliser*, 99.
64 Charnock, *Biographia Navalis*, V: 481. The entry on Montagu in the *ODNB* is silent on his role in the trial.
65 Jackson, *Minutes*, 10.
66 Ibid., 15.
67 Ibid., 35–6.
68 Ibid., 58–9.
69 Ibid., 75.
70 Ibid., 91.
71 Ibid., 92, 93.
72 For example, Jackson, *Minutes*, 27, 28, 29, 70, 97, and 161–2 for Hood's logbook.
73 Ibid., 58.
74 Ibid., 101–2, 166. See Banister, *Masculinity, Militarism and . . . Culture*, 172–6 for an account of the various published versions of the Keppel-Palliser trials.
75 Ibid., 115.
76 Ibid., 166–7.
77 Contemporary authorities upheld Palliser's claim; see Delafons, *A Treatise*, 230, 278–9 and John McArthur, *Principles and Practice of Naval and Military Courts Martial*, 2 vols, 4th edn (London: J Butterworth, 1813), II: 188.
78 Barnes and Owens, *Sandwich Papers*, II: 216–17, 11 Jan 1779.
79 Walpole, *Journal*, 331.
80 *General Advertiser and Morning Intelligencer*, 13 Feb 1779.
81 Ibid.
82 See Rogers, *Crowds, Culture, and Politics*, passim.
83 Walpole, *Journal*, II: 343.
84 Bedfordshire and Luton Archives, L30/14/333/170, ff3-4, 15 Jan 1779.
85 Rogers, *Crowds, Culture, and Politics*, 129.
86 See Gerald Jordan and Nicholas Rogers, 'Admirals as Heroes: Patriots and Liberty in Hanoverian England', *Journal of British Studies* 28, no. 3 (1989): 202.
87 William Hayley, *Epistle for Admiral Keppel* (London: Fielding and Walker, 1779), 12, 15.
88 *Keppel for Ever!* (London: sn, 1779).
89 *An Heroic Congratulation, Addressed to the Honourable Augustus Keppel, Admiral of the Blue* (London: the author, 1779), 4.
90 Cobbett, *Parliamentary History* XX: 130, 12 Feb 1779, 134, 135, 16 Feb 1779.
91 Fortescue, *Correspondence*, IV: 291, 25 Feb 1779.
92 Ibid., 298, 5 March 1779.
93 Keppel, *Life*, II: 226, 15 March 1779, 228, 18 March 1779, 229, 21 March 1779.
94 Fortescue, *Correspondence*, IV: 301, 8 March 1779.
95 Ibid., 309, 23 March 1779.
96 Rodger, *Insatiable Earl*, 250–1.
97 [John Stevenson] *An Address to the Hon Admiral Augustus Keppel . . .. With a Concluding Letter, Addressed to Right Hon the Earl of Sandwich*, 3rd edn (London: William Nicoll), 4.
98 Herbert, *Letters and Diaries*, 149, 18 Feb 1779.

Chapter 4

1 Barnes and Owens' comment in 1933 that 'no satisfactory explanation has yet been given of the Battle . . ., of the misunderstanding nor the quarrel' still holds for Palliser's role and his trial; G. R. Barnes and J. H. Owens, eds., *The Private Papers of John, Earl of Sandwich, First Lord of the Admiralty 1771–82*, 4 vols (London: Navy Records Society, 1932-), II: xi. With the exception of Julia Banister's work, the trial has been more mentioned than studied; see *Masculinity, Militarism and Eighteenth-Century Culture* (Cambridge: Cambridge University Press, 2018), 151–84. N. A. M. Rodger's dismissal of Palliser's statement of vindication in the House of Commons (praised by a contemporary historian as 'one of the ablest performances . . . ever heard within . . . the House of Commons') as 'long and boring' while nevertheless allowing its marked impact on those who heard and read it, epitomizes modern historians' reluctance to engage with Palliser's side of the affair; N. A. M. Rodger, *The Insatiable Earl: A Life of John Montagu, 4th Earl of Sandwich* (London: Harper Collins, 1993), 251; cf Robert Beatson, *Naval and Military Memoirs of Great Britain from 1727–1783*, 6 vols (London: Longman, Hunt, Rees and Orme, 1804), IV: 438.

2 N. A. M. Rodger, *The Command of the Ocean. A Naval History of Britain 1649–1815* (London: Penguin Books, 2005), 372.

3 NMM SAN/T/8, 29 June 1773.

4 Barnes and Owens, *Sandwich Papers*, II: 201–2, 8 December 1775.

5 NMM SAN/T/7 28 Dec 1777.

6 John Charnock, *Biographia Navalis*, 6 vols (London: R. Faulder, 1794–8), V: 496.

7 See Daniel A. Baugh, ' "Too Much Mixed in This Affair": The Impact of Ministerial Politics in the Eighteenth-Century Royal Navy', in *New Interpretations in Naval History . . . Fourteenth Naval History Symposium*, ed. Randy Carol Balano and Craig L. Symonds (Annapolis: Naval Institute Press, 2001), 38–40; Barnes and Owens ed., *Sandwich Papers*, II: 192–3; J. H. Broomfield, 'The Keppel-Palliser Affair, 1778–1779', *The Mariner's Mirror* 47 (1961): 195–207; Rodger, *The Insatiable Earl*, 248–50; Rodger, *The Command of the Ocean*, 337–8.

8 Broomfield, 'The Keppel-Palliser Affair', 201, 202, 207.

9 Rodger, *The Insatiable Earl*, 248.

10 Barnes and Owens, *Sandwich Papers*, II: 206, 28 Oct 1778.

11 Ibid., 207, 31 Oct 1778.

12 Ibid., 210, 11 Nov 1778.

13 Herein, 38–9.

14 William Cobbett, *Parliamentary History of England . . . to the Year 1803*, 36 vols (London: R. Bagshaw, 1806–1820), XIX: 1382–3, 2 Dec 1778, XX: 54, 11 Dec 1778.

15 Barnes and Owens, *Sandwich Papers*, II: 207–8, 5 Nov 1778.

16 Cobbett, *Parliamentary History*, XXI: 936, 4 Dec 1780.

17 Ibid., XXI: 937, 4 Dec 1780.

18 See John Delafons, *A Treatise on Naval Courts Martial* (London: s.n., 1805), 135 for this general condition.

19 Cobbett, *Parliamentary History*, XXI: 936, 4 Dec 1780.

20 Ibid., XX: 65, 11 Dec 1778.

21 Lord Herbert, *Henry, Elizabeth and George (1734–80). Letters and Diaries of Henry, Tenth Earl of Pembroke and his Circle* (London: Jonathan Cape, 1939), 1 Jan 1779,

from Dr Thomas Eyre, the Pembrokes' intimate; Barnes and Owens, *Sandwich Papers*, II: 193; Rodger, *The Insatiable Earl*, 247.
22 Rodger, *The Insatiable Earl*, 248, 247.
23 Cobbett, *Parliamentary History*, XX: 145, 19 Feb 1779; XXI: 919–20, 4 Dec 1780.
24 Cobbett, *Parliamentary History*, XX: 415, 420, 31 March 1779; Herbert, *Letters and Diaries*, 163, 2–8 April 1779.
25 Herbert, *Letters and Diaries*, 19, 18 Feb 1779.
26 Cobbett, *Parliamentary History*, XX: 410–14, 31 March 1779.
27 Barnes and Owens, *Sandwich Papers*, II: 222, 5 Feb 1779.
28 Ibid., 220–1, 4 Feb 1779, 231, 15 Feb 1779.
29 George Jackson, *Minutes of the Proceedings at a Court-Martial, Assembled for the Trial of Vice-Admiral Sir Hugh Palliser, Bart* (London: W. Strahan and T. Cadell, 1779), 1–2.
30 Barnes and Owns, *Sandwich Papers*, II: 222, 5 February 1779.
31 Ibid., 250, 22, 20 April 1779.
32 Jackson, *Minutes . . . Palliser*, 53ff.
33 Ibid., 46.
34 Barnes and Owens, *Sandwich Papers*, II: 128, 29 July 1778.
35 Jackson, *Minutes . . . Palliser*, 18, 44.
36 Ibid., 77–8.
37 Ibid., 15, 22.
38 Ibid., 8, 13, 28, and for *Formidable's* timing see *The Trial of Sir Hugh Palliser* (London: J. Murray and C. Etherington, 1779), 113–14, 167.
39 Jackson, *Minutes . . . Palliser*, 48, 51.
40 Ibid.
41 Ibid., 8, 14,15, 28, 30.
42 *Trial*, 49.
43 George Jackson, *Minutes of the Proceedings . . . Keppel* (London: W. Strahan and T. Cadell, 1779), 43.
44 Jackson, *Minutes . . . Palliser*, 25.
45 Ibid., 24, 79.
46 Ibid., 17.
47 *Norfolk Chronicle*, 8 May 1779.
48 John McArthur, *Principles and Practice of Naval and Military Courts Martial*, 4th edn, 2 vols (London: J. Butterworth, 1813), I: 292–3, 298–300, 322 and herein, 19–20.
49 *Gazetteer and New Daily Advertiser*, 7 May 1779.
50 Herbert, *Diaries and Letters*, 182, May 1779, fragment.
51 Cobbett, *Parliamentary History*, XX: 624, 627, 13 May 1779.
52 See McArthur, *Principles and Practices*, I: 226, 295.
53 Barnes and Owens, *Sandwich Papers*, II: 247 and note 1, 8? April 1779. For Spencer's epithet see J. S. Corbett, ed. *The Private Papers of George, 2nd Earl Spencer, 1794–1801*, 2 vols (London: Navy Records Society, 1913–14), II: 177.
54 Cobbett, *Parliamentary History*, XX: 626, 13 May 1779. Johnstone was a ministerialist but so prided himself on speaking his mind that Lord Sandwich appointed him to a string of special commands to keep him away from Westminster; *ODNB*.
55 NMM SAN/T/8, 13 April 1779. Pye did not have the power to remove Walters, and once appointed, he was not able to withdraw.
56 See McArthur, *Principles and Practices*, I: 259 for voting procedures.

57 T. O'Beirne, *Considerations on the Principles of Naval Discipline, and Naval Courts-martial &c* (London: J. Almon and J. Debrett, 1781), 106–10. Its title notwithstanding, this pamphlet is a highly partisan pro-Keppel treatment.
58 *ODNB;* John Fortescue, ed., *Correspondence of George the Third from 1760-December 1783,* 6 vols (London: Macmillan, 1927–8), IV: 226, November 1778.
59 Fortescue, *Correspondence*, IV: 225–7, Nov 1778; Barnes and Owens, *Sandwich Papers*, II: 229, no date.
60 See, for example, the entries on Palliser in the original *DNB*, 'More than Nelson' website and the editorial aside in R. V. Hamilton, ed., *Letters and Papers of . . . Sir Thomas Byam Martin,* 3 vols (London: Navy Records Society, 1898–1903), III: 295 n1. Interestingly, the authors of entries in near contemporary biographical dictionaries are far more circumspect.
61 Barnes and Owens, *Sandwich Papers*, II: 246, 4 May 1779.
62 Woods, *The Correspondence of Edmund Burke*, IV: 37, 12 Jan 1779.
63 Fortescue, *Correspondence*, IV: 225, Nov 1778.
64 *ODNB*; Fortescue, *Correspondence,* IV: 343, 17 May 1779, 424, 5 Sept 1779.
65 These proportions are derived from the questioners identified in *The Trial.*

Chapter 5

1 Richard Beatson, *Naval and Military Memoirs of Great Britain from 1727 to 1783*, 6 vols (London: Longman, Hunt, Rees and Orme, 1804), IV: 425–6; the analysis appeared originally in a pamphlet *A New and Distinct View of the Memorable Action of the 27th of July 1778 &c* (1791); this rare work was kindly brought to my attention by an anonymous reviewer of the manuscript.
2 For Lestock's trial, see Daniel A. Baugh, ' "Too Much Mixed in This Affair": The Impact of Ministerial Politics in the Eighteenth-Century Royal Navy', in *New Interpretations in Naval History . . . Fourteenth Naval History Symposium*, ed. Randy Carol Balano and Craig L. Symonds (Annapolis: Naval Institute Press, 2001), 30, and N. A. M. Rodger, *Command of the Ocean. A Naval History of Britain* (London: Penguin Books, 2005), 254.
3 It is curious that with the single exception of Julia Banister (see herein, 216 n. 51), historians' accounts of the Keppel-Palliser affair do not pay close attention to Palliser's trial or its aftermath.
4 George Jackson, *Minutes of the Proceedings at a Court Martial, Assembled for the Trial of the Honourable Admiral Augustus Keppel* (London: W. Straham and T. Cadell, 1779), 68.
5 Ibid., appendix VIII: 171, 12 Dec 1778.
6 Ibid., 52–3.
7 George Jackson, *Minutes of the Proceedings at a Court-Martial, Assembled for the Trial of Vice-Admiral Sir Hugh Palliser, Bart* (London: W. Strahan and T. Cadell, 1779), 26; *The Trial of Sir Hugh Palliser* (London: 1779), 53.
8 Jackson, *Minutes . . . Keppel*, 103–4.
9 Jackson, *Minutes . . . Palliser*, 86, 87–8.
10 G. R. Barnes and J. H. Owens, ed. *The Private Papers of John, Earl of Sandwich, First Lord of the Admiralty 1771–82,* 4 vols (London: Navy Records Society, 1932-8), II: 128, 29 July 1778.

11 Horace Walpole, *Journal of the Reign of King George the Third*, 2 vols, ed. Dr Doran (London: Richard Bentley, 1859), II: 319, Nov/Dec 1778.
12 *Trial*, 8.
13 Ibid., 13, 15–18.
14 Ibid., 8; Jackson, *Minutes . . . Palliser*, 14, 68.
15 Jackson, *Minutes . . . Keppel*, 129.
16 Thomas Keppel, *The Life of Augustus Viscount Keppel, Admiral of the White, and First Lord of the Admiralty, 1782–3*, 2 vols. (London: Henry Colburn, 1842), II: 164.
17 *Morning Post*, 10 October 1786.
18 *Morning Post*, 17 October 1786. This report came from an anti-Whig correspondent who found amusement in making mildly disruptive appearances at opposition dinners.
19 *General Advertiser and London Intelligencer*, 7 May 1779, 10 May 1779.
20 Ibid., 31 May 1779.
21 T. O'Beirne, *Considerations on the Principles of Naval Discipline, and Naval Courts-martial &c.*, 2nd edn (London: J. Almon and J. Debrett, 1781), 106–10, 112–13, 119.
22 The latter went through three editions in as many months.
23 *Thoughts on the Conduct of Admiral Keppel, Together with Reasons for Restoring Sir Hugh Palliser into the Full Confidence and Good Opinion of the Country* (London: Richardson and Urquhart, 1799), 6, 7–9, 11–14. Palliser's nineteenth-century biographer quoted extensively from this pamphlet, but it has been largely ignored by modern historians.
24 *The Conduct of Admirals Hawke, Keppel, and Palliser, Compared* (London: J. Bew, 1779).
25 William Cobbett, *The Parliamentary History of England from the Norman Conquest in 1066 to the year 1803*, 36 vols (London: R. Bagshaw, 1806–20), XX: 627, 13 May 1789.
26 Cobbett, *Parliamentary History*, XXI: 838, 84–3, 6 Nov 1780, 904, 6 Nov 1780.
27 Ibid., 916, 918, 4 Dec 1780.
28 NMM, SAN/1/8, nd 1780; copies were given to Lord Chancellor Thurlow, Lord North, William Pulteney and George Robinson (both independent MPs) and Sandwich. The statement was drafted on 22 June 1780; Barnes and Owens ed., *Sandwich Papers*, II: 198.
29 Cobbett, *Parliamentary History*, XXI: 922, 4 Dec 1780.
30 Ibid., 934, 4 Dec 1780.
31 Ibid., 924, 925, 933, 4 Dec 1780.
32 Ibid., 1116, 1 Feb 1781.
33 Ibid., 1121, 1 Feb 1781.
34 Ibid., 1131, 1 Feb 1781.
35 Ibid., 1133–4, 1 Feb 1781.
36 *Morning Post*, 11 October 1786.
37 Cobbett, *Parliamentary History*, XXI: 1145, 1148, 1 Feb 1781.
38 *Hereford Journal*, 16 Nov 1786.
39 *Morning Chronicle*, 5 Oct 1786; *Times*, 5 Oct 1786; *Northampton Mercury*, 21 Oct 1786; *Hereford Journal*, 26 Oct 1786.
40 *General Evening Post*, 19–22 March 1796; *Star and Evening Advertiser*, 22 March 1796.
41 Robert Adair, *Part of a Letter from Robert Adair, &tc* (London: J. Debrett, 1796), 21, 27–9, 53–4.

42 Lord Herbert, *Henry, Elizabeth and George (1734–80), Letters and Diaries of Henry, Tenth Earl of Pembroke and his Circle* (London: Jonathan Cape, 1939), 147, 14 Feb 1779, from Thomas Bromley, a master at Harrow.
43 Ibid., 367, 30 Dec 1779.
44 N. A. M. Rodger, *The Insatiable Earl. A Life of John Montagu, 4th Earl of Sandwich* (London: Harper Collins, 1993), 250–1, 254; J. H. Broomfield, 'The Keppel-Palliser Affair, 1778–1779', *Mariner's Mirror* 47 (1961): 206–7.
45 On Vernon, see Gerald Jordan and Nicholas Rogers, 'Admirals as Heroes: Patriotism and Liberty in Hanoverian England', *Journal of British Studies* 28, no. 3 (1989): 210.
46 See Margarette Lincoln, *Representing the Royal Navy. British Sea Power, 1750–1815* (Aldershot: Ashgate, 2002), 58–9.
47 [John Stevenson] *An Address to the Hon. Admiral Augustus Keppel . . . with a concluding Letter, Addressed to the Right Hon. The Earl of Sandwich* (London: William Nicoll, 1780), 46–7.
48 Herbert, *Letters and Diaries*, 183, 20 May 1779, 185, 24 May 1779.
49 *Morning Chronicle*, 6 Aug 1778; John Fortescue, ed., *Correspondence of George the Third from 1760 to* 1783, 6 vols (London: Macmillan, 1927–8), IV: 185–6, 9 Aug 1778; Barnes and Owens, *Sandwich Papers*, II: 141, 9 Aug 1778.
50 Fortescue, *Correspondence*, V: 158, 5 Dec 1780.
51 Julia Banister, *Masculinity, Militarism and Eighteenth-Century Culture* (Cambridge: Cambridge University Press, 2018), 183–4.
52 See Roger, *The Insatiable Earl*, 306.
53 *A New Form of Worship, for 27 July &c* (London: John Fowler, [1782?]), 9–10, 17–18.
54 Baugh, ' "Too Much Mixed in this Affair" ', 40.
55 Cf Broomfield, 'Keppel-Palliser Affair', 206; Rodger, *The Insatiable Earl*, 249.
56 John McArthur, *Principles and Practice of Courts Martials*, 4th edn, 2 vols (London: J. Butterworth, 1813), I: 432
57 NMM SAN/T/8, 16 June 1779; Keppel, *Life*, II, 213–20.
58 NMM SAN/T/8, 1 July 1779, 26 Oct 1779.
59 NMM SAN/T/8, 11 Feb 1784.
60 NMM SAN/T/8, 18 March 1780 for Palliser's hopes of the rear admiralship.
61 *Norfolk Chronicle*, 15 May 1779.
62 Barnes and Owens, *Sandwich Papers*, IV: 52, 1781, 278, 21 Jan 1782, 308–14.
63 J. S. Corbett, ed., *The Private Papers of George, 2nd Earl of Spencer, 1794–1801*, 2 vols (London: Navy Records Society, 1913-14), II: 239, 29 Jan 1798.
64 NMM MID/1/126, 17 Dec 1786.
65 Barnes and Owen, *Sandwich Papers*, IV: 424–5, 28 Jan 1783.
66 Ibid., II: 250, 22 April 1779.
67 Cf Rodger, *The Insatiable Earl*, 249, 371 notes 67, 68, quoting an early trial judgement in a post-trial context.
68 Hunt, *Palliser*, 448–9.
69 *ODNB*.
70 Cobbett, *Parliamentary History*, XX: 410–14, 31 March 1779.
71 *ODNB*.
72 Barnes and Owens, *Sandwich Papers*, II: 237–41, 29, 31 March 1779, 245, 3 April 1779.
73 Keppel, *Life*, II: 317, 2 February 1781.
74 R. V. Hamilton, ed., *Letters and Papers of Admiral of the Fleet Sir Thomas. Byam Martin*, 3 vols (London: Navy Records Society, 1898–1903), I: 292n.
75 *London Evening Post*, 30 Dec 1780–1 Jan 1781.

76 *Gazetteer and New Daily Advertiser*, 18 Aug 1780.
77 Christopher Ware, 'The Glorious First of June: The British Perspective', in *The Glorious First of June 1794. A Naval Battle and its Aftermath*, ed. Michael Duffy and Roger Morriss (Exeter: University of Exeter Press, 2001), 29–30.
78 John Bazely, More than Nelson, Officers' Biographies. https://morethannelson.com/officer/john-bazely-1/.
79 H. W. Richmond, ed., *The Private Papers of George, second Earl Spencer, First Lord of the Admiralty, 1794–1801*, 2 vols (London: Navy Records Society, 1924), III: 314, 19 May 1800.
80 Herein, 5, 10.
81 *Regulations and Instructions Relating to His Majesty's Service at Sea* (London: Admiralty, 1806), Section I ch. 1, VI: 3–4; ch. 2, VII: 12–14.
82 Barnes and Owens, *Sandwich Papers*, IV: 299, late 1781.

Chapter 6

1 N. A. M. Rodger, *The Insatiable Earl. The Life of the 4th Earl of Sandwich* (London: Harper Collins, 1993), 183; NMM SAN/T/8, 21 Dec 1776.
2 *ODNB*; see also Andrew Lambert, 'Sir William Cornwallis, 1744–1819', in *Precursors of Nelson. British Admirals of the Eighteenth Century*, ed. Peter le Fevre and Richard Harding (London: Chatham Publishing, 2000), 353–75, for an extensive recent scholarly evaluation of Cornwallis' career. There is a useful family life and letters: G. Cornwallis-West, *The Life and Letters of Admiral Cornwallis* (London: Robert Holden, 1927). See also John Morrow, *British Flag Officers in the French Wars, 1793–1815. Admirals' Lives* (London: Bloomsbury Academic, 2018), 95–9.
3 Cornwallis-West, *Life*, 514.
4 Alfred Spencer, ed., *Memoirs of William Hickey*, 4 vols (London: Hurst & Blackett, 1923), III: 361–3.
5 See Michael Duffy, *Soldiers, Sugar, and Sea Power. The British Expeditions to the West Indies and the War Against Revolutionary France* (Oxford: Clarendon Press, 1987) for the definitive account of the strategy, its rationale and the expeditions mounted in pursuit of it.
6 J. S. Corbett, ed., *The Private Papers of George, 2nd Earl Spencer, 1794–1801*, 2 vols (London: Navy Records Society, 1913–14), I: 58, 167–8, 169, 12 Oct 1795.
7 Ibid., 209–10, 2 Feb 1796, 215–16, 25 Feb 1796.
8 Ibid., 202, 5 Nov 1795; 209–10, 2 Feb 1796; 216, 25 Feb 1796; 217, 25 Feb 1796; NMM WYN/101, 28 February 1796, Curtis to Pole.
9 Corbett, *Spencer Papers*, I: 212, 15 Feb 1796.
10 Ibid., 221–2, 17 March 1796.
11 Duffy, *Soldiers, Sugar, and Sea Power*, 194–8.
12 Ibid., 41.
13 See Richard Middleton, *Cornwallis: Soldier and Statesman in a Revolutionary World* (London: Yale University Press, 2022), 11–12 for family relations and 262–3 for a succinct account of the court martial.
14 Charles Ross, ed., *Correspondence of Charles, First Marquis Cornwallis*, 3 vols, 2nd edn (London: John Murray, 1858), III: 515, 12 Aug 1804, II: 300, 18 March 1796. It has been suggested that Cornwallis was worried about the confidence and competence

of his rapidly promoted protégé; see Barry Jolly, *Mrs. Whitby's Lockett. The story of Captain John Whitby – England's Youngest Ever Naval Captain – and His Redoubtable Wife* (Milford-on-Sea: Historical Record Society, 2011), 23.

15 Ross, *Cornwallis*, II: 303, 22 March 1796.
16 NA PRO 30/11/275 f3a,'Thursday', 31? March 1796.
17 *True Briton*, 9 April 1796.
18 George Jackson, *Minutes of the Proceedings at a Court Martial . . . For Enquiring into the Conduct of The Honourable William Cornwallis* (London: John Stockdale, 1796), 30. These are the official minutes ordered to be printed by the Admiralty Board. Cornwallis did not sponsor the publication of verbatim transcripts, nor did he publish his Defence. The latter was, however, printed in the *Morning Post*, 13 April 1796, and the *Express and Morning Chronicle*, 15 April 1796.
19 Jackson, *Minutes . . . Cornwallis*, 30.
20 Ibid., 31 for a list of the judges.
21 Ibid., 6.
22 Ibid., 16–17.
23 Ibid., 26–7.
24 See Cornwallis-West, *Life*, 322, who assumes that Erskine played a major role in drafting the defence.
25 Jackson, *Minutes . . . Cornwallis*, 18.
26 Ibid., 21.
27 Ibid., 22.
28 Ibid., 21.
29 Ibid., 7, Admiralty Board to Cornwallis, 25 Feb 1796.
30 NMM COR/6, f6, 25 Feb 1796, f11, 25 Feb 1796.
31 Jackson, *Minutes . . . Cornwallis*, 15, Cornwallis to Nepean, 16 March 1796.
32 Ibid., 22.
33 Ibid.
34 Ibid., 24.
35 Ibid., 24–5.
36 Corbett, *Spencer Papers*, I: 205, 5 Nov 1795.
37 Jackson, *Minutes . . . Cornwallis*, 25.
38 Ibid., 21.
39 Ibid., 20.
40 Ibid., 26.
41 Ibid., 31.
42 *Times*, 9 April 1796, 4.
43 Sir John Barrow, *The Life of Richard Earl Howe &c* (London: John Murray, 1838), 314.
44 *Times*, 9 April 1796, 4.
45 *Evening Mail*, 8–11 April 1796.
46 *Hereford Journal*, 13 April 1796, *Chester Chronicle*, 15 April 1796.
47 *Morning Post*, 16 April 1796; *Star*, 16 April 1796.
48 *Hereford Journal*, 13 March 1796.
49 *Morning Post*, 16 April 1796.
50 Reported in *True Briton*, 22 April 1796.
51 Cornwallis West, *Life*, 341.
52 *Morning Post*, 11 April 1796, 15 April 1796.
53 *Times*, 9 April 1796; *Evening Mail*, 6–8 April 1796, 8–11 April 1796; *St James Chronicle or the British Evening Post, 7–9 April 1796; Lloyd's Evening Post*, 8–11 April 1796; *Star*,

8 April 1796; *True Briton*, 9 April 1796; *Morning Post*, 13 April 1796; *Hereford Journal*, 13 April 1796, *Chester Chronicle*, 15 April 1796.
54 Corbett, *Spencer Papers*, I: 223, 1 April 1796.
55 *Star*, 12 May 1796, reporting a debate that took place on 10 May.
56 NMM COR/6 f14, 25 April 1796.
57 R. G. Thorne, *House of Commons 1790–1820*, 5 vols (London: Secker and Warburg, 1986), III: 504.
58 NA PRO 30/11/275, f3a, 31 March 1796.
59 Corbett, *Spencer Papers*, I: 229, early April 1796.
60 NA PRO 30/11/275, f9a-10, 29 Jan 1797.
61 See Ross, *Cornwallis*, III: 515, 12 Aug 1804.
62 Nicholas Harris Nicolas, ed., *The Dispatches and Letters of Vice Admiral Viscount Nelson*, 7 vols (London: Henry Colburn, 1844–6) II: 164, 1 May 1796.
63 Michael Lewis, ed., *A Narrative of My Professional Adventures (1790–1839) by Sir William Dillon, KCH, Vice-Admiral of the Red*, 2 vols (London: Navy Records Society, 1953–6), I: 219.
64 Lambert, 'Sir William Cornwallis', 362.
65 Cornwallis-West, *Life*, 342; Duffy, *Soldiers, Sugar, and Sea Power*, 214–15.
66 Lewis, *A Narrative*, I: 177.
67 Ibid.
68 Cornwallis-West, *Life*, 342; *Morning Post*, 18 April 1796; NA PRO 30/11/275, f8, 7 Dec 1796.
69 NA PRO 30/11/275, f6, 6 Dec 1796.
70 Ibid., f9a-10, 29 Jan 1797.
71 D. Bonner Smith (ed.), *Letters of St Vincent*, 2 vols (London: Navy Records Society, 1921, 1926) I: 238.
72 See Lambert, 'Sir William Cornwallis', 365–75.
73 NA PRO 30/11/275, f4a, 31 March 1796.
74 Jolly, *Mrs Whitby's Locket*, 24–7.
75 NA PRO 30/11/275 f3a,'Thursday', 31? March 1796.

Chapter 7

1 R. G. Thorne, *The House of Commons, 1790–1820*, 5 vols (London: Secker and Warburg, 1986), II: 219.
2 J. S. Corbett, ed., *The Private Papers of George, 2nd Earl Spencer, 1794–1801*, 2 vols (London: Navy Records Society, 1913–14), II: 92, 22 Feb 1797.
3 Ibid., 98, 22 March 1797.
4 H. W. Richmond ed., *The Private Papers of George, Second Earl Spencer, First Lord of the Admiralty, 1794–1801*, 2 vols (London: Navy Records Society, 1924), III: 27–28, 28 May 1798.
5 E. Hughes, ed., *The Private Correspondence of Admiral Lord Collingwood* (London: Navy Records Society, 1957), 91, 16 Dec 1798.
6 BL Add Ms 31167, f3, 6 Dec 1798.
7 Richmond, *Spencer Papers*, III: 28–9, 13 Aug 1798.
8 BL Add Ms 31167, f25v, 27 March 1799.
9 BL Add Ms 31167, f 81, 24 July, 1799.

10 BL Add Ms 31167, f 112v, 2 July 1800.
11 *Times* 12 July 1800.
12 John Morrow, *The Naval Government of Newfoundland in the French Wars, 1793–1815* (London: Bloomsbury Academic, 2023), 33–4.
13 NA ADM2/139, Nepean to Parker 2 June 1800.
14 NA ADM 3/126, ff130-1, 25 April 1801.
15 NA ADM 3/126, Admiralty Minute, f129, 25 April 1801.
16 NA ADM 1/1529, Minutes, Parker to Board 7 Aug 1801, 10 Aug 1801.
17 See John R. Breihan, 'The Addington Party and the Navy in British Politics, 1802–5', in *New Aspects of Naval History. Selected Papers Presented at the Fourth Naval History Symposium, United States Naval Academy, 25–26 October 1979*, ed. Craig L. Symonds et al. (Annapolis: Naval Institute Press, 1981), 164, for the political context.
18 Herein, 109–10.
19 *Morning Chronicle*, 11 Nov 1801 and *Caledonian Mercury*, 14 Nov 1801.
20 *Morning Post*, 10 Nov 1801.
21 Hughes, *Collingwood's Correspondence*, 132, 8 Nov 1801.
22 NA ADM 1/1529, Minutes, f9
23 Ibid., f10.
24 Article XXII, emphasis added.
25 NA ADM 1/1529, ff12-13, Minutes of Parker's Court Martial, 'Parker's Defence'; the pagination of this document is separate from that of the rest of the Minutes.
26 Ibid., ff12-13, 15.
27 Ibid., ff5-7.
28 Ibid., f14.
29 Ibid., ff3-4, 11.
30 Ibid., ff7, , 9–10.
31 Ibid., f8.
32 Ibid., f1.
33 Ibid., ff12-13, 15.
34 Ibid., ff17-18.
35 Ibid., f17.
36 Ibid., f16.
37 Ibid., f18.
38 Ibid., f19.
39 Ibid., f20.
40 Ibid., ff20-1.
41 *Morning Post*, 16 Nov 1801, *Morning Chronicle*, 17 Nov 1801, *Times*, 17 Nov 1801.
42 See Oliver Warner, *The Life and Letters of Vice-Admiral Lord Collingwood* (London: Oxford University Press, 1968), 88 for Lady Parker's hospitality and Roger Morriss, *Naval Power and British Culture, 1760–1850* (Aldershot: Ashgate, 2004), 160–4 for St Vincent's campaign.
43 James Ralfe, *The Naval Biography of Great Britain ...*, 4 vols (London: Whitmore and Fenn, 1828), II: 56.
44 Arthur Aspinall, ed., *The Later Correspondence of George III*, 5 vols (Cambridge: Cambridge University Press, 1962–70), III: 627, 18 Nov 1801.

Chapter 8

1 For his appointment, see John D. Grainger, ed., *Papers and Correspondence of Admiral Sir John Thomas Duckworth. Volume 1: The French Revolutionary War, 1793–1802* (London: Routledge/Navy Records Society, 2022), 453, 467,
2 A. B. Sainsbury, 'Sir John Duckworth, 1748–1817', in *British Admirals of the Napoleonic Wars. The Contemporaries of Nelson*, ed. Peter Le Fevre and Richard Harding (London: Chatham, 2005), 165–95, provides a judicious account of Duckworth's career, which recognizes his foibles while making a case for his distinguished service (194–5).
3 Richard Hill, *The Prizes of War. The Naval Prize System in the Napoleonic Wars, 1793–1815* (Stroud: Sutton Publishing/Royal Naval Museum, 1998), 224–5.
4 BL Add Ms 31167, f4, 6 Dec 1798.
5 NMM DUC/8, ff7, 10, 12, 18 May–18 Oct 1802; D. Bonner-Smith, ed., *The Letters of Lord St. Vincent, 1801–1804*, 2 vols (London: Navy Records Society, 1922–27), I: 279–80, 12 Feb 1802.
6 NMM DUC/25, 13 July 1801.
7 John Marshall, *Royal Naval Biography*, 8 vols (London: Longman, Rees, Orme, Brown and Green, 1823–35), I, part 2: 784–97.
8 *ODNB*.
9 NMM DUC/10/2, 30 Oct 1804.
10 NMM DUC/25, 26 Jan 1805.
11 NMM DUC/25, 27 Jan 1805.
12 NMM DUC/25, 6 Feb 1805, 9 March 1805.
13 Philip Wright, ed., *Lady Nugent's Journal of Her Residence in Jamaica from 1801–1805* (Kingston: University of West Indies Press, 2002), 220, 11 Jan 1805.
14 NMM DUC/25, 9 March 1805.
15 NMM XDUC/21/9.
16 *Minutes of the Court Martial . . . For the Trial of Sir J. T. Duckworth, K. B. &c* (Portsmouth: J. C. Mottley, 1805), Appendix, 20-1; the trial minutes, appendices and Duckworth's defence are paginated separately. The judge advocate's record is in NA ADM 1/5369.
17 NMM DUC/25, 27 Feb 1805.
18 Grainger, *Papers and Correspondence*, 351, 357.
19 See Grahame Aldous, 'The Law Relating to the Distribution of Prize Money in the Royal Navy and Its Relation to the Use of Naval Power in War, 1793–1815' (PhD thesis, King's College, London, 2020), 194–7. These figures are indicative because freight rates for private bullion were a matter of treaty between the parties concerned. The freight was 460,000 silver dollars at a current rate of 4 to the pound sterling.
20 *Minutes*, Appendix, 17, 22 Feb 1805.
21 Ibid., 14, 17 Feb 1805.
22 *Minutes*, 12, 30, 44, 51, 54, 55, 56–7.
23 *Minutes*, Appendix, 17–19.
24 NA ADM 2/939, f118, 15 April 1805, responding to Duckworth's letter of 9 Feb.
25 Ibid., f120, 24 April 1805.
26 NA ADM 2/1092, ff 55, 57, 12, 18 June 1805.
27 J. K. Laughton, ed., *Letters and Papers of Charles, Lord Barham, 1758–1813*, 3 vols (London: Navy Records Society, 1907–1911), III: 373, 13 May.

28 See herein, 135.
29 *Minutes*, 12–14.
30 Ibid., 7–8
31 Ibid., 15–16.
32 Ibid., 16–18, 22–3. See Grainger, *Papers and Correspondence*, 404, 17 March 1801, for Headlam's earlier involvement in Duckworth's prize business.
33 *Minutes*, 19.
34 *Minutes*, Appendix, 19.
35 *Minutes*, 29–31, 33–4, 36.
36 Ibid., 56–7, 59–60.
37 Defence, *Minutes*, 1, 9.
38 Ibid., 1–2.
39 Ibid., 8.
40 Ibid., 5.
41 Ibid., 6–7.
42 Ibid., 7.
43 Ibid., 6–7.
44 Ibid., 10.
45 *Minutes*, 62, 63.
46 Ibid., 64–5.
47 Ibid., 74.
48 *Hampshire and Portsmouth Telegraph*, 29 April 1805.
49 NMM XDUC/35/2 f177, 27 April 1805.
50 Laughton, *Letters and Papers*, III: xi–xii.
51 Ibid., 372, 5 May 1805, 372, 13 May 1805. The meeting was reported in the *Hampshire and Portsmouth Telegraph*, 6 May 1805.
52 Ibid., 372, 5 May 1805.
53 NMM, DUC/25, 27 May 1805.
54 NMM DUC/27, 11 Nov 1806, 17 Nov 1806, 15 Dec 1806, 21 Dec 1806, 29 Dec 1806; DUC/28, 4 Dec 1807, 13 Dec 1807; DUC/15, 15 Dec 1809.
55 Bonner-Smith, *St Vincent's Letters*, I: 272, 273, 20 June 1801, 21 Aug 1801; NMM DUC/25, 13 July 1801.
56 NMM MID/1/51, 24 October 1805, DUC/11, 8 Oct 1805.
57 See John Morrow, *The Naval Government of Newfoundland in the French Wars 1793–1815* (London: Bloomsbury Academic, 2023), 58–9, 85–8, 151–5, 176–8, 198–201.
58 NLS Cochrane Papers, MS 2571, 27 March 1806.
59 NMM MID/1/25, 9 Feb 1806.
60 See Sainsbury, 'Duckworth', 181.
61 James Ralfe, *The Naval Biography of Great Britain*, 4 vols (London: Whitmore and Fenn, 1828), II: 288–9, 300–1. Captain Edward Codrington may have been referring to Duckworth when he complained that 'the same Admiralty' which 'wantonly destroyed' Sir Robert Calder's career allowed another officer to 'escape with impunity'; Lady Bourchier, ed., *Memoir of . . . Admiral Sir Edward Codrington* &c, 2 vols (London: Longmans, Green and Co, 1873), I: 93, 20 Jan 1806.
62 For the reaction see Sainsbury, 'Duckworth', 94. As in Rodney's case, disdainful views on aspects of an officer's character may be distinct from a recognition of professional merit.
63 *Hansard*, first series, 5, 209, 7 June 1805.
64 Ibid., 194.

65 Ibid., 200–1.
66 Ibid., 161, 31 May 1805.
67 Ibid., 202, 7 June 1895.
68 Ibid., 203.
69 Ibid., 204.
70 Ibid., 205–7.
71 Ibid., 208.
72 Ibid., 209.
73 Ibid., 843, 12 July 1805.
74 *Hansard*, First series, 11: 131–2, 285–9, 9, 16 May 1808; William James, *The Naval History of Great Britain*, new edn, 6 vols (London: Richard Bentley & Son, 1878), IV: 231.
75 Lords Commissioners of the Admiralty, *Regulations and Instructions Relating to His Majesty's Service at Sea* (London: Lords Commissioners of the Admiralty, 1806), 86–7.
76 NA ADM 2/939, f 189, 2 July 1800.
77 *Minutes*, 33–4.
78 *Hansard*, first series, 5, 201, 7 June 1805.
79 See Hill, *The Prizes of War*, 222–3, 228.
80 C. R. Markham, ed., *The Correspondence of Admiral John Markham, 1801–1807* (London: Navy Records Society, 1905), 84–5, 88, 2, 5 October 1802.
81 NMM DUC/22, 16 Oct 1805.
82 NMM DUC/28, 12 Dec. 1807.
83 morethannelson.com/officer/sir-john-thomas-duckworth/; Colonel Spencer Childers, ed., *A Mariner of England. An Account of the Career of William Richardson . . . As Told By Himself* (London: John Murray, 1908), 175–6, 178, 180–1, 186–7. 'Greedy Tommy' does not appear in Richardson's memoir but is consistent with his characterization of Duckworth. Richardson expresses a range of judgements on his superiors on merchant and Royal Naval vessels over a thirty-five-year period.
84 Wright, *Lady Nugent's Journal*, 63, 101, 148, 220–1; NMM DUC/25, 20 April 1801; National War Museum of Scotland, DUN/20f10, 7 Sept 1795.
85 W. C. Sellar and R. J. Yeatman, *1066 and All That. A Memorable History of England* (New York: E. P. Dutton, 1931), 69.

Chapter 9

1 Nicholas Tracy, 'Sir Robert Calder – 1745-1810', in *British Admirals of the Napoleonic Wars. The Contemporaries of Nelson*, ed. Peter Le Fevre and Richard Harding (London: Chatham Publishing, 2005), 204–5; Tracy's essay provides a very useful account of Calder's career and a discussion of his action and the court martial. The action and court martial are discussed in Peter C. Smith, *Sailors in the Dock. Naval Courts Martial Down the Centuries* (Stroud: The History Press, 2011), 111–19; Adam Nicolson, *Men of Honour. Trafalgar and the Making of the English Hero* (London: Harper Perennial, 2006), 185–9 provides a brief but insightful account of the aftermath of the action and the preliminaries to Calder's court martial. The *ODNB* entry on Calder is slight and not always reliable.
2 *Naval Chronicle*, XVII (1812), 91.

3 J. S. Corbett, ed., *The Private Papers of George, 2nd Earl Spencer, 1794*–1801, 2 vols (London: Navy Records Society, 1913–14), II: 37–8, 18 July 1796; D. Bonner-Smith, ed., *The Letters of Lord St Vincent, 1801–1804*, 2 vols (London: Navy Records Society, 1922–27), I: 200, 4 June 1801.
4 NMM MID/1/21, 23 July 1805, 17 Aug 1805. Only three of the junior officers named were promoted over the next six months.
5 See John R. Briehan, 'The Addington Party and the Navy in British Politics, 1801–6', in *New Aspects of Naval History. Selected Papers Presented at the Fourth Naval History Symposium, United States Naval Academy, 25–26 October 1979*, ed. Craig L. Symond et al. (Annapolis: Naval Institute Press, 1981), 179–80.
6 NMM, MID/1/21 17 Aug 1805.
7 Ibid., 22 Sept 1805.
8 Ibid., 30 Sept 1805. Nicholson's claim was reported in the *Morning Chronicle*, 5 Aug 1805.
9 J. Leyland, ed., *Papers and Letters Relating to the Blockade of Brest, 1803–1805*, 2 vols (London: Navy Records Society, 1899–1902), II: 336, 12 Aug 1805; Cornwallis to Marsden.
10 *Morning Chronicle*, 1 Aug 1805, 2 Aug 1805; *Times*, 5 Aug 1805; *Morning Post*, 3 Aug 1805, 9 Aug 1805.
11 *Cobbett's Weekly Political Register*, 3 Aug 1805.
12 James Grieg, ed., *The Farington Diary by John Farington, R. A.*, 5 vols (London: Hutchinson 1922–25), III: 95, 6 Aug 1805; *Morning Chronicle*, 5 Aug 1805.
13 Nicholas Harris Nicolas, ed., *The Despatches and Letters of Vice Admiral Lord Nelson*, 7 vols (London: Henry Colburn, 1844–46), VII: 5, 16 Aug 1805.
14 *Cobbett's Weekly Political Register*, 10 Aug 1805; *Morning Post*, 6 Aug 1805, 20 Aug 1805.
15 *Morning Chronicle*, 21 Aug 1805, *Morning Post*, 21 Aug 1805, *Cobbett's Weekly Political Register*, 7 Sept 1805.
16 *Morning Post*, 2 Sept 1805; *Cobbett's Weekly Political Register*, 7 Sept 1805.
17 Marianne Czisnik, ed., *Nelson's Letters to Lady Hamilton and Related Documents* (London: Routledge/Navy Records Society, 2020), 510, 4 Sept 1805; *Morning Post*, 6 Sept 1805.
18 *Morning Chronicle*, 28 Aug 1805.
19 Czisnik, *Nelson's Letters*, 513, 523, 2 Oct 1805.
20 Nicolas, *Despatches and Letters*, VII: 120n, 12 Oct 1805.
21 Ibid., 121, 14 Oct 1805, 126, 15 Oct 1805; Lady Georgiana Chatterton, *Memorials, Personal and Historical of Lord Gambier GCB*, 2 vols. (London: Hurst and Blackett, 1861), II: 3–6, 2 Oct 1805.
22 Cf Tracy, 'Sir Robert Calder', 216; Nicholas Tracy, 'Sir Robert Calder's Action', *Mariner's Mirror* 77, no. 3 (1991): 267.
23 Lady Bourchier, ed., *Memoir of the Life of Admiral Sir Edward Codrington. With Selections from His Public and Private Correspondence,* 2 vols (London: Longmans, Green and Co, 1873), I: 48, 10 Sept 1805.
24 See herein, 139–40.
25 *Hampshire and Portsmouth Telegraph*, 11 Nov 1805.
26 See, for example, Bourchier, *Memoir*, I: 52–3, 30 Sept 1805, 55, 16 Oct 1805.
27 *Minutes of the Proceedings at a Court Martial . . . For the Trial of Sir Robert Calder, Bart, Vice Admiral of the Blue. Published by Authority of the Vice Admiral* (Portsmouth: J. C. Mottley, 1806), 4.

28 NMM MID/1/21, 22 Sept 1805. He named eight ships, in addition to his flagship.
29 *Minutes of... the Trial of Sir Robert Calder*, 7–8.
30 Ibid., 13.
31 Ibid., 15–16.
32 Ibid., 14.
33 Ibid., 27.
34 Ibid., 27–8, 29.
35 Ibid., 29.
36 *ODNB*.
37 *Minutes Of... The Trial of Sir Robert Calder*, 33, 35.
38 Cambridge County Archives, Cotton Ms, MS 588/c70, 24 Aug 1805.
39 *Minutes Of... The Trial of Sir Robert Calder*, 36. St Vincent's post-trial comments on Calder are noticeably acerbic; BL Add Ms 29915, ff154-5, 20 Aug 1807, f245, 6 May 1808.
40 *Minutes Of... The Trial of Sir Robert Calder*, 36.
41 Ibid., 48.
42 Ibid., 64–5.
43 Ibid., 96.
44 Ibid., 98–102.
45 Ibid., 97.
46 Ibid., 102–4, 104–5.
47 Ibid. 108; see Greig ed., *Farington Diaries*, III: 96, 27 Dec 1805, for deliberation time.
48 *Morning Chronicle*, 27 Dec 1805.
49 Ibid. *Morning Post*, 27 Dec 1805; *Caledonian Mercury*, 30 Dec 1805; *Hampshire and Portsmouth Telegraph*, 30 Dec 1805; *Salisbury and Winchester Journal*, 30 Dec 1805; *The Scots Magazine*, 1 Jan 1806.
50 *Aberdeen Journal*, 1 Jan 1806.
51 *Caledonian Mercury*, 30 Dec 1805.
52 See herein, 132–3.
53 *Hampshire and Portsmouth Telegraph*, 30 Dec 1805.
54 Nicolson, *Men of Honour*, 189; Smith, *Sailors in the Dock*, 118–19; Tracy, 'Sir Robert Calder's Action', 267–8.
55 Breihan, 'The Addington Party', 181, notes a relaxation of the political focus on naval affairs following Trafalgar.
56 For Byng's case, see Margarette Lincoln, *Representing the Royal Navy. British Sea Power, 1750–1815* (Aldershot: Ashgate, 2002), 47–50.
57 *Morning Chronicle*, 1 Jan 1806.
58 *Minutes Of... The Trial of Sir Robert Calder*, 104.
59 Nicolas, *Dispatches*, VII, 84n; Collingwood, *Letters*, 169, 16 Dec 1805.
60 Duke of Buckingham and Chandos, *Memoirs of the Court and Cabinets of George the Third*, 4 vols (London: Hurst and Blackett, 1853–55), III: 446, 30 Sept 1805.
61 Bourchier, *Memoir*, 1: 56, 16 Oct 1805, 93, 20 Jan 1806.
62 Buckingham and Chandos, *Memoirs*, IV: 100, 25 Nov 1806.
63 NMM YOR/3, 14 Apr 1811.
64 NMM YOR/3, draft dated 17 Apr 1811.
65 NMM YOR/3, 22 Apr 1811.
66 Beinecke Rare Books and Manuscript Library, Yale University, James Marshall and Marie-Louise Osborn Collection, 71-8-62, 10 April 1811; Naval Chronicle, XVII (1812), 91.

67 Ibid., 27 January 1812.
68 Morrow, *British Flag Officers*, 179.
69 Beinecke . . . James Marshall and Marie-Louise Osborn Collection, 71-8-62, 7 Jan 1814.
70 Martin Robson, *A History of the Royal Navy: The Napoleonic Wars* (London: I. B. Tarus, 2014), 117.
71 Tracy, 'Sir Robert Calder's Action', 267–8; J. K. Laughton, ed., *Letters and Papers of Charles, Lord Barham, 1758–1813*, 3 vols (London: Navy Records Society, 1907–11), III: xxiv. The King acted precipitously in Hotham's case and much against Lord Spencer's and William Pitt's better judgement; see Morrow, *British Flag Officers*, 192.
72 Morrow, *British Flag Officers*, 3.
73 Bourchier, *Memoir*, I: 48, 10 Sept 1805.

Chapter 10

1 Anne Parry, ed., *The Admirals Freemantle* (London: Chatto and Windus, 1971), 77–8, 19 Nov 1805; *London Gazette Extraordinary*, #15858, 1366, 6 Nov 1805.
2 NA ADM 1/5396 Minutes of Harvey's Court Martial, f9, 22 Apr 1807.
3 James Grieg, ed., *The Farington Diaries by John Farington, R. A.*, 5 vols. (London, 1922–25), V: 173, 26 May 1809.
4 The Cocoa Club episode is from Horace Walpole, W. S. Lewis, ed., *The Yale Edition of Horace Walpole's Correspondence*, 48 vols (London: Oxford University Press, 1971), 25: 12 and n19; the claim that Harvey was the supplicant appeared in an account in the *London Chronicle*. The income figures are from the Harvey Papers in the Essex Records Office (ERO) D/DU 2057/1, Account Book, 1774–83 and D/DU 2531, Trustees' Account Book 1781–8.
5 *Caledonian Mercury*, 17 May 1809.
6 NA ADM 1/5396, Minutes of Harvey's Court Martial, ff2-4.
7 Ibid., f5.
8 Gareth Atkins suggests this reference may have been to Sir Charles Middleton's inheritance of an estate from a widow with whom his family lived and for whom he had acted as executor; see *Converting Britannia. Evangelicals and British Public Life, 1770–1840* (Woodbridge: Boydell and Brewer, 2019), 178 n7. Middleton was Gambier's uncle, patron and mentor. The most comprehensive account of evangelicalism in the Royal Navy is Richard Blake, *Evangelicalism in the Royal Navy 1775–1815. Blue Lights & Psalm Singers* (Woodbridge: The Boydell Press, 2008).
9 NA ADM 1/5396, Minutes, ff8-9.
10 NA ADM 3/168, 13 Apr 1809; ADM 1/5396, Minutes, f1.
11 *Caledonian Mercury*, 22 Apr 1809.
12 *Morning Post*, 15 Apr 1809.
13 *Norfolk Chronicle*, 15 Apr 1809; *Bury and Norwich Post*, 19 April 1809.
14 *Caledonian Mercury*, 17 Apr 1809.
15 *Bath Chronicle and Weekly Gazette*, 20 Apr 1809.
16 National Library of Wales (NLW), Ashton Hall Papers, 3121, f 79, 12 Apr 1899, 3122, f 77, 15 Apr 1809, 3123, 21 Apr 1809.
17 NA ADM 3/168, 13 Apr 1809.
18 *ODNB*.

19 ADM 1/5396, Minutes, f3. The proceedings, including Harvey's defence, were reported in the *Times*, 23 and 24 May 1809.
20 Ibid., f4.
21 See Atkins, *Converting Britannia*, 186–7 and Blake, *Evangelicals in the Royal Navy*, 174–224.
22 ADM 1/5396, 'Admiral Harvey's Defence', not paginated.
23 ADM 1/5396, ff5-7, 8, 9.
24 ADM 1/5396, 'Admiral Harvey's Defence'.
25 Ibid.
26 See the *Times*, 24 May 1809, and *Caledonian Mercury*, 27 May 1809, for the timing of the court's deliberation.
27 *Hampshire and Portsmouth Telegraph*, 29 May 1809; *Caledonian Mercury*, 27 May 1809.
28 *Morning Post*, 25 May 1809.
29 NLW, Aston Hall Papers, 3132, 21 Aug 1809.
30 NLW, Ashton Hall, Papers 2835, f448, 31 Aug 1809.
31 NA ADM 1/5210 Navy Privy Council Reports, ff79-80, 21 Mar 1810.
32 NLW Ashton Hall Papers, 2835, f452, 4 Apr 1810.
33 Arthur Aspinall, ed., *The Later Correspondence of George III*, 5 vols (Cambridge: Cambridge University Press, 1962–70), V: 541, 10 and 11 Mar 1810.
34 ADM 1/5210, Navy Privy Council Reports, ff72-72v, 12 Mar 1810.
35 Ibid., ff79-80, 21 Mar 1810.
36 The first report seems to have been in the *Times* on 2 Apr.
37 NLW Aston Hall Papers, 2835, f452, 4 Apr 1810.
38 A. M. W. Stirling, ed., *Pages and Portraits from the Past: Being the Private Papers of Sir William Hotham GCB*, 2 vols (London: H. Jenkins, 1919), II: 187.
39 Lady Harvey quoted in Richard Morris, *From Chigwell to Trafalgar. The Harvey's of Rolls Park* (Loughton: the author, 2005), 12–13. I am most grateful to Alison Jordan, Warden of St Mary's, Chigwell, for confirming the identity of the Mr Layton referred to in Lady Harvey's letter.
40 ERO, Harvey Papers, D/DGu C1/1/6, 15, 16, 20, 22, 23, 25 Mar 1821.
41 ERO, Harvey Papers, D/DGu C1/1/4, nd; Probate, D/DB/f F8, 16 Mar 1830.
42 ERO Harvey Papers, D/DGu C1/1/4, nd.
43 ERO Harvey Papers, D/DO E17, Abstract of the Agreement for partition of the Estates of the Heiresses of Sir Eliab Harvey deceased, nd.
44 ERO Harvey Papers, D/DGu, C1/6, 10 Mar 1821, 22 Mar 1821, 24 Mar 1824, 2 Aug 1827.
45 ERO T/G No 2; George Caunt, 'One of Nelson's Captains', *Chigwell Local History Society Transactions No. 1,* nd, 12.
46 ERO D/D Gu C1/1/6, 27 Feb 1826.
47 *Kent and Essex Mercury*, 23 Feb 1830, *Essex Herald* 23 Feb 1830, 2 Mar 1830; Caunt, 'One of Nelson's Captains', 13.
48 John Morrow, *British Flag Officers in the French Wars, 1793–1815. Admirals' Lives* (London: Bloomsbury Academic, 2018), 71–90 for acrimonious relationships between flag officers in the period.
49 Quoted John McArthur, *Principles and Practices of Courts Martial*, 2nd edn (London: J. Butterworth, 1805), II, 113–14.
50 Charles James, *A Collection of the Charges, Option and Sentences of General Courts Martial . . . from . . . 1795 to the Present Time* (London: Egerton, 1820), 140. I am grateful to Robert Burnham for referring me to James' compendium.

51 Cf. Caunt, 'One of Nelson's Captains', 12.
52 See Blake, *Evangelicals*, 115–24, for the court martial, some of the contemporary criticisms of Gambier and evaluation of them, and Morrow, *British Flag Officers*, 48–51, for their reputational implications.
53 Gareth Atkins, 'Religion, Politics and Patronage in the late Hanoverian Navy', c.1780-1820', *Historical Research* 88 (2015): 287; Morrow, *British Flag Officers*, 142.
54 R. V. Hamilton, ed., *Letters and Papers of Admiral of the Fleet Sir Thomas Byam Martin, 1783–1854,* 3 vols. (London: Navy Records Society, 1898–1903), I: 326–34; *Navy Chronicle*, XIX (1807), 68–69.
55 Aspinall, *Later Correspondence*, V: 573, 26 Apr 1810.

Chapter 11

1 See John E. Talbott, *The Pen & Ink Sailor. Charles Middleton and the King's Navy, 1778–1813* (London: Frank Cass, 1998).
2 Gareth Atkins, *Converting Britannia. Evangelicals and British Public Life, 1770–1840* (Woodbridge: Boydell and Brewer, 2019), 177–206; Richard Blake, *Evangelicals in the Royal Navy 1775–1815: Blue Lights and Psalm Singers* (Woodbridge: The Boydell Press, 2008), 62–3, 190–6.
3 See Christopher D. Hall, *British Strategy in the Napoleonic War, 1803–1815* (Manchester: Manchester University Press, 1992), 158–62.
4 William James, *The Naval History of Great Britain*, new edn, 6 vols (London: Richard Bentley & Son, 1878), IV: 210–11.
5 See 'Cathcart', *ODNB* for Copenhagen prize money.
6 For a recent account of the action, see James Davey, *In Nelson's Wake* (New Haven and London: Yale University Press, 2016), 282–8.
7 W. L. Clowes et al., *The Royal Navy: A History from the Earliest Times to the Present*, 7 vols (London: Samson Low, Marston and Company, 1898–1901), V: 258.
8 *Morning Post*, 22 Apr 1809; *Morning Chronicle*, 22 Apr 1809.
9 *Morning Post*, 24 Apr 1809.
10 Printed in W. B. Gurney, *Minute of a Court Martial . . . on the Trial of the Right Honourable James Lord Gambier, Admiral of the Blue* (Portsmouth: Mottley, Harrison and Miller, 1809), 22 Apr 1809.
11 *Morning Post*, 28 Apr 1809.
12 *Times*, 25 Apr 1809, 27 Apr 1809; *Morning Post*, 27 Apr 1809; *Times*, 5 May 1809.
13 *Morning Chronicle*, 5 May 1809.
14 *Morning Chronicle,* 4 May 1809, *Morning Post*, 5 May 1809; *Morning Chronicle*, 25 June 1809.
15 NA ADM 50/102, 30 May 1809, 3 June 1809.
16 *Caledonian Mercury*, 8 June 1809.
17 *Cobbett's Weekly Political Register*, 10 June 1809.
18 *Hampshire and Portsmouth Telegraph*, 26 June 1809, 3 July 1809.
19 *Morning Post*, 14 July 1809.
20 Gurney, *Minutes*, viii.
21 Clowes et al., *The Royal Navy*, V: 269, where the charge is restricted to Gambier's conduct on the 12th Apr.
22 Gurney, *Minutes*, 25, 27.

23 Ibid., 25.
24 Ibid., 27–8.
25 Ibid., 30.
26 Ibid., 31–69.
27 Ibid., 34–5, 37–9, 40, 42–3, 47–50, 54–6, 58–9.
28 Ibid., 70.
29 Ibid.
30 Ibid., 69, 74.
31 Ibid., 72–4, 81–2, 85–91.
32 Ibid., 107.
33 Ibid., 107, 108–9.
34 Ibid., 111.
35 See Blake, *Evangelicals*, 215–17, for the importance of information to hand.
36 Ibid., 120, 126, 128, 133–6.
37 Ibid., 154, 168, 170, 174, 208–9.
38 Ibid., 157, 163, 179.
39 Ibid., 195.
40 Ibid., 219–20, 221–2, 224.
41 Ibid., 231, 232.
42 For example, *Morning Chronicle*, 28, 28 July 1809, 2, 4, 5 Aug 1809; *Morning Post*, 28, 29 July 1809, 2, 3, 4, 5 Aug 1809; *Hampshire and Portsmouth Telegraph*, 31 July 1809, 2, 7 Aug 1809; *Aberdeen Journal* 9 Aug 1809, *Bury and Norwich Post*, 9 Aug 1809, *Northampton Mercury*, 5 Aug 1809. The *York Herald* reported the outcome on the following day thanks to a 'telegraphic dispatch' from the Admiralty, 5 Aug 1809.
43 *Hampshire and Portsmouth Telegraph*, 7 Aug 1809.
44 *Morning Chronicle*, 10 Aug 1809.
45 Lady Georgiana Chatterton, *Memorials, Personal and Historical of Lord Gambier GCB*, 2 vols (London: Hurst and Blackett, 1861), II: 328–9, 6 Aug 1809.
46 Ibid., 330, 331–5.
47 Ibid., 335–9.
48 See Robert K. Sutcliffe, *British Expeditionary Warfare and the Defeat of Napoleon, 1793–1815* (Woodbridge: Boydell Press, 2016), 209–13.
49 *Cobbett's Weekly Political Register*, 26 Aug 1809.
50 *Journal of the House of Lords*, 47, 422, 25 Jan 1810.
51 *Hansard*, 15, 348–9, 350, 8 Feb 1810.
52 As reported in the *Morning Chronicle*, 9 Feb 1810; the account of Holland's speech in *Hansard*, 15, 350–1, 8 Feb 1810 is less colourful.
53 *Morning Chronicle*, 9 Feb 1810.
54 *Hansard*, 15, 356, 9 Feb 1810.
55 *Hansard*, 15, 224–5, 29 Jan 1810.
56 Ibid., 230, 29 Jan 1810.
57 Ibid., 225–6, 29 Jan 1810.
58 Ibid., 226, 29 Jan 1810.
59 Ibid., 234–5, 29 Jan 1810.
60 Ibid., 242, 244, 29 Jan 1810.
61 *Morning Chronicle*, 30 Jan 1810; the reported reference to Hyde Parker in *Hansard*, 15:244, 29 Jan 1810 is blander.
62 *Hansard*, 15: 245–7, 29 Jan 1810.

63 Cf James, *The Naval History*, IV, 425–6. James had legal training but was often partisan in his historical judgements and in this instance criticized the verdict by reference to information that was not produced at the trial.
64 Gurney, *Minutes*, 49.
65 Chatterton, *Memorials*, II: 167 and Earl of Dundonald, *The Autobiography of a Seaman*, 2nd edn, 2 vols (London: Richard Bentley, 1861), II: 88.
66 See herein, 137.
67 Cf Clowes, *Royal Navy*, V: 269, who thought that Gambier was 'fortunate' when compared with Calder; that may be so, but not on the basis of the evidence at the court martial.
68 Arthur Aspinall, *The Later Correspondence of George III*, 5 vols (Cambridge: Cambridge University Press, 1962–70), V: 605, 16 July 1807; 24 Apr 1808; 574, 27 Apr 1810.
69 Third Earl of Malmesbury, *Diaries and Correspondence of James Harris, First Earl of Malmesbury*, 4 vols (London: Richard Bentley, 1844), IV: 403; quoted in Chatterton, *Memorials*, II: 90–1.
70 *London Gazette*, 2 Jan 1815.

Chapter 12

1 John Marshall, *Royal Naval Biography; or Memoirs of the Services of All the Flag Officers &c*, 8 vols (London: Longman, Hurst, Rees, Orme and Brown, 1823–35), I part 1: 405.
2 NMM, MID/1/180. There are brief accounts of the Stirling affair in Roger Knight, *Convoys* (New Haven: Yale University Press, 2022), 200–1, and John Morrow, *British Flag Officers in the French Wars, 1793–1815* (London: Bloomsbury Academic, 2018), 65–8. Cf Thomas Malcomson, *Order and Disorder in the British Navy, 1793–1815* (Woodbridge: The Boydell Press, 2016), 150–2, who assumes (contrary to the evidence presented in the trial, the verdict, Stirling's later statements and post-war civilian and service opinion in Jamaica) that Stirling was a party to ongoing corrupt transactions.
3 Marshall, *Royal Naval Biography*, I, part 1: 407 note.
4 James Ralfe, *Historical Memoirs of Admiral Charles Stirling: Extracted from the Fourteenth Part of The Naval Biography of Great Britain with Notes and Observation by Vice-Admiral Stirling* (London: L. Harrison, 1826), 63.
5 NMM WAR/82, f5, 4 Aug 1812; WAR/54, 16 Sept 1812.
6 For the strategic and operational context, see Andrew Lambert, *The Challenge: Britain Against America in the Naval War of 1812* (London: Faber and Faber, 2012), 198–259, and for general and particular issues of convoys, see Knight, *Convoys*, 11–52, 244–72.
7 NMM WAR/82, ff 18-20, 3 Dec 1812.
8 NMM WAR/53, f3, 20 February 1813, f16, 21 Feb 1813; for other instances see Lambert, *The Challenge*, 105–6, 112–14, 219–20, 258–9.
9 [Charles Stirling] *The Case of Vice Admiral Stirling. With an Appendix Containing the Minutes of the Court Martial and Mr Const's Observations* [1822] (Chertsey: William Slater Castell, 1821), 11–12.
10 Ralfe, *Historical Memoirs* (1826), vi–vii.

11 Rice University Library, Duckworth-Sterling Correspondence, MS304, nd but early 1804.
12 Ibid., nd July 1804, 29 Sept. 1804.
13 NA ADM 106/2034, 6 Sept 1812.
14 NA ADM 1/264, f34, 8 Feb 1813.
15 NA ADM 106/2034 25 Oct 1812, 24 Nov 1812, 27 Nov 1812, 16 Dec 1812.
16 NA ADM 1/264, f101, 2 July 1813, received 5 Sep 1813.
17 NA ADM 1/5442, 6 Nov 1813.
18 Stirling, *The Case*, 10, 36–7, 110.
19 Knight, *Convoys*, 25–52, 181–213; John Morrow, *The Naval Government of Newfoundland in the French Wars 1793–1815* (London: Bloomsbury Academic, 2023), 53–7.
20 NA ADM 1/264, f29, 29 Jan 1813; f48, 28 Feb 1813.
21 NA ADM 2/932, ff254-55, 10 Apr 1813.
22 NA ADM 1/264, f76, 18 June 1813.
23 NA ADM 1/264, f87, 20 June 1813.
24 Stirling, *The Case*, 14.
25 NMM WAR/35, f210, 3 Apr 1813.
26 NA ADM 1/5442, f14, 20 Feb 1813.
27 NA ADM 1/5442, f22, 28 July 1813.
28 Ibid., ff23, 28.
29 NA ADM 1/264, July-Aug 1813.
30 NA ADM 2/107B, f111, 12 Apr 1814.
31 NA ADM 1/5442, 6 Nov 1813.
32 Stirling, *The Case*, 22–3.
33 NA ADM 1/5442, 6 Nov 1813.
34 Stirling, *The Case*, 23.
35 NA ADM 1/5442, f3.
36 Stirling, *The Case*, 'Mr Const's Observations', 104–5.
37 Stirling, *The Case*, Minutes, 55, 58.
38 Ibid., 57, 67.
39 Ibid., 59.
40 NA ADM 1/5442, 'Stirling's Defence', f23.
41 Ibid., ff9, 15, 19–20.
42 Stirling, *The Case*, Minutes, 86–7.
43 NA ADM 1/5442, 'Stirling's Defence', ff15, 26–7.
44 Stirling, *The Case*, Minutes, 80–85.
45 Ibid., 74.
46 Ibid., 73.
47 Ibid., 9–10, 20, Minutes 75.
48 Ibid., Minutes, 89, 90.
49 Ralfe, *Historical Memoirs* (1826), 47.
50 NMM WAR/54, 27 Feb 1813.
51 Ralfe, *Historical Memoirs* (1826), 34 note.
52 *Norfolk Chronicle*, 4 Sept 1813. At the prevailing exchange rate of four shillings and sixpence to the dollar, a flag share of 1 per cent would enrich Stirling by close to £7000.
53 NA ADM 7/311 #49, 7 Sept 1803.
54 NA ADM 2/107B, ff187-8, 6 June 1814.

55 NA ADM 2/1096, f191, 8 Aug 1815.
56 Its circulation was so restricted that it is not in English copyright libraries, including the British Library, the Bodleian, or the Cambridge University Library. There is a copy in the Caird Library at the NMM; a friend of a senior staff member came across it in a second-hand bookshop during the Second World War and gave it to the library.
57 Ralfe, *Historical Memoirs* (1826), vii, viii–ix.
58 Ibid., viii–ix.
59 Ibid., ix.
60 Stirling, *The Case*, 'Mr Const's Observations', 104–5.
61 Stirling, *The Case*, 22, 35–6, 39–40.
62 'James Stirling'; 'Home Rigge Popham', *ODNB*.
63 Stirling, *The Case*, 38.
64 NA ADM 1/5442, note to J. W. Croker, 10 June 1821, to Hotham 14 Sept 1814.
65 Stirling, *The Case*, Letter to Sir Henry Hotham, 9 March 1822, 110.
66 Ralfe, *Historical Memoirs* (1826), xi.
67 James Ralfe, 'Historical Memoirs of Admiral Charles Stirling', in *The Naval Biography of Great Britain*, 4 vols (London: Whitmore & Fenn, 1828), III: 107.

Chapter 13

1 See Christopher D. Hall, *British Strategy in the Napoleonic War 1803–1815* (Manchester: Manchester University Press, 1992), 65–66, for the domestic political context and Rory Muir, *Wellington. The Path to Victory, 1769–1814* (London and New Haven: Yale University Press, 2013), 318–19 for Iberia and Austria.
2 BL Add Ms 31164, f129, 29 Nov 1806.
3 See Andrew Lambert, *The Challenge. Britain Against America in the Naval War of 1812* (London: Faber and Faber, 2012), 105–6, 112–14, 219–20, 258–9.
4 H. W. Richmond, ed., *Private Papers of George, 2nd Earl Spencer, 1794*–1801, 2 vols (London: Navy Records Society, 1924), IV: 23, 24 Dec 1800.
5 On Byng, see Daniel Baugh, ' "Too Much Mixed in This Affair": The Impact of Ministerial Politics in the Eighteenth-Century Royal Navy', in *New Interpretations in Naval History. Selected Papers Presented at the Fourteenth Naval History Symposium 23–25 September 1999*, ed. Randy Carol Balano and Craig L. Symonds (Annapolis: Naval Institute Press, 2001), and herein, 187 for Grenville's comment.
6 Cf Evan Wilson, *A Social History of British Naval Officers 1775–1815* (Woodbridge: The Boydell Press, 2017), 196–202.
7 See Adam Nicolson, *Men of Honour: Trafalgar and the Making of the English Hero* (London: Harper Perennial, 2006), 96.
8 See Geoffrey Best, *Honour Among Men and Nations: Transformations of an Idea* (Toronto: University of Toronto Press, 1982), 10 for honour and 'camaraderie' in military settings.
9 Quoted Thomas Keppel, *The Life of Augustus Keppel*, 2 vols (London: Henry Colburn, 1842), II: 98; herein, 87.
10 Herein, 146, 163.
11 Herein, 56, 149.

12 Herein, 87, 95.
13 Herein, 112–13, 117–19.
14 Herein, 132–3, 140–1.
15 Herein, 179–80.
16 John D. Byrn, *Crime and Punishment in the Royal Navy: Discipline on the Leeward Islands Station 1784–1812* (Aldershot: Scolar Press, 1989), 58, 123; Thomas Malcomson, *Order and Disorder in the British Navy, 1793–1815. Control, Resistance, Flogging and Hanging* (Woodbridge: The Boydell Press, 2016), 255–7, 260–1. Malcomson notes the tendency for heavy punishments on the North American station during the War of 1812; 235, 237.
17 Ross J. Dancy, *The Myth of the Press Gang* (Woodbridge: Boydell Press, 2015), 145–7.
18 The ratio is calculated from Brian Lavery, *Nelson's Navy: The Ship's, Men and Organisation, 1793–1815* (London: Conway Maritime, 1989), 328–9.
19 See Christopher Dandeker, 'The Old Navy and Social Change: Discipline, Punishment, and Authority in the Royal Navy, 1780–1860', in *New Aspects of Naval History. Selected Papers from the 5th Naval History Symposium* (Baltimore: US Naval Academy, Department of History, 1985), 93–7.
20 See Charles Consolvo, 'The Prospects of Promotion of British Sea Officers', *Mariners' Mirror* 91, no. 2 (2005): 135–59; Wilson, *A Social History*, 33–43.
21 Herein, 11.
22 See Morrow, *British Flag Officers*, 125. Dandeker's analysis (see note 19) mirrors these specifications.
23 Malcomson, *Order and Disorder*, 255, 262. I include articles II–IX, XI, XIV–XVI, XIX–XXIII, XXV–XXX, XXXIV–XXXVI in this category; some of these articles identify the responsibilities of officers but in relation to offences that might be committed by members of the lower deck.
24 John Delafons, *A Treatise on Naval Courts Martial* (London: s.n., 1805), 166–9; John D. Byrn, ed., *Naval Courts Martial 1793–1815* (Aldershot: Ashgate/Navy Record Society, 2009); N. A. M. Rodger, *The Wooden World. An Anatomy of the Georgian Navy* (London: Collin, 1986), 223–4.
25 V. A. T. Gatrell, *The Hanging Tree: Execution and the English People 1770–1868* (Oxford: Oxford University Press, 1994), 533; Peter King, *Crime, Justice and Discretion in England 1740–1820* (Oxford: Oxford University Press, 2000), 252ff.
26 Malcomson, *Order and Disorder*, 219 for variations in summary punishments.
27 Rodger, *The Wooden World*, 211–17.
28 Byrn, *Crime and Punishment*, 58, 123; Malcomson, *Order and Disorder*, 255, 262.
29 J. M. Beattie, *Crime and the Courts in England 1660–1800* (Oxford: Oxford University Press, 1986), 463–4; Markus Eder, *Crime and Punishment in the Royal Navy in the Seven Years' War, 1755–63* (Aldershot: Ashgate, 2004), 67.
30 See Eder, *Crime and Punishment in the Royal Navy*, 66–7. See Dandeker, 'The Old Navy and Social Change', 93–7 for the distinction between 'economic' and 'symbolic' sanctions.
31 James Greig, ed., *The Farington Diary by John Farington, R.A.*, 5 vols (London: Hutchinson, 1922–25), V: 173, 26 May 1809.

Conclusion

1 See N. A. M. Rodger, *The Command of the Ocean. A Naval History of Britain 1649-1815* (London: Penguin Books, 2005), 272, for the impact of Byng's execution.
2 See Roger Morriss, *Naval Power and British Culture: 1760–1850* (Aldershot: Ashgate, 2004), 20–1, 24, for the enhanced 'discipline of the Admiralty' across a range of areas.
3 See Brian Jolly, 'A Good Man in Every Sense of the Word: The Reputation of Admiral Robert Man', *Mariner's Mirror* 104, no. 2 (2018): 225–8; John Morrow, *British Flag Officers in the French Wars, 1793–1815. Admirals Lives* (London: Bloomsbury Academic 2018), 54–7.
4 The Army list for 1814 names 884 generals, lieutenant generals and major generals, of whom 10 were Royal Marines. The number of flag officers reached 223 following the valedictory promotion of 1814, but the boost in numbers had no bearing on flag appointments, which had peaked at thirty-seven in 1813. For the navy figures, see Morrow, *British Flag Officers*, 170. The army figures are from the *List of All The Officers of the British Army and Royal Marines* (London: War Office, 1814).
5 See J. W. Fortescue, *The British Army* (London: Macmillan and Company, 1906), VI, Part II: 878–80.
6 Rory Muir, *Wellington. The Path to Victory 1769–1814* (London and New Haven: Yale University Press, 2013), 280.
7 Ron McGuigan and Robert Burnham, *Wellington's Brigade Commanders. Peninsula and Waterloo* (Barnsley: Pen & Sword Military, 2017), 172–5.
8 Muir, *Wellington*, 276.
9 Ibid., 276–81.
10 See Martin Howard, *Walcheren 1809: The Scandalous Destruction of a British Army* (Barnsley: Pen and Sword Military, 2017), 201–11, for the enquiry and its aftermath.
11 Joseph Gurney, *The Sentence of the Court Martial . . . for the Trial of Hon Lieut. General James Murray* (London: M. Gurney, 1783), 1–10.
12 W. B. Gurney, *The Trial of Lieutenant General Sir John Murry, Bart. by a General Court Martial* (London: T. Egerton, 1815), 3.
13 See Sandy Anital, *Wampan Denied: Proctor's War of 1812* (Montreal and Kingston: Queen's McGill University Press, 2014), 377, 389 and cf. John R. Grodzinski, *Defender of Canada. Sir George Prevost and the War of 1812* (Norman: University of Oklahoma Press, 2013), 268–70.
14 W. B. Gurney, *Proceedings of a Court Martial . . . For the Trial of Lieut. Gen. Whitelocke*. two vols (London: Longman, Hurst, Rees, and Orme, 1808), I, 3–4, 237.
15 See *The Proceedings of a General Court Martial . . . on Major General Burton* (London: R. Faulder, 1804), 34, 16 Jan 1804; Charles James, *A Collection of the Charges, Opinions and Sentences of General Courts Martial . . . from 1795 to the Present Time* (London: Egerton, 1820), 140.

Bibliography

Manuscript Sources

Bedfordshire and Luton Records Office

L30/14 (Robinson)

Beinecke Rare Books and Manuscript Library, Yale University

James Marshall and Marie-Louise Osborn Collection, 71-8-62 (Calder)

British Library (BL)

Add Ms 29915 (Jervis)
Add Ms 31169 (St Vincent)
Add Ms 35196, 35200 (Bridport)

Cambridge County Archives, Cambridge

MS588 (Cotton)

Caird Library, National Maritime Museum, Greenwich (NMM)

COR/6 (Cornwallis)
DUC/ 8, 10, 11, 15, 22, 25, 27, 28; XDUC/21/9, 35/2 (Duckworth)
GRE/7
MID/1/21, 25, 51, 180 (Barham)
SAN/T/8 (Sandwich)
THO/2 (Thompson)
WAR/35, 53, 54, 82 (Warren)
WYN (Pole)
YOR/3 (Yorke)

Essex Records Office (ERO)

D/DU, D/DB, T/G (Harvey)

Devon Heritage Centre

153/M (Hood)

Melford Hall, Suffolk

Hyde Parker Papers, F42/2, F75/15, 25, F86/2, F94/1

UK National Archives, Kew (NA)

ADM 1/248, 264 (Letters from senior officers, Jamaica, 1797-8, 1813)
ADM 1/582, 583, 585, 591 (Letters from admirals unemployed, 1807-9, 1813, 1815, 1821)
ADM 1/3706 (Admiralty Solicitor, 1814)
ADM 1/5210 (Navy Report, Privy Council, 1810)
ADM 1/5529, 5369, 5396, 5442, (Courts martial)
ADM 2/107B (Admiralty Board out-letters, 1779)
ADM 2/139 (Admiralty Board out-letters, 1799-1800)
ADM 2/932, 933 (Admiralty Board out-letters, Mediterranean, North America, 1808-1813)
ADM 2/939 (Admiralty Board out-letters Jamaica, 1795-1807)
ADM 2/1091, 1092, 1094, 1096 (Admiralty Board out-letters consuls, admirals unemployed, miscellaneous, 1801-1815)
ADM 3/126, 168 (Admiralty Board Minutes and Rough Minutes, 1801)
ADM 7/311 (Law officers' opinions, 1813-14)
ADM 12/ 27C, 27D (Commissioned officers' convictions, 1794-1807, 1807-1815)
ADM 12/28A (Commissioned officers' trials, 1793-1803)
ADM 13/103 (Index, commissioned officers' courts martial)
ADM 50/54, 102 (Admirals' journals: Dacres 1805, Gambier, 1809)
ADM 106/2034 (Navy Board in-bound letters, Jamaica)
PRO 30/11/275 (Cornwallis)

National Library of Scotland

MS 2296 (Alexander Cochrane)

National Library of Wales

Aston Hall Papers 2835, 3121-3 (Harvey)

National War Museum of Scotland

DUN/20 (Duncan)

Rice University Library

MS 304 (Duckworth-Stirling).

Printed Primary Works

A New Form of Worship, for 27 July, Which is Ever to be held as a Day of Fasting and Humiliation &c. London: John Fowler, 1782[?].

Adair, Robert, *Part of a Letter from Robert Adair, Esq. to the Right Honourable Charles James Fox, Occasioned by Mr Burke's Mention of Lord Keppel, in a Recent Publication.* London: J. Debrett, 1796.

Admiralty Board, Lord Commissioners of, *Regulations and Instructions Relating to His Majesty's Service at Sea,* 13th edn. London: s.n., 1790.

Admiralty Board, Lord Commissioners of, *Regulations, and Instructions Relating to His Majesty's Service at Sea,* London: s.n., 1806.

Adye, Stephen Payne, *A Treatise on Courts Martial; also an Essay on Military Punishments and Rewards,* 8th edn. London: Vernon, Hood and Sharpe, 1810.

An Address to the Lords of the Admiralty, on Their Conduct Towards Admiral Keppel. London: J. Almon, 1779.

'An Interesting Trial. Vice-Admiral Stirling'. *The Weekly Entertainer; or, Agreeable and Instructive Repository,* 13 June 1814, 464–6.

Aspinall, Arthur, ed., *Later Correspondence of George III,* 5 vols. Cambridge: Cambridge University Press, 1962–70.

Barnes, G. R. and Owens, J. H., ed., *The Private Papers of John, Earl of Sandwich, First Lord of the Admiralty, 1771–82,* 4 vols. London: Navy Records Society, 1932–8.

Blanchard, W., *The Proceedings at Large of the Court-Martial, on the Trial of the Honourable Augustus Keppel, Admiral of the Blue ... Published By His Permission.* London: J. Almon, 1779.

Blandemor, Thomas, *The Trial of the Honourable Augustus Keppel ... At a Court Martial,* 2nd edn. Portsmouth: J. Wilkes, Breadhover and Peadle, 1779.

Bonner Smith, D., ed., *Letters of St Vincent, 1801–4,* 2 vols. London: Navy Records Society, 1921–26.

Buckingham and Chandos, Duke of, *Memoirs of the Court and Cabinets of George the Third,* 4 vols. London: Hurst and Blackett, 1853–55.

Byrn, John D. ed., *Naval Courts Martial.* Aldershot: Ashgate/Navy Records Society, 2009.

Childers, Spencer Colonel, ed., *A Mariner of England. An Account of the Career of William Richardson ... As Told by Himself.* London: John Murray, 1908.

Cobbett, William, *The Parliamentary History of England from the Norman Conquest in 1066 to the year 1806,* 36 vols. London: R. Bagshaw, 1806–20.

Corbett, J. S., ed., *The Private Papers of George, 2nd Earl Spencer, 1794–1801,* 2 vols. London: Navy Records Society, 1913, 1914.

Cunningham, Peter ed., *The Letters of Horace Walpole, Earl of Orford,* 9 vols. London: Henry G. Bohn, 1866.

Czisnik, Marianne, ed., *Nelson's Letters to Lady Hamilton and Related Documents.* London: Routledge/Navy Records Society, 2020.

Delafons, John, *Treatise on Naval Courts Martial.* London: s.n., 1805.

Falconer, William, *Universal Dictionary of the Marine,* 6th edn. London: T. Cadell, 1789.

Fortescue, John., *The Correspondence of George the Third from 1760 to December 1783,* 6 vols. London: Macmillan, 1927–8.

Gisborne, Thomas, *Enquiry into the Duties of Men in the Higher and Middle Classes in Society in Great Britain.* London: B. and J. White, 1794.

Grainger, John D., ed., *Papers and Correspondence of Admiral Sir John Thomas Duckworth. Volume 1: The French Revolutionary War, 1793–1802.* London: Routledge/Navy Records Society, 2022.

Greig, James, ed. *The Farington Diary by John Farington, R. A.*, 5 vols. London: Hutchinson, 1922–25.
Gurney, Joseph, *The Sentence of the Court Martial ... for the Trial of Hon. Lieut. General James Murray*. London: M. Gurney, 1783.
Gurney, W. B. *Proceedings of a General Court Martial ... For the Trial of Lieut. Gen. Whitelocke*. 2 vols. London: Longman, Hurst, Rees and Orme, 1808.
Gurney, W. B., *Minutes of a Court Martial ... on The Trial of the Right Honourable James, Lord Gambier, Admiral of the Blue*. Portsmouth: Mottley, Harrison, and Miller, 1809.
Gurney, W. B., *The Trial of Lieutenant General Sir John Murray, Bart. By a General Court Martial*. London: T. Egerton, 1815.
Hamilton, R. V., *Letters and Papers of Admiral of the Fleet Sir Thomas Byam Martin, 1783-1854*, 3 vols. London: Navy Records Society, 1898–1903.
Hannay, D., ed., *Letters Written by Sir Samuel Hood (Viscount Hood) in 1781–2*. London: Navy Records Society, 1895.
Hansard, UK Parliamentary Papers, Proquest.
Hayby, William., *Epistle to Admiral Keppel*. London: Fielding and Walker, 1779.
Herbert, Lord, ed., *Henry, Elizabeth and George (1734–1780). Letters and Diaries of Henry, Tenth Earl of Pembroke and his Circle*. London: Jonathan Cape, 1939.
Hildrop, John, *An Essay on Honour in Nine Letters*. Elizabeth-Town: s.n., 1791.
Hughes, E., ed., *The Private Correspondence of Admiral Lord Collingwood*. London: Navy Records Society, 1957.
Jackson, George, *Minutes of the Proceedings at a Court Martial, Assembled for the Trial of the Honourable Admiral Augustus Keppel*. London: W. Strahan and T. Cadell, 1779.
Jackson, George, *Minutes of the Proceedings at a Court-Martial, Assembled for the Trial of Vice-Admiral Sir Hugh Palliser, Bart*. London: W. Strahan and T. Cadell, 1779.
Jackson, George, *Minutes of the Proceedings at a Court Martial ... For Enquiring into the Conduct of The Honourable William Cornwallis, Vice Admiral of the Red*. London: John Stockdale, 1796.
Jesse, John Henage, *Memoirs of King George the Third, his Life and Reign*, 5 vols. Boston: L. C. Pye & Company, 1902.
Journal of the House of Lords, UK Parliamentary Papers, Proquest.
Keppel for Ever! London: s.n., 1779.
Laughton, J. H., ed., *Naval Miscellany 1*. London: Navy Records Society, 1901.
Laughton, J. H., ed., *Letters and Papers of Charles, Lord Barham, 1758–1813*, 3 vols. London: Navy Records Society, 1907–1911.
Lavery, Brian, ed., *Ship Board Life and Organisation, 1731–1815*. London: Navy Records Society, 1998.
Lewis, Michael, ed., *A Narrative of My Professional Adventures (1790–1839) by Sir William Dillon, KCH, Vice-Admiral of the Red*, 2 vols. London: Navy Records Society, 1953, 1956.
Lewis, W. S. ed., *The Yale Edition of Horace Walpole's Correspondence*, 48 vols. London: Oxford University Press, 1971.
Leyland, J., ed., *Dispatches and Letters Relating to the Blockade of Brest*, 2 vols. London: Navy Records Society, 1899, 1902.
List of All The Officers of the Army and Royal Marines. London: War Office, 1814.
Malmesbury, third Earl of, *Diaries and Correspondence of James Harris, First Earl of Malmesbury*, 4 vols. London: Richard Bentley, 1844.
Markham, C. R., ed., *The Correspondence of Admiral John Markham, 1801–1807*. London: Navy Records Society, 1905.
Mason, W., *Ode to the Naval Officers of Great Britain*. London: T. Codell, 1779.

McArthur, John, *Principles and Practice of Courts Martial*, 2nd. edn. 2 vols. London: J. Butterworth, 1805.
McArthur, John, *Principles and Practice of Courts Martial*, 4th edn. 2 vols. London: J. Butterworth, 1813.
Minutes of the Court Martial ... For the Trial of Sir J. T. Duckworth, K. B. Vice Admiral of the Blue. Portsmouth: J. C. Mottley, 1805.
Minutes of the Proceedings at a Court Martial ... For the Trial of Sir Robert Calder, Bart. Published by the Authority of the Vice Admiral. Portsmouth: J. C. Mottley, 1806.
Morriss, Roger, ed., *The Channel Fleet and the Blockade of Brest*. London: Navy Records Society, 2001.
Mountaine, William, *The Seaman's Vade-mecum and Defensive War by Sea*, 5th edn. London: Mount and Page, 1793.
Naval Chronicle, 40 vols., 1799–1818.
Nicolas, Nicholas Harris, ed., *The Despatches and Letters of Vice Admiral Lord Nelson*, 7 vols. London: Henry Colburn, 1844–46.
O'Breine, T., *Considerations on the Principles of Naval Discipline, and Courts-martial &c*, 2nd edn. London: J Almon and J. Debrett, 1781.
[Orde, Sir John], *Copy of a Correspondece, &c. Between the Right. Hon The Lords Commissioners of the Admiralty, The Right Hon The Earl of St. Vincent, KB, The Right Hon. Earl Spencer K.G. and Vice Admiral Sir John Orde, BART.* London: R. Faulder, 1802.
[Palliser, Hugh], *The Defence of Vice-Admiral Sir Hugh Palliser, Bart at The Court Martial Lately Held Upon Him, with the Court's Sentence*. London: T. Cadell, 1779.
Parry, Ann ed., *The Admirals Fremantle*. London: Chatto & Windus, 1971.
Proceedings of a General Court Martial ... on Major-General Burton. London: R. Faulder, 1804.
Ralfe, James, *Historical Memoirs of Admiral Charles Stirling: Extracted from the Fourteenth Part of The Naval Biography of Great Britain with Notes and Observations by Vice-Admiral Stirling*. London: L. Harrison, 1826.
Ralfe, James, 'Historical Memoir of Charles Stirling', *The Naval Biography of Great Britain*, 4 vols. London: Whitmore and Fenn, 1828.
Resolutions of the Court-Martial, Upon the Several Charges, Against Thomas Mathews, Esq. N.p., s.n., n.d.
Richmond, H. W., ed., *The Private Papers of George, second Earl Spencer, First Lord of the Admiralty, 1794–1801*, 2 vols. London: Navy Records Society, 1924.
Rodger, N. A. M., ed. *Articles of War*. Havant: Kenneth Mason, 1982.
Ross, Charles, ed., *Correspondence of Charles, First Marquis Cornwallis*, 2nd ed. 3 vols. London: John Murray, 1858.
Spencer, Alfred, ed., *Memoirs of William Hickey*, 4 vols. London: Hurst & Blackett, 1923.
Stirling, A. M. W., ed., *Pages and Portraits from the Past: Being the Private Papers of Sir William Hotham GCB*, 2 vols. London: H. Jenkins, 1919.
[Stirling, Charles], *The Case of Vice-Admiral Stirling. With an Appendix Containing The Minutes of the Court Martial and Mr Const's Observations* [1822]. Chertsy: William Salter Castell, 1821.
The Conduct of Admirals Hawke, Keppel, and Palliser, Compared. London: J. Bew, 1779.
The Sentence Pronounc'd by the Court Martial on Vice Admiral Lestock. London: M. Copper, 1746.
The Trial of Sir Hugh Palliser. London: J. Murray and C. Etherington, 1779.
Thoughts on the Conduct of Admiral Keppel, Together with Reasons for Restoring Sir Hugh Palliser into the Full Confidence and Good Opinion of his Country. London: Richardson and Urquhart, 1799.

Walpole, Horace, *Journal of the Reign of King George the Third*, 2 vols. Edited by Dr Doran. London: Richard Bentley, 1899.
Wheatley, Henry B., ed., *The Historical and Posthumous Memoirs of Sir Nathaniel William Wraxall 1772–1784*, 5 vols. New York: Scribner and Welford, 1884.
Woods, John A., ed., *The Correspondence of Edmund Burke*. IV. Cambridge: Cambridge University Press, 1963.
Wright, Philip, ed., *Lady Nugent's Journal of Her Residence in Jamaica from 1801–1805*. Kingston: University of West Indies Press, 2002.

Secondary works

Aldous, Grahame, 'The Law Relating to the Distribution of Prize Money in the Royal Navy and its Relation to the Use of Naval Power in War, 1793–1815'. PhD thesis, King's College, London, 2020.
Anital, Sandy, *Wampan Denied: Proctor's War of 1812*. Montreal and Kingston: Queen's McGill University Press, 2014.
Atkins, Gareth, 'Christian Heroes, Providence and Patriotism in Wartime Britain, 1793–1815'. *Historical Journal*, 58, no. 2 (2015): 393–414.
Atkins, Gareth, *Converting Britannia. Evangelicals and British Public Life 1770–1840*. Woodbridge: Boydell and Brewer, 2019.
Banister, Julia, *Masculinity, Militarism and Eighteenth-Century Culture 1689–1815*. Cambridge: Cambridge University Press, 2018.
Barrow, Sir John, *The Life of Richard Earl Howe*. London: John Murray, 1838.
Barton, Mark, 'Duelling in the Royal Navy'. *Mariner's Mirror*. 100, no. 3 (2014): 282–306.
Baugh, Daniel A., ' "Too Much Mixed in This Affair": The Impact of Ministerial Politics in the Eighteenth-Century Royal Navy'. In *New Interpretations in Naval History. Selected Papers Presented at the Fourteenth Naval History Symposium 23–25 September 1999*, edited by Randy Carol Balano and Craig L. Symonds, 21–43. Annapolis: Naval Institute Press, 2001.
Beatson, Robert, *Naval and Military Memoirs of Great Britain from 1727–1783*, 6 vols. London: Longman, Hunt, Rees and Orme, 1804.
Beattie, John, *Crime and the Courts in England 1660–1800*. Oxford: Oxford University Press, 1986.
Best, Geoffrey, *Honour Among Men and Nations: Transformations of an Idea*. Toronto: University of Toronto Press, 1982.
Blake, Richard, *Evangelicals in the Royal Navy 1775–1815: Blue Lights and Psalm Singers*. Woodbridge: The Boydell Press, 2008.
Bouchier, Lady, ed. *Memoir of the Life of Admiral Sir Edward Codrington, With Selections From His Public and Private Correspondence*, 2 vols. London: Longman's, Green and Co., 1873.
Bowman, James, *Honour. A History*. New York: Encounter Books, 2006.
Breihan, John R., 'The Addington Party and the Navy in British Politics, 1802–5'. In *New Aspects of Naval History. Selected Papers Presented at the Fourth Naval History Symposium, United States Naval Academy, 25–26 October 1979*, edited by Craig L. Symonds et al., 163–89. Annapolis: Naval Institute Press, 1981.
Brenton, Edward Pelham, *Life and Correspondence of John Earl of St Vincent, G.C.B, Admiral of the Fleet &c*, 2 vols. London: Henry Colburn, 1838.

Broomfield, J. H., 'The Keppel-Palliser Affair, 1778–1779'. *Mariner's Mirror* 47 (1961): 195–207.
Burnham, Robert and McGuigan, Ron, *The British Army Against Napoleon. Facts, Lists and Trivia 1805–1815*. Barnsley: Frontline Books, 2010.
Byrn, John D., *Crime and Punishment in the Royal Navy. Discipline on the Leeward Island Station, 1784–1812*. Aldershot: Scholar Press, 1989.
Caunt, George, 'One of Nelson's Captains', *Chigwell Local History Society Transactions No. 1*, n.d.
Charnock, John, *Biographia Navalis*, 6 vols. London: R. Faulder, 1794–8.
Chatterton, Lady Georgiana, *Memorials, Personal and Historical of Admiral Lord Gambier, G.C.B.*, 2 vols. London: Hurst and Blackett, 1861.
Clowes, W. L., et al., *The Royal Navy: A History from the Earliest Times to the Present*, 7 vols. London: Samson Low, Marston and Company, 1898–1901.
Colley, Linda, *Britons: Forging the Nation, 1707–1837* [1992]. London: Pimlico, 2003.
Consolvo, Charles, 'The Prospects of Promotion of British Sea Officers'. *Mariner's Mirror* 91, no. 2 (2005): 135–59.
Cornish, J. et al, *The Oxford History of the Laws of England 1820–1914*. Oxford: Oxford University Press, 2010.
Cornwallis-West, G., *The Life and Letters of Admiral Cornwallis*. London: Robert Holden, 1927.
Cox, Caroline, *A Proper Sense of Honour. Service and Sacrifice in George Washington's Army*. Chapel Hill: University of North Carolina Press, 2004.
Cuato, Sara, 'Mercenary Gentlemen? The Transnational Service of Foreign Quarterdeck Officers in the Royal Navy of the American and French Wars, 1775–1815'. *Historical Research* 94, no. 226 (2021): 806–26.
Dancy, J. Ross, *The Myth of the Press Gang. Volunteers, Impressment and the Naval Manpower Problem in the Late Eighteenth Century*. Woodbridge: Boydell Press, 2015.
Dandeker, Christopher, 'The Old Navy and Social Change: Discipline, Punishment and Authority in the Royal Navy, 1780–1860. In *New Aspects of Naval History. Selected Papers from the 5th Naval History Symposium*, 93–107. Baltimore: U.S. Naval Academy, Department of History, 1985.
Davey, James, *In Nelson's Wake. The Navy and the Napoleonic Wars*. New Haven and London: Yale University Press, 2016.
Dixon, Conrad, 'To Walk the Quarter Deck'. *Mariner's Mirror* 79, no. 1 (1993): 58–63.
Duffy, Michael, *Soldiers, Sugar and Sea Power: The British Expeditions to the West Indies and the War Against Revolutionary France*. Oxford: Clarendon Press, 1987.
Dundonald, Earl, *Autobiography of a Seaman*, 2nd edn, 2 vols. London: Richard Bentley, 1861.
Eder, Markus, *Crime and Punishment in the Royal Navy of the Seven Years War, 1755–63*. Aldershot: Ashgate, 2004.
Fortescue, J. W., *The British Army* IV, Part II. London: Macmillan and Co, 1906.
Gatrell, V. A. T., *The Hanging Tree: Execution and the English People 1770–1868*. Oxford: Oxford University Press, 1994.
Gilbert, A. N., 'Military and Civilian Justice'. *Journal of British Studies* 17, no. 2 (1978): 41–65.
Glass, R. E., 'Naval Courts-Martial in Seventeenth Century England'. In *New Aspects of Naval History. Selected Papers Presented at the Fourth Naval History Symposium, United States Naval Academy, 25–26 October 1979*, edited by W. B. Cogar et al., 53–64. Annapolis: Naval Institute Press, 1997.

Grodzinski, John R., *Defender of Canada. Sir George Prevost and the War of 1812*. Norman: University of Oklahoma Press, 2013.

Gwyn, Julian, *Frigates and Foremasts. The North American Squadron in Nova Scotia Waters, 1745–1815*. Vancouver: University of British Columbia Press, 2003.

Hall, Christopher D., *British Strategy in the Napoleonic War 1803–15*. Manchester: Manchester University Press, 1992.

Harding, Richard, 'Neglect or Treason: Leadership Failure in the Mid-Eighteenth-Century Royal Navy'. In *Naval Leadership and Management, 1650–1950. Essays in Honour of Michael Duffy*, edited by Helen Doe and Richard Harding, 43–57. Woodbridge: The Boydell Press, 2021.

Hill, Richard J., *The Prizes of War. The Naval Prize System in the Napoleonic Wars, 1793–1815*. Stroud: Sutton Publishing/Royal Naval Museum, 1998.

Hill, Richard J., 'Naval Discipline'. In *The Oxford Encyclopaedia of Maritime History*, I, edited by J. B. Hattendorf, 569–71. Oxford: Oxford University Press, 2007.

Hood, Dorothy, *The Admirals Hood*. London: Hutchinson & Co., 1934.

Howard, Martin, *Walcheren 1809. The Scandalous Destruction of a British Army*. Barnsley: Pen & Sword Military, 2017.

Hunt, Robert M., *The Life of Sir Hugh Palliser, Bart, Admiral of the White and Governor of Greenwich Hospital*. London: Chapman and Hall, 1844.

James, Charles, *A Collection of the Charges, Opinions and Sentences of General Courts Martial … from …1795 to the Present Time*. London: Egerton, 1820.

James, William, *The Naval History of Great Britain*, new edn, 6 vols. London: Richard Bentley & Son, 1878.

Jarrett, Dudley, *British Naval Dress*. London: J. M.Dent and Sons, 1960.

Jolly Brian, *Mrs Whitby's Locket. The Story of Captain John Whitby–England's Youngest Ever Naval Captain--and His Redoutable Wife*. Milford-on Sea: Milford-on-Sea Historical Record Society, 2011.

Jolly, Brian, 'A Good Man in Every Sense of the Word: The reputation of Admiral Robert Man'. *Mariner's Mirror* 104, no. 2 (2018): 225–32.

Jordan, Gerald and Rogers, Nicholas, 'Admirals and Heroes: Patriotism and Liberty in Hanoverian England'. *Journal of British Studies* 28, no. 3 (1989): 201–24.

Keppel, Thomas, *The Life of Augustus Viscount Keppel, Admiral of the White, and First Lord of the Admiralty in 1782–3*, 2 vols. London: Henry Colburn, 1842.

King, Peter, *Crime, Justice and Discretion in England 1740–1820*. Oxford: Oxford University Press, 2000.

Knight, Roger, *Britain Against Napoleon. The Organization of Victory 1793–1815*. London: Penguin, 2004.

Knight, Roger, *Convoys. The British Struggle Against Napoleonic Europe and America*. New Haven and London: Yale University Press, 2022.

Lambert, Andrew, 'Sir William Cornwallis, 1744–1819'. In *Precursors of Nelson. British Admirals of the Eighteenth Century*, edited by Peter Le Fevre and Richard Harding, 353–75. London: Chatham Publishing, 2000.

Lambert, Andrew, *The Challenge: Britain Against America in the Naval War of 1812*. London: Faber and Faber, 2012.

Lambert, Andrew, *Admirals: The Naval Commanders Who Made Britain Great*. London: Faber and Faber, 2012.

Lanbein, John H., *The Origins of Adversary Criminal Trial*. Oxford: Oxford University Press, 2003.

Lavary, Brian, *Nelson's Navy. The Ships, Men and Organisation, 1793–1815*. London: Conway Maritime, 1989.
Le Fevre, Peter, ' "Little Merit will be Given to me": Admiral Sir Hyde Parker (1739–1807) and the Diplomatic Build up to the Battle'. In *Battle of Copenhagen: 200 Years*, 1–29, edited by Stephen Howard. Shelton: The 1805 Club, 2003.
Lincoln, Margarette, *Representing the Royal Navy. British Sea Power, 1750–1815*. Aldershot: Ashgate, 2002.
Mackay, Ruddock and Duffy, Michael, *Hawke, Nelson and British Naval Leadership 1747–1805*. Woodbridge: The Boydell Press, 2009.
Malcomson, Thomas, *Order and Disorder in the British Navy, 1793–1815. Control, Resistance, Flogging and Hanging*. Woodbridge: The Boydell Press, 2016.
Marshall, John, *Royal Naval Biography; or Memoirs of the Services of All the Flag Officers &c.*, 8 vols. London: Longman, Hurst, Rees, Orme, and Brown, 1823.
McGuigan, Ron and Burnham, Robert, *Wellington's Brigade Commanders. Peninsula and Waterloo*. Barnsley: Pen & Sword Military, 2017.
Middleton, Richard, *Cornwallis. Soldier and Statesman in a Revolutionary World*. New Haven and London: Yale University Press, 2022.
Mitchell, Leslie, *Holland House*. London: Duckworth, 1980.
Morris, Richard, *From Chigwell to Trafalgar. The Harvey's of Rolls Park*. Loughton: the author, 2005.
Morriss, Roger, *Naval Power and British Culture, 1760–1850*. Aldershot: Ashgate, 2004.
Morrow, John, *British Flag Officers in the French Wars, 1793–1815. Admirals' Lives*. London: Bloomsbury Academic, 2018.
Morrow, John, *The Naval Government of Newfoundland in the French Wars 1793–1815*. London: Bloomsbury Academic, 2023.
Muir, Rory, *Wellington. The Path to Victory 1769–1814*. London and New Haven: Yale University Press, 2013.
Namier, Sir Lewis and Brooke, John, *The House of Commons, 1754–1790*, 3 vols. London: HMSO, 1964.
Nicolson, Adam, *Men of Honour. Trafalgar and the Making of the English Hero*. London: Harper Perennial, 2006.
Oldham, James, *The Varied Life of the Self-Informing Jury*. London: Selden Society, 2005.
Orde, Denis, *Nelson's Mediterranean Command*, 2nd edn. Barnsley: Pen and Sword Maritime, 2014.
Orth, Kathrin, 'Sir John Orde, 1751–1824'. In *British Admirals in the Napoleonic Wars*, edited by Peter Le Fevre and Richard Harding, 67–90. London: Chatham, 2005.
Palmer, M. A. J., 'Sir John's Action'. *Mariner's Mirror* 77, no. 1 (1991): 31–46.
Pope, Dudley, *The Black Ship*. London: Weidenfeld and Nicholson, 1988.
Robson, Martin, *A History of the Royal Navy. The Napoleonic Wars*. London: I. B. Tarus, 2014.
Rodger, N. A. M., *The Wooden World. An Anatomy of the Georgian Navy*. London: Collins, 1986.
Rodger, N. A. M., *The Insatiable Earl. The Life of John Montagu, 4th Earl of Sandwich*. London: Harper Collins, 1993.
Rodger, N. A. M., 'Honour and Duty at Sea'. *Historical Research* 77 (2002): 425–47.
Rodger, N. A. M., *The Command of the Sea. A Naval History of Britain 1649–1815*. London: Penguin Books, 2005.
Rogers, Nicholas, *Crowds, Culture and Politics in Georgian Britain*. Oxford: Oxford University Press, 1998.

Sainsbury, A. B., 'Sir John Duckworth, 1748–1817'. In *British Admirals of the Napoleonic Wars. The Contemporaries of Nelson*, edited by Peter Le Fevre and Richard Harding, 165–95. London: Chatham, 2005.
Schmidt, Patrick, 'Disobedient Officers in the Royal Navy, about 1680–1720'. *Mariner's Mirror* 188, no. 2 (2022): 159–76.
Sellar, W. C. and Yeatman, R. J., *1066 and All That. A Memorable History of England*. New York: E. P. Dutton, 1931.
Smith, Peter C., *Sailors in the Dock. Naval Courts Martial Down the Centuries*. Stroud: The History Press, 2011.
Smith, Russell G., *Medical Discipline. The Professional Conduct Jurisdiction of the General Medical Council, 1858–1990*. Oxford: Clarendon Press, 1994.
Sutcliffe, Robert K., *British Expeditionary Warfare and the Defeat of Napoleon, 1793–1815*. Woodbridge: Boydell Press, 2016.
Syrett, David and DiNardo, R. L., *The Commissioned Sea Officers of the Royal Navy 1660–1815*. Aldershot: Scolar Press/Navy Records Society, 1994.
Talbott, John E., *The Pen & Ink Sailor. Charles Middleton and the King's Navy, 1778–1813*. London: Frank Cass, 1998.
Thorne, R. G., *House of Commons, 1790–1820*, 5 vols. London: Secker and Warburg, 1986.
Tracy, Nicholas, 'Sir Robert Calder's Action'. *Mariner's Mirror* 77, no. 3 (1991): 259–70.
Tracy, Nicholas, 'Sir Robert Calder—1745–1810'. In *British Admirals of the Napoleonic Wars. The Contemporaries of Nelson*, edited by Peter Le Fevre and Richard Harding, 197–217. London: Chatham Publishing, 2005.
Tucker, Spencer C. and Reuter, Frank T., *Injured Honor: The Chesapeake-Leopard Affair, June 22, 1807*. Annapolis: Naval Institute Press, 1996.
Valle, James E., 'Discipline and Punishment'. In *The Oxford Encyclopaedia of Maritime History*, I, edited by J. B. Hattendorf, 564–8. Oxford: Oxford University Press, 2007.
Ware, Christopher, 'The Glorious First of June: The British Strategic Perspective'. In *The Glorious First of June 1794. A Naval Battle and its Aftermath*, edited by Michael Duffy and Roger Morriss, 25–45. Exeter: University of Exeter Press, 2001.
Warner, Oliver, *The Life and Letters of Vice-Admiral Lord Collingwood*. London: Oxford University Press, 1968.
Wilkinson, Clive, *The British Navy and the State in the 18th Century*. Woodbridge: Boydell Press, 2004.
Wilson, Evan, *A Social History of British Naval Officers 1775–185*. Woodbridge: Boydell Press, 2017.

Index

www.ingramcontent.com/pod-product-compliance
Ingram Content Group UK Ltd.
Pitfield, Milton Keynes, MK11 3LW, UK
UKHW020257051026
15470UKWH00020B/908

9 781350 467279